# International Economics

C000121252

We work with leading authors to develop the
strongest educational materials in economics,
bringing cutting-edge thinking and best learning
practice to a global market.

Under a range of well-known imprints, including
Financial Times Prentice Hall, we craft high quality
print and electronic publications which help
readers to understand and apply their content,
whether studying or at work.

To find out more about the complete range of our
publishing please visit us on the World Wide Web at:
www.pearsoneduc.com

# International Economics
## Theories, Themes and Debates

**Kevin Lawler**

**and**

**Hamid Seddighi**

with edited contributions

An imprint of **Pearson Education**

Harlow, England · London · New York · Reading, Massachusetts · San Francisco · Toronto · Don Mills, Ontario · Sydney
Tokyo · Singapore · Hong Kong · Seoul · Taipei · Cape Town · Madrid · Mexico City · Amsterdam · Munich · Paris · Milan

For Duo Qing, Arabella and Jemima
For Philip and Reza

**Pearson Education Limited**

Edinburgh Gate
Harlow
Essex CM20 2JE
England

and Associated Companies throughout the world

*Visit us on the World Wide Web at:*
http://www.pearsoneduc.com

_____

**First published 2001**

© Pearson Education Limited 2001

All rights reserved; no part of this publication may be reproduced, stored
in a retrieval system, or transmitted in any form or by any means, electronic,
mechanical, photocopying, recording, or otherwise without either the prior
written permission of the Publishers or a licence permitting restricted copying
in the United Kingdom issued by the Copyright Licensing Agency Ltd.,
90 Tottenham Court Road, London W1P 0LP.

ISBN 0 273 643312

All trademarks used herein are the property of their respective owners. The use of any
trademark in this text does not vest in the author or publisher any trademark ownership
rights in such trademarks, nor does the use of such trademarks imply any affiliation with
or endorsement of this book by such owners.

*British Library Cataloguing-in-Publication Data*
A catalogue record for this book is available from the British Library

*Library of Congress Cataloging-in-Publication Data*
Lawler, K. A.
    International economics : theories, themes, and debates / Kevin Lawler and Hamid
Seddighi with edited contributions.
        p. cm.
    Includes bibliographical references and index.
    ISBN 0-273-64331-2 (pbk.)
      1. International economic relations. 2. International trade. I. Seddighi, Hamid. II. Title.

HF1359 .L4 2001
337--dc21

                                                          00-050281

10 9 8 7 6 5 4 3 2 1
05 04 03 02 01

Typeset by 63
Printed and bound in Great Britain by T.J. International,
Padstow, Cornwall

In Memory of the recently deceased
Professor Brian Hillier
of the University of Liverpool
Department of Economics

# Contents

# List of contributors

Dr. Andrew Abbott
Dept. of Economics
Manchester Metropolitan University
*Chapter 15*

Professor H. D. Dixon
Dept. of Economics
University of York
*Chapter 14*

Mr. G. De Vita
The Oxford Brookes Business School
Oxford
*Chapter 21*

Dr. E. Katsoulie
Dept. of Economics
University of Macedonia
Greece
*Chapter 16*

Dr. M. Ling
Sunderland Business School
University of Sunderland
*Chapters 17, 18 and 22 with K. Lawler*

Professor A. O. Moscardini
CET
University of Sunderland
*Chapter 13 with K. Lawler*

Dr. K. Al Sabbah
Research Dept.
Kuwait Oil Ministry
*Chapters 8 and 9 with K. Lawler*

Professor R. Wilson
Centre for Middle-Eastern and Islamic Studies
University of Durham
*Chapter 11*

# Foreword

The topic of international economics is amongst the oldest in economics. As such, it is one of the best-established areas of research: many of the central results have a long pedigree, perhaps not all as long as Ricardo's theory of comparative advantage, but certainly dating over half a century. However, the last decades have seen many advances in trade theory. Most of the original bedrock of the theory was based on the assumption of perfectly competitive markets. Many of the more recent developments have arisen out of the realisation that markets are imperfect and that this is central to the pattern of many aspects of trade – from OPEC and oil to motor cars.

In the last decade, a number of new issues have arisen: the economics of transition in China and the ex-Soviet sphere, the new economy and e-commerce, globalisation and European monetary union. These are all important issues central to our understanding of the world economy today. This volume is unique and timely in bringing together all of these strands. It includes not only masterly exposition and surveys of traditional theory, but also wide-ranging and timely chapters on current issues and hot topics. The inspired editorship and contributions of Kevin Lawler and Hamid Seddighi provide advanced undergraduate and graduate students of international economics with a comprehensive and authoritative text that will have something in it for everyone.

In a rapidly-changing world, it is more essential than ever that economists try to develop economic science to embrace emerging and ever-more complex economic developments. Nowhere is this more important than in the context of the new world order, trade and globalisation. This book provides both a review of where we have come to and also a glimpse of where we are going in this enterprise. As such, it is a volume that is very much to be welcomed.

Huw Dixon
University of York

# Preface

This textbook focuses on three broad themes: theories, applications and global issues. Chapters 1–6 cover theoretical issues beginning with classical models of trade, income distribution and trade policy. Chapters 7–10 develop new approaches to the problem of imperfect competition and world trade. This area does not normally receive much attention in international texts as the theories are complex and the issues specific. However, imperfect competition has attracted a good deal of research effort in the past five years and these chapters help focus issues. The cases of oligopoly, product differentiation and OPEC behaviour are considered using game theoretical arguments. Chapter 13 develops dynamic theory of free trade based on the methodology of System Dynamics.

Chapters 10–13 address new developments and themes in world trade and focuses on the current controversy regarding multi-lateralism and the New Regionalism. Chapter 11 develops a case of new regionalism in the trade of the Gulf States. Thereafter the dominant rise-fall and rise of the East Asian 'Tigers' are discussed. Chapter 14 considers the issues relating to the transitional economies after the collapse of communism. Analysis focuses on a Balkan country – Albania, and a central Asian Republic – Kyrgyzstan.

Chapters 14–16 consider current research issues in exchange rate theory. Chapters 17–21 feature global issues presently acting on the world economy. Thus chapter 17 considers liberalisation in World Telecommunications and the world wide web and advertising. Chapter 18 considers issues of convergence with an application to IOR. Chapters 19–20 focus on a globalised industry – brewing – and its impact on emerging markets. Chapters 21–23 consider the key issues relating to FDI in general and specifically for China.

# Scope of the book

This book represents an attempt to provide a modern and accessible analytical framework for understanding international events in economic relations. The book focuses on the real and monetary sectors and attempts to deliver the fundamental teaching of classical analysis with the latest research and findings. The text eschews a thoroughgoing investigation of open economy macroeconomics and financial analysis as these two key areas are better handled in specialist texts.

For lecturers seeking a concise treatment of international economics issues in a one-semester module, we would recommend Chapters 1–5 and 16. A one-year graduate programme would need to include elements of these plus Chapters 13–16 and 21–23. Third-year undergraduates on European Economics modules and MBA, MSc and MA students will find Chapters 10, 11, 13 and 14 useful. Some chapters can be omitted by non-specialists, in particular Chapters 3, 4, 5, 7 and 8–9 are advanced and technical. Students seeking a concise treatment of the issues which affect oil-exporting countries will find Chapters 6, 8, 9, 11 very rewarding.

The text makes a real effort to cover global issues in some depth in Chapters 17–23. Here the latest research on new development in telecommunications, Internet advertising and global industry are tackled. Moreover, the economic vicissitudes of the East Asia 'Tigers' are considered and the debt crisis and the recent resurgence are analysed.

Finally, no international text nowadays could exclude transition economies and this is no exception. General issues of transition as well as detailed studies of European and central Asian transitional economies are considered.

# Acknowledgements

In the course of writing this book, we have received assistance from many people. We would gratefully like to thank Dr. Marcus Ling, Mr. K. P. Lee, and Jenny Kwok for the great efforts made in typing, proof-reading, and cross-checking the entire text. In addition to the chapters co-authored with Kevin Lawler, Dr. Ling initially typed the entire volume. Thereafter, Mr. K. P. Lee checked all formulae and equations for consistency and all tables and graphs for accuracy. Dr. Nuttall made many helpful suggestions at various stages, as did Professors Huw Dixon and Alfredo Moscardini. Paula Harris and Paula Parish made many useful suggestions and have been a constant source of encouragement. Finally, special thanks to Miss Jenny Kwok of Durham University for producing the master proof copy. As always, all errors that remain are ours.

Kevin Lawler
Hamid Seddighi

# PART ONE

# Theoretical issues and applications

## CHAPTERS

# 1 An overview of classical trade theories and pure theories of trade: Ricardo

## K. LAWLER and H. SEDDIGHI

## 1.1 An overview of classical trade theories

Economic development is associated with trade. As global economic linkages in the world become more pervasive, it would be difficult to find a country isolated from such linkages. The concept of a self-sufficient economy is based on autarky. This is very dated nowadays. Private firms are typically the economic agents for change and trade. Traditional economic theory views firms as primarily profit-driven, utilising specific production functions. Conversely, there are also strong non-profit maximisation strategic objectives pursued by governments. Such strategic moves can make trade flows perverse with resulting diverse impacts compared to traditional predictions. Moreover, governments and other bodies such as trade unions and political parties' organisations create other influential forces shaping the future trends for international trade. When globalisation processes intensify, production becomes increasingly strategically driven. Classical theories of trade stem from the endowment resource-based views. This is the typical starting point for Ricardian comparative cost analysis. Current trade patterns now involve more dynamic market-based processes, based on Product Life Cycle Theory. Whether trade flows follow the classical views or the contemporary principles, trade is a form of exchange which contributes to the increased wealth, rising living standards and the sustained economic development of trading nations. Hence, the World Trade Organisation (WTO) has been steadily easing the international trade environment and promoting multi-lateralism. So why do economic agents strive to conduct trade? Why do countries import goods that they can produce domestically? Why does an economy move away from traditional production systems? These are the key issues to be explained by trade theories old and new.

## 1.2 The historical development of classical trade theories

National relative comparative advantages are fundamental ideas used for analysing trade flows in classical economics. The theories were developed in the eighteenth century by Ricardo. The idea was simple but has proved striking in applications to the study of trade patterns. Ricardo's work was inspired by Adam Smith's (1776) famous work, *The Wealth of Nations*. Ricardo expanded Adam Smith's concept of the mutual benefits of trade and illustrated these via the concepts of comparative advantage. The predictive power of the comparative advantage principle was based on the theoretical framework of resource differentials. Given the fact that economies are always endowed with different natural resources and man-made production assets, the principle has strongest basic foundation for assessing actual trade patterns. After Ricardo's fundamental contribution, other

3

economists developed the theoretical implications. For instance, Heckscher, Ohlin and Samuelson use relative factor proportions as the cause of differences in comparative advantage and the origin of trade flows. Leontief (1953) used American data to focus on empirical testing of Heckscher, Ohlin and Samuelson (H-O-S) predictions. Rybczynski (1955) observed the power of shifting factor proportions in influencing trading patterns. More recently, Vernon (1966) stressed the importance of product life cycles in understanding trade between countries with similar economic structures.

## 1.3    The theory of comparative advantage

Trade is based on exchange. The basic aim of exchange is profit-driven. These underlying principles are well illustrated by the theory of comparative advantage. A simple example can be used to show these ideas. The example assumes that there are two countries and two products. Each country is endowed with 50 units of labour which is assumed for simplicity to be the only factor. The labour requirements per unit of production and the initial allocation of production are shown in Table 1.1.

In Table 1.1, based on factor requirements, a schedule for production possibilities is produced. At this stage, the total production is 34 cars and 40 pairs of shoes. Without trade, both countries adjust production possibilities to satisfy needs. However, if there exists perfect information and traders know all the comparative requirements for producing these two products, more efficient production schedules can be arranged. This makes both countries better off. This represents a Pareto improvement.

The situation shown in Table 1.2 assumes that country A uses all labour resources in producing cars whereas country B only produces shoes. Total production increases in both sectors. This represents a potential welfare improvement compared to the situation in

**Table 1.1  The labour requirement and the initial production schedule.**

| Country | Cars | | Shoes | |
| --- | --- | --- | --- | --- |
| | Labour requirement (unit) | Output (unit) | Labour requirement (unit) | Output (a pair) |
| A | 1 | 30 | 2 | 10 |
| B | 5 | 4 | 1 | 30 |
| Total | | 34 | | 40 |

**Table 1.2  The labour requirement and the production schedule after complete specialisation.**

| Country | Car | | Shoes | |
| --- | --- | --- | --- | --- |
| | Labour requirement (unit) | Output (unit) | Labour requirement (unit) | Output (a pair) |
| A | 1 | 50 | 2 | 0 |
| B | 5 | 0 | 1 | 50 |
| Total | | 50 | | 50 |

Table 1.3   The labour requirement and production schedules before complete specialisation.

| Country | Car | | Shoes | |
|---|---|---|---|---|
| | Labour requirement (unit) | Output (unit) | Labour requirement (unit) | Output (a pair) |
| A | 1 | 30 (50) | 2 | 20  (0) |
| B | 0.8 | 20  (0) | 1 | 34 (50) |
| Total | | 50 (50) | | 54 (50) |

Note: Figures in parentheses indicate production after complete specialisation.

Table 1.1. In fact this allocation of resources is the maximum production possibility taking account of relative efficiency. A reverse of this specialisation process would yield 10 cars and 25 pairs of shoes. However, this type of specialisation causes aggregate welfare to fall. Complete specialisation should raise welfare, therefore the reverse case of specialisation is not relevant. However, the outcomes for these two specialisations imply that firms need to specialise in production requiring less resources to increase welfare. This means, in this example, that country A is said to have comparative advantage in producing cars and country B has a comparative advantage in shoes.

Complementing the theory of comparative advantage is the principle of absolute advantage. The existence of absolute advantage for a country does not, however, imply the trade direction. For instance in Table 1.3, country B possesses an absolute advantage in producing both products. Country B requires less labour to produce both products. However, it is not possible for country B to specialise in both activities to generate maximum welfare. Absolute advantage does not indicate where the specialisation should be focused. The correct choice for specialisation is isolated by the concept of comparative advantage.

For example, country B requires only 0.8 units of labour to produce a car. However, complete specialisation for country B is realised in making shoes. This is because in relative terms country B forgoes 0.8 pairs of shoes for every car produced, whereas the corresponding figure for A is only 0.5 pairs of shoes. Under this relative condition, country A is more efficient in utilising resources to produce cars. Hence, complete specialisation for A is in car production. In short, comparative advantage is crucial for locating the right choices of specialisation, while absolute advantage measures the efficiency of utilising resources to produce a product in absolute terms.

## 1.4   The Heckscher-Ohlin-Samuelson (H-O-S) theory of factor proportions and trade

This theory of trade is focused on factor proportions to explain relative efficiency in production. The H-O-S principle is basically an explanation of comparative advantage. The H-O-S principle states that comparative advantage is crucially influenced by relative factor proportions in an economy. The key implication of the H-O-S model is that a country's trading pattern is determined by the society or abundance of factors of production. In developing countries, where cheap labour exists, exports are expected to be labour intensive, while a country rich in capital relative to labour tends to produce more capital-intensive products for export. Examples following the H-O-S principle can be identified.

Thus Silicon Valley in the US produces more high-tech computer software than anywhere else given a high level of human capital supply. By contrast, India has an abundance of cheap labour to produce textiles exports. Trade between India and the USA essentially follows H-O-S predictions.

The H-O-S model generates crucial implications for factor prices with complete specialisation. As capital-rich countries export more capital-intensive products to less capital-rich countries, the demand for capital increases. This leads to a rise in real prices for capital in the capital-rich country. By contrast, labour-rich countries can release more capital for better alternatives and import capital-intensive goods. This helps to lower capital prices in labour-rich countries. The process continues until factor prices are eventually equal. This is theoretically possible and results in the Theorem of Factor Price Equalisation introduced by Samuelson (1948). Hence, based on the H-O-S model, exports are equivalent to transfers of factor resources. Labour-rich countries transfer labour resources to a market with labour scarcity. On the other hand, capital-rich countries 'export' capital to countries short of capital. These kinds of transfer are possible provided that trade is frictionless and perfect information exists. However, these assumptions seldom occur in real-world situations.

The H-O-S model is mostly criticised in analysing intra-industry trade and trade between countries with similar endowments of factors. In fact, in a world with increased proliferation of product differentiation, factor endowments can indicate only the trade flows on a macro level. For a micro-level analysis, one can assume for simplicity that the factors that most affect the trade between firms in the same industry (and across different countries) are strategic motives and firm-specific. These assets include brand names, expertise and quality (vertical, horizontal) variations. The H-O-S model perhaps over-emphasises the initial endowment of factors. By contrast, it ignores accumulation and depreciation processes of factors of production. This means that the H-O-S model is not sufficiently dynamic to consider changes in factor availability and the degree of mobility attached to these. Owing to improvements in transportation and the speed of communications, factors are likely to become more mobile over time. For instance, East Asian iron and steel exports can be shipped to the West within a month, and Taiwanese computer chips sent to San Francisco within days. Moreover, the traditional theory of trade always tends to consider that exports are the only medium for trade activities. This ignores other media such as foreign direct investment, foreign production, other strategic joint ventures and alliances which are ever popular. The H-O-S model was developed in the 1920s and 1930s and at that time, these media were underdeveloped. Treatment of H-O-S allows, however, locational elements, differentiation in production functions and other quality aspects of factors to be used. Hence, these desirable geographical and climatic factors favouring rice production explain the strong export performance of Thai rice to many parts of the world. Moreover, expertise in mobile phone technology in Scandinavian countries has led to these countries manufacturing more handsets than other countries. Global brands such as Nokia and Ericsson enjoy scale economies in production.

## 1.5 Leontief Paradox

Leontief (1953) utilised American data in the 1950s to produce a statistical test of the H-O-S prediction. Leontief sought to test whether a capital-rich country would import relatively more labour-intensive goods and export relatively larger volumes of capital-intensive products. The results of this testing indicated that there was no sign that US trade followed the predictions of the H-O-S model. Instead, the statistical test on US data showed that capital-rich America's aggregate imports were relatively more capital intensive than her aggregate exports. The contradictory results were reconfirmed by Leontief with powerful testing procedures on US data in 1956. Other researchers such as Deardorff (1984) also drew the same paradoxical results based on US data. These perverse findings are called the Leontief Paradox. Vernon (ibid.) used a Product Life Cycle Hypothesis to argue that the paradoxical results are misleading if no account is taken of the product life cycle of export merchandise in the USA. He stressed that the labour inputs would be relatively high when large scales of mechanisation are introduced at initial stages. Capital-intensive production could therefore carry a relatively larger weight of labour inputs. As mechanisation progresses, so does the product life, the use of labour falls and more fixed capital is employed for expansion. This diffusive phenomenon is similar to Mansfield's (1961) model of technology diffusion. The rate of utilisation of technology is relatively low at first, then progresses as the importance of the related technology and the perceived risks of using technology reduce as the time horizon increases. Hence, despite these paradoxical results, the H-O-S model could hold for testing the long-term US trade patterns.

## 1.6    Rybczynski Theorem

The H-O-S model stresses relative factor proportions and employs a static view. By contrast, the Rybczynski Theorem is more dynamic and relates to changes in relative factor proportions. To a large extent, the Rybczynski Theorem is the corollary of the H-O-S model. There are many examples which show factor proportions altering comparative advantages and hence trade patterns in the world. A prominent example can be drawn from the development of the emerging South East Asian countries. Thus, Korea was an agricultural-based society shortly after World War II. As education improved and savings increased, with more accumulated capital, both human and physical, technology has been utilised to transform the country into a dominant world producer of household appliances. Other countries in the region focused on primary production that included rubber (Indonesia), rice (Thailand), coconut oil (the Philippines) and cotton (China) etc. Now these countries utilise more capital and advanced technology to assist production. Accumulated savings and manufacturing efficiency in the 1970s and 1980s enabled Taiwan to develop more advanced technology for its computer industry. Taiwan used to export light manufactured products with low value-added, but is now one of the biggest exporters of computer chips and microcomputer technology. Sometimes government policies are major influences in affecting factor proportions. For instance, the mainland Chinese government launched a large-scale '4 mechanisations processes' to stimulate economic growth using more efficient technology. Moreover, the Singaporean government argues that technology diffusion is the major cause of its ultimate success and sustainable growth of an economy. Barry (1997) shows how the Irish government reduced corporate taxes to create a supply-side condition to attract FDI. The resulting impact on Irish manufacturing has been huge as FDI increased to create around 45% of all employment in the manufacturing sector. Lipsey and Stevens (1992) argue that home and FDI are not necessarily independent. As FDI requires financial sums, an increase in overseas operations may require reductions in domestic capital investment. The major implication of the Rybczynski Theorem is that outward FDI interrupts the accumulation of factors of production and therefore reduces the long-term competitiveness of the home industries.

## 1.7 The pure theory of international trade: fundamental considerations

The key issue facing classical theorists like Ricardo and J. S. Mill was why international trade occurs as voluntary activity between trading partners. Essentially Ricardo's theory of comparative advantage explains the basis for trade in terms of differences between nations. Such differences might include disparities in technique, skill, knowledge, or all these elements combined.

In a general sense, trade depends upon differences between nations. Ricardo took differences between countries as given, then rigorously applied the principle of comparative advantage to determine the pattern of trade. The principle of comparative advantage, moreover, was simultaneously utilised by Ricardo and his followers to demonstrate the gains available to countries that adopted free-trade policies. Hence early trade theorists could use the principle of comparative advantage to both a positive and predictive aspiration: yet simultaneously construe and demonstrate the normative implications of that principle, to extol the benefits of free unrestricted trade. In short, that free trade between nations maximised global welfare. However, the deeper question, namely 'what constitutes the *minimum sufficient difference* between nations to explain the existence of trade?' was left unasked until the advent of the Heckscher-Ohlin theory (Ohlin, 1933) and Samuelson's later extension of this theory (Samuelson, 1948). In subsequent sections and chapters the following topics are analysed in detail:

1. The 'static Ricardian' theorem of comparative advantage

2. The gains from trade in a Ricardian world

3. A brief evaluation of the Ricardian model of trade

4. The Heckscher-Ohlin-Samuelson [H-O-S] theory of trade

5. Corollaries of the H-O-S theory of trade

6. The gains from trade in a general equilibrium context

7. The impact of tariffs and subsidies on trade

8. An evaluation of the static H-O-S theory of trade

## 1.8 The static Ricardian comparative advantage theorem

The Ricardian theorem can be derived from a basic model that includes two trading nations, two homogeneous goods, and a single homogeneous input (labour). Table 1.4 depicts the relative labour input cost (in work hours) for countries I and II producing commodities X and Y.

Inspection of Table 1.4 reveals that country I possesses an absolute production cost advantage in the production of both goods X and Y. However, country I has a comparative cost advantage in the production of good X since it can make a unit of good X for:

**Table 1.4  A relative production cost matrix for two countries producing two goods.**

|  | Work hours to produce 1 unit of X | Work hours to produce 1 unit of Y |
|---|---|---|
| Country I | 90 | 100 |
| Country II | 130 | 110 |

[90/130]*100 = 69% of the effort required by country II to produce the same quantity of that good, whilst for country I to produce a unit of good Y requires: [100/110]*100 = 91% of the effort of country II to produce the same amount of good Y. With the relative production costs displayed in Table 1.4, country II possesses an absolute disadvantage in both production activities. Although it requires [130/90]*100 = 144.4% of the effort required by country I to make a unit of X, country II only requires [110/100]*100 = 110% of the effort of country I to produce a unit of Y. Relatively speaking, country II has an absolute disadvantage in both lines of production, the disadvantage (cost penalty) is larger in good X than Y. Implicitly therefore, country II has a comparative advantage in the manufacture of good Y. The foregoing example depicts Ricardo's basic principle of comparative advantage: for example, once relative production cost ratios are compared for a single good in both countries (90:130), in good X and (100:110) in good Y, then as long as these two sets of ratios differ, one country will possess a comparative cost advantage in producing one of the two goods. Hence, when production cost ratios differ between countries, both may gain by free trade, notwithstanding the fact that one country might possess an absolute production cost advantage in producing all goods. In the example drawn in Table 1.4, Ricardo's comparative advantage principle predicts that the pattern of trade between countries I and II would be that country I specialises in producing good X and country II specialises in good Y. A pattern of trade on these lines minimises the opportunity costs of producing goods X and Y for both countries.

## 1.9  The gains from trade in a Ricardian world

Utilising the example given above, the gains from the specialisation of production in Ricardian terms may be deduced as follows. If country II requires 130 work hours to produce 1 unit of X whilst it takes only 110 work hours to produce a unit of Y, then the opportunity cost of a single unit of good X in country II prior to trade is: 130/110 = 1.20 units of Y. Whereas, if country I uses 90 work hours to produce a unit of good X and 100 work hours to make a unit of Y, then in country I, the manufacture of good Y will occur at a relatively larger opportunity cost per unit than good X. Hence, in country I good Y will cost 100/90 = 1.10 units of good X, or, a unit of good X in country I costs 90/100 = 0.90 units of good Y. Now should countries I and II establish trading links? If country II can get a unit of good X from country I for less than 1.20 units of Y, it can gain from such a trade. If country I can obtain more than 0.90 units of Y for exchanging one unit of good X, it too can gain from such a trade. Imagine further that countries I and II are both 'small' and cannot influence the world terms of trade between goods X and Y by unilateral or joint actions; then if the world terms of trade (WTOT) are between 1 unit of good X for 1.20 units of Y, and 0.90 units of good Y for 1 unit of good X, both countries gain from free trade. Assume that the WTOT are such that a unit of good X exchanges for a unit of Y, country II gains by exporting good Y and importing X, since under autarky country II would forfeit 130 work hours for every unit of good X produced. By trade, country II can instead expend 110 work hours' effort to produce a unit of good Y in exchange for a unit of good X. With autarky, the same production attainment of good X requires an additional 20 hours' labour effort. However, this additional 20 work hours can be usefully employed producing more units of good Y, or taken as leisure. Employing identical logic to country I with the same WTOT, there are clear gains from trading with country II.

Hence, the simple model outlined above demonstrates that free trade offers opportunities of specialisation in activities where comparative advantages are possessed such that a greater global supply of all goods is available. This raises world welfare. In our example, specialisation on the grounds of comparative advantage leads to greater outputs of goods X and Y, and hence larger real incomes in countries I and II.

## 1.10  An evaluation of the Ricardian theory of trade

It is evident, therefore, that the theorem of comparative (cost) advantage may be construed in two senses: either as a positive/predictive statement in the determinants of trade patterns between nations, or as a normative welfare precept of the gains attainable with free trade policies. The normative interpretation was clearly a dominant philosophy of the English liberal school of economics from Ricardo to Alfred Marshall. Neo-classicals, 'new'-classicals and the Austrian School of Economists would uphold the normative case of the gains available from free trade even today, though obviously on more polished bases (Ohlin, 1933).

However, the Ricardian positive theory of the determination of trade patterns is an over-simplified explanation of the basis of international trade patterns.

Ricardo based his theory of trade on the following assumptions:

a. two countries and two goods;

b. the labour theory of value – which implies that labour is the sole factor of production and/or the labour is utilised in constant fixed proportions in the production of all goods and that all labour inputs are homogeneous;

c. perfect competition existed in all markets in both countries;

d. labour inputs are perfectly mobile within a country but completely immobile across national boundaries;

e. no changes in technology or innovations occurred;

f. income distribution within a given country is not affected by trade;

g. constant returns to scale in the production of each good;

h. zero transportation costs and barter trade only.

Given these assumptions, Ricardo demonstrated that the pre-trade commodity price ratios in each country are then a function of the scale-free input/output ratios implied by the production function for each good. Hence, assumptions (b), (c), (e) and (g) imply constant production/opportunity costs. Assumptions (b) and (g) in each production activity ensure that neither the level of world demand, nor the quantity of available input supplies in either country makes any impact on the equilibrium pre-trade commodity price ratios for the closed economy. With an identical model/assumptions for 60 countries it follows that before trade, the commodity price ratios in each country and hence the pattern of trade are determined exclusively by international differences in production functions or input/output ratios.

So if $\psi_1$ and $\psi_2$ are the input/output ratios for country I and $\pi_1$ and $\pi_2$ are those for country II in production activities 1 and 2 respectively, then country I will export good 1 and import good 2; if $\psi_1/\psi_2 > \pi_1/\pi_2$, good 1 will be cheaper and good 2 will be more expensive in country I than in country II prior to trade. This factor/output condition may be written as:

$$\pi_1/\psi_1 > \pi_2/\psi_2$$

This equation puts the Ricardian theorem in terms of comparative input/output ratios. The Ricardian model can be generalised for an m-country, N-commodity case. Moreover, empirical tests of this version of the theory have been undertaken (Samuelson, 1948). But the major theoretical weaknesses of Ricardo's theory of trade pattern determination are:

a. the drastic utilisation of the labour theory of value;
b. the neglect of demand conditions completely, with a consequent exclusive focus on supply-side factors;
c. the absence of an explanation in the Ricardian theory as to why differences in production functions/factor:output ratios occur;
d. that the production possibility curves implied by Ricardian theory require constant opportunity costs of production.

Issue (d) above represents a serious weakness because it clearly does not square with the realities of international trade and production patterns. As will be shown, the constant nature of opportunity costs implied by the Ricardian model leads to the proposition that countries I and II in the previous example would maximise gains by each specialising completely in its comparative advantaged activity. Real-world trade patterns rarely feature total specialisation in production. Arguments such as these led later theorists to substitute the assumption of increasing opportunity costs for the Ricardian assumption regarding the constancy of opportunity costs. Rising opportunity costs imply that as one industry expands output at the expense of others, increasing quantities of other goods must be yielded to attain an incremental unit of the expanding output.

## 1.11 The Ricardian case of constant opportunity costs: linear transformation curves

A country's transformation curve shows all the alternative combinations of two goods that a nation can produce by full employment of its factors of production, with 'state of the art' technology. The gradient of the transformation curve refers to the marginal rate of transformation (MRT), or the marginal opportunity cost of producing an extra unit of one good at the expense of the other. Or, simply how much of the second good must be forgone to obtain an additional unit of the first good. In the Ricardian case the country faces constant opportunity cost or (MRT). Hence, the transformation curve for such a country is a straight line, the absolute slope of which equals the constant (MRT), and the relative commodity price ratios.

We can use Table 1.5 to illustrate these basic points. The data in the table relate to the maximum amount of goods A and B that countries I and II can produce, when all inputs are fully utilised with optimum technology available.

So with constant opportunity costs of producing A and B in both countries, the transformation curves for both countries are shown in Figure 1.1.

Table 1.5 Relative production possibilities: for two goods and two countries.

| | Country I | Country II |
|---|---|---|
| Units of A per period of time | 6 | 16 |
| Units of B per period of time | 12 | 8 |

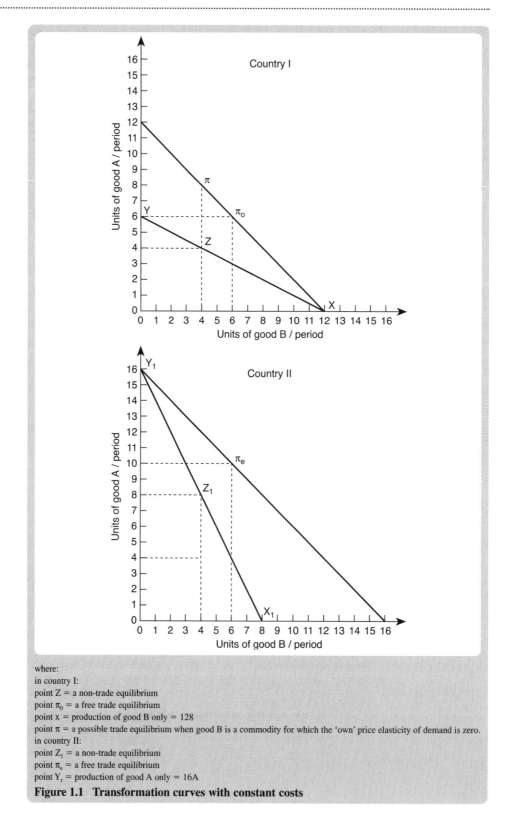

where:
in country I:
point Z = a non-trade equilibrium
point $\pi_0$ = a free trade equilibrium
point x = production of good B only = 128
point $\pi$ = a possible trade equilibrium when good B is a commodity for which the 'own' price elasticity of demand is zero.
in country II:
point $Z_1$ = a non-trade equilibrium
point $\pi_e$ = a free trade equilibrium
point $Y_r$ = production of good A only = 16A

**Figure 1.1  Transformation curves with constant costs**

Notice that any point on the transformation curves (YX for country I) and ($Y_1 X_1$ for country II) represents a unique production mix of goods A and B in each country. So point Z represents a production combination of 4A and 4B in country I. Whereas point $Z_1$ depicts a production mix of 8A and 4B in country II. The negative inclination of both transformation curves in both countries shows that the output of one in industry can only be expanded at the cost of contracting the other. The absolute slope of the transformation for country I in Figure 1.1 is: $6/12 = 1/2 = MRT_{B:A} = P_B/P_A$ which also stays constant. Notice that with constant costs the internal price equilibrium $P_B/P_A$ in each country is determined entirely by the nature of supply conditions in each country. This point was made above in the critique (point b) given of the Ricardian theory.

Geometrically, the Ricardian basis for trade and indeed the gains from free trade can be depicted on Figure 1.1. Under autarky, the transformation curves for countries I and II also represent each country's consumption frontier, meaning that the country can only consume a mix of commodities A and B that it can produce. If free trade is now permitted between countries I and II, each country specialises in the production of the good wherein lies its comparative advantage. Each country may then exchange part of its comparatively advantaged product for a portion of its comparatively disadvantaged product, and wind up consuming more of both goods A and B than without trade.

Imagine therefore, that in the absence of trade, country I consumes and produces at point Z in Figure 1.1, while country II is similarly engaged at point $Z_1$. These points (Z and $Z_1$) are determined by the demand condition (tastes) in each country. In the absence of trade, $MRT_{B:A} = P_B/P_A = 1/2$ (the slope of YX) in country I, while $MRT_{B:A} = P_B/P_A = 2$ in country II (i.e. the slope of $Y_1 X_1$). It is evident from these production cost ratios (price ratios) that country I has a comparative advantage in producing good B and country II has a comparative advantage in good A. Hence, mutually advantageous trade is possible within the parameters of: $1/2 < P_B/P_A < 2$. If the barter terms of trade between countries I and II are in equilibrium such that $P_B/P_A = 1$, country I can move from point Z to point X in production, exchange 6 units of its 12B (at point X) for 6 units of A. From country II, country I may then wind up consuming at point $\pi_0$ in Figure 1.1. This consumption point represents a gain of 2A and 2B over its non-trade equilibrium at Z. Country II, however, moves from point $Z_1$ to a production point $Y_1$; it can then exchange c units of good B from country I and ends up consuming at point $\pi_e$ in Figure 1.1. For country II, point $\pi_e$ represents a gain of 2A and 2B compared to its non-trading equilibrium at point $Z_1$. This example illustrates just one trading possibility with mutually beneficial gains from trade, when both countries specialise completely in the good(s) for which they possess a comparative advantage.

Before moving to consider the Heckscher-Ohlin-Samuelson theory of trade, it will be helpful for later discussion if the basis for and hence the gains from international trade under increasing opportunity costs is now considered. Generally, when transformation curves are either (a) straight lines or (b) concave to the origin mutually beneficial trade is possible when there is a disparity in the prior to trade relative commodity price ratios. When two countries' transformation curves are concave to the origin, however, as each country specialises in the production of the good for which it possesses a comparative advantage, it incurs larger and larger opportunity costs or MRT. Specialisation can continue until the increasing MRT in each country equates relative costs with the relative commodity price ratio at which international trade occurs. Through trade, each country can then finish up consuming outside and beyond its non-trade consumption and production boundary. It will become evident that in the case of increasing opportunity costs the equilibrium commodity price ratio in each country is determined by both supply and demand conditions in that country. Imagine that under autarky the relative price ratios $P_A/P_B$ in country I = 1/4, and 4 in country II, such that country I produces and consumes at point X, while country II produces and consumes at point $X_1$, in Figure 1.2. Now without trade the $P_A/P_B$ ratio is lower in country I than II, country I possesses a comparative advantage in producing good A, and country II has a comparative advantage in producing good B. Beneficial trade and exchange is feasible within the boundaries of: $\frac{1}{4} < P_A/P_B < 4$. If the net barter terms of trade between countries I and II equilibriate at 1A = 1B, or 1, country I can move from point X to point Z in production, and trade 6 units of its 12A (produced at Z) for 6 units of B from country II. Country I finishes consuming at point $\Psi$ with a gain A and B over point X. Country II conversely travels from point $X_1$ to $Z_1$ in production, and, via exchange, trades 6B to obtain 6A from country I. Country II can therefore attain $\Psi_1$ outside its production frontier. Point $\Psi_1$ represents a gain of A and B compared to non-trade point $X_1$. Inspection of Figure 1.1 shows that as country I specialises in good A it incurs increasing opportunity costs in production of good A. So the $MRT_{A:B}$ increases. Conversely, as country II specialises in producing good

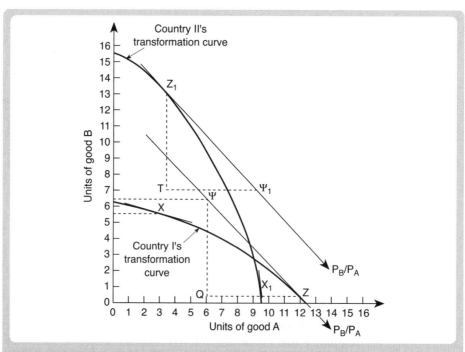

Note: country II exports $Z_1T$ of good B to import $T\psi_1$ of good A from country I. Country I exports ZQ of good A to import $Q\psi$ of good B from country II. The geometry illustrates that free trade is better than no trade for both countries.

where:

vectors PB/PA = the post-trade price ratios or terms of trade

For country I:

X = a non-trade point

Z = a production specialisation point with trade

$\psi$ = consumption point with trade; $\psi$ involves more units of A and B compared to point X.

For country II:

$X_1$ = a non-trade point

$Z_1$ = a production specialisation point with trade

$\psi_1$ = a consumption point with trade

**Figure 1.2   Trade with increasing opportunity costs**

B, hence the $MRT_{B:A}$ is higher. Or, the marginal costs of production of B are increasing as output expands from point $X_1$ in Figure 1.2. Specialisation in production will continue in each country until its $MRT_{B:A} = P_B/P_A = 1$. Moreover, notice from Figure 1.2 that neither country I nor country II specialises entirely in the production of a single good, in contrast to the constant cost (Ricardian) case. In trade equilibrium, both countries continue to produce both goods. Finally, as the geometric relation in Figure 1.2 indicates, balanced trade between countries I and II occurs at the terms of trade given by the $P_B/P_A$ vectors: country I's exports equal country II's imports and vice versa.

## Summary

- The Ricardian model shows how differences between countries give rise to trade and gains from trade. In this model labour is the only factor of production and countries differ only in the productivity of labour in different activities.

- In the Ricardian model, a country's production pattern is determined by comparative advantage and labour productivity differences.

- That trade creates benefits can be shown in two ways. First, we can think of trade as an indirect method of production. Instead of producing a good for itself, a country can produce another good and trade. Second, we show that trade enlarges a country's consumption possibilities, implying gains from trade.

- The gains from trade depend on the relative prices. To determine these relative prices it is necessary to look at the relative world supply and demand prices.

- Generalising the one-factor, two-products model to a world of many products does not alter the conclusion.

- If some of the predictions of the Ricardian model are unrealistic, the basic prediction – that countries tend to export goods in which they have relatively high productivity – has been confirmed by empirical work.

## Questions

1. What is the difference between linear and non-linear transformation curves? Does comparative advantage depend on the shape of the curves?
2. Why might relative labour productivities differ between nations?
3. What determines the distribution of gains from trade and specialisation?
4. What are main weaknesses in the Ricardian Model of trade?

## Key concepts

| | |
|---|---|
| comparative advantage | production possibility frontier |
| absolute advantage | relative wages |
| derived demand | gains from trade |
| general equilibrium analysis | Ricardian model |
| non-traded goods | opportunity cost |
| unit labour requirement | partial equilibrium analysis |
| transformation curves | |

## Bibliography

Barry, F., Bradley, J., Hannan, A., McCartan, J. and Sosvilla-Rivera, S. (1997) *Single Market Review 1996: Aggregate and Regional Aspects: the cases of Greece, Ireland, Portugal and Spain*, London: Kogan Page, in association with the Office for Official Publications of the European Communities, Luxembourg.

Deardorff, A. (1984) 'Testing trade theories', in R. Jones and P. Kenen (eds), *Handbook of International Economics*, vol. 1, Amsterdam: Elsevier, pp. 480–5.

Heckscher, E. (1949) 'The effect of foreign trade on the distribution of income', in *Readings in the theory of international trade*, H. S. Ellis and L. A. Metzler (eds), for the American Economic Association (Philadelphia: Blackston).

Leontief, W. (1953) 'Domestic production and foreign trade; the American capital position re-examined', *Proceedings of the American Philosophical Society*, vol. 97.

Leontief, W. (1956) 'Factor proportions and the structure of American trade: further theoretical and empirical analysis', *Review of Economics and Statistics*, vol. 38.

Lipsey, R. and Stevens, G. (1992) 'Interactions between domestic and foreign investment', *Journal of International Money and Finance*, vol. 11, no. 1, 40–62.

Mansfield, E. (1961) 'Technical change and the rate of innovation', *Econometrica*, vol. 29, pp. 741–66.

Ohlin, B. (1933) 'Interregional and international trade', *Harvard Economic Studies*, vol. 39, Cambridge, Mass: Harvard University Press.

Ricardo, D. (1817) 'Principles of political economy and taxation', reprinted as Vol. of Sraffa, P. (ed.) (1951) *The works and correspondence of David Ricardo*, London: Cambridge University Press.

Rybczynski, T. M. (1955) 'Faster endowments and relative commodity prices', *Economica*, p. 336.

Samuelson, P. A. (1948) 'International trade and the equalisation of factor prices', *Economic Journal*, vol. 58.

Smith, A. (1776) *The Wealth of Nations*, London.

Vernon, R. (1966) 'International investment and international trade in the product cycle', *Quarterly Journal of Economics*, vol. 80, pp. 190–207.

# 2 Comparative advantage and factor endowments

**K. LAWLER and H. SEDDIGHI**

## 2.1 The modern theory of trade: Heckscher-Ohlin-Samuelson theorem(s)

The Heckscher-Ohlin-Samuelson (H-O-S) theory of trade contrasts markedly with the Ricardian explanation of comparative advantage. It has been shown that the basis for international trade exists in a difference of pro-trade relative goods price ratios, between countries I and II. The H-O-S theory focuses on the disparities in relative factor endowments (and consequent factor/input prices) between countries as the single most significant cause of trade. The H-O-S theorem predicts that each country will export the commodity whose production is intensive in the use of that country's abundant factor(s) of production, and will import good(s) that are intensive in the use of that country's scarce factor(s) of production. The general reasoning behind the theorem is as follows. Different countries have different factor endowments; hence countries will possess comparative advantages in making those goods that utilise their relatively abundant factor/inputs more intensively; for this reason, each country will export the goods that are intensive in the use of their abundant factor inputs, and import those commodities that use scarce factor inputs more intensively. Moreover, the H-O-S theory predicts that free trade will completely eliminate (strong thesis) or reduce (weak thesis) differences in factor input prices between trading countries (Caves, 1976). Factor endowment differences between countries imply relative differences in income distribution. Therefore, trade and income distributions are linked uniquely.

## 2.2 The Heckscher-Ohlin-Samuelson theorem: in a $2 \times 2 \times 2$ general equilibrium system

To reiterate the H-O-S theorem predicts that a country's exports (imports) intensively use the country's abundant (scarce) factors of production. This theorem seems highly plausible. For it is reasonable to expect that a country should be able to produce more cheaply those goods that intensively use an input which is abundant in a physical sense, relative to the position in this respect confronting its trading partner.

However, the logical consistency of the H-O-S theorem depends upon various postulates; these latter vary with regard to the definition of relative factor abundance used. Indeed, there are two viable definitions of factor abundance. These are the so-called 'price' and 'physical' definitions. Given the physical definition, country I is rich in input $X_j$ and country II in input $X_i$, when:

$$(X_j/X_i)^{II} < (X_j/X_i)^{I}$$

where $X_i$ and $X_j$ refer to the physical quantities of factor inputs $X_i$ and $X_j$ and the roman numerals refer to countries I and II, whereas, under the price definition of relative factor abundance, countries I and II are similarly described if:

$$(\Psi X_j / \Psi X_i)^{II} < (\Psi X_j / \Psi X_i)^{I}$$

where $\Psi X_j$ and $\Psi X_i$ refer to the returns to factors $X_j$ and $X_i$ in countries I and II.

Given the physical definition, the truth of the H-O-S theorem is grounded, in a $2 \times 2 \times 2$ system, on the following assumptions:

a. perfect competition in all markets in both countries;
b. zero transportation costs;
c. identical production functions between countries for each good produced, hence all goods are produced with the same technologies in each country;
d. non-reversibility of factor intensities, such that a given good is input 'Z'-intensive at all feasible input price ratios;
e. constant returns to scale in production in the long run, but diminishing returns to the variable input in the short run, for tradable goods produced in both countries;
f. similar (tastes)/demand patterns between countries at any feasible commodity price-ratio.

So with perfect competition in all markets (assumption (a), the presence of constant returns to scale in all production activities (assumption (e)) and profit-maximising economic behaviour is sufficient to generate a convex transformation curve in each country. Consequently a $2 \times 2 \times 2$ model, identical production functions for every production activity (assumptions (c)) and non-reversible factor intensities means that each country will have a different capital:labour input ratio in aggregate, whence the capital-rich country will produce a higher ratio of capital-intensive to labour-intensive outputs at every feasible commodity price ratio. Hence given similar demand patterns in each country (assumption (f)), it follows that the pre-trade commodity price ratios will be such that the capital-intensive good will be cheaper in the capital-rich economy, thus the H-O-S theorem is logically consistent. However, given the price definition of relative factor abundance, the logical truth of the H-O-S theorem can be demonstrated without inclusion of assumption (f). This is because once assumptions (a) to (f) are met, a unique relationship between factor price ratios and commodity price ratios exists, such that the labour (capital) rich economy will necessarily produce a cheaper labour (capital) intensive output(s) prior to trade than its potential trading partners. On the price definition of relative factor abundance, therefore, the H-O-S theorem may be deduced with fewer assumptions. Though the price definition has this advantage compared to the physical definition, it correspondingly narrows the field of vision of the H-O-S theory and weakens the breadth of theoretical explanation. The H-O-S theorem holds also for an N-commodity two-country trade model, since all commodities may still be ranked from input supply data in terms of relative input ratios and thence exclusively ranked also in terms of comparative advantage on the supply side: demand conditions are then interposed such that outputs may be classified into exportables and importables. Demand conditions between the two countries in the N-commodity model influence, therefore, the point at which the chain of ranking into exportables and importables is reached; but demand conditions do not affect the order of ranking in the N-commodity two-country H-O-S model. Thus in this case, as in the Ricardian model, supply-side/production conditions determine the goods in which a country will have a comparative advantage.

The H-O-S hypothesis is not so easily extended to include a multi-country, N-commodity trading system. This difficulty has caused problems for researchers wishing to test the H-O-S prediction, since the international economy constitutes an N-commodity, multi-country system. The reasons for this difficulty are as follows: the sufficient conditions for the logical consistency of the H-O-S theorem in the N-commodity, 'many'-country context become blurred on critical issues regarding the appropriate comparison of relative factor endowments (Stern, 1975). In brief, the H-O-S theory is hazy on the issue as to whether the appropriate comparison of factor endowments is between: (a) country I and every other country on the globe; (b) country I and every other nation trading with it; (c) country I and each country directly trading with it on a strict bilateral basis, such that the H-O-S theorem might hold for each pair of trading nations. These alternative dimensions of factor endowment comparison have represented, therefore, serious problems for empiricists wishing to test the H-O-S theorem(s) in realistic trading systems. In a multi-country, N-commodity, trading framework the specific conditions necessary and sufficient to derive the H-O-S result differ significantly from those sufficient to obtain the H-O-S result in the simple $2 \times 2 \times 2$ context. However, the logical problems encountered by an extension of H-O-S propositions for an N-commodity, multi-country case approach an impasse. For example, if country I is input $(X_j)$-abundant relative to a potential trading partner country II, yet country I is input $(X_i)$ rich relative to some third potential trading partner country II; then if the H-O-S theorem holds for each pair of bilateral traders (countries I with II, and II with III), an Arrow-type impossibility case, or logical inconsistency, may be attained. Hence, as the importables and exportables of country I are ranked in terms of $(X_j:X_i)$ ratios such that all country I's exportables are $X_j$-intensive relative to all its importables, a potential logical impasse arises. But on general production assumptions, the exportable and importable commodities may inevitably switch and re-switch, breaking the links in the strictly ordered chains of potentially tradable goods, upon which the theorem(s) depend in the traditional $2 \times 2 \times 2$ model. However, if stringent assumptions are applied (e.g. assumptions (a), (d) and (e) above) and maintained, then the switching and re-switching between exportables/importables may be suppressed. To the extent that a bilateral interpretation of the (H-O-S) hypotheses is valid, empirical work has been undertaken many times since W. Leontief's famous studies. Generally, Leontief and other contributors have been meticulous in the assignment of input intensities, but typically the crucial issue as to the relative factor abundance of the country concerned has not been meaningfully quantified. Moreover, Leontief-type empirical investigations of H-O-S propositions have implicitly favoured the bilateral interpretation of relative factor abundance, yet frequently without a shred of theoretical justification. Analysis of some leading empirical studies of the H-O-S theory will be considered later. The discussion now moves to examine proofs of the H-O-S theorem in the traditional two-country, two-factor, two-commodity context.

## 2.3   Some geometric interpretations of H-O-S propositions

Now, the analysis is conducted on the basis of relative factor abundance defined in physical terms. To repeat: the H-O-S prediction maintains that disparities in relative factor endowments impart a supply-side bias such that a capital-rich economy's exports intensively use capital as a productive input, whereas a labour-rich economy's exports intensively use labour as a productive input. The nature of the bias created by differences in factor endowments is perceived in the relationship between the transformation curves of the two countries I and II. If these two countries had the same relative factor proportions, the constant returns to scale condition (assumption (e)) would be enough to ensure that the transformation curves of countries I and II were either exact reflections or radial expansions of each other. Disparities in relative factor endowments are reflected by transformation curves differing in shape. Imagine that country I is relatively capital rich. The transformation curve for country I must therefore be flatter than that of country II along any ray from the origin, if good X is a capital-intensive good in production and good Y is relatively labour intensive in production, as may be seen by inspection of Figure 2.1. Hence if both countries produce both goods (X and Y) in the same proportions, then relatively capital-rich country I will be able to increase its output of the capital-intensive good (X, in Figure 2.1) at a lower opportunity cost than country II, and vice versa for good Y in labour-rich country II. In this elemental sense, given similar demand conditions in both countries, the capital-abundant country I (labour-abundant country II) has a production bias in favour of its capital-intensive commodity X (labour-intensive good Y). However, trade patterns along the lines of the H-O-S prediction do not necessarily follow if sufficiently diverse demand conditions exist in either or both countries. Thus in the physical definition of relative factor abundance the assumption of similar tastes (assumption (f)) is required to deduce the H-O-S theorem.

We are now able to sketch a proof of the H-O-S theorem given assumptions (a) to (f) above; in Figure 2.1 the transformation curves of the two countries are drawn. Country I is relatively capital rich and good X is assumed to be the capital-intensive good in both countries: if both countries now produce good X and Y in the same proportion along vector $0\pi$, the slopes of the two transformation curves differ such that at $\Psi_1$ and $\Psi_2$ country I can expand its production of good X (the capital-intensive good) at a lower

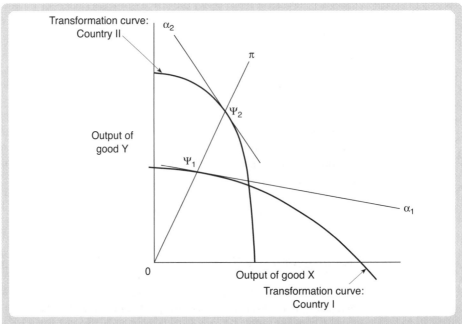

where $0\pi_i$ is a vector showing that prior to trade: both countries I and II produce both goods in the same proportion. Hence at pre-trade points $\psi_1$ and $\psi_2$, there is a basis for trade along the lines predicted by H-O-S.

**Figure 2.1  A simple proof of H-O-S: given the physical definition of relative factor abundance**

opportunity cost than country II, since the tangent $\alpha_1$ is flatter than tangent $\alpha_2$. Remember that the gradient of the transformation curve for any country at any point shows the Pareto-efficient production condition: such that tangents $\alpha_1$ and $\alpha_2$ depict the ratios of marginal costs of producing good Y relative to good X in both countries. The perfect competition condition guarantees that the ratio of marginal costs in both countries equals the pre-trade commodity price ratios; hence at $\alpha_1$: $P_x/P_y = MRT_D$ = marginal rate of substitution in consumption; and at $\alpha_2$: $P_x/P_y = MRT_D$ = marginal rate of substitution in consumption (MRS) in both domestic economies prior to trade.

Given trade on the basis of the H-O-S theorem, country I would move in a clockwise rotation along its transformation curve producing more of good X, and country II would move in a counter-clockwise rotation along its transformation curve producing more of labour-intensive good Y. Mutually advantageous trade then occurs and eventually the post-trade equilibrium can yield:

$$MRT_D = MRT_F = MRS \ldots \text{ for both countries}$$

where: $MRT_D$ is the slope of the transformation curve for both countries; $MRT_F$ is the world price ratio (terms of trade) $P_x/P_y$; and MRS is the ratio of substitution in consumption in both countries. Thus free trade produces a first best Pareto-optimality situation as previously suggested in Figure 1.2.

## 2.4 A more rigorous proof of the H-O-S theorem in a $2 \times 2 \times 2$ system

Given:

1. Assumptions (a) to (f).
2. Each country has fixed factor endowments.
3. Static technologies in both countries in both industries apply.
4. Any pair of countries may be represented by a pair of Edgeworth-Bowley Box diagrams drawn on equal scales with corresponding sides parallel.
5. Figure 2.2 shows such a pair of Edgeworth-Bowley Box configurations whence: XYZW and $X_1Y_1Z_1W_1$ correspond to the fixed inelastic amounts of basic inputs capital and labour in countries I and II respectively.

The pair of rectangles XYZW and $X_1Y_1Z_1W_1$ are depicted such that X and $X_1$ show the origins for the X isoquants, Y and $Y_1$ similarly representing the origins for Y isoquants. XZ, $X_1Z_1$ depict the endowments of capital in countries I and II, with XW and $X_1W_1$ the fixed endowments of capital respectively. In Figure 2.2 $XW > X_1W_1$; $XZ < X_1Z_1$; such that country I has relatively more labour and less capital than country II. Let $\Psi$ be a Pareto-efficient point on the contract curve of country I. In Box $X_1Y_1Z_1W_1$ draw vector $X_1\pi_1$ such that it is parallel to $X\Psi$ in XYZW. So $WX\Psi = W_1X_1\pi_1$. Now draw vector $Y_1\pi_2$ so that it is parallel to $Y\Psi$ in box XYZW. $X_1\pi_1$ and $Y_1\pi_2$ intercept each other at $\Psi_1$. The so-called theorem of 'corresponding points' now follows such that $\Psi$ and $\Psi_1$ form a 'pair' of such post-trade points (Lancaster, 1957). Because:

a. If $\Psi$ is Pareto efficient for country I, then $\Psi_1$ is Pareto efficient for country II.
b. The marginal productivities of labour and capital, in both industries x and y, are equal at $\Psi$ and $\Psi_1$.
c. The post-trade commodity price ratio at $\Psi$ equals that at $\Psi_1$.

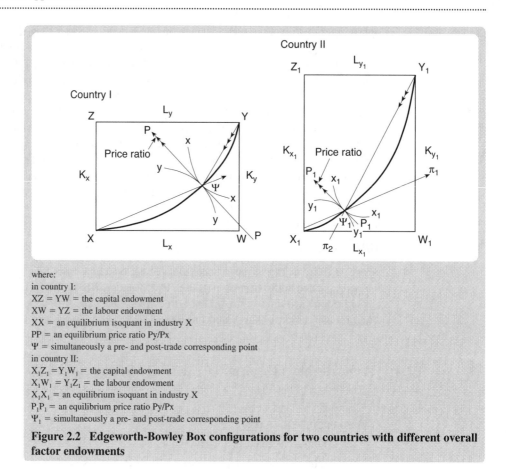

where:
in country I:
XZ = YW = the capital endowment
XW = YZ = the labour endowment
XX = an equilibrium isoquant in industry X
PP = an equilibrium price ratio Py/Px
$\Psi$ = simultaneously a pre- and post-trade corresponding point
in country II:
$X_1Z_1 = Y_1W_1$ = the capital endowment
$X_1W_1 = Y_1Z_1$ = the labour endowment
$X_1X_1$ = an equilibrium isoquant in industry X
$P_1P_1$ = an equilibrium price ratio Py/Px
$\Psi_1$ = simultaneously a pre- and post-trade corresponding point

**Figure 2.2  Edgeworth-Bowley Box configurations for two countries with different overall factor endowments**

d. The proportions in which the two goods X and Y are produced at $\Psi$ and $\Psi_1$ differ, to the extent that in each country a relatively greater amount of the good which is most intensive in its abundant factor is produced, with both inputs fully employed.

This theorem concisely restates the basic H-O-S prediction. Free trade equilibria in both countries will occur at the corresponding points $\Psi$ and $\Psi_1$ because this 'pair' of points satisfies internal general equilibria from condition (a), with a common price ratio/terms of trade in each country by condition (c). Exchange and trade will occur since both countries have similar tastes but produce goods X and Y in different proportions for any given price ratio via conditions (c) and (d). Moreover, at any pair of 'corresponding points' trade equilibria exist and input prices are equalised in both countries. Consequently, by condition (d) each country will export the commodity which is intensive in its abundant factor. In Figure 2.2, country I will export good X which is the relatively labour-intensive activity in both countries and country I is relatively labour rich compared to country II. Conversely, country II will export good Y which is a capital-intensive activity, and country II is relatively capital rich relative to country I. The formulation given here holds true for any pair of countries which satisfy the postulates of the model, but is also equally true for any number of countries which satisfy the conditions given above: producing two goods, using two inputs, labour and capital.

In Figure 2.2, due to the assumption of constant returns to scale (in production of both goods X and Y) in both countries, $X\Psi$ and $X_1\Psi_1$ intercept all X isoquants at an equal angle: hence the marginal product of labour in activity X ($MPL_x$) relative to the marginal product of capital in activity ($MPK_x$) is constant on both vectors. Given constant returns to scale, if the input ratio L/K is constant, output is proportional to the amount of either factor input unitised. Across $X\Psi$ the input ratio is constant. Therefore, the output of industry X along the vector $X\Psi$ is proportional to the distance $X\Psi$. Moreover, along $X\Psi$ the absolute values of marginal productivities of inputs labour and capital are constant given constant returns to scale in all activities. Hence: with production functions homogeneous of degree 1, Euler's theorem is valid, which yields:

$X = [(L_x)(MPL_x)] + [(K_x)(MPK_x)]$
where: $X$ = output of good x
$L_x$ = labour input in x
$K_x$ = capital input in x
hence: $X/L = MPL_x \{1 + (K_x/L_x)(MPK_x/MPL_x)\}$

which underpins point (b) of the theorem of 'corresponding points' and provides a strong clue to point (c). Given that the output:input ratio is constant for either input along $X\Psi$, it follows necessarily that $MPL_x$ and $MPK_x$ are constant on $X\Psi$. These conditions hold for Y isoquants too in both countries. Moreover, since points along the contract lines represent Pareto-optimal points given perfect competition in all activities, payments to labour and capital are the same in both industries. Thus, points (a), (b) and (c) of the theorem follow since:

$[(P_x)(MPL_x)] = [(P_y)(MPL_y)]$
$[(P_x)(MPK_x)] = [(P_y)(MPK_y)]$
which yields $P_x/P_y = MPL_y/MPL_x = MPK_y/MPK_x$;

which is an exchange and production optimality condition.

This condition exists pre- and post-trade in each country. With identical production functions and trade between countries I and II, all the properties of the X isoquants in country I apply equally to $X_1$ isoquants in country II, since $X\Psi$ is parallel to $X_1\Psi_1$. Since production functions are identical in each industry in each country, the same applies to all Y isoquants in country I and $Y_1$ isoquants in country II. The marginal productivities of both inputs are, in production of X, the same on $X\Psi$ and on $X_1\Psi_1$. Similarly, the marginal productivities of both inputs along $Y\Psi$ and $Y_1\Psi_1$ in production of Y are identical too. So the marginal productivities of both inputs in both activities are equalised at $\Psi$ and $\Psi_1$ since both lie respectively on $X\Psi$, $Y\Psi$ and $X_1\Psi_1$, $Y_1\Psi_1$.

Finally, production of good X in country I is proportional to $X\Psi$, and production of X in country II is proportional to distance $X_1\Psi_1$. Since $X\Psi$ and $X_1\Psi_1$ are uniformly comparable, it follows that production of X is larger in country I than in country II. Similarly, by inspection it may be seen that output of Y is less in country I than II, by comparing $X\Psi$ and $X_1\Psi_1$; earlier the model was developed with good X as the relatively labour-intensive commodity. Since country I is the labour-rich country, and country II is capital rich, the H-O-S theorem is proved. Each country's exports intensively use the country's relatively abundant factor input. The cause of trade, therefore, between countries I and II, with identical technologies, equal productive efficiencies in all activities, perfect competition in all markets and similar tastes, exists in differences in factor endowments shown by the differing dimensions of the Edgeworth-Bowley Box configurations in Figure 2.2. This disparity in factor endowments yields a sufficient condition for differences in comparative advantage and an elemental explanation of the pattern of trade. The reasoning above, moreover, underpins points (d) of the theorem of 'corresponding points' and provides invaluable insights to other corollaries of the H-O-S theorem. The theorem of 'corresponding points' yields the Pareto-optimality condition given above; specifically that $P_x/P_y = MPL_x = MPK_y/MPK_x$, this condition produces the price determination equilibrium for country I and country II as closed economies, but also exists with free trade between both countries.

Because the theorem of 'corresponding points' is a general equilibrium condition, instantaneous movement from no trade to free trade between countries I and II is presupposed. The geometry of Figure 2.2, though concise, hides the instantaneous reactions/movements to some extent. The very act of drawing vectors $X\Psi$ and $X_1\Psi_1$ subsumes a frictionless movement of inputs and outputs in both countries and in both industries towards free-trade general equilibrium. In its free-trade guise, the general equilibrium price condition above may be written as: $MRT_D = MRT_F = MRS$ as before. The price condition pre- and post-trade (with instantaneous frictionless reactions) may be derived as follows: For country I, with two inputs labour (L) and capital (K) with two outputs X and Y, to attain Pareto internal equilibrium requires:

$$dX = \partial X/\partial L_x \, (dL_x) + \partial X/\partial K_x \, (dK_x) \qquad \text{... industry X}$$

$$dY = \partial Y/\partial L_y \, (dL_y) + \partial Y/\partial K_y \, (dK_y) \qquad \text{... industry Y}$$

The Pareto efficiency locus requires:

$$\partial X/\partial L_x \div \partial X/\partial K_x = \partial L_y \, (dL_y) \div \partial Y/\partial K_y = \pi \qquad \text{... production optimality}$$

Given inelastic factor input supplies, or with both inputs fixed in aggregate supply:

$$dL_y = -dL_x$$
$$dK_y = -dK_x$$

So: $dX = \partial X/\partial L_x \, (dL_x + \pi dK_x)$
$\quad\quad dY = -\partial Y/\partial L_y \, (dL_{yx} + \pi dK_x)$

Hence the price ratio is $dX/dY = (-\partial X/\partial L_x) \div (\partial Y/\partial L_y) = -P_y/P_x$ ... for a consumption optimality.

*Mutatis mutandis*, the foregoing holds for country II, where also the marginal rates of substitution in consumption and production are equalised to the unique ratio of prices, given frictionless reactions of economic agents.

The final vital condition of the 'theorem of corresponding points', which also clinches the strong H-O-S prediction, may be readily revealed geometrically to underscore the 'proof' deduced above. In Figure 2.3, the configurations are rotated such that points W and $W_1$ now coincide. $X_1W_1$ now coincides with XW and $Y_1W_1$ with YW. The effect of such a transformation is shown in Figure 2.3.

Since $XW > X_1W_1$ and $XZ < X_1Z_1$, then in the transformation in Figure 2.3 ($W_1$ mapped to W) X is to the left of $X_1$, so $X\psi$ lies above $X_1\psi_1$ as in Figure 2.3. From previous analysis, the output of industry X at point $\psi$ in country I is directly proportional to distance $X\psi$ and output of $X_1$ in country II is directly proportional to $X_1\psi_1$. From Figure 2.3, since $X\psi$ and $X_1\psi_1$ are directly measurable, it follows that the output of X is larger in country I than in II. Conversely from Figure 2.3, output of Y in country I is less than $Y_1$ in country II, since $Y_1\psi_1 > Y\psi$. Thus it necessarily follows that output of X in country I relative to the output of $Y_1$ is larger in country I than in country II. Hence the labour-rich economy has larger output of labour-intensive good X than country II, yet a relatively

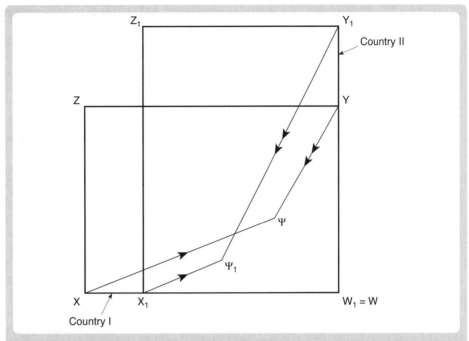

**Figure 2.3 A comparison of outputs for countries I and II: a geometric proof of the H-O-S theorem, using corresponding points analysis**

smaller aggregate output of capital-intensive good Y relative to capital-rich country II. This proves H-O-S via the notion of 'corresponding points' in general trade equilibrium. The proof may be generalised to include more than two countries, but with two inputs and two outputs. Such a 'proof' is complex diagrammatically but nonetheless covers cases where countries are of different sizes (Lancaster, 1957). Moreover, the theorem of 'corresponding points' of the type analysed represents a perfect 'equivalence' to a single country, whose input endowment of labour and capital equal the aggregate endowments of labour and capital in two separate countries. Hence: inter-regional trade patterns, within a given country, may be analysed using the same method.

## 2.5 Corollaries of the H-O-S theory of trade: the factor price equilibrium theorem (FPET)

Indirectly the theorem of 'corresponding points' implies that: given the conditions necessary for H-O-S to be true, then trade between two countries of differing factor endowments will ultimately lead to a complete equalisation of factor rewards in both countries, in both industries; providing that both countries trading on H-O-S lines continue to produce both traded goods. In other words, that post-trade for both countries remain incompletely specialised. The 'equivalence' condition noted above therefore implies factor price equalisation. Hence: at $\psi$ and $\psi_1$ in Figure 2.2, factor price equalisation occurs at these two corresponding points. Nonetheless a more detailed proof of factor price equalisation will be given now, since this exercise will assist and clarify later discussions.

## 2.6 Factor equalisation in a 2 × 2 × 2 general equilibrium system

To deduce FPET we require all the assumptions necessary and sufficient to prove H-O-S via the theorem of 'corresponding points'. In addition, the assumptions of (a) incomplete specialisation and (b) international factor immobility are required to deduce FPET. Factor mobility within each national boundary is retained, however; otherwise perfect competition in both industries in both countries could not necessarily exist. Perfect competition is required in both industries in both countries to guarantee the achievement of Paretian efficiency conditions in production and exchange in both industries prior to and post-trade (Samuelson, 1949).

Figure 2.4 shows two countries I and II with different relative overall factor endowments. The Edgeworth-Bowley Box diagrams XYZW and $X_1Y_1Z_1W_1$ depict relative capital and labour endowments, such that country I is labour rich relative to country II, country II being capital rich.

The factor endowments of labour and capital in both countries are different: since $XZ_1 > XZ$ and $XY_1 > XY$, $XZ_1$ and $XZ$ depict capital endowments, and $XY_1$ and $XY$ denote labour endowments in countries II and I respectively. It follows that, where K = capital endowments and L = labour endowments in I and II: $[K_{II}/L_{II} > K_I/L_I]$; exist such that, in physical terms, country II is capital abundant and country I labour rich. In Figure 2.4 outputs of good $[g_1]$ are measured from the south-western origin [0] and outputs of good $[g_2]$ are measured from the north-eastern origins $[0_2, 0_3]$. Since production functions are homogeneous of degree 1 and identical for each good $[g_1, g_2]$ in each

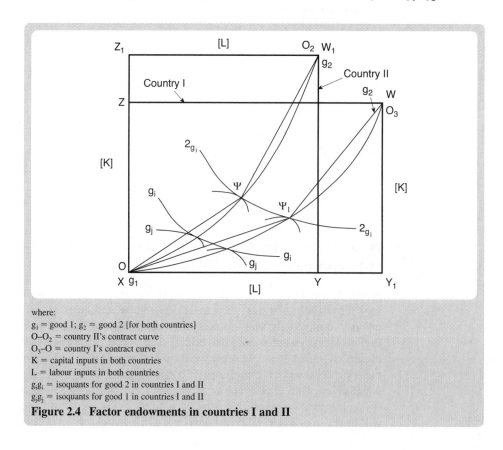

where:
$g_1$ = good 1; $g_2$ = good 2 [for both countries]
$O–O_2$ = country II's contract curve
$O_3–O$ = country I's contract curve
K = capital inputs in both countries
L = labour inputs in both countries
$g_ig_i$ = isoquants for good 2 in countries I and II
$g_jg_j$ = isoquants for good 1 in countries I and II

**Figure 2.4  Factor endowments in countries I and II**

country, the $[g_1]$ isoquants are identical in both countries, as are the $[g_2]$ isoquants, despite the fact that $[g_2]$ isoquants radiate outwards from different origins: $[O_2, O_3]$ respectively. Moreover, capital inputs are measured vertically $[XZ, XZ_1]$ and labour inputs horizontally $[XY, XY_1]$ in both countries. From the positions of the contract curves in both countries (both lie to the left of diagonals $XW_1$ and $XW$), and the way the respective isoquants are delineated, clearly good $[g_1]$ is the labour-intensive good and good $[g_2]$ the capital-intensive good in both countries.

## 2.7    Factor input prices without trade

In Figure 2.4, under autarky, countries I and II may produce goods $g_1$ and $g_2$ at any feasible point on their respective contract curves and meet the conditions necessary for Paretian production efficiency such that the marginal rates of transformation in production (MRT) for goods $g_1$ and $g_2$ are equal to the rates at which these goods are exchanged in the market ($P_{g_1}/P_{g_2}$; the internal price ratios). For the sake of clarity let $\psi$ and $\psi_1$ be the pre-trade internal equilibrium points in countries I and II respectively. At points $\psi$ and $\psi_1$, what are the implications for pre-trade input price? We may deduce immediately from Figure 2.4 that country II uses more capital-intensive methods of production than country I in both lines of activity $g_1$ and $g_2$. Since production functions are identical for each good in each country, and homogeneous of degree 1, it has been shown that respective marginal productivities of inputs are exclusively determined by factor input intensiveness utilised in production. So if country II uses more capital per unit of labour than country I, then the marginal productivity of capital inputs at point $\psi$ in country II will be less than the marginal productivities of capital $\psi_1$ in country I. Factor input prices are exclusively determined by marginal productivities. Hence the price of capital will be lower in country II than I and the wages of labourers will be higher in country II than in country I. This is valid when both countries produce and consume the goods $g_1$ and $g_2$ in isolation without trade.

## 2.8    Factor and goods prices with free trade between countries I and II

Given the H-O-S prediction, if the possibility of trade between countries I and II is available, country II will export its capital-intensive good $g_2$ and import $g_1$ from country I. Since $g_2$ is the capital-intensive good in both countries, and $g_1$ is the labour-intensive good in both countries, once trade occurs country I will travel along its contract curve from $\psi_1$ towards origin $O_3$ and country II will move along its contract curve from $\psi$ towards origin O. Feasible post-trade corresponding points for both countries are shown in Figure 2.5 at $\Omega$ and $\Omega_1$. Figure 2.5 is identical to Figure 2.4, except that country I now produces at point $\Omega_1$ and country II produces at point $\Omega$. Such a production pattern is entirely feasible given trade. But what has happened to factor input prices?

Given constant returns to scale, the theorem of 'corresponding points' demonstrates that the marginal productivities of labour and capital are constant along any given vector from the origin such as $(O, \Omega, \Omega_1)$ in Figure 2.5. Let the marginal productivity labour and capital in country I in industry $g_1$ and industry $g_2$ be respectively $MPL_{Ig_1}$, $MPK_{Ig_1}$, $MPL_{Ig_2}$, $MPK_{Ig_2}$. Similarly: let the marginal productivities in country II in corresponding industries be respectively $MPL_{IIg_1}$, $MPK_{IIg_1}$, $MPL_{IIg_2}$, $MPK_{IIg_2}$. With reference to Figure 2.5, earlier reasoning with the theorem of corresponding points showed that capital/labour

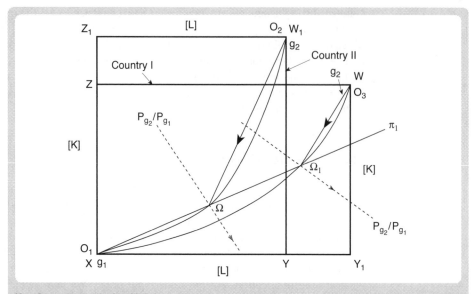

Note: Isoquants are omitted to aid clarity

where:

In country I:

$O-O_3$ = contract curve of efficient production point

$O-\Omega_1$ = output of exportables $g_1$ with trade

$O_3-\Omega_3$ = output of importables $g_2$ with trade

$XY_1$ and $XZ$ = labour and capital endowments

In country II:

$O_2-O$ = contract curve of efficient production point

$O_2-\Omega$ = output of exportables $g_2$ with trade

$O_3-\Omega$ = output of importables $g_1$ with trade

$XY$ and $XZ_1$ = labour and capital endowments

**Figure 2.5 Trade equilibrium and factor price equalisation**

input ratios are identical in industry $g_1$ in both countries at points $\Omega$ and $\Omega_1$ whence it follows that:

$$MPL_{Ig_1} = MPL_{IIg_1} \quad \text{and}$$
$$MPK_{Ig_1} = MPK_{IIg_1}$$

Since vector $O_2\Omega$ is parallel to vector $O_3\Omega_1$, this implies that inputs labour and capital are used in identical proportions in both countries in industry $g_2$ too. Whence it follows that:

$$MPL_{Ig_2} = MPL_{IIg_2} \quad \text{and}$$
$$MPK_{Ig_2} = MPK_{IIg_2}$$

Given perfect competition in (a) all goods markets ($g_1$ and $g_2$), (b) all factor markets, together with perfect mobility of inputs and outputs and no exit/entry barriers, then the wages of labour per unit of output must be the same in each industry $g_1$ and $g_2$ in each country prior to trade. Similarly, the return on capital in each industry prior to trade must be equalised by competition and free input mobility. Hence, prior to trade, factor returns in each industry are, for country I:

$$MPL_{Ig_1} \times P_{Ig_1} = MPL_{Ig_2} \times P_{Ig_2} \qquad \text{... [2.1]}$$
$$MPK_{Ig_1} \times P_{Ig_1} = MPK_{Ig_2} \times P_{Ig_2} \qquad \text{... [2.2]}$$

Equations [2.1] and [2.2] may be rearranged to yield:

$$P_{Ig_1}/P_{Ig_2} = MPL_{Ig_2}/MPL_{Ig_1} \qquad \dots [2.3]$$
$$P_{Ig_1}/P_{Ig_2} = MPK_{Ig_2}/MPK_{Ig_1} \qquad \dots [2.4]$$

Similarly, for country II:

$$MPL_{IIg_1} \times P_{IIg_1} = MPL_{IIg_2} \times P_{IIg_2} \qquad \dots [2.5]$$
$$MPK_{IIg_1} \times P_{IIg_1} = MPK_{IIg_2} \times P_{IIg_2} \qquad \dots [2.6]$$

$$P_{IIg_1}/P_{IIg_2} = MPL_{IIg_2}/MPL_{IIg_1} \qquad \dots [2.7]$$
$$P_{IIg_1}/P_{IIg_2} = MPK_{IIg_2}/MPK_{IIg_1} \qquad \dots [2.8]$$

whence: $P_{Ig_1}/P_{Ig_2}$ and $P_{IIg_1}/P_{IIg_2}$ are relative goods prices. From the theorem of corresponding points, implying instantaneous adjustments with no impediments to free trade, the relative goods price ratio is the same in both countries. Hence: $P_{Ig_1}/P_{Ig_2}$ and $P_{IIg_1}/P_{IIg_2}$ in trade which is shown in Figure 2.2 and subsumed in Figure 2.3 via corresponding points. By the theorem of 'corresponding points', it is true that at points $\Omega$ and $\Omega_1$:

$$MPL_{Ig_1} = MPL_{IIg_1} \qquad \dots [2.9]$$
$$MPK_{Ig_1} = MPK_{IIg_1} \qquad \dots [2.10]$$

whence:

$$MPL_{Ig_2} = MPL_{IIg_2} \qquad \dots [2.11]$$
$$MPK_{Ig_2} = MPK_{IIg_2} \qquad \dots [2.12]$$

which yields:

$$MPL_{Ig_1} \times P_{Ig_1} = MPL_{IIg_1} \times P_{IIg_1} = MPL_{Ig_2} \times P_{Ig_2} = MPL_{IIg_2} \times P_{IIg_2} \qquad \dots [2.13]$$
$$MPK_{Ig_1} \times P_{Ig_1} = MPK_{IIg_1} \times P_{IIg_1} = MPK_{Ig_2} \times P_{Ig_2} = MPK_{IIg_2} \times P_{IIg_2} \qquad \dots [2.14]$$

This last condition reveals that free-trade pairs of 'corresponding points' lead to a complete equalisation of factor rewards in both countries. Equations [2.1] to [2.14] are tantamount to a circuitous restatement of the theorem of corresponding points, hence similarities in the geometric configurations of Figures 2.4 and 2.5 are fairly pronounced if close inspection of the critical production vectors is made. Thus in Figure 2.5 vector $O\pi_1$ is the crucial vector producing a pair of feasible corresponding points. So if H-O-S is valid, FPET follows as a strict corollary (Meade, 1950).

## 2.9 The fundamental reasoning behind the factor price equalisation theorem

Prior to trade, capital is relatively inexpensive in country II compared to labour, whereas in country I labour is relatively inexpensive compared to capital. The dimensions of the Edgeworth-Bowley Box configuration in Figure 2.5 imply that country II is naturally abundant in capital resources relative to country I. Yet country I is naturally abundant in labour resources. From the H-O-S prediction therefore, country II has a comparative advantage in specialising in producing the capital-intensive good $g_2$ and country I has a comparative advantage in specialisation of the production of labour-intensive good $g_1$. When both countries trade freely, country II expands production of $g_2$, and country I expands its production of $g_1$. Country II exports $g_2$ and country I exports $g_1$. But to expand its production of $g_2$ country II must switch more factor inputs from industry $g_1$ toward industry $g_2$. In country II, entrepreneurs need relatively more capital and hence its price is bid up compared to the no-trade case. Hence the relative price of capital, prior to trade, was the cheap input, now rises. Similarly, in country I, entrepreneurs, facing no barriers to trade, produce more of $g_1$ for export. Since industry $g_1$ is a relatively labour-intensive activity, the demand for labour increases compared to the no-trade case. Thus free trade produces an increase, in both countries, in the price of the relatively abundant factor. Conversely, free trade on H-O-S lines produces a decrease in the price of the relatively scarce factor inputs in both countries. As long as 'corresponding points' like $\Omega$ and $\Omega_1$ as displayed in Figure 2.5 can be found, free trade leads to a complete equalisation of factor prices, given the conditions necessary and sufficient to deduce the H-O-S theorem. However, trade might take place between countries I and II in such a way that both countries specialise completely in their respective exportable. In this event complete factor price equalisation will not occur. Nonetheless, it can be shown via Edgeworth-Bowley Box analysis that free trade will produce a tendency towards factor price equalisation, because, in the labour-rich economy, trade will produce an excess demand for labour such that real wages will rise in exportable industry compared to the situation prior to trade. Similarly, in the capital-rich economy, trade will produce excess demands for capital inputs, and the price of these will be bid up compared to the case under autarky. Generally, free trade, even with complete specialisation, will raise the real return of the abundant inputs relative to the no-trade case. Trade benefits from the abundant inputs and penalises the returns available to relatively scarce inputs. Conversely, a movement from free trade to protection would normally produce the reverse. Normally protection benefits the scarce inputs and penalises the returns available to abundant factors.

Finally, complete specialisation in exportables, for any pair of trading nations, is more likely the greater the disparity between relative factor endowments. Likewise the probability of incomplete specialisation increases, the greater the similarity in techniques used in both lines of production, given some degree of disparity in overall factor endowments. Geometrically, this means that the contract curves in both countries would be closer to the diagonals of their respective Edgeworth-Bowley Boxes (Harrod, 1958).

## 2.10    Trade, poverty, and income equalisation

It has been shown that on stringent assumptions, trade will equalise factor input prices. In the trading system today, however, large differences in real wages can be observed. To what extent does this empirical fact undermine the logic of the factor price equalisation theorem?

It must be remembered that the factor price equalisation theorem does not imply income equalisation between trading nations. Real wages are not the exclusive source of real income. Capital obtains a real return via trade. Therefore the greater the capital endowment, for a given amount of labour resources, the higher average per capita real income will be. Even if factor returns were completely equalised via trade, so long as capital stocks differ between countries, real incomes will differ. Moreover, the factor price equalisation theorem is a static piece of reasoning which analyses the characteristics of a given general equilibrium situation at one instantaneous point in time. It produces a snap-shot result of a multitude of economic forces, and completely ignores the notion of technological change. The general equilibrium deduced at points [$\Omega$ and $\Omega_1$] in Figure 2.5 implies timelessness. So real trading systems are not stuck in a general equilibrium forever; technological factors operating over time may operate in such a way as to counteract the force free trade exerts on input prices.

Similarly, taxes, tariffs and subsidies affect real-world trading patterns in such a way that the tendency to import price equalisation is completely submerged via trade taking place at 'false' prices. In these cases, trading nations are not on their respective contract curves, and 'second best' results are to be predicted.

The factor price equalisation theorem is not directly amenable to empirical testing. This statement is true of much static marginalistic theorising in general. Theorising at this level of abstraction does, however, provide valuable clues and insights into the general equilibrium characteristics of economies. These insights provide essential foundations upon which theorising at the dynamic level may commence. Abstract reasoning, on which the factor price equalisation theorem is grounded, may lead to the clarification and development of testable hypotheses. Furthermore, abstract reasoning underpins the empirical testing of specific refutable hypotheses. Based on this reasoning alone, study of the factor price equalisation theorem is worthwhile.

## Summary

- The role of factor endowments in the H-O-S model is explained using two goods and two factors of production. The two goods differ in factor intensity.

- If a country produces two goods, there is a one-to-one relationship between the relative prices of goods and relative prices of factors used to produce the goods. A rise in relative prices of the labour-intensive good shifts the distribution of income in favour of labour.

- An increase in the supply of one factor of production expands production possibilities, but in a strongly biased way: at unchanged relative goods prices, the output of the good intensive in that factor rises while the output of the other good actually falls.

- A country that has a large supply of one input relative to the supply of others is abundant in that resource. A country will tend to produce relatively more of goods that use abundant resources intensively. The result is the basic H-O-S theory of trade: countries export goods that are intensive in the inputs with which they are abundantly endowed.

- Changes in relative prices affect relative earnings of resources, and because trade changes relative prices, international trade has strong income distribution effects.

- International trade may actually lead to equalisation of the prices of factors such as labour and capital. Complete factor price equalisation is not observed because of wide differences in inputs, barriers to trade, and differences in technology.

## Questions

1. 'Differences in factor endowments determine trade patterns.' Discuss.

2. How does trading on H-O-S lines affect income distribution and factor earnings?

3. What is the 'theorem of corresponding points'? Use the theorem to explain factor price equalisation.

4. Who gains most from trade in the H-O-S type of trading network?

**Key concepts**

| | |
|---|---|
| abundant factor | factor prices |
| expansion of production possibilities | factor proportions theory |
| | equalisation of factor prices |
| factor abundance | factor intensity |
| the H-O-S theorem | corresponding points |
| homogeneous production function(s) | Edgeworth-Bowley Box diagrams |

## Bibliography

Caves, R. E. (1976) *Trade and economic structure*, Harvard University Press, pp. 14–37.

Harrod, R. F. (1958) 'Factor price relations under free trade', *Economic Journal*, vol. 68.

Lancaster, K. (1957) 'The Heckscher-Ohlin trade model: a geometric treatment', *Economica*, vol. 24, pp. 19–39.

Meade, J. E. (1950) 'The equalisation of factor prices: the two-good, two-country, three-product case', *Metro-economica*, vol. 12.

Samuelson, P. A. (1949) 'International factor price equalisation once again', *Economic Journal*, vol. 59.

Shaikh, A. (1984) 'The laws of international exchange', in E. I. Nell (ed.), *Growth, Profits and Property*, Cambridge University Press, pp. 208–19.

Stern, R. M. (1975) 'Testing "Trade Theories" ', in P. B. Kenon (ed.), *International Trade and Finance; Frontiers for research*, Cambridge University Press.

# 3 The Stolper-Samuelson Theorem: protection and real wages[1]

**K. LAWLER and H. SEDDIGHI**

## 3.1 Introduction

As a 'special' case of the factor price equalisation theorem, analysis is now developed to demonstrate the Stopler-Samuelson Theorem (SST). The SST is founded on the assumptions sufficient to make the H-O-S prediction logically true. There are three versions of the SST. Each of these is stated. Thereafter, the implications of the alternative formulations are examined.

A The basic SST states that free trade necessarily reduces the real returns of the scarce factors of production in the standard (H-O-S) barter trade model. The real returns of the scarce factors may be expressed in terms of any good. Or, more succinctly, prohibitive protection necessarily raises the real return of the scarce input. In this guise, the basic SST restricts itself to the case of prohibitive protection.

B A more refined version of alternative A is: protection enhances the real return of the scarce factor inputs. Or, more precisely: protection (prohibitive and non-prohibitive) necessarily raises the real return of the scarce factors. Hence, alternative B is a more general version of the theorem than A.

C A more precise version of B might be termed the: 'Stolper-Samuelson-Metzler' case (Metzler, 1949). This version of the SST handles the Metzler case. This refines alternative B to read: protection (prohibitive or otherwise) normally enhances the real return of the scarce factor inputs. But non-prohibitive protection may lower the real returns of the scarce factors, when the elasticity of foreign demand for the tariff-imposing country's export good is less than the domestic marginal propensity to consume exportables. Or, more concisely: for the version of the SST given in B to be generally true the following condition must hold:

$$[E_f > (1 - c)] \qquad\qquad \dots (m)$$

where: $E_f$ is the foreign demand elasticity for the tariff-imposing country's exports, and $(1 - c)$ is defined as the tariff-imposing country's marginal propensity to consume its exportable good.

Hence, given the conditions necessary for the H-O-S prediction to be logically true, the SST is logically true when condition (m) is satisfied. Given condition (m), the generalised version of the SST stated in alternative B is logically valid. The analysis now focuses on the alternatives (A, B and C) of the SST and derives each version for the $2 \times 2 \times 2$ barter trade case (Bhagwati, 1959).

## 3.2    The analytical background of the restrictive and general versions of the SST

In all three guises, the, SST necessarily depends upon the effect that tariffs have on the domestic price of importables, which must rise with imposition of tariffs. Initially a partial equilibrium analysis of the effect of tariff imposition is examined. This provides a useful background for the general equilibrium analysis which follows. Figure 3.1 shows that the effect of a tariff is to raise the price of the importable good on which duty is levied. Prior to tariff imposition, the domestic price of the importable good is $P_1$ and $OX_5$ of this good is consumed in the domestic economy given free trade, ignoring secondary effects. Of the quantity $OX_5$ domestically consumed of the importable, $OX_1$ is produced by home producers, whereas the amount ($X_1$ to $X_5$) is imported. Let a tariff K now be imposed on the good. The domestic price of the importable now rises to $P_1 + K$. Home consumption of the importable drops now to $OX_4$, since the internal price of the good rises. However, domestic output of the importable simultaneously expands from $OX_1$ to $OX_2$ and the quantity imported falls from $OX_1$ to $OX_5$ to equal the amount ($OX_2$ to $OX_4$). The tariff levied at K is, however, non-prohibitive: a prohibitive tariff takes the domestic price of the importable to: $P_1 + K_1$. Such a tariff excludes imports completely; domestic consumption of the importable is now at $OX_3$ when domestic producers satisfy home demand completely and foreign imports are shut out. A prohibitive tariff curtails all imports.

Inspection of Figure 3.1 reveals that tariff imposition exerts an impact on prices, consumption and output. Implicit in Figure 3.1 is the proposition that free trade is superior to tariff-restricted trade in welfare terms. Hence, tariffs imply societal welfare costs. These costs are often termed the 'cost of protection'. With reference to Figure 3.1, imposition of a tariff K increases the domestic price of good X. This increase in price causes a loss of consumers' surplus equal to area ABCD. This loss is borne by consumers of the

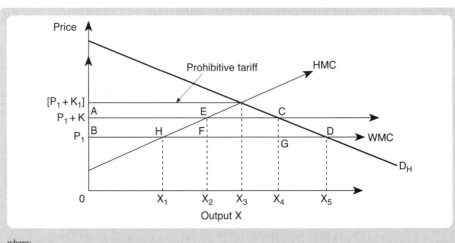

where:
WMC = world marginal cost/supply
HMC = domestic marginal cost/supply
DH = domestic demand for good X
$P_1$ = price in home market prior to tariff
$P_1 + K$ = domestic price of importable good X with a non-prohibitive tariff
$P_1 + K_1$ = domestic price of importable good X with prohibitive tariff

**Figure 3.1    Partial equilibrium aspects of tariff imposition**

importables. However, a portion of this loss in consumers' surplus passes to government in the form of tariff revenue – area FECG. Yet another portion of the loss goes to domestic industry in the form of enhanced producers' surplus – area ABHE. Hence, in Figure 3.1, two welfare loss triangles have not so far been calculated, and/or compensated – areas HEF and CDG; these two measure the production and consumption welfare losses of tariff imposition respectively. Jointly, areas HEF and CDG measure the aggregate cost of protection to the economies and aggregate output of exportables is not maximised, whereas area CDG measures the impact of the distortion that tariffs impose on consumption, since consumers in the domestic economy pay a price including the tariff which is higher than the world marginal cost of production of that good. Thus consumption decisions – given tariff distortions – are not optimised. For clarity, the foregoing discussion has been premised on the assumption that the domestic price of the good increased by the full amount of tariff duty levied. This assumption is frequently called the 'small country' case: whence the country's terms of trade are unaffected by the tariff. As such, the preceding analysis typifies partial equilibrium analysis. In a general equilibrium framework, only if the country levying the tariff is so tiny that a change in its demand is so minute as to leave world prices unaffected, or only if the foreign supply elasticity is infinitely large, will the terms of trade remain unchanged after imposition.

## 3.3 Tariff protection in a general equilibrium context: the impact of tariffs on real income(s) distribution: versions A and B of the SST

The Stolper-Samuelson Theorem (SST) can be analysed via an Edgeworth-Bowley Box diagram, such that the general equilibrium features of the impact of tariff protection can be highlighted. Figure 3.2 features the usual Box configuration for a country. In the interests of perspicuity, isoquants are removed. The labour input in production is measured horizontally, whereas capital inputs are measured vertically. Production of exportables is measured from origin O, whilst output of importables is measured from $O_1$.

Assume in Figure 3.2 that the country is enjoying free trade and attains internal general equilibrium at point $\psi$. From the theorem of 'corresponding points', it is clear that this country is relatively labour rich and produces, in equilibrium, a higher proportion of labour-intensive outputs (exportables) than capital-intensive outputs (importables). Now let a tariff be imposed on the importable good: the preceding analysis showed that normally the domestic price of importables rises (see Figure 3.1). Hence, domestic entrepreneurs switch production activities, such that with the new prices more importables and fewer exportables are produced after tariff imposition. This switch in production activities is shown in Figure 3.2 by the movement from $\psi$ and $\psi_1$. But now consider the impact of this movement in production on factor prices. Inspection of Figure 3.2 reveals that production activity in the exportables sector has become a more labour-intensive sector. The reasoning behind this change in factor intensities is that: entrepreneurs commence increasing production of importables which are capital intensive, hence more capital is needed and its price is bid upwards. Because capital prices are higher, cost minimisation dictates that entrepreneurs substitute more labour for capital, hence overall production methods become more labour intensive. The result of the tariff is therefore that the rent for capital increases and real wages fall in comparison to relative factor prices prior to tariff imposition. The tariff has caused income distribution to alter in favour of the scarce input capital and against the abundant input labour. More generally, the SST demonstrates

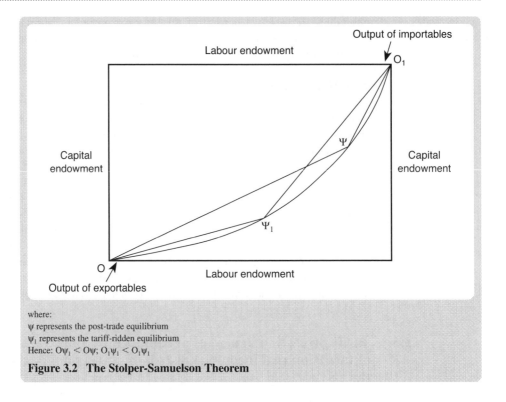

Figure 3.2  The Stolper-Samuelson Theorem

where:
$\psi$ represents the post-trade equilibrium
$\psi_1$ represents the tariff-ridden equilibrium
Hence: $O\psi_1 < O\psi$; $O_1\psi_1 < O_1\psi_1$

that the tariff favours the inputs used intensively in the import-competing sector. Given that the tariff raises the domestic price of importables, output of the import good expands. So the derived demand for the input used intensively in this industry rises, and its price rises. Hence, income distribution has altered unambiguously in its favour.

In Figure 3.2, when production switches from $\psi$ to $\psi_1$, the marginal productivity of labour falls whilst that of capital rises. The reasoning here runs as follows: as inputs are reallocated after the tariff imposition and shifted from the labour-intensive exportable sector to the capital-intensive importable sector, capital/labour ratios fall, more labourers are applied to proportionally less capital and the marginal productivity of capital rises whilst that of labour falls. But real returns to labour and capital are determined by respective marginal productivities. Since all inputs are fully employed at $\psi$ and $\psi_1$, it follows that labour's share of aggregate production (real national income) falls and that of capital rises.

Since production functions are homogeneous of degree 1 in this model, Euler's theorem dictates that factor rewards exhaust the aggregate product generated, where profits in equilibrium are normal/zero.

Let   X = national income/product
      L = the aggregate labour supply
      K = the aggregate quantity of capital
      W = the real wage of labour
      r = the real return on capital

Then $X = [L \times W] + [K \times r]$, in the case of free trade
hence, $[L \times W]$ = the share of labour in X
and: $[K \times r]$ = the share of capital in X.

With the tariff imposed the case at $\psi_1$ in Figure 3.2 may be written as:

$X_t = [L \times W_t] + [K \times r_t];$

whence    $X_t$ = the post-tariff national income

           $W_t$ = the post-tariff real wage

           $r_t$ = the post-tariff return on capital

But the marginal productivities and hence factor rewards are exclusively determined by factor intensities, as shown previously. Therefore, with the tariff at $\psi_1$ in Figure 3.2, $r_t > r$ and $W_t < W$. Hence, $[L \times W_t] < [L \times W]$ and $[K \times r_t] > [K \times r]$, such that labour's share of real aggregate income has fallen, whereas for capital it has risen in the post-tariff equilibrium. Finally, it must be noted that although the real national product, $X_t$, may have fallen because of the tariff imposition, the real reward for the scarce input (capital in this case) must rise in both absolute and relative terms compared to the case with free trade. Since the tariff causes a reallocation of inputs/outputs, this causes the marginal productivity of capital to rise in both sectors in the economy. Thus, whichever good is used to quantify the return on capital, its real reward will increase. Hence, given the assumptions necessary to maintain the H-O-S prediction, tariff imposition benefits the country's scarce factor, abundant input, unambiguously. This establishes the restrictive/general versions of the SST outlined above.

## 3.4    The Stolper-Samuelson Theorem: the Metzler case and offer curves[2]

The fundamental elements of both the restrictive and general versions of the SST are:

1. protection increases the domestic relative price of the importable;
2. an increase in the relative price of a good, in a $2 \times 2 \times 2$ general equilibrium system, increases the real return of the factor input used intensively in its production, given constant returns to scale and competitive conditions;
3. the importables, in the $2 \times 2 \times 2$ system, are intensive in the use of the scarce factor input, given the H-O-S prediction;
4. hence protection raises the real return of the scarce input.

As implied previously, prohibitive protection as depicted in Figure 3.1 necessarily raises the relative price of the importable. As observed in Figure 3.1, the free-trade relative price of the importable good is lower than under autarky, hence the basic restrictive version of the SST version A above is necessarily true. Non-prohibitive tariffs may either increase, leave unaltered, or reduce the internal relative price of the importable good, when the reasoning departs from the 'small country' assumption/conditions. The perverse case – specifically that protection may lower the domestic relative price of importables – was first demonstrated by Metzler. Metzler's 'perverse' case is perhaps most clearly seen via the use of offer curve analysis, which allows the general equilibrium implications of tariff imposition to be clearly observable.

Edgeworth/Marshall offer curves depict the impact of the terms of trade between two countries on the volumes exported and imported. The analysis now turns to consider the derivation of offer curves, prior to discussion relating to the Metzler case. A country/region/consumer's offer curve is exactly equivalent to either its supply curve for exports or its demand curve for imports. Offer curves depict exchange offers as a function of the international price ratio – the terms of trade.

Figure 3.3 demonstrates the derivation of offer curves from the standard transformation curve used heretofore. The country's transformation curve shows the production/consumption trade-offs. For any given terms of trade in Figure 3.3, the trading behaviour of the country is such that a given volume of exports/imports is voluntarily offered in

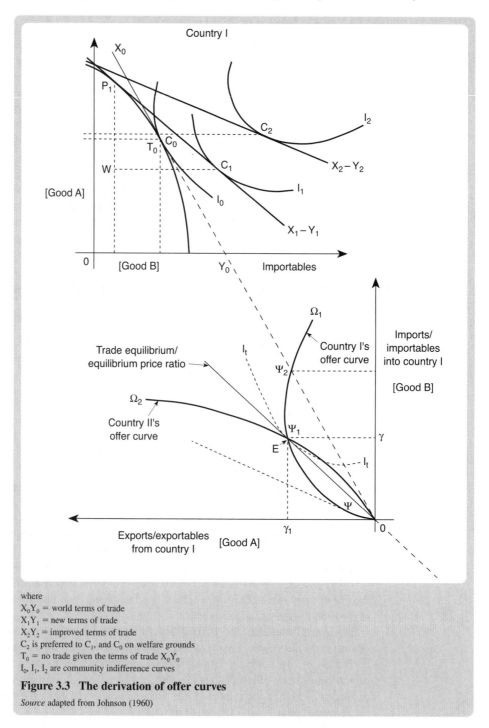

where
$X_0 Y_0$ = world terms of trade
$X_1 Y_1$ = new terms of trade
$X_2 Y_2$ = improved terms of trade
$C_2$ is preferred to $C_1$, and $C_0$ on welfare grounds
$T_0$ = no trade given the terms of trade $X_0 Y_0$
$I_0$, $I_1$, $I_2$ are community indifference curves

**Figure 3.3  The derivation of offer curves**

*Source* adapted from Johnson (1960)

exchange for imports at that price/terms of trade ratio. For example, at the terms of trade given by vector $(X_0, Y_0)$, the country does not wish to engage in any trade at all, as seen at $T_0$. The terms of trade are not favourable at this point – at $T_0$ the nation is self-sufficient. However, with the terms of trade given at vector $(X_1, Y_1)$, the country is willing to trade. Specifically, at these terms of trade the country is willing to produce efficiently at $P_1$ and consume $C_1$, thereby exporting $P_1W$ of good A and importing $WC_1$ of B. With better terms of trade at $(X_2, Y_2)$, the country is induced to offer more of its exportable good A for an even larger quantity of imports. Each particular trade/offer is plotted in the lower configuration of Figure 3.3, at points 0, $\psi$, $\psi_1$ and $\psi_2$. In the bottom configuration in Figure 3.3, the axes represent the quantities of exports/imports to be traded, and the gradient of any vector from the origin depicts the terms of trade/price ratios. The resulting locus $(0, \Omega_1)$ represents the country's offer curve. An offer curve for the country's trading partner could be similarly derived, locus $(0, \Omega_2)$. Where both the offer curves intersect the equilibrium, terms of trade are determined at point (E) on the lower segment of Figure 3.3. The slope of vector (OE) gives the equilibrium/unique terms of trade. In terms of gains from trade, country I in Figure 3.3 would prefer to see country II's offer curve move in a north-easterly direction: this movement represents an improvement in country I's terms of trade (country I offers less A for more B from country II). Conversely, country II would like to see country I's offer curve pushed in a south-westerly direction, because such a movement of country I's offer curve implies better terms of trade. Inspection of the trade indifference curves, in the lower configuration of Figure 3.3, brings out the 'welfare' implications of changes in the terms of trade for both countries. In this respect, offer curves provide useful tools for studying the impact of tariffs – shifts in offer curves – on 'welfare' and the terms of trade. Offer curves are useful analytical tools for examining the concept of optimal tariffs.

In Figures 3.4 and 3.5 offer curves so derived can now be used to examine the Metzler case of the SST.

In Figure 3.4 offer curves for countries I and II are displayed, for the case of free trade. Country I has a Heckscher-Ohlin-Samuelson comparative advantage in producing good A, whereas country II is similarly advantaged in production of good B. Hence, the free-trade offer curves are OI and OII respectively. Trade equilibrium is reached at point Z on Figure 3.4, where <u>OB</u> of good B is exchanged for <u>OA</u> of good A. The equilibrium terms of trade are given by <u>OZ</u>. Assume that country I now levies a 50% tariff. Consequently, country I's offer curve on Figure 3.4 shifts downwards to $OI_2$. Importers in country I now must pay a 50% duty, hence they are only willing to offer $OA_2$ of good A for OB of commodity B. The extra quantity $ZZ_2 = AA_2$ is now forfeited as tariff duty. This quantity, which is 50% of $Z_2B$ and previously went to exporters in country II, now goes as revenue to government in country I. $ZZ_2$ is equal to $\frac{1}{3}$ ZB, or $\frac{1}{2}$ $Z_2B$. A 50% duty causes all points on the tariff-ridden offer curve to lie 33.33% closer to the horizontal axis in Figure 3.4 than the former free-trade offer curve. Thus the exact locus of country I's new offer curve may be derived.

Consequent upon tariff imposition, a new trade equilibrium is determined at point $Z_2$ on Figure 3.4, where the tariff-ridden offer curve intercepts country II's unchanging offer curve. The volumes traded have diminished, because of the favourable movement in country I's terms of trade. Inspection of Figure 3.4 reveals that the ratio of exports to imports has fallen, since $B_2Z_2/A_3Z_3$ is less than BZ/AZ. This means that country I now gets more imports per unit of exports. This terms of trade improvement is also shown by the fact that vector $OZ_3$ lies to the right of free-trade vector OZ.

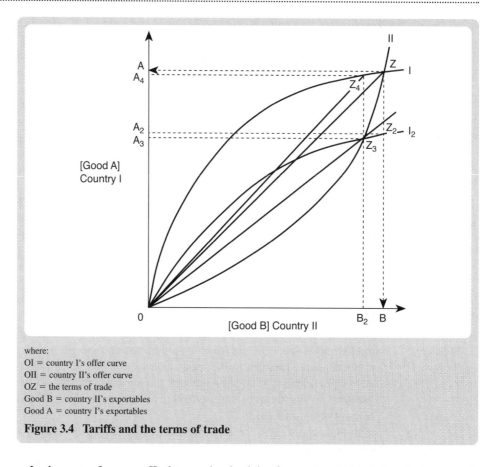

where:
OI = country I's offer curve
OII = country II's offer curve
OZ = the terms of trade
Good B = country II's exportables
Good A = country I's exportables

**Figure 3.4  Tariffs and the terms of trade**

In the case of country II, the supply elasticity for exports being infinitely large, such that country II's offer curve is a straight line, the equilibrium terms of trade are unaffected. Even in this case, the volume of trade shrinks as tariffs are imposed, despite the fact that the terms of trade are unaffected. The impact of tariffs on income distribution can now be examined. For the distribution of income, the significant variable that may be affected by the tariff is the domestic price of the importable. With reference to Figure 3.3, on world markets $OA_3$ of good A will exchange for $OB_2$ of good B. Domestic importers, however, will have to pay more in the home market: they pay $OA_4$ of good A for $OB_2$ of commodity B since they must pay the tariff, $Z_3Z_4$. Thus the domestic price of the import good will rise in the home market as can be seen by the fact that ratio $OA_4/OB_2 >$ ratio OA/OB. Or, that vector $OZ_4$ – the new domestic price of the importable – lies to the left of the free-trade price OZ. The result of this general equilibrium analysis implies that imposition of a tariff normally leads to an improvement in the terms of trade for the tariff-imposing country, providing that its trading partner does not retaliate with a rival tariff, hence the analysis thus far ignores the possibility of a trade war developing. For the normal case, as improvement in the terms of trade is not sufficient to offset the impact of the tariff on the domestic price of the importable, in Figure 3.4 the domestic price of the import good increased. This establishes the general [case B] version of the SST; namely, that the tariff raises the real reward of the input used intensively in the import substitution sector.

Metzler's contribution to tariff theory was to demonstrate that when the foreign offer curve is inelastic, the impact of the tariff on the domestic price of the import good may be

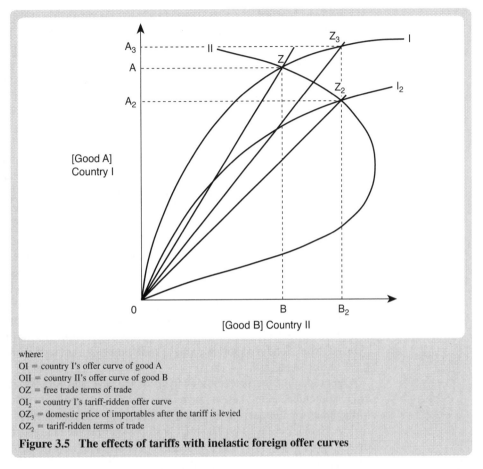

where:
OI = country I's offer curve of good A
OII = country II's offer curve of good B
OZ = free trade terms of trade
$OI_2$ = country I's tariff-ridden offer curve
$OZ_3$ = domestic price of importables after the tariff is levied
$OZ_2$ = tariff-ridden terms of trade

**Figure 3.5   The effects of tariffs with inelastic foreign offer curves**

to cause it to decrease rather than increase. This remarkable case can be explicated using offer curves. Figure 3.5 charts the offer curves for countries I and II. Usually, however, country II's offer curve is inelastic over the feasible range of trading prices. Free trade equilibrium is point Z, and country I exchanges OA of good A for OB of commodity B. The free trade terms are given by the slope of $OZ_1$ as before. Country I, as in Figure 3.4, now levies a tariff of 50% on imports from country II. Accordingly, its offer curve shifts down, from OI to $OI_2$. The new trade equilibrium is now at $Z_2$. Now $OA_2$ of good A exchanges for $OB_2$ of commodity B. Country II has a highly inelastic offer curve over the feasible trading range of prices, hence a massive improvement in country I's terms of trade results from the tariff. The gain in the barter terms of trade is large enough to enable the tariff-imposing country to obtain a larger quantity of imports for a smaller offer of exports. The new terms of trade are given by vector $OZ_2$. In the tariff-imposing country's home market, the domestic price of the exportable has risen whilst the domestic price of the imported good B has fallen. Domestic consumers now pay $OA_3$ of good A for $OB_2$ of commodity B. Since $OA_3/OB_2 <$ OA/OB, domestic consumers, even with a tariff included in the domestic price of imported good B, can obtain more of the imported good for a given unit of exportables A than was possible with free trade. This is revealed in Figure 3.5 by the fact that the vector representing the domestic price of importables, $OZ_3$, lies to the right of OZ. This case, where the domestic price of importables falls after tariff imposition, is exactly opposite to that predicted by the general version of the SST. This

41

demonstrates Metzler's perverse case of the SST. As the relative price of exportables rises, and importables fall, production of exportables becomes more profitable and the real return to the input used intensively in the export sector rises and income distribution turns unambiguously in that input's favour. In terms of the H-O-S prediction, the imposition of a tariff enhances the real return of the factor used intensively in the export sector – the physically abundant resource. However, the general SST is still valid, even in the case of an inelastic foreign offer curve, when the following condition exists:

$$E_f > (1 - C)$$

where $E_f$ is the foreign demand elasticity for the tariff-imposing country's exports, and $(1 - C)$ is defined as the tariff-imposing nation's marginal propensity to consume its exportable commodity. Logically it may be argued that, since any country's marginal propensity to consume its export good cannot exceed unity, and if the elasticity of foreign demand, $E_f$, is greater than unity, the general version of the SST necessarily holds (Bhagwati and Johnson, 1961).

The reasoning underlying the Metzler case runs as follows: the greater a country's marginal propensity to consume exportables, the greater is the incentive to spend tariff revenue on exportables. Thus an excess domestic demand for exportables may arise from this source. If the foreign country's reciprocal demand elasticity for the tariff-imposing country's exportables is low, then demand for the exportables falls marginally for a large price increase. Given these stringent conditions, imposition of a tariff may cause excess demand to develop for exportables in the tariff-imposing country, which in turn causes the price of imports to fall.

A good deal of the preceding analysis of the SST and Metzler effects hinges on the crucial point that an increase in the relative price of a commodity enhances the real return of the input used intensively in its production. This key relationship was first established by P. A. Samuelson in 1949. The relationship is entirely technological and demand factors do not figure at all in its establishment. The relationship may be proved with reference to Figure 3.6.

In Figure 3.6, $L_A$ and $L_B$ refer to the amounts of labour input applied in activities A and B respectively; $K_A$ and $K_B$ being the quantities of capital input so employed. The ratio W/R denotes the ratio of real wages to rents; the ratio L/K represents the factor endowment ratio of the country; and $P_A$ and $P_B$ denote the ratio of commodity prices. Good A is the labour-intensive industry, good B being the capital-intensive activity, at all feasible input price ratios. Hence: $L_A/K_A > L_B/K_B$ at all feasible ratios for W/R. As real wages fall relative to rents, the price of good B is seen to rise relatively to that of good A in a monotonic manner. The country's overall factor endowment ratio (L/K) determines the range of the diagram; $\pi$, being any given commodity price ratio $P_B/P_A$, may be altered to $\pi_1$, such that the relative price of good B rises. With this, the L/K ratios in both activities A and B rise too. The marginal product of capital in both activities rises as that of labour falls, hence the real return to capital unambiguously increases and the real wage of labour falls. Increases in the relative price of good B thus enhance the real return to capital, the input used intensively in its production, and lower the real wage of labour, the input used intensively in producing good A, the commodity for which the relative price has fallen. This analysis shows how the SST essentially follows from the analytical framework of the H-O-S theory of trade. To the extent that the SST is the converse of the factor price equalisation theorem, the SST is bound by the restriction that complete specialisation of production activity does not occur consequent upon tariff imposition. Complete specialisation destroys the logical validity of the analysis relating to Figure 3.6.

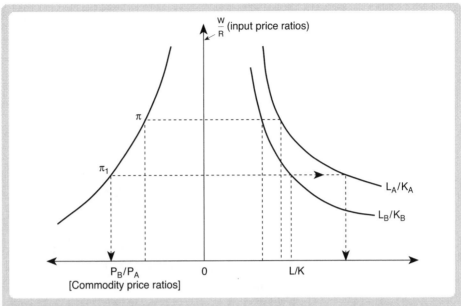

where:

$\pi$ = any given commodity price ratio, for goods B and A

$\pi_1$ = a new commodity price ratio; where the price of B is raised relative to the price of good A

W/R = the ratio of real wages to real returns to capital

L/R = labour to capital ratios in production of good A and/or good B

$L_A/K_A$ = input ratios in producing good A

$L_B/K_B$ = input ratios in producing good B

$P_B/P_A$ = the ratio of the price of good B relative to the price of good A

**Figure 3.6 The Samuelsonian relationships connecting commodity price ratios, input price ratios and factor/input proportions**

## 3.5   Trade patterns and changing factor endowments: The Rybczynski Theorem

The Rybczynski Theorem (RT) (Rybczynski, 1955) states that if one of the factor inputs increases in supply, the other factor being fixed in supply, then the output of the good that utilises the accumulating factor input intensively expands, and the output of the other good decreases in absolute terms, given that commodity prices and factor input prices are held constant. The RT, in this form, depends on nearly all conditions necessary to maintain the logical truth of the H-O-S prediction. To deduce the RT, however, it is not strictly necessary to assume that production functions are the same in both countries.

Imagine that two countries are engaged in trade and country I attains a trade equilibrium at point $\pi$ in Figure 3.7, prior to an increase in the supply of a factor input. The original factor endowments of the country are depicted by the Edgeworth-Bowley Box configuration ABCD. The capital endowment is measured by AB, the labour endowment by the vector AD. The contract curves have been deleted from Figure 3.7 to aid clarity. The output of exportables is measured from origin O, whereas that of importables is measured from origin $O_1$ prior to factor accumulation. Following the H-O-S prediction, the exportables are labour-intensive goods, whereas importables are relatively capital intensive. Point $\pi$ in Figure 3.7 is an efficient trade equilibrium for country I, following the reasoning which underpins the theorem of corresponding points.

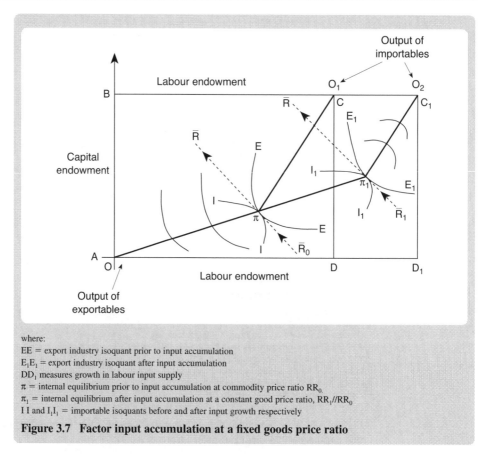

where:

EE = export industry isoquant prior to input accumulation

$E_1E_1$ = export industry isoquant after input accumulation

$DD_1$ measures growth in labour input supply

$\pi$ = internal equilibrium prior to input accumulation at commodity price ratio $RR_0$.

$\pi_1$ = internal equilibrium after input accumulation at a constant good price ratio, $RR_1//RR_0$

I I and $I_1I_1$ = importable isoquants before and after input growth respectively

**Figure 3.7   Factor input accumulation at a fixed goods price ratio**

Imagine now that country I experiences an absolute increase in the size of its labour force caused by either population growth or immigration of guest workers. The increase in size of the labour force is measured in Figure 3.7 by the distance D to D1. Now the new Edgeworth-Bowley Box is shown by the vertices $ABC_1D_1$. In this new situation, what are the implications for the volumes traded and the terms of trade? The (RT) stated above requires that commodity prices are held fixed. But to maintain the fixity of commodity prices, input prices too must be artificially kept constant. Nonetheless, to maintain constant input prices, marginal productivities of inputs must be held constant. This is evident if the analytical background of Figure 3.6 is remembered. Since production functions are homogeneous of degree 1, the ratio of marginal productivities is a function only of factor intensities. If factor intensities remain constant, the ratio of marginal productivities cannot change either. Hence, by the theorem of 'corresponding points', the only point in the enlarged Edgeworth-Bowley Box configuration in Figure 3.7, at which inputs are combined in constant/fixed proportions as at point $\pi$, is point $\pi_1$. The input intensity given by ray $O\pi_1$ is clearly identical to that along $O\pi$. Again, by the theorem of 'corresponding points', input intensity $O_1\pi$ (which is parallel to $O_2\pi_1$) is identical to that along ray $O_2\pi_1$ in Figure 3.7.

With reference to Figure 3.7, via the theorem of 'corresponding points', point $\pi_1$ lies on the contract curve since ray $O\pi_1$ intercepts all isoquants of the exportable industry, where the slopes of isoquants are equal. Since rays $O_1\pi$ and $O_2\pi_1$ are parallel, these too intercept the isoquants of the import-competing industry at points where those isoquants have equal gradients. Therefore, again via the logic of the theorem of 'corresponding points', the ratios of marginal productivities of labour and capital are identical at $\pi_1$ and $\pi$. Thus point $\pi_1$ satisfies the conditions of a Pareto-efficient production allocation, and lies on the contract curve of the new Edgeworth-Bowley Box $ABC_1D_1$.

Since production functions are homogeneous of degree 1, the quantity produced of each good may be measured by the distance along a ray from the origins, in the Edgeworth-Bowley Box. Clearly in Figure 3.7 distance $O_2\pi_1 < O_1\pi$, so that after input accumulation less of the import good is produced. Similarly, $\pi_1$ lies at a larger distance from origin O than point $\pi$, hence a larger quantity of exportables are produced at $\pi_1$ than $\pi$. If one factor input is fixed in supply – capital in the example above – whilst the other accumulates, then the commodity that intensively uses the accumulating input will experience an absolute increase in production, whereas the output of the other good decreases absolutely, provided commodity prices are fixed.

The foregoing logic therefore establishes the Rybczynski Theorem, which is seen to follow directly from the economic logic underpinning the theorem of 'corresponding points'. The maintenance of constant commodity prices in Figure 3.7 is merely a tool for examining the implications of the RT. Indeed, maintaining constant commodity prices is simply a special assumption and as such is not compatible with general equilibrium analysis. However, point $\pi_1$ might be a general equilibrium point under certain conditions, for example if a country experiences an increase in labour supply – full employment being maintained – *ceteris paribus* real national income (product must increase). But in Figure 3.7, at point $\pi_1$ fewer importables are consumed. As a result, the rise in real income caused a fall in demand for the importable good. For this to arise, the importable good must be an inferior good. Hence, the maintenance of constant commodity prices in the above is a special case and as such incompatible with general equilibrium analysis. The analysis may be cast in terms of transformation curves in Figure 3.8. Initially, prior to input accumulation, the transformation curve derived from the Edgeworth-Bowley Box (ABCD in Figure 3.7) is given as PP. The world terms of trade are denoted by TT in Figure 3.8; these are tangential to PP.

The new transformation curve based on Edgeworth-Bowley Box $ABC_1D_1$ might assume the shape shown by curve $P_1P_1$ in Figure 3.8. Real national income has risen. With unchanged terms of trade shown by $T_1T_1$, equilibrium tangency of $T_1T_1$ with the transformation curve $P_1P_1$ must reside beneath ZX, at point $Z_1$. For $Z_1$ to be a true general equilibrium, one of the goods (importables) must be an inferior good. Ruling out the possibility of inferior goods implies that once national income has risen due to import growth, the demand for both goods must increase, so the final equilibrium must lie somewhere in the zone YZX. The gradient of the new transformation curve $T_1T_1$, within the zone YZX, is less steep than the original transformation curve, TT, at point Z. This implies that exportable biased input growth leads to a deterioration in the terms of trade for the country since the relative price of importables – within zone YZX – is higher than previously.

An implication of the RT is that input accumulation leads to a diminution in the terms of trade for the commodity that utilises the accumulating input intensively. The key condition underpinning this reasoning is the existence of homogeneous production functions of degree 1. The RT cannot be generated for the case of more generalised/unconstrained production functions. For these production functions a specific result about the relative change in commodity prices can be established, without elaborate detail on second-order conditions being available.

Generally, the RT provides some powerful insights into possible effects of input biased growth. Thus, if the accumulating factor is used in the exportable industry intensively, the output of exportables must increase with linearly homogeneous production functions. The

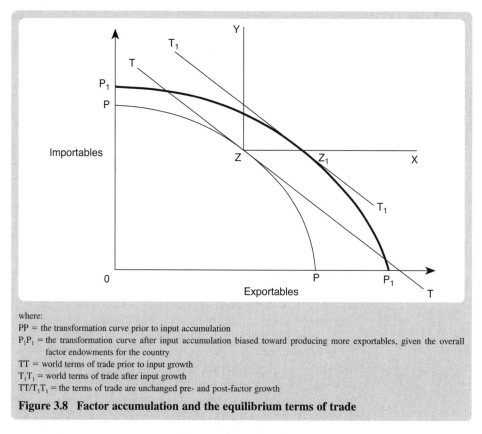

where:

PP = the transformation curve prior to input accumulation

$P_1P_1$ = the transformation curve after input accumulation biased toward producing more exportables, given the overall
  factor endowments for the country

TT = world terms of trade prior to input growth

$T_1T_1$ = world terms of trade after input growth

$TT/T_1T_1$ = the terms of trade are unchanged pre- and post-factor growth

**Figure 3.8  Factor accumulation and the equilibrium terms of trade**

impact of such factor growth on the production of importables is indeterminate. Conversely, if factor accumulation occurs in the input used intensively in the import-competing sector, the output of importables will normally rise. This effect is likely to lead to large gains for the country, since normally the country's terms of trade may improve as real national income increases. If factor growth occurs in the input used intensively in the exportable sector, the terms of trade may depreciate substantially, sufficiently perhaps for immiserising growth to occur. This latter is a highly undesirable possibility arising out of export-biased input growth. Finally, the RT implies specific possibilities for real factor incomes. If capital is the accumulating input, whilst the labour supply is constant, real wages will always rise relative to real returns to capital. Conversely, if labour is the accumulating input, whilst capital I in constant supply, real wages fall and returns to capital rise. In this circumstance, income distribution usually turns in favour of capital and against labour.

## 3.6    The Rybczynski Theorem and immiserising growth

An implication of the RT is that the export biased growth, which worsens the country's terms of trade, may make that country worse off than if no growth had occurred at all. Professor J. N. Bhagwati has underlined the deleterious effects of growth that worsens the country's terms of trade (Bhagwati, 1958). Imagine that a country expanded its supply of potential exportables at a rate in excess of its capacity to enhance import-substitution activities. For any given terms of trade, such a country will be willing to offer more exportables for more imports. Now if this country already possesses a significant world market share in its exportable good, enhanced supplies of its exportable, consequent upon export biased growth, bid down the world price of the good. A high world market share implies inelastic foreign demand, hence expanded supply of exportables bids down world prices. The impact on the country's terms of trade may be so severe that the country's improvements in supply capacity of exportables make it worse off than during the period prior to growth. This perverse result evokes shades of the Metzler case of the SST, in the sense that the country offers more exportables for fewer importables, as its terms of trade drastically worsen. In Figure 3.9, the case of growth for a trading country is depicted. Three conditions are necessary for immiserising growth to be obtained. These are: (a) The country's growth must be heavily biased toward the exportable sector. Specifically via the Rybczynski Theorem, this means factor growth in the input used intensively in exportable production. Or, that the accumulating factor absorbs a larger share of export costs compared to import-substitution costs and if additional real income does not reduce the country's demand for importables. (b) The foreign offer curve for the country's exports must be price inelastic, so that an increase in export supply causes a drastic fall in prices (refer to Figure 3.5). (c) The country must already have a considerable proportion of aggregate economic activity involved with trade, for the welfare losses associated with deteriorating terms of trade to be large enough to counteract the gains from being able to supply more exportables.

Some commentators have argued that Brazil may have faced the phenomenon of immiserising growth in the 1920s, when that country had a dominant share of the world coffee market, such that it encountered inelastic demand for its exports. This hypothesis

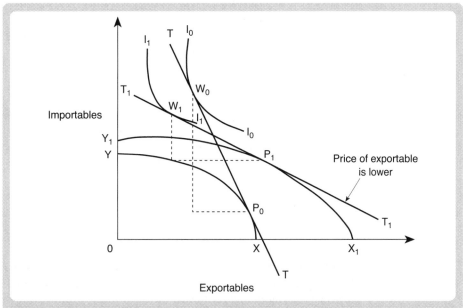

where:

YX = pre-growth transformation curve/$I_0I_0$ is the initial indifference curve

$Y_1X_1$ = post export-biased transformation curve/$I_1T_1$ is final indifferences curve

$P_0$ = pre-growth, free-trade production point, whence via exchange the country may consume at $W_0$.

TT = the initial pre-growth terms of trade

$T_1T_1$ = the post-growth, worsened terms of trade, because of enhanced supply of exportables, bringing lower prices

$P_1$ = post-growth, free-trade production point, whence via exchange the country consumes now at $W_1$. In welfare terms, $W_1$ is inferior to $W_0$.

**Figure 3.9  The phenomenon of immiserising growth in a trading nation**

has not been empirically tested via econometric analysis as yet. Immiserising growth is unlikely to be a common experience in LDCs, especially where exports of manufactures are concerned, because typically their world market shares are small in manufacturing activities. For the case of primary products, the possibility of immiserising growth occurring is more likely than for the case of manufactures, but still its occurrence in LDCs approaches the boundaries of improbability. Nonetheless, though an extreme case, the phenomenon of immiserising growth implies that governments in LDCs that are facing the problems of rapid population growth should consider discouraging investment in primary good production (which is a labour-intensive activity) and favour industry instead. Indeed, such policy advice is an implication of the standard RT too.

## Summary

The chapter has developed three special cases of the H-O-S model.

- Chapter 2 showed that trade benefits the abundant factor so the SST shows that under normal conditions protection benefits scarce inputs. The SST is in a sense the obverse of the factor price equation theorem.
- The predictions of the SST are reversed if conditions hold to allow for the Metzler paradox. This paradox requires exceptional special conditions for the marginal propensity to consume tariff revenue.
- The case of immiserising growth was discussed in the context of the H-O-S model with export biased growth. This case too is a very restrictive case.
- The Rybczynski Theorem shows how resource growth can have very strong income distributional effects in a H-O-S trading system.

### Questions

1. Is the SST prediction likely to be fulfilled given new regionalism trends in the world economy?
2. How does immiserising growth arise? Is it likely for an Asian Tiger?
3. Explain the main insights of the Rybczynski theorem.
4. Why is the Metzler Paradox an unlikely real world issue?

### Key concepts

| | |
|---|---|
| offer curves | the terms of trade |
| tariff-ridden offer curves | favourable and unfavourable terms of |
| factor accumulation | trade changes |
| the marginal propensity to consume tariff revenue | |

### Notes

1. Stolper, W. F. and Samuelson, P. A. (1941) 'Protection and real wages', *Review of Economic Studies*, vol. 9
2. Metzler, L. A. (1949) 'Tariff, terms of trade and the distribution of notional income', *Journal of Political Economy*, February, pp. 1–29.

# Bibliography

Bhagwati, J. (1958) 'Immiserising growth, a geometrical note', *Review of Economic Studies*, vol. 25.

Bhagwati, J. (1959) 'Protection, real wages, and real incomes', *Economic Journal*, vol. 69, pp. 733–44.

Bhagwati, J. and Johnson, H. G. (1961) 'A generalised theory of the effects of tariffs on the terms of trade', *Oxford Economic Paper*, vol. 13.

Johnson, H. G. (1960) 'Income distribution, the offer curve and the effects of tariffs', *Manchester School*, vol. 28.

Metzler, L. A. (1949) 'Tariff, terms of trade and the distribution of notional income', *Journal of Political Economy*, February, pp. 1–29.

Rybczynski, T. M. (1955) 'Factor endowment and relative commodity prices', *Economica*, p. 336.

Stolper, W. F. and Samuelson, P. A. (1941) 'Protection and real wages', *Review of Economic Studies*, vol. 9

# 4 Optimality and free trade: the gains from trade

**K. LAWLER and H. SEDDIGHI**

## 4.1 The gains from free trade in a general equilibrium context

Before the gains from trade are stated, equilibrium under autarky is initially examined. Essentially this chapter draws the threads of the preceding analysis together and restates precisely the gains from free trade. Later when tariff analysis is introduced, the argument here will provide a useful point of reference for readers.

In the case of isolation, the Pareto optimal point is found where a community indifference curve is tangential to the transformation curve as depicted in Figure 4.1. This is at point e, where the community indifference curve (CIC) and the country's transformation curve are tangential. The domestic terms of trade are given by (Pd, Pd). At point e, the following optimal conditions hold:

1. Optimal condition for exchange: to reach the Pareto maximum, the marginal rate of substitution (MRS) between any pair of consumer goods must be identical for all consumers who purchase both goods.

2. Optimal condition for input substitution: to reach a Pareto maximum, the marginal rate of technical substitution between any pair of inputs must be identical for all firms that utilise both inputs.

3. Optimal condition for production: to reach a Pareto maximum, the marginal rate of transformation (MRT) in production of exportables and importables must equal the marginal rate of substitution in consumption for every pair of goods, and for all consumers who purchase both.

Hence: at point e in Figure 4.1 the following condition holds: $P_E/P_I = MRT_D = MRS$, from conditions (1), (2) and (3) above, which is the Pareto welfare maximisation condition for a country under autarky. To attain the Pareto welfare maximisation condition the economy must exhibit the following characteristics:

a. perfect competition in all goods markets: exportables and importables;

b. absence of taxes or tariffs on domestic trade;

c. absence of public goods/free-ridership characteristics;

d. absence of production or consumption externalities;

e. constant returns to scale in all production activities: importables and exportables;

f. a fixed inelastic supply of factor inputs in aggregate/or a fixed overall factor endowment;

g. perfect mobility of inputs in response to market signals;

h. existence of 'twice' differentiable isoquants and indifference curves;

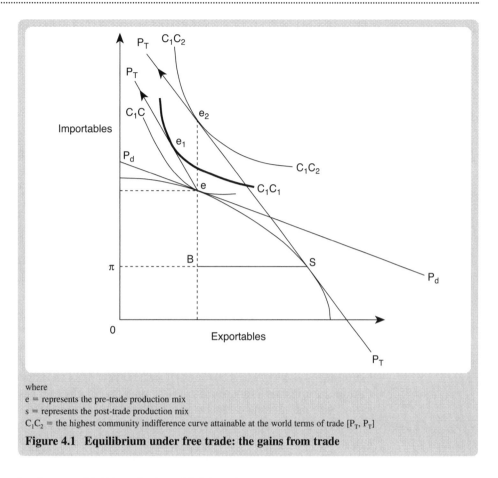

**Figure 4.1  Equilibrium under free trade: the gains from trade**

where
e = represents the pre-trade production mix
s = represents the post-trade production mix
$C_1C_2$ = the highest community indifference curve attainable at the world terms of trade $[P_T, P_T]$

i.  absence of joint products and joint costs;

j.  perfect competition in all factor markets.

If the country now starts trading it may specialise in the production of its exportable and move from point e to point s in Figure 4.1, whence via exchange at the world terms of trade given by $(P_d, P_d)$ it may achieve a superior position to point e by consuming at $e_2$. With reference to Figure 4.1, the free trade optimal condition now becomes:

$$MRT_d = MRT_f = MRS$$

where $MTR_d$ = the marginal rate of transformation in domestic terms
$MRT_f$ = the marginal rate of transformation through trade, or the world terms of trade: $P_E/P_I$, the price ratio on world markets for both goods
MRS = the marginal rate of substitution as before

Hence the logic of the preceding arguments leads to the conclusion that free trade is Pareto superior to no trade, since point $e_2$ is preferred to point e (Samuelson, 1948).

Inspection of Figure 4.1 reveals that the possibility of trade implies that the country may produce and consume at prices that are different from those available under autarky. The world terms of trade are given by $[P_T, P_T]$. The country may now reallocate its productive inputs and shift the aggregate mix to point S. The country has specialised in producing the good in which it possesses a H-O-S comparative advantage. The country will now export BS of its exportable and import $Be_2$ of importables from its trading partners, yet still produces $O\pi$ of importables domestically. At point $e_2$, the MRS in consumption is equated with the world terms of trade. Point $e_2$ represents the optimal point in commodity space that this economy can attain.

It is feasible to consider the pure gains from free trade in two stages:

1. stage one, which consists of new possibilities for exchange
2. stage two, which consists of gains from specialisation in production

This may be demonstrated with the aid of Figure 4.1. Imagine that due to inertia or government edict, the country could not change its production mix from e to point S. This means it would maintain the production mix at e. But the country could still achieve a pure exchange gain by trade at the new set of world prices shown by $eP_T$ in Figure 4.1, which is parallel to $[P_T, P_T]$. Pure exchange at the new price opportunities would put the country on commodity indifference curve $C_1C_1$ at point $e_1$, which too represents a higher level of utility than point e. Pure exchange gains could then be represented as the shift from point e to $e_1$. However, full optimality is still not available, since the MRT at point e does not equal the ratio of transformation in consumption at $e_1$. The country can improve its overall welfare position, by reallocation of inputs such that the production mix moves to S and thence via exchange to point $e_2$. The movement from e to point S may therefore be called a pure gain from the opportunity to specialise in production of exportables. It should be noted that the community indifference curves shown in Figure 4.1 ($C_1C$, $C_1C_1$, $C_1C_2$) are drawn on the assumption of a given/constant distribution of income, without this restriction meaningful comparisons of societal welfare situations are impossible. For example, if income distribution is allowed to vary, community indifference curves may intersect. If this occurs, meaningful comparisons of different levels of utility are impossible; the spectre of Arrow's impossibility case emerges. This is because the same commodity bundle may have different values according to how it is distributed. Thus it is feasible that for a given income distribution a pattern of consumption would be preferred to a second mix of consumption; but given a new income distribution, the second mix would be preferred to the initial consumption mix. This inconsistency is reflected by intersecting community indifference curves, whence it is impossible to conclude that one position is superior to another. Hence, without the restriction of a given distribution of income, community indifference curves encapsulate the impossibility of moving from individual preference rankings to societal preference rankings and demonstrate the nature of Arrow's (1963) Impossibility Theorem.

Instead of using the conceptual tool of community indifference curves to demonstrate the gains from trade, compensation test criteria may be utilised. Using this approach, a demonstration of 'potential' Pareto improvement in enhanced real income – caused by a movement from no trade to free trade – is made. The compensation test is then used to show that it is feasible for the gainers (from free trade) to compensate the losers, such that losers may be restored to the same level of real income they attained before the movement from autarky to free trade occurred, whilst the winners still retain some gains. In this new case the redistribution of gains/losses would be executed via lump sum taxes on the winners, and subsidies/transfers to losers. In terms of the H-O-S model, the winners in a movement from no trade to free trade are the owners of the abundant inputs used intensively in exportables, and the losers are the owners of scarce inputs used intensively in import-substitution activities. Such a redistribution policy produces a real income distribution where no one is left worse off and some are better off. A real income distribution of this type is called a Pareto-efficient distribution.

The compensation test requires a double-edged criterion: first, the winners from the policy change toward free trade must be able to compensate the losers, yet retain some gain; secondly, potential losers should not be able to compensate/bribe the potential winners for non-implementation of the prospective policy change from autarky/isolationism to free trade. Or, simply that those hit by removal of a tariff (think of the SST) should not be able to bribe those who gain from free trade to revert to protectionist policies. The first part of the compensation test is called the Hicks-Kaldor criterion, whilst the second is termed the Scitovsky-reversal criterion. The reversal to the free trade occurs if real income under autarky was distributed the same as with free trade. Hence, the double-edged criterion requires that it must be impossible to make all as well off under autarky, by any redistribution of actual amounts acquired via free trade. If the Scitovsky reversal criterion is not satisfied, it is feasible that, simultaneously, autarky should be preferred to free trade and free trade be preferred to autarky. Although the compensation test appears to alleviate the difficult restrictions imposed by the use of community indifference curves, the test has drawbacks too. These are (1) the compensation test possesses a stringently conservative bias toward 'do-nothing', or, it is 'worthy' to bring losers back to their initial position, which might represent a sub-optimal income distribution anyway; (2) the compensation test indicates only a potential Pareto improvement such that the indicated income distribution might be attained. Whether this is practically achieved requires an additional political choice. Thus if compensation is not paid in practice welfare need not have improved. Alternatively, if government does actually choose to impose necessary extra lump sum taxes and subsidies, the test assumes that redistribution is costless, that work incentives are unaffected, and that no distortions are created elsewhere in the system to reduce welfare. Economists of the Austrian persuasion would take issue on: (1) the enhanced role of government in the redistribution exercise, (2) the question whether redistribution could be costless for this implies the fallacy of the 'free lunch', (3) the fact that work incentives are not affected by lump sum taxes/subsidies, (4) that government had sufficient knowledge/data to determine that the necessary fiscal action/programme did not create further distortions in the economic system which undermined the desired objective of enhanced welfare.

Hence the use of the compensation tests for demonstrating the gains available from free trade compared to autarky can also be problematic. The test certainly lacks the neat clarity that community indifference curves bestow on the graphical/geometric solutions to the case in favour of free trade compared to autarky, once the restriction of a given distribution of income is admitted (Salvatore, 1986).

The arguments presented above demonstrated flaws in the basic Ricardian case in favour of free trade. Modern analytical welfare economics recognises that there is no guarantee that every individual consumer will be better off under free trade than autarky, but the country as a whole will be better off. The nature of the compensation test shows that only if a redistribution policy is pursued can free trade ensure each individual is better off. Hence, the logical arguments presented in the preceding analysis allow the following general statement to be made: specifically, that normally free trade will make the country as a whole actually better off and lead to a potential welfare improvement. Since free trade/laissez faire can only be theoretically justified if government intervention is operated concomitantly, Austrian economists would not perhaps accept this paradox, however. Austrian writers would dispute governments' ability to possess sufficient knowledge to operate interventionist/redistribution programmes efficiently. For Austrian economists, the danger ever-present in interventionist policies concerns the likelihood of government achieving, despite the finest intentions, negative-sum welfare outcomes. Austrians, therefore, would argue that because the case in favour of free trade is overwhelming in the aggregate, free trade must always be preferred to protection, despite changes in income distribution which the adoption of free trade might engender. The Austrian presumption in favour of free trade, though extreme, nonetheless provides a vigorous challenge to the tenets of modern analytical welfare economics.

## 4.2  The impact of tariffs and subsidies on trade and welfare

In practice, for various reasons, governments in rich and poor countries resort to policies to restrict the volume of foreign trade: import quotas, tariffs, voluntary export curbs, taxes, subsidies and exchange rate restrictions. Such trade restrictions/interventions are typical features of the trade regimes operated by many governments. In a large number of cases trade restrictions are applied to:

1. encourage exports

2. discourage imports

3. promote employment

4. ease the balance of payments problems

5. encourage industrialisation

6. retaliate against a foreign country.

But when are such trade restrictions optimal, or 'first best', in attaining a specific national objective? In practice, protectionist policies are likely to diverge considerably from what economists would specify as optimal policy interventions. In reality, policy measures to protect domestic trade are likely to produce second/third best results. More generally, what governments frequently purport to be arguments for trade protection are really non-arguments and amount to justifications for some other policy measure. Do optimal trade restrictions/interventions exist? The answer to this wide-ranging issue is best considered in the light of the conclusions offered by analytical welfare economics. These conclusions may be fairly summarised as follows:

a. Free trade is Pareto-superior to autarky for a given distribution of income. This is taken to be the 'optimum optimorum' case.

b. Restricted trade is Pareto-superior to autarky, for a given distribution of income.

c. But free trade is Pareto-superior to tariff-ridden/restricted trade, for a given income distribution.

d. However, an 'optimum tariff' is Pareto-superior to free trade when a particular country confronts world market distortions and the yardstick of welfare is national advantage only.

e. And an 'optimum subsidy' is Pareto-superior to a tariff when a country confronts domestic market distortions/externalities.

Briefly, welfare conclusions on protectionism reveal just one case where tariff protection produces a 'first best' result: specifically, that of the optimum tariff ([d] above). Other arguments for trade protection really amount to arguments for specific governmental interventions in the home economy; to utilise tariffs in such situations produces sub-optimal results (Bhagwati, 1968b).

## 4.3    Social/political arguments for protection and some fallacies

A case in favour of protection implies that a tariff situation is superior to free trade, if the compensation test is satisfied. Many arguments for protection can therefore be classified as social/political since welfare criteria are not met. Hence the typical social/political case for protection does not seek to enhance real national income but rather aims to change its composition, to attain a desired social/political end. Thus the plea for protection of national defence industries is common in many countries, but the criterion used, national defence capability, is not an economic one.

Similarly tariff protection to attain either (1) the cultural values of industrial society or (2) cultural simplicities of agrarian society as better ways of life are once more a social/ political/religious argument, for this is not consistent with an increase in real income over free-trade situations. Again, the common plea in many developing countries for self-sufficiency to remove all dependency on foreigners/ex-colonialists, for the attainment of nationalistic objectives, is a non-economic argument for tariff protection. Moreover, many 'arguments' in favour of protection turn out to be logical fallacies, despite being styled as economic arguments. A typically fallacious argument in favour of protectionism is that tariffs can stimulate and/or remove domestic unemployment. This argument can lead to more unemployment given foreign retaliation. Domestic involuntary unemployment is more efficiently removed via appropriate use of monetary policies and flexible exchange rates. Yet another common fallacy concerns the view that tariffs may alleviate Balance of Payments problems. In the long run a policy is doomed to fail, if the underlying cause of payments difficulty – perhaps domestic inflation, or an overvalued exchange rate(s) – is not eradicated (Bhagwati, 1968b).

## 4.4    Optimal interventions/restrictions on trade[1]

Returning now to the conclusions of analytical welfare economics, (a) to (e), it can now be recorded that:

1. the analysis underpinning Figure 4.1 demonstrates that free trade is superior to autarky, and establishes conclusion (a);

2. conclusion (b) may be established with reference to Figure 4.2, as follows: at price $P_1$, which equals the world marginal cost of production for good X, the country will consume $oX_4$ of the good, of which $oX_1$ is produced domestically, and $oX_4-oX_1$ of good X is imported. At price $P_1$, the country is trading freely. A non-prohibitive tariff at $P_2$ is now imposed on importables. Domestic consumers and producers now confront deadweight losses (refer to Figure 3.1) equal to areas W and Q respectively, in Figure 4.2. If a prohibitive tariff is now levied at $P_3$ in Figure 4.2, imports of good X cease. But welfare losses are greater now than in the case of restrictive trade, caused by tariff $P_2$. Because, if the prohibitive tariff $P_3$ is cut to $P_2$, pure welfare gains equal to area Z plus area G are available. The movement from the prohibitive tariff at $P_3$ to the non-prohibitive tariff at $P_2$ would, *ceteris paribus*, satisfy necessary compensation criteria. Hence point (b) is established, such that tariff-restricted trade is better than autarky imposed by a prohibitive tariff. Thus in terms of Figure 4.2, the free trade position at price $P_1$ is superior to both the restricted and no-trade cases. Free trade is thus a 'first best' policy, restricted trade is a second best alternative, whereas the prohibitive tariff represents a third best policy option. Figure 4.2 is circumscribed by being cast in a

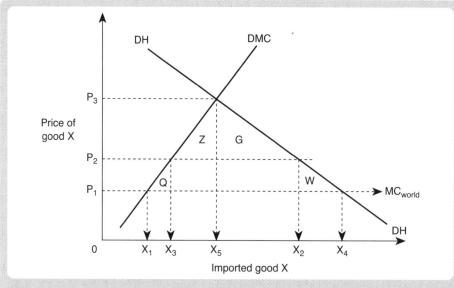

where

$D_H D_H$ = domestic demand for importable good X
DMC = domestic marginal cost of producing good X
$P_1$ = world marginal cost of producing good X
$P_2$ = domestic price of importable when a non-prohibitive tariff is imposed
$P_3$ = domestic price of good X when a prohibitive tariff is levied on imports of good X from the rest of the world
$oX_1$ = domestic output of good X with free trade
$oX_3$ = domestic output of good X with a non-prohibitive tariff
$oX_2 - oX_3$ = imports of good X when the non-prohibitive tariff is applied
$oX_2$ = domestic consumption of good X with the non-prohibitive tariff
$oX_5$ = domestic output of good X when the prohibitive tariff is levied. Home producers dominate the domestic market for X.

**Figure 4.2  The welfare implications of prohibitive and non-prohibitive tariffs**

partial equilibrium mould and subsumes the small-country assumption. However, the conclusion of point b is still valid for the general equilibrium case. With reference to Figure 4.1 autarky is represented by point e, restricted trade might be depicted by a movement from e to point $e_1$ and free trade is shown by point $e_2$. Point $e_1$ may be interpreted as a restricted-trade case since the no-trade production mix is maintained when trade occurs. Thus point B is logically valid for a given distribution of income (as assumed in Figure 4.2), and/or with the compensation test. Moreover, the preceding analysis automatically established the logical consistency implied by point c – hence free trade is superior to restricted trade.

## 4.5  The case of the optimum tariff

Points (d) and (e) of the preceding welfare conclusions can now be established. The case of the optimum tariff is considered first. An enduring argument for protection concerns the terms of trade (Bhagwati and Ramaswami, 1963). From the standpoint of national welfare, a nation with monopoly or monopsony market power in foreign trade may improve its terms of trade by taxing its exports (like OPEC if it possesses monopoly/cartel market power) or by taxing imports if the nation possesses monopsonistic/oligopsonistic market power. A tax on exports can be passed on to foreigners, whereas a tariff on imports can result in a reduced price of imports – calculated prior to duty – in order to maintain market share in the tariff-imposing country. In each event the commodity terms of trade improve. The nub of the 'terms of trade' argument for protection is that the 'foreigner pays the tax/duty'. By taxing exports, the monopolistic nation or cartel group raises its export price. Conversely, by levying duties on imports, the monopolistic nation encourages the foreign suppliers to reduce their export prices. The tax/duty is, therefore, absorbed by foreigners. Theoretically an optimum tariff is one that improves the nation's terms of trade up to the point where the marginal gain from enhanced terms of trade is equal to the marginal loss from the reduced volume of trade caused by the tariff. The case for seeking an optimal tariff arises out of the existence of distortions in world product markets. This means there exists a divergence between the marginal revenue or marginal cost and the market price available on world markets. As a monopoly firm selects optimal output where MC = MR, instead of where MC = price, so too should the nation (or group of nations in a cartel) with monopoly power. World market imperfections imply that the world market prices diverge from the $MRT_d$. Hence, there exists a world market distortion such that: $MRT_F$ not equal to $MRT_d$ = MRS becomes the case. Free trade gets the price ratio $MRT_F$ or average terms of trade equal to the ratio of marginal opportunity production costs $MRY_d$. However, the average terms of trade $MRT_F$ only equal the marginal terms of trade if national monopoly/oligopoly power is absent. The possession of national monopoly and/or cartel market power means that the exporting country can gain by equating its marginal terms of trade $MRT_F$, the marginal revenues from export sales, to its marginal opportunity cost in domestic production, $MRT_d$. The divergence may be corrected via a tariff which removes the market distortion. Since the distortion occurs in foreign markets, tariff imposition will be a first best intervention policy for it will equate $MRT_d$ and $MRT_F$ without distorting the equality between $MRT_d$ and MRS in the domestic economy. A second best option in this case would be a tax/subsidy policy on production. A key issue which arises concerns the optimum degree of trade restriction. The objective is to optimise the terms of trade. So long as the foreigner's demand function is not infinitely elastic, the terms of trade can always be enhanced by the exercise of national monopoly market power. It can be shown that there is perfect symmetry between export taxes and import duties (tariffs). More nations tend to possess monopoly power compared to monopsony market power and seek improvements in their terms of trade via export (pseudo) taxes, however.

Naturally the optimal tariff on imports (or exports) can be depicted using offer curve analysis. A country that taxes trade can use the tariff to shift its own offer curve until it reaches the point on the foreign offer curve which maximises the tariff-imposing country's welfare. Figure 4.3 depicts an optimal tariff for the country exporting good Y. The country exporting good Y shifts its offer curve rightwards by making the price of importables X in terms of units of good Y higher within the country than that price received by foreign suppliers of good X. At point W in Figure 4.3 domestic consumers pay for good X at the domestic price ratio QG/GW, giving up GQ of good Y for GW of good X. But foreign suppliers get only OG of good Y for GW of good X, because government collects tariff revenue at the rate QO/GW. Figure 4.3 shows that this particular rate of tariff duty is optimal because at point W, the foreign offer curve is tangent to $C_1C$, the optimal indifference curve attainable restricted via trade. The optimal tariff is positive since the foreign offer curve is not infinitely elastic. If it were perfectly elastic, the optimal tariff would be zero. Hence, the more elastic the foreign offer curve the lower will be the optimal tariff, and vice versa. A nation's offer curve elasticity may be defined as the

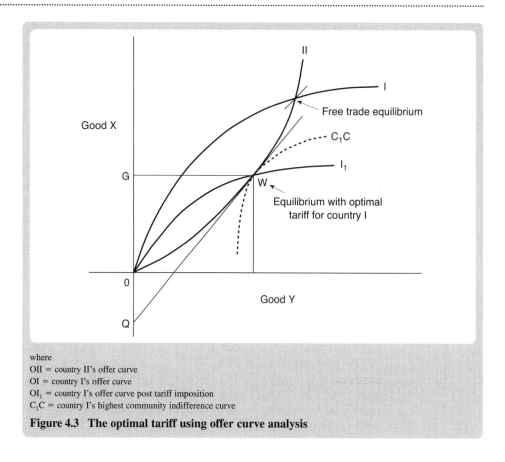

where
OII = country II's offer curve
OI = country I's offer curve
OI₁ = country I's offer curve post tariff imposition
C₁C = country I's highest community indifference curve

**Figure 4.3   The optimal tariff using offer curve analysis**

ratio of the percentage change of its import demand [X in Figure 4.3] to a percentage change with respect to the relative price of imports:

Hence, offer curve elasticity $[r] = -(\%\Delta X)/[\%\Delta (x/y)]$ ... [4.1]

where: $\%\Delta X$ = percentage in change in imports, X
   $\%\Delta(X/Y)$ = percentage change in relative price of imports

The price vector/ratio (X/Y) is difficult to perceive on the offer curves in Figure 4.3 so the definition in equation [4.1] may be written as:

$r = -(\%\Delta X)/[\%\Delta X - \%\Delta Y]$ ... [4.2]

$r = -1/\{[(\%\Delta Y)/(\%\Delta X)] - 1\}$ ... [4.3]

whence: $r = 1/\{1 - [(\partial Y/\partial X)(X/Y)]\}$ ... [4.4]

Equation [4.4] may now be connected with price vectors in Figure 4.3. Notice that it is the foreign offer curve elasticity which is being considered so analysis focuses on the offer curve for country II. Country II's export of good Y and import of good X at point W in Figure 4.3 occurs at the price ratio GW/GQ, whereas the world price of country II's imports of good X (X/Y) occurs at ratio GW/OQ. Hence, the elasticity of country II's offer curve may be written as:

$r = 1/\{1 - [(GW/GQ)(OG/GW)]\}$ ... [4.5]

Simplifying the denominator in equation [4.5] yields:

$$r = 1/\{1 - (OG/GQ)\} \qquad \qquad \text{... [4.6]}$$

whence further manipulation of equation [4.6] yields:

$$r = GQ/OQ \qquad \qquad \text{... [4.7]}$$

Thus the connection between the optimal tariff rate at point W in Figure 4.3 and the foreign offer curve elasticity may be written as:

$$T_0 = OQ/OG = 1/[(GQ/OQ) - 1] \qquad \qquad \text{... [4.8]}$$

Substitution of equation [4.7] into equation [4.8] gives the optimal tariff rate, whence:

$$T_0 = 1/(r - 1) \qquad \qquad \text{... [4.9]}$$

where: $T_0$ = the optimal tariff rate; r = elasticity of the foreign offer curve; country II's offer curve in Figure 4.3.

Equation [4.9] is equivalent to the reciprocal of country II's elasticity of demand for country I's export good Y. Finally, equation [4.9] yields any feasible tariff rate, not just the optimal rate. In Figure 4.3 the tariff rate is optimised at point W because country II's offer curve is at a point of tangency with country I's indifference curve, $C_1C$.

A final caveat is worth noting: the optimum tariff only potentially maximises a country's welfare. The optimum tariff will affect income distribution: some members of society are better off and others made worse off by the tariff. Hence, the imposition of an optimal tariff when there are world market distortions must be accompanied by a countervailing redistribution policy such that compensation criteria are satisfied. However, since by definition the optimal tariff enhances a nation's total welfare, it follows that compensation criteria will be satisfied, given no retaliation from trading partners. If, in Figure 4.3, we consider country I's gain and country II's losses, it must be said that country I's gain is not as great as country II's losses. From the standpoint of game theory, if retaliation by country II is permitted, the theory of the optimum tariff provides an example of a prisoner's dilemma variable-sum game. Competitive retaliation from both countries via tariff imposition might lead to negative-sum outcomes for both countries since a no-trade point could be reached at worst and potentially unstable trade patterns attained at best. However, in a time-constrained game, the Folk Theorem would produce a Cournot outcome. Cooperative outcomes emerge if this game is played endlessly.

In conclusion, the preceding analysis of arguments for protection permits the following generalisation to be made: only the optimum tariff provides an economic rationale for tariff protection, whence all other arguments for protection are essentially justifications for subsidies. Analysis now proceeds to consider the case of optimum subsidies: the welfare conclusion [point e] noted previously.

## 4.6    Domestic distortions: optimum subsidy/tax policies

If a world market distortion requires the use of an optimum tariff, a domestic distortion requires optimum subsidies as a first best remedial policy initiative. Domestic market distortions typically assume the form of a divergence between private marginal costs and social marginal costs of production because of: (a) externalities in product markets (Ghatak, 1986); (b) immobilities and/or imperfections in markets for factors. When distortions caused by either (a) or (b) above exist, domestic market prices do not reflect true social opportunity costs as given by $MRT_d$. The existence of a domestic distortion means that: $MRT_d \neq MRS = MRT_f$.

In this case the first best policy to equate $MRT_d$ with MRS will requires a domestic tax/subsidy policy targeted specifically at the source of the divergence between market prices in the home economy and marginal social opportunity costs. External economies of scale in product markets arise when the expansion of industry X produces a side benefit for industry Y, but when industry X cannot internalise the whole of the social benefit. If industry Y's long-run average costs fall as a result of increased output in industry X, there is an external economy from industry X's expansion of output. The system of market prices does not record this social benefit, and industry X cannot charge for the social benefit it has created. Industry Y then assumes the characteristics of a 'free-rider'. An example of an external benefit of this type occurs when industry X trains labour inputs that may become freely available to industry Y, or creates knowledge in its production techniques which are freely transferable to industry Y. In this event the output of industry X will be less than it should be if its private costs were reduced to the true social cost. Hence when domestic market prices do not represent true social marginal costs/marginal benefits, the domestic market distortion causes:

$$MRT_d < MRT_f$$

In Figure 4.4, the transformation curve for the two goods Y and X is depicted by AB. With free trade and the absence of any distortions, the country can specialise in production of good X, produce at point $G_1$ and consume at $U_1$. This represents the Pareto-optimal case where: $MRT_f = MRT_d = MRS$; as in Figure 4.1. Imagine that a domestic market distortion is now introduced in the labour market such that the social marginal opportunity cost of labour is less than the private cost, because industry X trains labour freely available to industry Y. This creates the divergence between $MRT_d$ and the ratio of private marginal costs of producing X and Y. The situation is displayed in Figure 4.4. The profit-maximising equilibrium for producers is at point G, yet consumers maximise utility at point $U_0$ since producers supply outputs according to the ratio of world market prices, and private marginal cost, whereas consumers equate the MRS to the $MRT_f$. Hence the Pareto optimal case is not attained since:

$$MRT_f = MRS \neq MRT_d$$

whence a first best remedial policy action means it is necessary to levy a tax on industry Y (to contract output) and subsidise the output of good X (to expand output of X) until the Pareto optimal welfare point is attained, at $G_1$ whence: $MRT_f = MRS = MRT_d$, and utility is maximised. Notice that a tariff could also enhance production of X. A tariff raises output of good X to point $G_3$. Equilibrium for production and consumption is now attained along the tariff-ridden price vector $T_1T_2$, reflecting that the tariff has improved the country's terms of trade. With the tariff, consumers get a higher level of utility at $U_2$ than at consumption point $U_0$ – free trade in the presence of domestic distortions – though this does not necessarily follow. Notice that at point $U_2$ welfare is not maximised since first best Paretian conditions are not satisfied. When a tariff is levied to alleviate the domestic distortion the following arises:

$$MRT_f \neq MRT_d \neq MRS$$

Hence the use of tariffs to correct domestic market distortions does not produce an optimal result. Alternatively the use of a domestic tax/subsidy option (in Figure 4.4, taxing industry Y and subsidising industry X) produces a welfare maximisation point

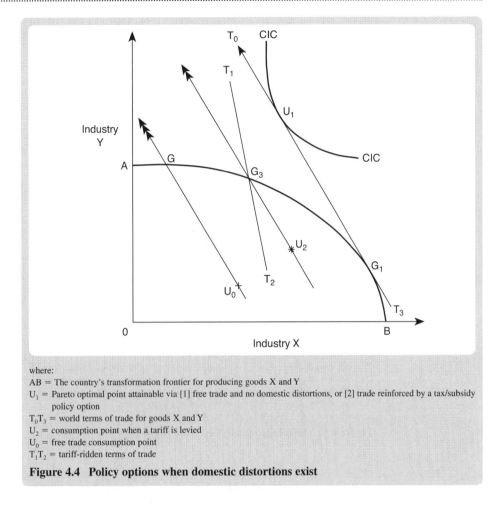

where:
AB = The country's transformation frontier for producing goods X and Y
$U_1$ = Pareto optimal point attainable via [1] free trade and no domestic distortions, or [2] trade reinforced by a tax/subsidy policy option
$T_0T_3$ = world terms of trade for goods X and Y
$U_2$ = consumption point when a tariff is levied
$U_0$ = free trade consumption point
$T_1T_2$ = tariff-ridden terms of trade

**Figure 4.4  Policy options when domestic distortions exist**

and represents a first best policy option for government, for given levels of income distribution.

## 4.7    The infant-industry case

Even classical economists allowed that in certain conditions, a nation's true comparative advantage might not develop due to the existence of domestic distortions. They argued that due to a divergence between marginal social and marginal private opportunity costs, trade could be protected on a temporary basis, such that high initial average production costs for the infant industry eventually fall via learning by doing, whence protection may then be removed and the true pattern of international specialisation attained. To enhance societal welfare, however, the infant industry must grow to maturity, and then compete on an equal basis with foreign manufacturers in home and world markets. J. S. Mill was unequivocal on this issue. Moreover, classicists argued that the infant industry must be able to cover the subsidisation costs of its immaturity by reducing absolutely its average production costs. Bastable too was unequivocal on this issue. Hence, classicists argued that protecting an infant industry was effectively an investment decision. The case of an

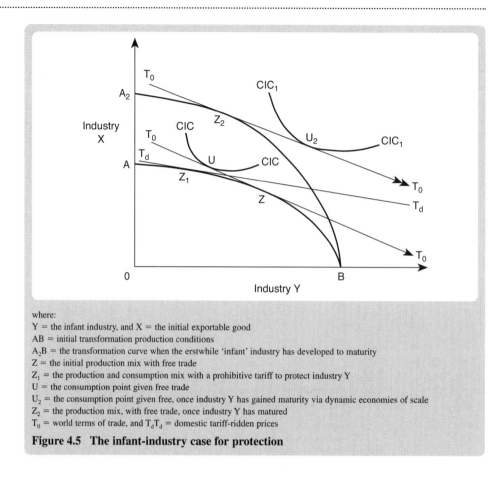

where:
Y = the infant industry, and X = the initial exportable good
AB = initial transformation production conditions
$A_2$B = the transformation curve when the erstwhile 'infant' industry has developed to maturity
Z = the initial production mix with free trade
$Z_1$ = the production and consumption mix with a prohibitive tariff to protect industry Y
U = the consumption point given free trade
$U_2$ = the consumption point given free, once industry Y has gained maturity via dynamic economies of scale
$Z_2$ = the production mix, with free trade, once industry Y has matured
$T_0$ = world terms of trade, and $T_dT_d$ = domestic tariff-ridden prices

**Figure 4.5   The infant-industry case for protection**

infant industry is represented in Figure 4.5. Industry Y is the infant industry and, given free trade, the nation produces at Z on the transformation curve AB, and consumes at U, at world terms of trade $T_0T_0$. A prohibitive tariff shifts production from Z to the mix at $Z_1$ where more of good Y is produced. With domestic prices shown by $T_DT_D$, $Z_1$ is also a consumption point. Compared to point U, societal welfare has fallen. If dynamic scale economies are achieved via tariff protection in industry Y, eventually the transformation curve may pivot at B and swing to $A_2$, where the nation now embraces free trade again, with the same terms of trade as previously, $T_0T_0$. The country now produces at point $Z_2$ and consumes at $U_2$, which is Pareto superior now than prior to protection.

To justify governmental intervention, neo-classical economists require that the following rules be applied: (1) the social rate must be larger than the private rate of return in the infant industry, and (2) the private return necessary to encourage investment in the infant industry must be greater than the private and social returns available on alternative investments in the economy, so as to ensure that private investment is unprofitable whereas public investment is socially profitable.

Generally, to justify the infant-industry argument for protection the whole country must gain from knowledge diffusion consequent upon its growth, such that it is reasonable for society to bear the welfare costs of its development. Once more a tariff is not the optimal protection instrument, for it involves unnecessarily harsh consumption losses in society compared to an optimal subsidy to the infant industry. To expand output to the correct level in industry Y, a tariff produces consumption losses that a subsidy designed to achieve the same output level in industry Y would not create.

Eventually the infant industry must attain maturity such that: $MRT_f = MRT_d = MRS$ is reached. Protection via a tariff yields: $MRT_f = MRT_d$ not equal to MRS, whereas an optimal subsidy to the infant industry gives: $MRT_f = MRT_d = MRS$ as required. However, new-classical and/or Austrian economists argue that subsidy protection is too selective in granting special advantages to some industries, compared to other domestic industries, whereas protection to all industries offers special protection to none. Such economists might well prefer policies involving monetary deflation and/or devaluation rather than use of tariffs and subsidies. Austrian and new-classical writers tend to be committed free-traders, so any governmental intervention is seen as sub-optimal action. Hence selective tariffs/subsidies might be regarded as anathema, in some schools of economic thought (Baldwin, 1969). Strategic subsidy policies introduced by protectionist governments create perverse trade patterns and Bertrand-Nash equilibria (see Chapter 13).

## Summary

- Trade often has strong effects on the distribution of income within countries, so that it often produces losers as well as winners.
- Trade nonetheless produces overall gains in the sense that those who gain could in principle compensate those who lose while still remaining better off than before. The Scitovsky criterion points to this case.
- The Pareto criterion shows why free trade is optimal. However, optimal interventions can be undertaken when full Pareto optimality is not available. The general equilibrium framework shows that specific policies can affect welfare. Generally when there are international distortions, such as market power, optimal tariffs boost individual country welfare but lower world welfare. Optimal subsidies are best applied in the case of domestic distortions.

## Questions

1. What is a domestic distortion? How does it affect trade?
2. When may an optimal subsidy be used?
3. What are optimal tariffs? How do they improve welfare?
4. Discuss two fallacious arguments for protection.

## Key concepts

optimum tariffs
optimal interventions
welfare criteria
market power

offer curve elasticity
prohibitive tariffs
domestic distortion

## Note

1. Baldwin, R. E. (1969) 'The case against infant-industry tariff protection, *Journal of Political Economy*.

## Bibliography

Arrow, K. J. (1963) *Social Choice and Individual Values*, New York: Wiley, second edition.

Baldwin, R. E. (1969) 'The case against infant-industry tariff protection, *Journal of Political Economy*, vol. 88, no. 6, May/June; see Rosefielde, S. (1974) 'Factor proportions and economic rationality in Soviet international trade, 1955–1968', *American Economic Review*, vol. 64, no. 4, September, pp. 670–81.

Bhagwati, J. (1968a) 'The gains from trade once again', *Oxford Economic Papers*, pp. 137–48.

Bhagwati, J. (1968b) 'Non-economic objectives and the efficiency properties of trade', *Journal of Political Economy*, vol. 75.

Bhagwati, J. and Ramaswami, V. K. (1963) 'Domestic distortions, tariffs and the optimal tariff', *Journal of Political Economy*, vol. 71.

Ghatak, S. (1986) *An Introduction to Development Economics*, Allen and Unwin, pp. 273–94.

Salvatore, D. (1986) *Micro-Economics, Theory and Applications*, Macmillan Publishing Company, pp. 591–683.

Samuelson, P. A. (1948) 'The gain from international trade once again', *Economic Journal*, reprinted in Bhagwati, J. N. (1969) *International Trade*, Baltimore: Penguin.

# 5 An evaluation of the static H-O-S theory of trade

## K. LAWLER and H. SEDDIGHI

## 5.1 Introduction

This chapter provides a two-stage evaluation of the H-O-S theory of trade. The first stage provides some theoretical limitations of the H-O-S theory. Thereafter a selective review of key empirical tests of the H-O-S prediction is presented. The survey of empirical literature on the H-O-S prediction, though not comprehensive in scope, nonetheless focuses on key theoretical issues thrown up by researchers.

## 5.2 The theoretical shortcomings of the H-O-S theory

Recall that the logical truth of the H-O-S prediction depends on the following conditions being met; specifically that:

1. perfect competition exists in all markets;
2. production functions exhibit constant returns to scale in the long run;
3. no factor intensity reversals occur;
4. trading countries possess similar tastes, when the physical definition of relative factor abundance is used

Releasing any (or all) of the foregoing may reverse the H-O-S prediction. For example, if we relax condition (i) above such that monopoly is allowed to enter the picture, trade between countries may still occur but on a pattern which is the reverse of the H-O-S prediction. In Figure 5.1, country I is assumed to be capital rich and good Y is assumed to be the capital-intensive good in both countries, whereas country II is labour rich, and good X is the labour-intensive good in both countries. The H-O-S theory predicts that country I has a comparative advantage in good Y and country II in good X. Good Y is country I's exportable good, whereas good X is country II's exportable good, by the H-O-S prediction. Imagine that industry Y in country I now becomes a state-trading monopoly. A monopoly industry structure in country I can now reverse the H-O-S prediction trade pattern. A profit-maximising monopoly in country I in industry Y means that the price of good Y will necessarily exceed the marginal cost of producing Y; hence:

$P_Y > MC_Y$
when $MC_Y = MR_Y$, profits are maximised
where: $P_Y$ = the price of good Y
$MC_Y$ = marginal cost of producing Y
$MR_Y$ = marginal revenue from sales of Y

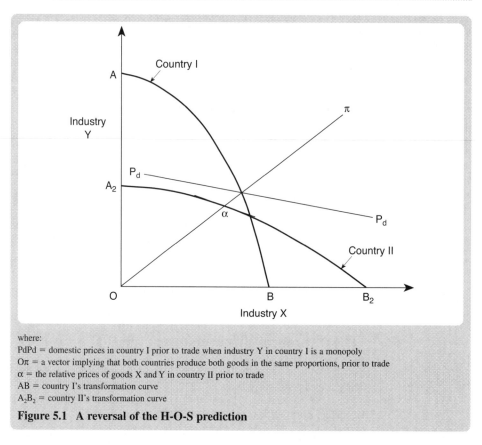

where:

PdPd = domestic prices in country I prior to trade when industry Y in country I is a monopoly

Oπ = a vector implying that both countries produce both goods in the same proportions, prior to trade

α = the relative prices of goods X and Y in country II prior to trade

AB = country I's transformation curve

$A_2B_2$ = country II's transformation curve

**Figure 5.1  A reversal of the H-O-S prediction**

Hence, it might be cheaper for country I to export X and import Y from country II, in which case the H-O-S prediction is reversed, due the existence of a monopoly market structure in the exportable sector of one country. So the relaxation of condition (1) above is sufficient to reverse the H-O-S prediction *ceteris paribus*. Along vector Oπ the H-O-S prediction is true when perfect competition exists in all markets, because the relative slopes of the two transformation curves imply that the opportunity cost of expanding Y production in country I is lower than in country II. But along vector Oπ, whence both countries produce both goods in the same proportion, a monopoly in country I in industry Y implies a domestic price ratio in country I which is not tangential to country I's transformation curve; trade will occur on a pattern which is now the reverse of the H-O-S prediction. Country II will export capital-intensive good Y.

Note: despite country I's production bias towards producing good Y, compared to X, this bias is outweighed by a monopolised industry in country I setting profit-maximising prices, prior to trade, when $P_Y > MC_Y$.

If condition (2) above is relaxed such that increasing and/or decreasing returns to scale are introduced, the H-O-S prediction can be reversed. Figure 5.2 shows the case where country I enjoys increasing returns to scale in the production of both goods Y and X, because its transformation curve is inward-bending. Country II is assumed to have a normal convex transformation curve. Once more it is assumed that country I is capital rich and good Y is a capital-intensive good in both countries. Country II is assumed to be labour rich, and good X is a labour-intensive activity in both countries. When both countries produce both goods in the same proportion – along vector Oπ in Figure 5.2 –

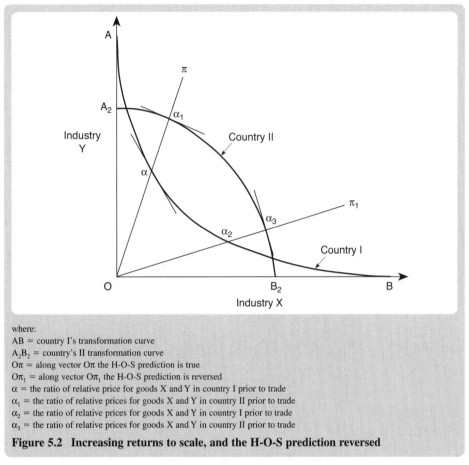

where:

AB = country I's transformation curve

$A_2B_2$ = country's II transformation curve

$O\pi$ = along vector $O\pi$ the H-O-S prediction is true

$O\pi_1$ = along vector $O\pi_1$ the H-O-S prediction is reversed

$\alpha$ = the ratio of relative price for goods X and Y in country I prior to trade

$\alpha_1$ = the ratio of relative prices for goods X and Y in country II prior to trade

$\alpha_2$ = the ratio of relative prices for goods X and Y in country I prior to trade

$\alpha_3$ = the ratio of relative prices for goods X and Y in country II prior to trade

**Figure 5.2  Increasing returns to scale, and the H-O-S prediction reversed**

trade along the lines of the H-O-S prediction might occur. However, at a different set of initial production conditions – along vector $O\pi_1$ in Figure 5.2 – the H-O-S prediction is reversed. Country II exports the capital-intensive good and country I exports the labour-intensive good Y. If condition (3) above is released such that the existence of factor intensity reversals is allowed, then fundamental damage is inflicted on the H-O-S prediction. For example, if factor intensities are reversed between two trading nations for exportables and importables, it is logically impossible for both countries' trade patterns to pass the H-O-S test, yet clearly either one can.

The existence of factor intensity reversals implies that at a given set of input prices a commodity is labour intensive, whereas at another set of input prices that same commodity becomes a capital-intensive production activity. Factor reversals are demonstrated in Figure 5.3. Hence, for a given input price ratio illustrated by the budget line BB, both industries X and Y combine inputs in the same ratio, that given by vector $O\pi$. If input prices vary, so that wage rates fall, both industries X and Y switch to more labour-intensive methods of production activities. But input substitution possibilities are easier in industry X than Y, so activity Y remains more capital intensive than X when wage rates fall. Similarly, if input prices vary such that wages rise relative to capital rentals, good X now becomes a more capital-intensive sector than industry Y, which will always be closer to the $\pi$ ratio in Figure 5.3 than will the factor intensity vector of industry X (Jones, 1956/7).

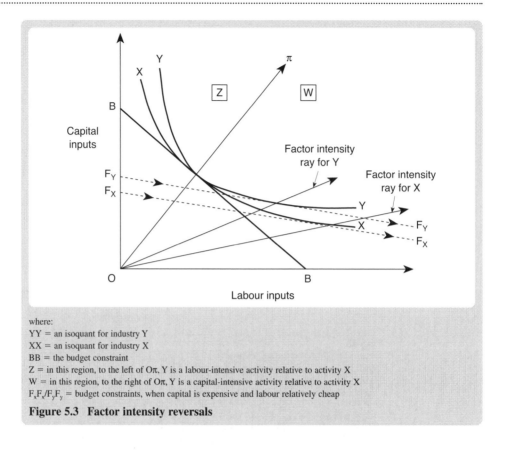

where:
YY = an isoquant for industry Y
XX = an isoquant for industry X
BB = the budget constraint
Z = in this region, to the left of Oπ, Y is a labour-intensive activity relative to activity X
W = in this region, to the right of Oπ, Y is a capital-intensive activity relative to activity X
$F_x F_x / F_y F_y$ = budget constraints, when capital is expensive and labour relatively cheap

**Figure 5.3   Factor intensity reversals**

The analysis underlying Figure 5.3 may now be applied to the case where: (1) factor endowments of two trading nations differ significantly; (2) given (1), the factor endowment proportions in both countries lie on different sides of the critical vector Oπ in Figure 5.3.

In Figure 5.4, the factor endowments of countries I and II differ significantly as inspection of the Edgeworth-Bowley Box configuration shows. Country I is relatively capital rich and country II labour rich, in physical terms. Isoquants in activities X and Y are the same as those drawn in Figure 5.3. Since the diagonal of country I is to the left of the vector Oπ, its contract efficiency locus lies entirely above the Oπ ratio of factor intensities. Hence, in country I good Y is a labour-intensive activity, whereas good X is a capital-intensive activity.

However, the diagonal of country II's Edgeworth-Bowley Box lies to the right of the crucial Oπ ratio of factor intensities. Hence, in country II the only input price ratios consistent with equilibrium are those where good Y is a capital-intensive activity – region W in Figure 5.3. Thus the contract efficiency locus for country II must pass above the diagonal of its Edgeworth-Bowley Box in Figure 5.4. Therefore, good Y is a labour-intensive activity in country I and a capital-intensive activity in country II, whereas good X is a capital-intensive activity in country I and a labour-intensive activity in country II.

What now are the implications for trade patterns and factor prices when factor intensity reversals, implicit in Figure 5.4, occur? When factor reversals occur it is not possible to infer anything unambiguously about comparative advantage from factor prices prior to trade between countries I and II. For example, imagine that prior to trade, good Y is

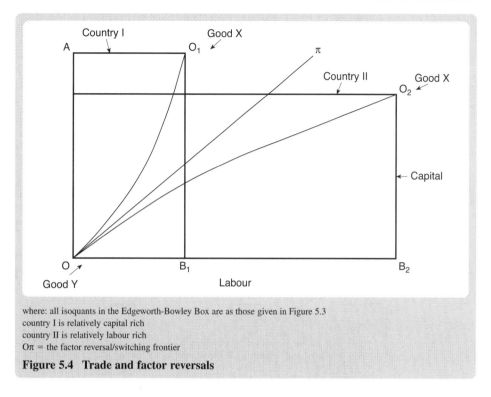

where: all isoquants in the Edgeworth-Bowley Box are as those given in Figure 5.3
country I is relatively capital rich
country II is relatively labour rich
$O\pi$ = the factor reversal/switching frontier

**Figure 5.4  Trade and factor reversals**

relatively expensive in country I and cheap in country II. If trade now occurs between countries I and II, country I will export good X and country II will export good Y in Figure 5.4. Hence country I, the capital-rich economy, exports its capital-intensive good, but country II, the labour-rich economy, also exports its capital-intensive good. So both countries export the respective capital-intensive goods and the H-O-S prediction is accordingly reversed. This must follow since both countries cannot export the same commodity. So given factor intensity reversals, if good Y is capital intensive in production in one country it is also a labour-intensive activity in the other trading partner, and vice versa. Thus, with widely different overall factor endowments and the presence of factor reversals, it follows that either both countries export their respective capital-intensive good(s), or both countries export their labour-intensive good(s). So the H-O-S does not hold when factor reversals are present, and the factor price equalisation theorem too is invalidated (Minhas, 1962).

If condition (4) above is relaxed such that widely different tastes are allowed between pairs of trading partners, the H-O-S prediction may also be reversed. In Figure 5.5, countries I and II have different overall factor endowments, as inspection of their respective transformation curves reveals. However, if, prior to trade, country I is in equilibrium at point $E_1$ and country II at $E_2$, then both countries possess a high propensity to consume their potential exportables under autarky. Hence the opportunity cost of expanding X production from point $E_2$ is higher than the relative cost in country I. Similarly, at point $E_1$, the opportunity cost of expanding Y production in country I is higher than in country II. So differences in tastes between countries I and II are such that the demand bias in consumption outweighs the production bias given by factor endowments. In Figure 5.5, country I might export good X and import Y, and country II would export Y and import X. Trade takes place on a pattern which is the reverse of that predicted by the H-O-S theorem.

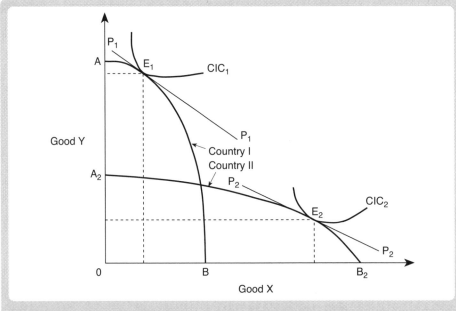

where:

$E_1$ = the production mix in country I prior to trade
$E_2$ = the production mix in country II prior to trade
$P_1P_1$ = domestic relative price ratio in country I prior to trade
$P_2P_2$ = domestic relative price ratio in country II prior to trade
$AB$ = the transformation curve in country I
$A_2B_2$ = the transformation curve in country II
$CIC_1$ = community indifference function in country I indicating the distribution of consumer tastes with respect to goods X
     and Y, before trade
$CIC_2$ = community indifference function in country II indicating the distribution of consumer tastes with respect to goods
     X and Y, before trade

**Figure 5.5   Trade based on demand rather than production bias, when tastes differ**

Finally, the H-O-S theory of trade may not provide a satisfactory explanation of the basis of trade between countries of similar economic structure/factor endowments as exists within the EU. Trade in manufactured goods between Germany, France and the UK may be dominated by demand characteristics caused by excessive product differentiation between oligopolised industries in these countries.

## 5.3   The H-O-S model in a many country/many commodity two-input trading framework

The preceding section analysed some crucial limitations of the H-O-S model within the framework of the basic $2 \times 2 \times 2$ system. Specifically it has been shown that when some production functions/demand conditions were introduced the H-O-S prediction may be reversed. Earlier it was argued that difficult issues arise when the H-O-S model/prediction is interpreted/extended to include a multi-country/multi-commodity trading system. In particular, it was noted that: because of difficulties and/or ambiguities in the relevant comparison of relative factor endowments in a many-good/many-country configuration, empirical testing of the H-O-S hypothesis has typically opted for a bilateral interpretation of the H-O-S prediction. Attention now turns to consider an extension of the H-O-S model to a many-good, many-country, two-input trading world. Once this extension is included, a complete theoretical background exists to provide a solid foundation for evaluation of the empirical tests of the H-O-S hypothesis.

## 5.4 Krueger's multi-country/multi-good interpretation of the H-O-S model

A. O. Krueger (1977) presents a many-country, many-good, two-factor version of the H-O-S model on the following assumptions:

a. Let there be 'N' industries producing 'N' different goods (manufacturers) which constitute each country's entire economy.

b. Let these 'N' industries produce 'N' separate goods utilising inputs of labour and capital only.

c. Let there be 'N' production functions in all 'N' industries which feature in the long run constant returns to scale, though exhibit diminishing returns to the variable input in the short run.

d. Let all goods in the trading network be ranked as follows: at a given/arbitrary input-price ratio, good 1 has the highest capital to labour ratio, good 2 the next highest and so on down to the 'Nth' good, which exhibits the lowest capital to labour ratio.

e. Let there be no factor intensity reversals, such that all 'N' production functions exhibit identical elasticities of substitution.

f. Let perfect competition exist in all industries.

g. Let perfect competition exist in all input markets.

h. Each country is 'small' and cannot unilaterally change world prices.

Assumptions (a) to (g) appear to guarantee that in all countries Pareto-efficient production relations obtain, such that the following exists: $MRT_d = P_i/P_j$ for any pair of two goods (i and j). Hence for any two produced goods $MRT_d$ is equated to the relative goods price ratio. So, as in the $2 \times 2 \times 2$ case, the crucial difference between each country is found by inspection of its overall capital to labour endowment, which is unchanging. In this static world the ratio of capital to labour endowments can be assigned for any country. Thus countries may be ranked such that the country with the largest overall capital to labour endowment is assigned number 1, the country with the next highest capital to labour endowment is assigned number 2, and so on for all countries. With assumption (d), goods are assigned numbers such that the highest number implies the highest labour to capital ratio in production, whence countries are numbered such that the higher number reflects a greater abundance of labour relative to capital.

For any country in this trading network, at an arbitrary set of relative prices the following options exist:

1. to produce only one good and maintain complete specialisation of inputs in its manufacture;

2. to produce just two goods, whence inputs are incompletely specialised;

3. to profitably produce three or more goods, whence the exact mix of final output cannot be determined, since the input price ratio is determined by the relative price of any

pair of goods. So for a given price vector, the country cannot necessarily make more profits by producing three goods instead of two, hence the exact mix of final output is unknown, but more on this anon.

In this multi-country/multi-good model, factor price equalisation across the system is unlikely, given option (1) above. However, if any two countries attain factor price equalisation they are counted as a single country. This might happen when industrial structures between any pair of traders are similar. Hence, in this trading system the possibility of option (1) occurring means that no pair of traders would produce two or more goods in common. So specialisation may occur such that some countries produce just one good using both inputs, whereas other countries may produce more than one good.

Krueger's interpretation of the H-O-S model for many goods and many countries allows the following hypotheses to be advanced:

1. The more capital-rich country specialises in producing more capital-intensive goods, given profit maximisation and perfect competition.

2. The more capital-rich country of any pair cannot manufacture any good more labour intensive than the least labour-using good manufactured in the other country, because it would be unprofitable to do so.

3. Two countries might manufacture one good in common, but the more capital-rich economy will utilise more capital-intensive methods in its manufacture than the labour-rich country, because it is more profitable to do so.

4. In a two-country/1000-good trading network the most capital-rich economy could feasibly manufacture the first 490 goods whilst the labour-rich economy manufactured the next 510 goods. Hence, hypotheses 1 to 3 seem unconnected with the number of goods being exchanged/produced.

A few observations on Krueger's multi-country, multi-good, two-factor interpretation of the H-O-S model can now be made:

a. The hypotheses derivable from the system do not differ significantly from those which can be proved unambiguously for the $2 \times 2 \times 2$ H-O-S model. This, however, is not surprising given the strong production bias. Assumptions of the $2 \times 2 \times 2$ model are common to the multi-good/multi-country model, specifically in that both versions of the H-O-S model production relations are bounded by the existence of: (1) non-reversibility of factor intensities, (2) constant returns to scale in all production activities, (3) identical production technologies in all countries for each separate good.

b. Serious difficulties may exist when the number of goods 'N' in the trading system do not equal the number of inputs. In Krueger's version of the H-O-S model, the number of produced goods 'N' exceeds the number of inputs utilised, such that in a deep sense, the general equilibrium system is underdetermined. The supply side in each country and/or demand in the system may be insufficient to determine the amounts produced. The basic Ricardian model with two outputs and a single input indicates what may go awry. The Ricardian world offers a linear transformation curve, whence for relative prices to equal the $\mathrm{MRT_d}$ the quantities produced are indeterminate.

c. Given the strong/restrictive assumptions of identical technology and homothetic preference functions, the H-O-S prediction in the general multi-good/multi-country system is not especially powerful. To be valid in the general case, the H-O-S hypothesis is bound by definitions of factor intensity based on general equilibrium derivatives (when the number of goods purchased is less than the number of inputs) rather than on directly observable input coefficients. Moreover, the H-O-S prediction may still not be valid when there are more goods produced than inputs. In the general case therefore, the H-O-S model may involve general equilibrium systems which are either over-determined or underdetermined, and where the definition of factor intensity becomes virtually non-operational/tautological.

Some of the preceding points may be highlighted if analysis of Krueger's feasible output patterns are examined. Inspection of Figure 5.6 allows examination of the sorts of production patterns that might emerge given Krueger's assumptions for the multi-good, multi-country, two-input version of the H-O-S model. In Figure 5.6 there are nine countries producing seven goods. The star in the yth row and xth column shows that output of a particular good is positive. A zero cell in Figure 5.6 indicates that output is zero for the particular good in question. The production system/patterns illustrated in Figure 5.6 may be understood as follows:

country 1: produces goods 1 and 2
country 2: produces goods 2, 3 and 4
country 3: produces good 4 only
country 4: produces good 4 only
country 5: produces goods 4 and 5
country 6: produces goods 4 and 5
country 7: produces goods 5 and 6
country 8: produces goods 5 and 7
country 9: produces good 7 only

Remember that country 2 produces goods 2, 3 and 4, and, by Krueger's definitions, country 2 is endowed with a higher labour to capital ratio than country 1, since it can

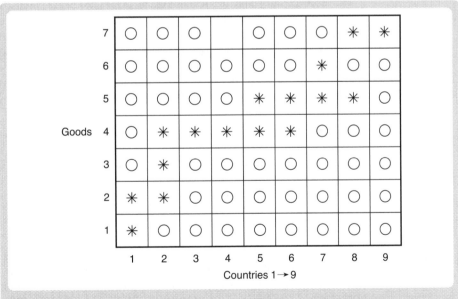

where:
countries are numbered in ascending order from the least labour abundant 1, to the most labour-rich country, 9
\* = positive production for the good in question
goods are numbered from the most (good 1) to least capital intensive

**Figure 5.6  Feasible production patterns for nine countries and seven produced goods**

produce good 4 in common with countries 3, 4, 5 and 6. Apparently the labour intensity of production of good 4 is higher in each higher numbered country. Factor price equalisation may occur between countries 5 and 6 since both produce two common goods. The most labour-abundant country is country 9 and this country produces the most labour-intensive good (i.e. good 7). However, country 8 produces good 5 with more labour-intensive methods than all other lower numbered countries that make good 5. Conclusions may be drawn from the production pattern displayed in Figure 5.6. If factor price equalisation occurs between a pair of trading countries then they are treated as a single economic entity.

Given the foregoing conditions, the following generalisations can be made:

1. The production mix in the most capital-rich economy will be concentrated on the most capital-intensive goods, and the production mix in the most labour-abundant economy will include the production of the most labour-intensive goods. Hence country 1 is sure to produce good 1, country 9 is certain to produce good 7, and so on. Because there are no factor reversals a relatively more capital-abundant country will not produce a more labour-intensive good than a relatively less capital-rich economy.

2. When a country produces more than two goods, the goods produced will be adjacent to each other in the factor intensity orderings.

3. When two countries produce a common good, the relatively more labour-abundant country uses more labour-intensive production techniques than a more capital-abundant economy.

4. Generally, the H-O-S factor proportions explanation of trade patterns emerges in the pattern of comparative specialisation of production, rather than in the factor intensity of exports. These generalisations seem plausible, if efficient resource allocation occurs in each country and the technological assumptions are valid. However, from these general observations on Krueger's model, deeper theoretical inconsistencies may flaw the model, since factor intensity definitions become blurred in each country where the number of inputs utilised exceeds the number of produced goods. The definition of factor intensity becomes tautological. Moreover, in each country where the number of inputs used exceeds the number of goods produced, changing the production mix is not by itself sufficient to ensure full employment of all inputs, or to maintain it in the face of enhanced factor supplies (consider the implications of the Rybczynski theorem for the Krueger model). In this latter case the concept of factor intensity is no longer a characteristic feature of technology, but of the entire general equilibrium system, including factor supplies within each country. The problem for efficient resource allocation occurring within each country prior to trade is worse if the number of goods produced is larger than the number of inputs utilised, because the amounts produced are indeterminate.

It is true that Krueger offers apposite critical comments on the limitations of Leontief-type tests of the H-O-S hypothesis. However, Krueger's suggestions concerning testing hypotheses derivable from the multi-country/multi-good system are also based upon the unwarranted 'a priori' assumption that the H-O-S factor proportions model is valid for the $2 \times 2 \times 2$ and/or the general multi-good, multi-country cases. Needless to say, if key assumptions relating to production functions and/or tastes are relaxed in Krueger's N-good multi-country model, the H-O-S hypothesis faces exactly the same problems as has already been demonstrated for the basis $2 \times 2 \times 2$ trading system. This is not to say that study of the H-O-S prediction is unhelpful, because sometimes a hypothesis of strictly limited ability is more useful for research than an all-embracing theorem. However, it seems reasonable to argue that the search for truly general theorems on the relationship between a country's factor endowment and trade patterns, as the Krueger version of the H-O-S model attempts, is of limited value. To this extent therefore, empirical testing of the H-O-S factor proportions hypothesis should perhaps be considered on a two-country basis where N goods are produced with M primary inputs, with N > M. The framework for such a test might be: designate country I a powerful trading nation, the USA or Japan for example, with country II being the rest of the world.

## 5.5    Empirical tests of the H-O-S hypothesis

MacDougall (1951) was the first writer to test the H-O-S hypothesis empirically. MacDougall used horse power as a measurement index for capital and hypothesised that the USA possessed more capital per worker than the UK. Hence, MacDougall's hypothesis was that the USA should be observed to have a higher world market share of capital-intensive goods than the UK. MacDougall did not detect any such systematic relationship; accordingly he rejected the H-O-S hypothesis as an explanation of comparative advantage.

Kravis (1956a) performed an indirect test of the H-O-S prediction. Kravis demonstrated that all wages are high in US export industries relative to import-competing industries. If these high real wages derived from comparatively more capital per unit of output per worker in such industries, this observation would be consistent with the H-O-S prediction. In the event, Kravis did not observe any connection between capital per unit of output and exports.

The most famous tests of the H-O-S hypothesis were those performed by Leontief (1953, 1956). Leontief postulated that the USA had more capital per unit of labour than any other nation with which it trades, hence the H-O-S prediction asserts that the USA has a comparative advantage in capital-intensive goods and should import labour-intensive goods. Leontief, using input/output analysis, tested the H-O-S hypothesis as follows: using the 1947 US input/output matrix he assumed that if the US reduced its output of exports and imports by an equal amount of $1m, this would change the aggregate production mix such that the H-O-S hypothesis could be tested. Thus when the output of exportables is reduced both labour and capital are released. Leontief reasoned that the export reduction should release relatively more capital and relatively less labour than would be absorbed (given fixed capital/labour input coefficients) by the import-competing industries.

Unusually, Leontief observed that a typical million dollars worth of US exports embodies considerably less capital and more labour than would be required to replace US competitive imports. Leontief's paradoxical finding was therefore that US exportables are typically labour- rather than capital-intensive goods. Leontief did not interpret these results as inconsistent with the H-O-S prediction, but instead maintained that the USA is relatively labour rich. Leontief argued that US workers are roughly three times more productive than foreign workers. Hence, on this interpretation, the US aggregate labour force may be multiplied by a factor of three to produce comparable labour 'efficiency' units; labour becomes thereby the relatively abundant productive input in the USA. Leontief thus tried to rescue the H-O-S prediction by arguing that the USA exports labour-intensive goods, which is consistent with the prediction of the H-O-S model.

Leontief's perverse result touched off a welter of activity among trade theorists and empiricists. Apart from Leontief's attempt at resolving the paradox, some economists, notably Ellsworth (1954), Becker (1962), Colbery (1963) and Kenen (1965) (see Rosefielde, 1974), argued that US exports were improperly 'identified' as labour intensive by Leontief. Instead these authors argued that US exports embody physical capital and human capital; once the 'human capital element' is properly included, the US export mix then becomes capital intensive which is consistent with the H-O-S hypothesis. On the issue of the 'human-plus-physical-capital' content of US exports, Kenen's work is notable for its thoroughgoing and comprehensive nature.

Several studies of a 'Leontief type' followed in the wake of Leontief's pioneering efforts. Tatemoto and Ichimura (1959), using the 1951 Japanese input/output table, found that, on average, a million yen's worth of Japanese exports embodies more capital and less labour than would be required for domestic Japanese replacements of imports of an equal quantity. Assuming that Japan could be classified as a comparatively labour-rich economy in 1951, the conclusion of this study was consistent with the 'Leontief Paradox', but at variance with the H-O-S hypothesis. The Japanese researchers were, however, able to mitigate doubts about the H-O-S hypothesis and dispel the paradox with a detailed analysis of Japanese imports and exports. Their argument ran as follows: in the 1950s Japan's overall capital/labour endowment was intermediate between an industrialised and a developing country. Accordingly, Japan in the 1950s should have a H-O-S comparative advantage in labour-intensive goods in trade with rich countries and in capital-intensive goods when trading with less developed countries. They demonstrated that three-quarters of Japan's export trade in the 1950s was with less developed countries, with the remaining 25% of her exports going to industrialised countries. Tatemoto and Ichimura found that Japan's exports to the USA were actually highly labour intensive, whilst her exports to other nations were relatively capital intensive. Hence, their findings were held to be consistent with the H-O-S hypothesis. This research was the first of several more detailed 'Leontief-type' studies which have looked specifically and carefully at the final destination of exports. Stolper and Roskamp (1961) performed an input/output study of trade in the former DDR. They concluded that East German exports were capital intensive and imports labour intensive. They took this finding as consistent with the H-O-S hypothesis and inconsistent with the Leontief Paradox. Wahl (1961) performed a similar study for Canadian manufactured goods. He found that Canadian exports were more capital intensive and imports potentially more labour intensive in specific bilateral trade with the USA in 1949. This finding was therefore consistent with the Leontief Paradox and at variance with the H-O-S prediction. A study by Bharadwaj (1962) of bilateral Indo-US trade produced, once more, results consistent with the Leontief Paradox, since Indian exports to the USA were demonstrated to be capital intensive whereas her imports from the USA were seen to be labour intensive. This was a startling result.

Baldwin (1971) surveys empirical studies on H-O-S to 1962. This article provides an excellent survey of the Leontief Paradox literature and reviews alternative hypotheses that have emerged as a result of Leontief's original findings. Moreover, Baldwin recalculated the Leontief results on the basis of the 1958 input/output coefficients and the US trade pattern in 1962. Baldwin also presents an extensive evaluation of the relative significance of a number of factors besides labour and capital in determining the commodity pattern of US trade. He concluded that application of a two-input H-O-S model is unsatisfactory for comprehending the pattern of commodity trade for the USA, and noted that the condition necessary for the H-O-S prediction to be logically true with respect to a nation's aggregate trade does not mean that the H-O-S model is necessarily valid on a strict bilateral basis, thereby undermining Leontief's original methodology. Rosefielde (1974) found that the basic H-O-S model prediction oddly produced good results in the context of state-monopolised trade in the Soviet Union. This study determined that in the 1950s and 1960s, the Soviet Union exported capital-intensive goods in exchange for labour-intensive goods when trading with developing countries both inside and outside the communist bloc. Simultaneously, the USSR tended to export relatively labour-intensive goods when trading with advanced nations.

Such a trade pattern would be expected from an application of the basic H-O-S model. Hence, Rosefielde's results in this study are similar to those obtained by Tatemoto/ Ichimura (ibid.) regarding Japanese trade patterns, insofar as both support the basic H-O-S predictions, though it should be borne in mind that the Japanese industrial structure in the early post-war period was not dominated by state/monopoly-trading organisations.

Hong (1975) produced an interesting empirical investigation of South Korean trade for the late 1960s. Hong's study is deeper and more extensive than many previous Leontief-type investigations. This is because the Hong study includes analysis of input accumulation and its impact on South Korean trade patterns. Broadly, the Hong study of South Korean trade patterns supports the H-O-S prediction.

Harkness (1978) offers a comprehensive econometric investigation of the H-O-S prediction. Harkness opted for a two-country, 'N'-good, 'M'-input trade model, and focused on US trade with the rest of the world, for which he rigorously demonstrates that the H-O-S hypothesis is normally valid.

Empirical investigations have therefore both retained and resolved the Leontief Paradox. The Leontief Paradox will perhaps always emerge whenever empiricists calculate simple capital/labour ratios, because then the USA will always appear as a net exporter of labour-intensive goods. Attempts down the years to account for the existence of the Paradox have done much to improve on the simple $2 \times 2 \times 2$ interpretation of the H-O-S model. There are several major sources of the 'Leontief paradox', specifically:

1. the existence of factor intensity reversals;

2. the existence of tariffs and non-tariff barriers to trade;

3. the existence of differences in skills and human capital;

4. the existence of large differences in natural-resource endowments internationally.

All of the above may to a greater or lesser extent account for the existence of the 'Leontief Paradox'. Perhaps a majority of trade theorists would argue that factors 3 and 4 above are more significant in explaining the existence of the Paradox than factors 1 and 2. However, due to the fact that the H-O-S hypothesis has enjoyed mixed success with respect to empirical verification down the years, some economists have argued that the H-O-S factor proportions explanation should be abandoned altogether. Such 'heretics' have argued that it is inappropriate in the modern world to retain a theory based on such strong/unrealistic postulates: for example, is it legitimate to assume:

a. that constant returns to scale exist in all activities?

b. international factor immobility in a world dominated by multinational corporations, which diffuse managerial skills and technical knowledge rapidly?

c. that the ranking of industries by capital/labour ratios is the same in all trading nations?

d. that all inputs are homogeneous in quality in all trading countries?

e. that demand conditions/tastes are similar in all trading nations, such that all theoretical analysis may be applied exclusively to supply-side conditions in trading nations?

Hence some economists have questioned both the predictive ability of the H-O-S explanation of trade patterns and the fundamental assumptions upon which the prediction rests. Indeed, as shown earlier, relaxation of any of the key assumptions underlying the H-O-S theorem can produce a 'new' theory of why trade occurs. Thus in the years since the original Leontief tests of the H-O-S hypothesis, 'new' theories of trade have been offered. Yet these so-called 'new' theories have often amounted to little more than the 'old H-O-S wine in new bottles'. Hence the 'new' theories, of Posner (1961), Vernon (1966, 1970), Kravis (1956b), Linder (1961), have involved not much more than a cataloguing of other additional factors that influence comparative costs. These 'new' approaches seem no better than starting with the Ricardian proposition that differences in labour productivity explain trade patterns. Thus a useful development on the empirical front would be availability of more sophisticated measures of the numerous factors which influence comparative advantages. The human capital and/or technology 'variables/factors' emphasise this requirement. Trade theory is now in a state of flux with respect to both formulation and empirical testing. Tests to date have produced mixed findings on which hypothesis/factors have the strongest explanatory power. It is hoped that some of the explanatory factors can be amalgamated into 'composite variables' which are theoretically valid. Given appropriate measurement techniques, each 'composite variable' may then be utilised to explain a distinctive 'segment' of trade. World trade is a highly complex phenomenon and it may be unreasonable to expect one theory to explain the totality of it. Trade theorists now possess additional factors/variables which could be used to improve the H-O-S approach (Kreinin, 1979). However, no theorist is certain about the relative significance of each factor, or how the factors link together. The basic and enduring appeal of the H-O-S factor proportions model is that it enables researchers to trace back the impact of price changes on the distribution of income in the economy. For this reason alone, the H-O-S model should continue to occupy the attention of theorists, researchers and students for years to come (Clegg, 1987). On the fundamental issue as to 'what provides the minimum sufficient differences between countries to explain the pattern trade', only the H-O-S theory provides a fully integrated, generalised explanation, the precision of which should increase given time.

## Summary

- Trade may not be the result of comparative advantage. Instead it may result from increasing returns or economies of scale. Economies of scale give countries an incentive to specialise and trade even in the absence of differences between countries in their resources or technology. Economies of scale can be internal depending on the firm or external depending on the industry.

- Economies of scale lead to a breakdown of perfect competition, so that trade in the presence of economies of scale must be analysed using models of imperfect competition.

- Imperfect competition reverses the H-O-S predictions, as also does the existence of factor reversals. Evidence exists that these are empirically possible.

- The H-O-S model has not stood up to empirical testing well either on US or global data. The Leontief Paradox is occasionally still found unless human capital arguments are introduced to resolve the paradox.

- Generally, empirical verification of the H-O-S model has not been established.

## Questions

1. How can the Leontief Paradox be resolved theoretically?

2. Show why trade between oligopolies in different countries reverses the H-O-S prediction.

3. Why is the H-O-S model incompatible with economies of scale?

4. What difficulties arise when H-O-S is extended to a many-country/many-good framework?

---

### Key concepts

| | |
|---|---|
| factor reversals | transformation curves and factor reversals |
| imperfect competition | intra industry trade |
| Leontief Paradox | |

---

## Bibliography

Baldwin, R. (1971) 'Determinants of the community structure of US trade', *American Economic Review*, vol. 61, pp. 126–46.

Bharadwaj, R. (1962) 'Factor proportions and the structure of Indo-US trade', *Indian Economics Review*, see Rosefielde, S. (1974) 'Factor proportions and economic rationality in Soviet international trade 1985–1988', *American Economic Review*, vol. 64, pp. 670–81.

Clegg, J. (1987) *Multinational enterprise and world competition: a comparative study of the USA, Japan, Sweden and West Germany*, Macmillan.

Harkness, J. (1979) 'Factor abundance and comparative advantage', *American Economic Review*, pp. 323–41.

Hong, W. (1975) 'Capital accumulation, factor substitution and the changing factor intensity of trade: the case of South Korea (1966–72)', in W. Hong and A. Krueger (eds), *Trade and Development in Korea*, Seoul, Korean Development Institute.

Ingram, J. and Dunn, M. R. (1993) *International Economics*, Wiley, third edition.

Jones, R. W. (1956/7) 'Factor proportions and the Heckscher-Ohlin theorem', *Review of Economic Studies*, vol. 10, pp. 1–10.

Kravis, I. B. (1956a) 'Wages and foreign trade', *Review of Economics and Statistics*, vol. XXXVIII, pp. 14–30.

Kravis, I. (1956b) 'Availability and other influences on the commodity composition of trade', *Journal of Political Economy*, vol. 64.

Kreinin, M. (1979) *International Economics: A Policy Approach*, Harcourt, Brace, Jovanovich, Inc., pp. 260–70.

Krueger, A. O. (1977) 'Growth, distributions and patterns of trade among many countries', *Princeton Studies in International Finance*, vol. 40.

Leontief, W. W. (1953) 'Domestic production and foreign trade: the American capital position re-examined', *Proceedings of the American Philosophical Society*, vol. XCVII, pp. 332–49.

Leontief, W. W. (1956) 'Factor proportions and the structure of American trade; further theoretical and empirical analysis', *Review of Economics and Statistics*, vol. XXXVIII.

Linder, S. (1961) *An essay on trade and transformation*, NY: John Wiley and Sons.

MacDougall, G. D. (1951) 'British and American exports: a story suggested by the theory of comparative costs, part I', *Economic Journal*, vol. LXI, pp. 687–724.

Minhas, B. S. (1962) 'The homohypallagic production function, factor reversals and the Heckscher-Ohlin theorem', *Journal of Political Economy*, vol. 70, pp. 138–56.

Posner, M. (1961) 'International trade and technical change', *Oxford Economic Papers*, Vol. 36, pp. 323–41.

Rosefielde, S. (1974) 'Factor proportions and economic rationality in Soviet international trade 1955–1968', *American Economic Review*, vol. 64, pp. 670–81.

Stolper, W. and Roskamp, K. (1961) 'An input/output table for East Germany with applications to foreign trade', *Bulletin, Oxford Institute of Statistics*, vol. XXIII, pp. 379–92.

Tatemoto, M. and Ichimura, S. (1959) 'Factor proportions and foreign trade: the case of Japan', *Review of Economics and Statistics*, vol. XLI, pp. 442–6.

Vernon, R. (1966) 'International investment and international trade in the product cycle', *Quarterly Journal of Economics*, vol. 80, pp. 190–207.

Vernon, R. (1970) *The Technology Factor in International Trade*, NY: NBER.

# 6 Application: Heckscher-Ohlin-Samuelson type trade

**K. LAWLER and H. SEDDIGHI**

## 6.1 National resource-intensive export behaviour: the case of Kuwait and the potential for immiserising growth

Since the first exports of oil in 1946, economic activity in Kuwait has been heavily influenced by activities (supply, demand and price) in the world oil market. As a Gulf State, Kuwait is one of a group of countries that possess major world oil reserves. With more than 60% of government revenues deriving from the oil industry, Kuwait's economic growth is closely linked to the changes in world oil prices.

The oil and gas industry is crucial to Kuwait's economy. Historically, revenues from oil exports account for the largest share of the country's export earnings. A significant part of this revenue is transferred to the government and represents the largest source of government income, making income taxes unnecessary. Furthermore, revenue is obtained from import tariffs and from various fees and profits from state-owned companies. In turn, government expenditure represents a significant portion of GDP. Taken together, the oil and government sectors account for about 95% of Kuwait's GDP, and oil exports are the main driving force for government expenditure.

## 6.2 The significance of the oil and gas industry in Kuwait

In 1995, the gross domestic product (GDP) at current prices amounted to KD 7952.3 million against KD 7349.1 million in 1994, representing a growth of KD 603.2 million or 8.2%. This growth was almost evenly distributed between the crude oil and natural gas production sectors and the non-oil sectors, whereby the value added by the non-oil sectors rose by 304 million (6.6%) in 1995, compared to the previous year, according to the Economic Report, Central Bank of Kuwait (1995).

The largest portion of the growth in the value added by the oil sector in 1995 is attributed to the relative improvement in the world oil prices during that period compared to 1994. The data for this period show that oil prices increased by 15%, from $13.53 per barrel of Kuwait's export blend in 1994 to about $15.56 in 1995. This increase was expected to be much larger for 1996, when the international oil prices soared to surpass the $20 mark (OPEC Bulletin, Oct., 1996).

The increase in the international oil prices in 1995, coupled with the increase in the production rates of the refined petroleum products industry, contributed to the growth in the value added by the oil industry to KD 580.6 million from KD 493.7 million in 1994, i.e. an increase of about 18%. Therefore the combined value added by the oil sectors (crude oil and natural gas production and refined petroleum products industries) grew in

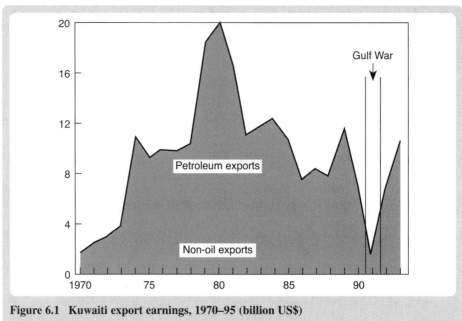

**Figure 6.1  Kuwaiti export earnings, 1970–95 (billion US$)**
*Source* adapted from Ministry of Planning – Foreign Trade Statistics (1996–99)

1995 by KD 394.2 million or 11.9% over its corresponding level of 1994, thus accounting for about 66% of the growth in GDP in 1995.

However, as the oil and gas industry dominates Kuwait's export earnings, non-oil
sectors exports have shown an upward trend since the 1970s (see Figure 6.1) and have
begun rising again since the end of the Gulf War. The value added by the non-oil sectors,
excluding the refined petroleum products industry, grew in 1995 by 217.1 million or
5.3%. This growth assumes a special importance for many reasons. From one perspective,
it represents the highest growth rate achieved in these sectors since the liberation of
Kuwait (Middle East Oil and Gas, IEA, 1995). Furthermore, a significant portion of the
revenue of the state-owned oil companies, Kuwait Petroleum Corporation and others, was
transferred to the government. Between 1970 and 1990, the share of oil export revenue
transferred to the government varied between 85% and 95%. The share tends to be highest in the years of high oil prices. In response to fluctuations in world oil prices, the share
of income derived from oil and gas has varied over time (see Figure 6.2). However, in
recent years the dominant pattern has resembled those of the early 1970s (Annual
Statistical Abstract, 1995). Since investments in oil and gas infrastructure have historically come from oil-generated cash flows, changing the share transferred to the government
may affect investment in the oil and gas sector. There has been concern that lower international crude oil prices since 1985, coupled with the government's financial requirements, have resulted in inadequate investment in the oil and gas sector, especially the
investment needed in order to expand Kuwait's crude oil production capacity. Thus, in
short, for Kuwait, higher oil prices are associated with higher government oil revenue, and
vice versa. After more than 50 years since the first shipment of crude oil from Kuwait, oil
is still the main source of wealth and the major force of the economic development of the
country (see Figure 6.3).

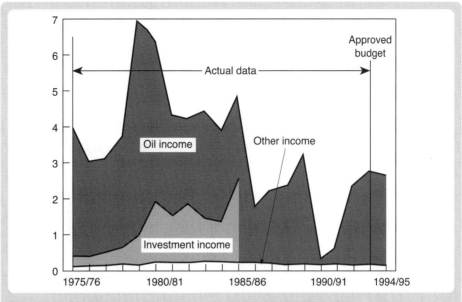

**Figure 6.2   Kuwaiti government revenue, 1975/76–94/95 (billion KD)**
*Source* adapted from Ministry of Planning – Central Statistical Office (1996)

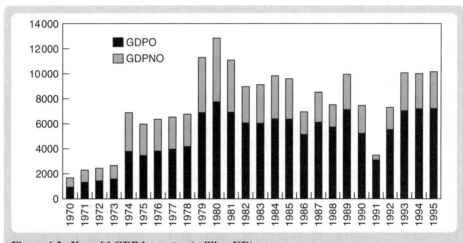

**Figure 6.3   Kuwaiti GDP by sector (million KD)**
*Source* adapted from Ministry of Planning – Central Statistical Office (1996)

## 6.3   The role of Gulf oil in the world energy market

The Gulf producers dominate the world energy market for several reasons. To begin with, the Gulf accounts for about 65% of global proven oil reserves (BP Statistical Review of World Energy, 1995).

Kuwait alone represents about 10% of world proven reserves. This constitutes a huge amount of oil, as is illustrated in Figure 6.4. Secondly, given the onshore location close to

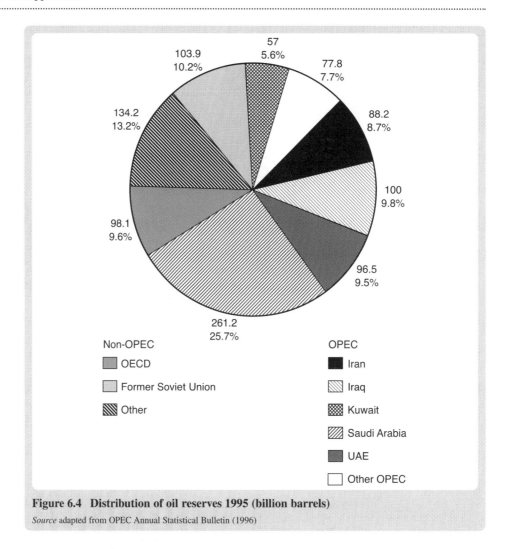

**Figure 6.4  Distribution of oil reserves 1995 (billion barrels)**
*Source* adapted from OPEC Annual Statistical Bulletin (1996)

deep water, the size of the fields and their geological formations (in which large volumes of crude oil were pressured by a layer of natural gas), the oil in place is extremely cheap to produce compared to that in the rest of the world. Figure 6.5 illustrates this point for 1995 rather well. Thirdly, the geographical location of the Gulf between the growing markets of both the East and the West provides excellent market opportunities. Figure 6.6 illustrates this point.

## 6.4  Kuwait economy and oil prices: an analysis

World demand for oil has grown steadily during the past four decades, except for short interruptions during the late 1970s and early 1980s, increasing from 22 million barrels per day in 1960 to 47 mb/d in 1970. This trend continued until 1979, when oil demand reached 64 mb/d in 1980. This decline lasted until 1983, when it reached a low of 58 mb/d. An upward trend started again after 1983 and, by 1992, demand was more than 65 mb/d. Demand declined slightly, by 200,000 b/d, to about 65 mb/d in 1995, due to

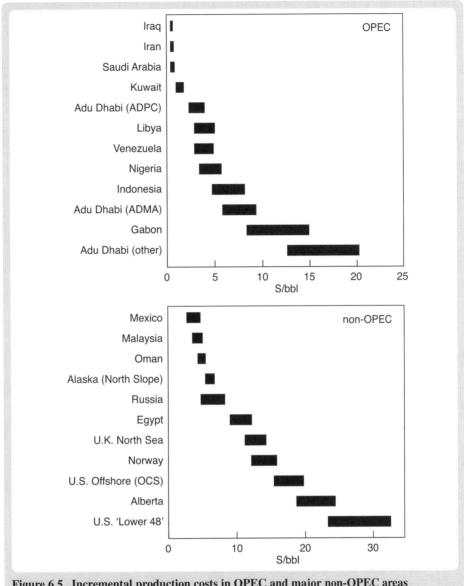

**Figure 6.5  Incremental production costs in OPEC and major non-OPEC areas**

*Source* adapted from OPEC Annual Statistical Bulletin (1996)

reduced world economic activity (see Figure 6.7). However, the demand has recovered since then and it is expected to grow steadily for the next few years (World Energy Outlook, OPEC Statistical Bulletin, 1995).

To balance the growth in world oil demand, both OPEC and non-OPEC producers were able, after substantial investment in the oil industry, to increase world supply from 22 mb/d in 1960 to 48 mb/d and 63 mb/d in 1970 and 1980 respectively. Supply declined to 57 mb/d in 1985, due to the fall in world oil demand, caused by energy conservation and substitution away from oil, before rising to more than 65 mb/d in the 1990s. OPEC crude production grew from about 9 mb/d in 1960 to 23 mb/d in 1997, due to reduced

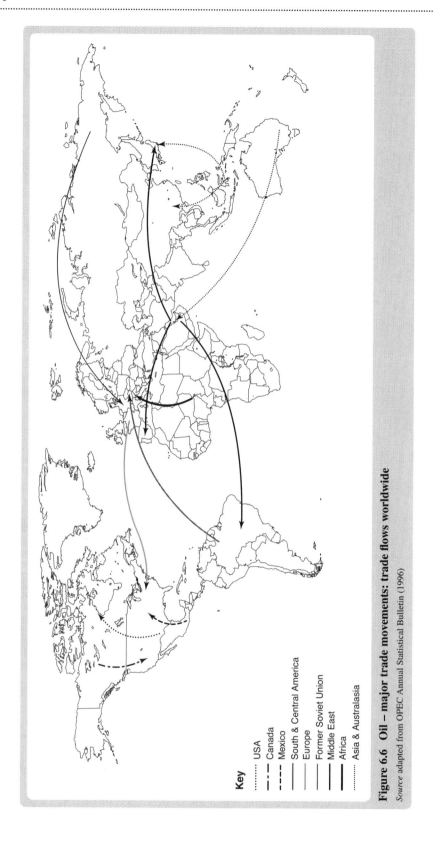

**Key**

USA
Canada
Mexico
South & Central America
Europe
Former Soviet Union
Middle East
Africa
Asia & Australasia

**Figure 6.6  Oil – major trade movements: trade flows worldwide**

*Source* adapted from OPEC Annual Statistical Bulletin (1996)

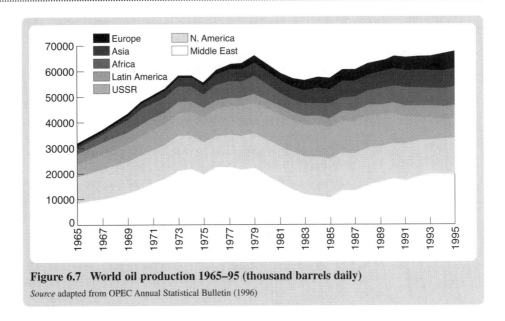

**Figure 6.7  World oil production 1965–95 (thousand barrels daily)**

*Source* adapted from OPEC Annual Statistical Bulletin (1996)

demand and increased supply from non-OPEC producers. After 1985, it rose gradually to about 23 mb/d in 1990 and to about 25 mb/d in 1995. Non-OPEC crude oil supply, on the other hand, increased from 13 mb/d in 1960 to 22 mb/d and 33 mb/d in 1970 and 1980 respectively. It peaked at 39 mb/d in 1988, before declining to about 35 mb/d in 1995 (see Figure 6.8).

The OPEC Gulf region has witnessed drastic output improvements in the past three decades. Production rose from around 5 mb/d, or 60% of total OPEC output, in 1960, and peaked at 21.6 mb/d, or 60%, in 1977, before declining to a low of less than 10 mb/d in

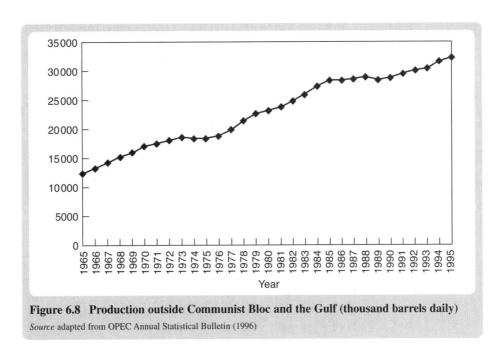

**Figure 6.8  Production outside Communist Bloc and the Gulf (thousand barrels daily)**

*Source* adapted from OPEC Annual Statistical Bulletin (1996)

1984. It started to improve again and reached 17.2 mb/d, or 69% of total OPEC output, in 1995.

Kuwaiti production began in 1946 with an initial output of 16,000 b/d. In the early 1960s, it was about 1.7 mb/d. It reached its highest level of 3.2 mb/d in 1972, before declining to only 190,000 b/d in 1991, in the wake of the Gulf crisis. Since that time, it has started to improve, averaging 2 mb/d in 1995, and reaching 2.1 mb/d in 1996.

Other Gulf countries experienced an upsurge in both production levels and production capacity. The evolution of the production output of the Gulf States is demonstrated clearly in Figure 6.9 (under Middle East production). It is interesting to note the peak in production from the Gulf around the mid-1970s and the collapse of production in the early 1980s. Its output in 1995 is still much lower than the mid-1970s peak.

The price of oil, now and in the future, is an essential issue in determining the level of investment for future oil supply expansion projects. This is important, not only to OPEC member countries, but also to the international oil companies operating in OPEC regions and for investment outside OPEC. For OPEC, low prices mean lower income for member countries and, consequently, there is not enough capital to be invested in future oil supply projects. For non-OPEC producers, low oil prices lead to deferments of the development of new oil fields, shutting off high-cost fields, with the consequence of steeper decline in non-OPEC supply.

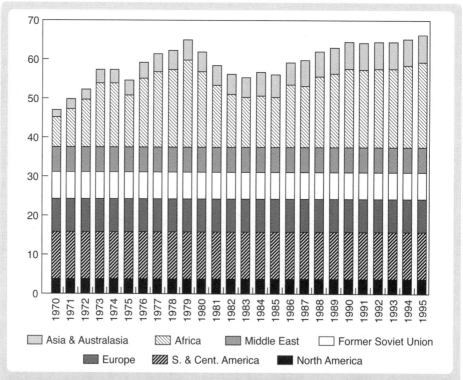

**Figure 6.9  Production by area (million barrels daily). Since 1987, falling oil production in the USA and the Former Soviet Union has been more than offset by greater output in other parts of the world**

*Source* adapted from OPEC Annual Statistical Bulletin (1996)

The evolution of oil prices has never been smooth. Looking at the history of oil prices since 1960, for example, it is interesting to note that, apart from relative stability during the period 1960–72, oil prices were never stable and fluctuated in a wide range, as illustrated in Figure 6.10 by the trend of the Arabian Light crude oil prices. The prevalence of price stability in the 1960s and early 1970s, an era characterised by abnormally low oil prices (less than $2/b), was due to the possession of oil resources by a group of multinational oil companies in almost all OPEC's member countries and the inclination of these oil companies to keep OPEC crude oil under-priced, so that more gains could be obtained from refined products, since these companies were vertically integrated (Zweifel and Bonommo, 1995). Major events, such as the Arab-Israeli war in 1973 and the limited and temporary embargo to the US that followed the Iran-Iraq War and the Gulf Crisis, all contributed one way or another to the instability in oil prices, as can be seen in Figure 6.10. In 1973–74 the real price of crude oil more than tripled. After declining slightly in 1975–78, it doubled again in 1979–80. But the 1979–80 price increase was eroded between 1981 and 1985, as price declined by nearly 40%.

Price then collapsed in the first half of 1986, falling by more than 50%. Within the period from 1981 to 1986, the real price of oil fell from more than a fivefold multiple of its 1970 value to less than a twofold multiple.

The new non-OPEC supply, such as production from the North Sea and Alaska, was the main reason for a significant impact, reducing oil prices. The oil price collapse in 1986 was a result of over-supply from both OPEC, mainly by Saudi Arabia, and non-OPEC producers (Griffin and Viehaber, 1994).

The world demand for oil, which had grown rapidly before the 1973–74 price increase, grew much less rapidly during 1973–78. It then fell by about 10% during 1979–83 and has grown only slightly since. The OECD had both the biggest demand growth before 1973 and the biggest decline.

There have been regional changes in world oil production since 1970. Until 1976 the non-OPEC oil supply grew quite slowly. Since 1977 there have been substantial increases

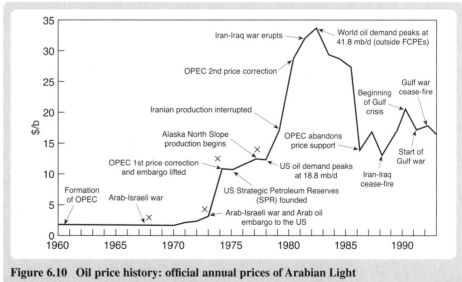

**Figure 6.10  Oil price history: official annual prices of Arabian Light**

*Source* adapted from OPEC Annual Statistical Bulletin (1996)

from Mexico, the North Sea, and a large number of small producers. (Between 1979 and 1985 five non-OPEC developing countries (Brazil, Egypt, India, Malaysia and Oman) doubled their output to a total of 3 million barrels per day (Ibrahim and Hurst, 1989). The 16% decrease in US output during 1970–76 was halted by an increase in Alaskan production starting in 1977. But total US output in 1985 was still 7% below its 1970 peak, despite much higher prices; without Alaska, US output would have been 25% lower in 1985 than in 1970.

OPEC, as the price-setting residual supplier, has the ability to reduce its output to support a given price level. It has seen the demand for oil fall by nearly 40% between 1979 and 1982. The changes in output within OPEC from 1970 to 1986 are depicted in Figure 6.7. Virtually all OPEC members shared in the burden of output restrictions from 1979 to 1985. But the greatest percentage cutbacks were borne by Saudi Arabia (more than 60% of its 1979 level), Kuwait (almost 60%) and Libya (almost 50%). From August 1985 through mid-1986, OPEC output increased by about 4 million barrels per day (bpd), or about 25%. More than half the increase came from Saudi Arabia, but some other members also had significant increases, especially Kuwait, the United Arab Emirates (UAE), Iraq and Nigeria. In the face of the price collapse, Iran and Mexico (a non-OPEC producer) cut output.

## 6.5 Future demand for energy

By 2002, world oil demand is forecast to be 75 mb/d; by 2020, it could reach a level of 86 mb/d, compared with the current level of around 66 mb/d as shown in Table 6.1.

The future growth in oil supply could therefore be as much as 80 mb/d in 2001, and 15 mb/d and 21 mb/d by 2010 and 2020 respectively. Several questions are raised here:

1. Is there a demand base available for this future huge expansion in supply?

2. What oil provinces will be most suitable for future development?

3. If non-OPEC oil supply diminishes in the future, will OPEC be able to supply the market with sufficient oil?

4. If low oil prices persist, will there be enough revenue and incentives for oil producers to invest in future oil projects?

5. Will technological advancement in the oil industry be able to recover more oil from depleted, existing and future oil fields?

6. What will be the impact of environmental measures, such as taxation and regulatory measures, on the future expansion of oil supply projects?

Table 6.1  World oil demand outlook (mb/d).

|            | 1993  | 1995  | 2000  | 2005  | 2010  | 2020  |
|------------|-------|-------|-------|-------|-------|-------|
| OECD       | 37.36 | 38.00 | 40.24 | 40.58 | 41.07 | 41.23 |
| DC's       | 18.14 | 18.92 | 21.58 | 23.65 | 25.93 | 30.67 |
| Former CPE | 9.41  | 9.58  | 11.05 | 12.71 | 12.71 | 13.64 |
| Total World| 64.91 | 66.50 | 72.28 | 76.07 | 79.71 | 85.63 |

*Source* adapted from OPEC Annual Statistical Bulletin (1997)

The world's proven recoverable crude oil reserves currently stand at more than 1000 billion barrels, with an additional undiscovered potential of around 500 billion barrels. At current production levels, the world's proven reserves could last for at least another 40 years. OPEC's share of this total exceeds 75%. The revolution of proven recoverable oil reserves by region during the past few decades is illustrated in Figure 6.11. It is evident from this graph that the Middle East witnessed the most growth during this period. OPEC added a huge volume of proven reserves estimated at more than 550 bn b, or 77% of the world total, compared with only 160 bn b, or 23% of the total, from non-OPEC. However, when oil production from OPEC and non-OPEC areas is compared, the picture changes; that is, in spite of the large volumes of proven reserves in OPEC, the production has been relatively small compared with non-OPEC (see Figure 6.7). This imbalance between reserves and production in OPEC and non-OPEC may need to be discussed thoroughly in future OPEC/non-OPEC meetings, to settle this disparity.

The resource base for the expansion of future oil supply is, therefore, available and oil will remain an important source of energy well into the twenty-first century. Future projects in oil supply expansion should take into consideration the economics of each oil province. That is, the cost of development and production from each region should be compared with other regions, and regions with lowest cost should be given priority.

Reserves in OPEC member countries, and particularly the Middle East, are the cheapest to develop and put on stream. This is demonstrated clearly in Figure 6.5. It is obvious from the figure that the cost of developing new reserves in the OPEC region is much cheaper than elsewhere. Therefore, OPEC and, in particular, the Middle East, will be the centre of attention in future oil developments.

Since regions outside OPEC have, in most cases, already matured and any future supply additions must come from high-cost areas, the expectation is that non-OPEC supply in the

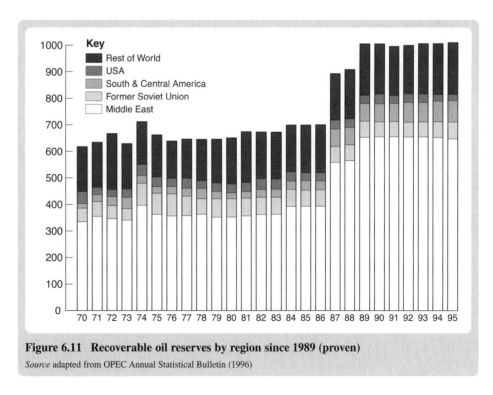

**Figure 6.11 Recoverable oil reserves by region since 1989 (proven)**
*Source* adapted from OPEC Annual Statistical Bulletin (1996)

coming decades will either maintain its current level or even decline slightly. Future investment in non-OPEC supply will be aimed at reducing the rate of production decline of existing fields and/or developing new marginal fields in order to offset part of this decline.

## 6.6 The future role of OPEC and Kuwait in oil markets

Oil demand will grow in future no matter what price scenario is assumed. The highest demand forecast is projected by the low price scenario ($14/b in real 1994 prices) (Figure 6.12). This scenario predicts that oil demand will increase from the current level by 9.1, 16.5 and 22.3 mb/d in the same three years. Therefore, future demand growth could range from 4.7 to 9.1 mb/d in the year 2000, rising to 8.8–16.5 mb/d in 2010 and 12.0–23.3 mb/d by 2020. Since non-OPEC supply will either decline or at best remain stable during this period, the additional supply must come from OPEC. The need for additional OPEC supply, therefore, compared with the 1994 average, is expected to range from 5.7 to 10.7 mb/d in the year 2000, increasing to 9.7–17.7 mb/d in 2010 and 14.7–24.7 mb/d by 2020, see Table 6.2.

The question here is: will OPEC be able to expand its production capacity to satisfy world future oil demand? The resource base for production capacity expansion in OPEC member countries is available and could be expanded to meet future oil demand, provided adequate investment is available (Lukeman, 1996). A huge sum of money, estimated at more than $100 bn, is required to expand OPEC production capacity by around 10 mb/d

**Table 6.2  Future supply scenarios.**

|  | 1995 | 2000 | 2005 | 2010 | 2020 |
|---|---|---|---|---|---|
| **1. Medium oil price** | | | | | |
| Real basket price ($bbl) | 17.0 | 17.0 | 20.2 | 24.0 | 33.8 |
| Normal basket price ($bbl) | 17.0 | 22.4 | 33.4 | 49.3 | 108.2 |
| World oil demand (mb/d) | 66.5 | 72.9 | 76.1 | 79.7 | 85.6 |
| Oil supply | | | | | |
| OPEC (mb/d) | 28.3 | 35.6 | 38.9 | 42.7 | 49.8 |
| Non-OPEC (mb/d) | 38.2 | 37.2 | 37.2 | 37.0 | 35.8 |
| **2. Low oil price** | | | | | |
| Real basket price ($bbl) | 14.0 | 14.0 | 16.6 | 19.8 | 27.9 |
| Normal basket price ($bbl) | 14.6 | 18.5 | 27.7 | 40.6 | 89.4 |
| World oil demand (mb/d) | 67.0 | 74.7 | 77.9 | 82.1 | 87.9 |
| Oil supply | | | | | |
| OPEC (mb/d) | 29.1 | 38.6 | 42.2 | 46.8 | 53.9 |
| Non-OPEC (mb/d) | 37.9 | 36.1 | 35.7 | 35.4 | 34.0 |
| **3. High oil price** | | | | | |
| Real basket price ($bbl) | 21.0 | 21.0 | 24.9 | 29.6 | 41.8 |
| Normal basket price ($bbl) | 22.1 | 27.7 | 40.9 | 61.1 | 133.3 |
| World oil demand (mb/d) | 66.0 | 70.9 | 74.2 | 77.2 | 83.3 |
| Oil supply | | | | | |
| OPEC (mb/d) | 27.5 | 32.3 | 35.3 | 38.2 | 45.5 |
| Non-OPEC (mb/d) | 38.5 | 38.5 | 38.9 | 39.0 | 37.8 |

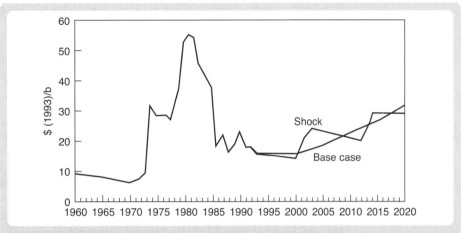

**Figure 6.12   Real oil price in the reference case and shock scenarios**
*Source* adapted from OPEC Annual Statistical Bulletin (1997)

**Table 6.3   OPEC oil production capacity and required investment.**

|  | Current capacity | | Future capacity | | Change % | Investment $bn |
|---|---|---|---|---|---|---|
|  | 1995 | 2000 | 2010 | 2020 |  |  |
| Kuwait | 2.00 | 3.00 | 4.00 | 3.80 | 1.00 | 5 |
| Algeria | 0.78 | 1.20 | 0.70 | 0.40 | 0.42 | 4 |
| Qatar | 0.44 | 0.54 | 0.50 | 0.40 | 0.10 | 2 |
| Indonesia | 1.40 | 1.30 | 1.00 | 0.80 | 0.10 | 15 |
| Iran | 3.80 | 4.50 | 5.00 | 4.80 | 0.70 | 12 |
| Iraq | 2.50 | 5.00 | 6.00 | 7.00 | 2.50 | 8 |
| Libya | 1.50 | 2.33 | 2.20 | 2.10 | 0.83 | 10 |
| S. Arabia | 8.50 | 10.00 | 11.00 | 12.00 | 1.50 | 17 |
| U.A.E. | 2.30 | 3.00 | 4.00 | 3.80 | 0.70 | 6 |
| Nigeria | 1.95 | 2.23 | 2.50 | 2.40 | 0.37 | 11 |
| Venezuela | 2.38 | 3.00 | 3.50 | 3.40 | 0.62 | 16 |
| Total Crude | 27.85 | 36.49 | 40.60 | 41.00 | 8.64 | 108 |

*Source* adapted from OPEC Annual Statistical Bulletin (1996)

in 2000, as shown in Table 6.3. The amount of investment required to raise it to 44 mb/d and 45 mb/d by 2010 and 2020 respectively would be much higher than this figure.

## 6.7   Conclusions

The importance of oil as a major source of income to the Kuwaiti economy is evident. For Kuwait, higher oil prices are immediately associated with higher government revenues, and vice versa. After more than 50 years since the first shipment of crude oil from Kuwait, oil is still the main source of wealth and the major force for economic development in the country.

The Gulf producers dominated the world energy market for several reasons. First, the Gulf accounts for about 65% of the global proven oil reserves of which Kuwait alone represents 10% of world proven reserves. Secondly, the oil in place is extremely cheap to produce compared to that in the rest of the world. Thirdly, the geographical location of the Gulf between the growing markets of both the East and the West provides excellent market opportunities.

World demand for oil has grown steadily during the past four decades, except for short interruptions during the late 1970s and early 1980s, increasing from 22 million barrels per day in 1960 to 47 mb/d in 1970. This trend continued until 1979, when oil demand reached 64 mb/d, before declining to 61 mb/d in 1980. This decline lasted until 1983, when it reached a low of 58 mb/d. An upward trend started again after 1983 and, by 1992, demand was more than 65 mb/d. Demand declined slightly, by 200,000 b/d, to 64.9 mb/d in 1993, due to reduced world demand economic activity. However, demand has recovered since then and it is expected to grow steadily for the next few years.

The pricing of oil is always a key issue in setting the economic policies against which Kuwait, among other Gulf producers, plan economic and social developments. This relationship will definitely continue for the future as expansion in world economic activity, driven by population growth worldwide, is expected to bring about more demand for energy, particularly oil. The various forecasts discussed in this chapter projected oil demand expansion of 5–9 mb/d in 2000, rising to 9–15 mb/d in 2010. To meet this demand growth, both OPEC and non-OPEC suppliers are expected to witness substantial growth in oil supply. The role of OPEC will certainly become more important in the future, as its share of the oil market grows substantially. Kuwait is among the OPEC countries that are expected to expand production to about 3 mb/d by 2000, rising to 4 mb/d in 2010. However, in order for the oil industry to meet future oil needs, substantial investment in production capacity expansion is required. The current higher oil prices definitely help. However, heavy taxes on oil and the environmental and regulatory measures to reduce oil use are all factors that could lead to reduced investment in the oil industry.

## Summary

- The Kuwait economy is hugely dependent on oil export. The world price of oil has critical impact on levels of activity in the Kuwait economy.

- Kuwait's natural resource-intensive trade is a classic case of H-O-S type trade. As the oil sector grew the government tried to encourage industrial development. This has largely failed for the obvious reasons that relative profitabilities in non-oil sectors of the economy are low. Kuwait's industrial development can be captured by the Rybczynski Theorem.

- Kuwait has characteristics that place it in a category which means it could experience immiserising growth if oil prices fell in real terms through time.

### Questions

1. Consider Kuwait's export behaviour in terms of the H-O-S model.
2. Link oil price changes to the Metzler Paradox, and show how Metzler's case can be interpreted for Kuwait and other Gulf states.

3. Explain why the Stolper-Samuelson theorem may carry insights for Kuwait and other oil exporters in the context of high or low world oil price scenarios.

4. Explain why new entrants in the world oil market undermine Kuwait's economic performance (See Chapter 8).

## Key concepts

natural resource-based trade        the Rybczynski Theorem
the H-O-S model        the Metzler Paradox

## Bibliography

Central Bank of Kuwait (1995) *Quarterly Economic Report*, Safat Kuwait, Central Statistical Office.

Central Bank of Kuwait (1995) *Quarterly Statistical Bulletin*.

Central Bank of Kuwait (1996) *Economic Report*.

Central Bank of Kuwait (1999) *Economic Report*.

*Middle East Economic Digest*, 21 February 1997.

*Middle East Economic Digest*, 29 August 1997.

*Middle East Economic Digest*, 3 October 1997.

*Middle East Economic Digest*, 7 November 1997.

Ministry of Planning (1995) 'Annual Statistical Abstract', *Annual Statistical Bulletin*.

Ministry of Planning – Foreign Trades and Statistics 1996–2000.

OPEC Annual Statistical Bulletin, 1996–2000.

Petroleum Institute (1995) *BP Statistical Review of World Energy*, Petroleum Institute, Washington.

Wilson, R. (1995) *Economic Development in the Middle East*, Routledge.

# 7 Oligopoly in new world markets: a case study of duopoly

## K. LAWLER and H. SEDDIGHI

## 7.1 Duopoly competition in new world markets, entry and price strategies – a study in duopoly in world trade: Strix and Otter

Background: Strix entered the market for electronic and electro-mechanised thermo-couples in the late 1960s based on patented innovations in the market for liquid boiling devices for use in coffee machines and kettles. By the mid-1970s Strix had established a market share in the UK of around 75% by sales. Strix's competitor was, and continues to be, Otter UK which has around 20–24% of the UK market. Potential entrants facing both duopolists are principally the end users/manufacturers of Strix's and Otter's products.[1] In world markets Strix has held a 70%+ market share for 20 country-specific markets.[2] Otter competes with Strix in all these markets. Price competition between the two duopolists is fierce in every market. Strix, the more innovative firm of the two, has twice successfully won patent infringement court battles against Otter. The last action, which involved Otter's direct copy of one of Strix's new products, resulted in a substantial patent for Otter and substantial compensation for Strix of several million pounds in 1997.

In this market the behaviour of the duopolists is best seen as a multi-stage game. Initially, Strix and Otter are involved in a Cournot capacity game with regard to the volume of advertising. Thereafter price competition becomes the feature of the competitive games. Here we see both firms fighting ever more bitter price warfare strategies. Sometimes they compete with each other by offering potential buyers production and tooling incentives, but these again can be seen as price competition. The fierce price-discounter is the smaller producer, Otter, and unusually, Strix tends to become a price follower when there are no capacity constraints. The model applied here is a version of the Bertrand game, with capacity constraints and buyers with rational expectations.

The models utilised discuss Strix and Otter's advertising/price strategies in new world markets. Strix is normally the incumbent in new markets and is typically a dominant firm price leader in Western Europe. Both firms are alternatively incumbents and entrants. The model developed assumes that Strix is an incumbent and Otter always enters new markets. Game models are developed which cover entry/advertising strategies and long-run price strategies which encompass observable data regarding competition. Initially a zero-sum game model is derived which focuses on the significance of marketing messages in the entry process. This game is Cournotesque in spirit since both firms fix an advertising budget consistent with a given volume of marketing messages. Thus each firm ignores the volume of messages/size of the advertising budget chosen by the rival. Thereafter, a game model is developed which typifies the type of price competition contemplated by both firms. In the development of this game price competition becomes a key strategic weapon and the emphasis switches to the Bertrand Paradox.

## 7.2 Competition in new markets: Strix (incumbent) vs. Otter (entrant)

In this chapter, three game models of duopoly are developed. Initially a zero-sum model is developed where a spatial monopoly incumbent faces entry from an equal-sized entrant. Entry and defensive strategies are considered for an elemental two-product-class entry game. Thereafter the results are generalised for an N-commodity entry game. These models derive optimal entry and defensive strategies. It is observed that once entry is established the duopolists must devise a rational business strategy for long-term success. The development of a viable long-run game which produces Nash equilibria is derived which links with consumer expectations and common knowledge regarding the initial entry battle. It is shown that certain types of pricing/competitive strategies are optimal, given the duopolists' advertising strategies. The discussion focuses on optimal strategies for new markets both as a multi-product incumbent (Strix) and as a multi-product entrant (Otter). The incumbent (Strix) must defend its market shares against significant attack from a single entrant (Friedman, 1977). This entry market share game is played using advertising outlays as the strategic weapon on both sides. Hence this game theoretic model focuses on optimal advertising budgets for both the incumbent and entrant.

## 7.3 Advertising volumes, messages and an entry game

The objective of the entrant (Otter) is to maximise market share in two product areas and the incumbent wishes to make these gains as small as possible. This is the familiar territory of the two-player zero-sum game. Each rival knows the strategies open to it and its rival and focuses on these. In this case advertising outlays to attack and defend market share are the strategic weapons. Each firm behaves rationally and delivers a best response to counter the other's actions. Initially the analysis concentrates on the two-product classes: namely the incumbent's defence of two product areas against entry (Kreps, 1991). Price competition is not contemplated at this stage. Further assume that consumers possess rational expectations as regards advertising and communicated messages, and that the number of time-constrained consumers is less than the number of non-time constrained (Kreps and Scheinkman, 1983).

Assume that the incumbent has two product groups $P_1$ and $P_2$ which yield profitability indices of $\pi_1$ and $\pi_2$, respectively. These product groups represent exclusive target areas for the entrant. Moreover, assume that the incumbent and the entrant possess equal economic strength and have equal advertising budgets 'A'.

A strategy for the entrant is an advertising budget of x aimed at product $P_1$, where:

$$0 < x < A$$

and the remainder of A − x is earmarked for $P_2$. A strategy for the incumbent is an advertising outlay of y to product $P_1$, where $0 < y < A$ and A − y is allocated to $P_2$, These strategies are summarised as:

|  | Product classes $P_1$ | Product classes $P_2$ |
|---|---|---|
| Profitability index | $\pi_1$ | $\pi_2$ |
| Entrant's advertising budget | x | A − x |
| Incumbent's advertising budget | y | A − y |

Let the payoff to the entrant be proportional to the number of advertising messages delivered to the targeted product and that product's profitability. Thus if $x \geq y$, then $A - x \leq A - y$, in which it can be assumed that $x - y$ units of messages are successful in product group $P_1$, and that none are successful in product area $P_2$. In this case the payoff to entry is $(x - y)$. If $x < y$, then $A - x > A - y$ and $y - x$ units of advertising messages are successful in target area $P_2$, while none are successful in product area $P_1$, The payoff can be summarised as follows:

$$E(x, y) = \pi_1(x - y) \text{ if } x \geq y \text{ and } \pi_2(x - y) \text{ if } x \leq y \qquad \text{... [7.1]}$$

$\pi_1$ can be interpreted to be the average payoffs per unit of advertising message that successfully penetrate the incumbent's product markets, $P_1$. Clearly $E(x, y)$ is a convex function of y for x. It consists of two curves in Figure 7.1. So:

$$\mathbf{K} = \min_{y} \max_{x} \dots E(x, y) = \min_{y} \max_{x} [(\pi_2 y, \pi_1)(A - y)] \qquad \text{... [7.2]}$$

The function $\max [(\pi_2 y, \pi_1)(A - y)]$ achieves a minimum at the level of y for which

$$\pi_2 y = \pi_1(A - y) \qquad \text{or } y^* = \pi_1 A/\pi_2 + \pi_1 \qquad \text{... [7.3]}$$

Thus the incumbent's optimal strategy is to allocate $\pi_1 A/\pi_2 + \pi_1$ advertising resources to product area $P_1$, and the rest, $\pi_1 A/\pi_2 + \pi_1$ of A to $P_2$. The value of the game is:

$$k = \pi_1 \pi_2 A/\pi_2 + \pi_1 \qquad \text{... [7.4]}$$

The entrant's optimal strategy is derived as follows: set

$$E [x, \pi_1 A/\pi_2 + \pi_1] = k$$

This equation yields solutions of $x_1 = 0$ and $x_2 = A$ $\qquad \text{... [7.5]}$

The solution of the game can be summarised as follows. The incumbent splits its fighting advertising budget adopting a fixed deployment: allocate $\pi_1 A/\pi_2 + \pi_1$ to product area $P_1$, and $\pi_2/\pi_2 + \pi_1$ of total resources to product area $P_2$. The entrant's optimal strategy is mixed. The entrant targets its advertising outlay on either $P_1$ or $P_2$, selected at random. The entrant selects $P_1$ with a probability $\pi_2/\pi_2 + \pi_1$ and picks $P_2$ with a probability $\pi_1/\pi_2 + \pi_1$. Hence if product $P_2$ is four times as valuable as product $P_1$, $4\pi_1 = \pi_2$, then the incumbent

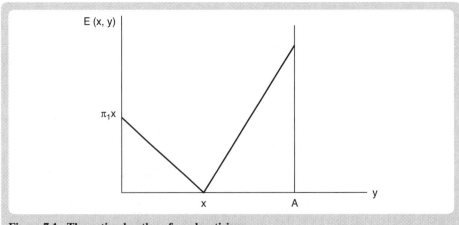

**Figure 7.1  The optimal outlays for advertising**

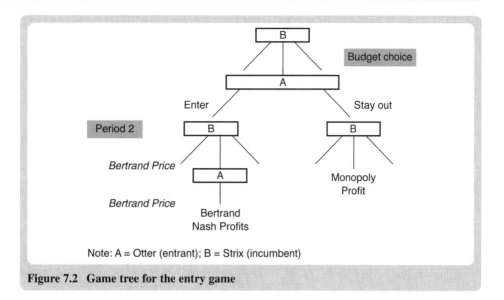

Note: A = Otter (entrant); B = Strix (incumbent)

**Figure 7.2  Game tree for the entry game**

(Strix) defends $P_2$ with 0.8 of its advertising allocation. The optimal strategy for the entrant (Otter) is to target $P_1$ with its entire advertising budget with a probability of 0.8. Figure 7.1 shows the optimal outlays for advertising. A game tree stylising this entry game is depicted in Figure 7.2. Generally, as the game tree shows, the entry game can have up to four moves. Seen sequentially these are: Strix's choice of advertising strategy to protect product classes $P_1$ and $P_2$. The second is Otter's decision to enter and the advertising budget if Otter enters. If Otter enters, then Strix and Otter play dynamic Cournot (budget setting) duopoly games. If Otter stays out, then Strix has the last move and stays a classic monopolist.

## 7.4    The N-product-entry case and the Nash equilibrium

These results can be generalised for n-product classes. Once more the problem is viewed as a two-player zero sum game. The entrant aims for maximum gains whereas the incumbent wishes to minimise these. This game can be analysed in a very simplified form in which each player has to make a single choice. The entrant must select an optimal volume of advertising resources among product targets and the incumbent chooses an allocation of defensive advertising resources for its product portfolio. Interesting questions arise when the game is stylised in this form. For example, should all products be defended by the incumbent? If the incumbent decides to defend some products, how will these be chosen? How should the entrant select its product areas? Consider the following model: assume both the incumbent and entrant have equal resources and are of equal size. The incumbent has Q units of advertising resources to allocate among n products, which are $P_1$, $P_2$, $P_3$ ... $P_n$. These products have relative profitability volumes of $\pi_1$, $\pi_2$, ... $\pi_3$ respectively and are ordered as follows:

$$0 < \pi_1 < \pi_2 < ... < \pi_n$$

The entrant has Z units of advertising resources to distribute among n product targets and $Z \geq Q$. A strategy for the entrant is an advertising allocation of resources $Z$ among $n$ product targets, so the entrant's strategy is a set of numbers:

$x_1, x_2, x_n$ such that $x_i \geq 0$ and $\Sigma x_i = Z$, for $i = 1$ to $n$.

A strategy for the incumbent is the set of numbers $y_1, y_2, y_n$

so that $y_i \geq 0$ and $\Sigma y_i = Q$, for $i = 1$ to $n$.

Each $y_i$ gives the volume of advertising allocated to defend product $P_i$.

## 7.5    Strix and Otter pay-offs in equilibrium for the Cournot game

It is assumed that one unit of defensive advertising from the incumbent can counter one unit of aggressive advertising from the entrant. Moreover, assume that the market penetration to any given target is proportional to the number of attacking messages which outnumber the defensive messages from the incumbent. Finally, assume that the pay-off is the sum over the targeted products of market penetration to each product area. The entrant's pay-off is:

$E(x,y) = \Sigma \pi_i \max (o, x_i - y_i)$, for $i = 1 \ldots n$

where

$x \geq 0, yi > 0$. $\Sigma xi = Z$ and $\Sigma yi = Q$, for $i = 1 \ldots n$

Clearly $E(x,y)$ is convex in $y$ for each $x$ and vice versa. The incumbent has a pure strategy which is optimal and the entrant has a mixed strategy which is optimal. It can be proved that it is optimal for the incumbent to allocate its defensive budget $Q$ to protect relatively high-profit products. Similarly, it can be proved that it is optimal for the entrant to choose one high-profit product at random, subject to a given probability distribution, then allocate its entire advertising budget to that target area. The entrant's optimal mixed strategy is never to enter low-value products $P_1, P_2 \ldots P_n$, and use the whole budget $Z$ on a product selected randomly. The incumbent's pure strategy is: leave low-profit products undefended and always defend high-profit products. If the incumbent has allocated its budget optimally there will be no soft targets. An entrant would get less than the value of the game if it attacked an undefended product. Given values for $\pi_1, \pi_2, \ldots \pi_3$, precise optimal strategies can be calculated for both players (Gertner, 1985). The firms compete in two unrelated markets, where the only link between the markets is that each firm's fixed advertising outlay can be allocated freely between the two markets. It is assumed that the firms compete only through advertising, and not through price competition. The entrant can gain market share by advertising more than the incumbent in one of the two markets. The difference between the incumbent and entrant in terms of strategy-space pay-offs is that the incumbent will sell to every customer who does not purchase from the entrant. Since in this case, the entrant will only sell in a market if it advertises more than the incumbent and only in proportion to how much more, this clearly is a difference. Here, if the duopolists split their advertising outlays in the same way in a market, the entrant will not sell anything, but the incumbent maintains the whole market. This could result from the incumbent's inherited stock of goodwill (Arrow and Nerlove, 1962). Hence, the difference between the duopolists lies not in objectives, but in relative payoffs. Inspection of Figure 7.3 reveals these counterfactuals. This graph has been plotted using Maple V to

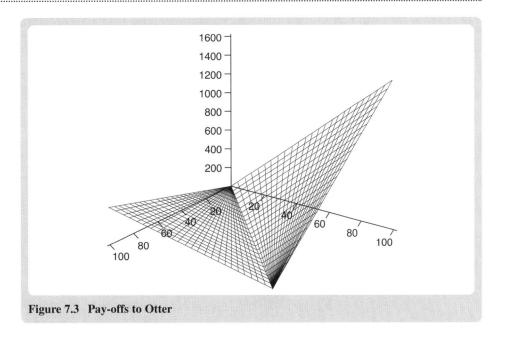

**Figure 7.3   Pay-offs to Otter**

generate a 3D output consistent with equation 2. As can be seen in Figure 7.3, when x = y the entrant's pay-off in either market is zero and increases vertically if x > y in product area $P_1$.

The models developed above and in subsequent sections are similar in approach to those developed by Kreps and Scheinkman (ibid.) in so far as we look at multi-stage games in which firms simultaneously choose advertising capacity, then knowing each other's capacity, simultaneously choose prices. Hence in our multi-stage game firms choose an investment/advertising decision which refers to choice in the product-space. The firms try to differentiate products for consumers to avoid intense Bertrand competition. Multi-stage games are useful in that they formalise the ideas that investment (advertising) decisions as generally made before price decisions since they are long-term choices whereas prices are flexible.

The previous model considers entry-incumbent battle strategies. Once established in the market, the duopolists now need to consider optimal long-run business strategies for survival. The next model considers this duopoly in a price competition.

## 7.6   The game model for Strix and Otter (price strategies: Bertrand-Nash equilibria)

Consider new markets where Strix and Otter compete. The interaction between these two firms is a multi-period game (Figure 7.4). Each firm chooses low prices or periodic high:low prices. This choice requires that specific information on seller data be communicated to buyers through advertising messages. The advertising message will either focus on 'good' value or may stress the availability of good deals in general or other attributes. Neither advertising message will convey specific price data. In other words,

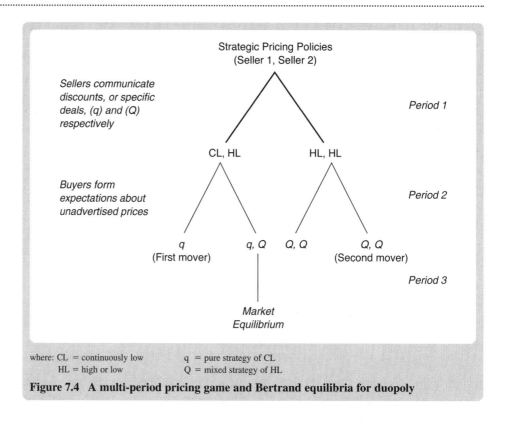

Strategic Pricing Policies
(Seller 1, Seller 2)

*Sellers communicate discounts, or specific deals, (q) and (Q) respectively*

*Period 1*

CL, HL          HL, HL

*Buyers form expectations about unadvertised prices*

*Period 2*

q                q, Q      Q, Q            Q, Q
(First mover)                              (Second mover)

*Period 3*

Market
Equilibrium

where:  CL = continuously low         q = pure strategy of CL
        HL = high or low              Q = mixed strategy of HL

**Figure 7.4  A multi-period pricing game and Bertrand equilibria for duopoly**

sellers choose first whether to aim for messages stressing 'savings' on goods or the availability of specific deals. In the second period, players must choose prices simultaneously and initiate long-term communication strategies. Otter's communication strategy involves advertising specific deals whereas Strix advertises specific savings relative to Otter. Thus if both choose periodic deals, then both announce specific deals in the second period. However, if one chooses periodic deals and the other chooses price competition, then Otter advertises deals and Strix advertises 'savings'. If, finally, both choose low prices, it is obvious that announcing relative savings is non-viable. Hence it is non-credible to have price competition since neither can claim to offer the 'best'/lowest prices. This discussion of the sequence of decisions includes the fact that both sellers simultaneously decide and communicate prices in period 2 and that the appropriate equilibrium concept is a Nash equilibrium. In this game, even though buyers can be aware of specific deals and savings at Strix's, they are not fully informed about all prices at all times for either firm.

## 7.7   Implications of the game model and the Bertrand Paradox

The initial entry game involved choosing an optimal advertising budget and communication strategy for messages such that entry into high-profit product groups was secured. Once entry has been accomplished, Otter maintains a credible communication strategy in advertising periodic good deals. The mixed strategy at the entry stage carries over into the post-entry game. The game models as such throw some light on the Bertrand

Paradox. Edgeworth (1925) solved the paradox by introducing capacity constraints for a given seller.

In our model it is clear that in equilibrium Strix's 'basket prices' are lower than Otter's. In this model the mixed strategy of Otter is interesting since it is consistent with its communication strategy on entry and is endogenous to the model. Thus its mixed high and low price strategy targets high-profit products, as did the advertising in the entry game, and ensures that Strix does not always have the lowest prices for all goods. Thus it is clear from the initial entry game that randomising messages over wide classes of product is preferable to deep price discounting. In the duopoly model, advertising across product ranges is a key observable feature of the industrial behaviour of players (Davis, 1998). These models capture the essence of world trade in electronic heating devices for both Strix and Otter's products. Both firms have world market shares of 65–70% (Strix) and 20–26% (Otter). Strix, the dominant firm price leader, always goes for continuously low prices in new and old markets. Otter enters via advertising, always offering periodic deals.

## Summary

- The case of two firms competing in world markets with technological/product advances is discussed using a game model with Bertrand and Cournot aspects.

- The entrants' strategy aims at profit maximisation with the use of advertising message volumes as the entry vehicle.

- The game models show that relatively low-profit markets will not be attacked or defended.

- The implications of the game model are that both firms must utilise advertising-based communication strategies based on product differentiation features of marketing strategies.

- Nash equilibria are shown on the game tree. Rational pairs are CL:HL; other rational pairs are HL:HL but not CL:CL.

## Questions

1. Why should Strix, the larger duopolist, follow Otter's price strategy?

2. Are the price strategies rational?

3. Why don't Strix and Otter cooperate?

4. Explain how exchange rate changes might affect Strix's demand in specific markets.

5. Explain how capacity constraints solve the Bertrand Paradox.

## Key concepts

| | |
|---|---|
| Bertrand Paradox | rational strategy |
| duopoly | rational expectations |
| capacity constraints | Bertrand-Nash Equilibria |

## Notes

1. End users are manufacturers of liquid boiling equipment devices such as Philips, Kenwood, Rowenta, Haden, Morphy-Richards and Russell Hobbs.
2. Principal markets among these are: Australia and New Zealand, Hong Kong and South China, Singapore, Brazil, the EU, South Africa and the Middle East.

## Bibliography

Arrow, K. J. and Nerlove, M. (1962) 'Optimal advertising policy under dynamic conditions', *Economica*, vol. 29.

Beggs, A. W. (1994) 'Mergers and malls', *Journal of Industrial Economics*, vol. 44, pp. 419–28.

Berry, S., Levinsohn, J. and Pakes, A. (1995) 'Automobile prices in market equilibrium', *Econometrica*, vol. 63, pp. 841–90.

Blundell, R., Pashardes, P. and Weber, G. (1993) 'What do we learn about consumer demand patterns form Micro Data?', *American Economic Review*, vol. 83, no. 3.

Davidson, C. *et al.* (1986) 'Horizontal mergers and collusive Bertrand', *International Journal of Industrial Economics*, vol. 17, no. 3, p. 404–14

Davis, P. (1998) 'Spatial competition in retail markets: motion theaters', Discussion Paper, Yale University.

Dublin, J. A. and McFadden, D. L. (1984) 'An econometric analysis of residential electric appliance holdings and consumption', *Econometrica*, vol. 54, pp. 345–62.

Edgworth, F. Y. (1925) 'Papers relating to political economy', *Economic Journal*, vol. 2, pp. 32–36.

Friedman, J. W. (1977) *Oligopoly Theory*, Cambridge University Press.

Friedman, J. W. (1991) *Game Theory With Application To Economics*, Oxford University Press, New York, second edition.

Gertner, H. (1985) Simultaneous move price–quantity games, mimeo, MIT.

Goldberg, P. K. (1995) 'Product differentiation and oligopoly in international markets: The case of the US automobile industry', *Econometrica*, vol. 63, no. 4.

HSBC, James Capel (1997) *Sector Report: Food Retailing, June 1997*, HSBC, London.

Klemperer, P. D. and Padilla, A. J. (1997) 'Do firm's product lines include too many varieties?', *Rand Journal of Economics*, vol. 28, pp. 427–88.

Kreps, D. M. (1991) *Game Theory and Economic Modelling*, Oxford University Press.

Kreps, D. M. and Scheinkman, J. (1983) 'Quantity pre-commitment and Bertrand competition yield Cournot outcomes', *Bell Journal of Economics*, vol. 14, pp. 326–37.

Mankiw, N. W. and Whinston, M. D. (1996) 'Free entry and social efficiency', *Rand Journal of Economics*, vol. 17, pp. 48–58.

de Palma, A., Lindsey, R., von Hohenbalken, B. and West, D. S. (1994) 'Spatial price and variety competition in an Urban retail market: a nested logit analysis', *International Journal of Industrial Organisation*, vol. 12, pp. 331–57.

Porter, M. E. (1976) *Interbrand Choice, Strategy, and Bilateral Market Power*, Harvard University Press, Cambridge MA.

Stahl, K. (1987) 'Urban business location', in E. S. Mills (ed.), *Handbook of Regional and Urban Economics, Vol. II*, Elsevier Science Publishers EV.

Smith H. (1998) 'Supermarket choice, supermarket competition in market equilibrium', *Oxford Institute Research*, Oxford Discussion Paper 207.

Smith, H. and Hay, D. (1999) 'Competition in retailing: one stop shopping', Oxford Institution of Economics and Statistics.

Tirole, J. (1988) *The Theory of Industrial Organisation*, MIT Press, Cambridge MA.

# 8 Oligopoly and world trade: OPEC

## K. LAWLER and K. AL SABBAH

## 8.1 Oil prices and OPEC's role in the 1990s

### 8.1.1 Introduction

The fundamental question which continually arises in the minds of all those concerned with energy in general, and oil in particular, is: what determines the price of internationally traded oil? In the 1980s the conventional answer to this question was simply 'OPEC'. Hence, the considerable interest manifested during that decade on the OPEC phenomenon, an interest that extended from a fascination with the behaviour, psychology and statements of oil ministers to research on the political economy of an organisation perceived by many as an oil cartel. The price of oil was construed as an OPEC affair, but the question of how and why OPEC use this or that price in any relevant instance was rarely, if ever, answered in a satisfactory manner.

Gradually in the 1980s, and increasingly in the 1990s, the answer to the question of what determines the price of oil became encapsulated in two deceptively simple words: 'the market'. But this answer, like the previous one, straightforward and almost self-evident as many may perceive it to be, does not have much explanatory content. As before, it only points to a major phenomenon. In the 1970s the OPEC cartel possessed the power to set the price of oil without fear of new entry. However, the 1990s saw the advent of new entry.

At a most basic level, answers that appear initially to single out first OPEC and then the market, in fact raise issues as to their interrelationships, which have undergone significant transformation in the past ten years. The 'self-evident' truths that the determination of oil prices was in the past an OPEC affair and more recently the market's, like many assertions that are accepted without question, are not evident at all. These are not definitive conclusions, thoroughly argued and solidly established truths, merely preliminary statements that on close examination open a research agenda.

The purpose of this case study is to review and examine OPEC's behaviour in the 1980s, focusing on the cartel's pricing problems which did not occur. Chapter 9 brings the OPEC story up to date by considering market influences.

### 8.1.2 The role of the Gulf oil in the world oil market

At the end of 1995, the Gulf accounted for about 65% of the global proven oil reserves (BP, 1995). In other words, the amount of oil in place is huge.

Moreover, because of the onshore locations close to deep water, the size of the fields and their geological information, where large volumes of crude oil were pressured by a layer of natural gas, the oil in place is extremely cheap to produce compared to the rest of the world. Finally, the geographical location of the Gulf between the growing markets of both the East and the West provided excellent market opportunities for oil exporters.

By the 1960s Gulf oil dominated the world's export markets and Gulf producers gradually became the main inventory for the international oil industry. However, inter-fuel substitution and oil conservation were triggered partly by the higher crude oil prices brought about by the Arab oil embargo of 1973 as a consequence of the Arab-Israeli war. But, for the most part, this trend continued for years afterwards because of continued expectation of higher oil prices coupled with the security of supply issue which became highly important to many industrial nations. The tremendous increase in oil supplies from non-OPEC sources was a reflection of a frantic search for 'secure' oil. However, much of the reduction required in demand fell upon the Gulf, with Saudi Arabia and Kuwait in particular bearing most of the drop.

As oil prices plummeted in 1986, the demand for oil began to recover; however, it was driven partly by the growing needs of the newly developing countries such as Korea, Singapore, Hong Kong, Taiwan and Brazil. Nevertheless, supplies from non-OPEC sources remained strong with the result that Gulf supplies grew moderately and remained well below 1970s peak levels.

## 8.2  OPEC's quota problems: a brief history of the 1980's oil price collapse

A decade after OPEC quadrupled oil prices, 1983 saw the cartel under considerable pressure to cut total production to 17.5 million barrels per day. The scale of OPEC's production losses from 1979 is revealed in Table 8.1. Compared to 1979, individual production quotas have been drastically curtailed. Throughout 1984 the cartel was under more pressure to reduce quotas and prices as Norway and Britain (non-cartelised producers) sold light crude oils at competitive prices. Eventually, in November 1984, Nigeria reduced official marker prices by 4.5%. Apparently OPEC's grip on world oil prices diminished as internal discipline receded and discounts increased. By December 1984, OPEC's Geneva meetings sought only to stabilise prices and eradicate competitive behaviour. From 1985 OPEC assigned a new overall output ceiling, reduced individual quotas, and aimed to attain pricing uniformity. This section attempts: (1) to explain that it was in the

**Table 8.1  The scale of OPEC's production losses 1979–85.**

| Year | OPEC crude oil production 1000 barrels per day (a) | Saudi Light official prices $ per barrel (b) | Saudi Light spot price $ per barrel (c) |
|------|------|------|------|
| 1979 | 30,037 | 17.26 | 29.89 |
| 1980 | 26,086 | 28.67 | 35.69 |
| 1981 | 21,984 | 32.50 | 34.30 |
| 1982 | 18,269 | 34,00 | 31.74 |
| 1983 | 17,092 | 29.50 | 28.80 |
| 1984 | 16,972 | 29.00 | 28.08 |
| 1985 | n/a | 28.09 | 27.55 |

*Source* adapted from
(a) *Oil and Gas Journal*, various issues
(b) *OPEC Annual Statistical Bulletin* (1985) plus *Petroleum Intelligence Weekly*, various issues. (in nominal terms)
(c) *Petroleum Intelligence Weekly*, various issues, obtained from arithmetic means of quarterly data. (in nominal terms)

interests of most OPEC members to 'cheat' as long as they were certain that Saudi Arabia would alter production to maintain the cartel's overall quota; (2) to suggest that revenue pooling among OPEC members would have been a more effective way of operations.

## 8.3 'Prisoners' dilemma' issues/was OPEC unstable?

Given that a group of oil producers can form an agreement on prices and output levels, can such a cartel survive in the long run? Economic theory provides a definite answer: due to innate contradictions, cartels are inherently unstable (Osborne, 1976).

Once a cartel is formed, the controlling body must be able to persuade members to stick to the agreement. Open price cutting can obviously lead to the break-up of the cartel. However, if a member finds out that it can covertly cut prices and increase profits without the others finding out, there will be a great incentive to actually do so. Consider the pay-off matrix below which encapsulates the problem (Table 8.2). Suppose there are two producers in the cartel who have two options, either to cheat or to adhere to the rules. The number on the left of each cell in the matrix shows the profit pay-off to producer 1 if both colluders adhere to the agreement, i.e. producer 1 gets £1,000 and producer 2 receives £800.

These numbers are purely illustrative but reflect the following principles:

1. The worst thing to do is to adhere to the agreement when the other cheats. It can be seen that if producer 2 cheats he will gain the highest profit of £900 while producer 1, who adheres to the agreement, will get the lowest, that is £750.

2. The best action is to cheat while the other member adheres. This is clear from (1). Moreover, (1) underlines the core problem facing cartelised sellers – namely, the temptations to offer secret price cuts producing the classic 'prisoners'-dilemma' problem. Or, each cartel member is tempted to gain a 'free ride' on the anti-competitive behaviour of the others. In a multi-stage game oil producers behave in a Cournot manner, setting quotas, then in later stages Bertrand-type price cutting emerges. Any stage game is a Prisoners' Dilemma with multiple Nash equilibria.

It is rational, therefore, for one member to cheat if the probability of getting caught is not very high. Clearly, there is a dilemma. Both producers are worse off if they cheat simultaneously than if they adhere, yet they are better off if only one cheats without detection. What would be done? The dilemma is one of deciding between individual and collective rationality, i.e. whether to put producer self-interest or the cartel's interests first. Economic theory provides the answer that individual rationality will prevail (Osborne, ibid.).

The overall output ceiling (Table 8.3) for oil production (1985) was 16 million barrels per day, a drop of 1.2 million barrels per day from 1984, with Saudi Arabia absorbing the largest individual output loss. Even in 1982 the prospect of output restrictions would, through the mechanism of panic buying, have sent oil prices soaring. But 1984 witnessed

**Table 8.2  Pay-off matrix.**

|  |  | Producer 2 Don't cheat | Cheat |
|---|---|---|---|
| Producer 1 | Don't cheat | £1,000, £800 | £750, £900 |
|  | Cheat | £1,200, £500 | £900, £700 |

**Table 8.3   Oil production 1985 and 1984 (million barrels/day).**

|              | 1985  | 1984  |
|--------------|-------|-------|
| Saudi Arabia | 4.35  | 5     |
| Iran         | 2.25  | 2.5   |
| Venezuela    | 1.55  | 1.5   |
| Nigeria      | 1.40  | 1.13  |
| Indonesia    | 1.15  | 1.3   |
| Iraq         | 1.10  | 1.3   |
| Libya        | 1.00  | 1.05  |
| UAE          | 1.00  | 1.05  |
| Kuwait       | 0.95  | 1.04  |
| Algeria      | 0.70  | 0.71  |
| Qatar        | 0.20  | 0.26  |
| Ecuador      | 0.20  | 0.22  |
| Gabon        | 0.15  | 0.14  |
| Total:       | 16.00 | 17.20 |

*Source* adapted from *Petroleum Intelligence Weekly* (1985)

a considerable increase in the volume of oil flowing to spot markets. In 1978 spot markets accounted for roughly 5% of oil transactions, whereas in 1984 these markets involved 40% of oil transactions. Consequently, spot oil prices diverged from OPEC prices continually through 1984 by as much as $2 per barrel. Spot markets operate as follows: oil refineries purchase oil from OPEC on the basis of long-term contracts. Now these same refineries can also trade on spot markets where prices fluctuate daily. Excess supplies reaching spot markets immediately weaken prices, unlike OPEC prices which are changed at intervals following a meeting of OPEC members. Hence, favourable spot prices create strong market opportunities for refiners. Spot prices are clearly very sensitive to gluts, as experience in 1986 proved. Moreover, the recurrent collapse of 'spot' prices had, to a large extent, been due to OPEC members overshooting quotas and unloading oil not required for long-term contracts on spot markets.

The gradual deterioration of OPEC's power over the market in the last three years is evident when considering the trends in official Saudi light prices. For example, the official price of Saudi light crude was $24 per barrel in December 1979, whence it reached $30 per barrel by 1 August 1980. This price endured until 1 November 1980, whereupon it became $32 per barrel. Official prices rose to $34 per barrel on 1 October 1981 before dropping to $30 per barrel from 1 February 1983. By 1 March 1983 the price of light crude oil was at $29 per barrel. On 1 February 1985 official light crude prices were down to $28 per barrel. Hence, the erosion of official light crude prices is clearly observable. These prices represented a very significant real fall on the prices obtained from 1980 to 1986. Accordingly, the business press made much of this apparent undermining of OPEC's market power.

## 8.4   OPEC's quota problems in the 1980s

Since negotiation costs are negligible, OPEC aimed to select individual production quotas such that joint profits are maximised. The cartel's problem was identical to that facing the textbook case of a multi-plant dominant firm oligopoly. Accordingly, optimality dictates that the cartel's marginal revenue be equated to individual marginal costs. Normally this would fix the cartel's optimal market price but in practice its agreements must do more than this, because at the cartel optimal price each participant wants to produce more oil than is demanded (Layard and Walters, 1978). Overshooting quota targets had been commonplace among some cartel members with foreign exchange problems when the desire to sell more oil than is possible under long-term contracts has been prominent. If this pricing disarray continued indefinitely, spot markets would get large enough to further undermine OPEC's price-making powers. To stabilise long-run oil prices OPEC sought to achieve an optimal overall ceiling output. However, OPEC would not be shorn of all market power if quota discipline failed, even for extended periods, since the oligopolistic nature of the world oil market creates an enduring incentive to collude, after spasms of price cutting. This did not necessarily mean that OPEC's quota discipline failed. It was the 13 members of OPEC who later managed to collude. Clearly internal conflicts arose and the future lack of discipline might ultimately lead to the disintegration of OPEC's membership. However, what could happen in the future might be a new oil cartel based around, say, Saudi Arabia, Kuwait and other GCC states.

## 8.5   Quotas vs. revenue pooling

OPEC allocates individual production quotas to quell internal competition, suppression of which is necessary for short-run price stability. Individual quotas seek to confer the security that each cartelised member produces no more than the allocated quantities. Each participant can fix its own policies within its quota, on the assumption that, if it adjusts its own output, others may not alter theirs (in Cournot fashion). This alleviates, to a degree, the market uncertainty inherent in the oligopoly. The quota system utilised by OPEC was not without problems, however. Quota breaking by member states was a key issue at OPEC's meeting in July 1985, leading to the resolution that 'the OPEC price structure will be defended … OPEC is now discussing ways of making the output quota seasonally adjustable and how certain malpractices can be stopped' (*The Times*, 8 July 1985, p. 17). For example, it is revealing to consider how a simplified version of OPEC's quota system operated in theory. This simplified case is considered with the aid of Figure 8.1. Let us assume that the members of OPEC can be separated into two groups of producers. We could call these the dominant group (DM) and a second group of other leading producers (OLPs). The dominant group might be Saudi Arabia and Kuwait, the second group of leading producers might include Iran, Abu Dhabi and Nigeria. Now consider Figure 8.1 – the dominant group's output quota can be found once the other leading group has assigned a production quota. Assume, therefore, that the OLPs are allowed to produce in total no more than $(X_i)$. Once this market share has been agreed the dominant group (DM) can establish its portion of industry demand. In Figure 8.1, R to $D_0$ is the effective demand curve confronting the dominant group (DM). Hence, this segment of the aggregate industry demand schedule $(RD_0)$ is that portion remaining after the market share of the other leading producers, $X_i$, has been subtracted. So the marginal revenue curve facing the dominant group is $RMR_1$. Where SMC is member marginal cost, profit is maximised when each member produces $X_f - X_i$ at P. If the cartel wanted to produce less, say $X_t - X_i$, marginal revenue would exceed the (OLP's) marginal cost at the point where this group exhausts its quotas. The OPEC price would be at P or $P_c$ depending on market conditions (Figure 8.1).

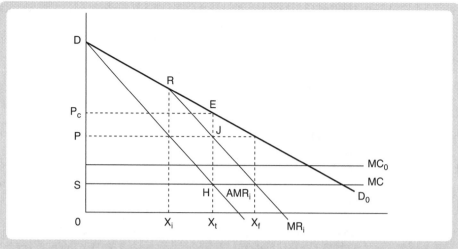

Notes:
1. With MC constant the cartel's price optima may be P or PC, under a quota regime depending on demand conditions
2. With higher marginal costs – $MC_0$ – optimal price would normally exceed P but be $\leq P_c$.
3. A pooling arrangement adjusts MR, from J say with no pool, to H with a pool: rather than truncating the function the revenue pool displaces MR, as shown by $AMR_i$.
4. $DD_0$ – the market demand curve facing the cartelised group.

**Figure 8.1  A simplified version of OPEC's quota system**

How, then, might quotas be fixed? In principle, they could be set to maximise joint profits where the quantities produced would give each member the same marginal cost. Maximum profit is where MC = MR from total sales and each member would, therefore, produce where its individual MC equals the aggregate MR. However, in the face of changing demand and cost conditions, continuous profit maximisation is unlikely as it requires constant and seasonally adjustable quotas. Moreover, OPEC's quota problems were enhanced by supplies from outside sources.

## 8.6  The algebra of collusive price formation: the collusion models

The cartel model frequently used in the 1970s and early 1980s for analysing the oil market was one where OPEC behaved as a dominant producer price leader confronting fringe competitors, who acted as price followers. Though obviously stylised, this model appeared reasonably accurate in reflecting behaviour in the world oil market (Clarke, 1985). However, since OPEC's first serious effort to drastically cut production in October 1984, utilisation of this model to analyse competitive behaviour in the market seems less attractive now. Hence, a persuasive case can be made for the view that OPEC price formation is likely to follow a pattern which can be more accurately represented by overt multi-producer collusion models. Accordingly, two collusion models are offered here which seek to capture the critical variables that OPEC (and non-OPEC) producers need to balance to attain maximisation of joint profits. Moreover, these mathematical models may be interpreted in two ways: (i) optimal quota-based cartel models: specifically indicating the mathematics of optimal quota determination between cartel members – OPEC's endemic problem; or (ii) full collusion models between oil suppliers (OPEC and non-OPEC sources) bent on joint profit maximisation. On both interpretations mutual dependence is recognised between relevant producers.

## 8.7  Model I. Cartel quota allocations: a full collusion model

Here the cartel or colluding group's problem is to allocate production quotas from two sources of supply such that joint profits may be maximised. This is called locating the contract surface. Let:

$Q$ = total output of oil per period

$Q_1$ = amount of oil from producers in Group (1)
$Q_2$ = amount of oil from producers in Group (2)
$C_1 = C_1(Q_1)$ = production costs for producers in Group (1)
$C_2 = C_2(Q_2)$ = production costs for producers in Group (2)
$\pi$ = profits
$\pi_1$ = profits for Group (1)
$\pi_2$ = profits for Group (2)

Total costs of oil production and total revenue for both the colluding groups may be written as follows:

$C = C_1(Q_1) + C_2(Q_2)$
$R = R(Q)$

The cartel's, or colluding group's, objective is to maximise joint profits, i.e. maximise

$$\pi = R(Q) - C_1(Q_1) - C_2(Q_2)$$

The first-order conditions are:

$$\pi_1 = \frac{\partial \pi}{\partial Q_1} = MR - MC_1 = 0$$

$$\pi_2 = \frac{\partial \pi}{\partial Q_2} = MR - MC_2 = 0$$

Yielding: $MR = MC_1 = MC_2$

Solution of the above simultaneous equations yields the profit-maximising quotas from each source of supply. According to the first-order condition for a maximum, the cartel or colluding group must ensure that the marginal cost from all sources of supply is equal to the level of common marginal revenue. Hence quotas once allocated on this principle must not be exceeded, despite the fact that a producer in the cartel now has an individual incentive to exceed its quota. When production costs differ between groups significantly, tensions in maintaining the fixed output quotas are exacerbated.

### Second-order conditions

To ensure that the cartel or colluding group actually attains a maximum profit, the relevant Hessian determinant must satisfy the following conditions (i) and (ii) below:

$$H = \begin{bmatrix} \Pi_{11} & \Pi_{12} \\ \Pi_{21} & \Pi_{22} \end{bmatrix}$$

(i) $|H_1| = \Pi_{11} < 0$
(ii) $|H_2| = \Pi_{11}\Pi_{22} > \Pi_{12}^2$

where the elements in H are the second-order partial derivatives of the profit function, evaluated at profit-maximising levels of output. Conditions (i) and (ii) imply that:

$$\frac{\partial MR}{\partial Q} < \frac{\partial MC_1}{\partial Q_1} \text{ and } \frac{\partial MR}{\partial Q} < \frac{\partial MC_2}{\partial Q_2}$$

So at the optimal quota levels, the marginal cost from each source of supply must be increasing at a faster rate than the common marginal revenue. The contract surface is therefore located.

The foregoing cartel/collusion quota-based model indicates the fine balance of variables that the collusive organisation must maintain to maximise profits over the long run. If quotas are exceeded the conditions for a maximum profit are destroyed. If this happens, competitive price cutting, and massive output expansions, force profits to the competitive level and the Bertrand solution to oligopoly is achieved.

## 8.8    Model II. Cartel quota fixing: a full collusion with multi-products

We now turn to consider the additional complication of a multi-product cartel, or multi-product collusive group.

Imagine the cartel is producing two goods, $Q_1$ and $Q_2$ from two separate sources of supply, hence group (1) and group (2) produce $Q_1$ and $Q_2$ respectively. Demand functions for each good may now be written as:

$Q_1 = Q_1 (P_1, P_2) \dots$ for good (1)
$Q_2 = Q_2 (P_1, P_2) \dots$ for good (2)

Inverse demand functions are given as:

$P_1 = P_1 (q_1, q_2)$
$P_2 = P_2 (q_1, q_2)$

Clearly both products may be substitutes or complements for each other. The total cost function for each supplier is:

$C_1 = C_1 (Q_1) \dots$ for group (1)
$C_2 = C_2 (Q_2) \dots$ for group (2)

The objective of the cartel is to maximise profits:

$$\pi = R_1 + R_2 - C_1 - C_2$$

where $R_1$ and $R_2$ are the total revenues associated with production of each good, respectively.

The profit function may be written as:

Maximise: $\pi = R_1 (q_1, q_2) + R_2 (q_1, q_2) - C_1 (Q_1) - C_2 (Q_2)$

First-order conditions:

$$\frac{\partial \pi}{\partial Q_1} = \frac{\partial R_1}{\partial Q_1} + \frac{\partial R_2}{\partial Q_1} - \frac{\partial C_1}{\partial Q_1} = 0$$

$$\frac{\partial \pi}{\partial Q_1} = \frac{\partial R_1}{\partial Q_2} + \frac{\partial R_2}{\partial Q_2} - \frac{\partial C_2}{\partial Q_2} = 0$$

or

$$\frac{\partial R_1}{\partial Q_1} + \frac{\partial R_2}{\partial Q_1} = \frac{\partial C_1}{\partial Q_1} = MC_1 \dots \text{Good (1) Group (1)}$$

$$\frac{\partial R_1}{\partial Q_2} + \frac{\partial R_2}{\partial Q_2} = \frac{\partial C_2}{\partial Q_2} = MC_2 \dots \text{Good (2) Group (2)}$$

Assuming that the second-order conditions are satisfied, the solution to the foregoing simultaneous equations yields profit-maximising production quotas. With multi-product production the cartel/colluding group must again equate the marginal revenue of each product to its marginal cost. With multi-product production a quota-based system becomes more ponderous and temptations for individual members to cheat may be stronger than in a single product case. In fact, OPEC pricing practice in the 1970s consisted of Saudi Arabia setting a market price for crude and leaving other members to fix their own prices. Oil varies in quality/grade and members set prices to reflect quality differences with reference to the market price. At this time any OPEC member dissatisfied with its market share could adjust price, hence oil of similar quality/grade would be priced similarly, so a small change in price could lead to a large change in sales. Hence in the 1970s OPEC's multi-product-pricing system allowed some flexibility for members since market shares could vary in buoyant demand conditions. Once recession struck the oil market in the 1980s and quota systems were imposed, the complications of multi-product production intensified strains among members.

Revenue pooling is self-explanatory. Each member gives up a certain portion of its revenue to a pool and then each is allotted a share of this pool. The amount placed in the pool is usually uniform but it does not follow that all get an equalised percentage share-out. Suitable choices of the proportions pooled and shares withdrawn induce each cartel member to produce the quota allocated. When accurately selected each member's MR curve is distorted to intersect with the MC at the target output. In Figure 8.1 this is shown by the movement from J to H. Here, adjustment marginal revenue (Amr) equals MC at an output of $X_t$.

Revenue pooling effectively restricts output by operating like an *ad valorem* tax on all members of the cartel. Essentially, therefore, the proceeds of the tax are then distributed in lump-sum payments to producers. In the past, firms operating pools passed over to the pool a fraction of their gross revenue. If the price and the fraction of receipts handed over are both correctly calculated, the effects of the pooling system are identical to optimally stabilised quotas. Comprehensive revenue pools have been operated successfully in the ocean liner trade, and by international airlines (see Bennathan and Walters, 1969). Detailed case histories of such pooling systems are sparse, hence most of the work in this area is largely theoretical. Pools have existed in British industry in the past, but for some specific purpose. For example, in the metal window manufacturing industry in the UK prior to 1956, larger firms operated a pool to provide funds for small firms to transport window frames to galvanising plant. Thus, the pool was a subsidy to small firms.

The significant difference, however, between quotas and revenue pooling in this context is that revenue pooling adjusts marginal revenue, unlike quotas which slice it off. The (AMr) does not become zero until elasticity of demand exceeds $-1$. For a given (AMr) a decrease in MC leads cartel members to expand output and vice versa. The amounts placed in the pool and shares taken out do not have to be changed to allow flexibility. Revenue pooling therefore permits the expansion of low-cost producers and enables contraction of less efficient producers. Due to this flexibility, pooling arrangements are more suited to circumstances involving seasonally changing demand and costs, unlike the pure quota system which requires a renegotiation before adjustments may occur. For OPEC, therefore, a pooling system would be less problematic than its quota system. A mathematical analysis of a revenue pooling system which (i) illustrates these critical points and (ii) may also be compared to the mathematics of the quota-based system given above is as follows.

## 8.9 Revenue pooling in OPEC

In general, for profit maximisation MC must equal MR: Case A: No revenue pooling: Current OPEC practice. In this case revenues are simply a function of price and quantities produced:

where:

$\pi_i$ = profits of ith member

$q_i$ = output of ith member

$C_i(q_i)$ the cost function of ith member

$p$ = price

$g_i$ = share of pool received by ith member

$t$ = fraction of revenue placed in the pool

$E_i$ = demand elasticity for ith member

$TR_{1i}$ = total revenue of ith member

$E$ = world market elasticity of demand

Hence: $TR_{1i} = pq_i$; revenue as a function of price and quantity; therefore:

$$MR_{1i} = \frac{p\partial q_i}{\partial q_i} + \frac{q_i\partial p}{\partial q_i} = p + \frac{q_i\partial p}{\partial q_i}$$

The own price elasticity of demand is:

$$E_i = \frac{p}{q_i}\frac{\partial q_i}{\partial p}$$

so that:

$$MR_{1i} = p\left[1 + \frac{1}{E_i}\right]$$

Case B:

With a revenue pooling system producer (I) will get the same revenue as in Case A plus an adjustment factor from the revenue pool; thus,

$$TR_{2i} = pq_i + [g_ipq - pq_i] \quad \text{where } q = \sum_{i=1}^{n} q_i$$

$$MR_{2i} = \left[\frac{p\partial q_i}{\partial q_i} + \frac{q_i\partial p}{\partial q_i}\right] + \left[g\left(\frac{p\partial q}{\partial q_i} + \frac{q\partial p}{\partial q_i}\right)_i - \left(\frac{p\partial q_i}{\partial q_i} + \frac{q_i\partial p}{\partial q_i}\right)\right]$$

Therefore $MR_{2i} = p(1 - t)\left[1 + \frac{1}{E_i}\right] + ptg_i\left[1 + \frac{1}{E}\right]$

If $U = \left[1 + \frac{1}{E}\right]$ and $U_i = \left[1 + \frac{1}{E_i}\right]$

Then, $MR_{2i} = p(1 - t)U_t + ptg_iU = pU_i\left[(1 - t) + tg_i\dfrac{U}{U_i}\right]$

Moreover, $MR_{1i} = pU_i$

Therefore, $MR_{2i} = MR_{1i}\left[(1 - t) + tg_i\dfrac{U}{U_i}\right]$

Or adjusted marginal revenue = marginal revenue $\times$ adjustment factor and, for $\dfrac{U}{U_i} \leq 1$ and $E \leq 1$, $E_i \leq 1$, we have $E_i \leq E$.

It has been assumed in both cases that marginal costs are identical. For a given distortion (of adjustment) in the producer's MR curve a fall in marginal costs will lead to a seller increasing production. No change in t or $g_1$ is required. Price, p, will fall and unless the marginal cost of other members has fallen too, their outputs will decrease. So long as $E \leq 1$, $U/U_i$ will vary from unity downwards, t will be unity or less, and $g_i$ is less than unity. For a given MR, $MR_{2i}$ will be lower and the adjustment greater, the smaller is $g_i$. In this comprehensive 'perfect' revenue pooling system, different shifts in costs of producers are to be expected. Some producers may improve their performance whilst others do not. If demand for oil stays the same, and one member's costs remained the same whilst others' fell, this pooling system automatically leads to the expansion of the low-cost producer.

If $MR_{2i} = MR_{1i}\left[(1 - t) + ptg_i\dfrac{U}{U_i}\right] = MC_i$

then after a fall in $MC_1$, $MR_{2i}$ would exceed the lower $MC_i$. Efficient producers thus expand output and the less efficient would reduce output. With the correct proportions pooled one may intuitively expect that the quantity:

$$\left[(1 - t) + ptg_i\dfrac{U}{U_i}\right]$$

would be greater than unity, if pooling is to offer benefits to members. A concept which helps intuitive understanding concerning this condition is the notion of the core. No producer could be expected to join a revenue pooling cartel not offering him at least as much as he could obtain without its help, given pessimistic assumptions about rivals', and outside producers', behaviour. This quantity is the maximum the producer could be certain to get, if he was coerced to play a non-cooperative game whilst all rivals acted in collusion (Bacharach, 1976). Revenue pooling cartels can attain goals of joint profit-maximising equilibria more easily than quota-based cartels. Indeed, it is perhaps possible to argue that revenue pooling cartels have possible points available to them on the contract surface which are not options for quota-based cartels. Surely, given the current demise of OPEC's quota-based system, even a limited/specific pooling system would commend itself as a viable option given the current uncertainty in the oil market.

## 8.10   Conclusions

The foregoing analysis shows that an optimal pooling arrangement could remove most of OPEC's endemic quota problems, producing greater price uniformity and long-term maximised foreign exchange earnings, but clearly to the detriment of the oil-importing nations. Moreover, the analysis suggests that a pooling system would remove the incentive among cartel members to offload excess oil supplies on spot markets, so avoiding the

**Table 8.4  World proved reserves of crude oil (1996).**

|  | Billion barrels |
|---|---|
| Saudi Arabia | 175 |
| Kuwait | 100 |
| former Soviet Union states | 75 |
| Mexico | 50 |
| Iran | 47 |
| Iraq | 46 |
| UAE | 31 |
| USA | 28 |
| Venezuela | 26 |
| Libya | 25 |

*Source* adapted from *American Petroleum Institute Statistical Bulletin* (1997)

potential erosion of the organisation's market power. Again, the pooling analysis illustrates how OPEC could maintain a considerable mark-up on production costs even if it diminished in size to include merely the countries of the Arabian Peninsula, given the latter's distribution of 'proved' world reserves (Table 8.4). In fact OPEC may continue to wield considerable world market power for years, despite its present quota system and the instability inherent in its operation.

If Saudi Arabia and Kuwait operated a system of direct side-payments to cartel members experiencing short-term liquidity crises (e.g. Nigeria and/or Venezuela), even the current quota system would operate more efficiently. To reinforce the conclusion drawn here, it seems apposite to quote an important though frequently overlooked comment from George Stigler (1950):

> The most recent and reasonable stopping point short of complete collusion is that proposed by Fellner. He finds pooling of profits necessary to complete maximisation, and deems pooling impossible for reasons of long-run uncertainty of the relative strengths of firms and because of anti-trust policy. Fellner's stopping point is … arbitrary and rests on too literal a view of pooling. It is possible to pool by dividing market areas, by dividing products, by asymmetrical patent royalties – by many devices of variable durability and detectability. (p. 64)

## Summary

- The chapter considers in detail how the world price of oil is determined and how OPEC's role has changed in the past 20 years.

- OPEC no longer has a dominant role in oil price making, though its market power is evident.

- OPEC's occasional price turmoil and cheating activity undermines its power. The case of full collusion with a revenue pooling model is developed to show OPEC's market potential strength.

- Entry into the world oil market can still weaken OPEC's market position. This erosion in market power will continue in the next five years as new global entrants appear from the new republics in Central Asia formed by the break-up of the USSR.

## Questions

1. Why does OPEC experience price breakdown scenarios?
2. How does revenue pooling remove incentives to cheat for OPEC?
3. Why should 'formula pricing' be so popular with oil producers? (Read Chapter 7)
4. Explain how new entry weakens the oil-based cartel.

### Key concepts

| | |
|---|---|
| revenue pooling | quota-breaking behaviour |
| full collusion | profit maximisation |
| prisoner's dilemma | quota-based cartels |
| free-ridership cases | |
| marginal revenue adjustment factors | |

## Suggested further reading

Krugman, P. and Obsfield, M. (1997) *International Economics*, Addison Wesley, second edition.
Griffiths, A. and Walls, S. (1996) *Intermediate Microeconomics*, Longman.
*The Economist* (6 July 1985)
Peter F. Drucker, 'The decline of the OPEC cartel', *Wall Street Journal*, 26 November 1982.
The following issues of *The Economist* are relevant here: 22 December 1979; 6 October 1984, 27 October, 1984; 3 November 1984; 1 December 1984; 29 June 1985; 6 July 1985.
Moreover, at OPEC's Spring 1986 meeting, five non-OPEC producers, Mexico, Egypt, Malaysia, Angola and Oman, accepted a cut in their daily combined total output of 500,000 barrels (see *The Times,* 16 April 1986, p. 21).

## Bibliography

American Petroleum Institute, 1985–1999, Statistical Bulletin.
Bacharach, M. (1976) *Economics and the Theory of Games*, Macmillan, London.
Bennathan, E. and Walters, A. (1969) 'Revenue pooling cartels', *Oxford Economic Papers*, pp. 161–76.
BP (1995) *Annual Statistical Report 1995*.
Clarke, R. (1985) *Problems and Price Theory*, P. Allan, Oxford.
Hirschey, M. (2000) *Managerial Economics*, Dryden, Chapters 10 to 12.
Layard, R. and Walters, A. A. (1978) *Microeconomic Theory*, Macmillan, London.
Lindert, P. H. (1993) *International Economics*, Irwin, second edition.
*OPEC Statistical Bulletin*, Vienna, 1995–2000.
Osborne, D. (1976) 'Cartel problems', *Journal of Political Economy*, vol. 8, pp. 56–9, Chicago.
*Petroleum Intelligence Weekly* (1985), vol. 88, pp. 15–42.
Stigler, G. (1950) Symposium on oligopoly discussions: comments, *American Economic Review*.

# 9 OPEC's dominant strategy and potential entry

## K. AL SABBAH

## 9.1 A Cournot game

In the pure theory chapters, the main propositions of the H-O-S framework are developed. In this section the analysis switches focus to consider applications of the major implications. In Chapter 6 we considered the Kuwait economy as an example of H-O-S trade patterns. Remember that the main H-O-S proposition is that a country's exports (imports) make intensive use of the country's abundant (scarce) factor. Kuwait is a classic example of natural resource-based trade where above 90% of the country's exports make intensive use of oil. The dependence of the Kuwait economy on oil provides another serious problem. The Metzler Paradox has obvious implications for Kuwait and the Kuwaiti Government's publication expenditure reform programmes. Indeed, most of the Gulf States are oil dependent but none to the same extent as Kuwait. This application features Kuwait and other oil exporters and considers pricing formulae used by oil states. An interesting feature regarding oil price determination in world markets concerns the fact that the entry of new oil producers from the former Soviet bloc has meant that OPEC-based producers find themselves in a multi-stage pricing game with Cournot and Bertrand type features. In this game, OPEC always has a dominant accommodation market sharing strategy.

It is evident from this study that initially OPEC producers play a Cournot capacity game (based on quotas), and that when these are established Bertrand price competition breaks out. The oil game can be modelled as follows:

Stage 1    Cournot capacity games where OPEC and new entrants decide capacity volumes of oil
Stage 2    Bertrand price games

OPEC and entrants decide the pricing strategy formula: OPEC's (Mexico derived) market formula pricing model implies that entrants and OPEC find themselves in a chain-store paradox game. OPEC can accommodate or fight entry. Given that entry occurs, a fighting policy leads to competitive outcomes. Hence OPEC should accommodate entry in every stage even though this appears to be a paradox. Given OPEC's internal competition, fighting entry would not be sub-game perfect.

The pricing formulae featured in this study imply High:Low pricing strategies based on entry decisions. In the context of declining world demand for OPEC-based oil, this implies that OPEC's former price leadership qualities are now impaired as world price competition weakens export prices.

In the game tree shown in Figure 9.1, the entrant choosing low capacity can go for low or high prices in the second stage. Low capacity would result in an Edgeworth game with price cycles if the game were played repeatedly. Entry with high capacity would imply

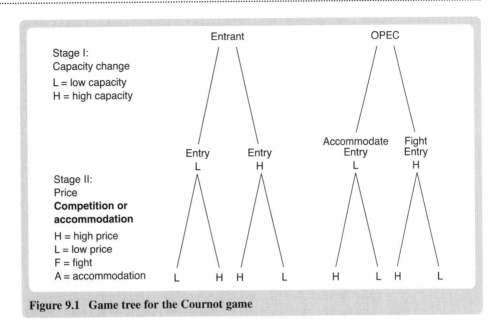

**Figure 9.1  Game tree for the Cournot game**

low prices and a Bertrand game. The dominant strategy for OPEC in the game tree is to accommodate and share high profits with high prices. This is true whatever capacity the entrant chooses. This is yet another instance of the Chain Store Paradox Game (Kreps and Wilson, 1982). Accommodating entry attains a Bertrand-Nash outcome, which is sub-game perfect.

## 9.2    OPEC current pricing systems: formula pricing

Formula pricing is a method for defining the sale price of an export crude by relating it to the spot or forward price of another crude taken as a reference. This method, now applied by most oil-exporting countries, was adopted as early as March 1986 by Mexico. By 1998 it had become a common and widely accepted pricing method.

The adoption of pricing ushered in a new chapter in the history of oil price determination. The 1986 crisis was the watershed that separated this episode from a radically different one during which the international price of crude oil was strongly influenced, if not almost fully determined, by a reference price set by OPEC at meetings of its oil ministers. Oil-exporting countries then fixed official selling prices for their own crude varieties related through some estimate of relative values (taking into account API gravity, sulphur content and location) to the OPEC reference price, that of Arabian Light 34 API, the market crude. The period during which world oil prices were subject to OPEC's administration began in late 1973 and ended in 1985; this episode therefore lasted 12 years. It was preceded by a much longer period of price administration by seven or eight major oil companies.

The 1986 crisis brought to an end the period of OPEC's price administration and introduced the era of market-related price formulae. The old system collapsed because the burden of holding the oil price line, as administered by OPEC, had become intolerably heavy on Saudi Arabia which saw its production dwindling from a peak of some 11 mb/d in 1980 down to 3.0–3.5 mb/d in 1985 (OPEC, 1986). In fact total OPEC production fell during the first half of the 1980s from a peak of some 31 mb/d to a low of 16 mb/d. This was due to three major factors: (a) the coming on stream of additional non-OPEC oil production, mainly from the former Soviet Union, the North Sea, Alaska, Mexico, West Africa and Oman; (b) a world economic recession causing a decline in the demand for energy and therefore oil; (c) inter-fuel substitution against oil and energy conservation measures which affected oil demand more significantly than other fuels.

The oil price shocks of 1973–74 and 1979–80 were blamed, almost exclusively, for all these developments (OPEC, 1988). The true story is naturally more complex. It has been shown by Seymour (1990) that more than half of the increase in non-OPEC oil output of the period 1975–85 would have obtained regardless of the price increases because irreversible investment decisions had already been made before the shocks. Furthermore, the economic recession which reduced energy demand was due to many factors besides the oil price rises; and the energy efficiency and inter-fuel substitution drive owed some of its momentum to security rather than economic considerations.

In short, the problems faced by OPEC in the mid-1980s cannot be attributed totally to the rise in oil prices. A number of other factors – geological, political, fiscal, economic and strategic – played a part. More importantly, it was the manner in which prices were administered rather than the principle of price administration, which can be conceived and implemented in many different ways, that caused some of the problems (see Chapter 8).

## 9.3 OPEC's current pricing techniques: a case study

Many within OPEC, and most authorities outside the organisation, concluded from the experience of the early 1980s that the principle of price administration is inherently flawed. The year 1986 was a watershed because it witnessed the wholesale rejection of the old oil pricing system. Interestingly, a system different from both OPEC price determination and its successor, market-related pricing, was tried for a short time. This was netback pricing, introduced by Saudi Arabia and quickly adopted by most oil-exporting countries in a competitive race for market shares. The short experiment was traumatic as it led to a price collapse in later 1986 and early 1987.

Market-related price formulae thus emerged as the only viable option. Market price formulas were pioneered by Mexico in March 1986 as an alternative to netback pricing which Pemex (Mexico Petroleum Company) disliked. This spread during that year and in 1987, and soon became almost universal. It is now established practice among most oil exporters.

The methodology of OPEC's market-related price formula has three objectives:

1. To relieve exporting countries from the burden of discovering the 'economic' price of oil. 'The market performs this task best when left on its own' is the widely accepted wisdom.

2. To ensure, through the formula, that the exporter realises the prices which reflect movements in the general oil price level in the world petroleum market.

3. To ensure competitiveness between the export crude, which a country wants to sell, and the set of close substitutes which other countries also sell in the same market, or even more narrowly, to the same refiner.

The method chosen to achieve these objectives appears very simple at first sight. It is a method of differential pricing expressed by the formula:

$$P_x = P_R +/- D \qquad\qquad [9.1]$$

where X is the export crude (say, Arabian medium); R is the crude chosen as a market reference in a particular area; and D is the value of the price differential between X and R as estimated from time to time by the exporting country. It is known as the adjustment factor and is sometimes broken up into two or three elements. This, however, should not detract attention from the fact that the critical part of (9.1) is the difference, however expressed, between $P_X$ and $P_R$.

It is useful to discuss the relationship between this simple method and the objectives of market-related pricing. The comparison of means with aims can provide insights into the economic significance of this system and at the same time explain several features of pricing as applied in practice by oil-exporting countries today.

### 9.3.1  Economic prices for oil

Formula pricing raises the question of whether the spot, forward or other type of market in which the reference crude R is traded is the focus where supply and demand balance at the margin and yield the economic price of oil for the region. A positive answer to this question is tantamount to making very strong assumptions about the structure and per-formance of markets. The purist will always be inclined to say that they can never be satisfied. To stick to this position is clearly futile since imperfections are inherent features of all markets and indeed any institution. The more positive approach is to recognise that while one may have to accept recourse to the reference crude markets, there are essential tasks to be continually performed to identify imperfections, to attempt to remove some of them, to improve the structure and mode of operations of markets, and to create, if necessary, more representative and economically meaningful ones.

The current practice is to take Brent (North Sea Oil) as the reference crude for sales to Europe; ANS (the Alaskan North Slope), sometime in combination with LLS (Light Louisiana Sweet), WTS (West Texas Sour) or Brent for sales to north America; Dubai, Oman or an average of the two for the Far East. It is possible to argue that Brent has a central role in this system, because of its significance for crude oil prices and its use by some exporting countries as a partial or full reference crude for sales to the USA.

Brent is the only reference crude in this list that is traded in a market which displays many of the essential economic characteristics required for eligibility. It is an active, multi-layered market, centrally placed in the heart of a large oil-consuming region, and is well linked through active arbitrage to WTI in the USA and Dubai in the Gulf. Its imperfections and peculiar features raise interesting economic issues but do not affect its rank at the top of the merit order of reference crudes.

#### Price equivalence with the reference crude and competition with substitute crudes

The exporter's dual purposes are: to track as closely as possible the general movement of oil price, and at the same time, to set the price of his crude X in line with the prices set by close competitors for crudes with similar characteristics. There would be no problem reconciling these two objectives if (1) refiners were able to switch easily from one crude variety to another irrespective of how far apart they lie on the (multi-dimension) quality spectrum, and (2) if, partly as a result of this substitutability, the relative prices of any pair of crudes reflected at all times the correct economic valuation of their characteristics.

In practice, the set of export crudes traded in the world is segmented and competition is to a large extent limited to subsets which include crudes of fairly similar gravity and

**121**

sulphur characteristics. Thus, Arabian Heavy is not in the same subset as Brent; Arabian Light competes more closely with Iranian Light, Dubai, Kuwait, USW, Iraq and Egyptian crudes and murals than with north and west African or with North Sea crudes.

Furthermore, the relative prices of crudes in different subsets do not usually move in very close harmony in the short period. In other words, the equilibrium condition that relative prices are such as to make a refiner indifferent as between buying this or that crude is an ideal towards which the market may tend but which is naturally never realised. In a market context, distortions give rise to arbitrage. But in setting in advance the value of D, the differential or adjustment factor, the exporting country cannot easily reconcile strict adherence with the principle of equivalence between the price of its export crude X and that of R and the main competitive objective which is to price X in relation to that of [Y], the subset of close substitutes.

Put differently, formula (9.1) implies that an oil-exporting country needs to be concerned only with the differential between R and X, while in reality it has to watch very closely how its competitors are pricing their crude Y in relation to R. As the decisions of different countries are made separately, the dates at which everyone announces the chosen value of D for the formula acquires significance. A country that announces its formula first is at a competitive disadvantage. If undercut by its competitors it may respond in the next round by adjusting its new price downward, or by delaying the announcement, or both. This produces a potential for Bertrand-style competition.

In sum, the setting of a value for D would rarely reflect at first the economic differential between the prices of W and R but may involve a complex process of lagged adjustment. The notion of equivalence through differential pricing of X and R, or X and Y (as the case may be), for the marginal buyer raises the complex issue of the relevant location where this equivalence should be sought. A very strict application of this principle would multiply the number of relevant locations and therefore the number of formulae for every export crude. It would involve discriminatory pricing on a large scale, which is both undesirable and impractical.

The current practice is to distinguish three (and sometimes four) broad regions: North America or Korea, broadly the Western Hemisphere, Europe (sometimes Northwest Europe and the Mediterranean separately) and the Far East. Because the set of markets across the world is incomplete and the transport infrastructure not always fully adequate, arbitrage is not absolutely perfect. This provides some opportunities for a bit of price discrimination between the regions supported by destination restriction on some sales contracts and naturally gives rise to some buyers' complaints.

Thirdly, the 'equivalence to the buyer' principle means that the point of comparison must be close to the destination rather than to the point of origin. This is tantamount to CIF pricing. Yet many oil-exporting countries wish to retain the notion that their export crudes are sold FOB and their pricing formulae states that the point of sale is at a certain port or terminal FOB. In practice, the way around this apparent contradiction is found by (a) stipulating a time lag between the loading and the pricing dates and (b) by including freight rate elements in the computations that set D, the differential parameter, in the price (as generically expressed by equation (9.1)). The time lags can be as long as 50 days, as in the Saudi formulae for sales to the USA. In important cases, however, like Saudi Arabia's sales to the Far East or Mexico's to the western hemisphere, there is no time lag. This means the risks of price changes during the haul period are carried by the buyer.

The key parameter of the price formula D in equation (1) is in certain cases set some time in the month preceding the months in which the formula is applied, and in some cases only quarterly. The first step in the process that leads to the choice of a value for D is to estimate it in a way that reflects as accurately as possible the difference in GPWs (Gross Product Worth) obtained from refining the two crudes (X and R), the difference in freight costs involved in moving these two crudes from their respective origins to the point of comparison (e.g. Brent from Sullom Voe to Rotterdam and Arabian Light from Ras Tanura to Rotterdam) and differences in refining costs (RC). The equivalence implies,

$$D = P_R - P_X$$

$$D = (GPW_R - GPW_X) + (freight_X - freight_R) + (RC_X - RC_R) \qquad [9.2]$$

The setting of D at a value that reflects fairly exactly (9.2) at the time and point of delivery involves certain practical problems. The first arises because of the time discrepancy between the date at which D is usually set and announced (two or more weeks before the beginning of the applicable month) and the day at which the crude reaches its destination. Although the time lag in pricing covers for possible changes in the level of the reference price during the haul, the pre-setting of D means that the differential in the formula is always bound to be out of date. The time discrepancy between the date at which D is set and the date of arrival of a cargo can be very long in the extreme case when D is set at the beginning of the month preceding the applicable month on the basis of data of say the previous two or three weeks, the cargo lifted at the end of the applicable month for a destination involving a six-week haul. In this case the time discrepancy can be as long as 15 or 16 weeks.

This second is a classical measurement problem. Since a price usually applies to a whole region, the setting of D involves the choice of a typical point of destination for computing the freight element and that of a marginal refinery, or of a particular refining model for calculating GPWs. This means that the value set for D will never be identical to the relative valuation put by individual refiners in the region on the two crudes. The circumstances of various refiners naturally differ.

The second step is to compare the resulting value with the behaviour of competitors and make accordingly an adjustment based on marketing experience and judgement. It is also likely that the setting of D will often involve some attempt to look at conditions expected to prevail two or three months ahead; and in many instances oil-exporting countries sound the views of their main customers before finally setting D.

Problems arising from the pre-setting of D are probably ironed out to some extent by the pattern of sequential adjustments as mentioned earlier. Thus if D is set in January for lifting in February at a level that yields too high a price $P_X$ relative to $P_R$ at the time of arrival in March, there will be buyers' pressure to adjust the value of D set in March for April lifting. It is possible, of course, that this adjustment yields a price $P_X$ for April that turns out to be too low in the circumstances prevailing in May or June at the time of delivery. This will induce the seller to adjust upward in the subsequent month.

For these and other reasons the pattern of changes in the values of D for any given formula may sometimes seem erratic when compared *ex post* with the actual movements of GPWs and freight differentials; but this does not prove that attempts to set D as close as possible to its expected market value are not continually made through a mixture of forecasting, analysis of recent data, consultations and adjustments for past discrepancies.

Biases introduced by measurement problems (the choice of reference location and of the marginal refining yield) against crude X for particular refiners are perhaps removed, albeit partially or occasionally, through individual bargaining. It may be, however, that in a buyer's market, the most common state of affairs, the exporting country will set D at a level that makes its crude X competitive with the reference crude for the refiner that values

X least (relatively to R). In practice, this means that crude X will be undervalued relatively to R for all buyers except one when uniform pricing is applied.

Finally, market-related pricing inevitably involves compromises between (a) the seller's main objectives, which are to offer their crudes at prices that are both comparable (after all adjustments for quality, transport costs and so on are made) with that of a reference crude taken to represent the market and in line with competitors' prices, and (b) their desire to price as uniformly as possible (within every broad region) and to retain the appearance of an FOB base.

### 9.3.2 Saudi Arabia's pricing system

We start with Saudi Arabia partly because it is the largest oil exporter and partly because of a greater availability of data. Most of the details of the pricing formulae are considered a highly confidential matter with very little officially mentioned. The introduction of formula pricing by Saudi Arabia did not follow immediately the end of the 1986 crisis. In early 1987 Saudi Arabia returned for a while to official pricing and this was associated with a rather strict adhesion to quotas. This position, however, could not be held for very long considering that many oil-exporting countries were adopting the much more flexible system of formula pricing, thus threatening Saudi Arabia's market share. Sometime during the first half of 1987 Saudi Arabia began to show flexibility in setting contract terms and in pricing. The explicit adoption of price formulae dates probably from October 1987 although this was initially done secretly and press reports about their introduction were strenuously denied.

Published data on Saudi Arabia's price formulae provide information starting in October 1987 for Arabian Light sales to Aramco partners for US destinations; in December 1987 for other crude varieties also to Aramco partners for the USA; and as late as April 1988 for sales to Aramco partners for Europe and the Far East.

All the Saudi price formulae are of the general form

$$P_x = P_R +/- D$$

There is only one reference crude in all formulae for European and US destinations, Brent and ANS respectively, and now the average of Oman and Dubai is used in formulae for Far Eastern destinations. The latter case amounts to having Dubai alone as the reference crude because the Dubai/Oman differential as assessed by Platt's tends to remain constant for very long periods of time. The relevant Brent price in the formulae has been changed from dated to first month forward in January 1989 and back to date in May 1991. It seems that in the past some customers were allowed to opt for either a dated or forward Brent pricing formula, but that Saudi Arabia now wishes pricing with reference to dated Brent to become universal.

The basic formulae are for sales to Aramco partners. In these the point of sale is stated as FOB but the formulae involve long time lags for sales to Europe (40 days) and the USA (50 days). There is no time lag in formulae for the Far East, as mentioned earlier on. The market quotas of the reference price are, however, averaged over ten days around the pricing date for Europe and the USA, and over the calendar month that includes the loading date for the Far East.

The D term in the Saudi pricing formulae for Europe and the USA consists in fact of two parts, the first termed the adjustment factor and the second the freight adjustment factor. The former is supposed to reflect differences in GDWs between the relevant export and the reference crude, differences in refining costs and the difference between the

**Table 9.1  Saudi Arabia's main oil pricing formulae.**

| Crude/Destination | Period | Formulae |
|---|---|---|
| 1. All crudes/Aramco Europe | Apr. 88 – Dec. 88<br>Jan. 89 – Apr. 91<br>May 91 – Present | Dated Brent − Adj. Factor<br>Forward Brent − Adj. Factor<br>Dated Brent − Adj. Factor |
| 2. All crudes/Aramco USA | Oct. 87 – Present | ANS − Adj. Factor − freight |
| 3. All crudes/Aramco Asia | Apr. 88 – May 88<br>June 88 – Present | Dubai − Adj. Factor<br>0.5 (Dubai + Oman) − Adj. Factor |

*Source* adapted from *OPEC Statistical Bulletin*

freight rate involved in moving the reference crude say, in the case of Brent, from Sullom Voe to Rotterdam, and a basic freight rate for the haul of the export crude from Ras Tanura to the oil-consuming region. The latter was set in the past at WS40, and since December 1990 at a fixed level of $7.39 per long ton for Europe. The second element, the freight adjustment factor, adds to or subtracts from the price the difference between the freight rate and the base rate depending on whether the actual rate is below or above the base.

The formulae applied to non-Aramco sales are less well documented (Table 9.1). The important point is that since mid-1989 these formulae involve a CIF point of sales, which means that the pricing date is the actual delivery date. The general principle of Saudi oil pricing in this context is the specific prices yielded by formulae despite differences in the way these algorithms are specified. Although some flexibility may be involved to suit the circumstances of individual customers, it is generally said that small differences in formulation are not allowed to yield, other than in an insignificant manner, non-uniform pricing.

In short, oil-exporting countries, as exemplified in this illustration by Saudi Arabia, attempt to fulfil a competitive marketing objective with a combination of means: an analysis of theoretical price relativities, a continual reference to the behaviour of exporters of crude varieties that are close substitutes, an attention to the desiderata of their customers, and unavoidably trials and errors that lead to long, and at first unavoidable, sequences of adjustments. The customers put up with errors that may affect them from time to time because they can seek subsequent corrections. The term is available for adjustments and corrections. A further consideration is that moving in and out of term supply contracts involves costs. This means that a company with an established relationship with an important exporting country will be reluctant to give it up when the exit costs exceeds costs occasionally incurred through imperfect pricing.

### 9.3.3  Pricing formulae in other Gulf countries

#### UAE, Oman and Qatar

The major market in the Gulf is the Dubai forward market, to which the other Gulf markets are either directly or indirectly linked. While the Gulf is the major oil-exporting area in the world, comparatively little oil from the region is sold on a spot basis. The volume spot traded, other than that trade through the Dubai market, normally lies between 0.5 mb/d and 0.7 mb/d compared to 12.4 mb/d produced in the Gulf countries. The bulk of the Gulf exporters is sold on formulae-priced term contracts. Limited amounts of Saudi Arabian grades are currently sold spot (BP, 1996).

There has been in the past some trade in Kuwaiti and Iraqi grades. However, the major sources of oil for spot trade in the Gulf have been the two countries with the most active equity participation by the international oil companies – Oman and UAEs (Abu Dhabi in particular). There is also limited trade in production of Qatar oil and an emerging market in the currently limited volumes of Yemeni grades.

Price formation for the Gulf spot trade is one of the most complicated in any region of the world. It owes much to the mechanics of the derivation of official sell prices (OSPs) in Oman, Qatar and Abu Dhabi. The OSP for particular grade represents the price for all transactions with state oil companies, as well as representing the taxation or royalty reference price. In all three countries OSPs are announced retroactively, and apply to all cargoes loaded in the previous month.

The Omani retroactive price is known as the MPM price (after the Omani oil ministry) or the PDO price (after the state oil company). The Qatari Oil Company, QGPC, announces retroactive prices for both Qatar Marine and Qatar Land. In Abu Dhabi the state oil company, ADNOC, announces prices for each of its four grades (Upper Zakum, Murban, Lower Zakum and Umm Shaif). The exact method of derivation for MPM, QGPC and ADNOC prices has never been revealed, but it is relatively easy to infer the general principles involved as all are based on the Dubai crude prices.

The retroactive OSP system has come to mean that most spot trade is currently conducted as a differential to OSPs. For example, Table 9.2 shows the evolution of price formation in the market for Oman. After the abandonment of fixed reference price OSPs in 1986, there was a broad following of Dubai, Brent or Oman market prices before the current system of OSPs was introduced in late 1987. Since then virtually all spot trades have been conducted on the basis of differentials to the relevant MPM prices, which is of course unknown when the deal is struck. Trades are then discussed as differentials to the expected average price of Dubai in the next month plus a relatively stable premium.

Similar patterns hold in the other Gulf spot markets. Table 9.3 shows the price basis of Abu Dhabi spot price sales. By 1991, nearly all trade was conducted on the basis of differentials to the ADNOC retroactive price, with little outright or direct market trade taking place. Table 9.4 shows the evolution of pricing for Qatar spot trade. As with Omani and Abu Dhabi spot sales, trade is currently conducted as a differential to official prices, with no outright trade observed since 1987. Hence, trade is conducted relative to expected average Dubai prices over the next month, plus the expected level of two unknown premia, the premium of MPM over average Dubai prices, and the premium of AGPC prices over the MPM.

### Table 9.2 Pricing basis of Omani crude deals (% of total deals).

|  | 1986 | 1987 | 1988 | 1989 | 1990 | 1991 |
|---|---|---|---|---|---|---|
| Outright price | 37.2 | 80.7 | 5.9 | 0.5 | 0.4 | – |
| Differential price to |  |  |  |  |  |  |
| MPM | 44.6 | – | 78.0 | 97.3 | 94.2 | 99.1 |
| Dubai | 16.5 | 11.3 | 12.7 | 0.5 | 2.1 | – |
| Brent | 1.1 | 1.3 | – | 0.9 | 0.4 | 0.4 |

*Source* adapted from *Petroleum Argus* (1986–1991)

Table 9.3 Pricing basis of Abu Dhabi crude deals.

|  | 1986 | 1987 | 1988 | 1989 | 1990 | 1991 |
|---|---|---|---|---|---|---|
| Outright price | 48.3 | 54.9 | 3.5 | – | – | – |
| Differential price to |  |  |  |  |  |  |
| ADNOC | 17.8 | 45.1 | 45.6 | 98.0 | 91.8 | 98.2 |
| MPM | 28.0 | – | 24.6 | – | – | – |
| Dubai | 4.1 | – | 3.5 | – | 5.1 | – |
| Brent | 0.8 | – | 0.7 | 2.0 | 1.0 | 1.2 |

*Source* adapted from *Petroleum Argus* (1986–1991)

Table 9.4 Pricing basis of Qatari crude deals.

|  | 1986 | 1987 | 1988 | 1989 | 1990 | 1991 |
|---|---|---|---|---|---|---|
| Outright price | 50.5 | 36.6 | – | – | – | – |
| Differential price to |  |  |  |  |  |  |
| ADNOC | – | 61.0 | 79.1 | 94.4 | 100.00 | 100.00 |
| MPM | 33.7 | – | 7.0 | 3.7 | – | – |
| Dubai | 12.7 | 2.4 | 2.3 | – | – | – |
| Brent | – | – | 7.0 | – | – | – |

*Source* adapted from *Petroleum Argus* (1986–1991)

To sum, the prices paid in the Gulf spot market are related to the three sets of OSPs represented by MPM, QGPC and ADNOC prices. These in turn are related to average Dubai prices over each calendar month, and hence the Dubai market does not have the same immediate daily transmission to other spot prices inherent in the relationship between dated Brent and spot trade elsewhere in the world.

While there is some limited flexibility in the retroactive prices, the determination of Dubai prices by western rather than eastern trading conditions means that OSPs in the Gulf are also primarily driven by western factors. Thus, the characteristics of Dubai prices feed through to a much greater volume of crude oil. They affect all term sales priced off Dubai, i.e. Saudi, Iranian, Kuwaiti, and Iraqi crudes, and all term sales oil OSPs, i.e., Abu Dhabi, Oman, Qatar, and Gulf spot trade.

Kuwait's pricing formula for sales to the Far East is of the standard type. The reference price is the average of Oman and Dubai plus or minus an adjustment factor. Kuwait, however, has a clause in its contracts providing for price revisions (quarterly) that take into account the prices generated by Saudi formulae for Arabian medium.

Iran has experienced difficulties in the marketing of its crude oil largely because of disruptions caused by the revolution and the long war with Iraq. Logistical bottlenecks put FOB sales at a disadvantage, and the practice now is to sell CIF Some Iranian pricing formulae reflect this fact with prices set on a CIF basis at the date of delivery.

In so far as we can ascertain, the formulae for CIF sales of Iranian Light (34 API) and Iranian Heavy (31 API) for Europe are dated Brent minus an adjustment factor. The pricing date is that of delivery, and prices are averaged over five days. The FOB formulae also take dated Brent as a reference minus the adjustment factor. The pricing date is the 25th after loading and the market quotes are averaged over five days.

### 9.3.4 The formulae for sales to the Far East

The reference crude for Iranian Light (34 API) is Oman and for Iranian Heavy (31 API) Dubai. Market quotations for the reference crude are averaged over the month loading. This is the common practice of Gulf countries for sales to the Far East.

### 9.3.5 Iraq

The price formulae for FOB sales of Kirkuk (37 API) and Basrah (35 API from Ceyhan) to Europe, before the Gulf crisis of 1990–91, were dated Brent minus an adjustment factor. Interestingly, the pricing date was set at only five days after loading, with market quotes averaged over ten days. Formulae for the Far East took the Oman/Dubai average as reference plus or minus an adjustment factor. The usual monthly price averaging applied. Formulae for the USA had ANS and sometimes in the past the average of WTI, WTS and ANS as reference price, minus an adjustment and sometimes an additional freight discounting factor. The unusual feature is a short lag between loading and pricing date which as initially between ten and 15 days and further reduced to five days in 1990.

Although Iraqi pricing formulae were officially expressed as FOB and naturally in a unique form, the Iraqi marketing approach was known to be flexible with prices often agreed cargo by cargo and buyers' preference for CIF sales accommodated in many instances.

### 9.3.6 North Sea's Brent crude oil pricing formulae

Apart from Saudi Arabia which, as seen in Table 9.1, uses Brent as the reference price for sales to Europe, all of the following oil-exporting countries include Brent in pricing formulae:

1. Algeria, for Saharan Blend (44 API) and Zaraitine (42 API)
2. Libya's price formulae for all crudes were based on 50% Brent and 50% products net-backs until the second quarter of 1989. Then, the full price reference was Brent.
3. Kuwait for the Kuwaiti Blend to Europe.
4. Iran for all crudes to Europe.
5. Russia prices Urals on dated Brent for term contracts.
6. Egypt currently uses Brent with a 60% weight as a base for setting the price of Suez Blend.
7. Syria initially used Brent, then switched to Es Sider whose price is in any case related to Brent.
8. Nigeria, for all crudes, both to Europe and the USA. This practice is probably followed by all West African exporters.
9. Mexico includes Brent in its pricing formulae for sales to both Europe and USA.
10. Yemen currently uses Brent as a reference for sales of Marib light (40.4 API) to both Europe and USA.

In 1991, world crude oil trade was estimated at just over 30 mb/d. OECD Europe total imports in 1991 (including intra-regional international trade) amounted to 10.9 mb/d, and Eastern European imports (not including the states of the CIS), amounted to 1.2 mb/d. Total European imports, all Brent linked or Brent derived, were 12.1 mb/d. About

1.4 mb/d of US imports were solely linked to Brent (there is also 0.7 mb/d of Mexican exports that are linked to Brent or other crudes). Thus there are about 13.5 mb/d linked to Brent or some 45% of world trade. When one considers Brent-linked trade within Africa, and between the states of the CIS, we believe what happens in the Brent market directly affects the pricing of over 50% of world trade in crude oil, or more than 15 mb/d.

It has been shown that the determination of the Dubai price, which serves as reference for exports to Asia (26.5% of world trade), is the result of arbitrage on the Atlantic Basin where Brent is the linchpin. Ignoring Brent influences on the price of ANS, the third world crude marker, one can safely say that, in a rather close sense, the prices of some 75% of internationally traded crude oil are predicated on Brent.

### 9.3.7  Mexico's oil-pricing formulae

Mexico was the first major oil-exporting country to adopt a price formula system. This was introduced in March 1986 and represented Mexico's alternative to netback pricing, the method applied by several oil-exporting countries at that time, which Pemex, for good reasons, strongly disliked. Mexico's reluctance to abandon the official pricing system at the beginning of 1986 when almost everybody else was competing for market share through the netback system cost it a significant loss of export volume. It tried to retrieve the situation with formula pricing; in the circumstances of 1986 this alternative idea may not at first have yielded better export prices than the netback system (because crude oil prices fell for a while faster than product prices which determined the netbacks). Nevertheless Mexico can claim that it pioneered the new system, whatever its merits and drawbacks.

The Mexican formulae are more complex than those offered by other countries as they use more than one reference crude (in the case of Western Hemisphere sales) and involve in some instances a link with fuel oil prices. The use of several reference crudes is an insurance against the effects on occasions of erratic performance in particular markets. The reference crudes used during the period 1987–91 were a varying combination of WTI (West Taxes Intermediate), WTS, LLS, ANS and dated Brent. WTI, however, was abandoned in August 1989 because of a realisation that WTI spot price movements are sometimes strongly influenced by local factors and thus become separated from the general movements of world oil prices.

Pipeline crudes are prone to accidental squeezes arising from logistical difficulties. The view that pipeline crudes are unsuitable for use as reference is widespread (hence the inclusion of ANS in the pricing formulae for Western Hemisphere sales of other countries). Mexico tries to mitigate the problem by retaining a mixture of pipeline crude (WTS and LLS), a US non-pipeline crude (ANS), and an international marker (Brent). The closeness of Isthmus properties to WTS makes it difficult to discard WTS as a reference crude; and the importance of the US Gulf Coast to Mexican sales makes the resource as reference to Texas and Louisiana crudes, whatever the qualms, almost unavoidable.

It is in this context that the introduction of Brent as reference for sales of such different crude as Maya in the Western Hemisphere can be explained. The inclusion of Brent, however, increases the volatility of the formula and places a burden on the adjustment factor.

The formulae are constructed in a way that seeks to equalise the refinery yield of the relevant Mexican crude with the composite yield of the set of reference crudes (given the weights attributed to them) included in the formula. The fuel oil element in the pricing formula is there to bring the two sets of yields to full equivalence and to correct for

**Table 9.5   Mexico's pricing formulae, 1987–95.**

| Period | Formula |
|---|---|
| 1. Isthmus 34 API Western Sales | |
| Jan 87 – Jul 95 | 0.33 (WTI + WTS + ANS) − 0.15 (fuel oil 1% S − fuel oil 3% S) − Adj. Factor |
| 2. Isthmus 34 API European Sales | |
| Jan 87 – Mar 88 | 0.85 (dated Brent) + 0.5 (fuel oil 3.5% S) − 0.21 (fuel oil 1% S) − Adj. Factor |
| Apr 88 – Present | 0.887 (dated Brent) + 0.113 (fuel oil 3.5% S) − 0.16 (fuel oil 1% S) − Adj. Factor |
| 3. Maya 22 API Western Sales | |
| Jan 87 – Jul 89 | 0.21 (WTI + WTS + ANS) + 0.37 (fuel oil 3% S) − 0.28 (fuel oil 1% S)) − Adj. Factor |
| Aug 89 – Apr 90 | 0.33 (WTI + ANS) + 0.335 (fuel oil 3% S) − Adj. Factor |
| May 90 – Present | 0.246 (WST) + 0.147 (ANS) + 0.099 (LLS + dated Brent) + 0.394 (fuel oil 3% S) − Adj. Factor |
| 4. Maya 22 API European Sales | |
| Jan 87 – Mar 88 | 0.47 (dated Brent) + 0.13 (fuel oil 3.5% S) − 0.17 (fuel oil 1% S − fuel oil 3.5% S) − Adj. Factor |
| Apr 88 – Present | 0.527 (dated Brent) + 0.467 (fuel oil 3.5% S) − 0.25 (fuel oil 1% S) − Adj. Factor |

*Source* adapted from PEMEX (Petroleos Mexicanos), PIW and MEES

sulphur contents. These tasks are performed imperfectly by the fuel oil element and the resulting discrepancies are mitigated by changes in the adjustment factor. The freight rate element is also dealt with by the adjustment factor. Whether changes in this factor are used, in addition, as a competitive instrument cannot be established from the data.

Table 9.5 presents the formulae offered for Isthmus and Maya sales to the Western Hemisphere and Europe during the period 1987–92. The European formulae take dated Brent as the only reference crude. They involve a 15-day time lag, which approximates the duration of the haul across the Atlantic.

The Western Hemisphere formulae do not involve time lags. There is also a pricing formula for Olmeca 39 API for Western Hemisphere sales introduced in August 1988 soon after the discovery of this crude. Since May 1990 it defines the Olmeca prices as a simple average of the prices of WTS, LLS and dated Brent with a small adjustment factor. Mexican sales to the Far East did not use pricing formulae until October 1992. Retroactive pricing (at the end of the month) was used instead. There is little doubt that Dubai/Oman prices influenced the setting of these retroactive prices.

## 9.4   Conclusion

The old OPEC system of administered oil prices had some merits and major defects. One merit was that a reference price was posted for all producers. But its more important advantage for all producers – be it OPEC, non-OPEC countries or companies with upstream equity – is that it sought to provide an insurance against an oil price fall towards the very low levels set by the cost floor in the short or medium term. But it can only provide this insurance if the exporting countries that administer the price are able to absorb adverse swings in demand.

In this respect OPEC proved to be very successful between 1974 and 1978, that is for a relatively short period of five years. It struggled to prevent a sharp fall in oil prices in 1980 and this uneasy period lasted another five years, that is between 1981 and 1985. The major problem with the price administration system is not, as the conventional wisdom wants us believe, the determination of price differentials with the marker crude. As we have seen, formula pricing as now practised is inherently a system of differential pricing. And we have seen that despite many internal difficulties and inconsistencies, it is made to work through trial and error, and compromises.

The fundamental problem of the old OPEC pricing system was that the volume of residual demand for OPEC oil is a wild variable whose movements are not entirely due to prices but to a combination of other factors (economic, geological, political). The ability to hold stable prices comes under severe strain because of large variations on the call for OPEC oil. If this demand exceeds the volume of capacity available to OPEC (as happened in 1979 and in August/September 1990, for example), prices immediately rise and OPEC loses control over their levels.

Whenever demand falls short of capacity by a very significant amount (as happened between 1982 and 1989), the burden put on the residual supplier in terms of revenue and market share losses becomes intolerable. This could cause a loss of control, as happened in 1986.

The alternative system, netback, used extensively in 1986, is entirely geared to securing a positive refinery margin to the buyer of crude oil. Contrary to a commonly held opinion it is not netback pricing as such that causes prices to collapse, but its use in combination with a marketing policy aiming at volume maximisation without any supply restraint. The main defect of netback pricing, apart from insulating one set of agents (the refiners) from the vagaries of the market, is that the absolute crude oil price emerges only *ex post* as a residual. This hinders the fulfilment of its normal economic role as the signal that helps determining *ex ante* supply and demand decisions.

The current OPEC system of market-related formula pricing enables exporters to set their prices close to those of competitors in the place where crude oil is refined. In this sense it has commercial merits for both buyers and sellers. Refiners are not as fully and exclusively protected under this system as under netback pricing but are less exposed to risks of significant price discrimination. Exporting countries can more easily protect their market shares under this system than under the old OPEC price administration arrangements. Its main disadvantage, however, is that it does not afford by itself any protection against a significant oil price fall. The producers have no direct influence through production policies whose effects on prices always prove uncertain, sometimes perverse and almost always widely different (because of inevitable under- or over-shooting) from the intended result.

## Summary

- The argument about what determines oil prices is discussed with reference to OPEC's behaviour and formula pricing.

- Formula pricing varies between each Gulf and non-Gulf oil producer. The individual systems are very similar to one another.

- An oil game is modelled where OPEC-based producers play a Cournot capacity game, with new entrants and then Bertrand games. OPEC's dominant Nash Equilibrium strategy is to always accommodate entry.

## Questions

1. Compare and contrast the old OPEC price fixing system with the modern formulae.

2. How do the new systems compensate for cyclical changes in demand?

3. Why is OPEC inherently unstable? (See Chapter 8.)

4. Does formula pricing bypass problems of Bertrand-type price cutting behaviour?

5. Why does OPEC use 'Brent Oil' as the reference crude oil? (Hint: think of Barometric price leadership.)

6. Why did OPEC lose 'market power', and do pricing formulae avert the potential for Bertrand price competition among oil exporters?

7. Construct, using diagrams, a 'general equilibrium' analysis of oil price changes linked to changes in the oil-exporting country's terms of trade – refer to Chapters 2–5.

8. Indicate how government policies in oil-exporting countries like Kuwait might influence the terms of trade. (Hint: consider the case of immiserising growth.)

9. Do the pricing formulae used by oil exporters represent cooperative or conflicting oligopoly price strategies? Illustrate your answer using game theoretical arguments (refer to Chapter 7).

### Key concepts

| | |
|---|---|
| formula pricing | terms of trade |
| price fixing | general equilibrium |
| cyclical demand charges | Brent pricing |
| market power | Saudi Arabian light crudes |
| Bertrand games | |

## Bibliography

BP (1996) *Annual Statistic Report 1996*.

Butter, D. (1997) 'Arabs seek common economic cause', *Middle East Economic Digest*, 4 July, pp. 2–3.

Central Bank of Kuwait (1996) *Economic Report*.

Central Bank of Oman (1997) *Quarterly Statistical Bulletin*, vol. 23, no. 1.

Dubai Chamber of Commerce (1995) *Annual Report*.

Kreps, D. M. and Wilson, R. (1982) 'Reputations and imperfect information', *Journal of Economic Theory*, vol. 27, pp. 253–79.

*OPEC Annual Statistical Bulletin*, vol. 6, Vienna.

*OPEC Annual Statistical Bulletin*, vol. 8, Vienna.

*OPEC Statistical Bulletin*, vol. 48, Vienna.

*OPEC Statistical Bulletin*, 1994–2000, vol. xxxiv, Vienna.

# PART TWO

# New developments and themes in world trade

# 10 Customs unions, regionalism vs. multilateralism

## K. LAWLER and H. SEDDIGHI

Economic integration is defined as 'the diffusion of boundaries of segmented economies in order to create a bigger more coherent economy.[1] In essence, there are six stages, beginning with the abolition of trade barriers in visible and invisible goods. Once these two stages are completed, a free trade area exists. Within a free trade area, there are no internal trade restrictions, but each member state is free to set its own external tariff. The use of a Common External Tariff (CET) represents the third stage of economic integration to form a customs union. The idea of a CET is crucial. This issue became the focus of the work of Jacob Viner (1950) when he contested the previously unchallenged ideas that customs unions were welfare improving by suggesting that there was potentially a significant 'trade diversion' caused by external barriers. This concept is important to the discussion in Section 10.2.

The General Agreement on Tariffs and Trade (GATT) was formed in 1947 in order to ensure that the protectionist policies of the pre-war 1930s, where tariff competition generally resulted in reduced volumes of trade and reduction in welfare, would not return. Indeed, during the war, the allies developed the International Trade Organisation (ITO). The failure to agree upon the future of ITO resulted in GATT assuming responsibility for multilateral trade liberalisation.

Since 1947, GATT continued attempts to reduce tariff barriers and in 1994 developed into the World Trade Organisation (WTO). However, the path of multilateral trade liberalisation has not been smooth. It has had to cope with regionalism and new-protectionism, which in the 1970s undermined GATT. Throughout the 1990s, the WTO seems to have faced a second or 'new regionalism'. We later consider the strength of this phenomenon and attempt to conclude whether the existence of preferential trading arrangements (PTAs) create an impetus towards the development of new customs unions, and present potential threats to multilateral trading relations. These latter aim to 'provide the common institutional framework for the conduct of trade relations'.[2]

## 10.1  The theory of customs unions since Viner

Customs unions represent fundamental issues in world trade, insofar as they constitute a movement towards free trade areas. However, there are crucial differences between free trade areas and customs unions. Within a free trade area, members are free to set their own external tariff. 'A customs union consists of two or more countries which have no tariff between themselves and a common tariff against the rest of the world.'[3] The idea is to create an area of free trade, so that once goods enter into it, or if they are produced within it, they are free to circulate without tariffs. Moreover, the Common External Tariff strengthens barriers against external countries, supporting the industries of members and discriminating against non-members. Hence the main similarities between customs unions and free trade areas are that they are both represent discriminatory trading arrangements.

Little work on free trade areas existed until the formation of the North American Free Trade Association (NAFTA) involving the USA, Canada and later Mexico. However, the formation of this prompted new research which attempts to show that free trade areas are in fact inferior to customs union. The research focus points out that problems arise in free trade areas as goods enter through the country with the lowest external tariff and then circulate through members. This may alter the distribution of production, consumption, welfare, income and investment. Thus, the advantage of a customs union, with common external tariffs, is clear as such problems do not arise. Equalisation of rents, wages, profits and interest rates may occur as the convergence process continues.

Static approaches tend to observe the 'once and for all effects' of a customs union and accommodate two points in time, before and after unionisation. Dynamic approaches analyse impacts taken over a period of time. The theory of customs unions can be developed using an example involving the production costs of commodity $X^4$ (Table 10.1).

The formation of a customs union between countries A and B depicts a fall in prices of good X. Moreover, the population of country A would now purchase the imported product from country B. Therefore, country B might now specialise in the production of good X. Furthermore, country B, by forming an alliance with country A, has protected its industry from country C, which produces the cheapest products. What happened here can be divided into production and consumption effects.

Prior to the customs union, the consumers of country A were buying good X at a price of 160. However, now they can be purchased at a price of 140. Fundamental theory dictates that if price falls, demand will expand, as will supply to meet the demand, creating a production effect. The consumer makes a saving of 20 by purchasing imported good X, and spends the savings on other goods; a consumption effect. The extra 'money' brought about by the 'saving' accumulates and multiplies throughout the economy and forms a small virtuous circle. Both the production and consumption effects exhibit the advantages reaped from the union.

The dynamic effects of customs unions occur through time. Balassa (1961) views dynamic effects as one of the many ways that a customs union may affect the rates of growth of countries involved. The 'orthodox' customs union theory implicitly and strictly assumes perfect competition. However, more recent work relaxes such assumptions in order to analyse the effects in terms of the following factors, namely, economies of scale, monopolies, terms of trade and increased efficiency.

Economies of scale involve internal specialisation which encourages efficiency. This is because, within any area of free trade, only the most efficient survive, and previously tariff-protected industries suffer. The formation of a customs union increases the market

**Table 10.1  A price data for good X: before and after unionisation.**

| | Price before the customs union | | | Price after the customs union | | |
|---|---|---|---|---|---|---|
| Country | A | B | C | A | B | C |
| Cost of production | 160 | 140 | 100 | 160 | 140 | 100 |
| 100% tariff imposed by A | 0 | 140 | 100 | 0 | 0 | 100 |
| Price in A | 160 | 280 | 200 | 160 | 140 | 200 |

size. In response, supply expands and unit costs fall. In essence, this creates higher levels of economic welfare, from the union member point of view. Internally, there is more efficient use of machinery and better division of labour. Indeed, the EU estimated a £61bn increase or 2.1% rise in EC GDP within member states in 1981 due to economies of scale.[5] Economies of scale can be viewed from the firm level (internal) and from the industry level (external). Corden (1972) considers two effects of economies of scale as a cost-reducing benefit (internal) and a trade-suppressing consequence (external). He argues that in most cases, particularly when the common external tariff is lower than pre-union individual tariffs, the internal effect is likely to outweigh the external effect so net benefits are gained.

National monopolies are exposed to competition not previously experienced. A group of monopolies become subject to oligopolistic competition in an area of free trade. Thus ICI was exposed to competition from Hosech and BASF in the EU. Increased competition creates increased efficiency, and traditionally, a monopolistic firm does become inefficient over time. The results of trading alliances are normally increases in economic welfare, especially in the long run. Such increases in economic welfare may be large. Increased market share should not reduce the gains yielded by economies of scale as the new market size should be sufficient to support all players. Moreover, increasing market sizes induces better technological progress as investment and R&D are stimulated. This implies better quality machinery and products.

The terms of trade of a country compare the price paid for imports with the prices attained for exports. These should improve with economic union due to falling import prices. Moreover, the abolition of tariffs and quota barriers significantly diminishes import prices, and thus terms of trade improve. However, the effect on exports is quite different. Prices received for exports fall and in this case, there is a worsening in the terms of trade. It can be deduced from this that the more import-biased a country is the more benefits they potentially derive from customs unions, whereas export-biased countries may lose welfare in free trade arrangements in the short run.

Whilst the static, or 'once and for all' effects are apparent with a fall in price of imports, the effects over time, or dynamic effects, reach deeper into the economy in terms of welfare and economic growth.

## 10.2 Tariffs, unions and trade

Scitovsky (1958), using a partial equilibrium study, assumes that the differences in marginal costs between countries are a direct reflection of the import tariffs in the importing country. Under this assumption, the gains from union are the resource gains equalisation of the marginal costs. Baldwin (1992) constructed a dynamic general equilibrium model to evaluate dynamic effects of the EU. He concluded that dynamic welfare effects from the trade liberalisation (removal of tariff barriers) increases welfare by a further 15–90% of the static gains.[6] Although this study was not based around the static gains calculated by Scitovsky, many static calculations are similar and smallish. Baldwin's work indicates that there might be small additions to the static gains as each time period passes, and in some cases, the dynamic gains received will almost equal the static gains compounded. Other dynamic studies argue that Baldwin's evaluation is conservative, and indeed, the dynamic gains are potentially larger.

The prospective gains and losses of union's theory divide into two areas, namely, initial static gains and dynamic gains over time. The static gains are simple to examine, but the dynamic effects reach deeper into the economy and thus are more difficult to evaluate. The main gains/losses involved relate to economies of scale, monopolies, terms of trade and increased relative efficiencies. With all these factors combining, the dynamic gains may be substantial. If countries possess the option to specialise, they can focus on the production of certain products, allowing for the possibility of better production techniques and technological advancement.

Empirical evaluations indicate that there are indeed static gains and dynamic gains present in the EU. Scitovsky's study provides evidence of static gains and Baldwin suggests that the dynamic gains differ between countries. The study by Hamilton and Whalley (1985) asks whether there can be multiple trading alliances in place simultaneously. They conclude that it is possible and argue that the EU is potentially the most competitive trading bloc and always gains from trading alliances.

## 10.3    Viner's conundrum: trade creation and trade diversion?

We now isolate welfare effects of customs unions and question the validity of the view that there is potentially a considerable welfare improvement arising from economic integration. The analysis focuses mainly upon the insights of Jacob Viner (1950), who was the first theorist to question the conventional view that trading alliances were unambiguously welfare improving. Other economists have also contributed to and extended Viner's argument and their views too are explored.

The argument begins with the separation of the two effects of customs unions. Thus trade creation 'is the replacement of expensive domestic production by cheaper imports from a partner country'.[7] It relates to the increased volume of trade flows internally. Hence, new supplies of goods within the union replace higher-priced external goods, which were previously protected by tariff barriers. Thus, trade occurs which would not have happened without the union. External trade creation is also possible provided the common external tariff is lower than previous individual tariffs. This, however, is unlikely as trading alliances are discriminatory; they discriminate in favour of members and against non-members. It is this discriminatory dimension which leads to trade diversion.

Trade diversion 'is the replacement of cheaper imports from the outside world by more expensive imports from a partner country'.[8] There is an assumption here that the trade diversion is harmful to welfare patterns. When customs unions are formed there is a removal of internal barriers to trade, but also a strengthening of the external barriers via the common external tariff. It is the external barriers that cause trade diversion as trade flows are shifted away from non-member states. Viner considered this as a step towards protectionism.

Trade diversion refers to members being forced to purchase more expensive internal goods because a lower-cost foreign source is being discriminated against by means of tariff barriers. Trade diversion reduces the efficiency of world production as more resources are required to produce the same quantity as before. In our example, a union between countries A and B with a common external tariff of 100% results in a diversion of trade as the cheapest producer is now discriminated against.

To show evidence that trade diversion takes place, Viner used an example involving one good and three countries[9] (Table 10.2).

Here, unit costs are assumed to be fixed. It is evident that country C is the lowest-cost producer and country A is the least efficient producer. Under free trade, country A imports the good from C. However, if the tariff of 100% was imposed, the domestic market for the

Table 10.2 Trade diversion, involving one good and three countries.

| Country | A | B | C |
|---|---|---|---|
| Price (= unit costs) | 35 | 25 | 20 |
| Price in A include 100% tariff | | 50 | 40 |
| Price in A include 50% tariff | | 37.5 | 30 |

good is comparatively cheaper. Country A meets the entire domestic demand but at higher production costs. Now, assume a union between countries A and B, maintaining the 100% tariff against C. Country A stops production of the good and imports all supply from B. The formation of the union has enhanced international trade, a trade-creating effect. There is a gain in welfare as the good is purchased for 25 rather than 35.

Consider, instead, only a 50% tariff on A's imports. Production of the good in country C is cheaper than domestic production, so A imports the good from country C. However, when the union is formed, the tariff is imposed against country C but not against B. Comparatively, B's products are now cheaper than C's, so A imports excessively from B. This is a trade-diverting effect, as country A pays a price of 25 for the product in comparison to the 20 it was paying before under free trade. The increase in price indicates a loss of welfare from forming a customs union. This is a static loss but it is unambiguous and hurts consumers in country A.

Lipsey (1957) disputed Viner's arguments. He divided the effects of a union into production and consumption effects. Even if total consumption was fixed, there would be some changes in consumption patterns. Lipsey uses a three-country model with the countries consuming two products, wheat and clothing. Country A produces wheat only and trades with country C for clothing which produces a cheaper product. Country A now forms a union with country B, meaning country B's clothing is comparatively cheaper. Trade is diverted and production is shifted from a low- to a high-priced source.

## 10.4    Consumption effects of trade-diverting customs unions

Lipsey uses indifference curves and production possibility frontiers to illustrate welfare effects (Figure 10.1).[10]

As country A specialises in wheat, it produces OD wheat and no clothing. The line DE represents the price ratio between the two products when trading with country C. Line DF represents the domestic price ratio, clearly lower than line DE. Now, the union is formed. The price ratio with country B lies between DE and DF, line DV. The price ratio with country C falls to some level below DV because of import tariffs. Clearly, the welfare yield on the indifference curve tangential to DV is less than the indifference curve tangential to DE prior to the union, so welfare is lost because of a switch from a low- to a high-cost source. Trade is diverted. However, in a second best world, Lipsey shows, even trade-diverting customs unions can be beneficial if the consumption substitution effects, post-union, are positive and outweigh the welfare-reducing trade-diverting tendency. To achieve this, consumers post-union need better terms of trade than previously obtainable.

In the first case, pre-union tariffs meant that there was no trade. The prices at home and abroad were $P_h$ and $P_f$ respectively. After the union is formed, a common external tariff is imposed, and for this analysis assume that it is the average of pre-union tariff rates. This

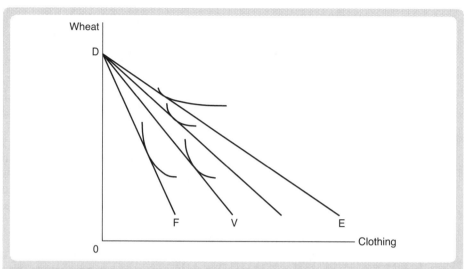

**Figure 10.1  Indifference curves and production possibility frontiers illustrating welfare effects**

is denoted by $P_{CET}$ on Figure 10.2. The price causes demand abroad to rise to OS whilst supply abroad contracts to OR. In the home country, demand falls to OA whilst supply expands to OB. Obviously, the extra supply at home is exported to meet the extra demand abroad. From one point of view, there is a trade gain. Consumer surplus has risen by $P_{CET}VTP_f$, whilst producer surplus has lowered by $P_{CET}UTP_f$. The net value is a gain of TUV. In the home country prices rise. Consumer surplus falls by $P_hEGP_{CET}$ whilst producer surplus rises by $P_hECP_{CET}$. Clearly, the producer surplus gain outweighs the consumer surplus loss, and delivers a welfare gain.

A second case is where only the home country has a prohibitive tariff whilst the foreign country has lower tariff rates allowing trade with the rest of the world. The initial price abroad, including the tariff, was $P_F$. This allows PQ imports from the rest of the world

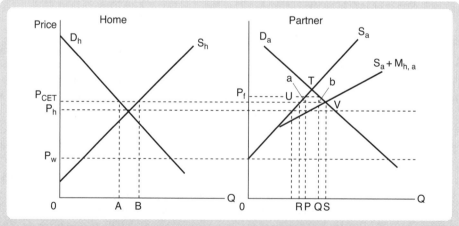

**Figure 10.2  Consumption and production substitution effects can outweigh welfare-reducing trade-diverting tendencies**

with OP production domestically. The revenue collected would be $PQP_WP_F$. The customs union results in a universal tariff of $P_{CET}$. Demand abroad rises to OS and domestic production falls to OR. Triangle (a) represents saved costs from reducing the scale of inefficient production and triangle (b) represents the gain in consumer surplus. Together, these represent all gains. However, the union has shifted the imports of the foreign country from a low-cost producer (the rest of the world) to a high-cost producer (the home country); there is thus a trade-diverting effect. Unit costs rise by $P_WP_{CET}$, and this multiplied by PQ exhibits the total trade diversion abroad. Collectively, trade diversion outweighs trade creation so there is an overall trade-diverting effect, but this could go in reverse, either in [a] general equilibrium change, or [b] if b > a in the diagram.

Johnson (1962) also widened the concept of diversion to include overall consumption effects. He suggested that unions, more than anything, changed consumption patterns. This would either increase or decrease the consumer surplus depending on whether there was a shift to higher- or lower-cost sources of production. Sources of production with higher costs reduce the quantity of goods purchased. The area which denotes the consumer surplus is therefore reduced. The opposite is true for lower-cost sources.

Krauss (1972) argued that the view of Viner conceals some 'general conditions' of trade creation/diversion, and welfare effects. He relaxes some of Viner's initial assumptions, such as that of constant costs and fixed consumption patterns. However, despite obtaining various results, no 'universal law' of customs unions was derived. Few conclusions of practical importance can be substantiated theoretically on the pros and cons of static trade creation and diversion effects.

Meade (1955) and Johnson (1962) following Viner established a set of practical criteria which would indicate whether a custom union was generally trade creating. They argued that, for a union to be trade creating, there should be many members, who trade only a small proportion of their domestic production abroad, and undertake a large proportion with other union members. Once countries export a large share of production or if exports are highly non-union orientated, this opens possibilities of trade diversion.

Moreover, Meade and Johnson contend that there is a general necessity for low common external tariffs, especially compared to previous tariff levels. Moreover, the areas which are covered by the tariff should frequently overlap. However, without overlaps, there is no possibility of specialisation and therefore no trade-creating effects. The greater the overlap present, the less likely it is that there are trade-diverting effects. Finally, in order to ensure competitiveness, a necessary condition for trade creation is that there is a requirement for wide differences in costs of production between potential union members.

Although the conditions set out by Meade and Johnson at first appear unrealistic, the underlying ideas are valid. The conditions set out appear to imply that less developed countries would be less likely to gain by membership of unions. This is because less developed economies produce a narrower range of commodities and these goods are more export-orientated. However, a yet unexplained paradox has recently emerged as groups of less developed economies continue to develop preferential trading arrangements.

### 10.4.1 Regionalism or multilateralism?

The process of multilateral tariff elimination is one which the General Agreement on Tariffs and Trade (GATT) has been attempting to enforce since its formation in 1947. Its work is now continued by the World Trade Organisation (WTO). The ratification of the North American Free Trade Association (NAFTA) between the USA, Canada, and later Mexico seems to have indicated the onset of a new wave of regional integration.

Throughout the 1990s, there seems to be a rebirth of regionalism or new-regionalism which presents threats to the efforts of the WTO.

Regionalism is seen to 'be a tendency towards some kind of Preferential Trading Arrangement between a number of countries belonging to a particular region'.[11] The term Preferential Trading Arrangements (PTAs) includes free trade areas and customs unions. One of the main characteristics of the 'new'-regionalism is that the countries involved in each PTA belong to a particular region. Moreover, there seems to be a tendency for smaller countries to attach themselves to large neighbouring countries to obtain trade advantages. This attachment requires quite deep economic integration on the part of the smaller countries. In effect, these smaller countries are 'purchasing' links with larger neighbouring countries through means of moderate trade concessions. Examples of this recently are NAFTA's expansion to include Mexico, and Austria, Finland and Sweden joining the EU.

The problem with regionalism is that despite the trade created, there is also some trade diversion. It is the trade diversion that makes regionalism inferior to multilateral tariff reductions, as shown by Cooper and Massell (1965). Their work suggests that the latter reaps all the benefits of the former without the costs. The formation of regional trading blocs restricts inter-regional trade and therefore restricts multilateral free trade. Thus, it can be said that the existence of regionalism in comparison to the alternatives lowers welfare in the world. Hindley and Messerlin (1993) and Bhagwati (1993) show that regionalism may cause significant trade diversion.

Multilateralism is the term given to the aim of GATT and the WTO to unilaterally reduce tariff barriers. To explore this fully, it is necessary to examine the principles which have been used in order to gain unilateral tariff reductions. There are three main principles. The first is a non-discriminatory principle. The 'most-favoured-nation' principle is critical and is the keystone of GATT agreements. It ensures that the reduction of tariffs or quotas are non-discriminatory; or that reductions in tariffs are the same for all countries.

The principle of reciprocity is one that makes sure that countries which receive tariff cuts must also reduce tariff barriers. This principle ensures that there are no 'free-trade' and/or political disputes brought about by the system. The final principle permits concessions. Most notably, exceptions are allowed for countries that wish to create free trade areas or customs unions and for developing countries. In effect, by allowing for the existence of PTAs, GATT has allowed 'regionalism' to emerge. The concern now is that the world is dividing into three competing blocs focused around the United States, the European Union and East Asia. This initiation for this trend appears to be the ratification of NAFTA in the late 1980s and its expansion to include Mexico, and continued integration in Europe and Asia. Indeed, it is estimated that there are nearly 100 preferential arrangements currently in the world.[12] The key question is discussed by Bhagwati (1991) who asks 'will the existence of PTAs be stumbling blocks or building blocks in the freeing of trade multilaterally?'[13] This he considered to be the dynamic 'time path' question.

Bagwell (1998) too attempts to answer this same question. Bagwell suggests there are two sides to the argument; namely those who argue that PTAs complement the multilateral efforts and encourage their existence, and those who consider that PTAs are a threat to multilateral efforts. Bagwell supports the view that there is a real threat posed to the multilateral trading system by regionalism. He considers the appeal of the GATT principles for governments, why governments are attracted to such systems and whether PTAs are consistent with reciprocity and non-discrimination. The term PTA divides into free trade areas and customs unions (Bagwell, ibid.). He concludes that free trade areas cannot be consistent with the multilateral 'principles', since countries involved in free trade areas, such as the United States, frequently exercise rights to trade preferentially under the aegis of the exceptions principle. These violate non-discriminatory principles and create barriers which affect world prices. However, for the case of customs unions, common external barriers may still be consistent with the multilateral 'principles'. Bagwell concludes that a tension between PTAs and multilateralism is ever present.

Bagwell (1997) proposes that PTAs and multilaterism can co-exist with multilateral tariff reductions. There is a 'honeymoon' period in the early stages of the formation of a customs union. However, as the union becomes completely implemented, conflicts emerge. This is due to non-members recognising that sooner or later, members will raise tariffs because of increased market power. Thus, a trade war begins. Once the customs union is operational, market power is realised. Here, co-existence is only possible if multi-lateral tariffs rise, which violates the principles of multilateral trading systems.

Wilfred Ethier (1998) discusses how the new-regionalism emerged. However, he argues that there is a critical need to accept that the new-regionalism emerged in a different era from the old-regionalism and so methods used to combat old-regionalism are now ineffective. The environment, according to Ethier, now differs in three dramatic, funda-mental and critical ways. First, the multilateral trade liberalisation in manufactured goods is now more effective than before. Indeed, in the several bouts of GATT talks since the 1970s much tariff elimination has occurred. Ethier states that 'scores of economically less advanced countries have abandoned the basically-autarkic, anti-market policies followed during the times of old regionalism and are now actively trying to join the multilateral trading system'.[14]

A third reform proposed by Ethier is that Foreign Direct Investment (FDI) has become much more of a two-way process, and is now growing faster than trade. Formerly, the patterns of FDI saw developed countries investing in developing countries in order to obtain cheap labour and natural resource advantages. Recently and most especially in East Asia, there is a tendency for the economically less-developed countries to begin investing in developed economies. The point here is that regionalism has re-emerged as a result of the success of the multilateral trading system. In essence, regionalism occurs when groups of countries, such as the former communist countries, join the multilateral trading system and by competing among themselves for investment opportunities create a benign environment.

A crucial difference between the two different waves of regionalism is the way they have been viewed. In the era of old regionalism, the concerns centred around the static welfare effects of the regional integration. Now the controversy focuses on the dynamic 'time path' consequences. However, Bhagwati (1988) attempts to assess the static effects of new regionalism. First, Bhagwati asks whether trade diversion is a 'red herring' and condemns recent views which revert to pre-Vinerian analysis, whereby freeing trade by means of reducing tariffs was considered to be unambiguously welfare improving. It follows that trade diversion occurred with NAFTA when it raised tariffs against non-members.[15]

The second issue contemplated by Bhagwati (ibid.) is that PTAs are formed among natural trading partners. This is dismissed by some with evidence from NAFTA which cites that the majority of US trade is from outside states, whereas for Canada and Mexico, the reverse is true. Bhagwati proposes a method where trade diversion reflects the elasticities of substitution and constructs a model where each country specialised in dif-ferent imperfect substitutes with the preferential tariff gradually being reduced (Bhagwati and Panagariya (1996)).[16] Thus the initial tariff of country A on B is $t_b$ (equal to the tariff of external country C). As the tariff is reduced, the volume of trade of country A with B increases absolutely and relatively compared to country C. Thus Bhagwati (ibid.)

provides a case where trade diversion exists with the formation of a regional trading bloc. In the case of unilateral tariff reductions, trade diversion is unrealistic as the reductions are on a non-discriminatory basis. This work shows that PTAs are harmful to welfare patterns and the implications are very similar to those of Cooper and Massell (1965) and Johnson (1965).

It seems clear that regionalism does pose a threat to the multilateralism system. The analysis now considers what can be done to diminish the threat. Bagwell (1998) considers enforcement mechanisms of the multilateral system to be self-enforcing, and that the WTO provides guidelines for cooperative trade policies and acceptable retaliatory measures. In the light of recent regional integrations (NAFTA's expansion to include Mexico), current enforcement mechanisms may be inadequate. Bagwell concludes that the efficiency of the multilateral system is only compromised by the existence of PTAs if the enforcement mechanisms are sufficiently weak. 'Further strengthening of the enforcement mechanisms of the GATT/WTO will undercut the case for preferential agreements.'[17]

The Uruguay Round saw GATT develop into the WTO. At its peak 117 countries participated by the end of the round.[18] These figures indicate the commitment of the countries of the world to multilateral tariff liberalisation. Moreover, the WTO is a permanent arrangement, unlike the GATT. Indeed, the GATT was simply an understanding between countries but the newly formed WTO is an international institution. Although there are no new arrangements, structures or major changes to the system since WTO replaced GATT, there are a number of differences.

Among new additions is a dispute Settlement Board, and in general, the WTO is now 'actively seeking to resolve trade disputes'.[19] Moreover, the trade rules are now clearer than before. There appears to be in essence a strengthening of the enforcement/policing mechanisms. The Uruguay Round has been seen by many as a departure from all others, as little concern was placed upon tariff reductions and more concern focused towards strengthening the system and restoring consistency with the multilateral principles. Bagwell (ibid.) contends that the threat of regionalism can be weakened by invigoration of the enforcement mechanisms.

Moreover, the WTO extended the scope of areas covered. Much of the criticism of the GATT was that the tariffs were reduced only in some areas whilst others were ignored or at least given less attention, such as textiles. However, the Uruguay Round saw the WTO move into new areas, for example intellectual property rights. In general, the scope of the WTO is much broader than that of the GATT.

Considering the principles of a multilateral trading system, the WTO established in 1995 argued that developing countries should be given additional tariff aid as part of the exceptions principle. Ethier (1998) points out that regional integration occurs as a result of the success of the multilateral trading system. The recent high degree of Asian integration is due to the fact that most are developing economies, being given additional tariff advantages. For many goods, e.g. textiles and raw materials, tariff reductions have not applied as these are the main industries in developing countries. Hence, the additional advantages given to developing countries may have caused further regional integration. Therefore it follows that a way to stem the new momentum of regionalism would be to reduce the additional aid given to developing countries.

In conclusion, the multilateral tariff elimination efforts of the GATT and the WTO seem to be under threat from the phenomenon of regionalism. Regionalism increases the welfare of member states, but considerably harms welfare in the world. By contrast, tariff elimination on a unilateral basis does not raise external barriers and thus is superior to regional tariff elimination. The controversy between the two views is not new, and has returned in recent years as areas of the world have become more integrated.

Bhagwati (1991) raised issues of the dynamic 'time paths' outcomes and much attention has been focused in this area. Bagwell (1998) considers the principles underlying the multilateral trading system. By considering these principles, he argues that a threat is posed by regionalism. Strengthening the enforcement mechanisms would undercut the case for PTAs. An earlier paper by Bagwell (1997) proposes that a co-existence of the two (regionalism and multilateralism) is only possible in the early stages of customs union formation. As time passes, the two types of organisations become contradicting so co-existence is not possible long term.

Ethier (1998) points out the need to consider the global economic environment. The point here is that regionalism emerged as a result of the multilateral trading system. It follows from this that integration in Asia may be due to the success of the multilateral system. Bhagwati *et al.* (1998) move away from the dynamic approach and attempt to assess the static effects of regionalism. They conclude that trade diversion does exist and that initially, the tariff reductions of customs unions complement the multilateral system up to a point. These begin to undermine multilateral efforts. This argument is consistent with Bagwell (1997).

Considering all the views in this debate, some of the arguments are consistent. It is apparent that regionalism may complement the multilateral system initially but as it becomes more advanced, a conflict, essentially caused by trade diversion, exists. Indeed, the economic environment has changed since the last wave of regionalism, but the most powerful argument is that the threat of regionalism can be undermined by strengthening enforcement mechanisms in the multilateral system. The WTO is now adopting measures to strengthen the system. Further strengthening of the enforcement mechanisms will ensure that the multilateral system does not founder upon the principles on which it was built.

## Summary

- Regionalism vs. multinationalism has been a major controversy in economics since Viner's seminal work in the area.

- Trade diversion and trade creation can arise under a variety of circumstances. Supply-side concepts based on Viner's analysis are limited in a general equilibrium setting.

- Pressures of the new regionalism are undermining the development of the world multilateral trading system and creating pressures for new regional trading blocs. The WTO's position on regional developments is occasionally unclear except that its overriding mission is to promote a free multilateral world trading system.

### Questions

1. Can trade-diverting customs unions be beneficial?

2. How do consumption issues influence welfare outcomes for a customs union?

3. Is economic integration preferable to free trade zones?

4. How should the WTO approach the rise of the tendencies towards new protectionism?

5. How will China benefit from WTO membership? Will China's accession benefit the global trading system?

## Key concepts

customs unions                                World Trade Organisation (WTO)
general equilibrium                           trade creation
multilateral trade systems                    trade diversion

## Notes

1. Neilsen, J. U. M. *et al.* (1991) *An Economic Analysis of the EC*, UK: McGraw Hill, p. 3.
2. World Trade Organisation Web site (1999) [online] The Agreement Establishing the World Trade Organisation, Available from http://www/wto.org, p. 1.
3. Eatwell, J. *et al.* (1998) *The New Palgrave Dictionary of Economics*, New York: Macmillan, p. 743.
4. Barnes, I. *et al.* (1995) *An Enlarged European Union*, New York: Longman Ltd, p. 54.
5. Linter, V. *et al.* (1991) *The European Community: Economic and Political Aspects*, UK: McGraw Hill, p. 37.
6. Mimic, M. (1998) *International Trade*, Basingstoke: Macmillan, p. 477.
7. El-Agraa, A. M. (1990) *Economics of the European Community*, Cambridge: Phillip Allan, p. 80
8. El-Agraa, A. M. (1988) *International Economic Integration*, Basingstoke: Macmillan, p. 17.
9. Neilson, J. M. *et al.* (1991) *An Economic Analysis of the EC*, UK: McGraw Hill, p. 16.
10. Lipsey, R. G. (1957) The theory of customs union: trade diversion and welfare, *Econometrica*, vol. 24, p. 43.
11. Lahiri, S. (1998) 'Controversy: regionalism vs multilateralism', *Economic Journal*, vol. 108, p. 1126.
12. Lahiri, S. (1998) 'Controversy: regionalism vs multilateralism', *Economic Journal*, vol. 108, p. 1126.
13. Bhagwati, J. (1991) *The World Trading System at Risk*, New York: Princeton University Press, p. 12.
14. Bhagwati, J. *et al.* (1996) *Preferential Trading Areas and Multilateralism: Strangers, Friends or Foes?*, Washington: AEI Press, p. 25.
15. Ethier, W. (1998) 'The new regionalism', *Economic Journal*, vol. 108, p. 1149.
16. Bhagwati, J. *et al.* (1998) 'Trading preferentially: theory or policy', *Economic Journal*, vol. 108, p. 1131.
17. Bagwell, K. *et al.* (1998) 'Will preferential agreements undermine the multilateral trading system?', *Economic Journal*, vol. 108, p. 1181.
18. Whalley, L. *et al.* (1955) *The Trading System after Uruguay Round*, London: Longman, p. 33.
19. World Trade Organisation Web site (1999) [online] The Agreement Establishing the World Trade Organisation, Available from http:// www.wto.org, p. 2.

## Bibliography

Bagwell, K. and Staiger, R. W. (1997) 'Multilateral tariff co-operation during the formation of a customs union', *Journal of International Economics*, vol. 42, pp. 91–123.
Bagwell, K. and Staiger, R. W. (1998) 'Will preferential agreements undermine the multilateral trading system?', *Economic Journal*, vol. 108, pp. 1162–82.

Balassa, B. (1961) *The Theory of Economic Integration*, London: Allen & Unwin.

Balassa, B. (1967) 'Trade creation and trade diversion in the European Common Market', *Economic Journal*, vol. 77, pp. 4, 9 & 20.

Baldwin, R. E. (1992) 'Measurable dynamic gains from trade', *Journal of the Political Economy*, vol. 100, pp. 162–74.

Barnes, I. *et al.* (1995) *An Enlarged European Union*, New York: Longman Ltd, p. 54.

Bhagwati, J. and Panagariya, A. (1996) *Preferential Trading Areas and Multilateralism: Strangers, Friends or Foes?* Washington: AEI Press, p. 25.

Bhagwati, J. (1991) *The World Trading System at Risk*, New York: Princeton University Press.

Bhagwati, J. (1993) 'Regionalism and multilateralism: an overview', in J. De Melo and A. Panagariya (eds), *New Dimensions in Regional Integration*, New York: Cambridge University Press.

Bhagwati, J., Greenaway, D. and Panagariya, A. (1998) 'Trading preferentially: theory or policy', *Economic Journal*, vol. 108, p. 1131.

Cooper, C. A. and Massell, B. F. (1965) 'A new look at customs union theory', *Economic Journal*, vol. 75, pp. 742–47.

Corden, W. M. (1972) 'Economies of scale and customs union theory', *Journal of Political Economy*, vol. 80, pp. 465–75.

Eatwell, J. *et al.* (1998) *The New Palgrave Dictionary of Economics*, New York: Macmillan, p. 743.

Ethier, W. (1998) 'The new regionalism', *Economic Journal*, vol. 108, pp. 1149–61.

El-Agraa, A. M. (1988) *International Economic Integration*, Basingstoke: Macmillan, p. 17.

El-Agraa, A. M. (1990) *Economics of the European Community*, Cambridge: Phillip Allan, p. 80.

Hamilton, R. and Whalley, J. (1985) 'Geographically discriminatory trade arrangements', *Review of Economics and Statistics*, vol. 67, pp. 446–55.

Hindley, B. and Messerlin, P. (1993) *Guarantees of Market Access and Regionalism*, New York: Harvester Wheatsheaf.

Johnson, H. G. (1965) 'An economic theory of protectionism, tariff bargaining and the formation of a customs union', *Journal of Political Economy*, vol. 73, pp. 256–83.

Johnson, H. G. (1962) *Money, Trade and Economic Growth*, London: Allen & Unwin.

Krauss, M. (1972) 'Recent developments in customs union theory: an interpretative survey', *Journal of Economic Literature*, vol. 10, pp. 424–30.

Lahiri, S. (1998) 'Controversy: regionalism versus multilateralism', *Economic Journal*, vol. 108., p. 1126.

Lintner, V. *et al.* (1991) *The European Community: Economic and Political Aspects*, UK: McGraw Hill, p. 38.

Lipsey, R. G. (1957) 'The theory of customs union: trade diversion and welfare', *Econometrica*, vol. 24, pp. 40–6.

Meade, J. E. (1955) *The Theory of Customs Union*, Amsterdam: North-Holland.

Mimic, M. (1998) *International Trade*, Basingstoke: Macmillan, p. 477.

Neilsen, J. U. M. *et al.* (1991) *An Economic Analysis of the EC*, UK: McGraw Hill, p. 3 & 16.

Ricardo, D. (1817) 'Principles of Political Economy', reprinted as vol. 1 of Sraffa P (1951) *The works and correspondence of David Ricardo*, London: Cambridge University Press.

Robson, P. (1987) *The Economics of International Integration*, London: Unwin Hyman Ltd.

Scitovsky, T. (1958) *Economic Theory and Western European Integration*, London: Allen & Unwin.

Viner, J. (1950) *The Customs Union Issue*, New York: Carnegie Endowment for International Peace.

World Trade Organisation Web site (1999) The Agreement Establishing the World Trade Organisation, available from http://www/wto.org

Whalley, J. *et al.* (1995) *The Trading System after Uruguay Round*, London: Longman, p. 33.

# 11 New regionalism and GCC trade: new directions

## R. WILSON

## 11.1 The changing composition and direction of GCC trade

Trade diplomacy has become increasingly important for the West, but for most Arab countries, economic interests have always been secondary to political goals. The four GCC states which are OPEC members, Saudi Arabia, Kuwait, the UAE and Qatar, have of course tried to influence export earnings through oil pricing and production policy, but little consideration has been given to wider long-term trade strategy issues. Diversification into oil products and petrochemicals was examined in technical and marketing terms, but once the decisions were made to invest, companies such as SABIC, the Saudi Arabian Basic Industries Corporation, were given little government diplomatic support, even though they were largely under state ownership.

The GCC states have seldom used their import purchasing power as a lever in trade negotiations, even though Saudi Arabia is the 25th largest world importer, accounting for around 0.7% of world imports, while the UAE is the 26th largest world importer, accounting for 0.6% of world imports.[1] In negotiations with the European Union, the GCC has achieved little, as despite its opposition to the EU tariffs on petrochemicals, the policy remains unchanged. Membership of the World Trade Organisation has proved a divisive issue for the GCC, with Bahrain and Kuwait admitted as founder members on 1 January 1995, Qatar and the UAE in January and April 1996 respectively, and Oman only in 2000. Saudi Arabia remains outside, with its negotiations largely stalled.

The aim of this study is to examine GCC trade trends to discover what issues are significant, and need to be brought to the attention of policy makers in the region. Development plans in the GCC are usually formulated with purely domestic economic policy in mind, but more attention needs to be given to the regional context, and the changing global environment. This presents both challenges and opportunities for the GCC states which need to be identified. As the millennium approaches, the GCC faces a very different world economy to only a decade ago. Trade with South and South East Asia has become much more significant, and trade with Europe has declined relatively. International exchange rate changes have had a major impact on import sourcing, notably in the case of Japan.

The GCC states have tended to be passive observers of all these developments, yet they affect vital Gulf economic interests. The GCC may only be able to influence international economic events at the margin, but it is important to appreciate what is happening and assess how to react. Political and country risk appraisals are made with respect to the GCC states by their Western trading partners. Yet the GCC states themselves do not conduct similar appraisals in the light of their own economic interests. This study attempts to suggest some avenues which deserve further exploration. Detail matters in trade diplomacy, as sound analysis can only be based on a careful study of the facts.

## 11.2    GCC export trends

The GCC countries trade composition is asymmetrical, as exports are highly concentrated, largely in crude oil and petroleum products, while imports are diversified, ranging from foodstuffs to consumer items and military supplies. This means a vulnerability to pricing developments in international commodity markets, and oil markets in particular, over which the Gulf states have only limited control through OPEC, and by Saudi Arabia's role as a swing producer of oil. Such vulnerability to external pricing developments is not new in the Gulf, as even before oil some of the states, notably Bahrain and Qatar, were dependent on pearl exports, the prices of which were subject to international demand and supply factors which producers in the Gulf could do little to control.[2] Even the prosperity of trading Emirates such as Dubai depended on the economic conditions in the countries with which it traded, including the Indian subcontinent and Iran, while Oman with its close trading links with East Africa was affected by the spice trade in the Indian Ocean, and in particular economic activities on the island of Zanzibar which was ruled by traders of Omani origin.

Invisible export earnings were also affected by economic conditions outside the region. The prosperity of the Hijaz was influenced by its relations with the Ottoman Empire and the flow of pilgrims to Mecca, which was determined by the financial circumstances in which potential pilgrims found themselves.

Yet the vulnerability of the Gulf states to external developments should not be exaggerated, and it certainly did not result in an aversion to trade and commerce. Far from being closed and backward economies, historically the Gulf states have always prospered through their links with the outside world, and the deserts and oceans have served as channels for transportation and communications rather than barriers. What has changed is the scale of the transactions involved as the Gulf economies themselves have grown. Saudi Arabia is the world's 16th largest exporter, accounting for 1.3% of global exports, the largest exporter in the Middle East, and leading oil exporting country worldwide. The UAE is the 23rd largest exporter in the world, while the GCC states collectively occupy the tenth position in the world exporting league table.[3]

Saudi Arabia accounts for around half of GCC exports, as Table 11.1 shows, its share being significantly higher since the Gulf War when it raised the volume of oil exports to

**Table 11.1  GCC merchandise exports, $ million.**

|      | Bahrain | Kuwait | Oman  | Qatar | Saudi Arabia | UAE    |
|------|---------|--------|-------|-------|--------------|--------|
| 1985 | 2,879   | 10,487 | 4,972 | 3,419 | 27,481       | 16,780 |
| 1986 | 2,200   | 7,383  | 2,842 | 1,849 | 20,185       | 10,640 |
| 1987 | 2,430   | 8,264  | 3,776 | 1,985 | 23,199       | 12,380 |
| 1988 | 2,411   | 7,661  | 3,268 | 2,210 | 24,377       | 12,040 |
| 1989 | 2,831   | 11,476 | 3,933 | 2,686 | 28,382       | 15,010 |
| 1990 | 3,761   | 7,042  | 5,508 | 3,529 | 44,417       | 20,730 |
| 1991 | 3,513   | 1,088  | 4,871 | 3,186 | 47,797       | 22,160 |
| 1992 | 3,465   | 6,660  | 5,428 | 3,499 | 50,280       | 21,220 |
| 1993 | 3,710   | 10,248 | 5,299 | 3,082 | 42,395       | 19,670 |
| 1994 | 3,454   | 11,614 | 5,545 | 3,052 | 42,614       | 19,000 |
| 1995 | 3,930   | 13,036 | 6,260 | 3,365 | 48,150       | 21,700 |

*Source* adapted from World Trade Organisation, *Annual Report* (1996)

compensate for the shortfall in Iraq's oil exports. Kuwait's exports are subject to the same oil pricing factors as Saudi Arabia's, with their respective export values being closely correlated, but Kuwait's exports ceased during the Iraqi occupation, and it took almost two years for production to return to normal after the destruction of key oil installations. By 1995 Kuwait's exports were back at their highest level for over a decade, and the economic legacy of the Gulf War had finally passed. The value of exports has also been significantly higher for the UAE and the other smaller Gulf states in the 1990s, although UAE exports appear to be falling relatively to those of Saudi Arabia. Most of this reflects the earning from oil and natural gas from Abu Dhabi rather than the trends with Dubai's re-exports and service earnings which will be dealt with in later sections. The UAE remains a more significant exporter than the three smaller Gulf economies combined, Bahrain, Qatar and Oman. Bahrain has overtaken Qatar with respect to its export earnings, but Oman has increased its export earnings by a much greater amount than the two smallest GCC economies, Bahrain and Qatar.

Not surprisingly, there is a close correlation between export fluctuations and gross domestic product growth for all the GCC states. In the case of Saudi Arabia, for example, the rapid rise in export earnings following the Gulf War was accompanied by real rises in GDP of 10.7% in 1990 and 8.4% in 1991, but as export revenue levelled off in 1992 growth fell to 2.8%, and in 1993 with falling exports, real GDP declined by −0.6%.[4] Similar trends were apparent for the other Gulf states, especially Kuwait, where there was a sharp contraction in economic activity in 1990 and 1991 followed by an even more dramatic revival in 1992 and 1993.[5] Interestingly, for all the GCC states there appears to be a closer correlation between export revenue increases and GDP growth than between falling revenue and GDP contraction, indicating that there is a type of ratchet effect, with upward flexibility but downward stickiness.

Crude oil is the major export commodity for all of the GCC states, but the attempts to diversify into oil products, gas and petrochemicals have affected export composition. Exports are much less dominated by crude oil than they were in the 1970s, which demonstrates at least the partial success of the diversification plans. In Saudi Arabia crude oil still accounts for almost three-quarters of total exports, while refined products and petrochemicals account for 16% and 5% of the total value of exports respectively.[6] The shares of non-energy-related exports, construction materials and grains, account for less than 1% of the total each. In Kuwait crude oil exports account for around 55% of the total, with refined oil and liquefied gas accounting for 36% and 4% of the total respectively.[7] Of the remaining 5 per cent of Kuwait's exports, most is accounted for by fertiliser production.

In the case of the United Arab Emirates the share of crude petroleum to total exports has fallen from 62% in 1990 to only 43% by 1997, and most forecasters expect this trend to continue.[8] Gas exports have increased steadily, exports from Abu Dhabi's Das island being especially significant, while Dubai's exports even include textiles and clothing from its duty-free zone at Jebel Ali. In the case of Qatar crude oil accounts for around 80% of exports, and gas for much of the remainder, although some petrochemical products and fertilisers are exported. Omani exports are less diversified, with crude oil accounting for over 90% of the total,[9] but there are some fish exports, and there would seem to be much scope for lessening dependence on oil. In Bahrain crude oil accounts for two-thirds of exports, but the island's aluminium smelter and ship repair yard make significant contributions to foreign exchange earnings, as does the offshore banking sector, which will be discussed in the section dealing with commercial services.

During the period up to 2005 there will be much greater export diversification by the GCC states. The value of Saudi Arabian petrochemical exports rose by over 50%

during the 1993–96 period.[10] SABIC is pressing ahead with its third major expansion programme in petrochemicals with the construction of three new ethylene crackers powered by local natural gas.[11] This should increase the value of ethylene and other petrochemical products in its total exports to 8% by 2002, but much will depend on petro-chemical prices, as the expanded capacity in the Gulf could have a detrimental effect on the world market. The market is already suffering from the effect of the Asian crisis, and weakening demand for petrochemical products,[12] although this is probably short term and cyclical.

Qatar, Oman and Abu Dhabi are still pressing ahead with the building of new petro-chemical plants, and in the case of the latter existing ethylene capacity is also being expanded at Ruwais. An ammonia and urea complex is also being planned for Fertil near Abu Dhabi, together with a methanol capability.[13] In the case of Oman progress on petro-chemical developments has been slower, with the decision still to be taken over whether its proposed plant should be at Sohar or Sur. Gas is available at Sur, but a new industrial port is being developed at Sohar which gives it an advantage. A ferro-chrome and ferro-silicone plant is to be built at Sohar, and a hydrochloric acid project is being discussed. Oman's major development outside the petrochemical field is to be a sugar refinery, the aim being to export regionally to Iran and Yemen.[14]

## 11.3    Merchandise imports

The GCC economies are amongst the most open in the world, with no foreign exchange controls and very limited tariff and quota protection. The share of trade in GDP was over 191% in Bahrain in 1995, the corresponding figures for the UAE, Kuwait, Oman and Saudi Arabia being 139%, 104%, 89%, and 70% respectively, with no figure quoted by the World Bank for Qatar.[15] Given the very limited breadth of the manufacturing sector and the restricted scope for agriculture, this dependence on imports is both natural and inevitable. Given the sizes of their domestic markets, GCC states were precluded from pursuing ambitious import substitution strategies, and in retrospect this may have been fortunate given the experiences elsewhere in the Arab World. Egypt and Syria would seem to have paid a heavy price in terms of lost economic growth for the structural distortions resulting from their protectionist policies in the 1950s and 1960s, policies which the GCC states were wise not to emulate.

The policy of export specialisation on the basis of the existing resource base in accord-ance with classical notions of comparative advantage has served the Gulf states well. The development of petrochemicals and energy-related industries makes sense in terms of dynamic comparative advantage, whereas trying to establish production facilities in areas where there is no expertise or resource advantage would be nonsense. Furthermore, the GCC states are global players in energy, and can become so in energy-related activity, but in other areas they have little real economic power, and competitive imports make more sense than potentially very high cost domestic production.

The growth of GCC imports and the relative significance of each market is illustrated in Table 11.2. Saudi Arabia is the largest market, but the gap between it and the UAE has narrowed significantly in recent years. This is largely accounted for by the rapid growth of re-exporting from the UAE, and Dubai in particular. In Saudi Arabia, in contrast, most imports are locally consumed, and import growth is closely correlated with non-oil GDP growth which tends to be less erratic than overall GDP growth given oil price and volume fluctuations.

**Table 11.2  GCC merchandise imports, $ million.**

|      | Bahrain | Kuwait | Oman  | Qatar | Saudi Arabia | UAE    |
|------|---------|--------|-------|-------|--------------|--------|
| 1985 | 3,107   | 6,005  | 3,153 | 1,139 | 23,622       | 6,549  |
| 1986 | 2,405   | 5,717  | 2,402 | 1,099 | 19,112       | 6,422  |
| 1987 | 2,714   | 5,493  | 1,823 | 1,161 | 20,110       | 7,226  |
| 1988 | 2,593   | 6,143  | 2,202 | 1,267 | 21,784       | 8,522  |
| 1989 | 3,134   | 6,295  | 2,255 | 1,326 | 21,154       | 10,010 |
| 1990 | 3,712   | 3,972  | 2,681 | 1,695 | 24,069       | 11,199 |
| 1991 | 4,115   | 4,761  | 3,194 | 1,720 | 29,079       | 13,746 |
| 1992 | 4,263   | 7,261  | 3,769 | 2,015 | 33,698       | 17,410 |
| 1993 | 3,858   | 7,036  | 4,114 | 1,954 | 28,198       | 19,520 |
| 1994 | 3,737   | 6,697  | 3,915 | 1,991 | 22,796       | 20,500 |
| 1995 | 3,581   | 7,139  | 4,340 | 2,165 | 27,180       | 22,800 |

*Source* adapted from World Trade Organisation, *Annual Report* (1996)

The other prime import level determinant in Saudi Arabia is government spending, as although successive development plans have emphasised the role of the private sector, it is government fiscal policy that still drives demand. As tax changes are not used as an instrument of fiscal policy in Saudi Arabia, this leaves expenditure variation as the main instrument. Deficits therefore prompt expenditure cutbacks, which immediately get translated into import cuts, not least because capital budgets are much easier to curtail than current spending on salaries. Stock adjustments by traders would also appear to be related to government expenditure, which magnifies the impact of spending changes on imports.[16] Indeed, commercial bank financing of imports appears to vary more than government spending, indicating that multiplier effects are at work.

The table also shows how Kuwait's imports were drastically affected by the Gulf War in 1990 and 1991. The value of imports has since recovered, and by 1995 it was at its highest-ever level. Bahrain's import market was the largest of the smaller GCC states in the 1980s, but it has been overtaken by Oman. This reflects the strength of local demand in Oman, as the Sultanate has insignificant transit trade. The import market in Qatar also appears to be increasing relatively to that of Bahrain, as it was less than one-third as large as the latter in the early 1980s, but by the mid-1990s this proportion had risen to over 60%.

Around one-third of Saudi Arabian imports are financed directly by the government or state corporations such as SABIC. This accounts for many major items of capital equipment for the petrochemical industry and some of the imported items relating to infrastructure development and maintenance. Defence equipment also constitutes a major element of government import spending, and although there are offset agreements relating to military aircraft purchases, the saving in foreign exchange is minimal as the main motivation is technical transfer.

Private sector imports financed through Saudi Arabia's commercial banks are shown in Table 11.3 which has been compiled from Saudi Arabian Monetary Agency data. Motor vehicles are the largest single commodity category, followed by foodstuffs and textiles and clothing. The consistency in the shares from year to year is notable, the only difference being the decline in the share of motor vehicles over the 1992–94 period. This decline was attributed to a rise in the imports of lower-priced used cars at the expense of new models, and the tendency of car owners in Saudi Arabia to replace their vehicles less

**Table 11.3  Private sector imports in Saudi Arabia.**

|  | 1991 | 1992 | 1993 | 1994 | 1995 | 1996 |
|---|---|---|---|---|---|---|
| Motor vehicles % | 19 | 21 | 18 | 16 | 11 | 14 |
| Foodstuffs % | 12 | 12 | 11 | 14 | 14 | 16 |
| Textiles and clothing % | 10 | 10 | 10 | 10 | 9 | 8 |
| Appliances % | 8 | 8 | 8 | 9 | 8 | 7 |
| Construction materials % | 6 | 7 | 7 | 8 | 6 | 6 |
| Machinery % | 6 | 6 | 6 | 6 | 5 | 5 |
| Other % | 39 | 36 | 40 | 37 | 47 | 44 |
| *Total $ US billion* | *19* | *20* | *19* | *15* | *16* | *17* |

*Source* adapted from SAMA, *Annual Report* (1995 and 1997)

often due to pressures on consumer expenditure. Given that the decline in the share of motor vehicles was accompanied by a decline in total imports, this indicates a very substantial fall in expenditure on vehicles. In fact expenditure declined by 17% in 1993 and 28% in 1994.[17]

As households spend more on education, health and consumer non-durables rather than the acquisition and replacement of durables, this tends to reduce the leakages from consumer expenditure into imports. As the age of household heads rises in Saudi Arabia and the other GCC countries, such trends are likely to become more pronounced, which should have favourable implications for the trade balances. Spending on local services may have a multiplier effect as the recipients purchase imported goods, but the overall effect will be limited as recipients will also purchase locally produced goods and services.

## 11.4  Entrepôt trade

Import figures for some GCC states, notably the UAE, are greater than local demand would indicate due to significant re-exporting. Although there is some re-exporting from Bahrain and Kuwait to other GCC states, it is Dubai that is the major re-exporting centre for the entire region. It was Dubai's creek, the best natural harbour in the Gulf, that accounted for the Sheikhdom's economic growth and prosperity for hundreds of years as a crossroads for Gulf trade. The advent of modern shipping meant the Creek had to be dredged so that larger vessels could be accommodated as well as traditional dhows, but by the 1970s the capacity of the Creek itself was inadequate and substantial new port facilities were built at Mina Rashid and Jebel Ali. The two new ports, which are 35 kilometres south of Dubai city, were merged in 1991 under the Dubai Port Authority. It now controls over one hundred deep-water berths, which have enabled Dubai to become the world's twelfth largest port in terms of container traffic.[18]

The duty-free zone at Jebel Ali, which was established in 1985, has become by far the largest and most successful in the Middle East, with over 600 international companies operating distribution and processing facilities. As a consequence, Dubai has become for West Asia what Singapore is for South East Asia. International companies can take advantage of Dubai's position in the GCC to ensure there is tariff-free, or reduced tariff, access to other member states, including Saudi Arabia. To qualify there must be 40% GCC value added, but this figure can be based on redistribution margins to cover wage costs in both Dubai and the ultimate export destination. Certificates of origin are also needed, but these can be obtained easily without administrative difficulties from the Dubai Chamber of Commerce.

The growth of re-exports from Dubai based on Chamber of Commerce figures is shown in Table 11.4. There has been almost a trebling in re-exports over the 1986–95 period by volume, and more than a trebling by value. Re-exports far exceed exports, although there has been much fluctuation from year to year in the ratio of re-exports to exports, varying from 270% to almost 400%, with an average of around 300%, but no identifiable trend.

Iran is by far the most important destination for re-exports, accounting for over one-quarter of the total by both volume and value, followed by India and Saudi Arabia.[19] Given GCC preferences, the high volume of re-exports destined for Iran may seem surprising, but this reflects Dubai's traditional strengths as an entrepôt centre for both the northern and southern shores of the Gulf, and the many family and business connections of its merchant community.[20] Hong Kong, Afghanistan and Pakistan are the fourth, fifth and sixth ranked destinations for Dubai's re-exports, ahead of Qatar, and both Azerbaijan and Russia rank in the top ten destinations ahead of Kuwait.[21] The economic difficulties in Iran resulted in a dramatic reduction in re-exports from Dubai to the Islamic Republic, with the value falling from $1,140 million in 1995 to $781 million in 1996. However, re-exports to oil-rich Azerbaijan rose by 63% to $185 million in 1996, and re-exports to Afghanistan doubled to $225 million in spite of the continuing civil war which even affected Kabul.[22]

Dubai Chamber of Commerce deals effectively with trade disputes, and the World Trade Centre which was established in Dubai as long ago as 1979 has generated much business. The exhibition halls have been extended over the past 18 years, with the seven halls now providing 33,100 square metres of exhibition space. Around 40 major exhibitions are staged annually under the auspicious of the Dubai World Trade Centre, including many regional exhibitions on an annual basis. These include the Gulf Information Technology Exhibition, the Middle East Cable and Satellite Show, the Middle East Consumer Electronics Exhibition and the Middle East International Car and Boat Shows. Orders placed during these exhibitions and subsequently usually boost Dubai's re-exports, as does hosting sporting events such as the Dubai Desert Classic and the Power Boat Racing Championships.[23]

**Table 11.4  Re-exports and exports from Dubai.**

|  | Re-exports<br>*Million kilos* | Re-exports<br>*$US million* | Exports<br>*$US million* | Re-exports/exports<br>*Percentage* |
|---|---|---|---|---|
| 1986 | 562 | 943 | 351 | 268 |
| 1987 | 961 | 1,427 | 359 | 397 |
| 1988 | 594 | 1,385 | 469 | 295 |
| 1989 | 941 | 1,774 | 567 | 312 |
| 1990 | 950 | 2,070 | 625 | 331 |
| 1991 | 851 | 2,049 | 758 | 270 |
| 1992 | 1,050 | 2,451 | 899 | 272 |
| 1993 | 1,178 | 2,799 | 964 | 290 |
| 1994 | 1,185 | 2,906 | 891 | 326 |
| 1995 | 1,485 | 3,560 | 1,276 | 278 |

*Source* adapted from Dubai Chamber of Commerce *External Trade* figures

Dubai re-exports to the other United Arab Emirates, notably Abu Dhabi, the major oil and gas exporter, but the latter has some re-exporting trade in its own right. Although Abu Dhabi's re-export trade is less than 10% the value of Dubai's, the former's is more orientated to other GCC countries, notable Qatar which receives almost 40% of Abu Dhabi's re-exports and Saudi Arabia and Kuwait which receive around 10% each.[24] Monthly re-export figures for Abu Dhabi seem rather erratic, however, and are often related to particular projects. Re-exports to Italy soared in February 1997, for example, but this was accounted for by Italian involvement in desalination and power generation in the Emirate, and the need to send expensive equipment to Italy for modification. This highlights the fact that not too much significance should be attached to monthly trade figures when the values are comparatively small.

Dubai faces some potential challenges to its position as a re-exporter from other Arabian Peninsula states, notably Oman, which is developing a large container complex at Salalah, and Yemen, which has ambitious plans to reactivate the port of Aden. The latter was a major transit port serving British imperial trade with India and beyond coming through the Suez Canal when Aden itself was a British protectorate. However, even when the initial development phase of Salalah and Aden is completed by 2000, they will have only a combined capacity which is one-quarter of that of Dubai. Subsequent developments will depend on how competitive they are as re-exporters, but Dubai with its head start, considerable experience and freedom from bureaucratic hassle should be able to maintain its lead.

Saudi Arabia's re-exports are very limited, and mostly are sourced from its import substitution industries that cater predominantly for the local market, but which have some spare capacity to supply other GCC states. A typical example is the corrugated paper and cardboard industry which manufactures packaging and cartons for soft drinks and ice cream which are supplied to Bahrain, Qatar and Kuwait. Saudi Arabia's imports and re-exports of corrugated paper and cardboard products are shown in Table 11.5, the difference between imports and re-exports being accounted for by domestic value added in production and domestic consumer demand.[25]

The value of imports of corrugated paper and cardboard products reflects timber and paper prices in international markets which fluctuate considerably. This has implications for stock holding policy, which is reflected in import volumes. Prices of re-exports are more stable, however, a result of the greater value added and the longer-term supply contracts won by Saudi Arabian producers. As a result of this greater certainty there has been a steady rise in re-exports of corrugated paper and cardboard products, with re-exports doubling in value over the 1991–95 period. Despite such successes, re-exporting does not

**Table 11.5  Saudi Arabia's imports and re-exports of corrugated paper and cardboard.**

|  | Imports (tons) | Re-exports (tons) | Imports $ 000 | Re-exports $ 000 |
|---|---|---|---|---|
| 1991 | 6,373 | 2,919 | 8,846 | 3,332 |
| 1992 | 8.351 | 477 | 11,189 | 3,789 |
| 1993 | 5,596 | 3,854 | 6,726 | 4,115 |
| 1994 | 3,145 | 3,841 | 4,699 | 4,372 |
| 1995 | 7,143 | 5,386 | 9,134 | 6,895 |

*Source* adapted from *Al-Nashra al-Sanai'yah*, No. 21 (1996)

seem to be a priority in Saudi Arabia, rather it is seen as a residual outlet after domestic demands have been met. In Saudi Arabia the stress is on production and supplies, whereas in Dubai more attention is paid to marketing and the changing nature of wholesale trade and retail demand.

## 11.5 Trade in commercial services

While Dubai can be described as the mercantile capital of the Gulf, Bahrain aspires to be the region's financial hub. Although Bahrain is a very small oil exporter in comparison to the other GCC states, and re-exports are minimal, it is the only state in the region to enjoy a substantial balance of payments surplus in commercial services, an increasingly important element of international trade, as worldwide invisible exports are increasing at twice the rate of visible merchandise trade. While Bahrain's oil exports were worth $2.2 billion in 1994, its earnings from commercial services amounted to over $1.3 billion, as Table 11.6 shows.[26] The only other GCC country to report its earnings from commercial services to the World Trade Organisation is Kuwait, but it has a large deficit in its invisible earnings, despite the international activities of its banking sector and the size of its local shipping companies.

Bahrain's major source of invisible earnings are its offshore banking sector, tourist revenues and to a much lesser extent its ship repair yard, the largest in the Gulf apart from the dry dock facilities in Dubai. Tourism largely involves weekend visitors from Saudi Arabia, both local nationals and expatriates, who cross over on the Saudi-Bahrain causeway which has been open since 1986. An estimated 300,000 visitors come each month,[27] many for leisure, although Bahrain's four and five star hotels have also become major venues for business conferences in the Gulf and the main rivals to Dubai.

The offshore banking sector provides deposit and lending facilities as well as a wide range of financial services to non-residents, mainly Saudis. By 1997 the sector had over $65 billion in assets, making it the largest single such centre between Singapore and Europe.[28] In the 1980s there were over one hundred foreign banks with offices in Bahrain which had been attracted by the business resulting from the oil price rises of 1979. As foreign banks were unable to operate in Saudi Arabia unless they incorporated

Table 11.6  GCC trade in commercial services, $ million.

|  | Bahrain exports | Bahrain imports | Kuwait exports | Kuwait imports |
|---|---|---|---|---|
| 1985 | 875 | 295 | 944 | 3,315 |
| 1986 | 731 | 347 | 847 | 3,142 |
| 1987 | 860 | 433 | 815 | 3,413 |
| 1988 | 896 | 493 | 943 | 3,649 |
| 1989 | 808 | 535 | 1,124 | 3,530 |
| 1990 | 874 | 660 | 1,054 | 2,804 |
| 1991 | 934 | 730 | 756 | 3,074 |
| 1992 | 1,254 | 861 | 1,269 | 3,274 |
| 1993 | 1,244 | 751 | 1,087 | 3,412 |
| 1994 | 1,347 | 870 | 1,287 | 3,675 |
| 1995 | na | na | 1,263 | 4,021 |

*Source* adapted from World Trade Organisation, *Annual Report* (1996)

domestically and had majority local ownership, Bahrain's offshore banking laws were the best means of securing access to potential Saudi Arabian clients.[29] By the late 1980s, however, many foreign banks had pulled out of Bahrain, as the oil price falls reduced business and the relatively high operating costs could not be covered.

The revival of offshore banking business in Bahrain since the Gulf War has partly reflected firmer oil prices and higher revenue levels for Saudi Arabia. In addition, the banks themselves, which currently number around 50, have become more specialised and focused. Foreign exchange business is especially active, and the island is the major centre for exchange rate quotations in regional currencies. A forward market has developed in both the dollar and regional currencies, with rates also quoted against the German mark and Japanese yen. Investment banking and fund management have become significant, and Bahrain has its own regional stock market. At the same time niche banking areas have been developed, notably Islamic banking, with Bahrain being the largest financial centre worldwide for transactions based on the *Shariah* Islamic law. Islamic banks operating from the island include Al Baraka Islamic Investment Bank, the Arab Islamic Bank, the Bahrain Islamic Bank, Citi Islamic Investment Bank (a subsidiary of Citibank) and the Faisal Islamic Bank of Bahrain.[30] A number of conventional banks in Bahrain also offer Islamic banking services, including the Arab Banking Corporation.

Despite such success with offshore banking, commercial services are likely to remain in deficit for the GCC states. Other states cannot emulate Bahrain in financial services, as the Gulf market is only large enough to support one centre, and although the Saudi Arabian authorities are willing to tolerate the loss of business to Bahrain, as the resultant income flows contribute to political stability on the island, any further outflows to other Gulf states are less likely to be acceptable. The scope for tourist development is limited, with Bahrain already having much of the market for GCC nationals on excursions, and Dubai having established itself as the major centre for non-Arab visitors, even from Europe and beyond. Gulf shipping could be developed further, but most states already have locally owned tanker fleets, and the acquisition of vessels for the wide variety of types of imports with different transportation requirements may not be economically viable.

With most GCC airlines losing money apart from Emirates, the Dubai-based carrier, an expansion of airline fleets to reduce dependence on foreign carriers is unlikely to be a satisfactory means of reducing the deficit in commercial services. Table 11.7 shows passenger load factors for Gulf airlines, the key factor in determining profitability.

The financial position of the state-owned airlines such as Saudia is not helped by the fact that purchasing decisions are made on political grounds rather than on the basis of value for money. Agreements were concluded for the purchase of 61 new American

**Table 11.7  GCC airline performance 1996.**

| Carrier | International passengers | Domestic passengers | Passenger load factor | Number of aircraft |
|---|---|---|---|---|
| Saudia | 3,872,907 | 7,833,408 | 64.8 | 112 |
| Gulf Air | 3,488,422 | 1,312,753 | 66.7 | 27 |
| Emirates | 2,863,195 | 14,364 | 70.4 | 20 |
| Kuwait Air | 2,130,039 | 101,992 | 68.2 | 20 |

*Source* adapted from World Air Transport Statistics and International Air Transport Association (IATA) as reported in *Middle East Economic Digest*, 7 November 1997

aircraft by Saudia in 1995, including five Boeing 747, 23 Boeing 777, 29 McDonnell Douglas MD 90s and four MD 11s for cargo.[31] The MD 90 aircraft are rather dated variants of the DC9 which are to be phased out of production once the Saudi Arabian order is completed, as Boeing has now taken over the company. The main reason for the order was simply to temporarily safeguard jobs at the McDonnell plant in the United States in recognition of the company's contribution to the Kingdom's defence effort. Arguably the Boeing 777 are unnecessarily large and expensive aircraft, as Saudi passenger traffic rose by a mere 1.8% in 1996,[32] and cheaper Boeing 767 aircraft might have been adequate. Furthermore, some in the airline itself would have preferred European Airbus aircraft, but these were ruled out in the interests of Saudi-American relations.

## 11.6　Trade between GCC states and Arab regional integration

There have been many attempts at Arab regional integration since the 1950s dating from the early efforts of the Arab league, but the GCC is arguably the only Arab economic grouping that has enjoyed some measure of success. The attempt in the 1960s by President Nasser of Egypt to forge a common market between his own country, Syria, Jordan and Iraq, failed largely due to political differences.[33] At the beginning it was suggested that Kuwait might join, but in the end it refused, as there was no commercial advantage in restricting the choices of local purchasers to higher-cost and often poorer-quality goods from protected infant industries rather than sourcing imports from the best value for money location worldwide. In other words, there was concern over the costs of trade diversion, especially when there were no offsetting advantages on the exporting side, as it was unlikely to result in significantly higher oil export volumes.[34]

Despite these failures there has been a revival of discussion on wider Arab economic integration by the GCC states.[35] A dialogue was started between the GCC states, Egypt and Syria at a meeting hosted by the Syrians in Latakia on 24 June 1997. GCC foreign ministers attended and there were renewed calls for an Arab common market.[36] This is probably unattainable, however, as a common market provides for free mobility of factors of production, notably labour and capital, and not merely the removal of restrictions on mercantile trade. The GCC countries are unlikely to want to remove their systems of work and residence permits with respect to Egyptian or Syrian nationals given the potential impact on their labour markets and the increasing difficulties of GCC citizens themselves in securing employment in their own countries. As both Egypt and Syria operate work and residence permit systems themselves, any creation of a common market in labour is even more improbable, although preferences extended to GCC nationals would present few problems, as few are likely to want to work in Egypt or Syria in any case given prevailing wage levels. Progress would be most likely if restrictions were lessened or even removed for work permits for high-level rather than low-level workers, with for example work permits immediately issued or not required for doctors or qualified engineers. Selective liberalisation may be the best way forward, such as the electronic passport system to be introduced for GCC nationals from 2000 onward which should facilitate more rapid transits at regional airports.[37]

Foreign exchange controls are used to restrict capital exports in the case of both Egypt and Syria, but the GCC countries have fully convertible currencies for capital as well as current account transactions. Arguably liberalisation would be easier to achieve in the case of capital movements, as even the original 'open door' policy which Egypt adopted in 1974 to attract Arab Gulf capital has provision for repatriation of profits free from foreign exchange controls. Selective liberalisation already exists with respect to potential capital movements from the GCC for inward investment in both Egypt and Syria.

It is at the intra-GCC level that the greatest degree of trade and investment liberalisation has already been achieved. As just indicated, the GCC countries have no foreign exchange restrictions on payments for traded goods or controls on capital transfers, although nationality laws are applied to ensure local citizens control domestic businesses. Removal of tariffs on traded goods between GCC member states was easily achieved, as tariffs were at generally low levels in any case. Hence a transition period of less than two years was required from the foundation of the GCC on 25 May 1981 for the complete removal of tariffs.[38] By 1 March 1983 customs duties were abolished on intra-GCC trade in all agricultural products and manufactured goods, with the provision that at least 40% of the value added had to originate from within the GCC in the case of manufactures, and that these had to be produced in a company at least 51% owned by GCC nationals. This 40% provision has already been discussed with respect to Dubai's re-export trade.

The GCC Unified Economic Agreement also provides for exemption of products passing in transit from one state to another from fees and taxes, as well as free access for national ships to the ports of all GCC states. There is also a clause providing for freedom of movement of GCC citizens which was especially important during the Iraqi occupation of Kuwait when many Kuwaiti nationals took refuge in other GCC states. Professionals such as those engaged in medicine, law, engineering, accountancy and business consultancy services can practise freely throughout the GCC subject to local standards being met, although this clause does not apply to non-GCC nationals working within the GCC.

There is also provision in the GCC Unified Economic Agreement for joint business ventures which are subject to a lower 25% host country ownership requirement provided the other participants are GCC nationals, companies or governments.[39] The dry dock in Bahrain was built as a GCC joint venture under this provision, and with the Gulf Investment Corporation playing the major role in such projects. This Kuwait-based organisation has been capitalised by the GCC governments at over $1 billion, and its subsidiary, the Bahrain-based Gulf International Bank, is a major provider of corporate financial services on behalf of Gulf clients.[40] The Gulf International Bank has overseas branches in London and New York, and representative offices in Singapore, Beirut and Abu Dhabi.

Part-privatisation share issues by GCC countries are open to other GCC nationals, but not to foreigners. An early example of such a part-privatisation was the sale of $10 billion of stock in the Saudi Arabian Basic Industries Corporation (SABIC) in 1985, representing 20% of the total capital of the company.[41] Kuwaiti, Bahraini and UAE nationals all purchased holdings as well as Saudi Arabian citizens, although the latter are believed to hold most of the shares. As privatisation gathers momentum in the Gulf, this privileged access to shares by GCC nationals is likely to prove increasingly significant.

The GCC finance ministers agreed on 1st September 1997 that their countries should have a unified external tariff of 4%, rising to 20% in the case of competing imports. Although this in theory means that the GCC is a customs union rather than merely a free trade area, in practice tariff discrepancies remain, with for example the UAE applying the 4% rate of tariff to foodstuffs and agricultural produce, while the duties in Saudi Arabia remain at 10%, as Table 11.8 shows.

It is the competing industry provision which has been most widely used, with Kuwait and Saudi Arabia applying the highest rates of duty in the GCC to ensure their domestic producers are protected, whereas countries such as Oman and the UAE have taken a much more liberal stance, largely because they have less to protect and no domestic producer interests seeking to lobby for protection. These issues were addressed at the GCC summit

**Table 11.8  Tariffs imposed by GCC states on selected imports.**

|  | Agricultural produce | Chemicals | Processed food | Textiles and clothing | Machinery and equipment |
|---|---|---|---|---|---|
| Bahrain | 5.0 | 5.0 | 10.0 | 10.0 | 10.0 |
| Kuwait | 4.0 | 20.0 | 25.0 | 15.0 | 20.0 |
| Oman | 5.0 | 5.0 | 5.0 | 5.0 | 5.0 |
| Qatar | 4.0 | 20.0 | 4.0 | 4.0 | 4.0 |
| Saudi Arabia | 12.0 | 20.0 | 20.0 | 12.0 | 20.0 |
| UAE | 4.0 | 4.0 | 4.0 | 4.0 | 4.0 |

*Source* adapted from Jamal Eddine Zarrouk, 'Intra-Arab trade: determinants and prospects for expansion', in Saad El-Naggar (ed.), *Foreign and Intratrade Policies of the Arab Countries,* International Monetary Fund, Washington, 1992

in Kuwait in December 1997, when there was further discussion of the unified customs tariff,[42] but a substantial list of exemptions is likely to remain for the foreseeable future.

Although the proportion of intra-GCC to extra-GCC trade is less than 4% when oil trade is included, the share of imports from other GCC countries to total imports is over 8%. This share has risen in recent years, although it does include re-exported goods, mainly from Dubai, which are subsequently imported by other GCC states. Saudi Arabia accounts for around half of all intra-GCC trade, its main regional trading partner being the United Arab Emirates, as Table 11.9 shows, with imports worth over $1 billion coming into the Kingdom annually from the Emirates. Although Saudi Arabia runs a trade deficit with the UAE and Bahrain, it maintains a trade surplus with Kuwait and modest surpluses with Oman and Qatar. Saudi Arabia's major exports to these countries include construction supplies and processed foodstuffs, as well as equipment for the oil industry that is serviced and maintained in the kingdom.[43]

In the future there may be increased intra-GCC trade in utility services, especially if the electricity grids are all connected into a unified system, and gas and even water pipeline links established. In the case of electricity there is the possibility of peak load sharing, which would bring benefits in terms of capacity utilisation, and would ultimately be reflected in lower prices. Discussions on a regional grid are well advanced.[44] Telephone systems are of course already linked, but there is the issue of regional fibre optic networks for Internet communication and teleconferencing, and the question of telephone call centre support for utilities and telesales. It is more efficient to provide such services on a regional basis rather than for often limited national markets, so that duplication can be avoided.

**Table 11.9  Saudi Arabia's non-oil trade with GCC states, $ million, 1996.**

|  | Imports | Exports | Balance |
|---|---|---|---|
| UAE | 1,142 | 735 | −407 |
| Bahrain | 538 | 180 | −358 |
| Kuwait | 189 | 455 | 266 |
| Qatar | 98 | 202 | 104 |
| Oman | 67 | 118 | 49 |
| Total | 2,034 | 1,688 | −346 |

*Source* adapted from Saudi Arabian Monetary Agency, *Annual Report* (1997)

## 11.7    The GCC and the WTO

World Trade Organisation membership has proved a divisive issue for the GCC states. The states have negotiated individually with the WTO rather than as a group, and consequently the pace of negotiations and entry has varied. Bahrain, Kuwait, Qatar, Oman and the United Arab Emirates have all become members of the WTO, as already indicated, but Saudi Arabia has not. This division within the GCC is potentially damaging, as the organisation is supposed to promote economic cooperation amongst its members and bring some measure of harmony in external trade relations. The contrasting stances of Saudi Arabia on the one hand, and the smaller GCC states on the other, reflects both differing attitudes towards western companies that trade with Israel and differences in economic interests.

On 29 and 30 May 1997 the WTO working party on Saudi Arabia's membership application met again, but little progress was made. The United States had threatened to block Saudi Arabian accession to the WTO unless it changed its position on the secondary boycott of firms doing business with Israel. As a consequence, Saudi Arabia's negotiations with the WTO over its membership application have proved extremely protracted and complicated. The Minister of Commerce, Osama Bin Jafar Bin Ibrahim al Faqih, made intensive diplomatic efforts to get Saudi Arabia admitted by the end of 1997, but both political and economic obstacles have prevented this happening.[45] This is unfortunate, as Saudi Arabia risks being marginalised on international trading issues if it continues to be excluded from the world body, and the external negotiating position of the GCC will be weakened if its membership continues to be divided into those enjoying WTO privileges and those excluded. Countries belonging to other regional groupings such as the European Union, the North American Free Trade Area (NAFTA) and the Association of South East Asian Nations (ASEAN) have all of their membership in the WTO rather than being divided.

It is paradoxical that the United States, which wishes to see more GCC cohesion, has divided the organisation through its stance over Saudi Arabia's membership application to the WTO. As guardian of the holiest shrines of Islam, Saudi Arabia feels particular concern over violations of Muslim rights in Jerusalem. King Fahd could not ignore matters such as the tunnelling work under Muslim areas of Jerusalem, and the new settlement activity that threatens to surround the Islamic core of the city. In these circumstances, given the stance of the Israeli government, a guarantee not to support any secondary boycott of Israel could not be given. When the smaller Gulf states were admitted to the WTO the Middle East peace process appeared to be making good progress with Rabin and Peres, and there was little controversy about adhering to WTO obligations with regard to non-discrimination. By 1997, however, with a tense atmosphere prevailing between the Likud government and the Palestinians, it had proved impossible to make any concessions.

There are many vested domestic interests at stake with Saudi Arabia's WTO membership bid. The WTO is a much more cohesive organisation than its predecessor, the General Agreement on Tariffs and Trade (GATT), and demands much more of its members. The high degree of economic openness required poses few problems for small economies with only limited industrial capacity geared to the domestic market such as the smaller Gulf states, but for Saudi Arabia, which has a much larger economy and numerous protected industries, much more is at stake.

The Ministry of Industry and Electricity has supported the development of new manufacturing ventures for over 25 years through its industry licensing system, which gives protection to local firms under majority Saudi Arabian ownership.[46] New entrants, even locally owned companies, are not allowed into the market if this would threaten the position of existing producers. The protected firms have enjoyed access to subsided credit from the Saudi Industrial Development Fund, and their local monopoly power ensures that they are seen as a low risk for commercial bank lending.

Tariffs, which are generally low in Saudi Arabia as already indicated, are less of an issue than the commercial presence of foreign service providers, which is restricted under the Kingdom's laws. Firms with a permanent presence in the Kingdom are obliged to incorporate under majority Saudi Arabian ownership, this being designed to provide business opportunities for local merchants. At the same time the local stock market, the largest in the Arab world, is closed to foreign investors.

Yet there are some signs of economic liberalisation which have been noted by the WTO working party considering Saudi Arabia's membership bid. While foreign direct investment still has to be channelled through locally controlled companies, the market for portfolio investment was opened up in March 1997 when the Saudi Arabian Monetary Agency agreed that the Saudi American Bank could launch a mutual fund designed to attract foreign investment into local equities. Furthermore, the need to raise capital for utilities such as the electricity industry has resulted in a new willingness to attract foreign interest, and in April 1997 bids were invited for the Kingdom's first build operate transfer (BOT) power project at Shuaiba.

The WTO for its part is prepared to allow lengthy transition periods for countries to adhere to new agreements. The agreement in March 1997 on telecommunications was a major breakthrough, yet only four Middle Eastern countries have given telecommunications market access commitments to the WTO: Israel, Morocco, Tunisia and Turkey. The Gulf states which are WTO members are still considering their position, although they are increasingly aware of the advantages of ratification. The agreement, involving 69 countries, is opening up 75 per cent of the world telecoms market in 1998, and much of the remainder by 2003.

Saudi Arabia should have no problems with respect to the WTO provisions on items such as textiles and clothing, but surprisingly the rules on subsidies to agricultural exports could cause some problems given the Kingdom's grain surpluses. Trade-related aspects of intellectual property rights (TRIPS) could also result in problems for Saudi Arabian producers of pharmaceuticals because of restrictions on the local manufacture of generic products. This issue was raised by the working group on WTO accession in November 1996, and is certain to be considered again if talks on entry proceed.

It is evident that Saudi Arabia faces both political and economic obstacles in its bid for WTO membership. The economic obstacles can be overcome, but the political difficulties may prove more intractable unless there is a revival of the Middle East peace process, which seems unlikely. For Saudi Arabia one of the greatest benefits of WTO membership would be its access to the organisation's trade settlement procedures. As an outsider, Saudi Arabia cannot take its disputes before the arbitration panels. Yet this could sort out the problems over petrochemical exports, and prove a more fruitful avenue to pursue than the bilateral negotiations with the European Union and other interested parties that have yielded meagre results. These difficulties will be explained in the latter section where trade relations with the European Union are discussed.

## 11.8    Commercial relations with Asia

The GCC has no formal dialogue with ASEAN, the Association of South East Asian States, or APEC, the Asia Pacific Economic Cooperation countries. The main formal links are at national level with Muslim states in Asia such as Iran, Pakistan, Bangladesh, Malaysia and Indonesia. Bilateral relations with these states are supplemented at multi-lateral level through the Organisation of the Islamic Conference, but the main initiative of this organisation has been in finance rather than in trade, as it resulted in the founding of the Jeddah-based Islamic Development Bank.[47]

GCC trade with Asian countries has been affected by their relative growth rates, exchange rate changes and oil price developments, all of which have moved trade in different directions. Table 11.10 illustrates the trends in Saudi Arabia's exports to leading Asian markets, the trends for other GCC countries being rather similar. Japan remains the major Asian trading partner of GCC states, but its importance as a market has declined relative to other Asian countries, notably South Korea. Most of Japan's imports from the GCC are accounted for by oil and gas, the oil price falls resulting in a decline in the value of imports in the mid-1980s. Since then, sluggish economic growth and a falling income elasticity of demand for energy have contributed to the lower value of oil imports. South Korea's higher growth rate accounts for its rising share of Asian oil imports, although by the late 1990s its economic growth had also slowed. Singapore imports crude oil for its refinery complexes, the largest in South East Asia, but capacity is no longer being expanded, as the city state concentrates more on services and highly specialist activities rather than processing and manufacturing.

India is a market of increasing significance for GCC oil exports, a trend that is likely to continue as liberalisation policies result in higher economic growth. As much of the expansion in India is in basic manufacturing, this should raise energy demand. Turkey has become Saudi Arabia's major Middle Eastern trading partner and links between the two states are likely to become closer in the years ahead, reflecting both useful complementarities in trade and a number of common diplomatic interests for these two Muslim states. Indeed, Turkey has arguably more to offer Saudi Arabia than any of its Arab neighbours both politically and economically.

The rise in the yen against both the dollar and European currencies in the 1980s and early 1990s adversely affected the share of Japan in GCC markets, although much of the loss was to a large number of supplying countries, including European Union states, rather than simply to other Asian exporters. The Saudi Arabian Monetary Agency reports on imports from Taiwan but not from mainland China. It is likely that some of the re-exports going through Dubai to Saudi Arabia originated from mainland China, but are recorded as imports from the UAE. Imports from Indonesia and Malaysia show the highest increase of those from Asia, illustrating the increasing significance of trade with

**Table 11.10  Saudi Arabia's exports to leading Asian destinations, $ million.**

|             | 1984   | 1986  | 1988  | 1990  | 1992  | 1994  | 1995  |
|-------------|--------|-------|-------|-------|-------|-------|-------|
| Japan       | 11,234 | 4,036 | 4,111 | 8,415 | 8,210 | 6,792 | 8,114 |
| South Korea | 1,086  | 411   | 460   | 1,667 | 3,405 | 3,466 | 4,927 |
| Singapore   | 1,877  | 540   | 1,416 | 2,377 | 2,361 | 2,062 | 2,666 |
| India       | 1,117  | 293   | 682   | 1,097 | 1,431 | 1,249 | 1,562 |
| Turkey      | 199    | 227   | 177   | 756   | 1,447 | 1,213 | 1,332 |
| Philippines | 298    | 107   | 97    | 590   | 653   | 710   | 978   |
| Pakistan    | 520    | 267   | 344   | 448   | 514   | 465   | 534   |
| Indonesia   | 723    | 68    | 110   | 165   | 763   | 489   | 500   |

*Source* adapted from Saudi Arabian Monetary Agency, *Annual Report* (1997)

Table 11.11  Saudi Arabia's imports from leading Asian sources, $ million.

| | 1984 | 1986 | 1988 | 1990 | 1992 | 1994 | 1995 | 1996 |
|---|---|---|---|---|---|---|---|---|
| Japan | 6,285 | 2,968 | 3,479 | 3,654 | 4,690 | 2,738 | 2,490 | 1,956 |
| S. Korea | 954 | 774 | 1,026 | 989 | 888 | 660 | 883 | 786 |
| India | 265 | 212 | 225 | 273 | 410 | 421 | 510 | 599 |
| Taiwan | 862 | 672 | 724 | 525 | 558 | 373 | 405 | 413 |
| Indonesia | 82 | 61 | 166 | 211 | 349 | 264 | 386 | 412 |
| Thailand | 213 | 174 | 310 | 272 | 326 | 204 | 286 | 325 |
| Turkey | 455 | 328 | 358 | 298 | 359 | 460 | 420 | 300 |
| Malaysia | 93 | 58 | 108 | 128 | 220 | 193 | 275 | 241 |

*Source* adapted from Saudi Arabian Monetary Agency, *Annual Report* (1997)

other Muslim countries which the Islamic Development Bank tries hard to promote (Table 11.11).

## 11.9  The GCC dialogue with the European Union

Since the oil price rises of the mid-1970s the European Union has maintained a sporadic dialogue with Arab countries, much of which has concerned the Mediterranean Arab countries rather than the GCC. The European Union has cooperation agreements with many of these states, including the Magreb countries, Egypt and Jordan,[48] and a series of free trade agreements were negotiated in the mid to late 1990s providing European Union exporters with duty-free access to these markets from 2012, once tariffs are eliminated over a 12-year transition period starting in 2000. In exchange the Mediterranean Arab countries are receiving a limited amount of aid.[49]

The European Union has special policies towards its geographical neighbours such as the Arab Mediterranean states, not least because of past labour inflows from these countries and the possibility of further migratory flows in spite of restrictions on immigration. The GCC countries are regarded as rather different, not least because when their citizens come to the European Union they are usually in a position to support themselves financially, and are not seeking work. Most GCC visitors are either on business or on holiday, or wanting medical treatment for which they pay.

Since the mid-1980s there has, however, been a dialogue between the GCC and the European Union, and the GCC maintains a small office in Brussels to provide secretarial and other support services for its negotiators. The European Union wants to maintain links with other regional groupings worldwide such as the GCC, and at the same time recognises the importance of the Gulf region as a source of energy, and as a market for its exporters. Saudi Arabia alone was the fifth largest market for European Union exports in 1991, and the seventh major source for imports, although by 1995 it had declined to 20th rank in terms of external export markets and 16th rank as a source of imports.[50] The UAE was the European Union's 24th largest export market.

The major dispute between the GCC and the European Union has been over petrochemical exports, mainly from Saudi Arabia. Brussels argued that these were unfairly subsidised through low feedstock prices, and that the GCC was 'dumping' petrochemicals on the European Union market to the detriment of European producers. No formal dumping procedures were instigated, but the European Union imposed a 13.5% tariff on GCC petrochemical exports in 1984 which has remained in place.

The GCC has argued on behalf of its members that its comparative advantage is in feed-stocks which are inherently cheap in the Gulf, but that transport costs bring prices into line with those of competing producers in Europe in any case, and therefore no protection can be justified. The GCC is only supplying basic petrochemicals, which allows ample opportunities for European purchasers to add value in their own plants. Furthermore, the GCC itself has very low tariffs on imports from the European Union, and is a major market for European exports. GCC negotiators argued that the region should be accorded most favoured nation treatment as provided for by the United Nations Conference on Trade and Development (UNCTAD), as although GCC countries have high per capita GDP and GNP levels they remain developing countries in terms of their structural characteristics. Hence their manufactures should be accorded preferential treatment, whereas as far as the European Union was concerned, the reverse was the case, the negotiators argued.[51]

The European Union negotiators have not given way to these arguments, pointing out that Saudi Arabia has still been able to secure a share of the European basic petrochemical market, and that a tariff is preferable to a quota. The issue could potentially be resolved by a World Trade Organisation arbitration panel, but this would only be possible if Saudi Arabia was admitted to membership.

There is an increasing trade imbalance between the European Union and the GCC, as Table 11.12 shows, as although the share of the European Union in GCC imports increased, the proportion of GCC exports going to the European Union fell substantially. There was increasing European Union import penetration in the markets of Bahrain, Kuwait, Oman and Qatar, and in Saudi Arabia and the UAE the share remained around one-third. Yet only Saudi Arabia and Kuwait exported oil volumes of any significance to the European Union, and in the case of Saudi Arabia the European Union accounted for less than a fifth of the total, and in the case of Kuwait less than one-sixth.

As a consequence, the European Union has an increasing trade surplus with GCC states, as Table 11.13 shows, the overall surplus exceeding ECU 9 billion ($11 billion) in 1995. The most substantial surplus is with the UAE, but even in the case of Saudi Arabia trade is in approximate balance. In reality, increasingly the surplus the GCC enjoys with Asia and the United States gets translated into a deficit with the European Union, which is a major turnaround from the situation in the 1970s. There is, however, enormous pressure on Saudi Arabia to purchase from the United States rather than the European

**Table 11.12  European Union's share of GCC trade, %.**

|  | Imports | | Exports | |
| --- | --- | --- | --- | --- |
|  | **1980** | **1995** | **1980** | **1995** |
| Bahrain | 13.0 | 18.8 | 0.5 | 1.4 |
| Kuwait | 34.5 | 46.8 | 26.1 | 13.7 |
| Oman | 34.7 | 39.1 | 22.4 | 2.6 |
| Qatar | 43.9 | 54.1 | 41.2 | 1.8 |
| Saudi Arabia | 39.4 | 35.6 | 41.1 | 19.0 |
| UAE | 37.4 | 33.0 | 33.1 | 3.7 |

*Source* adapted from Eurostat, *Basic Statistics of the European Union*, 33rd edition, (1996)

Table 11.13 European Union's trade balance with the GCC, million ECU (1 ECU = $US 1.16).

|  | 1991 | 1992 | 1993 | 1994 | 1995 |
|---|---|---|---|---|---|
| Bahrain | 597 | 591 | 505 | 499 | 393 |
| Kuwait | 588 | 955 | 681 | 207 | 1,057 |
| Oman | 623 | 805 | 920 | 1,222 | 1,183 |
| Qatar | 533 | 404 | 572 | 703 | 1,054 |
| Saudi Arabia | −751 | 608 | 271 | 67 | −62 |
| UAE | 2,401 | 3,135 | 4,679 | 5,324 | 5,649 |

Source adapted from Eurostat, *External and Intra-European Union Trade, Monthly Statistics*, No. 12 (1996)

Union, as typified by the contract in 1997 to buy Boeing and McDonnell Douglas aircraft worth $7.5 billion which Saudi Arabian Airlines could ill afford.[52]

Most European Union exports to the GCC countries are capital goods such as machinery and equipment for the oil and petrochemicals industries or manufactured goods, largely consumer items. Table 11.14 shows this export composition for the three largest GCC markets. Food exports to Saudi Arabia, mainly from France, remain substantial. Table 11.15 illustrates how energy continues to be the dominant export from Saudi Arabia to the European Union.

Table 11.14 Composition of European Union exports to major GCC partners, million ECUs (1 ECU = $US 1.16).

|  | SITC* | Kuwait | Saudi Arabia | UAE |
|---|---|---|---|---|
| Food & beverages | 0+1 | 177 | 1,060 | 489 |
| Raw materials | 2+4 | 18 | 160 | 42 |
| Energy | 3 | 7 | 37 | 79 |
| Chemicals | 5 | 194 | 1,168 | 553 |
| Machinery & equipment | 7 | 1,095 | 3,188 | 2,875 |
| Manufactured goods | 6+8 | 590 | 2,625 | 2,107 |

Source adapted from Eurostat, *External and Intra-European Union Trade, Monthly Statistics*, No. 12 (1996)
*SITC = Standard International Trade Classification.

Table 11.15 Composition of European Union imports from major GCC partners, million ECUs (1 ECU = $US 1.16).

|  | SITC* | Kuwait | Saudi Arabia | UAE |
|---|---|---|---|---|
| Food & beverages | 0+1 | 0 | 14 | 27 |
| Raw materials | 2+4 | 2 | 38 | 13 |
| Energy | 3 | 1,256 | 7,216 | 118 |
| Chemicals | 5 | 0 | 434 | 17 |
| Machinery & equipment | 7 | 61 | 667 | 241 |
| Manufactured goods | 6+8 | 31 | 246 | 380 |

Source adapted from Eurostat, *External and Intra-European Union Trade, Monthly Statistics*, No. 12 (1996)
*SITC = Standard International Trade Classification.

## 11.10    Trade prospects

It would be wrong to be excessively pessimistic about the trade prospects for the GCC states. As has been noted, much has been achieved in terms of diversification already, as Saudi Arabia has a world-class petrochemical industry, gas exports have increased from Qatar and Abu Dhabi, Dubai has become a major re-exporting port, building on its earlier entrepôt role, and Bahrain has emerged as a regional financial centre.

These achievements have not been easy, as difficulties have often thwarted the best intentions. Petrochemical pricing and marketing has proved a much greater challenge than the technical and engineering problems of actually getting the industry going in the first place. In Bahrain the offshore banks and financial services companies had to re-focus their activities to give the island a greater competitive edge in specialist areas as the more favourable business climate of the oil boom years came to an end. Dubai has needed to adapt not only to the changed trading conditions in the GCC following the Gulf War, but also to the many policy changes in Iran, its major re-export market. As gas exporters, Abu Dhabi and Qatar have had to respond to changes in Far Eastern markets, in particular the economic slowdown in Japan, and further adaptation will be needed given the new financial circumstances faced by the former Asian 'tiger' economies.

It is at the institutional level where trade policy has been weakest, however, or even lacking entirely. This applies at both national and regional level. Governments do little to assist their own exporting companies despite the rhetoric about the need for diversification. A survey of Saudi Arabian exporting companies revealed that there was a lack of government export promotion programmes. Competition failure in transport resulted in both high costs for imported raw materials and high costs for exporting the subsequent output. Export financing programmes were also deficient, the commercial banks preferring to finance imports, with the goods themselves serving as collateral.[53] There is a need for further studies of this type in other GCC countries to identify deficiencies in terms of government support for exporters and potential exporters.

It is at the level of trade diplomacy, however, that the failure has been greatest. Negotiations with the WTO have been conducted on a bilateral basis rather than through the GCC, with the consequence that some GCC members have been admitted, while others have not. Admittedly the GCC itself has achieved little in trade negotiations, as the stalled negotiations over petrochemical exports show. Nevertheless, the GCC would seem the appropriate forum for external trade negotiations, given the greater economic power of the organisation collectively than its individual members, even Saudi Arabia. This is highlighted by the fact that the GCC market for imports is continuing to expand, but Saudi Arabia's relative share is falling. This purchasing power can be translated into bargaining strength, but the GCC has first to develop a coherent external trade strategy, and address the problem of trade imbalances.

This does not mean that national governments have no role to play in Gulf trade and exports. The GCC must ultimately be accountable to Gulf governments for its actions. Governments themselves can organise and sponsor trade missions to Europe, Asian capitals and the United States. The United Kingdom sent a high-level trade mission to the Kingdom in November 1997, as Saudi Arabia is the United Kingdom's second largest customer outside the Organisation for Economic Cooperation and Development (OECD). British exports to the Kingdom were worth $3.5 billion in 1996, including defence exports under the Yamamah programme, and it is hoped to raise the amount to at least $4.6 billion by 2000.[54] The GCC states need to be thinking in similar terms, setting targets for non-oil exports, which are at present barely discussed in most of the development plans.

In the Holy Koran the virtues of trade are extolled. One passage urges believers not to hoard, but to trade: 'O ye who believe, eat not up your property amongst yourselves in vanities, but let there be amongst you traffic and trade by mutual goodwill'.[55] Another passage speaks of the 'hope for a commerce that will never fail'.[56] Such themes were taken up by early Islamic jurists and scholars, notably Ibn Taimiyah in the eighth century after *Hijra*.[57] These themes deserve to be revisited, as the gains from trade which most western economists have pointed to since Adam Smith's *Inquiry into the Wealth of Nations*[58] were expounded long before in Islamic economic writing.

## Summary

- The GCC is an important example of the new trends in the world economy for pressures toward greater regionalism which to an extent runs counter to the proper development of the world multilateral trading system.
- The changing nature of GCC trade with the EU and the wider world are analysed from a political economy and diplomatic viewpoints.
- Prospects for enhanced GCC trade are analysed against the background of the WTO recent policy initiatives in the area regarding all GCC members with respect to individual countries' sensibility.

### Questions

1. How might Saudi Arabia liberalise its trade systems to allow full membership of the WTO?

2. How do cultural issues in the GCC impact on trade?

3. GCC countries have small non-oil exports. How can this be explained? (Refer to Chapters 2–4.)

4. What are the future trade prospects for the GCC members and their roles with respect to the WTO?

### Key concepts

GCC export trends                            merchandise imports
entrepôt trade                               trade in commercial services
trade prospects                              the GCC and the WTO
commercial relations with Asia
trade between GCC states and Arab regional integration
the GCC dialogue with the European Union

### Notes

1. World Trade Organisation, *Annual Report*, 1996, Geneva, Vol. 2, table 1.6, p. 4.
2. Rodney Wilson, *The Economies of the Middle East*, Macmillan, London, 1979, pp. 74–5.
3. World Trade Organisation, *Annual Report*, 1996, Geneva, Vol. 2, table 1.6, p. 4.
4. Real GDP growth figures from the Economist Intelligence Unit accessed by *Datastream*.

5. Statistical work using regression techniques and covariance was undertaken for export and GDP growth data and the results confirmed the high association of these variables.

6. Saudi Arabian Monetary Agency, *Annual Report*, 1995, pp. 66–7.

7. Estimated from figures in the Central Bank of Kuwait *Economic Report* for 1996, pp. 124–5.

8. Economist Intelligence Unit figures accessed through *Datastream*.

9. Central Bank of Oman, *Quarterly Statistical Bulletin*, Volume 23, No. 1, 1997, p. 33.

10. Saudi Arabian Monetary Agency, *33rd Annual Report*, Riyadh, 1418 (1997), p. 101.

11. *Middle East Economic Digest*, 3 October 1997, p. 3.

12. Henry T. Azzam, 'Saudi Arabian economy: the outlook for 1998', *Saudi Economic Survey*, 8 and 15 April 1998, p. 11.

13. *Middle East Economic Digest*, 21 February 1997, pp. 2–3.

14. *Middle East Economic Digest*, 29 August 1997, pp. 2–3.

15. World Bank *Atlas*, 1997, pp. 36–7. Qatar is also not cited in the World Bank *World Development Indicators*, Washington, 1997. Figures on trade growth and structure are provided for the other GCC countries: table 4.7, pp. 154–6 and table 4.8, pp. 158–60.

16. Saudi Arabian Monetary Agency, *Annual Report*, 1995, op. cit., p. 69.

17. Ibid., p. 71.

18. Angus Hindley, 'Dubai ports ready for regional tussle', *Middle East Economic Digest*, 24 October 1997, p. 2.

19. National Bank of Dubai, *Annual Report*, 1995, p. 16.

20. Robin Allen, 'New strategy for a different era', *Financial Times Survey on Dubai*, 3 November 1993, p. 2.

21. Data from Dubai Chamber of Commerce *Annual Report* for 1995, pp. 228–9.

22. Angus Hindley, op. cit.

23. National Bank of Dubai, *Annual Report*, 1995, pp. 20–1.

24. Estimated from figures supplied by the Abu Dhabi Chamber of Commerce, January 1997.

25. *Al-Nashra al-Sanai'yah*, Riyadh, No. 21, 1996, pp. 8–11.

26. Bahrain Monetary Agency, *Quarterly Statistical Bulletin*, Vol. 23, No. 2, 1997, p. 23.

27. Arab Banking Corporation, *The Arab Economies*, 4th revised edition, Bahrain, 1994, p. 21.

28. Bahrain Monetary Agency, *Quarterly Statistical Bulletin*, Vol. 23, No. 2, 1997, p. 2.

29. Rodney Wilson, *Banking and Finance in the Arab Middle East*, Macmillan, London, 1983, pp. 110–19.

30. Rodney Wilson, *Islamic Finance*, Financial Times Publications, London, 1997, pp. 135–6.

31. Saudi Arabian Monetary Agency, *33rd Annual Report*, Riyadh, 1418 (1997), p. 164.

32. Ibid., p. 103.

33. Rodney Wilson, *Economic Development in the Middle East*, Routledge, London, 1995, p. 169.

34. Elias T. Ghantus, *Arab Economic Integration*, Croom Helm, London, 1982, pp. 60–1.

35. For a detailed explanation of the reasons for failure see Nemat Shafik, 'Learning from doers: lessons on regional integration for the Middle East', in Hanaa Kheir El-Din, *Economic Co-operation in the Middle East: Prospects and Challenges*, Dar Al-Mostaqbal Al-Arabia for Cairo University, Faculty of Economics and Political Science, 1995, pp. 281–306.

36. David Butter, 'Arabs seek common economic cause', *Middle East Economic Digest*, 4 July 1997, pp. 2–3.

37. *Saudi Economic Survey*, 31 December 1997, p. 7.

38. United Nations Economic Commission for Western Asia, *Economic Integration in Western Asia*, Frances Pinter Publishers, London, 1985, p. 16.

39. Ibid., p. 17.

40. Gulf Investment Corporation and Gulf International Bank, *GCC Business and Finance Guide, 1996/97*, Bahrain, 1997, p. 3.

41. Alan Richards and John Waterbury, *A Political Economy of the Middle East: State Class and Economic Development*, Westview Press, Boulder, Colorado, 1990, p. 239.

42. *Saudi Economic Survey*, 31 December 1997, op. cit., p. 7.

43. Rodney Wilson, *Economic Development in the Middle East*, op. cit., p. 170.

44. *Saudi Economic Survey*, 31 December 1997, op. cit, p. 7.
45. Rodney Wilson, 'Saudi Arabia: WTO Membership', *Oxford Analytica Daily Brief*, 14 May 1997.
46. Ali D. Johany, Michel Berne and J. Wilson Mixon Jr., *The Saudi Arabian Economy*, Croom Helm, London, 1986, p. 144.
47. Rodney Wilson, 'The Islamic Development Bank as an aid agency for Muslim countries', *Journal of International Development*, Vol. 1, No. 4, 1989, pp. 444–66.
48. Saleh Al-Mani and Salah Al-Shaikhly, *The Euro-Arab Dialogue*, Frances Pinter, London, 1983, pp. 78–93.
49. Werner Weidenfeld, *Europe and the Middle East*, Bertelsmann Foundation, Gütersloh, 1995, pp. 39–41.
50. Source: Eurostat, *External and Intra-European Union Trade, Monthly Statistics*, No. 12, 1996, table 2B, pp. 44 and 48.
51. Rodney Wilson, *Euro-Arab Trade*, Economist Intelligence Unit, Report 1105, London, 1988, pp. 88–92.
52. *Middle East Economic Digest*, 7 November 1997, pp. 11–12.
53. Abdulrahman Yousef Al-Aali, 'Saudi Arabian export strategy: a micro-level analysis', in J. Wright (ed.), *Business and Economic Development in Saudi Arabia*, Macmillan, London, 1996, pp. 152–69.
54. Michael Binyon, 'Big trade drive in Saudi Arabia', *The Times*, 11 November 1997, p. 35.
55. *Sûra*, 4:29.
56. *Sûra*, 35:29.
57. Abdul Azim Islahi, *Economic concepts of Ibn Taimiyah*, Islamic Foundation, Leicester, 1988, pp. 39–42 and 230.
58. Adam Smith, *An Inquiry into the Nature and Causes of the Wealth of Nations*, Everymans Library, 1910, pp. 340 ff.

# Bibliography

Al-Aali, A. Y. (1996) 'Saudi Arabian export strategy: a micro-level analysis', in J. Wright (ed.), *Business and Economic Development in Saudi Arabia*, Macmillan, London, pp. 152–69.

Allen, R. (1993) 'New strategy for a different era', *Financial Times Survey on Dubai*, 3 November.

Al-Mani, S. and Al-Shaikhly, S. (1983) *The Euro-Arab Dialogue*, Frances Pinter, London.

*Al-Nashra al-Sanai'yah*, Riyadh, No. 21, 1996.

Arab Banking Corporation (1994) *The Arab Economies*, 4th revised edition, Bahrain.

Azzam, H. T. (1998) 'Saudi Arabian economy: the outlook for 1998', *Saudi Economic Survey*, 8 and 15 April 1998, p. 11–20.

Bahrain Monetary Agency (1997) *Quarterly Statistical Bulletin*, vol. 23, no. 2.

Binyon, M. (1997) 'Big trade drive in Saudi Arabia', *The Times*, 11 November, p. 35.

Butter, D. (1997) 'Arabs seek common economic cause', *Middle East Economic Digest*, 4 July, pp. 2–3.

Central Bank of Kuwait (1996) *Economic Report*.

Central Bank of Oman (1997) *Quarterly Statistical Bulletin*, vol. 23, no. 1.

Dubai Chamber of Commerce (1995) *Annual Report*.

El-Din, H. K. (1995) *Economic Co-operation in the Middle East: Prospects and Challenges*, Dar Al-Mostaqbal Al-Arabia for Cairo University, Faculty of Economics and Political Science.

Eurostat (1996) *External and Intra-European Union Trade, Monthly Statistics*, no. 12.

Ghantus, E. T. (1982) *Arab Economic Integration*, Croom Helm, London.

Gulf Investment Corporation and Gulf International Bank (1997) *GCC Business and Finance Guide, 1996/97*, Bahrain.

Hindley, A. (1997) 'Dubai ports ready for regional tussle', *Middle East Economic Digest*, 24 October, p. 2.

Islahi, A. A. (1988) *Economic concepts of Ibn Taimiyah*, Islamic Foundation, Leicester.

Johany, A. D., Berne, M. and Mixon, J. W. Jr. (1986) *The Saudi Arabian Economy*, Croom Helm, London.

*Middle East Economic Digest*, 21 February 1997.

*Middle East Economic Digest*, 29 August 1997.

*Middle East Economic Digest*, 3 October 1997.

*Middle East Economic Digest*, 7 November 1997.

National Bank of Dubai (1995) *Annual Report*.

Richards, A. and Waterbury, J. (1990) *A Political Economy of the Middle East: State Class and Economic Development*, Westview Press, Boulder, Colorado.

Saudi Arabian Monetary Agency (1995, 1997) *Annual Reports*, Riyadh.

*Saudi Economic Survey*, 31 December 1997.

Shafik, N. (1995) 'Learning from doers: lessons on regional integration for the Middle East', in H. K. El-Din (ed.), *Economic Co-operation in the Middle East: Prospects and Challenges*, Dar Al-Mostaqbal Al-Arabia for Cairo University, Faculty of Economics and Political Science, pp. 281–306.

Smith, A. (1910) *An Inquiry into the Nature and Causes of the Wealth of Nations*, Everymans Library.

United Nations Economic Commission for Western Asia (1985) *Economic Integration in Western Asia*, Frances Pinter Publishers, London.

Weidenfeld, W. (1995) *Europe and the Middle East*, Bertelsmann Foundation, Gütersloh.

Wilson, R. (1997) *Islamic Finance*, Financial Times Publications, London.

Wilson, R. (1997) 'Saudi Arabia: WTO Membership', *Oxford Analytica Daily Brief*, 14 May.

Wilson, R. (1995) *Economic Development in the Middle East*, Routledge.

Wilson, R. (1989) 'The Islamic Development Bank as an aid agency for Muslim countries', *Journal of International Development*, vol. 1, no. 4, pp. 444–66.

Wilson, R. (1988) *Euro-Arab Trade*, Economist Intelligence Unit, Report 1105, London.

Wilson, R. (1983) *Banking and Finance in the Arab Middle East*, Macmillan, London, pp. 110–19.

Wilson, R. (1979) *Economies of the Middle East*, Macmillan, London.

World Bank (1997) *Atlas*, pp. 36–7.

World Bank (1997) *World Development Indicators*, Washington.

World Trade Organisation (1986) *Annual Report*, Geneva.

Wright, J. (ed.) (1996) *Business and Economic Development in Saudi Arabia*, Macmillan, London.

# 12 Trade and development: the Asian 'Tigers'

## K. LAWLER and M. LING

## 12.1 Introduction

Over the past quarter of a century, eight economies in East Asia have experienced growth rates in incomes per head of nearly 6% a year. This figure contrasts dramatically when compared with Organisation for Economic Cooperation and Development (OECD) countries which have, on average, recorded yearly GDP growth rates of around 2% over the same period. These eight, so-called, 'Tiger' economies have been led by Japan which has been a major player on the world stage since the 1960s. However, Japan's rapid growth has been mirrored by the economies of South Korea, Taiwan, Singapore and Hong Kong, all of which really started to develop in 1960s. These countries in turn were pursued by Indonesia, Malaysia and Thailand. These latter seven countries are generally termed the Newly Industrialising Countries (NICs).

All these countries were poor agricultural economies in the 1950s. Within 20 years much of the industry in the NICs has reached the technological standards of the West. Though this study concentrates on the development of South East Asia, the giant economy of China should not be forgotten. Like most of the other economies of S. E. Asia, the Chinese economy is growing rapidly. As mentioned in the World Bank Review, The East Asian Miracle (1993), China recorded an average annual GNP growth of 9.4% from 1979 to 1989, with an increase to 11.4% between 1982 and 1988. After falls to 4.4% and 4.1% in 1989 and 1990 respectively, the economy recorded a 12% growth rate in 1992. Indeed, economic development in East Asia has been so great that between 1970 and 1990, according to the World Bank Review (1992), the number of desperately poor people in East Asia as a whole has been reduced from 400m to 180m. What is more remarkable is that this reduction in poverty has occurred simultaneously with the population of East Asia growing by about two-thirds over the same period. According to the World Bank, between now and the year 2000, Asia as a whole will account for half of the growth in world trade.[1] The population of this region is expected to register around 3.5 billion people by 2001. The total world population is predicted to be approximately 6.2 billion in 2000.

A major Western concern is the rapid rise in the economic profiles of these very competitive NICs and other low-wage East Asian economies, which could potentially bring about a fall in Western wages and employment as the world moves towards greater levels of free trade. This Western concern first became evident in the mid-1970s and was highlighted in particular due to the poor economic performance of OECD countries in general after the first oil shock.[2] The increase in imports of manufactures from the NICs intensifies the problems of the deterioration of trade balances, the slowdown of growth and the rise of unemployment. The challenge from the NICs for the OECD countries was reflected in the difficulties of industrial adjustment due to structural deficiencies in specific sectors such as shipbuilding, steel and the car industry.

The classical Ricardian theory of comparative advantage predicts that freer trade brings benefits to all. The West benefits from cheaper, less technically advanced, labour-intensive products and therefore, its resources can be concentrated in the manufacture of more technologically advanced, capital-intensive products. Hence, a more efficient, worldwide, allocation of resources is achieved. Thus, calls for protectionist measures against Far Eastern imports are not needed. Theory implies that such policies would bring about slower, or even a decline in, total world economic growth.

Furthermore, as the SE Asia region continues rapid development, the rise in consumer real incomes and the investment in infrastructure that is needed provide gains to the West. Equally, increasing financial opportunities are achieved by the West in services. For example, the need for bigger and better banking services increases in relation to the region's economic growth. Obviously, one particular comparative advantage that the West possesses lies in supplying the world with banking, commercial and insurance services.

## 12.2  Economic development in East Asia

Thirty years ago, few observers could have predicted the massive rise in wealth of the Pacific Rim countries. Thus in the quarter of a century after the Second World War, much of the world destruction and poverty was situated in East Asia. For example, India and Pakistan fought three wars in those years. Korea was devastated by the civil war between 1950 and 1953. Indochina and Vietnam saw much conflict, as did ethnic Indonesia which went through bouts of 'ethnic cleansing' in the mid-1960s. Finally, Thailand, Malaysia, Burma and the Philippines all saw guerrilla uprisings and political instability. In China, in the mid-1960s the Cultural Revolution pushed back economic advance. This major draw-back which afflicted China was to some extent mirrored, though on a smaller scale, in Cambodia where perhaps 15–20% of the educated population were destroyed.

Asian economic performance in the 1950s and 1960s was not impressive. The richest country, Japan, had a GDP per head of around $380 which was about one-eighth that of the USA. South Korea's GDP per head in 1962 was $110 and Taiwan's was $160, which were comparable at the time to any country in sub-Saharan Africa. China's GDP per head was $60, the world's eleventh lowest. This large country was still recovering from Mao's new economic policy called the 'Great Leap Forward', which took place from 1964–1969. Between 30 and 50 million Chinese starved to death.

From the 1950s onwards things started to improve. For example, Japan had already begun its revolution in the 1950s, where emphasis on export-led growth increased real income per head four times between 1960 and 1985. Japan's rapid development was followed about ten years later by South Korea, Taiwan, Hong Kong and Singapore, with real GDP doubling roughly every eight years from 1960 to 1985. In the late 1970s, growth in Malaysia, Thailand, Indonesia and eventually China began to speed up. All in all, these eight economies, during the 1980s, grew three times as fast as any economy in the developed world, excluding Japan.

The economies of the East-Asian Pacific region can be classified into three main groups (four if Japan is included). To begin with, there are the Newly Industrialising Countries of South Korea, Singapore, Hong Kong and Taiwan, and although not quite at the same stage of development, Malaysia and Thailand are included in this group. The second group comprises the developing economies of China, Indonesia and the Philippines. Finally, the less-developed countries (i.e. those in the Pacific Rim area) are not included in the above two groups. These are the countries of North Korea, Laos, Vietnam, Cambodia and

Table 12.1  Population and income distribution of East Asian countries.

| Country | Population (1998) | GDP per capita ($US) (1995) | Distribution of GDP (%) | | |
|---------|------------------|----------------------------|-------------|----------|----------|
| | | | Agriculture | Industry | Services |
| Bangladesh | 124,043 | 246 | 31 | 18 | 52 |
| Cambodia | 10,751 | 276 | 51 | 14 | 34 |
| China | 1,255,091 | 572 | 21 | 48 | 31 |
| India | 975,772 | 346 | 29 | 29 | 41 |
| Indonesia | 206,522 | 1,003 | 17 | 42 | 41 |
| Japan | 125,920 | 40,846 | 2 | 38 | 60 |
| Loas | 5,358 | 361 | 52 | 18 | 30 |
| Malaysia | 21,450 | 4,236 | 13 | 43 | 44 |
| Myanmar | 47,625 | – | 63 | 9 | 28 |
| Philippines | 72,164 | 1,903 | 22 | 32 | 46 |
| Singapore | 3,491 | 25,156 | 0 | 36 | 64 |
| Sri Lanka | 18,450 | 720 | 23 | 25 | 52 |
| South Korea | 46,116 | 10,142 | – | – | – |
| Thailand | 59,612 | 2,868 | 11 | 40 | 49 |
| Vietnam | 77,896 | 276 | 28 | 30 | 42 |

*Source* adapted from United Nations 'World Resources' (1998–99)

Myanmar. The varying levels of income can be seen in income distribution statistics and GDP data in Table 12.1.

## 12.3  Why was economic growth so rapid?

An extensive debate currently exists as to the reasons which brought about the rapid rise in industrialisation of the Pacific-Rim countries. More fundamentally, the debate is directed towards the roles that free-market policies or government-led intervention played in bringing about such growth. The economic success of the NICs is seen by the Neoclassical school as evidence that minimal state intervention and strong free-trade policy is the answer to rapid economic growth. However, the eight 'Superstars' of Hong Kong, Indonesia, Japan, Malaysia, Singapore, South Korea, Taiwan and Thailand have followed a mixture of policies, each with varying degrees of intervention. Hong Kong has pursued the most extensive free-market liberalism policies of any country in the world, whereas Japan and South Korea have seen high levels of government intervention.

Substantial research provides evidence against the neoclassical explanation of growth, with the exception of the ultra free-market economy of Hong Kong. This different approach to that suggested by the Neoclassical school, in explaining the success of the NICs, has been called the 'developmental statist' approach. This sees state intervention as the fundamental cause of the NICs' rapid economic growth. For example, Alice Amsden (1989), in her study of the development of the South Korean economy, points out that instead of firms being allowed to develop in a competitive market structure, the government intervened with a large degree of market control and initially protected the economy from foreign competition. She argues that in fact, 'not only has Korea gotten relative prices right, it has deliberately gotten them wrong'. That is, in order to create profitable opportunities for industry, the state intervened on a large scale to establish multiple prices in the same market. Amsden believes that 'late developing' countries require large amounts of intervention to enable them to overcome the 'harsh justice' previously imposed upon them by market forces. For example, she argues that the South Korean government created low interest rates to stimulate investment, and at the same time, kept other interest rates high to encourage people to save. Equally, exchange rates were undervalued to boost exports and simultaneously overvalued so as to minimise the cost of foreign debt repayment and of imports. Also, the government provided infant-industry protection but also had to advocate free trade so that import needs could be satisfied.

In the same vein, it is stated by McDermott (1992), who looked at the subject of the internationalisation of the South Korean and Taiwanese electronics industries, that the governments of both countries have largely contributed to their countries' economic development. Although McDermott notes that the role of government has been different in each country, in South Korea government intervention took place to ensure industrial concentration. Thus *chaebols* (large conglomerate enterprises) were created. Although the government lured firms to enter new industries with protectionist policies and subsidies, it also limited the number it allowed to enter, thus ensuring that scale economies and the rise of these mammoth *chaebol* business empires were created. The government foresaw these groups as necessary to build basic industry. In contrast, however, McDermott notes that the Taiwanese government adopted a more 'laissez-faire' approach. The government's role here was primarily to provide the best conditions and incentives for the entrepreneurial spirit to flourish. As a result, Taiwan's industry has a fragmented structure based largely on small and medium-sized enterprises. The World Bank (1992) suggests that rapid economic growth occurred because the Asian economies implemented free-market policies and yet maintained stable growth by pursuing strict macroeconomic policy. Thus the World Bank takes a neoclassical view and believes that various governmental interventions in the S. E. Asian NICs have, on the whole, 'cancelled each other out'. Prices 'have been got right', more or less at free-market levels, and the report also states that trade policies have in fact turned out to be neutral between the domestic market and exports, therefore they have been 'out-orientated'.

## 12.4    Factors facilitating rapid growth in the NICs

### 12.4.1  Government intervention

The OECD Report (1988) argues that one factor which all the NICs share has been the ability to concentrate their energies towards the goal of greater industrial growth. A large degree of government intervention, particularly in South Korea and Taiwan, has helped to strengthen and provide support to the NICs in their pursuit of high levels of industrial development. The common industrial path taken by the NICs has been as follows: first, import substitution running in parallel with protective barriers. This was later followed by export-orientated strategies when the disadvantages of import substitution, such as under-utilisation of installed capacity and other and poor export growth due to artificially high exchange rates, were bearable no longer. Moreover, with the exception of Hong Kong and Singapore, all other East Asian economies relied on import barriers to protect 'infant industries'. Indeed, as the Report argues, even by the late 1980s, most of South Korea's industry was still protected by some combination of tariff and non-tariff barriers.

Although it has been argued successfully that government industrial policy played a major role in fostering the NICs' economic development, this does not mean that government intervention is necessarily always successful. Indeed, typical government failures predicted by neoclassicists, such as infant industries that do not mature and incentives that encourage unproductive activities, are recognised by the developmental statist approach. For example, the OECD (1988) reports that, due to current world overcapacity, the South Korean shipbuilding industry, which entered the world market at the end of the 1970s, is feeling the strain of declining world prices.

Rhys Jenkins (1995), in a paper examining the political economy of industrial policy in the Asian and South American NICs, looks specifically at the automobile industry, and addresses the question as to what circumstances lead to successful intervention and what factors determine the effectiveness of industrial policy. He found that four of the economies covered in his study: South Korea, Taiwan, Brazil and Mexico, all adopted highly interventionist policies to develop their car industries. Moreover, Jenkins states that South Korea, the most successful of the four, used the most highly interventionist policies. On the other hand, the Taiwanese car industry, in which government seldom intervened, was the least successful.

Jenkins also notes that the domestic car markets in all four countries are highly protected, and South Korea, Brazil and Mexico have all promoted automobile exports with considerable success. He concludes that the results obtained are consistent with the developmental statist approach, with industrial performance explained by the effectiveness of state intervention. However, Jenkins does note that the failure of the Taiwanese car industry contrasts sharply with its successful policies in developing other industries, such as steel, shipbuilding, chemicals, petrochemicals and electronics.

According to the World Bank (1992), export promotion and directed credit were two types of intervention that were successful. Most NIC nations implemented aggressive export promotion policies, such as subsidies and favoured access to foreign borrowing and foreign exchange. This targeting on foreign markets imposed a high level of discipline on firms and encouraged efficiency. Amsden (1989) suggests that the manipulation of interest rates has played a role in the creation of growth. Governments in Japan, South Korea, Malaysia, Taiwan and Thailand all intervened so as to reduce the cost of capital to firms and directed credit to favoured industries. Indeed, the World Bank argues that low interest rates were the key to the NICs' directed credit programmes. Thus, low interest rates on loans resulted in excess demand for credit, which permitted governments to take an active role in credit rationing. This, in turn, gave governments strong leverage with which to influence the behaviour of firms. The World Bank puts forward two reasons as to why it may not be feasible to use such policies now: for example, (1) in the increasingly integrated global capital markets of today, governments wishing to attract foreign investment cannot close their financial markets to the outside world. Therefore it is much more difficult to hold down interest rates. In the past, ceilings on interest rates encouraged investment in Japan, South Korea and Taiwan. (2) Developing countries looking to boost trade face greater pressure today from other trading nations and trade organisations (e.g. GATT) to open domestic markets than the pressure that was imposed upon the East Asian NICs.[3] Again, direct subsidies to exporters, which are generally against GATT rules, are likely to provoke retaliation from industrial economies too.

However, all forms of intervention in the structure of protection or interest rate control carry costs, either in the form of direct fiscal costs of subsidies or revenues forgone, or in the form of implicit taxation of households and firms. But the report also mentions the fact that, although price distortions were present in many NICs' policies, they were not excessive. For example, interest rate controls generally had international interest rates as benchmarks and explicit subsidies were also kept within bounds. Finally, the World Bank argues that success also depended upon a somewhat unique institutional factor: the competence and relative lack of corruptness of civil servants in countries like Hong Kong, Japan, South Korea, Singapore and Taiwan. These countries were successful in creating professional and honest bureaucracies. In other developing economies, where exacting institutional demands cannot be met, the same policies have failed.

## 12.5   Foreign Direct Investment (FDI)

Foreign direct investment refers to various forms of capital investment from the OECD countries in the industrialising NICs and lesser developed Asian countries. Such investment, albeit in different forms and degrees, has had a significant impact bringing about the rapid economic development of NICs and other S. E. Asian nations. Table 12.2 shows the size of FDI flows in selected Asian economies. Clearly, the NICs and China have received the majority of such investments. The reasons behind this trend are explained below.

According to the Transnational Corporations in World Development (1988), FDI flows to S. E. Asia tend to be heavily concentrated in a few countries. The leading eight of the 20 or so East Asian nations: China, Hong Kong, Indonesia, Malaysia, South Korea, Singapore, Taiwan and Thailand, received 92% of FDI during the 1981–85 period. FDI plays a significant role in Hong Kong and Singapore since it contributes to more than half of the external financial resources.

The main reasons why these eight countries attract large volumes of FDI are:

1. relatively large domestic markets, for example China, Indonesia and Thailand, with large potential increases in consumer spending power also advantageous;

2. the favourable conditions necessary for low-cost export-orientated manufacturing industries such as low-cost labour costs, skilled labour and well-developed infrastructure, e.g. Hong Kong, Malaysia, Singapore and Taiwan;

3. petroleum and other natural resources, e.g. Indonesia and Malaysia.

**Table 12.2   Foreign direct investment.**

| Country | 1986 | 1988 | 1990 | 1992 | 1994* | 1996* |
|---|---|---|---|---|---|---|
| Bangladesh | 2 | 2 | 3 | 1 | 11 | 9 |
| China | 1,875 | 3,194 | 3,489 | 4,366 | 33,787 | 42,300 |
| Hong Kong | – | – | 1,597 | 2,051 | 2,000 | 2,500 |
| Indonesia | 258 | 576 | 1,093 | 1,482 | 2,109 | 7,960 |
| India | 208 | 287 | 112 | 200 | 1,314 | 2,587 |
| Malaysia | 489 | 719 | 2,514 | 3,454 | 4,342 | 5,300 |
| Pakistan | 105 | 186 | 244 | 257 | 419 | 690 |
| Philippines | 127 | 936 | 530 | 544 | 1,591 | 1,408 |
| Singapore | 1,710 | 3,655 | 3,861 | 3,584 | 5,480 | 9,440 |
| Sri Lanka | 30 | 46 | 43 | 98 | 166 | 170 |
| South Korea | 435 | 871 | 715 | 1,166 | 809 | 2,308 |
| Taiwan | 326 | 959 | 1,330 | 1,271 | 1,375 | 1,402 |
| Thailand | 263 | 1,105 | 2,444 | 2,014 | 1,322 | 2,426 |

*Source* adapted from Asian Development Bank Handbook (1993)
* Figures from the World Investment Report, 1997

However, it should be argued that without the appropriate policies and attitudes of the host countries with respect to foreign investment such a high level of flows would not have taken place. For example, the World Bank (ibid.) states that Japan, although not a developing country, provides a good example nonetheless, has been quite openly hostile to foreign investment but very good at recognising what the overseas consumer wants, copying foreign innovations or buying foreign technology licences and then supplying the new goods to the market. Taiwan has allowed foreign direct investment flows only on the condition of technology transfer. Taiwanese entrepreneurs now bring back to the nation high-technology skills and business practices fresh from the USA. Hong Kong and Singapore, on the other hand, have had very liberal policies towards FDI and such policies have interacted positively.

Examining the South Korean economy, Amsden argues that, from the end of the Japanese occupation, FDI, in the form of equity ownership by foreigners of Korean production facilities, has been kept to a minimum so that the *chaebols* would be able to develop without any major form of foreign control. Investors were welcome to enter the light manufacturing export sector, but were discouraged from investing in import-substitution sectors such as pharmaceuticals and heavy industry. In 1983, the government finally began to encourage FDI in the high-technology industries, but interestingly, Amsden finds that in fact, even though the absolute quantity of FDI increased, it actually accounted for a lower percentage of GNP in 1985 than 1965[4] (Table 12.3). According to Amsden, this provides evidence that Korea has industrialised mainly on the basis of national enterprise. South Korea's relatively independent rise to industrialisation is examined in depth later.

In 1992 the Korean government implemented its first five-year plan which set the country's industrial growth in motion. The government welcomed FDI investment but projects had to meet two conditions: (a) that investors' ownership-specific advantage was transferred to a local partner or that (b) the investor agreed to comply with the government's performance requirements, which were generally export-related. Consequently,

Table 12.3  South Korea and FDI in relation to GNP.

| Year | FDI (in US$ 000) | % of GNP |
|---|---|---|
| 1965 | 20,671 | 0.73 |
| 1970 | 13,642 | 0.16 |
| 1975 | 169,398 | 0.81 |
| 1976 | 72,160 | 0.25 |
| 1977 | 65,915 | 0.18 |
| 1978 | 107,312 | 0.17 |
| 1980 | 140,751 | 0.25 |
| 1981 | 145,327 | 0.23 |
| 1982 | 187,791 | 0.28 |
| 1983 | 267,753 | 0.36 |
| 1984 | 419,049 | 0.52 |
| 1985 | 531,720 | 0.65 |
| 1990 | 705,000 | 0.30 |
| 1992 | 727,000 | 0.27 |
| 1994 | 809,000 | 0.22 |
| 1996 | 2,308,000 | 0.36 |

*Source* adapted from Amsden (1989)

due to condition (a), joint ventures with overseas partners facilitated technology transfer to Korean manufacturers. Licensing also proved another important way of obtaining the use of foreign technology and thus provided a stimulus for a wide spectrum of industries such as motor cars, electronics, petrochemicals and textiles. McDermott suggests that, on the whole, it was the combination of foreign technology and cheap hard-working labour that resulted in the domestic manufacturers of South Korea, and the other NICs, becoming 'the world's lowest cost, reliable manufacturers of numerous low-tech products'.

He adds that this rapid industrialisation can also be explained by local manufacturers experiencing rapid growth as a result of supplying the original equipment manufacturers (those that were developed by foreign investment), aided by the fact that the South Korean won was generally weak against the US dollar over this time period, so many foreign multinationals found it cheaper to obtain supplies from local manufacturers.

## 12.6　High domestic investment and saving rates

Economists view investment as a driving force behind economic growth. In a closed economy, domestic savings are the only source of investment, but in an open economy, investment can be financed by borrowing abroad, using foreigners' savings, too. If a country possesses inadequate domestic savings and if therefore a large proportion of capital has to be financed from abroad, then the continued build-up of foreign liabilities, which have to be ultimately paid for by domestic savings, may eventually pull down total investment rates. Thus, an industrialising nation will benefit greatly if a high level of domestic saving rates exists within that country.

The World Bank found that between 1960 and 1990 both savings and investment increased rapidly in the NICs, outperforming other developing regions. In 1990, the S.E. Asian NICs' gross domestic investment as a percentage of GDP stood at around 35%; for all the other developing regions of the world (Latin America and the Caribbean, South Asia and Sub-Saharan Africa), this proportion stood at less than 20%. As for gross domestic savings, that ratio for the Asian NICs in 1990 was around 36% of GDP. The rates for the other developing regions were again much lower; around 8% for South Asia and Sub-Saharan Africa and 18% for Latin America. Indeed, the East Asian NICs are the only group of developing countries in which savings exceed investment, making them net exporters of capital.

Governments of the NICs have attached great importance to maintaining savers' confidence in financial institutions, even to the extent of bailing out troubled financial institutions through financial and management assistance or mergers with stronger banks. This continues to be a feature in Japan too over the past five years. However, controls are widespread. South Korean investors have been subject to controls on capital flight, or the remittance of liquid capital overseas. Legislation passed in the 1960s stipulated that any illegal overseas transfer of $1m or more was punishable with a minimum sentence of ten years' imprisonment and a maximum sentence of death.[5]

## 12.7　Education

The NICs of East Asia have basically followed the USA's late nineteenth- and early twentieth-century profile. Thus, although the USA was a pioneer in mass production techniques, it was to a large extent a technological follower for much of the nineteenth century, borrowing 'know-how' from Britain. The relatively large amounts of funds invested in the economy over this period definitely helped the USA to industrialise. According to World Bank data, the USA's gross fixed investment averaged 21% of GDP between 1887 and 1910. The UK on the other hand invested 13% over the same period. In the mid-1990s, South Korea invested around 35% of its GDP, more than double the USA's capital spending. Moreover, the NICs, and especially South Korea, have invested heavily in physical capital and the education of the workforce – often referred to as 'human capital'.

Education is very important if the development of skills is to occur in order to master new technologies. The USA was a pioneer, Amsden suggests, in the introduction of universal literacy and primary education. In the same way, the NICs' considerable success has been partly caused by their investment in human capital.

The World Bank argues that the Tiger economies of S.E. Asia have thrived because their prospective governments have allocated a large amount of education investment to basic primary and secondary education, which is vital for skilled workforce development, rather than to more glamorous levels of education such as universities. Indeed, the World Bank (ibid.) adds that primary and secondary enrolment rates are positively correlated to income per capita rates. Nonetheless, the World Bank found that NICs' enrolment rates have tended to be well above those predicted by even their levels of income. For example, in 1987, the predicted mean secondary enrolment rate for middle-income economies was 36%, whereas the actual mean was 54%. South Korea and Indonesia registered enrolment rates of 88% and 46% respectively. Only Thailand with 28% was below the predicted rate.

The advantages to an economy of such an educational spending ratio are that, first, the productivity of the mass of the workforce is increased, which obviously leads to a greater comparative advantage, especially in semi-skilled industries such as light manufacturing, as South Korea certainly realised. Second, income equality occurs more quickly in this way. Third, in South Korea, the income of the richest 20% of households is eight times that of the poorest 20%. In the South American NICs of Brazil and Mexico, the richest fifth have at least 20 times as much income as the poorest fifth.

Amsden suggests that the relative status and salary a society attributes to the teaching profession acts as a barometer of the importance it attaches to education. She finds that in 1984, the average Korean monthly salary for teachers (539,000 won/month) was below the average of managers (630,000 won/month) but above the average of all professional, technical and technically related workers (432,000 won/month).

## 12.8    Globalisation

The massive expansion of world trade in the past 30 years is another important factor in explaining the rapid growth of Asian NICs. Owing to the growth of multinational corporations and international communications, worldwide diffusion of technology is becoming quicker than ever before. This suggests that a firm or nation that invents a new product, or innovates an existing one, will only possess a 'head-start' or an advantage over other firms or nations for a much shorter time period than previously. Firms can now, owing to the advance in communications, learn, examine and copy leading firms over an ever-decreasing time period. However, taking the lead requires the ability to be a technological innovator rather than a 'copy-cat'. This is one reason why the USA forged ahead in the 1950s. In order to achieve this position, heavy spending on research and development and pure science was necessary. This is the main reason why innovating nations tend to be situated in the developed world, since only relatively rich countries can afford massive expenditure on R&D.

Thus, even though the East Asia NICs are currently developing at a faster rate than the developed economies of the West, this does not mean that the Western economies have lost the ability to adapt to changing economic and technological conditions. Indeed, as argued by OECD (1988), although the leading NICs (South Korea and Taiwan in particular) have increased R&D and training efforts, it is generally believed that it may be some time yet before the NICs have the ability to create a scientific and technological infrastructure capable of generating basic innovation to an extent comparable with the more advanced industrialised countries.

## 12.9    NICs and LDCs: South Korea and Indonesia

When the economic challenge from the NICs first became apparent to the OECD countries in the mid-1970s, as the result of the phenomenon of large increases in exports of manufactured goods from these countries, the traditional trade theory in the form of Heckscher-Ohlin-Samuelson (H-O-S) was challenged. It became obvious that forms of international specialisation were changing. The product life-cycle theory of trade was developed to explain trends in world trade which did not easily fit the H-O-S paradigm. However, the patterns of trade existing between NICs, and those of less developed countries (e.g. Indonesia), appear to fit within the H-O-S framework and can be viewed from the vantage point provided by the Rybczynski Theorem.

To recapitulate, the H-O-S theorem of trade states that a nation will export those goods that use that particular country's most abundant factor of production intensively in the manufacture of that good, and it will import those goods that have been manufactured using intensively that factor of production which is relatively scarce in that country. A country with a greater physical amount of labour relative to capital will normally possess comparatively cheap labour and expensive capital. Its comparative advantage will lie in the manufacture of relatively labour-intensive goods. The H-O-S model suggests that comparative advantage will tend to be determined by factor proportions and not just natural differences, as advocated by David Ricardo.[6] In high-wage countries it is not advantageous to manufacture goods that require large inputs of expensive labour when such goods can be imported from cheap-labour countries. Therefore, scarce, expensive capital will be used efficiently, if it is used to manufacture capital-intensive goods in high-wage countries. Obviously, the reverse is true for low-wage economies. As a country develops and production becomes more capital intensive, wages will rise relative to capital costs (i.e. any previous comparative advantage in terms of low wage costs will be lost), and exports and imports will reflect this change. This new advantage will, therefore, lead to an increase in the export of capital-intensive products, whereas home manufacture of labour-intensive products will decrease, as imports of these products increase. A good example of this pattern of development is provided by the history of the Japanese textile and clothing industry.[7] This labour-intensive industry accounted for around 51% of all Japanese exports in 1990. This ratio had fallen to around 38%, as levels of cheaper imports increased, in 1950 and in 1980 the ratio stood at around 4%.

Data in the GATT handbooks (1993) reveals that a pattern of decline, or slowing growth rates, in the relatively labour-intensive industries such as textiles and clothing, and an increase in the capital-intensive production of goods, have occurred in South Korea.

However, as an LDC, not at the same stage of development as South Korea, Indonesia still possesses a relatively large textile and clothing industry, which is still expanding. The Republic of Korea was ranked fifth largest textile exporter in the world in 1992. The share of textiles in relation to total export merchandise fell from 12.6% in 1980 to 10.7% in 1992. Indonesia was ranked 14th largest textile exporter but its share of total export merchandise has increased from 0.2% in 1980 to 9.7% in 1995. In particular, there has been a marked decline of the clothing industry in South Korea (the share of the country's total exports fell from 16.8% in 1980 to 8.8% in 1992), and a large growth of the industry in Indonesia (the share in the economy's total merchandise exports has increased from 0.4% to 10.8% over the same period). This increase can be explained to some extent by NICs relocating their clothing/textile plants to the lower (labour) cost Asian economies, such as Indonesia. For example, according to data obtained from the UN *Handbook of Industrial Statistics 1992* (1993), the average manufacturing employee wage per annum in Indonesia was $600 in 1989 in the Spinning, Weaving and Finished Textile categories, and $7,200 in South Korea.

Obviously, with such low relative and absolute wages, Indonesia possesses a comparative advantage in low-cost labour at this particular stage of its development. South Korean wage levels in the Spinning category increased to the $7,200 stated from $2,700 in 1983. This large increase reflects the rapid development of the economy, although, obviously, these wages are still not comparable to Western earnings.

The relative low cost of labour in Indonesia encouraged a sharp rise in foreign investment, especially from 1989 when foreign investment restrictions were significantly reduced (Table 12.3). According to the *Asian Development Bank Yearbook* (1993), in 1990 Japan invested a total of $2.24bn in the Indonesian economy. The next major investors were Hong Kong ($993m) and South Korea, whose total planned investment by industry in value terms went firstly into chemicals, with around $2bn invested, and then textiles ($1.1bn), which incidentally saw the largest number of foreign projects approved. Thus, the high level of South Korean direct investment in Indonesia can partly explain the fall in South Korean exports of textiles. In effect, Indonesia is actually exporting South Korean textiles.

The OECD (1988) report finds that the focus devoted by the NICs to moving further up market, to high value added product manufacture, has been strengthened by increased competition at the more labour-intensive end of the product cycle, from lower-wage countries, such as Indonesia. One consequence of this strategy has been an increase in licensing, joint ventures and other contractual arrangements with OECD multinational enterprises, in exchange for greater technology transfer and managerial 'know-how' going to NIC firms. At the same time, OECD producers in sectors such as textiles and semi-conductors are increasingly finding a diminishing cost advantage in investing in the NICs due to rising labour costs as workers become more skilled, factories become more automated and more flexible manufacturing systems are introduced. Thus, the NICs are gradually losing their initial comparative advantage in relatively labour-intensive manufacturing processes.

For manufactured goods, UN data (1992) shows that Indonesia's total exports of manufactured goods increased notably, rising from 31.5% of total exports in 1986 to 58.1% in 1992. This suggests that Indonesia was industrialising very quickly, and like South Korea, the development of certain intermediate and heavy industries had also been encouraged by the government. Indeed, the value of manufactured exports (1996) exceeds the value of oil and gas exports, of which Indonesia possesses abundant reserves and which are major export products.

Manufactured products comprise textiles, petrochemicals, cement, fertilisers, basic metals, motor cycles, chemicals, paper and household goods (especially electronic products). However, most of these products are for domestic consumption. According to SITC classification (UN, 1992), all exports of electrical products (SITC 750 to 778) increased dramatically between 1989 and 1992 for Indonesia. This increase in the level of exports of electronic and telecommunication products provides some evidence against the predictions of the H-O-S model. This is because Indonesia is seen now to be a large exporter of capital-intensive goods with seemingly relatively high levels of technology involved in production. The H-O-S theorem would predict, owing to the highly developing nature of the country, that Indonesia's comparative advantage should be more heavily concentrated towards the manufacture of relatively labour-intensive products requiring a relatively low level of technology. This anomaly can be explained by the fact that the actual manufacture of the majority of Indonesian electronic and related goods are, in fact, relatively labour-intensive assembly processes, requiring relatively little knowledge or human capital. Frequently, the more industrialised nations, such as Japan and South Korea, use low labour cost nations as an assembly base for products, especially in cases where these products are mass produced for mass consumer markets, such as radios and simple tape recorders.

The UN *Handbook of Industrial Statistics* (ibid.) shows that in 1981, the average Indonesian wage per employee in the electrical industrial machinery sector (SITC 3831) was very low when compared to the average for the NIC, e.g. $1,300 in 1981, and this only rose to $1,400 in 1989. Whereas for Korea, the average wage in this sector was $3,800 in 1983 and this increased dramatically to $8,800 in 1989. Thus, this seems to provide evidence of the relatively unskilled assembly-process nature of Indonesian industry.

The highly differing levels of technology of goods involved in trade between a high growth NIC, such as South Korea, and that of a developing economy, such as Indonesia, are clearly shown in the 'Trade in Manufactures by End-Use, Stage of Processing and Research Intensity' in the UN *Handbook* (1993). If we focus in particular on research intensity in 1990, goods classified as low research products made up 50.4% of South Korean exports. The same figure for Indonesia stood at 40.5%. However, when the two countries are compared in terms of medium and high research intensity products, much greater differentials appear between the two. In 1990, 5.1% of Indonesia's total exports were classified as medium research and only 1.5% as high research products, whereas medium research products made up 24.1% of South Korean total exports and low research products accounted for 22.4% of total exports. Hence, these statistics seem to agree with the H-O-S principle. That is, Indonesia, being relatively less developed and therefore expected to possess an abundant supply of relatively cheap labour, exports a much greater proportion of low research composition products (i.e. relatively labour intensive), when compared to more industrialised nations such as South Korea.

The growth rates for each of these research intensity categories show that over the period 1980–85, Indonesia experienced a relatively high 35.6% growth rate in high research products. However, the period 1985–90 period saw an 8% decline in this category. This phenomenon, together with the fact that the largest growth in the three categories in Indonesia from 1985–90 occurred in low research products (27.9%), suggests that the government may have decided to concentrate, to a certain degree, on specialising in the production of relatively labour-intensive goods. This may be because the government realised that as the NICs become more industrialised and thus switch to more capital-intensive methods of production (generally involving the use of higher levels of technology), the greater scope there is for lesser developed countries like itself to gain more of a trade advantage by concentrating resources and therefore strengthening comparative advantages in industries which are relatively labour intensive. Aided by greater levels of competition from countries like Indonesia, South Korea's comparative advantage has shifted quite considerably away from the manufacture of relatively labour-intensive to capital-intensive products. Indeed, in South Korea, the growth rate of exports is highest in the high research intensity category: 30.2% over the 1985–90 period, with 25% and 10.2% growth rate of exports in medium and low research products respectively over the same period.

A reasonable indicator showing the increasing capital-intensive nature of South Korean industry can be seen by examining the value of capital-intensive product trade flows.[8] Hence, according to the GATT handbook (1993), South Korea is placed among the leading world exporters of office machines and telecom equipment. The value of this particular category of goods exported by South Korea stood at $1.7bn in 1980. In 1992, this figure had increased to $17.4bn. The country's share in total world exports in this category increased from 2% to 5% over this period. Another example of South Korea's high level of industrial development is that exports of machinery and transport equipment products, which obviously involve a relatively high degree of capital-intensive production methods, have risen from a value of $32.5bn in 1992 to $64bn in 1998. The nation's share in world exports has risen from 0.7% to 2.4% over the same period. This category comprises a vast range of products, such as all forms of electrical goods, from freezers to sophisticated telecommunications equipment.

Indonesia possesses many natural resources, such as tin, nickel ores, bauxite and copper, and huge reserves of oil, gas and coal. Obviously, a large proportion of industry in Indonesia is specialised in mineral and fuel production. However, owing to falling world commodity prices, the mining and quarrying sector has declined rapidly (UN *Handbook*). Moreover, the role of oil and gas peaked in the 1980s when it contributed over four-fifths of total exports. This contribution has now fallen to around a third.[9] However, as is evident in the listings of exports by commodities, the actual values of exports of crude materials and minerals (SITC 2), in particular copper ores (SITC 28711) and mineral fuels (SITC 3) and particularly coal (322), oil (33) and gas (341), have actually increased. Therefore, for the percentage value of the mining and quarrying sector as a whole to decline by such large amounts over the 1986–92 period shows to what extent, in comparison, the level of exports of other products, such as textiles and manufactured goods, must have increased over recent years. This provides evidence again of just how rapidly less developed economies such as Indonesia are industrialising. However, although the country has successfully developed a growing non-oil sector, it remains heavily dependent on oil. The country is Asia's largest oil exporter (World of Information, 1991).

## 12.10 Trends in the Asia-Pacific Region

As the Asian Development Bank handbook (1993) notes, the high degree of acceleration of industrialisation of the Chinese economy stands out from the recent trends of the Asia-Pacific region. It is a major source of intra-regional trade growth. In accordance with the H-O-S model (and therefore tending to suggest a certain degree of inter-regional trade), Korean exports to China are mainly manufactured and processed products such as textiles, ferrous metals, machinery and chemical products. Imports from China tend to be basic primary products, agricultural products, yarn, coal and oil. However, South Korea's lack of natural resources explains, to a large degree, such a composition of Chinese imports. Owing to the establishment of diplomatic relations between the two countries in 1991, the handbook states that Korean exports to China rose to $439m for the first half of 1992, from a value of $44m for the same period in 1991.

Whilst the handbook mentions that there has been some slowing down in the industrial performance of the NICs, the transitional economies of Asia have experienced quite substantial patterns of growth.

The strong economic performance of these lesser developed countries (i.e. Indonesia, Malaysia and Thailand) has been aided by increases in the level of domestic demand and export growth. Government policy reforms of recent years, increases in disposable incomes and a rise in private investment and public spending on infrastructure have helped an increase in growth.

In the NICs of South Korea, Malaysia and Thailand there was a notable slowdown in domestic demand and the growth rates of investment by 1993. This has been induced by respective government efforts to dampen inflationary pressures which were building up in these economies, by introducing tight monetary and fiscal policies.

Until 1997, increased levels of inter-regional trade and intra-regional trade helped to protect the economies of the region from the slow growth in the world economy. These patterns of trade have developed due to the ongoing processes of specialisation within the region, the influence of foreign direct investment and the relocation of production capacity mainly from Japan and the NICs to the developing economies of China and the Philippines, in particular.

According to McDermott, both South Korea and Japan since the mid-1980s ceased to be attractive locations for subcontracting (i.e. for direct investment from OECD countries). This is mainly due to rising production costs as a result of labour acquiring higher levels of pay and better working conditions.

Asian Development Bank (1993) states that, in the face of rapid domestic wage increases and the emergence of competitors with lower labour costs, many South Korean firms have been forced to increase their rate of investment abroad. This process has occurred since 1986. The major recipients of this investment have been China, the Philippines, the USA and Europe. The UK, in particular, has seen the highest level of investment of any country in Europe. South Korean investment in China has mainly been directed towards light industries in which South Korea's comparative advantage has been eroded, such as the manufacture of shoes, leather goods, textiles and toys.

Large amounts of direct investment have come to the NICs themselves from the USA, Japan and Europe. This investment tended to be focused in the manufacturing sectors, particularly chemicals, electrical and the electronics industries. Since 1997, this investment level from Japan to developing countries was due to the slowdown in the Japanese economy. Also, balance sheet adjustments in financial institutions have been limiting outward spending by Japanese banks. Such lending plays a major role in aiding the FDI flows from Japan. Also, due to the recession, Japanese corporations experienced a large squeeze on their profits and capital base. There is currently strong evidence to suggest that this recession affecting the Japanese economy is now coming to an end.

## 12.11    South Korea

Generally, therefore South Korea's industrial development has been characterised by a high degree of state intervention. Such intervention began in 1958 with a series of five-year economic plans (OECD, 1988). From 1958 to 1964 an import substitution policy was implemented to nurture the country's light manufacturing industries by employing such methods as strict import controls, multiple exchange rates and foreign aid (mainly from the USA) to pay for imports.

In 1964, the South Korean government introduced an export-led industrialisation programme by directly intervening in the main industrial sectors at the time, textiles and consumer electronics. Moreover, the won was devalued and a number of financial and fiscal incentives for exporters (and producers of intermediate goods used in export goods) were also introduced. In 1996, large reductions in customs duties occurred for imports of capital goods used in the production of exportables.

In 1973, the government focused on the development of heavy industry, in particular steel and non-ferrous metals, chemicals, petrochemicals, machinery and shipbuilding. Indeed, today, South Korea is a very efficient producer of steel (with the plant at Posco being one of the most efficient in the world), and was also given a strong impetus in the late 1970s.

State intervention and a general export-orientated development have contributed to an average 7% growth rate over the past 25 years. However, a significant slowdown in growth occurred in late 1992, when GDP fell to 0.5% after recording 7.4% in 1991 (Asian Development Bank Review, 1993). This slowdown was due to the government's efforts to reduce the speed of activity in the economy, which was leading to high rates of inflation. In order to do this, tight fiscal and monetary policies were imposed.

Also, owing to such factors as the slowness of the world economic recovery, relatively high wages and interest rates, tight liquidity in financial markets and domestic political uncertainty, investor confidence in the country declined, adding to the slowdown in growth which has, since 1997, plunged along with other Asian Tigers.

As a result of the induced slowdown in aggregate demand, inflationary pressures eased towards the end of 1992, with the inflation rate falling to 6.2% after recording an average of around 9% throughout 1991. The deficit on the external current account also fell.

Indeed, until 1986, South Korea ran considerable deficits on its trade and current accounts. The shortfall was made up by hidden soft loan borrowing from overseas and the World Bank. South Korea's total foreign indebtedness hit a peak in the mid-1980s with a value of $47m, which actually made the country the fourth largest indebted country in the world. But Korea's heavy investment eventually paid off and the huge deficits on both the trade and current accounts were both turned into credit of about $10bn in 1987.

Heavy tariffs on manufactured goods and a multitude of consumption taxes were major factors which facilitated the government's export-orientated development. Since 1987, when Korea moved into the black on its trade and current accounts, the USA (Korea's major export market) declared that the protected infant industries had now matured into efficient industries in their own right and since then, has constantly demanded that South Korea reduce its many tariff barriers. Indeed, the average tariff fell from 18.1% in 1990 to 8% in 1992.

South Korean government intervention in the economy, therefore, has been on a large scale, comparable to the government intervention in Japan. This intervention has traditionally been directed mainly at the octopus-like, family-run conglomerates or *chaebol* which include such well-known multinational companies as Samsung, Hyundai, Lucky-Goldstar and Daewoo. Around 90% of South Korean GNP comes from these conglomerates. In fact, World of Information (1991) stated that the sales of these top four companies combined came to W97.86 trillion ($135bn), equivalent to more than half of South Korean GNP.

## 12.11.1  Trade in South Korea

According to the UN *Handbook of Industrial Statistics 1992* (p. 524), South Korean total exports, FOB, in 1992 amounted to $76.6bn. The value of total exports stood at $47.3bn in 1987 and $21.9bn in 1982. This shows the extent of the success achieved by the South Korean export-oriented development drive, especially when developing countries' exports are compared to those of South Korea. For example, the value of Indonesia's total exports in 1982, 1987 and 1992 were $22.3bn, $17.1bn, and $29.1bn respectively. Thus, clearly, the Indonesian economy, especially when its larger population size is taken into account, still has some ground to make up before it can rival the South Korean level of exports.

During 1992, South Korea's main export, in terms of value, was machinery and transport equipment (SITC 7), with $32.5bn worth of such goods exported, which amounted to 42.4% of all exports. The fast rate of development and industrialisation of the South Korean economy is also shown by the fact that in 1989, the value of total exports of machinery and transport equipment was $23.5bn, which then accounted for 38% of all exports. The percentage of exports of this category in relation to total exports has therefore increased less (from 38% to 42.2% = 11.5%), compared to the actual increase of machinery and transport exports over the same period (from $23.5bn to $32.5bn = 38%). Thus, for such a relatively small increase in exports of machinery and transport equipment in relation to total exports to occur, when there has been a much larger increase of total exports, shows just how fast exports of other product categories grew.

This group (SITC 7) comprises a huge range of products. Electrical goods make up a large proportion of the category, such as:

- office machines, SITC 75, $3.09bn worth of products exported in 1992;
- telecommunications equipment, SITC 76, $6.5bn exported in 1992;
- electrical machinery, SITC 77, $10.7bn exported in 1992;
- consumer goods (such as household appliances), SITC 775 (a sub-category of SITC 77), $1.09bn exported in 1992;
- electronic circuitboards, transistor valves, SITC 776 (a sub-category of SITC 77), $7.7bn exported in 1992;
- road vehicles, SITC 78, $4.3bn exported in 1992 – this figure has increased from $3.5bn in 1989;
- ships and boats, SITC 793, $4.1bn exported in 1992. Exports have increased dramatically from the $1.7bn worth of products exported in 1992.

Exports of television and radio transmitters (SITC 7643) have decreased from $255m in 1989 to $209m in 1992. This shows the results of increasing competition from lower wage, less developed S. E. Asian countries.

The values of exports within the miscellaneous manufactures category (SITC 8), according to the statistics given in the UN (1993) yearbook, fell over the 1989–92 period, from $18.9bn to $15.7bn, or from 30.5% of total exports to 20.5%.

The decline has mainly been due to a large decline in the export of clothing and accessories (SITC 84), from $9.2bn in 1989 to $6.9bn in 1992. Indeed, most exports of clothing products declined, in terms of both weight and value, over this period. This is partly a result of Korean manufacturers setting up production bases in cheaper labour-cost Asian countries.

Also, Hong Kong and Singapore, although classed as NICs, are major locations for other NICs and OECD countries to establish production facilities. Indeed, international trade statistics reveal this trade pattern. Imports of clothing into South Korea have been increasing steadily over the past decade (GATT Handbook, 1993); there was a particularly large increase from 1991 to 1992, when imports rose from $183m to $270m. At the same time, retained imports (i.e. imports exclusively for the domestic market) have been falling in Hong Kong over the past decade. For example, in 1987, imports of clothing to Hong Kong were $3.3bn, whereas retained imports amounted to $994m. In 1992, total imports were $10346m, retained imports just $256m. Thus, obviously, Hong Kong is importing an increasing volume of products which are actually just assembled, or just have the labour-intensive production stage performed in Hong Kong, before being re-exported.

Basic manufactures classified by material (SITC 6), such as leather, rubber, textiles and iron/steel products, have increased steadily over the same period, 1989–92, from $13.9bn to $18.7bn. An interesting point here, however, is that, unlike clothing, general exports of textile manufactures have increased from a value of $5.4bn in 1989 (8.7% of total exports), to $8.2bn in 1992 (10.7% of total exports). This phenomenon may be explained if such textile manufactures have been produced using high levels of synthetic fibres which involve a relatively large degree of capital bias and advanced technological production processes. Less developed economies (for example, Indonesia), through lacking either the technology or available capital for the production of these goods, do not yet possess the means to produce such goods as efficiently as South Korea. Therefore, following the H-O-S model of trade, South Korea seems to possess a comparative advantage in the synthetic fibre industry. For example, the relevant data in the UN *Handbook of Industrial Statistics 1992* (p. 523) shows that exports of woven man-made fabrics (SITC 651), which are relatively labour intensive, were much smaller in comparison and have also increased over the same time period to a much smaller degree, from $903m to $1,046m.

Thus, as labour costs rise in South Korea, due to the increase in capital-intensive production processes, the economy loses its initial comparative advantage held in the labour-intensive, mass-produced, standard clothing industry. However, South Korea's losses are other, less developed countries' gains.

South Korea has become a leading producer and exporter of consumer electronics and the economy has moved upstream to more sophisticated electronics. Indeed, the electronics industry has grown faster than any other sector (McDermott, ibid.).

At the same time, there has been a rapid growth of electronic imports. This reflects, in part, the large supply of advanced parts and components, as well as of industrial electronic equipment from the USA and Japan.

Although South Korean electronics production is largely geared to exports, the domestic market itself has grown rapidly, due to increasing national income. The increasingly important role of the domestic electronics market is shown by the fact that in 1979 exports accounted for 56.3% of total electronics production, but in 1983 this figure had fallen to 53.6% (OECD, 1988).

The desire to expand and develop the higher-technology production processes in South Korea, especially in electronics-associated production, should ensure the country's rising requirements for foreign technological cooperation. This desire for knowledge is reflected in the increase of South Korean outlays for overseas technological acquisitions. Payments for obtaining such technology in the electronics and electronic equipment sector increased from $8.9 million in 1980 to $30.6 million in 1983 (OECD, 1988).

The transfer of technology, Amsden suggests, is a major factor in explaining the rapid Korean real wage growth (Table 12.4), but not in the sense that H-O-S theory predicts.

**Table 12.4  Wages in manufacturing selected sectors (in won).**

| Economic activity | 1983 | 1987 | 1992 |
|---|---|---|---|
| Textiles | 183 | 272 | 658 |
| Footwear | 156 | 225 | 532 |
| Industrial chemicals | 341 | 514 | 1,168 |
| Transport equipment | 327 | 437 | 1.085 |

*Source* adapted from *UN Handbook of Industrial Statistics* (1992)

One would expect initially that once the process of industrialisation has begun, a late industrialising country, such as South Korea, would experience a shortage of relatively skilled labour (managers, engineers and technicians) and an abundance of relatively unskilled labour. The wage levels of the former would then be expected to pull up the overall average. Amsden found that (Table 12.5) over four sub-periods, from 1965–1984, wage rates increased more for production workers than for the higher-skilled employees. Thus, Amsden puts forward the view that scarcity value and supply and demand factors are not in themselves sufficient to explain the rapid rise in real wages.

The fast rate of growth of wages, Amsden suggests, was assisted by an especially intense learning process. However, as Table 12.4 shows, the lowest-paid workers, those in textiles and footwear, as admitted by the state-dominated labour federation, are earning little more than subsistence wages. Workers in the more capital-intensive activities, chemicals and transport, are much more highly paid.

Such a learning process has occurred historically due to less industrialised countries copying and then innovating borrowed technology from the industrialised world and finally commercialising new product variations. However, Amsden finds that the learning process operated somewhat differently in Korea due to the government's policy of developing the economy from within, via the large *chaebol* enterprises, without the direct influence of foreign firms.

She suggests that because South Korea's experience in textiles dates back to the Japanese colonial period, modernisation in the 1950s posed no real problems for the industry. The huge fixed-capital investments in the heavy-industry-oriented *chaebols*, such as oil refining and steel industries, relied on turnkey technology transfers. Managers thus faced the problem of trying to understand processes that, Amsden notes, the foreign experts themselves did not even fully understand. In such circumstances, different styles of management to those practised in the industrialised world were developed in order to deal with Korea's inexperience in working with new technologies.

**Table 12.5  Rate of wage increase for production and professional-managerial workers.**

| Period | Production workers | Professional, technical and managerial workers |
|---|---|---|
| 1965–70 | 12.8 | 6.6 |
| 1971–74 | 7.1 | 6.1 |
| 1975–79 | 16.8 | 15.3 |
| 1980–84 | 5.3 | 2.5 |

*Source* adapted from from Amsden (1989)

In short, this new style of management involved placing a large degree of emphasis upon motivating all workers, even if they possessed little formal education, to 'exercise the most important skill of all, intelligence'. Hence in all of the new capital-assembly industries, production workers were motivated with relatively high wages, first to increase output, then to improve quality.

However, Amsden points out that, because firms were managed as though higher wages alone could generate higher worker productivity levels, inflationary pressures were created within the economy. Also, due to strong competition from 'learners', less developed, lower-cost economies, the more labour-intensive South Korean industries, namely textile production and light manufacturing, had to be either phased out or forced to move to lower-cost Asian economies.

## 12.12    FDI flows and the international movement of technology

The H-O-S model suggests that in a perfectly functioning world of free trade, with incomplete specialisation and no factor-intensity reversals,[10] there would be few incentives for international factor movements, since free trade would equalise relative factor prices. In practice, the failure of factor prices to fully equalise, due to various forms of trade barriers and the existence of transport costs, provides an explanation for foreign direct investment (FDI). For example, multinational companies establish foreign subsidiaries to take advantage of lower labour costs in other countries. A more common cause of differences in factor prices that may generate FDI is that the assumption of common production functions (technologies), central to the H-O-S model, is not met. The differences in production functions may be due to, for example, the technical knowledge (or the level of 'human capital') that a country possesses, difference in management skills or different social attitudes between nations towards the role of work.[11]

New theories of international trade are primarily connected to technology and, in particular, explain the phenomenon of 'intra-industry trade',[12] something that the H-O-S model cannot do.

As suggested by Vernon in his work on the product cycle hypothesis, a firm will tend to develop into some form of multinational corporation when it reaches the stage of investing abroad. Even though Asia still needs Western investment since this incorporates the latest technology, it is common practice for Asian multinationals to invest in the industrialised world.

### 12.12.1  New theories of international trade: the product cycle theory of trade

The product cycle theory of trade attempts to provide explanations of the empirical observations that:

- innovations are usually concentrated in the more developed countries and that the production of the good, in the early stages of its development, usually takes place in the innovating country;

- the innovating firm which actually developed the new product may eventually switch production to a country where its resource endowments are more suited to the production of this good in the longer term. Evidence of this is provided by Western FDI flows to S. E. Asia and the more recent NIC FDI flows to the less developed Asian economies.

As most inventions and innovations are the result of large amounts of investment in research and development (R&D), although some innovations may occur as the result of good fortune or inspiration, it is generally the case that the main sources of new product inventions and innovations occur in the richer, more developed economies. The observation that R&D expenditure is concentrated more in some countries than in others may be due to the existence of effective and long-running product patents, favourable tax structures, or the availability of specialist equipment in the particular country, all of which lead to a relatively R&D-abundant environment.

Vernon argues that because innovation is a risky undertaking, only rich firms will be able to afford to run product development programmes. Such risks can be reduced, by proximity to the market. This explains why the development of the good should occur in the innovating country.

As the product and the manufacturing process become more standardised and any product patents run out, manufacturers in other countries will attempt to enter the market, especially if such countries possess more favourable factor endowments which give them a cost advantage over the original producer.

Vernon then proposes that the original firm, which developed the new product, will seek to keep up production facilities in other countries in order to benefit from possibly more advantageous prices.

If the technology for the new product becomes completely standardised, so that relatively unskilled labour may be used in its manufacture, the production base may well switch to relatively lower labour-cost nations. Moreover, it may be the case not only that factor inputs are less expensive abroad, but that greater scale economies from longer production runs may be obtainable as well through the allocation of component production and assembly to different plants. Thus, production may come from newly established domestic companies in lower labour-cost countries, or from existing companies transferring production plant abroad.

At this stage, the model suggests that the foreign (less developed) country will now export this erstwhile innovated product back to the innovating (developed) country.

Vernon's product cycle hypothesis can explain trade flow and FDI as an integrated process. FDI itself, however, provides an explanation for the rapid rise in exports of manufactured goods by the NICs.

Multinational corporations generally use FDI instead of licensing technology for foreign firms since FDI allows a firm to capture all the possible rents in foreign markets. FDI allows the exercise of control over decision making in an enterprise located in one country by investors located in another. Therefore, certain access to patented and generally unavailable technology can be kept restricted, team-specific management skills can be maintained and developed, plant economies of scale and skills can be extended and the benefits of a wider recognition of a brand name can be reaped. However, disadvantages of FDI include communication problems and lack of understanding of a nation's institutions, customs and tastes. The costs and gains must be weighed up before a firm invests abroad.

Interestingly, for the Korean economy, the government decided initially to restrict foreign FDI flows conditional upon technology transfer or control of the industry staying in Korean hands. By doing this, the Korean government brought about a high degree of autonomy within Korean industry and thus the conglomerate *chaebols* and more efficient styles of management were created. Therefore, in the Korean case, the importance of FDI flows in providing the impetus for industrialisation and rapid development was somewhat restricted, although Korea relied very much upon foreign borrowing to create adequate investment funds. However, Korea's recent move, in the 1980s, into high-tech industry was very dependent upon a solid Japanese base technology.

The product cycle hypothesis seems to explain the actual East/West patterns of trade. The USA, and the West in general, import, on a large scale, consumer goods such as radios, hi-fis, televisions and video recorders from South Korea and South East Asia as a whole. The last phase in the process, when the 'pioneer' nation becomes a net importer in the mature phase, is rather controversial, since it suggests that the country, to a large degree, loses all or most of its initial advantages. But of course, due to the highly advanced technological industries of the West and the large expenditures on R&D, such advantages are not likely to disappear quickly. Indeed, the NICs still tend to be good imitators of processes and products invented in the West.

As an example, the percentage of total UK exports to the Asian region has experienced a period of slight decline, from 16% in 1983 to 14.3% in 1992 (UN, 1992).

## 12.13   Krugman's model of innovation and technology transfer

Paul Krugman (1979) developed the Vernon model of the product cycle. the basic assumptions of Krugman's model are:

1. Even if labour in two countries is equally productive in similar industries, wages will still be higher in the North due to the rent the North is able to obtain due to the monopoly position it holds in the creation of new goods.[13]

2. Innovation, which is assumed to take place only in the North, by extending the range of new goods, increases the demand for Northern goods at any given relative price. Therefore, as the relative price of Northern goods rises capital will move from South to North; assuming that capital will move until it earns the same return in both countries. Thus, due to this reallocation of capital and the relative prices of Northern goods rising, the income of Northern workers increases relative to Southern workers.

3. In the same way, technology transfer tends to shift demand towards goods produced in the South. This will cause a southwards movement of capital and the relative income of Southern workers to increase.

Thus, the model shows that technological change will be associated with capital movement, and that the region that experiences the most rapid technological advance will also experience capital inflows.

The important point Krugman makes is that, due to the technological process that causes the marginal product of capital to increase, this provides an incentive for foreign investment, the causation will only run from technological change to capital movement and will not occur the other way around.

Thus, Krugman's model implies that the decline of industries in developed countries and their emergence in the less developed countries (due to increasing levels of world technological transfer) will be a recurrent phenomenon.

The other implication of the model is that technical change is even more important than the conventional theory predicts since now developed countries must continually innovate, just to maintain their real incomes, and not simply just to maintain growth, as argued by Vernon.

Thus, Krugman suggests that technology transfer can bring about an improvement in a less-developed country's terms of trade, whereas greater success by the less-developed countries in adopting the new techniques of the developed countries, he predicts, will slow the economic growth of developed countries and may even bring about a decline in real incomes.

South Korean strategy has two aims: first to modernise traditional industrial activities and secondly to become more competitive internationally in upmarket, high-technology products. Moreover, by 1988 South Korea had actually started to move from the 'learner', or 'borrower of foreign technology' category, to that of 'creator of new products and processes'. This is definitely an extension of the product cycle hypothesis in the Krugman form, since this suggests that the 'imitator' eventually replaces, or at least is able to match, the 'pioneer' or other leading industrial nations in terms of producing new, high-technology products.

The implications of Krugman's model concern the distinct possibility of world economic dominance eventually accruing to the Asia-Pacific region becoming ever more likely. Clearly the transition from 'learner' to 'creator' takes some time to fully achieve, and Western industrial powers are not going to stay idle in the meantime. However, the amount of expenditure that Korea is pouring into R&D and technological education is rapidly increasing. Amsden (ibid.) finds that R&D as a percentage of GNP was 0.39% in 1970, whereas by 1986 it stood at 2% even though GDP had risen rapidly. Such investment is predicted to rise to around 5% in 2000.

Returning to Vernon's product life cycle hypothesis, this suggests that, in general, for industrialising countries to acquire the capacity to develop new product variations or even new products, a close relationship with developed countries is necessary. However, Amsden's view is that, 'because learning in itself turns out to be a highly creative process', especially in the case of Korea, where the country devised its own management industrial organisational structures and thus was allowed to maximise the benefits of industrialisation with a lesser degree of foreign control than otherwise could have been the case, eventually 'learners' will become 'creators' (Amsden, ibid.).

The main destination for South Korean exports is the USA, which account for 23.8% of 1992 total exports. This share has fallen dramatically from the 40% share it accounted for in 1986 (and 33.9% in 1983).

Japan was the destination for 15.2% of total South Korean exports in 1992. This proportion has also fallen quite dramatically since 1989, when Japan accounted for 21.6% of South Korean exports (19.9% in 1983).

Likewise, South Korean exports to other leading developed economies, such as Germany (3.7% of 1992 total South Korean exports, compared to 3.9% in 1988), the UK (2.4% of 1992 total, 3.1% in 1988) and Canada (2.1% of 1992 total, 2.8% in 1988, 4.1% in 1985), all show a declining trend, in comparision to the total Korean exports, over the past decade.

The share of South Korean exports to the S. E. Asian NICs or developing countries all show an increasing trend over the same period. For example, 7.6% of total South Korean exports in 1992 were exported to Hong Kong. This share has increased from 3.3% in 1983. Equally, exports to Singapore, Indonesia and Thailand accounted for 4.2%, 2.5% and 1.9% of South Korean exports in 1992; these shares have all increased from 2.3%, 0.7% and 0.8% respectively in 1988 (UN, Handbook of Industrial Statistics, 1993).

Thus, it seems reasonable to conclude from this evidence that South Korean trade with the neighbouring countries of S. E. Asia, either NICs or developing countries, in comparison to trade with the rest of the world, is becoming larger and more important as these nations become more industrialised and richer.

Indeed, 'the dynamics of intra-regional trade played a key role' in helping to protect the S. E. Asian economies from the general world recession which appeared in 1992. In fact, intra-regional trade accounted for 35% of the region's developing countries' exports in 1992 and is becoming increasingly important. Trade among developing countries grew by 23% in 1991, while their exports to the rest of the world grew by only 14.8% (Asia Development Bank, 1993).

The report suggests that intra-regional trade has generally benefited from the ongoing process of specialisation within the region, the role of FDI and the relocation of production mainly from Japan and the NICs, and in particular since 1992, from the boom in the Chinese economy. Indeed, trade by Asians amongst themselves has been growing so fast that it now exceeds Asia's trade with the USA. Moreover, it is generally recognised that China's large purchases of steel from Japan and cars from South Korea saved these industries from collapse.[14]

The Asian Development Bank (1993) argues that since 1991 there has been a trend of decline in FDI flows to the lesser developed S. E. Asian countries. For instance, in 1991, investment commitments from traditional sources, such as Japan and the NICs, fell at rates of between 20 and 60%. The possibility of the less-developed Asian economies eventually assuming the role of 'creators' would seem to be reduced. Especially in the current context of crisis and decline in Asia, the key factor bringing about the decline in intra-Asian investment commitments is due to, in terms of the product life cycle hypothesis, the decline of labour-intensive processes in the investor country, or in accordance with the Rybczynski Theorem, such processes being phased out altogether in the S. E. Asian NICs.

In general, a large proportion of intra-Asian trade is actually in sub-units of products for which the final demand is in the West. For instance, in 1991, more than half of Hong Kong's trade with its Asian partners was ultimately dependent upon the size of demand in the USA. This is because most of Hong Kong's trade with China involves processing (sub-contracting) for re-export to the USA. Moreover, Japan is a major supplier of electronic components and sub-assemblies to the Asian NICs for assembly and export, mainly to the USA. Hence, in this context, the NICs are intermediary participants in trade flows.

Indeed, as a result of the long-term rise in the yen against the dollar, which began in the late 1980s, Japanese component manufacturing declined and grew in the NICs, notably South Korea. This was due to South Korea's highly skilled workforce. This process of transference to South Korea intensified in the mid-1990s.

Early evidence of this phenomenon is provided by the general fall in the level of South Korean imports originating from Japan since 1992. The main source of imports to South Korea is Japan, but the percentage has fallen dramatically from 34% of total imports in 1986, to 18% in 1995 (UN, 1996).

## 12.14   Intra-Asian trade

A study by Muscatelli et al. (1994) focuses directly on 'intra-less developed country' competition in export markets. They focused directly on the exports of manufactures from Asian NICs, particularly the four 'tigers' of South Korea, Taiwan, Singapore and Hong Kong. Moreover, they examined the extent to which some of the newly emergent Asian economies were following these leading developing Asian economies.

Muscatelli found that the 'four tigers' have experienced a steady decline in the relative importance of 'traditional' exports and a movement towards higher technology products, while such a trend has not yet appeared in the East Asian 'late industrialising arrivals'. This pattern of specialisation and trade can be explained by the product life cycle hypothesis.

The similarity in areas of specialisation by the NICs demonstrated by Muscatelli implies that a substantial amount of intra-NIC competition must exist. This study also found that by concentrating on the elasticity of substitution between a single NIC's produced goods and its principal trading partners (mainly the OECD countries), most empirical studies ignore the effects of intra-NIC competition on NICs' exports. Muscatelli therefore put forward the view that this factor may be vital in determining the export revenues for the NICs as a whole.[15]

Moreover, Muscatelli's results show that cross-price effects in estimated models were a significant factor in determining NIC export demand. Indeed, the results show that intra-NIC competition is possibly stronger in many cases than OECD–NIC competition in world export markets. Finally, Muscatelli examined the extent of NIC non-price competition in determining market penetration. This form of competition was also found to play a significant role in determining the volume of export demand.

The implications of Muscatelli's findings suggest that if the NICs decided collectively to introduce fully outward-oriented development strategies, then perhaps the increase in employment and output that would be gained by such countries would be less than those results predicted by previous studies which ignored intra-NIC competition.

Furthermore, if a single NIC economy decided to undertake outward-oriented strategies, this would be more harmful to the other NICs rather than to the NIC-trading OECD countries, such as Europe, Japan and the USA.

Finally, this study implies that as industrial development and technology become more widely diffused from more developed economies, such as South Korea, to the emerging Asian manufacturing countries such as Indonesia, Malaysia and the Philippines and therefore as more nations join the NIC group, such cross-price effects identified by Muscatelli get stronger.

However, instead of relying purely on outward export-oriented strategies, the NICs have, at an increasing rate over the past two decades, implemented an FDI strategy directed towards the West, in order to expand markets and therefore continue their rate of development.

## 12.15    The Asian crisis: the fall and rise of South East Asian economies

During the second half of the twentieth century, various countries in South East Asia experienced different stages of growth and development. During the 1990s, the economic relationships of these countries, both internally and externally, underwent phenomenal changes. There are obviously several reasons for these economic and political changes. For instance, the political and economic relationships of China and Taiwan experienced several phases of military tension. The very uneven distribution of income and increasing poverty created racial movements in Indonesia. Frequent riots in Indonesia damaged the leadership for promoting its constructive trade cooperation within the Association of South East Asian Nations (ASEAN). Moreover, the excessive lending and corruption that occurred in Indonesia made economic relationships with other countries very unhealthy, resulting in the largest-ever International Monetary Fund bail-out package in August 1997.

The regional debt crisis also exerted additional long-lasting burdens. Similarly, several domestic problems such as elections and unemployment preoccupied Malaysia and gave less room for economic momentum. In June 1997, Anwar Ibrahim, the acting Prime Minister, cracked down on corruption in government. In South Korea, the tradition of family-owned consortia (*Chaebols*) has been experiencing an ever-increasing challenge from economic downturns and reforms urged by the public. Japan, which was a major economic power in the world for decades, also faced recession. Most Japanese blamed corrupt government officials who had been hiding the real crisis for too long. This created detrimental domino effects on the Japanese economy. Hong Kong, a financial hub in South East Asia, also suffered severe plunges in stock market values and joined the economic contagion. After two decades of sustainable boom across South East Asia, all the big economies were on the verge of collapse in the 1990s. Owing to their geographic proximity and trade linkages, the chain effect moved at catastrophic speed through the region.

## 12.16    China

### 12.16.1    Political background

China suffered heavily in terms of geography and human resources from internal civil wars, which resulted in continuous political struggles between Taiwan and the Mainland. The *Kuomintang* political party migrated to Taiwan and started its own version of Chinese civilisation. Taiwan in recent decades has displayed substantial development in economic growth and is now the biggest world producer of microcomputer chips. However, the One-China policy employed by China and other crucial members of the World Trade Organisation, including the USA, confirms the provincial status of Taiwan. This East Asian Tiger still finds it hard to develop its ambitious political status on the international stage to maximise economic gains in trade and from globalisation. China was transformed by the Cultural Revolution, the 'Four Mechanisations' and the 'Open Door Policy' engineered by Deng Xiaoping. The forward-thinking liberalisation initiated by Deng created crucial reforms to assist growth. The most obvious economic success can be seen in the coastal regions running from the north eastern part of China (Shanghai) to the south eastern provinces (Gougzhou). Economic growth increases reached double figures during the early 1990s. Despite this, most Asian economies suffered heavy downturns in the recent economic crisis, but China was largely unaffected. In July 1997, Hong Kong was a colony. It returned to Mainland China in December 1999. Macau, the former Portuguese colony, was returned to China too. These two landmark political events ended colonial power in Chinese territories. Moreover, they add impetus to the future economic development in Mainland China and achieve part of the One-China policy. Owing to colonial influence, Hong Kong and Macau evolved different systems compared with the type of socialism prevailing in China. Hong Kong is based on capitalism, Western democratic thinking and the British legal system. Owing to the vast gulf in economic life, the Hong Kong government and the UK signed a joint declaration with China in 1987 to create a political and social model, the so-called 'One Country, Two Systems', to maintain business confidence in Hong Kong. This means that China may still adopt its own socialism, while Hong Kong and Macau enjoy their own types of capitalism. This method of operating two conflicting social systems was created by Deng when he saw the need to cope with different economic development trends. The problems in Tibet and Mongolia, however, constitute barriers for China's future growth.

### 12.16.2 WTO Membership

In recent years, as economic development in China involved foreign direct investment and globalisation, the basic thrust of socialism in China was directed towards a more open and Westernised liberalisation framework. For instance, the recent success in trade talks with the USA ended the long-lasting conflicts in crucial trade issues. For example, cotton products are still a highly problematic area for the USA and China. The USA practised import restrictions and allowed certain import quotas for Chinese exports to protect the domestic garment manufacturing industry and the cotton producing industry. The USA has always complained that the communist system of food distribution and agricultural cooperation units blocks market entry for American suppliers. China's successful application to join the WTO signifies that China must open trade sectors for foreign countries and fulfil its responsibilities in accordance with WTO multilateralism. In recent years, global development in the telecommunications network and microcomputer Internet applications have been advancing at an unprecedented pace. In 1998, European countries carried out large-scale liberalisations in the telecommunications market and received large inward investment. This facilitates economic growth and rising living standards. The Chinese government saw the potential in this area and globalisation has been a norm for sustainable success. Hence a more open attitude was used in negotiating WTO membership. Indeed, future development in China in many trading areas is expected to see much foreign participation. Many infrastructural investment programmes may bring in more foreign expertise and better project management. Within banking and financial institutions, the biggest challenge will be to open up foreign exchange markets. Undoubtedly, farm income may be one of the biggest worries for China in getting WTO membership. Many Western countries which depend on farming significantly still practise trade restrictions. This is why the Common Agricultural Policy has been the most crucial issue for trade talks between member countries within the EU. On the other hand, if Chinese farmers foresee intense competition from other countries, they may upgrade production and invest more capital to become more competitive. This may be a positive feedback for Chinese farming. As China is huge in terms of population and geography, a better organisation for planting, distributing and storing food products is vital. Government subsidies are unavoidable. However, with the forthcoming WTO member status, this type of public funding may violate WTO rules and will become impossible in the longer term. Each year, unpredictable diseases, severe climatic changes or the regular flooding of the Yellow River destroys massive amounts of farmland and this interrupts normal food supplies. WTO membership is important to China, especially now when it is experiencing rapid economic growth. Indeed, China's membership is important for other well-developed economies such as the USA and the EU. Without China, which currently represents one-fourth of the world's population, the benefits of world trade cannot be said to be truly redistributed to the world market. Thus trade talks can be regarded as a successful outcome of political and economic tensions.

### 12.16.3 Internal inefficiency

To tackle national inefficiency, many developing countries have been engaged in large-scale investment for infrastructural development. For instance, to protect the rich farmland along the Yangtze River and other riverbed areas of the Yellow River, China is building the largest dam in the world, investing £20 billion. In recent years, the Chinese government has actively promoted home ownership and national banks provide mortgage services with relatively low interest rates for the public. This improves living standards and reduces brain-drain problems among the better educated. In China, compared to neighbouring countries, especially the developed countries, the labour-intensive phenomenon still prevails. At the operational and manufacturing levels, market power is driven by cheap labour. Low (labour) cost production in China results in larger profit margins for bigger scales of reinvestment and in turn attracts more FDI. This is an opportunity for China to experience increases in productivity to enhance general efficiency. Liberalisation of trade in China improves labour productivity. However, unskilled labour is still abundant. This means that low-cost labour-intensive activities remain crucial to economic development in China. It does not follow that capital-intensive economic activities are impractical in China. In fact, they are essential to the overall infrastructural efficiency. For example, although natural resource supplies in China are abundant, efficiency in producing electricity and natural gas is relatively low. Foreign investment in these areas should foster the development of the power supply industry. Moreover, corruption among government officers has been very serious. *Guanxi*, which literally means relationship, is often regarded as crucial for success. This traditional custom in Chinese society could be the most difficult barrier for the economy in moving towards a genuine open economic system. Indeed, this custom is the fundamental cause of inefficiency at every level across different sectors in China.

Since the mid-1990s, China has been actively transforming its economic structure. Zhu Rongji, the present Prime Minister, is eager to address new initiatives for promising reforms. When he took charge of the Chinese government, he focused on WTO membership, constructive market liberalisation and home ownership, and treated technological advance as the backbone of the future Chinese society. On the production side, to bring earnings in line with world manufacturers, preferential tax breaks were removed to increase government revenues. For instance, the government aims to improve infrastructural standards to raise international competitiveness. Domestically, there will be increased government expenditure on welfare. The direct effect will be a slowdown in capital inflows in certain low-margin economic activities. In substantial infrastructural programmes, foreign investments may still earn profitable margins as in transportation, computer equipment and the telecommunications industries. Capital inflows are likely to stay high. WTO membership will more than offset the slowdown of inflows due to the elimination of tax breaks. In fact, these preferential tax concessions may soon become a barrier to trade. Moreover, the Chinese authorities will use a range of reforms for taxation. For instance, they will focus on eliminating tax evasion by foreign companies. These measures are crucial for China to prepare a desirable business environment for (WTO) liberalisation processes to transpire.

## 12.17　Japan

As the Asian crisis rumbled on, Japan suffered deeper and deeper economic setbacks. Owing to its economic leadership in the region and because it is the world's largest creditor, several major and G7 countries urged the Japanese government to take steps to improve the economic atmosphere in the region. During the first quarter of 1998, Japan was reluctant to take action and indeed its internal economic stagnation was worrying. Since Japan suffered a serious credit crunch, these incidents created hard times for internal adjustments between money, labour and product markets simultaneously. Given that there was no sign of recovery in Japan in early 1998, external problems in other economies were of lower priority. In fact, when a booming nation suddenly fell from grace, the aftershocks would take time to restore fragile equilibrium in various markets. Like other Asian countries involved in the financial crisis, the economic bubble burst and rationalisation gradually started. This is a natural sequence. Despite this economic logic, Japanese economic performance picked up more slowly than expected. There were some key underlying factors. First, when other Asian countries sought ways to get out of the debt trap, regional demand still remained low; this normally represents around 40% of Japanese exports. The poor intra-regional trade volume resulted in slower growth in exports. Secondly, the adjustment in labour markets created a lack of confidence. The reluctance was the outcome of the chain effects of bankruptcies and downsizing practices. Thirdly, price-cutting effects are limited by anti-dumping policies in foreign countries. Thus the American government warned Japan and other steel producer nations to avoid dumping. Without doubt, Japanese consumers benefit from decreasing prices and the rise in real purchasing power. But the low marginal propensity to consume could not create sustainable growth in recession. Given these potential detrimental effects, surprisingly the Japanese government raised VAT by 2% in 1997. However, the vicious cycle continued in Japan. Even though large-scale expansionary policies were employed, they were slow-acting. The root of these economic problems seems to remain partly unsolved.

Declining price levels in Japan enabled policy makers to utilise strategic inflation to pull the economy out of the doldrums by means of an expansionary policy. In July 1998, the Economic Planning Agency (EPA) in Japan suggested monetary laxity to ease the credit crunch in Japan. Before the crisis, interest rates were low in Japan and the process of money creation via lending within the society was discouraged. The process relied heavily on overseas investment and loans. After the crisis, monetary expansion brought down real interest rates, which helped to stimulate domestic investment, thus stimulating growth. The cost of expansionary monetary policy is higher inflation and the creation of future inflationary expectations. Ironically, the lowered general price levels caused by bearish economic trends provided a buffer absorbing the unfavourable impacts of supply shocks. In fact, this is what the EPA hoped to test in the 'coordinated inflation' strategy (Matsunaga, 1998).

At the start of 1999, the Japanese economy was viewed as stagnant and the marginal propensity to spend was low. The government initiated a plan to bolster the multiplier effect within the economy by giving cash to taxpayers. This policy is primarily aimed at the middle classes to boost spending. Unfortunately, the plan failed and most people put the money into bank accounts. However, tax cuts have a direct impact by increasing purchasing power, though this is still subject to the degree of permanent income expectation. Equally likely, however, is a persistent reluctance to spend. What is more harmful is the reluctance to lend, which hinders long-term development. Ironically, the chicken-and-egg problem of creditworthiness versus demand effects emerges.

## 12.18   Other Asian economies

The 1997 debt crisis in South East Asia created enormous effects in the region. The crisis started in Thailand when the Baht, the official currency, could no longer maintain its peg with the US dollar. The exchange rate system was unable to hold the value of the Baht as bad debt accumulated to more than $90 billion. The trigger point was the loans to the property market where ambitious investors thought that there were good opportunities. However, the market was not sustainable and they failed to produce sufficient profits to cover their loans. The debt-laden phenomenon spread quickly to other sectors and within the financial institutions. Share prices plunged as foreign investors responded by repatriating funds. The crisis eventually emerged when high interest rates and currency controls failed to work. This resulted in devaluation of the Thai Baht and a rescue plan initiated by the International Monetary Fund. Creditors of Thai businesses came from investment banks and financial institutions across the region, especially Japan, South Korea, Malaysia and Indonesia. Hence, the chain effects dispersed quickly like a game of dominoes. Liquidation and bankruptcies followed, which created high levels of unemployment. For instance, Japan, a country used to having low unemployment levels with a tradition of lifetime employment systems, experienced around 6% unemployment.

The debt crisis resulted in serious currency discounting effects within the region. The Malaysian Ringit collapsed despite a $61.9bn support programme. The government response was to float the Ringit. The problems of financial weaknesses in South Korea had accumulated for a period of time well before Thailand's debt crisis. The exchange rate significantly depreciated from March 1997. After a series of rising bankruptcies and mounting foreign debt caused by its poor performance in sales and exports, the problem of stagflation reached its peak in November 1997. The stock market plummeted and the IMF eventually offered a rescue package. The cumulated job losses by January 1998 were reported at half a million. In Japan, the effects felt resulted in economic confidence sinking to its lowest point when the exchange rate for the Japanese Yen against the US dollar dropped below 125 Yen in February 1998. However, in terms of the exchange rate system, the Japanese Yen is flexible. This prevents the economy from continuous overheating or undergoing long depressions. Financial shocks automatically adjust via the depreciation and appreciation of exchange rates and increased interest rates. By contrast, the crawling peg exchange rate system is primarily fixed against other international currencies, and is vulnerable to speculation in foreign exchange markets. For instance, the Hong Kong dollar suffered from serious speculative attacks by an American consortium in 1997. There were rumours about devaluation of the Chinese currency as well as the Hong Kong dollar. This resulted in government intervention and US$15 billion of foreign reserves were used to avoid heavy selling in the stock market in August 1997. The natures of the flaws causing economic failure in the region are different. However, on the whole, the Asian debt crisis shows that there is a need for comprehensive financial reforms. International organisations such as the IMF were urged to monitor the standards of international capital flows and to assess members' commitment to improve financial systems. Undoubtedly, the Asian crisis stemmed from Asian capitalism. On one hand, speculators like to see fluctuations in market performance because this provides profitable scope to seek gains. On the other hand, interventionists are afraid to see dramatic upturns and downturns which affect stability. These tensions are basically contradictory within a free-trade market system. What is needed is healthy global capitalism with effective international measures to monitor capital flows and risk assessment exercises. At the national level, government or supervisory authorities should pay close attention to private capital flows to increase transparency and to maintain financial probity. Flawed government policies are certainly crisis initiators. However, investors, speculators and other market participants should accept responsibility for their decisions. Indeed, after a long period of economic boom, they may forget how to carry out sensible risk judgements, assess liquidity and other crucial criteria for measuring prices. These are key factors leading to the fragile nature of Asian capitalism in the past decade.

After the Asian debt crisis, the resulting impacts on the region and other economies are serious. Within the region, recessionary pressures have been mounting. Trade surpluses were becoming important to ASEAN members. In 1997, the surplus for South Korea and the other four member nations reached $30 billion. In 1998, the corresponding figure exceeded $70 billion. The deflationary effects in the region worsen current accounts. The current account figures were expected to deteriorate by more than $100 billion between 1997 and 1999 in the USA. The corresponding data for the EU and Japan are $47 and $34 billion respectively (Chote, 1998). Moreover, as the expected demand for oil in South East Asia will continue to slow down, oil prices in the US reached their lowest benchmark of $12 a barrel in 1998q2 as compared with its peak $26+ a barrel in 1996q4. This reduction in oil prices helped lots of industries, particularly consumers in the USA, which offset trade deficits. However, as the largest importers are Continental Europe and Japan, the real beneficiaries are other non-American petroleum users. Owing to the higher import prices in Japan caused by the falling exchange rate against the US dollar, corresponding gains fell. To prevent the declining oil price and profit, Saudi Arabia, Mexico and Venezuela responded by asking oil-producing countries to cut back production. The agreement partly succeeded and now oil prices are pushing to $30 a barrel.

In terms of interest rate regimes, as a recessionary atmosphere and low inflationary expectations were clouded in the region, there are likely to be long periods of low interest rates across the region. This will ensure a relatively low exchange rate against the US dollar. The declining exchange rates recorded in East Asian countries, in theory, should have created a bounce-back effect for their trade volumes and industry performance. This was because Asian products became more price competitive and export booms were expected. In reality, there were daunting obstacles. For instance, despite the Indonesian Rupiah depreciating by 80%, trade data continued to decline in early 1998. This was largely because of the acute shortage of credit in the region as the debt crisis erupted. In most cases, foreign suppliers refused to ship oil supplies unless they received letters of credit issued by foreign banks. The currency devaluation was so deep that business confidence in Asian traders was completely destroyed and credit became crucial. The unexpected blows to export trade further hindered the recovery of the debt-laden economies. In response to this credit crisis, different Asian economies took different measures to correct the severity. In South Korea, the government urged its central bank to provide more loans to small businesses and discussed with foreign banks how to reschedule loan payments to ease the liquidity problems of domestic exporters. In Indonesia, the central bank gave assurance for letters of credit refused by commercial banks. The most effective way to restore confidence and safeguard imports of essential supplies is to offer foreign exchange guarantees from the central bank. In rescuing joint ventures in Thailand, Japan provided funds to Thailand's Export-Import Bank. In Korea, mountains of debt in large Korean conglomerates resulted in bigger barriers preventing an export boom. As Korean production relies heavily on imported components and equipment, as the rising demand due to devaluation accelerates sales, costs of production rise more than proportionally. The net effect results in losses. Does it mean that the theory is wrong or that something strange was happening in the region? There was a modest recovery shortly after the blow, but the degree of advancement was not as dramatic as believed. Some industries enjoyed better prospects, especially those relying on domestic raw materials and engaging in primary production, for instance the rubber plantations in Indonesia and Malaysia. Thailand's rice and sugar industries experienced relatively higher exports. The crisis, therefore, enabled income redistribution across different sectors in the world. As textile production in Thailand became cheaper after the crisis, rivals such as China and Vietnam were believed to lose orders to Thai production. Needless to say, a similar effect occurred in the USA and European countries. According to the law of one price and the theory of purchasing power parity, when Asian products become cheaper, consumers in importing nations should eventually enjoy better prices. An export boom is expected over the medium term across South East Asia. This should provide better cash flows. As in the case of Korean industries such as car manufacturing and electronic sectors, cost cutting seems to be vital for survival. Korean industries should find ways to outsource supplies from cheaper locations. Moreover, an alternative to cost cutting is to improve productivity by providing redundancy packages for unnecessary staff. Cutting back on staff results in higher unemployment, which has been common across South East Asia in recent years. In South Korea, company unions used to be very powerful in protecting the welfare of unionised labour, but have failed recently to avoid job losses. The unemployment rate in South Korea jumped by more than 100% within six months of the crisis, from 2.3% to 4.7%. In Indonesia and Thailand, low levels of unionisation reduced the chances of constructive negotiations. According to the International Labour Organisation (ILO), the sharp rise in unemployment may create social unrest (Ridding and Taylor, 1998). These are indeed very important negative externalities. The potential social cost is huge. Even in Hong Kong, financial turmoil resulted in massive unemployment, reaching 6% in 1998. The Hong Kong government used to avoid interventionism to create a welfare state. However, since the crisis emerged, income support policies were established to ease public tensions. This creates social protection. In many Asian countries, this type of redistribution of income via the tax system is still not the norm. Owing to lagged effects of the crisis, downturns in some major industries may be recorded soon. There have been a series of casualties within the region. Cathay Pacific, a favoured carrier in Asia, eventually reported its first loss since 1963. Like other airlines, Cathay benefited from low oil prices, but it was unable to avoid downsizing. In 1998, Cathay cut staff levels by 12.5%. Similarly, in order to maintain a competitive position, Singapore Airlines slashed prices after the regional crisis. Singapore is the least affected city within the region. This is due to its sound financial structure and the high transparency of its financial system. During 1998–99, Singapore bypassed Hong Kong as the most attractive city for foreign investment and the busiest container port in the world. Its favourable factors supporting this outcome are efficiency, reliable insurance, quality management and maturity of financial infrastructures. However, links to the crisis were under-reported. Aggregate loans to the regional five, namely, Indonesia, Malaysia, Korea, Thailand and the Philippines, were £14.6 billion, disregarding the amount lent to Singaporeans who eventually invested in these hard-hit economies (McNulty, 1998).

Another Asian Tiger which largely weathered the debt crisis is Taiwan. It suffered currency devaluation by around 20% and falling share prices at the onset of the currency turmoil. Taiwan was able to experience overall growth of more than 4%. This shows that Taiwanese consumers were resilient and relatively optimistic. This is in sharp contrast to Japan in terms of economic atmosphere and consumer demand. There are reasons for these differences. In recent years, Taiwanese society has carried out much infrastructural investment, such as the express rail links and an underground mass transit system. This constructional boom was more or less like the Japanese fiscal expansionary policies used in the past two decades. Job prospects were healthy and unemployment was kept low, despite corruption. Hence, the marginal propensity to consume in Taiwan was relatively high and stable, which helped economic growth and sustainability. Regarding the technology cycle, the Taiwanese economy was in the early stages. Replacements needed for technological advance and equipment were ever-increasing. This fostered growth with increasing orders and investment. However, this was not the case in Japan as its technology cycle was at higher levels of maturity. For instance, Japan had more advanced and mature telecommunications. In microcomputers, electronics and electricals and other heavy industrial sectors, Japan was advanced. Thus investment was not necessary and there was excess capacity.

A key feature of the turmoil was the capital flight conducted by Western firms. The aggregate corporate investment from the top ten acquiring countries exceeded US$217 billion in 1997, with US$59.8 billion spent by the USA and US$53.0 billion used by UK companies (Harris and Ford, 1998). According to some market reports, some assets in the region were sold at a rate of discount equivalent to replacement cost values. This was because some companies suffered deeply in the slump. Corporate funds were urgently needed and vital for restructuring; hence, firms traded at low prices. This crisis stimulated global merger and acquisition activities. Obviously, hard-hit economies dogged by the liquidity crisis were unable to provide funds for inward corporate acquisitions. Thus Western companies continued acquiring assets while the intra-regional corporate acquisitions kept falling. For instance, investment funds for inward M&A were US$4.78 billion in 1996 for Japan. The corresponding statistic plummeted to US$800 million in 1997. Owing to this severity and turmoil in Korea and Thailand, foreign buyers concentrated on acquisitions. For instance, Yamaichi was acquired by a Taiwanese financial corporation in early 1998. In terms of business strategies, the turmoil in South East Asia provided a golden opportunity for aggressive investors to expand. In other words, it assisted the globalisation process.

Shelter is a basic necessity which represents a significant proportion of a society's asset values and household spending. Since the early 1990s, countries across South East Asia have experienced staggering increases in housing asset values. This was first seen in Japan, and then in Hong Kong, Singapore and Kuala Lumpur. Soaring prices are significant for income redistribution processes. Spillover effects from the property sector to others are essential for overall credit creation systems. An overheated property sector is a crucial symptom of deep economic crises. This is because escalating house prices favour speculation and reckless transactions in the market. When speculative motives focus on an industry, there is no sensible judgement on prices, returns and risks. The prices created by excessive speculation are unsustainable equilibria which consist of too many uncontrollable elements. In most cases, properties were bought via mortgages which needed loans and income streams to support repayments. If speculators took up a large proportion of the market, the long-run cost (risk) of buying an asset, by a non-speculator user who needs a shelter, rapidly increases. This is simply because speculators care only about short-term prospects. This creates a divergence in market expectations (expected equilibria) and overvalued assets. This is why an overheated economy is so vulnerable to any economic shocks. The 'property bubble' burst in these booming markets as the debt crisis emerged in late 1997. The resulting effects were large volumes of bad debts and liquidations as properties became 'negative assets'. This means that mortgage payments far exceed the resale market values. In Hong Kong, the crisis produced an asset plunge of more than 50% in property prices. In Japan, the property market was also seriously damaged, particularly in Tokyo. There, many discounted office blocks were acquired by foreigners.

## 12.19    Asian world economic dominance?

As the NICs develop and concentrate on more technically advanced products instead of traditional labour-intensive goods, rising wages may mean that some potential exports became uncompetitive. This, in turn, benefits the lesser developed nations who possess a comparative advantage in the production of labour-intensive goods. The comparative advantage of low wages thus seems to be an increasingly transitory phenomenon. The loss of the South East Asian NICs' original comparative advantage in producing labour-intensive manufactured goods is shown by the fact that in 1964, 82% of these countries' manufactured exports to the developed world were classified as low-technology products and only 2% as high-technology. As these countries acquired more technical knowledge and wages have risen, the low-technology proportion of exports fell to 53% in 1985 and high-technology exports rose to 25% (NICs OECD, 1988).

Indeed, the momentum of innovation within the leading NICs is altering the position of some industries in the product cycle, since they are moving from obsolete or standardised product manufacture to the new product manufacturing phase. The product cycle hypothesis effectively accounted for the dynamics of the OECD–NIC relationships in the 1970s but is no longer appropriate for interpreting trade flows. Some industries that had been relocated in the NICs, such as textiles and electronics, are beginning to move back to certain OECD countries (as factor endowments, i.e. mainly a cheap labour supply, become less favourable). The reversal has been further intensified by the appearance of direct investment flows from the NICs towards the OECD countries, e.g. investment in the advanced countries by Korean and Taiwanese producers of consumer electronics or automobiles in order to obtain direct access to markets or to circumvent trade barriers.

McDermott (ibid.) argues that since 1986 the South Korean electronics industry has completely revamped its thinking towards marketing strategies for the European market. It can be assumed that the same process is occurring in other industries, which are also facing high levels of competition from neighbouring, less developed South East Asian nations.

As South Korea and the other NICs continue to invest in Europe and the USA, the international market supply from these Asian nations has fallen. For example, South Korean exports of television picture tubes (SITC 7761), after increasing from a value of $624m to $780m, then to $940m in 1989, 1990 and 1991 respectively, fell to a value of $886m in 1992 (UN, 1992). This period, 1991–92, coincides with a particularly heavy Korean investment phase in Europe and in the UK.

Equally, owing to the relatively low-tech foreign product competition, South Korean domestic production is becoming more focused on high-value-added branded products. In order words, price differentials between South Korea and the OECD countries are falling, conforming to the Rybcynski theorem, because this expenditure on promotion of brands has greatly increased so as to attempt to create global brand-awareness.

With respect to FDI flows, the UK is the leading European recipient of NIC investment, especially from South Korea and Taiwan, mainly as a result of the UK's flexible labour market. For example, the four leading Korean *chaebol* have been very active in the UK. Hence, in 1994, Samsung decided to invest £450m in an electronics plant in Billingham. The same company announced in 1996 that it had plans to expand its empire into car manufacture by building a plant in Europe. Moreover, Lucky Goldstar plans to invest £1.5bn in the UK, in a semiconductor and consumer electronics plant, and Daewoo are planning to team up with Texas Instruments to build a £700m microchip plant in Northern Ireland. Furthermore, Hyundai is planning to open a British microchip plant costing £850m.

Likewise, in November 1995, the Taiwanese Chunghwa group announced plans for a £260m development in Lanarkshire which will produce television tubes. The Asian crisis has put a brake on these developments but some are going ahead.

The IMF World Economic Outlook (1995) argues that the output growth of the developing countries of the world has consistently been higher than that of the developed world since the mid-1960s. Average GDP per capita rates for the Asian NICs, for example, are around 6%. Those for the OECD members are approximately 2%. However, as these NICs and more 'less developed' nationals of the world continue their development, and as their population increases as opposed to the general decrease in the developed world, this output growth gap is expected to widen.

Currently, the industrialised countries of the world produce around 58% of the world's output and developing countries produce around 40%. An output estimate by the IMF for 2004 puts the developing countries on 48% and the industrialised world on 47%.

These are purely estimates and, even if such rates do materialise, the IMF argues that output per head and standards of living will still tend to be lower in Asia on average than those of the industrialised world. However, the more advanced developing economies, Asian NICs, certainly should have achieved OECD standards of living by then. Thus, they will cease to be 'industrialising countries'. Their views will certainly have to be taken into account at G7 meetings and the West may lose the economic power it has held for the past two centuries. In certain areas the West will actually be 'learning' from these newly developed Asian economies.

This does not mean that the West should fall behind in the economic development race. The development of technology and innovation has been emphasised particularly by the OECD countries, so that their comparative advantages in high-tech industries may be strengthened. Although this comparative advantage will certainly be reduced and indeed equalled by various Asian 'newly developed' countries, the West will still provide substantial competition for the Asian-Pacific region. Indeed, the West stands to benefit greatly from the ever-increasing Asian consumer spending power and demand for improvements to existing as well as development of new infrastructures.

The Asian growth miracle was not based on economic bubbles or financial bubbles in recent years. It has its supporting factors as shown by the Korean case study, including education, higher saving rates, skilful labour forces, FDI, R&D programmes and other desirable government policies. During the debt crisis, various Asian countries suffered different levels of losses, largely depending on the level of prudence in terms of provision of loans. Among the Asian Five, South Korea, Thailand and Indonesia suffered the most, while the Philippines and Malaysia weathered the crisis with their more prudent lending systems. Strangely enough, there are also distinctive internal factors contributing to severe downturns, such as reluctance to spend in Japan, property speculation in Hong Kong, threat of devaluation in China, production inefficiency in South Korean large conglomerates, etc. The devaluation of the currencies of these countries resulted in a serious credit crunch. Some countries even suffered more shortly after currency devaluation, as evident in South Korea. However, most of them were picking up later, at various paces. Those initially hit hardest rebounded by a bigger magnitude. The speed of recovery was also stimulated by many acquisitions of bargain assets which injected funds into different sectors facing financial difficulties. Indeed, Western acquirers and Asian companies which were on the edge of collapse mutually benefited from this rationalisation process. More importantly, the debt crisis was so timed that it helped to slow down the overheated US economy as Asian demand slipped away dramatically. Entrepreneurs across the region are flexible in adapting to change. To a large extent, these debt-laden nations have undergone a satisfactory recovery and they are trying to establish more sustainable prosperity. To catch up with the globalisation process and technological advances, various designated programmes were initiated. The explosive Internet growth has already migrated into the Asian region from North America, and so have the induced bubbles. This may be a big test of the effectiveness of Asian financial systems if they can maintain prosperity after liberalisation and transformation since the crisis.

## Summary

- The view that economic growth must occur via import substitution – and the pessimism about economic development that spread as import-substituting industrialisation seemed to fail – have been confounded by the rapid economic growth of a number of Asian economies. These high-performing Asian Tigers have industrialised via exports of manufactured goods. They are characterised both by very high ratios of trade to national income and by extremely high growth rates. Some point to the fact that, while they do not practise free trade, they do have lower rates of protection than other developing countries. Others assign a key role to the interventionist policies pursued. Research suggests, however, that the roots of success may lie largely in domestic causes, especially high savings rates.

- The high-growth Asian Tigers experienced a severe decline in incomes in the debt crisis. This disappeared to some extent by 1999, though low growth seems to have enveloped Asian's star economy of Japan. In most 'Tiger economy' cases FDI has played a significant role, as well as government subsidy strategies.

- Recent improvements in growth are lifting formerly developed economies such as South Korea out of recession. However, in all Tigers, higher levels of unemployment are a new economic characteristic of the millennium.

## Questions

1. For at least two of the four Tiger economies, discuss the validity of the following statement: 'Foreign Direct Investment has proved essential for economic success in South East Asia.'

2. For any of the Tigers, assess the claim made by Young, Krugman and others that the only remarkable feature of the high rates of investment was that the investment was not in Research and Development.

3. Assess the validity of the following assertion: 'The Tiger economies' success is primarily the result of their success in implementing *import*-substituting rather than *export*-promoting policies.'

4. Analyse the view that the high levels of economic growth enjoyed by SEA countries prior to 1997 constitutes support for the arguments of those economists who argue that government intervention in national economies should be kept to a minimum.

5. Assess the validity of the following claim: 'The economic crisis of 1998–9 was a direct result of poor lending decisions made by South East Asian banks in 1997–8.'

### Key concepts

| | |
|---|---|
| Tiger economy | capital transfers |
| import substitution | Foreign Direct Investment (FDI) |
| technology and growth | |

## Notes

1. In this example, people living on the Asian continent (including Japan), east of Iran but outside the former Soviet Union.

2. The OECD countries comprise the leading industrialised economies of the world. The main purpose of this group is to achieve sustainable economic growth and employment in member countries.

3. However, many NICs like Japan have invested heavily in the West, especially in the UK and the USA, as a means to jump over tariffs and other trade restrictions that may be imposed by the West in retaliation against Asian governmental intervention, e.g. via tariffs and subsidies, in protecting industry from Western trade.

4. With the aptly named 'Revised Foreign Capital Inducement Law'.

5. Policies were also introduced to increase interest rates on savings, which previously, due to actually quite low rates, were leading to a low saving ratio. This meant that South Korea was becoming very dependent upon foreign borrowing to finance much of its investment expenditure (NIC:OECD, 1988).

6. In the famous English/Portuguese, Cloth/Wine example of comparative advantage.

7. Indeed the British textile industry suffered a very similar decline over approximately the same time period.

8. Although, of course, relative country size and particularly US dollar exchange rates must be taken into consideration.

9. However, Iraq's invasion of Kuwait brought windfalls, even if only temporary gains to the country.

10. i.e. no ambiguity exists about which is the labour-intensive good and which the capital-intensive good.

11. World Review (1991); in the Asian-Pacific region, the Korean worker is renowned for being hard-working, even more so than the Japanese.

12. The simultaneous import and export of similar goods.

13. Old goods are assumed to be those developed some time ago, thus their technology is common property and therefore they can be produced in any country, developed (Northern) or less-developed (Southern). New goods are those which have been recently developed and therefore can only be produced in the developed country.

14. See Asian survey, *The Economist*, 30 October 1993.

15. Even if additional cross-price elasticity of substitution terms were added to allow for this, Muscatelli suggests that other types of intra-NIC competition, which do not necessarily show through the additional price variable, such as commodity comparison effects (i.e. changes in the technological composition of commodities) and changes in the quality of the product, may not be accounted for fully.


## Bibliography

Amsden, A. (1989) *Asia's Next Giant; South Korea and Late Industrialisation*, New York: Oxford University Press.

Asian Development Bank (1993) *Asian Development Bank Handbook*, vol. 15.

Asian Development Bank (1993) *Asian Development Outlook*, Oxford: Oxford University Press.

Chote, R. (1998) 'Asia's financial crisis is forecast to have long knock-on effect', *Financial Times*, 9 April, p. 4.

GATT (1993) 'International Trade Statistics', *GATT Handbook*, Geneva: GATT.

Harris, C. and Ford, J. (1998) 'Asian Pacific countries attract bargain hunters', *Financial Times*, 19 January, p. 22.

IMF World Economic Outlook (1995) *World Economic Outlook 1996*, Washington DC: International Monetary Fund.

Jenkins, R. (1995) 'The political economy of industrial policy: automobile manufacture in the newly industrialising countries', *Cambridge Journal of Economics*, vol. 19, pp. 625–45.

Krugman, P. (1979) 'A model of innovation, technology transfer and the world distribution of income', *Journal of Political Economy*, vol. 87, no. 2.

Matsunaga, S. (1998) 'Editorial: Study idea of strategic inflation', *The Daily Yomiuri*, 18 July, p. 6.

McDermott, M. (1992) 'The industrialisation of South Korea and Taiwanese electronic industries: the European dimension', in S. Young and J. Hamill (eds), *Europe and the Multinationals: Issues and Responses for the 1990s*, Aldershot: Edward Elgar.

McNulty, S. (1998) 'Singapore's strengths keep it from turmoil', *Financial Times*, 9 February.

Muscatelli, V., Stevenson, A. and Montagna, C. (1994) 'Intra-NIE competition in exports of manufactures', *Journal of International Economics*, vol. 37, pp. 29–47.

OECD (1988) *Newly Industrialising Countries – OECD Report*, 1988, Paris: OECD.

Ridding, J. and Taylor, R. (1998) 'ILO warns of social unrest risk in Asia', *Financial Times*, 16 April, p. 4.

The Economist (1993) 'Asian Survey', *Economist*, 30 October.

The World Bank (1993) 'The East Asian Miracle', *World Bank Review*.

The World Bank (1992) *World Bank Report 1992*.

United Nations (1993) *Handbook of Industrial Statistics, 1992*, Industrial Development Organisation, New York: UNIDO.

United Nations (1993) *International Trade Statistics Yearbook 1992*, New York: UNIDO.

United Nations (1996) *UN Statistical Year Book*, New York: UN.

United Nations (1999) 'World Resources', *UN Statistical Year Book 2000*, New York: UN.

World of Information (1991) *The World and Business Review 1991*. Oxford: Blackwell.

World Investment Report 1997, vol. 15, New York.

# 13 Transition economies

## K. LAWLER and A. O. MOSCARDINI

With the collapse of communism in the former Soviet Union between 1989 and 1992 came 22 former Soviet republics experiencing a plethora of economic ills and disadvantages. These countries were either large potential market economies such as Kazakstan and the Ukraine or smaller countries such as Kyrgyzstan in central Asia and the Baltic Republics. These economies in the Soviet era had remarkably strange trading patterns, governed by the parameters laid down by central planning. Given World Bank and IMF assistance to achieve transition and economic transformation, some progress has been made in some of the former Soviet Republics in eastern central Europe. Thus Poland, Hungary and the Czech Republic have achieved growth and opened up trade with the EU and the wider world. These three transition economies have benefited from substantial FDI from Germany and other EU states. Consequently, there are signs that trade between Hungary, Poland, the Czech Republic and the EU follows H-O-S lines in so far as exports from the Soviet economies appear to be in low-technology labour-intensive goods whereas imports tend to be in goods with human capital content such as computing hardware and digital system technologies. It could be argued that trade between the more advanced former Soviet economies and the West represents Vernon-type trading patterns given the flow of FDI or indeed Posner-type trade given clear technological gaps. However, a careful analysis of relative factor productivity in the former eastern/ central Europe Soviet Republics by Myant (1999) and Hoen (1998) shows that the former Soviet economies possess low levels of capital and labour productivity. Trading patterns therefore, abstracting from the enclaves created by substantial FDI, follow H-O-S lines.

In the poorer transition economies such as Russia, Kyrgystan and Kazakstan, trade export performance is largely dependent on natural resource-intensive activity. Exports from these countries tend to be in oil and gas, timber, semi-precious stones and gold. The poor transition economies have dependency on a narrow range of exports all of which are highly resource intensive. Imports from the West tend to be in high-tech manufactures and computing technologies. As such, these poorer transition economies are prone to the same difficulties as Kuwait in so far as world prices for their exports are governed by world supply and demand for exportable homogeneous goods. Swings in the terms of trade and bouts of rampant inflation seriously undermine the terms of trade in these countries. The case study on Kyrgyzstan indicates these features in some detail, as does that on Albania.

## 13.1 Transitional issues

Joseph Stiglitz (1999) discusses a number of fundamental issues which he considers delineate the distinguishing characteristics of the republics of the former Soviet bloc. He presents, moreover, some interesting data, which displays the economic performance of the former communist countries. These data indicate that only Poland has managed to exceed in 1999 its gross domestic product of 1989, ten years after the collapse of the Soviet system. Other 'successful' transition economies (Hungary, the Czech Republic and Slovakia) have 'nearly' recovered the levels of activity they attained in 1989. Still other transitional economies, namely Russia, the Ukraine and the Central Asian republics, have fared badly, recording massive and progressive decreases in overall activity compared to the 1989 benchmark. Stiglitz's focus of attention is Russia, which he compares with China. Stiglitz notes that China's 20-year transitional experience has delivered high export and GDP growth, whereas the ten-year experience in Russia has seen GDP fall by over 40% and industrial production reduced by 50% in the past five years. In terms of overall economic activity, China outdistanced Russia in 1992 (Stiglitz (ibid.)). Stiglitz argues that these different transitional experiences in two large countries are difficult to explain. He nonetheless concludes that Russia's failure to benefit from the Western model of market capitalism stems from the fact that there is no rule of law for the effective enforcement of commercial contracts and no legal framework encompassing the concept of bankruptcy in Russia and in other former Soviet republics. He thus concludes that the 'Washington Consensus' model of transition is inadequate.

That the transition to market capitalism has been a 'failure' in Russia is, according to Stiglitz, due to the fact that the assistance given by the West to Russia and other transition economies has been based on what he calls the 'Washington Consensus model' of functioning markets. This model of the 'market' used by agencies in the West is not appropriate for former communist states because it subsumes a concept of bankruptcy, the entry and exit of firms and price signalling. He argues that in the former Soviet states such concepts as these were never understood nor consequently applied by policy makers, managers or consumers.

Stiglitz's paper (ibid.) provides a useful background/commentary, which assists in considering three studies examined here. These three timely publications provide useful commentaries charting 'successes' and 'failures' in the former Soviet economies in Eastern Central Europe and Russia. None of the studies considered are as pessimistic in tenor as Stiglitz's paper. In particular, the volume edited by Simon Clarke consistently chides the World Bank's pessimistic view of Russian labour market performance/flexibility (pp. 9–87), and takes a sanguine view of Russia's potential for growth.

In *The Transformation of Economic Systems in Central Europe*, Hoen (ibid.) focuses on the transformation of the economic systems in Hungary, Poland, the Czech Republic and Slovakia. Given Stiglitz's benchmark, these countries are relatively 'successful' transitional economies compared to Russia and the Central Asian Republics. However, this study provides a comprehensive overview of different theoretical approaches to transformation, these being Neoclassical, Post-Keynesian and Austrian. Hoen challenges the dichotomous Shock treatment vs. Gradualism controversy, which hides the key features of the transformations from planned to market economies. Thus Hoen, considering Hungary's transformation, dubs this as 'Hidden Shock Therapy' rather than an example of gradualism. The Neoclassical Paradigm views transformations as 'invisible jumps' whereas Post-Keynesians view transformations as 'unpredictable journeys'. The Austrian evolutionary school views transitional transformations as best achieved by the slow creative destruction of former planned systems.

Thus the Neoclassical School propound policy prescriptions for transition based upon the rational behaviour of agents within the framework of the Walrasian General Equilibrium Model. However, despite the fact that Neoclassical theory is static, the approach nonetheless yields a view on economic transformations, which is that rational optimising agents will respond to newly created rules of the game and these may be successful. Thus, the Neoclassical instantaneous adjustment to stimuli by agents in this purist world results in transformations being seen as jumps from one equilibrium to another. The pace at which this can be achieved is dependent on the speed at which property rights may be transferred from the state to individuals. The choice of device for the privatisation mechanism follows the Coase Theorem, which argues that, however bad the initial distribution of property rights looks at the beginning, it always results in the most efficient method. The pre-Stiglitz World Bank view on transformations adopts this approach, as witnessed in the writings of Commander (1995).

Post-Keynesians by contrast, by rejecting Walrasian General Equilibrium and taking an historical view of time, view the transformations of former planned economies as a gradualist process given historical legacies implying irreversibility and path dependencies (Pheby, 1989).

Austrian thinking on evolutionary theories focuses on selection processes, entry, exit and innovation which generate economic development and reject Neoclassical preoccupations with allocative inefficiency. Thus the Austrian evolutionists reject Neoclassical Shock Therapy as inappropriate for transitional economies, either for macroeconomic stabilisation or microeconomic restructuring. The Austrian principle of organic change views transformations as slow continuous processes (Murrell, 1991, 1992). Stiglitz (ibid.) comes very close to this perception by strongly advocating incrementalist policies for transition, based on views emanating from the classic Austrian traditions laid down by Schumpeter and Von Hayek.

*Structural Adjustment without Mass Unemployment*, edited by Clarke (1998), reviews the turbulence evident in Russian labour markets in the years of transition since 1990. The introductory article by Simon Clarke is the most useful one, because it impinges on the issues raised by Stiglitz (ibid.) and challenges the mid-1990s World Bank view that structural adjustment in Russia has been impeded by labour market rigidity caused by the hoarding of labour by worker-controlled firms. Thus Russia presents economic researchers with many challenges and paradoxes. An interesting Russian paradox explored by Clarke is this: given the collapse of Russian industrial production since 1993 and the sharp decrease recorded in GDP since 1990 (40 and 50% reductions respectively), how is it that registered unemployment in Russia in June 1997 was a mere 3.79%? Do these low rates of unemployment indicate a failure of industrial structural adjustment, which is the World Bank view, or are these rates indicators of an extremely flexible labour market? Clarke tests this paradox, whereupon the Bank's views are remorselessly undermined to the extent that they appear to be unrealistic perversions of the true state of Russia's labour market performance since 1990.

*Industrial Competitiveness in East-Central Europe*, edited by Martin Myant (1999), adopts a different perspective, in so far as the contributors seek to clarify the specific issues relating to the comparative efficiency of manufacturing in Hungary, Poland, the Czech Republic, Slovakia and East Germany. Hence it covers the 'successful' transformations. The primary pervading aim of this study is to provide an evaluation of the hypothesis espoused by the EU Commission which is that the 'success' economies in East Central Europe should have little difficulty in meeting competitive pressures caused by enlargement and integration in the EU. In challenging this proposition, the study ranges over issues relating to levels of investment, sources of growth and levels of competitiveness in regions and countries. Myant concludes that although the basic structures of the market economy are deeply rooted – and this contrasts starkly with Stiglitz's view for

Russia and the Ukraine – he counsels against a too rapid harmonisation of macro-economic conditions with the EU. Instead, they argue that in East Central Europe, the transition has not developed high-tech R&D-based activity to any significant degree, so a policy framework targeted at enhancing East Central European competitiveness in R&D-intensive activity is needed.

## 13.2   Economies in transition: Albania

### 13.2.1  Introduction

The 1990s have seen drastic developments in the countries of Central and Eastern Europe. The way the rest of the world deals and trades with these countries has also changed. This change has simultaneously brought along greater risks and new opportunities. Investigations seeking to gain insights from these opportunities, however, must conduct a thorough examination of the prevailing situation in the country in question, in order to lower potential risks. Both analysts and entrepreneurs need to take into consideration the socio-economic activities and the local production potential, as well as the institutional frameworks (trade and labour legislation, privatisation, foreign investments, etc.). This section investigates primarily the case of Albania within the general socio-economic situation of the Balkans and the prospects for cooperation with developed countries.

**Background**

The socio-economic developments observed during the past few years (1989–96) in the countries of Central and Eastern Europe have had a profound influence on the social structure of the modern world. The procedures employed in the transformation of these countries from centrally controlled economies towards open market economies have changed the way the Western countries conduct business with them. The opening up of these countries has led to the formation of a new era of economic development. At the same time, though, it led to the creation of a series of conditions that allows strategic involvement in the transformation procedures of their economies (United Nations, 1992).

The countries of the European Union, given their proximity to the area, are facing perhaps their greatest challenge in taking up direct investments in these countries. For Greece, in particular, taking into consideration its geopolitical position in the Balkans, the prospect of new markets consisting of millions of consumers lying just across its northern borders, in conjunction with the technological and economic developments that are taking place there, forms the basis of a new geoeconomic role (Bank of Macedonia and Thrace, 1995).

The needs of the new markets cover almost the whole range of the available services and products. The business world must act with both daring and prudence. Daring is needed in putting to use the comparative advantages and opportunities that exist at this point of time, while prudence must be exercised due to the economic and political situation of the country and the speed with which changes are happening. These factors create an atmosphere of great uncertainty, especially for potential investors. Consequently, direct investment must be based on careful study. Generally, in the Balkan states, special importance must be paid to the present state of the economies, as well as of the level of the existing political institutions.

Albania, a Balkan state lying to the north-western border of Greece, was the last of the centrally planned economies to move towards a market economy. After an era of both political and economic isolation that lasted decades, Albania has initiated a procedure of opening up towards the outside world (Dana, 1996). Albania is the poorest of all the countries in Europe. The per capita income is estimated to be around $340 per year. In addition, the existing regional differences are great. At the same time all the indices reflecting the social and economic infrastructure are very low (Daoulas, 1995). This section presents a detailed examination of the socio-economic identity of Albania, based on the latest developments, highlighting useful material for those entrepreneurs considering direct investment.

### Key socio-economic indicators in Albania

Albania is a relatively small country covering an area of 28,748 km$^2$, with a population of 3,256,000, of whom 36% live in urban or semi-urban areas and the remaining 64% in rural areas (1990 data) (Papas *et al.*, 1994). The population density is 114/km$^2$ (compared to Greece's 78/km$^2$) (Hellenic Export Promotion Organisation, 1995; National Statistical Service of Greece, 1994). However, Albania has the highest population growth rate compared to the rest of Europe (Economist, 1992). The rate of growth is 2.15% per year, twice as much as Poland's rate, for example. About 50% of the population is of an age less than 26 (1990 data). The high rate of population growth can be attributed to the religious composition of the country. Approximately 70% of the total population is Muslim (Ermidis and Egyptiadis, 1993). Of the remaining 30%, 20% are Orthodox and 10% are Catholics. With respect to the ethnic composition of the country, 86% are native Albanians, 12% are Greeks and 2% are other minorities.

According to the latest available data, the rate of change for the Gross National Product (GNP) was −27.7% for 1991, −9.7% for 1992, +11.0% for 1993 and +8.0% for 1994 (Daoulas, 1995). The GNP composition according to the sectors of the economy (1993 data) are: 14% for industry, 56% for agriculture, 9% for construction, 3% for transportation and the remaining 18% represent other smaller sectors. It is obvious that agriculture holds a central, if not somewhat disproportionate, position in the economy. Following the political changes of 1991, efforts have been made, not always wholly successful, to carry out transformations affecting land ownership status, cultivation and operation of the agricultural sector (Pata and Osmani, 1994).

Albania's foreign debt was $539 million in 1996 (representing 24% of the GNP). Inflation was at 18.5% p.a. in 1994 (while in 1992 it reached 236.6% p.a.). Despite this drastic decrease, attention must be paid to the especially low income of the workers and pensioners. In 1995 the average monthly salary was $48, while the average monthly pension in the cities was $25 but just $7 in the rural areas. Hence, the majority of Albanians live in conditions of poverty (Hellenic Export Promotion Organisation, 1995).

The transitional period that started in 1991 was followed by many economic and social problems. The total lack of any infrastructure caused severe problems in all fields. In 1998, for every 1000 people, there are 14 telephones installed. Until 1990, there were only 300 telex connections in the whole country (Economist, 1992). Electricity supply is, even in the big cities, at best, erratic. Environmental pollution is high and the unemployment rate is very high. According to the country's Statistical Institute, at the end of 1993 the number of the unemployed reached 467,000 people compared to the 555,000 that had employment (454,000 of these are employed in the public sector). The unemployment benefit for those ones entitled to it is $15 per month.

In 1991, the collapse of all productive sectors was total. Entire factories, that were working before the removal of the old political regime, have closed. These plants were denuded by looting (Daoulas, 1995). Albania used to export agricultural products, but now it imports about 50% of the products it needs. In 1996, trade was completely deregulated. In short, Albania is a country situated in Europe with a Third World socio-economic identity. The conditions enforced by the previous regime, in conjunction with the anarchic procedures employed in the transition to democracy and new open market rules, have contributed to this present scenario. This identity is radically different from those of the other Central and Eastern European countries with which comparison could be made (Bank of Macedonia and Thrace, 1995). Raising per capita income in Albania will be a long slow process based on large imputs of FDI.

**Productive sectors**

The productive sector of the economy has always been riddled with problems. Though Albania is, mainly, an agricultural country, its agricultural efficiency is very poor. The main products produced are wheat, corn, beans and tobacco. The respective cultivation yields, though, are very low, partly because of the present bad state of the infrastructure and partly because of the inaccessibility of the land (mountain ranges cover 76% of the total land space). The Albanian government enacted a law (1501/19.7.91) distributing to farmers land previously belonging to the state. However, the farmers faced financial difficulties and this caused difficulties in the cultivation of the acquired land. In addition, strong disagreements as to how this distribution should take place and who was entitled to it, have led to many problems, resulting in subsequent drastic production falls. The inability of existing production levels to satisfy the needs of the country can be attributed, in great measure, to this factor. The effort to distribute land lots was, nevertheless, intensified during 1993, when 92% of the land that was exploited by cooperatives and 62% of the state land was returned to the private sector. Around 86 Private Farmers' Associations (PFA) were formed in total. The average lot per farmer is now 1.5 acres (Hellenic Centre of European Studies, 1995a).

The situation in the livestock sector was better until 1989. According to the data available, in 1989 there were 699,000 cattle, 2,745,000 sheep/goats, 5,630,000 hens, 181,000 pigs and 86,000 beehives. These figures are, however, no longer true. Most of the animals were slaughtered to cover the immediate food needs of the population or because they could not be fed. The existing extensive woodlands have not, till now, been widely exploited due to technical difficulties as well as the bad road conditions through which the products would have to be transported. With respect to aquaculture sectors, despite the rich potential and the favourable laws that the government enacted in 1995, production is still non-existent.

The sector with the highest possible potential, from the production point of view, is mining. Albania has a soil rich in petrol, nickel, coal, asphalt, copper, salt, chrome (it actually holds the number three slot in world production of chrome) and natural gas. The secondary production sector is in a very weak state. During 1990–92 most of the factories closed down due to lack of materials, spare parts or available markets for the products. As a result the greater part of the workforce emigrated to Western countries (mostly to Greece). The capital stock that still remains is considered obsolete and unproductive. The industrial problems have become more acute due to the lack of specialised know-how in fields such as foreign trade, marketing and sales. Whole sectors of the economy were either destroyed or are threatened with closure (Economist, 1992). The lack of infrastructure is evident in the banking and insurance sectors too. The lack of specialised personnel is very acute.

Tourism is a significant industry in Balkan states such as Turkey, Greece and Bulgaria. In particular, the tourism industries in Turkey and Greece are performing extremely well.

**Table 13.1  Tourism expenditure by country in US$ million.**

|         | 1991 | 1992 | 1993 | 1994 | 1995 |
|---------|------|------|------|------|------|
| Albania | 3 (0.00) | 5 (0.00) | 6 (0.00) | 4 (0.00) | 5 (0.00) |
| Bulgaria | 128 (0.10) | 313 (0.21) | 257 (0.18) | 244 (0.15) | 195 (0.10) |
| Greece | 1015 (0.80) | 1186 (0.79) | 1003 (0.71) | 1130 (0.68) | 1322 (0.67) |
| Turkey | 592 (0.46) | 776 (0.52) | 934 (0.66) | 866 (0.52) | 912 (0.46) |
| Romania | 143 (0.11) | 260 (0.17) | 195 (0.14) | 449 (0.27) | 695 (0.35) |

*Source* adapted from World Tourism Organisation
Parentheses show corresponding shares in European tourism (in %)

**Table 13.2  Number of tourist arrivals by country (in 000).**

|         | 1991 | 1992 | 1993 | 1994 | 1995 |
|---------|------|------|------|------|------|
| Albania | 13 (0.00) | 28 (0.01) | 45 (0.01) | 28 (0.01) | 40 (0.01) |
| Bulgaria | 4000 (1.41) | 3750 (1.23) | 3827 (1.23) | 3896 (1.19) | 3466 (1.03) |
| Greece | 8036 (2.83) | 9331 (3.06) | 9413 (3.02) | 10713 (3.26) | 10130 (3.01) |
| Turkey | 5158 (1.81) | 6549 (2.15) | 5904 (1.89) | 6034 (1.84) | 7083 (2.11) |
| Romania | 3000 (1.06) | 3789 (1.24) | 2911 (0.93) | 2796 (0.85) | 2608 (0.78) |
| Yugoslavia | 379 (0.13) | 156 (0.05) | 77 (0.02) | 91 (0.03) | 100 (0.03) |

*Source* adapted from World Tourism Organisation
Parentheses show corresponding shares in European tourism (in %)

Both countries are in the top 20 ranking of tourist destinations. For example, Greece and Turkey rank 17th and 19th respectively in 1997. For Greece, the growth of tourism can be represented by a healthy 11% increase in arrivals and 2.1% increase in tourism receipts in 1997 compared to 1996 data. Correspondingly, the figure for the healthy growth of Turkish tourism is illustrated by the 13.5% rise in arrivals and an amazing 17.4% increase in tourism receipts in 1997. The recent trends for other Balkan states in the tourism industry are indicated in Tables 13.1 and 13.2. If Albania could develop its tourist resorts and other attractions for world travellers, the economic impact could be huge, and similar to other Balkan states.

Moreover, like other economic sectors, effective application of the communication superhighway and informational networks and other advanced technological systems are vital to the success of enhanced growth in key development projects. The economic impact of such applications, for instance the installation and comprehensive use of super-information networks, has provided real benefits for the general economic growth in various developed and emerging markets.[1]

**Foreign trade**

The lack of funds and the state of the economy in conjunction with the lack of expertise, of know-how and of specialised personnel have had an adverse effect on Albania's foreign trade. The trade deficit in 1993 reached $509 millions. Despite the fact that during 1994 the level of exports increased, the imports were four times as much. The private sector is responsible for 48% of the total volume of exports and for 78% of the imports (Hellenic Centre of European Studies, 1995a). For 1995 the available data shows a further increase in export-import data. The private sector increased its share of exports to 60% and it accounts for 82.4% of the imports. Regarding the countries to which Albania exports, Italy is the recipient of 63.48% of these, Greece 7.78%, Germany 5.97% and the USA 4.39%. The bulk of these exports cover chrome and other ore products. During the first three months of 1995, 82.15% of all the exports were directed to European Union countries (INSTAT, 1995).

Imports cover foodstuffs (23.96% of the value), machines and transport goods (24.38%), other industrial products (20.34%), and chemical products (7.95%). It must be noted that in addition to these products a large number of products arrive in the country in the form of external assistance (39.40% are foodstuffs and drinks, 33.84% are machines etc., in the first three-month period of 1995). The main countries from which Albania imports are: Italy (38.25% of the volume), Greece (23.60%), Bulgaria (10.50%) and Germany (4.48%). In total, 73.55% of Albania's imports arrive from European Union countries. Greece represents 32% of the EU's exports to Albania, with Italy at 52%. More particularly, Greece's exports to Albania increased by 242% during the 1992–93 period, whereas during the 1993–94 period they increased by another 66.11% (Agora, 1995). Greece's imports from Albania show an increase of 110.92% for the same period. The level of Greece's imports from Albania, though, is low compared to the exports there, since these represent only 13.42% of the total trade volume between the two countries. Greece exports foodstuffs, drinks, petrochemical products, machines, textile products, clothes, etc. In order to address the issues related to the organisation of foreign trade and the movement of goods, the Albanian government has enacted a series of laws and regulations. But this legal framework is in a state of constant evolution and adaptation.

**Institutional development measures**

The Albanian government, in its effort to promote the transition of the economy towards a free market, took a number of policy measures and enacted many laws aiming to create an institutional framework (trade and labour legislation, privatisation, etc.), within which economic activity could occur. Among the laws enacted were the 7512/10.8.91 on private ownership and privatisation of the state property, the 7638/19.11.92 on trade companies, and the 7703/11.5.93 on social security. The overall responsibility for the coordination of the necessary measures that have to be taken in order to privatise the state property lies in the hands of the National Organisation for Privatisation. Privatisation can take place through an auction, share selling or through distribution of the public shares. The National Organisation for Privatisation fixes the prices of the shares and organises the auctions, and at the same time supplies information with respect to the financial status of the companies to be privatised.

Despite all efforts, though, the privatisation of the big productive units in the country has been delayed. The units that attract the interest of the public are very few. Nevertheless, in 1994, 2500 small and medium companies were privatised. Of these, 33.4% were awarded to domestic investors, 41% to the employees of the companies, 25.4% to the owners of the land surrounding the buildings where those companies were housed and only 0.2% to foreign investors (Hellenic Centre of European Studies, 1995b). According to the present laws, foreigners cannot buy property but only lease the use of land (urban or rural) or a building (law 7501/19.7.91 and Ministerial Decision

365/5.10.91). The duration of the leases can be up to 99 years. Regarding social insurance, the workers in the private sector contribute 10% of their monthly salaries and employers contribute a further 26%.

### Foreign investment

It is self-evident that for the Albanian economy to get modernised and to move towards the median standard of a European free market, foreign investments are imperative. The introduction of foreign capital, know-how and expertise will revitalise those elements in the economy that will move forward the development factors leading to a vibrant economy. A number of laws were enacted with respect to foreign investments on issues such as the conditions that must be satisfied by investors wishing to start a business in Albania (7496/4.8.92 and 7764/2.11.93). Special issues related to tourism (7665/2.11.93) and to exploitation and production of petrol and natural gas (7746/28.7.93) were also addressed (Hellenic Centre of European Studies, 1995a).

Albania's legal framework, with respect to foreign investments, is complemented with legislation connected to the operation of joint ventures. This type of collaboration is particularly favourable to both Albania and Greece thanks to a bilateral agreement between the two countries. The World Bank, the International Monetary Fund and other organisations have undertaken a series of studies and are already providing the funds for a number of economic enterprises. Despite the keen interest showed by the Albanian government in attracting foreign investments and despite the very favourable legal frameworks (in fact more favourable than in any of the other Balkan states), foreign investment has occurred on rather a small scale. Albania is still a high-risk investment country. The difficulty in securing appropriate local partners, the political and social conditions alongside the long preparation periods necessary, the delays and the tendency of the Albanian state to protect the newly emerging class of domestic investors, are the main reasons for this. However, the main foreign investments have come from Italy (50%), Greece (20%), Germany (8%) and the USA (2%). The greater part of these cover industry (30%), construction (17%), agriculture and stock-breeding (10%), fisheries (7.5%), foodstuffs and drinks (13%). In 1994 the main bulk of the investment came from Canada and Italy in the fishery and telecommunications fields. Tirana has absorbed 45% of these investments with the rest being distributed in other areas (Hellenic Centre of European Studies, 1995b).

### Conclusion

Despite the low socio-economic indicators in Albania, the country is entering into a new developmental period. The strong presence and support afforded by the international community and in particular by many organisations, such as the World Bank, the International Monetary Fund, the European Union and the OECD, have contributed to the creation of favourable perceptions for the country. A number of independent international companies, after conducting extensive research in the country, conclude that Albania must be considered a strong candidate for future investments in the Balkans. International investors are, for the time being, showing signs of hesitation in undertaking large investment initiatives. Nevertheless, many of them are working on and establishing networks that will assist them in future investment plans. It can be claimed with certainty that lately there is a keen interest in investing in the country by both international bodies and private companies (Tzen, 1993). The European Union is already providing financial support for a series of investments through programmes such as PHARE and JOPP (Hellenic Export Promotion Organisation, 1995; Vlahos, 1994). In addition, the World Bank organisation

MIGA is offering insurance coverage of all investments in Albania in case of political upheavals, wars, and nationalisation.

## 13.3    Economies in transition: Kyrgyzstan

### 13.3.1  Introduction

Transitional economies have always existed but, in the past ten years, since the fall of the Berlin Wall and the subsequent collapse of the Soviet Union, many states, several of them large and potentially economically powerful, are struggling to transform from centrally planned economies to the vagaries of the free market. This is causing large oscillations in global economic dynamics. We describe the principal features of such economies and select Kyrgyzstan as a particular example.

### 13.3.2  Transitional economies

**Definitions**

It is well known from economic history that different countries, during their epoch of development, experienced processes of transition. These processes are defined as follows:

- *classical transition* (the extensions of democracy in advanced capitalist countries between 1860 and 1920);

- *neoclassical transitions* (refer to the process of democratisation in capitalist countries after World War II);

- *market-oriented reforms* in non-communist countries after World War II (South Korea and Taiwan in the early 1960s; Chile in the 1970s; Turkey and Mexico in the 1980s, etc.);

- *Asian post-communist transitions* (China since the late 1970s and Vietnam since the late 1980s) and *post-communist transition in Central and Eastern Europe*.

Comparative analysis undertaken by Balcerowicz (1995) demonstrated essential features which distinguish post-communist transition in Central and Eastern Europe from the other types. The major features are:

- Simultaneous changes in economic and political systems. Included in these changes are problems of defining territorial, social and cultural boundaries. Balcerowicz underlined the unprecedented scope of changes in Eastern and Central Europe which encompassed both political and economic systems. Such challenging widespread reforms had never happened before and were either political or economic. They brought about 'an extreme information overload for top decision-makers'.

- In spite of the largely simultaneous beginnings of political and economic reforms it is misleading to consider them as developing simultaneously. 'It takes more time to privatize the bulk of the state-dominated economy than to organize free elections … This asymmetry in speed produces a historically new sequence: mass democracy … first, and market capitalism later.'

- Balcerowicz states that this *sequence* implies that market-oriented reforms, which must be exceptionally comprehensive because of socialist economic legacy, have to be introduced under democratic, or at least pluralistic, political arrangements. Such conditions complicated the process of transition.

There is a consensus on a number of conditions which have to be met in order to accomplish transition reform from centrally planned economy to market economy. For the post-communist countries, such as Kyrgyzstan, this process of reform would involve the following changes:

- Privatisation and competition – the West advised the transition economies that they would have to start selling off state enterprises if they wished to establish a free market economy. After all, you cannot have a free market if all property and industry is owned by the state. Private ownership of enterprises would hopefully lead to a more efficient allocation of resources with competitive forces determining the direction of resource allocation. In order to facilitate privatisation, the right to own and transfer property (private property) will have to be enshrined in law. This is the only way that individuals will be able to buy state-owned property legally. Allied with privatisation was competition policy.

- Competition policy – measures to stimulate competition and protect consumers against monopoly will have to be adopted. This would involve some sort of regulatory mechanism to monitor the market behaviour of privatised enterprises and those which maintained their monopoly status.

- System of civil law – contracts and company law would have to be established in order to allow private firms to operate effectively in a market environment. In other words, codes of company conduct would have to be established and enforced.

- Redefining the role of the state – state involvement would have to be greatly reduced. The state will be required for the purpose of transferring certain things from public to private ownership. But the state cannot be allowed to intervene heavily, or manipulate the working of the economy as before. There is also the matter of changing the role of the state as it takes on new functions related to the market economy.

- Liberalisation of foreign trade – in order that the economy can be integrated into the world trading system; the opening of frontiers to capital and labour (though not needed at an early stage) and to international trade and competition. Related to this would be the need to establish convertibility of the currency, and a meaningful exchange rate policy: undervaluing the currency would be a viable strategy to promote growth and exports, and to limit imports to allow trade outside the former communist bloc. The currency could be anchored to a hard currency or a market basket of currencies.

- Price liberalisation – removal of state control of prices, and subsidies to enterprises. The forces of demand and supply would determine the level of prices. Also, there would be the need to remove subsidies to consumers.

- Macroeconomic stabilisation – budgetary and monetary discipline is crucial for financial stabilisation, and controlling inflation. Macroeconomic restraint through restrictive macroeconomic policy at the start of a transition programme would be viewed as a necessary condition of the programmes credibility.

- Creation of private financial institutions such as commercial banks, as well as a wide range of financial markets.

The case of Kyrgyzstan is somewhat unique given its small size, its potential mineral wealth and stable ethnic and cultural traditions. However, in transitional economies intrinsic inertia still leaves the microeconomic base as largely monopolistic/oligopolistic.

### 13.3.3 An economic profile of Kyrgyzstan

Kyrgyzstan is a small country of 4.5 million people in Central Asia, bordering with Kazakhstan, Uzbekistan, Tadjikistan and China. It was once one of the major trading countries on the 'great silk road'. Major assets are large mineral resources, especially gold, agriculture and potentially tourism. Kyrgyzstan is often referred to as the Switzerland of Central Asia (Table 13.3).

Since 1990, Kyrgyzstan has been actively engaged in reforming its economic system. Thus it was the first country of the Commonwealth of Independent States (CIS) to introduce its own currency in 1993, the first to agree to a Systematic Transformation Facility (STF) programme and a standby arrangement, also in 1993, and the first to enter into a three-year Enhanced Structural Adjustment Facility arrangement in 1994 (IMF Reports, 1996).

The nation's early reform efforts had to contend with difficult conditions.

Following sharp increases in prices in 1993, the annual inflation rate declined from an average of 278% in 1994 to 43% in 1995. By late 1995, however, a broad-based recovery in output had started and official statistics indicated an increase in real GDP of about 2% per annum in the first quarter of 1996 relative to the same period in 1995 (Goskomstat, 1995–96). However, inflation rose in 1996, mostly as a result of increases in world market prices for imported grain and in electricity and heating tariffs (see Table 13.4).

After stagnating in 1994, external trade expanded rapidly in 1995. Overall, exports in US dollars rose by 20% in 1995 compared to 1994, while imports increased by 47%. This rise in imports largely related to the construction of a large foreign-financed gold mining project. The trade deficit more than doubled to US$ 263 million in 1995 (16% of GDP), while the current account deficit (including grants) rose from US$ 124 million in 1994 (12% of GDP) to US$ 288 million (18% of GDP). Excluding imports and services related to the gold project, the current account deficit was US$ 133 million in 1995 (8% of GDP), compared with US$ 99 million in 1994 (10% of GDP). Borrowing by the Kyrgyz Republic on concessional terms increased sharply in 1995, but

**Table 13.3 Macroeconomic indicators: Kyrgyzstan.**

| | 1991 | 1992 | 1993 | 1994 | 1995 | 1996 | 1997 |
|---|---|---|---|---|---|---|---|
| Nominal GDP (in m US$) | 9.26 | 74.13 | 535.47 | 1106.00 | 1493.00 | 1740.94 | 1848.87 |
| Growth rate of real GDP (in % of the previous year) | 92.20 | 86.10 | 84.50 | 79.90 | 94.60 | 107.10 | 110.40 |
| Index of real GDP (in %, base 1990=100) | 92.20 | 79.40 | 67.10 | 53.60 | 50.70 | 54.30 | 59.90 |
| Unemployment rate (official unemployment in % of the econ. active population) | – | – | 0.20 | 0.70 | 2.90 | 4.40 | 3.10 |

*Source* adapted from National Statistics Committee

**Table 13.4  Annual and average monthly inflation rates as measured by prices: Kyrgyzstan (in % for the period).**

| | Jan.–Dec. 1995 | Jan.–Dec. 1996 | Jan.–Dec. 1997 | Aver. monthly (Jan.95–Dec.95)** | Aver. monthly (Jan.96–Dec.96)** | Aver. monthly (Jan.97–Dec.97)** |
|---|---|---|---|---|---|---|
| Consumer price developments | 31.9 | 35.0 | 14.8 | 2.3 | 2.5 | 1.2 |
| of which: | | | | | | |
| food products | 43.7 | 39.1 | 17.4 | 3.1 | 2.8 | 1.3 |
| non-food items | 7.2 | 20.0 | 7.3 | 0.6 | 1.5 | 0.6 |
| services | 28.0 | 45.8 | 15.4 | 2.1 | 3.2 | 2.1 |

* *Source* adapted from National Statistics Committee data
** average indices are derived from annual root indices as the radical of the 12th power

**Table 13.5  Investment: Kyrgyzstan (in m US$).**

| | 1994 | 1995 | 1996 | | | 1997 | | |
|---|---|---|---|---|---|---|---|---|
| | Total | Total | H1 | H2 | Total | H1 | H2 | Total |
| Fixed assets launched | 23.49 | 57.74 | 3.79 | 102.9 | 106.7 | 6.59 | 338.27 | 344.87 |
| Investment from all sources of financing | 82.08 | 258.02 | 97.99 | 217.96 | 315.95 | 45.53 | 147.65 | 193.17 |

*Source* adapted from National Statistics Committee data

foreign direct investment (with the exception of the gold project) remained low. The overall balance of payments recorded a deficit of US$ 29 million in 1995 (Goskom-invest Reports, 1996). Significant progress on investment was achieved in 1995 (see Table 13.5).

The GDP (US$ 1.740 billion in 1996) growth rate for 1997 was expected to reach the targeted level of 6.2% per year, while consumer price inflation for the year has been brought down to a tolerable level of 14.8% per annum in 1997. Government expenditure cuts were applied in 1997 such that expenditure fell up to 5.7% of GDP in that year; moreover, for 1998 the government is considering cutting expenditure by further 0.5% (see Tables 13.6–13.8).

Almost all of the enterprises included in the 1994–95 Privatisation Programme had been offered at coupon auctions by the end of the year, and the state shares were entirely divested from more than half of these enterprises. In early 1996 the government approved the 1996–97 Privatisation Programme, which included large enterprises operating in monopolistic markets as well as enterprises remaining from the earlier programme. Progress was also made in the restructuring of enterprises and land reform. The diagnostic studies of all enterprises under the Enterprise Restructuring and Resolution Agency (ERRA) programme were completed by the end of 1995 (IMF Reports, 1997). The economic programme for 1997 envisaged the completion of a wide range of structural reforms

**Table 13.6  GDP structure by value added in sectors of the Kyrgyz economy.**

| | 1996 | | 1997 | |
|---|---|---|---|---|
| | m US$ | % of total | m US$ | % of total |
| **Total GDP** | **1740.99** | **100.0** | **1848.87** | **100.0** |
| industry | 192.55 | 11.1 | 287.10 | 15.5 |
| agriculture | 805.07 | 46.2 | 801.51 | 43.4 |
| construction | 103.91 | 6.0 | 81.52 | 4.4 |
| transport and communications | 34.50 | 2.0 | 39.95 | 2.2 |
| trade | 180.50 | 10.4 | 199.78 | 10.8 |
| others | 426.46 | 24.4 | 438.19 | 23.7 |

*Source* adapted from National Statistics Committee data

**Table 13.7  GDP structure by income: Kyrgyzstan.**

| | 1993 | | 1994 | | 1995 | | 1996 | |
|---|---|---|---|---|---|---|---|---|
| | m US$ | % of total | m US$ | % of total | m US$ | % of total | m US$ | % of total |
| Total GDP | 535.47 | 100.0 | 1112.88 | 100.0 | 1494.91 | 100.0 | 1740.94 | 100.0 |
| wages and salaries | 186.66 | 34.8 | 379.29 | 34.1 | 565.18 | 37.8 | 584.36 | 33.6 |
| taxes on production and import | 44.93 | 8.4 | 109.15 | 9.8 | 166.22 | 11.1 | 180.97 | 10.4 |
| subsidies on production and import (−) | 8.94 | 1.7 | 5.66 | 0.5 | 15.36 | 1.0 | 14.89 | 0.9 |
| households' income from entrepreneurial activities and other sources | 312.89 | 58.4 | 630.10 | 56.6 | 778.87 | 52.1 | 990.57 | 56.9 |

*Source* adapted from National Statistics Committee data

covering privatisation, de-monopolisation, enterprise restructuring and governance, and agriculture. To address the issue of corporate governance, the government initiated a programme to improve the management and accountability of public enterprises. The legal framework for private firms was strengthened. Moreover, the budget process and inter-governmental financial relations are being restructured, together with substantial reforms to the financial sector (IMF Reports, 1997).

The recovery that started in 1995 was reflected in most components of aggregate demand. While public consumption remained almost unchanged in real terms, private consumption expanded along with the increase in agricultural production, and was reflected in increases in the purchase of consumer durables. Exports rebounded, growing by about 15% in volume terms, for the most part due to strong performance in agricultural and light industry exports. Private investments also surged primarily due to construction work on the new foreign-financed gold mining project; however, there was little indication of a recovery in investment in other sectors of the formal economy

**Table 13.8 GDP structure by expenditures: Kyrgyzstan.**

|  | 1993 | | 1994 | | 1995 | | 1996 | |
|---|---|---|---|---|---|---|---|---|
|  | m US$ | % of total | m US$ | % of total | m US$ | % of total | m US$ | % of total |
| GDP, used | 535.47 | 100.0 | 1112.88 | 100.0 | 1494.91 | 100.0 | 1740.94 | 100.0 |
| of which: | | | | | | | | |
| Total final consump. of goods and services | 513.93 | 96.0 | 1082.76 | 97.3 | 1413.43 | 94.5 | 1751.85 | 100.6 |
| – households* | 389.78 | 75.8 | 839.45 | 77.5 | 1089.04 | 77.0 | 1391.60 | 79.4 |
| – government* | 108.62 | 21.1 | 210.37 | 19.4 | 292.07 | 20.7 | 322.40 | 18.4 |
| – non-commerc.instit. | 15.53 | 3.0 | 32.93 | 3.0 | 32.30 | 2.3 | 37.84 | 2.2 |
| Gross investment | 62.48 | 11.7 | 100.30 | 9.0 | 274.17 | 18.3 | 438.69 | 25.2 |
| Net export | −40.93 | −7.6 | −70.18 | −6.3 | −192.69 | −12.9 | −499.52 | −25.8 |

*Source* adapted from National Statistics Committee data
* in percentage of the final consumption of material wealth and services

as business confidence remained weak and financial intermediation limited (IMF Reports, 1997).

### 13.3.4 Economic policy options for transition in Kyrgyzstan

What type of policies and processes should be implemented in transition to attain the goals of steady employment levels and stable growth? There are at least three key elements of policy bearing on effective transition. The first of these concerns implementation of credible monetary policy by competent agencies. Thus, if a country inherits hyper-inflation, the safest approach is to introduce radical therapy, as it is the most likely way to reduce inflationary expectations.

For Kyrgyzstan the macroeconomic objectives for 1997 were: 'Economic and financial policies for 1997 will be implemented in compliance with the indicative plan of social and economic development for 1996–1998. The Government and the National Bank of the Kyrgyz Republic have strong intentions and will make all the required efforts in order to keep the inflation target in 1997 at 17 percent per year. Growth of real GDP is expected to be 106 percent, compared with 1996, that of industrial output – 124 percent of 1996. By contrast, agricultural output will remain at its 1996 level. Basic social and economic policy objectives for 1997 aimed at fostering stable economic growth. To achieve this goal it is intended: –to further the progress in financial and agricultural sector reforms; –to restructure enterprises and develop efficient management' (National Bank of the Kyrgyz Republic (NBKR), Annual Report, 1997).

A second key element is the microeconomic liberalisation process. Thus, all bureaucratic and fiscal restrictions on founding and developing private firms should be removed as fast as possible. In addition, a comprehensive price liberalisation should be introduced in order to remove the inherited shortages in the economy and the related inefficiency.

A third key element is privatisation of activity in the economy – that is, increasing the share of the private sector in economic activities. The growth of the private sector should be as fast as possible, as it is the main engine of growth and flexibility in the transition to a market economy. A more disputed question is the optimal pace of privatisation given increased structural unemployment. However, one should always compare the development of unemployment in the longer run under alternative speeds of privatisation, especially in the larger Former Soviet States (Balcerowicz, 1995).

The second and third key elements are effectively policies aimed at the supply side of the transition economy and seek to remove or nullify the effects of wage rigidities and bureaucratic inertia. Clearly, such supply-side policies have links with new-classical thinking. As the quotation above implies, the Kyrgyz economy is experiencing all three types of policy initiative to varying degrees.

### 13.3.5 Macroeconomic policy and transition

Post-Keynesians might argue that the choice of strategy for economic transition depends in part on the initial conditions and especially on the degree of inherited macroeconomic instability. A radical and comprehensive economic programme introduced in former socialist countries undergoing extremely difficult macroeconomic conditions could still be successful in spite of powerful external shocks. The fluctuations inherent in a free market cause uncertainty about future aggregate demand, aggregate supply and prices. This uncertainty reduces private investment and hence reduces growth. Government, therefore, should intervene much more to stimulate growth and investment. Post-Keynesians frequently refer to the cases of Japan, France and Germany, where there has been a much closer collaboration between government and industry than there has been in the UK and the USA. A substantial increase in aggregate demand may be necessary initially if unemployment levels are very high in transition periods. The best way of achieving this is for the government to increase its expenditure on public works such as roads and housing, since these projects have a relatively low import content and therefore increased expenditure does not lead to balance of payments problems. Thereafter, the government should maintain a high and stable demand, by appropriate demand management policies. Any policies aimed at reducing long-term unemployment must be focused on the supply side of the economy; e.g. reducing natural unemployment by increasing labour mobility and retraining, although Keynesians argue that there is no automatic mechanism to eliminate demand-deficient unemployment even in the long run. Under the given circumstances of difficulties in transition, governments might lead recovery. By raising government expenditure and cutting taxes, the transitional nation may move quickly out of recession. Yet, it is very important for the government to maintain high levels of demand in transition; not only will this achieve low unemployment and keep actual income close to potential income, but it will also provide the most favourable environment for future development, and investment generally. Thus potential income grows more rapidly.

### 13.3.6 Eclecticism in policy formulation in transition

Economic policy is an art that requires making timely decisions with incomplete and imperfect information. This is especially true of a radical transition to a market economy during periodic economic crises. External shocks intensify these difficulties (Moumouras and Su, 1995). In such circumstances new-classical theory is virtually irrelevant since markets cannot clear due to lack of effective communications infrastructure and inadequate market-signalling processes.

### 13.3.7 Conclusions

Keynesian policy prescriptions can be usefully envisaged as trying to stabilise the economy. Thus in the expansionary phase of the business cycle unemployment falls so that unemployment in the current year is less than in the previous year, whereas in recessionary periods of the cycle unemployment rises with appropriate shifts in the capital stock and investments as described by Kalecki (1971).

However, the potential for disorder in Kyrgyzstan is clear if the government in Kyrgyzstan attempted to apply proactive demand management systems. Non-linearities in the economic system could wreck such well-intentioned demand manipulation strategy. Oddly, we find ourselves in the paradoxical position of recommending effectively a new-classical set of policy prescriptions targeted at removing supply bottlenecks, rigidities and controls. Although we argue that the new-classical perceptions of an orderly stable market system are not appropriate for Kyrgyzstan and other transitional economies, nonetheless supply-side policies, properly focused, are less likely to lead transition economies like that of Kyrgyzstan to the brink of economic crisis. This paradox results in part from the fact that Keynesians and New-Classicals conduct debates on matters of macroeconomic policy assuming the economy is in some 'stationary state', or debates focus on static models and at best consider comparative static cases. The Kyrgyz authorities state that they take an eclectic view too of the post-transition policy mix, which is perhaps understandable given the political climate: 'The Government of the Kyrgyz Republic and the National Bank of the Kyrgyz Republic are strongly committed to take every necessary effort to keep the inflation target at not more than 15 percent in 1998. The real GDP growth for 1998 is expected to be about 103.6 percent, that of industrial output – 107.5 percent, agricultural output – 102.6 percent, higher compared to 1997. The basic objective of the social-economic policy in 1998 is to ensure stable economic growth. To this end, the authorities intend to further reforms in the financial sector, agriculture; restructure enterprises, develop efficient management, and take other measures under the indicative plan for 1998' (National Bank of the Kyrgyz Republic, Annual Report, 1997). This seems a wise view and is consistent with Stiglitz's view (ibid.) on effective transition policy.

## 13.4 Free trade zones, duopoly and strategic trade policy

This section develops generic System Dynamics models to explore various scenarios when there is an entrant attempting to capture part of a monopolised market. The models developed are first tested against a classical duopoly model, the Cournot Model, and then used to test government attempts to boost exports via subsidies or defend industry with tariffs. The models yield interesting results regarding the pattern of trading outcomes with government intervention to protect or defend domestic producers operating with delay lags in the presence of linear and non-linear demand patterns. A 'Prisoner's Dilemma' type game is revealed where both traders are better off when working together rather than pursuing independent trading patterns. This modelling study is relevant to transition economies, many of which have free trade zones.

### 13.4.1  Introduction

Much trade policy is piecemeal in nature, involving tariffs and subsidies to make politic-ally powerful industries more profitable, to keep beleaguered industries afloat or allow governments to maintain high agricultural support prices. Beyond these basically reactive policies are national policies to establish and strengthen comparative advantage in certain areas at the expense of foreign trade. Such designs carry various labels, including strategic trade policy, trade targeting, managed trade and 'picking winners'.

All these names describe some sort of collaboration and cooperation among businesses and governments, to alter more quickly than the free market would the existing pattern of relative trade efficiencies. The tools for doing this usually involve a combination of sub-sidies and/or home market protection by means of tariffs, quotas, VERs and so on to accelerate the development of some chosen industry. The subject has caused a lengthy debate among economists and represents a new challenge for the proponents of free trade (Spencer and Spencer, 1984).

We initially develop a version of the Brander-Spence trading model of duopoly with homogeneous goods. The basic model is initially developed algebraically then contrasted with a Systems Dynamics model simulated in Powersim. The systems model is validated against the basic linear mathematical model and then used to explore various scenarios involving non-linearities, delays, subsidies and tariffs. The power of the Systems Dynamics methodology is revealed once non-linear demand configurations and delay lags are introduced. The models show the maximum profits to be obtained when strategic trade policy initiatives are introduced first in one country via subsidy and then with retaliation by tariffs from the trading partner. Hence the system framework is ideal for displaying potential instabilities in the trading world of duopoly.

### 13.4.2  The Cournot model

This model assumes that the only decision variable is output. In the classic Cournot model, price is not the strategic decision variable. Each player adjusts output to maximise profit assuming the rival's output is fixed. Price in the Cournot model is simply the market clearing vector resulting from successive additions or reductions in output from the duopolists.

We illustrate this by the following example. Assume that there are two countries, the UK and the Ukraine (UKR), with one coal producer in each country: British Coal (BC) and Donbass coal (DC). Each country uses the same technology and has identical linear cost and demand curves. Initially there is no trade between the countries. The profit-maximising condition for each monopolist under autarky can be calculated mathematic-ally as follows:

The monopolists total revenue and costs can both be expressed as functions of output:

$$R = R(q) \quad C = C(q)$$

The monopolist profit, $\pi$, is thus given by $\pi = R(q) - C(q)$ ... [13.1]

To maximise $\pi$ we set the derivatives of (1) to zero thus obtaining

$$R'(q) = C'(q)$$ ... [13.2]

Simple algebra will then predict that with a linear demand function, maximum profit will be obtained when the monopolist supplies half the market.

### 13.4.3 The Systems Dynamics model

This behaviour is now replicated by using System Dynamics. Figure 13.1 is the causal loop diagram for a simple monopolist in the UK. It can be noted that there are two positive loops P1 and P2 and three negative loops B1, B2 and B3. The initial behaviour of the model will thus be one of growth but because of the effect of the decreasing linear demand function (represented by B1) the long-term behaviour will be an equilibrium state. Figure 13.2 shows the System Dynamics model resulting from the causal diagram. It has the further assumption that everything produced is sold. The form of the demand function was taken as:

$$P = a - b\,Q \qquad\qquad \dots [13.3]$$

Initially we took a = 6 and b = 1/80 which results in a market of 480. The model introduces a weekly production rate per employer and the number employed is set at 100. Sales are calculated monthly and these are used as the value of the variable Q in equation 3 to calculate the price for the next month. The demand function was input using the graphical tool.

This model was built using Powersim which does not have a maximising function. The model was therefore run via the spreadsheet Excel. The production rate was set at 0 and increased to a maximum of 1.2 (maximum production of 480) in steps of 0.1. At each step, Excel called Powersim, ran the program and recorded the profit.

This model showed that a maximum profit of 8640 occurs when the monopolist took 240 units (half the market share) at a price of 3 units (which matches the mathematical solution). The model was then run for various values of a and b. These values were then graphed to give Figure 13.2. In all cases, maximum profit occurs at half market share.

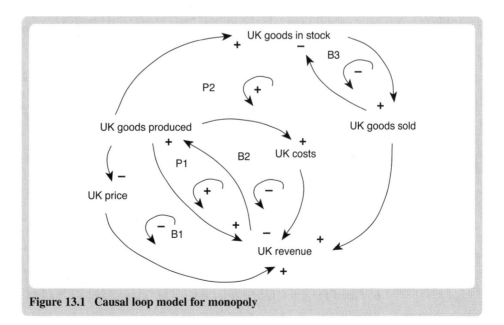

**Figure 13.1  Causal loop model for monopoly**

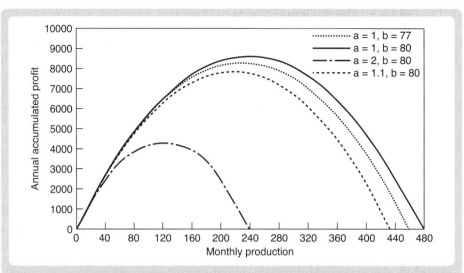

**Figure 13.2  Profit curves for various forms of linear demand – sensitivity analysis for different price/monthly sales line slope**

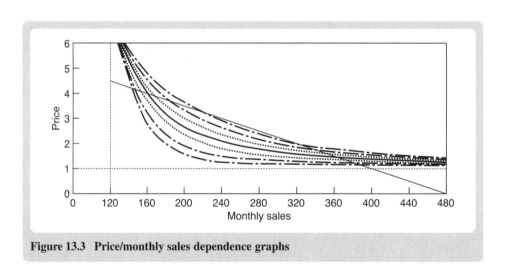

**Figure 13.3  Price/monthly sales dependence graphs**

As the model behaves as predicted by the mathematics, one is confident to perform 'what if' experiments when assumptions are relaxed which might be mathematically more difficult. The linear demand curve was therefore replaced by the curves shown in Figure 13.3. Here, it is assumed that there is a quantity of coal that must be sold and there is a price below which it is impossible to go.

The results are shown in Figure 13.4. There is a local maximum at 8640 as before but once the price reaches the minimum, profit increases indefinitely with increased production.

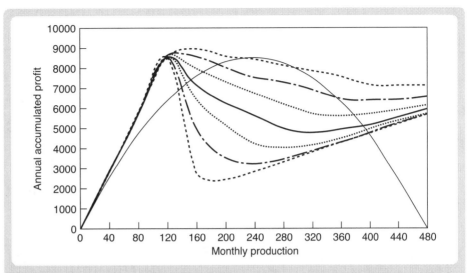

**Figure 13.4 Profit curves with non-linear demand – sensitivity analysis for different price/monthly sales dependence graphs**

### 13.4.4 A Cournot model of duopoly

If now trade between the UK and UKR is opened via say the development of a free trade zone, then a duopoly in each countries' coal market is established as both countries export coal to each other. Hence the domestic demand in each country is now satisfied by both the domestic monopolist and the foreign importer. Entry into each other's domestic market occurs given the drive for profit maximisation, expanding revenues and constant costs.

The duopoly trade case is illustrated by Cournot's classical solution. Now each duopolist maximises profit on the assumption that the quantity produced by its rival is invariant with respect to its own quantity decision.. The duopolist A maximises $\pi_A$ with respect to $q_A$ treating $q_B$ (B is the rival) as a constant, whereas duopolist B behaves in a similar fashion. The total revenue for each duopolist depends on its own output and that of its rival:

$$R_A = q_A\, f(q_A + q_B) \qquad R_B = q_B f(q_A + q_B) \qquad \ldots [13.4]$$

Thus

$$\pi_A = R_A(q_A, q_B) - C_A(q_A) \qquad \pi_B = R_B(q_A, q_B) - C_B(q_B) \qquad \ldots [13.5]$$

Taking partial derivatives and equating to zero gives the equilibrium position which occurs when each duopolist takes one-third of the market share. Hence the Cournot solution delivers a stable equilibrium for duopoly for linear demand curves where output changes are both instantaneous and simultaneous.

### 13.4.5 A System Dynamics model of duopoly

The causal diagram in Figure 13.5 shows an extension of the previous model when the UKR coal producers (DC) become an entrant to the UK coal market. Identical

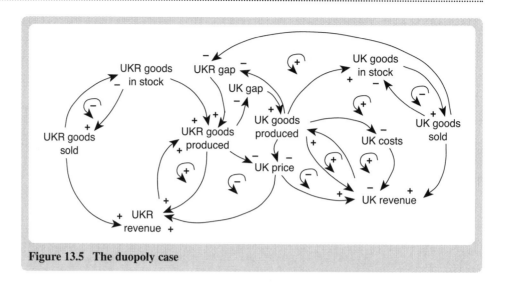

**Figure 13.5   The duopoly case**

assumptions are made for each producer with regard to costs, production, etc., and initially the previous linear demand function is used, making the available market equal to 480 units. The UK price is now determined by the goods produced by both the UK and the UKR. It is also assumed that the UKR has enough coal to easily satisfy its domestic market and is trying to sell its excess on the UK market. The modelling interest arises in the interplay between the two producers. Using the results of the previous model, producers will maximise profit when taking half the market available to them.

In the UK, BC is the incumbent trader taking half the market. This leaves a market gap, named UKGap, and this gap will become the target market for the UKR which will maximise its profit when producing half. The UK then retaliates, attacking what is named UKRGap. There are two positive loops in opposition to each other. Again the initial behaviour of the model is expected to be oscillatory but eventually the balancing loops arising from the demand function should produce long-term stability. Figure 13.6 shows each eventually taking one-third of the market as predicted by Cournot.

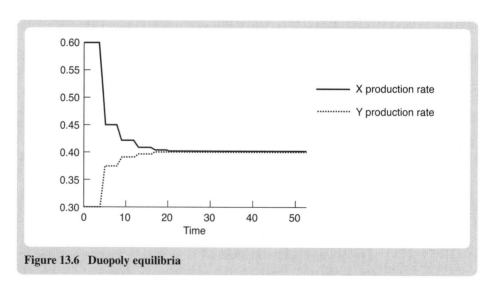

**Figure 13.6   Duopoly equilibria**

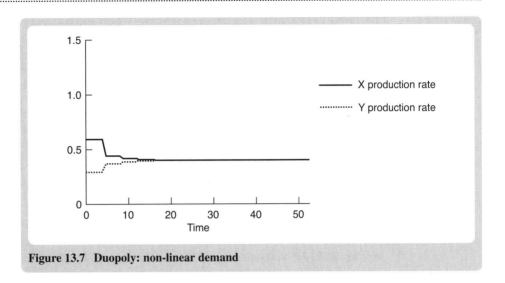

**Figure 13.7  Duopoly: non-linear demand**

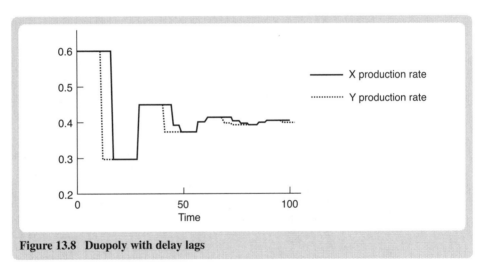

**Figure 13.8  Duopoly with delay lags**

Figure 13.7 shows the results when the non-linear demand function in Figure 13.3 is used. There is a small period of uncertainty but then the same equilibrium point is reached at one-third of the market.

It is interesting to see the effect of delay lags. DC and BC cannot respond instant-aneously so a delay lag of three months is introduced and the results shown in Figure 13.8.

It is observed that equilibria are reached but it takes a long period to do so. If, in that time, one of the producers loses its nerve and starts to take extraordinary actions then instabilities may occur.

### 13.4.6  Strategic trading

#### Subsidies

Suppose the UKR wants to set an export subsidy for coal in the free trade zone to stabilise employment for miners and raise profitability. Assuming no retaliation initially from the

UK, a direct subsidy to coal production in the Ukraine raises coal export production by cutting artificially Ukrainian pit-head production costs. The Systems Dynamics model shows this boost in coal exports to the UK and the loss of market share in the UK coal market for British Coal. Paradoxically, we see here that, on the platform of a palpable free trade zone, a government can maximise national industrial profitability by capturing in a sense some of the foreign monopoly profit. The Ukrainian decision to subsidise the production costs of coal to enhance exports to the UK seeks to enhance the Ukrainian coal industry's profit by more than the costs of the subsidy (Flamm, 1981).

Effectively, the subsidy allows for the Ukrainian coal industry to lower its price in the UK. Consequently, BC loses market share. Profits for DC rise since costs fall. Achieving success with the subsidy policy depends on a number of conditions:

- The policy has to be credible. If BC does not believe the subsidy will actually be paid, or will be paid for only a short while, it may not contract its output and thus DC will not capture additional profits.

- The subsidy should only be paid where high monopoly profits are earned abroad.

- An industry with initially high capital requirements forming substantial entry barriers is most suited to export subsidies.

- Subsidies paid to a declining industry might stave off foreign rivals for a time but result in no advances at their expense.

- The optimal outcome of subsidy policy would be if foreign rivals had many other alternative markets because then foreign output would fall consistently as prices fall. It would be most favourable if the DC model moved quickly down steep cost and learning curves as its output expands. This would create additional employment (Krueger, 1992).

The System Dynamics models are thus developed as quantity adapter output models so we assume that if a subsidy of 30% is granted to, say, the Ukrainian producers, they can increase output by this amount without affecting prices.

The causal model for this case is shown in Figure 13.9 and some results are shown in Figure 13.10. DC has managed to boost sales from 160 to 230 whilst decreasing BC sales

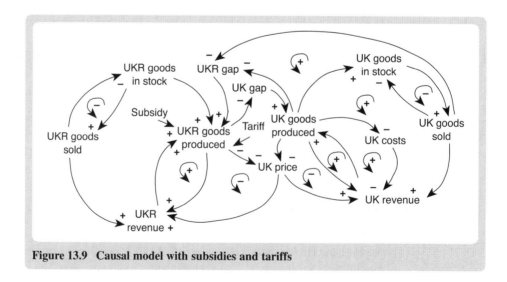

**Figure 13.9 Causal model with subsidies and tariffs**

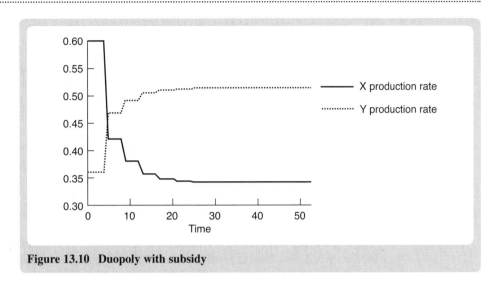

**Figure 13.10  Duopoly with subsidy**

**Table 13.9  Delays in responding to subsidy.**

| Subsidy | Delay in BC response | BC sales | DC sales | Price | BC profit | DC profit |
|---|---|---|---|---|---|---|
| 0 | 0 | 240 | 0 | 3 | 8640 | 0 |
| 0 | 0 | 160 | 160 | 2 | 3840 | 3840 |
| 20 | 0 | 137 | 206 | 1.71 | 2811 | 4227 |
| 20 | 12 | 146 | 200 | 1.67 | 2925 | 4008 |
| 20 | 26 | 168 | 187 | 1.56 | 3144 | 3149 |
| 20 | 52 | 240 | 144 | 1.2 | 3456 | 2073 |

to 125 at a common UK price of 1.56. DC's profits are then more than the equilibrium position but BC's are well below. BC would not allow this to continue for long and would retaliate.

It can be seen that DC increases its market share from 160 to 206 at the expense of BC which decreases from 160 to 137. The UK price has now dropped from 2 to 1.71 pounds. This model assumes that BC will respond to the increase in DC imports instantaneously and according to the previous rule of taking half the available market. Table 13.9 shows the effects of BC delaying its response to the entrant. The last row corresponds to BC ignoring the entrant completely and continuing to produce at the monopoly rate. Because of the increase in DC's sales, the price reduces and so although BC can keep its production rate (and thus avoid redundancies) its profits fall by almost 50%. According to the Cournot model, it should decide on market share alone.

If both countries play a subsidy game for their coal industries, then BC and DC find themselves playing a four-player subsidy game. In this game, the two governments move first and simultaneously decide subsidy rates for export production. The duopolists then observe the subsidy rates granted by both governments and play a Cournot game in each market (Krugman, 1987).

### 13.4.7  BC defence against predatory subsidies

The predatory nature of an export subsidy to Ukrainian exports of coal designed to capture profits at the expense of BC means that the UK, facing such an active policy, needs to consider how to retaliate (Gray and Licklider, 1985). A major aim of UK policy might be to convince the UKR government that a predatory strategy is dangerous and uncertain. Thus the UK might retaliate with its own pit-head or hidden subsidies to the producer hurt by foreign strategy or could impose protection against the subsidised goods. Indeed, game theorists have shown that in these circumstances, a 'tit for tat' strategy may be the most effective defence (Elliott, 1994). The Systems Dynamics model shows that if the UK replies with tariff protection for BC, this countervails the UKR subsidy strategy. By contrast, a direct subsidy in the UK for coal production simply raises the cost of trading, though consumers in the UK would gain from lower prices in the short run.

If a retaliatory tariff of 40% is added to the previous model with a subsidy of 30%, DCs trade falls to 140 whereas BC is boosted to 170 at a price of 2.13. This is on the assumption of an instantaneous response and using half the available market strategy. BC recaptures its share of the market at the expense of DC. The results so far are summarised in Table 13.10.

We can now use the model to investigate the effect of delays in the response of BC to DC's behaviour, DC's response to BC's behaviour and the case when they both delay their responses. These results are summarised in Tables 13.11, 13.12 and 13.13.

A similar analysis was performed as before. Table 13.11 shows that by ignoring DC's behaviour, BC keeps its market share but at a lower price.

**Table 13.10  BC recaptures its share of the market at the expense of DC.**

| Subsidy | Tariff | BC sales | DC sales | Price | BC profit | DC profit |
|---------|--------|----------|----------|-------|-----------|-----------|
| 0 | 0 | 240 | 0 | 3 | 8640 | 0 |
| 0 | 0 | 160 | 160 | 2 | 3840 | 3840 |
| 30 | 0 | 125 | 230 | 1.56 | 2415 | 4306 |
| 30 | 40 | 170 | 140 | 2.13 | 4328 | 3288 |

**Table 13.11  BC delays in responding to DC.**

| Subsidy | Tariff | Delay in BC response | BC sales | DC sales | Price | BC profit | DC profit |
|---------|--------|----------------------|----------|----------|-------|-----------|-----------|
| 0 | 0 | 0 | 240 | 0 | 3.00 | 8640 | 0 |
| 0 | 0 | 0 | 160 | 160 | 2.00 | 3840 | 3840 |
| 20 | 30 | 0 | 170 | 140 | 2.13 | 4345 | 3578 |
| 20 | 30 | 12 | 174 | 138 | 2.10 | 4385 | 3478 |
| 20 | 30 | 26 | 186 | 132 | 2.02 | 4508 | 3200 |
| 20 | 30 | 52 | 240 | 108 | 1.65 | 4752 | 2138 |

**Table 13.12  DC delays in responding to BC.**

| Subsidy | Tariff | Delay in DC response | BC sales | DC sales | Price | BC profit | DC profit |
|---|---|---|---|---|---|---|---|
| 0 | 0 | 0 | 240 | 0 | 3.00 | 8640 | 0 |
| 0 | 0 | 0 | 160 | 160 | 2.00 | 3840 | 3840 |
| 20 | 30 | 0 | 170 | 140 | 2.13 | 4345 | 3578 |
| 20 | 30 | 12 | 168 | 140 | 2.16 | 3641 | 3396 |
| 20 | 30 | 26 | 162 | 156 | 2.07 | 3102 | 3644 |
| 20 | 30 | 52 | 132 | 216 | 1.67 | 2423 | 3854 |

**Table 13.13  Both delay in responding to each other.**

| Subsidy | Tariff | Delay in response | BC sales | DC sales | Price | BC profit | DC profit |
|---|---|---|---|---|---|---|---|
| 0 | 0 | 0 | 240 | 0 | 3.00 | 8640 | 0 |
| 0 | 0 | 0 | 160 | 160 | 2.00 | 3840 | 3840 |
| 20 | 30 | 0 | 170 | 140 | 2.13 | 4345 | 3578 |
| 20 | 30 | 12 | 172 | 132 | 2.02 | 3470 | 2632 |
| 20 | 30 | 26 | 132 | 183 | 1.83 | 2560 | 1960 |
| 20 | 30 | 52 | 240 | 216 | 0.30 | 846 | 761 |

The more important factor in this case would be DC's response to the tariff. Table 13.12 shows the outcomes for varying degrees of indifference. DC can bear the tariff and increase imports but at a lower price.

If they both attempt to continue as before but with the subsidy tariff existing, then it is disastrous for them both. This is then a 'prisoners' dilemma' type game as each will do better by cooperating with each other than by ignoring each other.

The power of the Systems Dynamics methodology and the clear counterintuitive insights revealed are evident in the analysis presented in tables 13.11, 13.12 and 13.13. If both duopolists delay their 'best' response to either the subsidy or the tariff, the strong elements of conflict and potential instability are clear. Thus with reference to Table 13.13, both BC and DC have a vested interest in lobbying their respective governments for a return to free trade with no subsidies and tariffs. However, if this was accomplished, stable free trade could be compromised by either party using hidden tariffs or subsidies. If this happened, both BC and DC could be once again on the horns of a prisoners' dilemma as both duopolists have dominant strategies to increase output in all markets. Prices would drop drastically until capacity constraints in both countries were reached. At this point, both producers would want to cut production down to 160 units. Price would return to maximum profit levels. Once again, at this point, a whole new round of output expansion could arise, causing market prices to permanently fluctuate from 3 to 0.3. This is Edgeworth instability. This instability reduces with quick response times and increases with slower response times. The System Dynamics methodology shows that even in the context of the inherently stable Cournot model, permanent oscillations in prices and outputs can occur in dynamic games. Hence the zero-sum nature of the Cournot game becomes the variable-sum game of the prisoners' dilemma. Stability can only come from a WTO-brokered peace.

### 13.4.8 Conclusion

The models developed show the reasoning behind the general popularity of free trade zones and export subsidies. They also show the paradoxical desire of governments in the WTO to negotiate bilateral trade agreements with major trading partners. The dynamic runs of the Systems Dynamics model show the potential for instability and collapse of trading arrangements if subsidies and 'tit-for tat' retaliations via tariffs with variable leads and lags occur. Pricing chaos and Edgeworth-type instability would occur if capacity constraints were placed on domestic or foreign production in either market.

If both countries play a subsidy game, this resembles the prisoners' dilemma. Hence, the strictly dominant strategy equilibrium in which both subsidise exports results in both countries being worse off than if they had not intervened in the market. Clearly, balanced reductions in subsidies/tariff in the WTO can make both countries better off (Hufbauer and Schott, 1984). The present trade war between the USA and the EU could easily spiral out of control since the USA regards the EU policy of banning imports of US beef as protectionist since it effectively protects the domestic market for EU farmers. The USA could easily reply to this with prohibitive tariffs placed on EU producers. In the end, this issue would need to be resolved by the WTO.

## Summary

- The transition economies could not easily offset the contractionary effects of reduced demand via devaluation or monetary expansion because they were also suffering from high inflation. The excess capacity created by the decline in investment and military spending did not restrain inflation.

- Observers expected the transition economies to attract large inflows of capital; in practice, the first several years after the end of communism were marked by only small inflows, in large part because of political uncertainty.

- Albania and Kyrgyzstan both experienced severe macroeconomic instabilities after 1992.

- FDI probably remains the best hope for future growth now that inflation is subsiding.

### Questions

1. Suppose you were elected President in either Albania or Kyrgyzstan, what trade policies would you follow?

2. Kyrgyzstan was the first former Soviet Republic to join the WTO. What benefits might it expect?

3. Why did former Soviet Republics suffer rampant inflation and umemployment in 1992–1996?

4. Should former Eastern European planned economies join the EU? What might be the effects?

## Key concepts

| | |
|---|---|
| central planning | trade policy |
| inflation | balance of payments |
| recession | growth |
| unemployment | duopoly |
| FDI | |

## Note

1. A case study regarding the application of the hypermedia digital library aiming to meet the educational and informational needs of Greek beekeepers can be found in Batzios *et al.* (1997). The study highlights the economic and social effects of the use of an efficient information system. The information framework is accessible through the Internet which is expected to generate greater productivity and profitability.

## Bibliography

*AGORA* (1995) 'Commercial trade between Greece and the countries of the Balkan Peninsula', *AGORA of Food and Drinks in Northern Greece*, Edition for Industry, Exports and Trade.

Balcerowicz, L. (1995) *Socialism Capitalism Transformation*, Central University Press, p. 377.

Bank of Macedonia and Thrace (1995) 'Investment strategy', *Economical Bulletin for the Balkans and East Europe*, vol. 1, pp. 10–11.

Batzios, C. A., Salampasis, M., Liakos, V., Tait J. and Androulidakis, S. (1997) 'A hypermedia digital library for the education and extension training of Greek beekeepers', *Proceedings of the First European Conference for Information Technology in Agriculture*, Copenhagen, 15–18 June.

Chen, P. (1988) 'Empirical and theoretical evidence of economic chaos', *System Dynamics Review*, vol. 4, nos. 1–2, pp. 81–108.

Clarke, S. (ed.) (1998) *Structural Adjustment with Mass Unemployment: lessons from Russia*, Edward Elgar.

Clower, R. W. (1984) *Money and Markets*, Cambridge University Press.

Commander, S. and Coricelli, F. (eds) (1995) *Unemployment, Restructuring and the labour market in Eastern Europe and Russia*, Washington, DC, EDI World Bank.

Dana, L. P. (1996) 'Albania in the twilight zone: the Perseritje model and its impact on small business', *Journal of Small Business Management*, January, pp. 64–70.

Daoulas, D. (1995) 'A country of organised disorganisation', *Newspaper LOGOS*, 4 August.

Economist (1992) *103 Checklists for Successful Operations in E.E.*, Business International Limited.

Elliott, K. A. (1994) *Trade Protection in the United States*, Institute for International Economics.

ÉNSTAT (1995*) Statistika 1. Informations, Analyses and Periodical Statistical Data*, NSTAT, Tirana.

Ermidis, P. and Egyptiadis, A. (1993) *Albania – Bulgaria – Rumania. Economic and Commercial Issues Today*, A Hellenic Export Promotion Organisation edition, Branch of Northern Greece, Thessaloniki.

Flamm, K. (1981) *Creating the Computer: Government, Industry and High Technology*, Brookings Inst.

Fleissner, P. (1994) *The transformation of Slovakia: The Dynamics of Her Economy, Environment, and Population*, Verlag, Dr. Kovac.

Fleissner, P. and Ludwig, U. (1992) *East German economy in transition – computer simulation by means of a system dynamics model*, Braunschweig/Weibaden: Vieweg, Verlag.

Ghosh, S. (1978) 'Is Central Bank independence desirable?', The University of Wales, Aberystwyth Economic Research Paper, 95-07, 1995.

Goskominvest (Kyrgyz National Committee on Foreign Investments and Economic Aid) (1996) *Annual Report*.

Goskomstat (National Statistical Office) *Annual Report*, 1995–1996.

Gray, H. P. and Licklider, R. E. (1985) 'International trade warfare: economic and political strategic considerations'. *Euro. Journal of Political Economy*, vol. 1.

Hellenic Centre of European Studies (1995a) Semi-annual Review of the Balkan States, *periodical edition of the Hellenic Centre of European Studies*, June 1995.

Hellenic Centre of European Studies (1995b) *Balkan Review*, 1995 Bulletins.

Hellenic Export Promotion Organisation (1995) *A Business Guide for Albania*, a survey by M. Porikis, Hellenic Export Promotion Organisation, Ioannina Branch.

Hoen, H. W. (1998) *The Transformation of Economic Systems in Central Europe*, Edward Elgar.

Holden, A. V. (1986) *Chaos (Non-linear science: Theory and Applications)*, Manchester University Press.

Hufbauer, G. C. and Schott, J. J. (1984) *Economic Sanctions Reconsidered: History and Current Policy*, Institute for International Economics.

International Monetary Fund Reports on Kyrgyz Republic, Recent Economic Developments, 5 July 1996; 10 December 1997.

Kaldor, N. (1940) 'A model of the trade cycle', *Economic Journal*, March.

Kalecki, M. (1971) *Selected Essays on the Dynamics of the Capitalist Economy, 1933–71*, Cambridge University Press, Cambridge.

Kay, J. and Thompson, D. (1986) 'Privatisation: a policy in search of rationale', *The Economic Journal*, vol. 96.

Kemp, J. (1997) 'New methods and understanding in economic dynamics? An introductory guide to chaos and economics', *Economic Issues*, vol. 2, p. 1, pp. 1–26.

Keynes, J. M. (1936) *The General Theory of Employment, Interest and Money*, Macmillan, London.

Krueger, A. O. (1992) 'Free Trade is the best policy'. *Journal of Economic Literature*, vol. 30, no. 2.

Krugman, P. (1987) 'Is free trade passè?' *Economic Perspectives*, vol. 1, no. 2, Fall, pp. 131–44.

Leamer, E. and Stern, R. M. (1970) *Qualitative International Economics*, Chicago, Aldine Publishing Co.

Moscardini, A. O. and Lawler, A. K. (2000) 'An alternative pedagogy for economic modelling', *Economic Issues*, vol. 5, part 2, September.

Mosekilde, E. (1992) 'Non-linear mode-interaction in the macroeconomy', *Annals of Operations Research*, J.C. Baltzer AG, vol. 37, pp. 185–215.

Moumouras, I. A. and Su, D.-M. (1995) 'Central Bank independence, policy reforms and the credibility of public debt stabilisations', *European Journal on Political Economy*, vol. 11, pp. 189–204.

Murrell, P. (1991) 'Can neoclassical economics underpin the economic reform of centrally planned economies?', *Journal of Economic Perspectives*, vol. 5.

Murrell, P. (1992) 'Evolutionary and radical approaches to economic reform', *Economics of Planning*, vol. 25.

Myant, M. (ed.) (1999) *Industrial Competitiveness in East-Central Europe*, Edward Elgar.

National Bank of the Kyrgyz Republic (1988) *Annual Report 1997*, Kyrgyzstan.

National Statistical Service of Greece (1994) *Greece in Figures*, Special edition, Athens.

Ormerod P. (1994) *The Death of Economics*, Faber and Faber, London and Boston.

Parker, D. and Stacey, R. (1994) *Chaos Management and Economics: Implications of Non-linear Thinking*, IEA, London.

Papas, H. P., Mantzios, A. S. and Malatou-Bontini, E. (1994) *The Agricultural Sector and Agricultural Industries of Albania*, National Foundation of Agricultural Research, Institute of Milk of Ioannina, Greece.

Pata, K. and Osmani, M. (1994) 'Albanian agriculture: a painful transition from communism to free market challenges', *Sociologia Ruralis*, vol. XXXIV, no. 1, pp. 84–101.

Pheby, J. (ed.) (1989) *New Directions in Post-Keynesian Economics*, Edward Elgar.

Rowthorn, R. (1981) 'Demand, real wages and economic growth', *Thames Papers in Political Economy*, Autumn.

Salvatore D. (1996) *National Trade Policies*, OECD Economic Studies.

Sinclair P. J. N. (1987) *Unemployment: Economic Theory and Evidence*, Basil Blackwell, Oxford, UK, p. 312.

Spencer, B. and Brander, B. J. (1984) *Tariff Protection and Imperfect Competition, Monopolistic Competition and International Trade Journal*, OUP.

Stiglitz, J. (1999) *Whither Reform? Ten years of transition*, World Bank Annual Bank Conference on Development Economics, Washington, DC.

Tzen, I. (1993) 'The prospects for investment activities in Albania are encouraging', *NAYTEMPORIKI*, September, 58th HELEXPO.

United Nations (1992) 'Economies in transition, growth of foreign investment', *East-West Investment and Joint Ventures News*, No. 14, United Nations, Economic Commission for Europe, Geneva, December.

Vlahos, D. (1994) 'Direct investments in the Central-East European countries and the ex-Soviet Union countries', *The Social Science Tribune*, vol. 5, no. 15, pp. 177–212.

# 14 Exchange rates: fundamentals, random walks and volatility

## HUW DIXON[1]

## 14.1 Introduction

An exchange rate[2] between two currencies is a price ratio of two nominal values. Are exchange rates ultimately tied down by economic fundamentals, or are they free to drift at random on a sea of speculation? This is of course an interesting question both on the theoretical and the empirical levels. If fundamentals play no empirically significant role in the data, then this is something that needs to be explained and taken into account when writing models and understanding how the economy works. At the time of writing (January 2000), most economic commentators believe the UK currency (£ Sterling) to be overvalued relative to the European currency, the Euro. Indeed, the Monetary Policy Committee has expressed some surprise at the continuing strength of Sterling despite relatively low UK interest rates. This is seen as something of a mystery. Going back almost two decades, the exchange rate between the £ Sterling and the $US ranged from about $2.40 in mid-1980 to below $1.20 in 1984. Such a massive change in the Sterling/dollar exchange rate gave rise to much debate at the time, but was not easily linked to clearly identifiable 'fundamentals'.

Most theoretical open economy models make strong theoretical assumptions regarding nominal exchange rates, for example:

- purchasing power parity (PPP) must hold every instant or at least in the long run;
- current and capital accounts must be in equilibrium in the long run.

If these basic theoretical restrictions are found to be absent from the data, what is to be done? In this chapter I will focus on theoretical and empirical issues raised by this issue. The empirical aspects are the most crucial to understand, and can be divided into two. Is the *mean* exchange rate determined by fundamentals over time? This has to do with the *level* of the exchange rate. The second issue is the *variance* of the exchange rate: is the variation of the exchange rate consistent with the efficiency of the exchange rate markets? This is a question of *volatility*: is the volatility of the exchange rates consistent with them being determined by fundamentals?

## 14.2 Fundamentals: what determines the level of the exchange rate?

We will refer to the view that in some sense the fundamentals of the economy determine the exchange rate in the long run as the *fundamentalist* view. Since the exchange rate is a ratio of two nominal values, the fundamentals might include not only real variables such as output or productivity growth, the discovery of a natural resource, but also nominal factors (money supply growth, inflation, financial liberalisation). Furthermore, the policy regime might also be important: is there a fixed or floating regime, is monetary policy devolved to an independent central bank, what are the fiscal/monetary preferences of the government and so on?

One of the simplest examples of a fundamentalist theory is the international monetarist view. Suppose that the path of output in economies is fixed by real factors to follow the 'natural' growth path. The level of nominal prices in each economy is then determined by the quantity theory (at least in the long run). Now, suppose that we assume that there is purchasing-power parity (PPP). Under PPP the exchange rate is assumed to ensure that the purchasing power of a currency (the $) is the same in the home country (the USA) as it would be if it were exchanged into another currency (the Euro) and used to buy goods in the foreign country (the Euro zone). This determines the level of the exchange rate at an instant of time. Changes in the exchange rate are then determined by relative money supply and inflation. If inflation is higher in the USA than in Europe, the $ will decline in value. The theory can be expressed in simple form in the following way. First we have the PPP equation, which says that the price of goods are the same when expressed in the same currency

$$P = S.P*$$

where $P$ and $P*$ are the domestic and foreign currency prices of goods respectively and $S$ the home currency price of foreign currency. The right-hand side gives the foreign price in terms of domestic currency. This simple equality implies the following relationship between the rate of growth in the exchange rate $\hat{S}$ and the differential of the inflation rates at home and abroad, $\pi$ and $\pi*$ respectively

$$\hat{S} = \pi - \pi*$$

What this relationship says is that if the domestic inflation rate is 10% higher than the foreign rate, then the exchange rate must go up: i.e. it devalues so that more domestic currency is required to buy the foreign currency. To see why this is, suppose that we start off with a $/Euro exchange rate of 1. Now suppose that inflation in the USA is 5% and in Euroland 0. If prices started off satisfying PPP, after the inflation, the US goods are now 5% more expensive at the original exchange rate. In order to keep PPP, the dollar price of a Euro needs to rise by 5%, to $1.05.

Some notion of PPP is central to any fundamentalist view of ER. The driving force behind this theory is the notion of *arbitrage*: if goods have different prices, then there is a potential arbitrage opportunity. Arbitrage will bring together prices, at least in the long run, it is argued. Just to state it in this way is to realise why PPP may not hold. There are transport costs. Just because a good is cheaper in the USA does not mean that it makes sense to import it into Europe. If the price difference is large enough, then arbitrage may happen, but for many products the costs are prohibitively large. Furthermore, there are transactions costs: changing from currency to currency incurs a cost. Furthermore, products are differentiated and there is market power. Let us take an example: cars in Europe. British cars have the driving wheel on the right-hand side: Continental cars on the left.[3] Now, there is a substantial premium on UK car prices: the same model will often be 10–20% more expensive in the UK than on the continent. This provides a large incentive for UK car owners to buy from the continent, and indeed some do. However, most do not: it is difficult to organise and time consuming, involves language problems and so on. Take another example: music CDs. The price variation here is substantial, particularly comparing the USA to the UK. Imperfect competition in the UK retail market is probably a major factor here. Although the wholesale price of CDs is similar in the USA and UK (as can be seen from similar prices for mail-order and online prices in different countries), the markup of retailers is much larger in the UK: the same CD often costs 30–50% more in the UK than the USA (although this differential is diminishing with the growth of online ordering). However, even with cheap transatlantic airfares, you would need to buy a lot of CDs in order to make a round trip pay!

In fact PPP has become one of the most intensively scrutinised empirical relationships in applied macroeconomics in the 1990s. Although the intensity of this research has been driven more by a desire to implement recently developed econometric methods – such as multivariate cointegration and panel unit root tests – than any new interest in PPP *per se*, this work has, nevertheless, thrown up some interesting findings. The key finding in this literature is that real exchange rates are mean-reverting (which is a key requirement of PPP), but the magnitude of such reversion is far too slow to be consistent with a traditional form of PPP such as that formulated by Gustav Cassel (1928). Should PPP be abandoned, therefore? Some would argue in the affirmative and propose that equilibrium exchange rates can only be understood if the key real determinants of real exchange rates are modelled. However, die-hard proponents of PPP would argue that the concept may be saved if the importance of transaction costs in imparting non-linear adjustment is recognised. If it is, estimated adjustment speeds turn out may be consistent with a more traditional view of PPP.

Most tests of PPP express it in the following terms, taking logs of the previous PPP relationship

$$s_t = p_t - p_t^*$$

where $p_t$ and $p_t^*$ are the log of domestic prices and $s_t$ is the home currency price of foreign currency. In effect, this PPP equation says what $s_t$ should be if PPP were true. Deviations from PPP can be expressed in terms of the real exchange rate $q_t$

$$q_t = s_t - p_t + p_t^*$$

The following equation can then be estimated

$$q_t = \rho q_{t-1} + \alpha + \varepsilon_t$$

where $\rho \leq 1$ and $\varepsilon_t$ a white noise error. If $\rho < 1$, then we have Cassellian PPP: there is a long-run tendency for deviations from PPP to die away (at least to some fixed level $\alpha$ that may reflect other factors such as transport costs, interest rate differentials, etc.). Alternatively if $\rho = 1$ then the deviations away from PPP are persistent: we have a random walk. There is some evidence for PPP in the long run, in the sense that deviations in competitiveness tend to die away. However, the decay of deviations is very slow: even the most optimistic estimates find half-lives of 4 years, whilst most find significantly longer, up to 20 years (MacDonald, 1999). A *half-life* gives the time taken for a given deviation to be reduced by half. Thus, if £ Sterling is currently 30% overvalued, then it could take up to 20 years to halve that to 15%.

Now here we have a basic issue. Intertemporal arbitrage (speculation) requires that the exchange rate will be random walk: otherwise currency speculators can make money by predicting the future exchange rate.[4] However, the fundamentalist view implies that there is some sense in which the future currency can be predicted. For example, if there is a long-run tendency towards PPP, then if a currency is currently overvalued it would tend to drift down in value. *There is thus a contradiction between the predictability of the exchange rate as implied by a theory of the exchange rate (such as PPP) and the operation of arbitrage in speculative markets.* It is to this issue that we now turn.

## 14.3    Outperforming the random walk?

In 1983, Meese and Rogoff (1983) made what seemed at the time a startling discovery. What they did was to take a variety of exchange rate models and test them against a simple random walk model. The random walk model was one with a drift term $\kappa$:

$$s_t = s_{t-1} + \kappa + \varepsilon_t$$

This says that the best predictor of the next period's exchange rate is the current exchange rate possibly plus a constant or 'drift' term (the error term $\varepsilon_t$ is white noise).

Meese and Rogoff found that a comprehensive range of exchange rate models were unable to outperform a random walk. In particular, they found no model outperformed the random walk model within sample or as a 12-month forecasting model. The exchange rate models were in the following general form (all variables in logs):

$$s = a_0 + a_1(m - m^*) + a_2(y - y^*) + a_3(r - r^*) + a_4(\pi - \pi^*) + a_5 TB + a_6 TB^*$$

where the following 'economic fundamentals' were employed:

| | |
|---|---|
| $(m - m^*)$ | the ratio of US/foreign money supply |
| $(y - y^*)$ | the ratio of US/foreign real income |
| $(r - r^*)$ | the ratio of US/foreign real interest rates |
| $(\pi - \pi^*)$ | the ratio of US/foreign expected inflation |
| TB and TB* | US and foreign cumulated trade balances. |

The various models of exchange rates can be obtained by imposing restrictions on the coefficient parameters. For example, PPP implies that $a_4 = a_5 = a_6 = 0$; the Dornbusch model implies that $a_5 = a_6 = 0$ and so on. The amazing result was that none of these fundamentals was able to improve upon the simple random walk model. The implication was that perhaps macroeconomics does not matter in determining exchange rates!

Since Meese and Rogoff, the role of traditional macroeconomic variables in explaining exchange rate movements has been a hotly contested issue. Some researchers have interpreted the evidence that has accumulated since Meese and Rogoff as reinforcing the original result, whereas others are more favourably inclined towards fundamentals. Ken Rogoff summarized the evidence:

> Today, the Meese-Rogoff (1983) results no longer seem quite so crazy. Despite longer data sets on modern floating rates, and the application of more sophisticated econometric techniques, researchers have continued to find it very frustrating to firmly demonstrate any systematic relationship between exchange rates and macroeconomic fundamentals, at least for the cross rates between the dollar, DM (euro) and yen. It is true that researchers have occasionally found particular sub-samples where certain models seem to perform noticeably better than the random walk model but, as a rule, these results wilt under sustained out-of-sample testing. Surveying the evidence in their survey for the *Handbook of International Economics*, Frankel and Rose (1995) conclude that numerous attempts to overturn the Meese-Rogoff results have failed. (Rogoff, 1999)

Whilst the shorter-term perspective has tended to show that you cannot beat the random walk, this is not so if one extends the horizon to 24–36 months. Mark (1995) finds that there is a statistically significant improvement over the random walk at longer horizons. However, this has been challenged on largely econometric grounds – e.g. Kilian (1997) and Berkowitz and Giorganni (1997). Perhaps in order to understand why it is that the fundamentals do badly, at least in the short run, we need to understand the issue of *volatility*, so we move from the first moment to the second.

## 14.4    Exchange rate volatility: too much of a bad thing?

Two issues relate to volatility or, more precisely, the second moment. The first is simply to do with the fact that it seems that the degree of ER volatility under floating rates is simply too high. The second is a comparison between fixed and floating regimes: it appears that whilst floating regimes have greater ER volatility, there is no gain in stability of the real economy in terms of output and employment. To put it another way, a fixed regime means that there is no less real stability but there is a clear gain in terms of a stable exchange rate. Let us look at these issues in turn, dealing with the issue of comparing the volatility of fixed versus flexible exchange rate regimes.

There has been a widely held view that the overall degree of uncertainty in an economic system is in some sense 'objectively' determined (by, for example, tastes, technology and so on). The way that this uncertainty manifests itself is affected by the type of exchange rate regime, but not the underlying volatility itself. Volatility and uncertainty are a bit like air in a balloon: you can squeeze the balloon and make different shapes, but the volume remains the same. In the same way, you can configure an economic system in different ways, by floating or fixing the ER regime, but this simply means that the underlying volatility will show up differently: with a floating regime there is ER volatility, with a fixed regime real volatility (i.e. volatility in output, interest rates, etc.). Flood and Rose summarise this viewpoint (not their own):

> Exchange rate regimes differ in the mechanisms through which this underlying volatility is channelled. For instance, 'money supply' or 'liquidity' shocks affect the nominal exchange rate when rates float, but the money supply if rates are fixed. Underlying systemic volatility cannot be *reduced* by the regime, only *channelled* to one locus or another. The economy can be thought of as a balloon; squeezing volatility out of one part merely transfers the volatility elsewhere. Flood and Rose (1999)

If we take this view, then there is a trade-off between fixed and floating regimes. In a floating regime compared to a fixed regime, there will be volatility in the ER, but less in the real sector. This sort of view is quite common in the current discussion in the UK about membership of the Euro (and previous discussions of the whole project of monetary union in the EU): being free to float means that a country can rapidly adjust to real shocks, whilst being locked in a fixed regime means that more painful adjustment must occur.

However, a number of researchers have demonstrated that the variability of observable macroeconomic variables such as money, output and consumption do not differ systematically across exchange rate regimes. In any case, it is simply hard to believe that the post–1973 (floating) era has been so much more volatile from a macroeconomic perspective than the pre–1973 (fixed) period. Indeed the *magnitude* of the increase in exchange rate volatility following the breakup of Bretton Woods in 1973 was a surprise to many who accepted the Balloon analogy, e.g. Mussa (1986) or Obstfeld (1995). However, the evidence has been largely self-evident and uncontested.

Baxter and Stockman (1989) looked at both exchange rates and other macroeconomic variables. Using data for a selection of both OECD and developing countries, Baxter and Stockman examined the variability of output, trade variables, private and government consumption. They were

> unable to find evidence that the cyclic behaviour of real macroeconomic aggregates depends systematically on the exchange-rate regime. The only exception is the well-known case of the real exchange rate. (Baxter and Stockman, 1989)

The flavour of Baxter and Stockman's results is best illustrated by looking at an example. Let us look at the variability of industrial production in the OECD countries (variability is measured by the standard deviation relative to a linear trend). This is shown for the more important economies in Table 14.1.

Out of the 14 OECD countries, only three showed a decrease in volatility post-1973: the USA, Japan and Italy. All the others showed increases in the variability of industrial production. A similar pattern was found in terms of trade and the real exchange rate: '… changes in trade variability and real exchange variability appear to be independent of the exchange rate system' (Baxter and Stockman, *op.cit.*, p. 391).

Flood and Rose (1995) found comparable cross-country results. The conclusion is clear:

> It is easy to summarise. Exchange rate volatility differs with the exchange rate regime. Macroeconomic volatility doesn't. To our knowledge, no one has identified macroeconomic fundamentals that exhibit dramatically different volatility across exchange rate regimes *other than the exchange rate*. (Flood and Rose, 1999)

Whilst the level of uncertainty and volatility under floating exchange rates has been large, a word of caution must be struck. First, the increase in volatility post-1973 was due to many factors. Few would argue with the fact that the post-war reconstruction period (1950–70) was one of exceptional stability: a golden age for many Western European economies of high employment and high growth with little or no inflation. The oil shocks and productivity slowdown in the 1970s represented something new.

One implication, however, if one accepts the advantages of a fixed rate is that the Euro will generate mainly benefits. The costs that most commentators have alleged of the system is that the Euro will prevent individual countries from stabilising their own economies. However, the Flood and Rose argument would imply that the opposite may well be true: output and employment may well be no less stable for individual countries within the Euro. It is interesting to look at the case of the UK at the time of writing. Whilst being outside the Euro gives the UK monetary authorities the power to vary the exchange rate or the interest rates, in practice this freedom has not bought the UK any obvious benefits: just high interest rates and an overvalued currency. Future readers will be in a better situation to determine how things will have turned out.

**Table 14.1 The variability of industrial production under fixed exchange rate and floating regimes. Column 2 shows the s.d. of industrial production pre-1973; column 3 post-1973.**

| Country | Fixed | Flexible |
| --- | --- | --- |
| US* | 8.0 | 6.9 |
| France | 9.9 | 12.7 |
| Canada | 8.3 | 11.4 |
| Italy* | 10.8 | 10.5 |
| Netherlands | 10.4 | 16.4 |
| Ireland | 6.3 | 6.7 |
| Japan* | 17.3 | 13.9 |
| UK | 6.5 | 7.2 |
| Sweden | 14.8 | 14.9 |
| Spain | 14.7 | 19.9 |

*Source* adapted from Baxter and Stockman (1989). Those countries with reduced volatility are marked with an asterisk.

## 14.5 Resolving the paradox

Much of the most influential work in international finance during the 1970s and 1980s was geared towards rationalising the apparently high level of floating exchange rate volatility. Dornbusch (1976) is the classic example. The Dornbusch overshooting model explains the volatility of real exchange rates in terms of their reaction to nominal rates; the volatility of nominal rates are, in turn, due to the interaction of sticky prices with liquidity impulses. Suppose that there is a restriction in the money supply. In an economy with perfectly flexible prices, there would be an immediate and proportionate fall in nominal prices and wages and appreciation of the currency. However, if wages and prices are inflexible, then the monetary contraction leads to a real contraction in output and employment. However, as wages and prices fell, the real economy would return to its natural rate. What Dornbusch also showed was that there would be overshooting of the ER: the exchange rate would jump from its initial level to a level above the new level, and then fall gradually to its new higher level.

The Dornbusch model clearly gives an account of how the interaction of nominal rigidity with real or nominal shocks can cause a greater degree of volatility in the nominal exchange rate. Indeed, it was held up as an explanation of the high UK £ Sterling rate in the early 1980s (Buiter and Miller, 1981).

An alternative theory is put forward by Flood and Rose (1999) based on the possibility of a non-linear model with multiple equilibria. Rather than focusing on macroeconomic forces to explain this difference, they suggest modelling the changing structure of the foreign exchange market in the move from fixed to floating exchange rates. In essence they argue that it is important to incorporate a form of *risk premium* when comparing expected interest rate yields across financial centres, adjusted for the expected exchange rate across countries. The changing market microstructure generated by the move to flexible exchange rates attracts agents into the foreign exchange rate market with a high appetite for risk and this, in turn, can impart considerable volatility to exchange rates.

More formally they argue that there are significant non-linearities in a floating exchange rate system to do with the behaviour of investors. If investors are risk averse and have a home-currency preference, nominal ER volatility matters to them. In particular, there is no longer a linear relationship between the rate of return on assets and the exchange rate: the variance is inherently non-linear. This leads to the possibility of multiple equilibria given real variables. Volatility may thus be the result of switching between equilibria.

Another theory of exchange rates which can yield volatility is the notion of exchange rate 'bubbles'. A speculative bubble happens when (rational) investors continue to invest in an appreciating asset despite the knowledge that the bubble will collapse. What keeps the bubble going is the short-term speculative gain: this balances the probability that the bubble will burst. Eventually the bubble bursts, of course, but the precise timing is uncertain. It is this uncertainty that keeps the bubble going (no one wants to be left out of the short-term gains to be made). A bubble is consistent with rational expectations and can occur even if fundamentals remain unchanged.

## 14.6 Conclusion

In this chapter, we have examined the view that there are fundamental problems with the way we understand and model exchange rates. In essence, these can be reduced to two ideas which have found widespread empirical support.

- If we are looking at exchange rate movements in the period of 12–24 months, then it is not possible to outperform the random walk model, either for the purpose of *ex post* modelling or prediction.

- Exchange rates are more volatile than we would expect. The volatility of nominal ERs under a floating regime does not lead to a reduction in real volatility as compared to a fixed regime.

The lesson we can draw from these conclusions is that we have been looking at the wrong sort of models to understand exchange rates. In particular, it is essential to model the speculative nature of agents in the FOREX markets. Nearly all of the trading in FOREX markets is speculative: less than 5% is related to trade and non-monetary transactions. These markets are dominated by the short term.

FOREX markets are similar to equity markets in that they are dominated by speculation. However, there is a clear and very important difference. In the equity market one can think of a 'true' value for a share in terms of the net present value of current and future dividends: if one held onto a share forever, one would get that present value. From that present value, one can work back: it acts like a terminal condition that to some extent ties down the share value. Clearly, no one lives forever and there are many imperfections which make this condition weaker: however, it is there in the background even for the most short-termist speculator. There is no such terminal condition in the FOREX market: if you held a dollar bill forever, it would still just be a piece of paper, having an unknown and indeterminate purchasing power. This makes the nominal exchange rate very different from a share value.

There are those politicians who look at the value of a currency in terms of a measure of confidence in the economy or measure of economic virility. Nothing could be more stupid. In the 1920s and 1930s, millions of lives were blighted by politicians who wanted to have high 'symbolic' exchange rates: Winston Churchill's return to the gold standard in Britain and Poincaré's 'Strong Franc' policy. The irrational attachment to a highly valued currency persists in Europe today: French and German politicians were sensitive to the decline in the Euro in its first year. Since it was almost certainly initially overvalued against the $, its decline was if anything to be welcomed.

The fundamental economic relationships emphasised by economists seem to be very weak. PPP is the prime example: it may be present but there is only a very weak pull towards PPP which operates in the medium to long run. However, whilst the notion of PPP does not give us a theory of the actual exchange rate, it does give us a measure of *competitiveness*. A currency which is way above PPP is overvalued and will probably be in trouble unless it has some large natural resource (such as oil). Its firms will find it hard to sell on the international markets profitably, whilst imports of foreign firms will flood in to take advantage of the easy money.

The Meese and Rogoff finding that the random walk is the best model of the exchange rate is not surprising if we accept that it must be so in a speculative market where all arbitrage opportunities are exhausted. However, perhaps it points to a need to take finance theory more seriously in our modelling of exchange rates.

If there is no clear theory of how exchange rates are determined, it becomes possible for governments to influence them in the long run. Clearly, government policy might be an additional source of volatility. However, if the exchange rate is not tied down by fundamentals, then perhaps the government can move it from an undesirable level towards something better. There will of course be an interaction between the markets and the government (or its delegated central bank), but this can be managed.

## Summary

- For exchange rate movements over a two-year period, the random walk model cannot be surpassed for *ex-post* modelling or forecasting.
- Exchange rates are volatile. With floating rates, real volatility does not decline compared to fixed ER regimes.

## Questions

1. What causes changes in the real exchange rate?
2. Are fundamentals crucial for ER determination in the long run?
3. What is the purchasing power parity puzzle?
4. Why might the PPP not hold in reality?

## Key concepts

| | |
|---|---|
| real rate of return | real appreciation |
| Fisher equation | real depreciation |
| PPP | exchange rate volatility |
| random walks | FOREX markets |

## Notes

1. The author would like to thank Kevin Lawler, Linda Jordan and Bipasa Datta for their comments. The chapter was written whilst the author was an ESRC research fellow.
2. This is sometimes called the *nominal* exchange rate. Another related concept is the *real* exchange rate. This measures the cost of (traded) goods in two countries in a common currency, and is more a concept of *competitiveness*.
3. Other right-hand drive countries include Japan and India, but these are rather far away from the UK.
4. This omits the interest rate differential across currencies. These are often small relative to currency fluctuations and can often be ignored as a first approximation.

## Bibliography

Baxter, M. and Stockman, A. (1989) 'Business cycles and the exchange-rate system', *Journal of Monetary Economics*, vol. 23, pp. 377–400.

Berkowitz, J. and Giorgianni, L. (1997). 'Long-horizon exchange rate predictability?' *International Monetary Fund*, Working Paper 97-6.

Buiter, W. and Miller, M. (1981) 'Monetary-policy and international competitiveness – the problems of adjustment', *Oxford Economic Papers*, vol. 33, pp. 143–75.

Cassel, G. (1928) *Foreign Investments*, University of Chicago Press.

Dornbusch, R. (1976) 'Expectations and exchange rate dynamics', *Journal of Political Economy*, vol. 84, pp. 1161–76.

Flood, R. P. and Rose, A. K. (1995) 'Fixing exchange rates: a virtual quest for fundamentals', *Journal of Monetary Economics*, vol. 36, pp. 3–37.

Flood, R. and Rose, A. (1999) 'Understanding exchange rate volatility without the contrivance of macroeconomics', *Economic Journal*, vol. 109, pp. F660–72.

Frankel, J. and Rose, A. (1992) 'Empirical research on nominal exchange rates', in G. Grossman and K. Rogoff (eds), *Handbook of International Economics*, pp. 1689–729, Amsterdam: Elsevier Science Publishers BV.

Killian, L. (1997). 'Exchange rates and monetary fundamentals: What do we learn from long-horizon regressions?', *Mimeo*, University of Michigan.

MacDonald, R. (1999) 'Exchange rate behaviour: are fundamentals important?', *Economic Journal*, vol. 109, pp. F673–91.

Mark, N. (1995) 'Exchange rates and fundamentals: Evidence on long-horizon predictability', *American Economic Review*, vol. 85 (March), pp. 201–18.

Meese, R. and Rogoff, K. (1983) 'Empirical exchange rate models of the seventies: Do they fit out of sample?', *Journal of International Economics*, vol. 14 (February), pp. 3–24.

Mussa, M. M. (1986) 'Nominal exchange rate regimes and the behaviour of the real exchange rate', *Carnegie-Rochester Series on Public Policy*, pp. 117–213.

Obstfeld, M. (1995) 'International currency experience: new lessons and lessons relearned', *Brookings Papers on Economic Activity* 1, pp. 119–220.

Rogoff, K. (1999) 'Monetrary models of the Dollar/Yen/Euro nominal exchange rates; dead or undead?', *Economic Journal*, vol. 109, pp. F655–9.

# 15 Exchange rate variability and trade[§]

**ANDREW ABBOTT**

## 15.1 Introduction

With the move to floating exchange rates in 1973 concern arose that exchange rate volatility could be harmful to international trade. The switch to floating exchange rates has generally been characterised by a higher degree of exchange rate variability (Kumar and Whitt, 1992; Macdonald, 1988). These concerns led to further international monetary policy cooperation to limit exchange rate fluctuations. Formal policy regimes, such as the European Currency Snake (1972–1978) and the European Exchange Rate Mechanism (1979–1999), were established to coordinate intervention among member states to limit movements of currencies within fixed bands. In the recent past, the Plaza and Louvre accords led to coordinated intervention to reverse observed misalignments of the US dollar. More recently, the introduction of the Single European Currency (the Euro) eliminated all currency fluctuations between the member states.

Economic theory suggests that exchange rate variability creates uncertainty regarding the prices importers would have to pay, or exporters would receive, in their domestic currency terms, at some date in the future. Assuming risk aversion, participants in international trade would tend to prefer the relatively certain profits from domestic trade compared to foreign markets, where uncovered profits earned are subject to exchange rate fluctuations. The uncertain revenue would thus encourage them either to switch away from foreign markets to domestic economic activities or attempt to insure (at a cost) against exchange rate fluctuations through hedging techniques.

Despite a large amount of empirical research, over a wide range of countries and sample periods, ambiguity still remains as to the direction and strength of the exchange rate variability effect on trade volumes and prices (McKenzie, 1999). This ambiguity appears to have arisen for two reasons. Firstly, there is little consensus regarding the measurement of exchange rate variability. A range of measures have been suggested, although it is not apparent which is the most appropriate measure to be used and under what circumstances one measure is more appropriate than another. In measuring exchange rate variability researchers are attempting to depict the uncertainty that exporters and importers face regarding the future movements in the exchange rate. Thus some studies have used measures which capture movements in the unanticipated exchange rate, such as the average deviation of the spot rate from the lagged forward rate (Justice, 1983; Cushman, 1988a) and the variance of the exchange rate around its estimated trend (Kenen and Rodrik, 1984; Thursby and Thursby, 1987; Perée and Steinherr, 1989). Many studies have used the standard deviation (or variance) of the exchange rate (or its percentage changes) measured either in nominal or real terms (see Abbott *et al.*, 2000; Bahmani-Oskooee, 1991).

A second factor is that recent research has tended to rely less on traditional estimation methods, such as Ordinary Least Squares. For example, since the late 1980s researchers have adopted estimation techniques such as Zellner's Seemingly Unrelated Regression Estimator (SURE) (de Grauwe, 1988; Stokman, 1995); Polynomial distributed lag models (Anderson and Garcia, 1989; Bailey, Tavlas and Ulan, 1987); Vector Autoregressions (Koray and Lastrapes, 1989; Lastrapes and Koray, 1990); and the Johansen Cointegration Methodology (Chowdhury, 1993; Holly, 1995; Arize, 1997).

However, the use of new econometric techniques in this field has not generally been accompanied by significant developments of the underlying theory. Many studies still utilise simple linear trade models which usually include: a proxy for economic activity (e.g. GNP; GDP or industrial production); possibly a definition of capacity utilisation; a proxy for relative prices; and a measure of exchange rate variability. Further developments in economic theory and modelling could therefore be necessary to clarify the debate as to the sign and magnitude of exchange rate variability effect.

The chapter is structured as follows: Section 15.2 considers the main economic arguments as to why exchange rate variability should influence international trade; Section 15.3 discusses the mean–variance framework; Section 15.4 provides an empirical framework; Section 15.5 provides a survey of the main themes and studies in the empirical literature. Section 15.6 provides conclusions of the chapter.

## 15.2    Why should exchange rate variability influence international trade?

In attempting to demonstrate a link between exchange rate variability and international trade, economists are essentially concerned with illustrating how uncertainty regarding future exchange rate movements influences the decision making of exporters and importers. Exchange rate uncertainty arises because many trade contracts are not denominated in domestic currency. Table 15.1 presents evidence by Tavlas (1997) on the currency denomination of export and import contracts for a selection of countries. The data suggest that significant proportions of trade contracts are denominated in foreign currency. For example, the US dollar invoicing of imports varies from 18.1% (Germany) to 28.0% (Italy), up to 70.4% (Japan). The percentage of imports denominated in home currency for all countries except the USA, varies from 22.5% (Japan) to 53.3% (Germany). The US dollar maintains a strong position as a currency frequently used for invoicing trade contracts. We can see that 98% of US exports and 88.8% of US imports are denominated in US dollars. Thus by virtue of the fact that a far higher proportion of trade contracts are denominated in domestic currency, US exporters and importers are less affected by currency volatility.

Most trade contracts incorporate a payment lag from the contract date to allow time for delivery or to provide trade credit. For example, an importer may have to pay a trade contract in foreign currency at some future date. If the price of foreign currency increases then import costs will rise, which could influence the profitability from importing if the higher costs cannot be passed on to the final consumer. Uncertainty over the future price of foreign currency will generate uncertainty about the importer's own profits, given the potential for fluctuations in the cost of importing due to exchange rate movements.

The extent of the variability effect on trade will generally depend upon the size and predictability of the exchange rate fluctuations; the degree of risk aversion; the degree of market power (and thus to what extent the variability costs can be passed on to the final

**Table 15.1  Currency denomination of exports and imports for selected countries, 1992–96 (percentage terms).**

### EXPORTS

|  | US Dollar | Deutsche Mark | Japanese Yen | Pound Sterling | French Franc | Italian Lira | Other |
|---|---|---|---|---|---|---|---|
| United States | 98.0 | 0.4 | 0.4 | 0.3 | – | – | 9.0 |
| Germany | 9.8 | 76.4 | 0.6 | 2.4 | 2.8 | – | 8.0 |
| Japan | 52.7 | – | 35.7 | – | – | – | 1.6 |
| United Kingdom | 22.0 | 5.0 | 0.7 | 62.0 | 3.5 | 1.7 | 5.1 |
| France | 18.6 | 10.6 | 1.0 | 4.2 | 51.7 | 3.1 | 10.8 |
| Italy | 23.0 | 18.0 | – | – | 7.0 | 40.0 | 3.0 |

### IMPORTS

|  | US Dollar | Deutsche Mark | Japanese Yen | Pound Sterling | French Franc | Italian Lira | Other |
|---|---|---|---|---|---|---|---|
| United States | 88.8 | 3.2 | 3.1 | – | – | – | 4.9 |
| Germany | 18.1 | 53.3 | 1.5 | 1.9 | 4.4 | – | 20.8 |
| Japan | 70.4 | 2.8 | 22.5 | – | – | – | 4.3 |
| United Kingdom | 22.0 | 11.9 | 2.4 | 51.7 | 5.3 | 2.2 | 4.5 |
| France | 23.1 | 10.1 | 1.0 | 2.9 | 48.4 | 3.7 | 10.8 |
| Italy | 28.0 | 13.0 | – | – | 8.0 | 37.0 | 14.0 |

*Source* adapted from Tavlas (1997).

consumer); the presence of goods and markets with more stable exchange rates; and the price elasticity of demand and supply for exports (imports).

Foreign exchange risk can be covered through a number of internal and external hedging techniques. The most common form of external mechanism is the use of forward exchange markets. This allows exporters and importers to buy or sell foreign currency at an agreed rate now for delivery at some specified date in the future. Forward contracts are usually available for fixed lengths, e.g. 1 month, 3 months.

However, there may be a number of reasons why forward markets aren't used to hedge foreign exchange risk. First, exporters (importers) may be risk loving or have a sufficiently low degree of risk aversion that they choose not to cover forward. Secondly, forward markets can only provide complete cover if the foreign currency denominated sales receipts are known with certainty. If the foreign currency price is allowed to vary over the contract period, forward markets may provide only limited cover. Thirdly, forward contracts are typically only available for contracts up to 12 months. This may make providing cover for longer-term trade contracts or investment appraisal more difficult, unless financial engineering methods are adopted to provide continuous cover. There is also usually a risk premium attached to covering forward which can mean that the cost of forward cover is prohibitive if profit margins are small on trade contracts.

Internal hedging techniques are generally used by multinational firms and involve a subsidiary company being used to cover the foreign exchange risk exposure. For example, a parent company may use the funds of a foreign subsidiary, so that it can pay for a contract in the subsidiary's currency. Parent companies may also provide a loan of their domestic currency to a foreign subsidiary to pay contracts, which could be repaid in the foreign subsidiary's currency. Such a technique is known as a swap loan. Companies may also use leads and lags, whereby the timing of payments and collections is adjusted in anticipation of favourable currency movements. The use of this technique is dependent upon a number of factors, including market expectations, the invoicing currency position, and the degree of stability of the invoicing currency.

The costs of exchange rate variability may also be greater for smaller firms. Larger firms tend to have more market power to pass hedging costs on to the final consumer. They also tend to have a more comprehensive organisational structure (e.g. financial departments and financial management structures), as well as greater financial reserves, which can be used to minimise foreign currency risk exposure. Furthermore, a wider selection of products and markets may be available to larger firms to diversify away their currency exposure. If raw materials are also imported, the greater degree of market power to renegotiate contracts with suppliers enables larger firms to absorb uncertainty costs into the negotiated prices, or to switch to suppliers in markets with more stable exchange rates. Each of these factors could mean that smaller firms are deterred from entering foreign markets or could cause them to leave foreign markets and switch to domestic economic activities. This could lead to a rise in industrial concentration and possible reduction in trade volumes. Companies may also tend to specialise in products or services for which they have sufficiently large profit margins so as to cover the costs of hedging.

Persistent exchange rate variability may also generate a tendency for governments to resort to protectionist policies, either in the form of direct quantitative restrictions such as tariffs, quotas or other forms of assistance, e.g. infant-industry assistance for exporters. Alternatively, governments may undertake competitive devaluations of their own currency. Indirectly they may simply slow down the pace of free trade reforms through signing fewer free trade treaties and agreements. Such policies have been termed 'the political economy of exchange rate variability' (De Grauwe, 1988), which result in markets becoming more protected, so that opportunities for international trade to take place are reduced.

The above arguments have presupposed that exchange rate variability will be detrimental to trade flows. However, a number of authors have produced theoretical models which prove that under certain assumptions a positive exchange rate variability effect can be obtained (De Grauwe, 1988; Demers, 1991; Franke, 1991). For example, De Grauwe (1988) considers a model of a representative exporter who faces the choice between supplying goods to domestic and foreign markets. The only source of risk faced by the exporter is assumed to be the price received from export sales (in domestic currency terms) due to fluctuations in the exchange rate. Whether increases in exchange rate variability are expected to lead to an increase or reduction in export volumes is shown to depend upon the concavity or convexity of the marginal utility function and therefore the degree of risk aversion. Exporters with a small degree of risk aversion will export less in the face of higher exchange rate variability. Intuitively, given the exporter is not concerned with the worst possible outcome, the marginal utility falls, since the negative substitution effect from higher exchange rate variability outweighs the positive income effect, so that the quantity of trade falls. By contrast, a very risk averse exporter would have a negative substitution effect resulting from higher exchange rate variability outweighed by a positive income effect. The very risk averse exporter worries about the worst possible outcome and exports more so as to allow for the lost possible revenue resulting from higher exchange rate variability.

## 15.3     A theoretical framework: mean-variance analysis

The mean-variance analysis (Tobin, 1958; Markowitz, 1959) is the framework that is most commonly used to analyse the impact of exchange rate uncertainty on international trade. Agents are assumed to maximise utility U($\pi$), which is a function of expected profits ($\mu_\pi$) and the standard deviation (or variance) of the profits ($\sigma_\pi$):

$$U(\pi) = \mu_\pi + \gamma/2 \, (\sigma_\pi^2)^{1/2} \qquad\qquad \dots 15.1$$

The mean of a normal distribution of profits[1] is used to reflect the firm's expected profits and the standard deviation or variance used to characterise the uncertainty. The utility function is assumed to be of a quadratic form, with respect to $\pi$. $\gamma$ is a constant coefficient of risk aversion, which characterises the firm's risk preferences. Typically it is assumed that the firm is risk averse, which means that $\gamma < 0$, so that certain profits are preferred to those which are subject to exchange rate uncertainty.[2]

Ethier (1973) uses the mean-variance framework to demonstrate how exchange rate uncertainty influences the amount of forward hedging undertaken by firms rather than the level of trade directly. A perfectly competitive firm imports goods for delivery $n$ periods into the future, and covers a fraction of the transactions on the forward market, exposing the remainder to fluctuations of the spot exchange rate. It is assumed that perfect cover is available (i.e. forward cover is available for every possible length of import contract) and the importer either covers forward completely or partly exposes the profits to spot rate fluctuations. This model investigates the relationship between expected profits and the standard deviation of the profits. As the firm exposes itself to higher exchange rate uncertainty, expected profits will increase. The firm can hedge against this risk but the higher costs of forward cover reduce the profitability of international trade. Thus the objective of the firm is to find the combination of expected profits and standard deviation of profits that maximises utility and determines the optimal amount of forward cover.

Some of these issues have been addressed by Clark (1973) who examines the effect of exchange rate uncertainty on the demand for exports produced by a perfectly competitive firm. Clark shows that even if a firm can hedge perfectly on the forward exchange market it will still be exposed to uncertainty regarding movements in the forward exchange rate. This occurs, first, because the forward exchange market may not be sophisticated enough to ensure complete cover, when the length of the exporter's contract period is greater than the maximum forward contract available. Secondly, the firm may be uncertain as to the amount of forward cover needed until the end of the contract period if the foreign price is a random variable. It is assumed that the exporter knows the mean and variance of the export earnings, but only knows how much forward cover is needed a fixed period before payment is due. Thus a fraction of the foreign earnings is hedged in anticipation of the amount of forward cover required and another fraction is covered when the required amount of forward currency becomes known with certainty, towards the end of the contract period. The exporter is exposed to foreign exchange risk because of uncertainty about future movements in the forward exchange rate, since complete hedging is not available.

More recently Gagnon (1993) has extended the traditional expected utility framework by using dynamic optimisation to analyse the response of a representative exporting firm who faces exchange rate variability between the contract and settlement dates. Again the exporter is assumed to maximise expected utility, but adjustment costs and rational expectations are incorporated into the decision-making process.

## 15.4    An empirical framework

One of the first attempts to empirically model the impact of exchange rate uncertainty on international trade came from the work of Hooper and Kohlhagen (1978). Their theoretical model considers the case of profit-maximising exporters and importers who maximise utility via a mean-variance framework. The optimal conditions for import demand and export supply are derived, from which the price and volume equations can be obtained. The model for representative exporters and importers is then aggregated to derive the reduced form price and volume equations for trade flows between economies.

Hooper and Kohlhagen estimate the impact of a measure of nominal exchange rate uncertainty[3] on bilateral and mutlilateral trade flows for the USA and West Germany with France, Japan, the UK and Canada for the period 1965 Q1 to 1975 Q4. The empirical research suggests that the variability measure had a significant positive influence on trade volumes in 1 out of 16 cases, while for trade prices a significant positive influence was found for 2 cases and a significant negative effect in 6 cases.

Since the publication of the Hooper and Kohlhagen study a large amount of empirical research has taken place to discover whether exchange rate variability is detrimental to international trade. Studies have focused either on estimation of a single trade volume equation, reduced form price and volume equations or on a structural system of export demand and supply, as follows:

$$p_t = \delta_0 + \delta_1 c_t + \delta_2 v_t^e \qquad \qquad \dots 15.2$$

$$x_t = \beta_0 + \beta_1 p_t^x + \beta_2 p_t^* + \beta_3 y_t^* + \beta_4 v_t^e \qquad \qquad \dots 15.3$$

where $p_t$ is the logarithm of the price of exports in domestic currency terms; $c_t$ is the log of unit costs of production; $v_t^e$ is the chosen measure of exchange rate variability. In 15.3, $x_t$ is the log of the volume of exports; $p_t^x$ is the log of the price of exports in foreign currency terms;[4] $p_t^*$ is the log of the price of foreign substitutes and $y_t^*$ is the log of foreign income, both denominated in foreign currency terms. The nature of the structural system infers an infinitely price elastic export (import) supply schedule, so that export (import) prices are determined independently of export (import) volumes.

## 15.5    Empirical research

In order to proceed to an evaluation of the empirical literature it is useful to classify studies, so that papers from similar methodologies can be compared more effectively. Four categories are proposed: Aggregate trade studies; Bilateral trade studies; Disaggregated/Industry specific studies and Cointegration analysis. An appendix summarising some of the major studies is provided at the end of the chapter.

### 15.5.1  Aggregate trade studies

One of the most conventional approaches is to test for the effect of exchange rate variability on aggregate trade flows of a particular country or even a collection of economies. A significant number of studies have adopted this approach, primarily for convenience, since aggregate data is usually far more plentiful for longer periods of time and a larger number of countries. Studies of this kind often require a 'global' measure of variability, which is usually calculated by trade weighting the relevant exchange rates, according to the percentage of trade occurring with the country being analysed.

This methodology, however, has its difficulties since, as the IMF (1984) note, it may fail to take account of switching trading patterns, as trade is diverted from countries of high volatility to those of low volatility within the aggregate measure. Moreover, a particular country may be trading with a large number of economies, with a variety of exchange rate agreements and regimes, which introduces interpretation difficulties into the analysis of the exchange rate variability effect. Bini-Smaghi (1991) also notes that data aggregation constrains the variability elasticities to be similar across countries and indeed sectors of the economy. Aggregate studies may fail to recognise that the response of importers and exporters to a change in variability may be different for economies experiencing a high degree of exchange rate volatility compared to one with relatively stable exchange rates. Furthermore, some sectors may have less market power to pass the costs of exchange rate variability on to the final consumer, depending upon the price elasticity of demand. Aggregate data studies also face the difficulty of finding appropriate proxies for the other independent variables in the model to the exchange rate variability measure. For example, proxies for world income and price indices for substitute goods from the rest of the world have to be found.

Akhtar and Hilton (1984) examine the influence of exchange rate variability on the prices and volumes of US and West German exports and imports, over the sample periods 1974Q1–1981Q4 and 1974Q1–1982Q4. Akhtar and Hilton specify a two-equation structural system, modelling export (import) demand as a function of foreign (domestic) income; relative prices and a measure of nominal exchange rate variability.[5] Export (import) supply is assumed to be a function of unit costs and exchange rate variability. For the 1974Q1–1981Q4 period, Akhtar and Hilton found a statistically significant negative variability effect on West German export and import volumes and US export volumes, but no significant effect on US import volumes. The US export price equation had a negative variability coefficient, with a positive coefficient for West Germany, although neither was statistically significant. A positive variability coefficient was also found in the West German export and import price equations, although again no statistically significant results were found. When the sample period was extended to 1982 all of the results remained robust, except that a statistically significant, positive variability coefficient was found in the West German import price equation.

The empirical methodology of Akhtar and Hilton, however, has been strongly criticised by Gotur (1985), who extends their original work to include exports of France, Japan and the UK, specifically because Akhtar and Hilton systematically applied a one-step Cochrane–Orcutt (CO) procedure to all regression equations, without pre-checking for serial correlation. When the Akhtar and Hilton regression results were re-examined, the results for the US export volume equation suggested no serial correlation; moreover, the variability coefficient was no longer significant. Gotur also raises the difficulty that since an eight-quarter lag structure was imposed on the exchange rate variability measure, the estimation period of 1974Q1–1984Q4 ranges over both fixed and floating exchange rate periods, since the estimation period began in 1972Q1. Consequently, when the sample period began in 1975Q1, Gotur found that there were significant changes in the sign and magnitude of the variability coefficients for the US and West Germany. The empirical results from the Akhtar and Hilton study were also found to be sensitive to the order of polynomial lag used. Failure to correctly specify the correct order of polynomial could have rendered the estimates to be biased and inconsistent, as well as possibly leading to standard hypothesis tests giving misleading conclusions. Akhtar and Hilton use a second-order lag polynomial for all cases. Gotur shows that with the use of a third-order lag polynomial the significant 'variability' effect on US export volumes and US import prices disappears.

The Akhtar and Hilton model was consequently re-estimated taking account of the above modifications, over the sample period 1975Q1–1983Q4, calculating the quarterly standard deviation from the daily observations of an alternative effective exchange rate index.[6] The modified results suggest only the German export volume equation remains robust. Results for France, Japan and the UK suggest no effect on trade volumes or prices.

Bailey, Tavlas and Ulan (1986) have also estimated the effect of the absolute value of the quarter to quarter changes in the nominal effective exchange rate using a similar group of countries and sample period to that used by Akhtar and Hilton (1984). The results suggest no significant effect on aggregate trade volumes. In a later study, Bailey, Tavlas and Ulan (1987) consider the effect on aggregate exports by extending the original sample of countries from their 1986 study, by using the absolute value percentage changes in the nominal and real effective exchange rate plus an eight-quarter moving average standard deviation of the percentage changes in the effective exchange rate, both in nominal and real forms. In only three out of 40 cases analysed were the estimated variability co-efficients negative and statistically significant, while five variability coefficients were positive and significant.

More recently, Bahmani-Oskooee (1991), Bahmani-Oskooee and Ltaifa (1992), Chowdhury (1993), Kroner and Lastrapes (1993) and Caporale and Doorodian (1994) have all demonstrated a statistically significant negative relationship between a variety of exchange rate variability measures and aggregate trade flows. To measure exchange rate variability Kroner and Lastrapes (1993) and Caporale and Doorodian (1994) use conditional heteroscedasticity processes; Bahmani-Oskooee (1991) and Bahmani-Oskooee and Ltaifa (1992) use a standard deviation measure, and Chowdhury (1993) adopts an eighth-order moving average standard deviation. The difference in conclusion from these studies, compared to the work of Akhtar and Hilton (1984), Gotur (1985) and Bailey, Tavlas and Ulan (1986, 1987), could therefore possibly be explained by examination of a wider sample of countries, longer sample periods, use of different variability measures and use of other estimation techniques than OLS.

## 15.5.2  Bilateral trade studies

In order to avoid some of the problems associated with using aggregate trade data, some studies have analysed trade flows between two specific countries. This approach, however, does not avoid the problem of there being separate variability effects for different sectors of the economy.

Cushman (1983, 1986 and 1988b) attempted to test the robustness of the empirical results found in Hooper and Kohlhagen (1978). Cushman (1983) adapts the Hooper and Kohlhagen framework by assuming that the utility of exporters and importers depends upon real rather than nominal profits. Consequently, this study attempts to examine how sensitive the results of Hooper and Kohlhagen are to a different choice of exchange rate variability based on movements in the real exchange rate and denoting the majority of the independent variables in real terms. The proxy of exchange rate variability used is a four-quarter moving average standard deviation of the changes in the real exchange rate. The rationale for using the real exchange rate is that movements in the exchange rate which influence international trade may be offset by movements in relative prices. The sample period used is 1965Q1–1977Q4, which is two years longer than that used by Hooper and Kohlhagen. A number of lag structures were also tried, on the basis that the effects of exchange rate uncertainty will be extended beyond the firms' current planning horizon. The more flexible dynamic specification was successful in solving some of the serial correlation problems found in the Hooper and Kohlhagen study, where a one-period distributed lag was applied to all cases.

Cushman's empirical results somewhat contradict those of Hooper and Kohlhagen, in that 6 out of 16 cases for the US and West Germany show a negative relationship between real exchange rate variability and real export volumes. Three out of 16 cases show a significant effect on real trade prices, one case being negative and two cases being positive. However, it can be difficult to compare directly the results of Cushman with Hooper and Kohlhagen. Cushman's moving average standard deviation proxy can only directly measure exchange rate variability rather than uncertainty. By contrast, the uncertainty proxy used by Hooper and Kohlhagen measures the dispersion between a proxy for the market's expectation of the future spot exchange rate (the current forward rate) and the actual spot rate one period in the future.

In Cushman (1988b), the sample period, measures of exchange rate variability, and number of countries used in the Hooper and Kohlhagen study are extended. The focus of the paper is the robustness of the variability effect to a wider spectrum of measures.[7] Cushman (1988b) examined the influence of each variability (uncertainty) measure on the US export and import volumes with the UK, the Netherlands, France, West Germany and Japan, for the period 1974Q1–1983Q4. A total of 60 trade flows were examined. Significant negative exchange rate variability effects were found in five out of six US import flows, and robust conclusions for the various proxies were found for the Netherlands, UK and Japan. US exports to the UK and Canada were the only two cases where negative 'variability' effects were found.

One of the main difficulties of bilateral trade studies is that the variability measure included often ignores the influence of uncertainty from other trading partners. In an important contribution, Cushman (1986, 1988a) examines the effect of the co-variance between two bilateral exchange rates on bilateral trade,[8] or what he terms third-country risk. Cushman estimated an econometric equation, similar to that specified by Hooper and Kohlhagen, for bilateral trade flows to and from the United States with a number of countries, over a period of fixed and floating exchange rates. Over the fixed rate period, 1965Q1–1977Q4, in three out of six cases, coefficients were negative and significant when third-country risk was included; in four out of six cases the coefficients were negatively signed and significant when the third-country risk variable was excluded. From 1973Q1 – 1983Q4, for two out of six cases the variability coefficients were negative and significant when third-country risk was included. Three out of six cases were negatively signed and significant when third-country risk was excluded.

A difficulty, however, for the third-country risk measure is that it can only consider the interrelationship between two bilateral exchange rates. Some firms may be able to diversify their risk exposure to a number of currencies. Furthermore, for individual countries or sectors of the economy, a wider portfolio of currencies need to be accounted for.

### 15.5.3  Disaggregated industry-specific studies

A number of authors have examined the influence of exchange rate volatility on trade for individual industries or sectors of the economy. This approach has the advantage of avoiding the problem of data aggregation mentioned earlier, where the variability elasticities are constrained to be similar across industries. Furthermore, disaggregated trade data allow external factors, which are specific to a particular industry, to be incorporated into a regression equation. For example, a period of very bad weather could possibly account for a significant reduction in the exports of agricultural produce. If these products account for a large proportion of an economy's total exports, we might incorrectly infer that a decline in aggregate external trade was caused by exchange rate variability.

Industry-specific data also enables researchers to examine the relationship between industrial concentration (and hence market power) and the influence of exchange rate variability on international trade. As Gosling (1987) notes, in markets which are significantly price competitive, higher exchange rate variability would force exporters invoicing in foreign currency to raise export prices, and as a consequence of the high price elasticity of demand, experience a reduction in the volume of exports, if the costs of hedging are significant. If, however, firms have some market power by which they can raise their export price or are able to invoice in their own currency, and the own price and cross price elasticities are relatively low, the costs of higher exchange rate uncertainty are likely to be borne by the consumer, with little effect on the volume of international trade.

Coes (1981) analysed exports of 22 products for Brazil ranging from agricultural products such as Beef and Fish to Metals and Machinery, using annual data over the sample period 1957 to 1974. An interesting feature of this paper is that it adopts a non-conventional measure of exchange rate variability, in the form of the integral difference between the cumulative distribution of the monthly real exchange rate and a 'certain' exchange rate. Coes presents evidence to suggest that the exchange rate variability proxy used had a significant negative effect on trade volumes in 16 out of 22 cases at the 95% significance level and in an additional two cases at the 90% level. Furthermore, the evidence indicates that there were significant differences in the variability effect across sectors of the Brazilian economy. In one case, for example, the overall elasticity of export volumes with respect to exchange rate variability (i.e. the sum of the variability elasticities for the contemporaneous and three lagged variables) for Rice was $-0.24$ compared to an overall elasticity of 0.028 for Electrical and Communications equipment.

A number of authors have concentrated on aggregate trade within the manufacturing sector of the economy (see Justice, 1983; Kenen and Rodrik, 1986 and Bini-Smaghi, 1991). Gosling (1987) analysed UK manufactured exports for seven products, over the period 1977Q2–1988Q2. Using a quarterly standard deviation calculated from the daily observations of the nominal effective exchange rate, in five out of seven cases analysed, the variability measure had a significant negative effect, whilst one product suggested a positive relationship between variability and trade. For the price equation, two out of seven cases suggested a significant positive variability effect, and four cases indicated the presence of a significant negative variability effect. This study also demonstrates that there were significant differences in the estimated variability coefficients across different sectors of the economy. The effect on trade volumes was strongest for the Chemicals sector, with an elasticity of $-0.23$, compared to the Textiles sector, with an elasticity of $-0.091$. The variability elasticity in the price equation was largest for the Road Vehicles sector (0.07) and smallest for Manufactures ($-0.004$).

Stokman (1995) uses trade data for five European countries, over the period 1980Q1 to 1990Q4, and examines the influence of a standard deviation measure of exchange rate variability on aggregate exports to the EU in Food, Raw Materials, Chemicals, Manufactures and Machinery sectors. Using a SURE estimation method, the empirical results indicate the presence of a significant negative influence on export volumes in 23 out of 25 cases. However, the direction and magnitude of the variability effect varies across sectors and countries. For example, Food Products generally tend to have a larger variability elasticity than capital goods, such as Machinery and Manufactured Products. Stokman partly explains this result by the fact that producers of capital goods tend to be less risk averse, due to their greater market power. Furthermore, for these producers, short-term exchange rate variability is likely to be less relevant, given that they usually have longer delivery and contract payment lags.

A difficulty, however, for this study is that the aggregate export data used extends across countries operating under both fixed and floating rate periods. This is likely to influence the characteristics of the exchange rate variability measure used, since the distribution of the exchange rate is likely to change between periods of fixed and floating exchange rates (Vlaar and Palm, 1993). Also, an interesting extension to this paper would have been to consider the percentage of trade accounted for by the products examined in the study. The policy conclusions derived from the Stokman paper could then be considered in the light of the negative variability effect on the total trade of a particular country. The logical extension of this conclusion is that some products may be more relevant to some countries, rather than using a fixed category of products. It is also useful to consider the interlinkages between the different sectors, and the impact of a decline in trade in one sector on other sectors of the economy, particularly if some products are used as raw materials in the production of final goods. Some sectors may also be able to cushion the effects of exchange rate variability through higher profit margins, or their market power enabling them to pass the hedging costs on to the final consumer.

### 15.5.4 Cointegration analysis

A lot of studies in the empirical literature have made the assumption that the data used for estimation were stationary, i.e. I(0) (the time series fluctuates around a constant mean with a finite variance). It is now apparent, however, that many economic time series may in fact be non-stationary or I(1) (where the mean, variance or co-variance of the series fluctuates over time), thus making standard inferential methods inappropriate. In an attempt to overcome these problems recent research has utilised the Johansen Cointegration procedure (Johansen, 1988), which accommodates non-stationary variables and permits multiple cointegrating vectors.

Chowdhury (1993) uses the Johansen procedure to examine the impact of an eight-quarter moving average standard deviation of the changes in the real effective exchange rate on the volume of real exports. The aggregate export volume equation was estimated for the G7 countries over the period 1973–1990. In each case a unique cointegrating vector was found together with a statistically significant, negatively signed long-run normalised coefficient for the variability measure. Interestingly, the long-run variability coefficients were similar across the G7 countries. Chowdhury also found a statistically significant negative relationship between the movements in export volumes and movements in exchange rate variability, when a short-run error correction model was estimated.

Arize (1995a) also uses the Johansen approach to examine the influence of an ARCH measure of exchange rate variability on the volume of US real aggregate exports, over the period 1973Q2–1991Q3. A unique cointegrating vector is found and a long-run normalised variability elasticity of $-0.066$. Hypothesis testing also suggests that the variability measure plays a significant role in the determination of the long-run equilibrium relationship, when an exclusion restriction is imposed on the relevant coefficient. The short-run movements in exchange rate variability also played a significant role in determining the movements in real export volumes from an estimated error correction model. Arize (1995b) estimates the previous model of real aggregate export volumes for Denmark, the Netherlands, Sweden and Switzerland. The estimated unique cointegrating vectors indicate that an eighth-order moving average standard deviation of the changes in the real effective exchange rate had a significant influence on export volumes. The measure of exchange rate variability also had a significant influence on short-run movements in export volumes.

Arize (1997) later tested the robustness of the model used in earlier papers for the UK, USA, Denmark, Germany, Italy, Japan and Switzerland. The results confirm the findings of the 1995 papers, where in each case a unique cointegrating vector and statistically significant negative long-run variability coefficient are found. However, in comparison to Chowdhury (1993), the magnitude of the long-run variability coefficient varies significantly across countries, for a similar sample period and range of countries. For example, Switzerland has a long-run variability coefficient of $-0.72$, compared to $-3.72$ for Japan. Arize also compares the performance of the ARCH measure of variability with a moving average standard deviation. He concludes from the empirical work that the moving average standard deviation understates the 'true' degree of exchange rate uncertainty, as originally suggested by Pagan and Ullah (1986).

One of the difficulties associated with applying the Johansen procedure in this literature arises when the variability measure used is found to be I(0). The testing procedure used to identify the number of cointegrating vectors can be sensitive to the incorporation and treatment of I(0) variables. Abbott et al. (2000) found that the standard deviation measure was I(0) when applied to the case of UK sterling and the impact of its volatility on UK exports. Abbott et al. (ibid.) estimate a model of UK export volumes using the recently developed Bounds test/ARDL approach to Cointegration. This allows the testing and estimation of a single cointegrating vector incorporating both I(1) and I(0) variables. From this research Abbott et al. (2000) found no significant impact from the standard deviation measure on UK exports.

## 15.6    Conclusion

The move to floating exchange rates resulted in a rise in inter-temporal exchange rate volatility. These currency fluctuations were believed to be the source of instability and uncertainty in the operation of the international trading system. It is still widely believed that exchange rate variability will be detrimental to foreign trade for the reasons outlined in the chapter. This uncertainty can be covered or 'hedged' against, using a variety of techniques. However, such uncertainty usually incurs costs to firms either in the form of forward risk premiums or additional management costs as firms use internal accounting methods to avoid risk exposure.

Despite a large empirical investigation it is still unclear whether exchange rate uncertainty is detrimental to international trade. Our survey of the literature has shown that different results can be obtained using similar research methodologies, so it is unclear what generally the direction of the variability effect is, let alone the strength of any impact.

The most obvious reason is the apparent lack of guidance provided as to the most appropriate means of measuring exchange rate variability, in particular its ability to accurately characterise the exchange rate uncertainty that exporters and importers face in their decision making. A fruitful area of future research would be to compare the characteristics and performance of the plethora of variability measures used to determine a set of guidelines by which variability measures would be most appropriately used.

## Summary

- Arguments are considered as to why variability in the exchange rate influences trade flows.
- Theoretical models and empirical investigations are explained and the large volume of empirical work in this area surveyed.
- Despite voluminous empirical research, it is still not clear if exchange rate uncertainty is detrimental to trade flows.
- No agreed method of assessing exchange rate volatility exists.

## Questions

1. 'Exchange rate variability should influence trade flows.' Discuss.
2. Consider the main advantages and disadvantages of the main measures of exchange rate variability.
3. 'Industry-specific studies provide more insights on the impact of exchange rate variability than other types of study.' Comment.
4. 'Hedging can avert most elements of risk that importers and exporters face with floating rates.' Discuss with respect to empirical models.

## Key concepts

| | |
|---|---|
| OLS | mean-variance analysis |
| cointegration | expected utility |
| aggregate trade studies | industry specific studies |
| risk aversion | bilateral trade studies |
| exchange rate variability | Johansen procedure |

## Acknowledgement

§ The author gratefully acknowledges the comments of Professor George Zis (Manchester Metropolitan University) on an earlier draft of this chapter.

## Notes

1. The normality assumption is problematic since recent evidence suggests that in some cases the distribution of the exchange rate can be non-normal, in particular leptokurtic (has 'fat tails'). Non-normality means that information concerning the degree of skewness and kurtosis in the distribution would have to be included in the estimation of expected profits. The standard deviation can act as an erratic and misleading measure if the exchange rate distribution is leptokurtic, since it gives more weight to the extreme observations (McFarland, Petit and Sung, 1982; Rana, 1981 and Westerfield, 1977).
2. If $\gamma > 0$ then the firm is risk loving, while if $\gamma = 0$ the firm is risk neutral.
3. The uncertainty measure used is the average over a given quarter of the 13 weekly absolute deviations between the current spot rate and the lagged forward rate.
4. $p_t^x = (p_t/e_t)$, where e is the exchange rate, which is defined as the price of foreign currency per unit of domestic currency. The export price in exporter's currency is assumed to be constant over

the contract period, so that uncertainty about the domestic currency price only occurs because of fluctuations in the exchange rate.

5. The measure of exchange rate variability used is the standard deviation of the daily observations in the nominal effective exchange rate for a given quarter.

6. Specifically, the effective exchange rate index is calculated from weights derived from the IMF Multilateral Exchange Rate Model. Akhtar and Hilton simply use trade weights.

7. Cushman (1988b) uses a fourth-order moving average standard deviation of the percentage changes in the real exchange rate and measures that capture exchange rate uncertainty through the deviation of the spot rate from the lagged forward rate, where the lagged forward rate acts as a proxy for the expected future spot rate.

8. The co-variance is usually calculated by using the exchange rate from the bilateral trade flow being estimated and the bilateral exchange rate of a close trading partner.

# Bibliography

Abbott, A., Darnell, A. C. and Evans, J. L. (2000) 'The influence of exchange rate variability on UK exports', *Applied Economics Letters*, forthcoming.

Akhtar, A. M. and Hilton, R. S. (1984) 'Effects of exchange rate uncertainty on German and US trade', *Federal Reserve Bank of New York Quarterly Review*, Spring, pp. 7–16.

Anderson, M. and Garcia, P. (1989) 'Exchange rate uncertainty and the demand for US soybeans', *American Journal of Agricultural Economics*, vol. 71, No. 3, pp. 721–9.

Arize, A. C. (1995a) 'The effects of exchange-rate volatility on United States exports – an empirical investigation', *Southern Economic Journal*, vol. 62, No. 1, pp. 34–43.

Arize, A. C. (1995b) 'Trade flows and real exchange-rate volatility: an application of cointegration and error – correction modelling', *North American Journal of Economics and Finance*, vol. 6, No. 1, pp. 37–51.

Arize, A. C. (1997) 'Conditional exchange-rate volatility and the volume of foreign trade: evidence from seven countries', *Southern Economic Journal*, vol. 64, No. 1, pp. 235–354.

Bahmani-Oskooee, M. (1991) 'Exchange rate uncertainty and trade flows of developing countries', *The Journal of Developing Areas*, vol. 25, pp. 497–508.

Bahmani-Oskooee, M. and Ltaifa, N. (1992) 'Effects of exchange rate risk on exports: cross-country analysis', *World Development*, vol. 20, No. 8, pp. 1173–81.

Bailey, M. J., Tavlas, G. S. and Ulan, M. (1986) 'Exchange rate variability and trade performance: evidence for the big seven industrial countries', *Weltwirtschaftliches Archiv*, pp. 466–76.

Bailey, M. J., Tavlas, G. S. and Ulan, M. (1987) 'The impact of exchange rate variability on export growth: some theoretical considerations and empirical results', *Journal of Policy Modelling*, vol. 9, No. 1, pp. 225–43.

Bini-Smaghi, L. (1988) 'Exchange rate variability, trade and capital mobility', Phd Dissertation, University of Chicago, Department of Economics.

Caporale, T. and Doorodian, K. (1994) 'Exchange rate variability and the flow of international trade', *Economics Letters*, vol. 46, No. 1, pp. 49–54.

Chowdhury, A. R. (1993) 'Does exchange rate volatility depress trade flows? Evidence from error-correction models', *Review of Economics and Statistics*, vol. 75, No. 4, pp. 700–6.

Clark, P. B. (1973) 'Uncertainty, exchange risk and the level of international trade', *Western Economic Journal*, vol. 11, pp. 302–13.

Coes, D. V. (1981) 'The crawling peg and exchange rate uncertainty' in J. Williamson (ed.), *Exchange Rate Rules: The Theory, Performance, and Prospect of the Crawling Peg*, St. Martin's Press, New York, USA.

Cushman, D. O. (1983) 'The effects of real exchange rate risk on international trade', *Journal of International Economics*, vol. 15, pp. 45–63.

Cushman, D. O. (1986) 'Has exchange risk depressed international trade? The Impact of third country exchange risk', *Journal of International Money and Finance*, vol. 5, pp. 361–79.

Cushman, D. O. (1988a) 'The impact of third country exchange risk: a correction', *Journal of International Money and Finance*, vol. 7, pp. 359–60.

Cushman, D. O. (1988b) 'US bi-lateral trade flows and exchange risk during the floating period', *Journal of International Economics*, vol. 24, pp. 317–30.

De Grauwe, P. (1988) 'Exchange rate variability and the slow-down in growth of international trade', *IMF Staff Papers*, vol. 35, pp. 63–84.

Demers, M. (1991) 'Investment under uncertainty, irreversibility and the arrival of information over time', *Review of Economic Studies*, vol. 58, pp. 333–50.

Ethier, W. (1973) 'International trade and the forward exchange market', *American Economic Review*, vol. 63, No. 3, pp. 393–503.

Franke, G. (1991) 'Exchange rate volatility and international trading strategy', *Journal of International Money and Finance*, vol. 10, pp. 292–307.

Gagnon, J. E. (1993) 'Exchange rate variability and the level of international trade', *Journal of International Economics*, vol. 34, pp. 269–87.

Gosling, S. (1987) 'Effects of exchange rate volatility on UK exports', *National Economic Development Organisation, Economics Working Paper*, No. 24.

Gotur, P. (1985) 'Effects of exchange rate volatility on trade: some further evidence', *IMF Staff Papers*, vol. 33, pp. 475–512.

Holly, S. (1995) 'Exchange rate uncertainty and export performance: supply and demand effects', *Scottish Journal of Political Economy*, vol. 42, No. 4, pp. 381–91.

Hooper, P. and Kohlhagen, S. W. (1978) 'The effect of exchange rate uncertainty on the prices and volume of international trade', *Journal of International Economics*, vol. 8, pp. 483–511.

International Monetary Fund (1984) 'Exchange rate volatility and world trade', *IMF Occasional Paper*, No. 28, July.

Johansen, S. (1988) 'Statistical analysis of cointegrating vectors', *Journal of Economic Dynamics and Control*, vol. 12, pp. 231–54.

Justice, G. (1983) 'The impact of exchange rate variability on international trade flows', *Bank of England, Discussion Paper*, No. 4.

Kenen, P. B. and Rodrik, D. (1984) 'Measuring and analyzing the effects of short term volatility in real exchange rates', *Working Papers in International Economics*, G-84-01, Department of Economics, Princeton University, Princeton, USA.

Koray, F. and Lastrapes, W. D. (1989) 'Real exchange rate volatility and US bi-lateral trade: a VAR approach', *The Review of Economics and Statistics*, vol. 68, pp. 311–15.

Kroner, K. F. and Lastrapes, W. D. (1993) 'The impact of exchange rate volatility on international trade: reduced form estimates using GARCH-in-mean model', *Journal of International Money and Finance*, vol. 12, pp. 298–318.

Kumar, V. and Whitt, J. A. (1992) 'Exchange rate volatility and international trade', *Federal Reserve Bank of Atlanta, Economic Review*.

Lastrapes, W. D. and Koray, F. (1990) 'Exchange rate volatility and US multi-lateral trade flows', *Journal of Macroeconomics*, Summer, vol. 12, No. 3, pp. 341–62.

Macdonald, R. (1988) *Floating Exchange Rates: Theories and Evidence*, Unwin Hyman, London.

Markowitz, H. (1959) 'Portfolio selection', *Journal of Finance*, vol. 7, pp. 77–91.

Mckenzie, M. D. (1999) 'The impact of exchange rate volatility on international trade flows', *Journal of Economic Surveys*, vol. 13, No. 1, pp. 71–106.

McFarland, J. W., Pettit, R. R. and Sung, S. K. (1982) 'The distribution of foreign exchange price changes: trading day effects and risk measurement', *Journal of Finance*, vol. XXXVII, No. 3, pp. 693–715.

Pagan, A. and Ullah, A. (1986) 'The econometric analysis of models with risk terms', *Centre for Economic Policy Research, Discussion Paper*, No. 127, July.

Perée and Steinherr, A. (1989) 'Exchange rate uncertainty and foreign trade', *European Economic Review*, vol. 33, pp. 1241–64.

Rana, P. B. (1981) 'Exchange rate risk under generalized floating: eight Asian countries', *Journal of International Economics*, vol. 11, pp. 459–66.

Stokman, A. C. J. (1995) 'Effects of exchange risk on exports', *De Economist*, vol. 143, No. 1, pp. 41–54.

Tavlas, G. S. (1997) 'The international use of the US dollar: an optimum currency area perspective', *World Economy*, vol. 87, pp. 85–103.

Thursby, J. C. and Thursby, M. C. (1987) 'Bi-lateral trade flows, the Linder Hypothesis and exchange risk', *The Review of Economics and Statistics*, pp. 488–95.

Tobin, J. (1958) 'Liquidity preference as behaviour towards risk', *Review of Economic Studies*, vol. 25, pp. 65–86.

Vlaar, P. J. G. and Palm, F. C. (1993) 'The message in weekly exchange rates in the European Monetary System: mean reversion, conditional heteroscedasticity, and jumps', *Journal of Business and Economic Statistics*, vol. 11, No. 3, pp. 351–60.

Westerfield, J. M. (1977) 'An examination of foreign exchange risk under fixed and floating rate systems', *Journal of International Economics*, vol. 7, pp. 181–200.

**Appendix: A summary of empirical literature on the relationship between exchange rate variability and international trade volume and prices.**

| Author | Sample period | Countries | Measure(s) of variability | Estimation technique | Dependent variable | Result |
|---|---|---|---|---|---|---|
| Hooper and Kohlhagen (1978) | 1965Q1–1975Q4 | West Germany, France, Japan, UK; US and Canada | Average absolute deviation between current spot rate and the lagged forward rate, using 13 weekly observations for a given quarter. | OLS | Bilateral trade volumes and prices for US and West Germany | *Price Equation*: significant negative influence in 6 cases, significant positive influence in 2 cases. *Volume Equation*: significant positive influence in 1 case. |
| Coes (1981) | 1957–1974 (Annual Data) | Brazil | Integral difference in cumulative distribution of monthly real exchange rate and a 'certain' exchange rate. | OLS with Cochrane-Orcutt Iterative Technique where appropriate | Exports as a fraction of Production for 22 products* | Significant effect on trade volumes for 18 out of 22 cases. |
| Cushman (1983) | 1965Q1–1977Q4 | UK, US, France, West Germany, Canada and Japan | Four-quarter moving average standard deviation of the percentage changes in the real exchange rate. | OLS | Bilateral trade volumes and prices | Six out of 16 cases show evidence of a negative relationship between real exchange rate variability and trade volumes. Two out of 16 cases show a significant effect on trade prices. |
| Akhtar and Hilton (1984) | 1974Q1–1978Q4 and 1974Q1–1982Q4 | West Germany and US | Standard Deviation of daily observations of the Effective Exchange Rate for a given quarter. | OLS | Aggregate exports and imports; prices of aggregate imports and exports | Significant negative effect except for US imports. No significant effect on export prices. Extended sample period presents some evidence of a significant negative effect. |
| International Monetary Fund (1984) | 1959Q1–1982Q4. Sub-periods: 1962Q1–1982Q4; 1967Q1–1987Q4; 1959Q1–1991Q4; 1974Q1–1987Q4. | Canada, France, Italy, West Germany, Japan, UK and US | Standard deviation of a seven-country trade-weighted average of quarterly real effective exchange rates. | OLS | World Trade Index and 42 bilateral trade flows of imports and exports between countries | Insignificant results and positively signed for world trade. Two out of 42 bilateral trade flows significant and negatively signed. |
| Gotur (1985) | 1975Q1–1983Q4 | US, West Germany, France, Japan and UK | Standard deviation of the Effective Exchange Rate Index weighted from the IMF Multilateral Exchange Rate Model (MERM). Daily observations used to calculate quarterly measure. | OLS and Cochrane-Orcutt correction procedure where appropriate | Aggregate import and export volumes and prices | One out of ten trade volume equations have significant variability elasticities which are negatively signed. Four out of ten price equations have significant variability elasticities. |

* The products analysed include non-metallic mineral products; metals; machinery; electrical and communications equipment; transportation equipment; paper and paper products; rubber products; leather and leather goods; textiles; clothing and footwear; food processing; beverages; tobacco products; beef; fish; seafood; cashews; wool; rice; corn; peanuts; soybeans.

| Author | Sample period | Countries | Measure(s) of variability | Estimation technique | Dependent variable | Result |
|---|---|---|---|---|---|---|
| Bailey, Tavlas and Ulan (1987) | 1962Q2–1974Q4 and 1975Q1–1985Q3 | Canada, France, Germany, Italy, Japan, UK, US, Australia, the Netherlands and Switzerland | The absolute quarterly percentage change in the effective exchange rate (nominal and real forms); eight-quarter moving average standard deviation of the effective exchange rate (nominal and real forms). | Polynomial distributed lag model | Volume of Aggregate Exports | Overall significant effect but not very strong. Direction of the variability effect inconclusive. |
| Gosling (1987) | 1977Q2–1988Q2 | UK | Quarterly standard deviation of the daily nominal effective exchange rate. | Polynomial distributed lag model | Aggregate manufactured exports for seven products: Manufactures; Chemicals; Clothing & Footwear; Scientific instruments; Textiles; Machinery; Road Vehicles | *Volume Equation:* 5 out of 7 cases significant and negative; 1 case significant and positive. *Price Equation:* 2 out of 7 cases significant and positive; 4 cases significant and negative. |
| Cushman (1988b) | 1974Q1–19783Q4 | US, UK, the Netherlands, France, West Germany, Canada and Japan | Four-quarter moving standard deviation of recent changes in bilateral real exchange rates; forward exchange rate measures; forward risk premium measures. | OLS | US bilateral trade flows | Five out of six cases have significant negative risk coefficients for imports. Two out of six cases have a significant risk coefficient for exports. |
| De Grauwe (1988) | 1960Q1–1969Q4 and 1973Q1–1984Q4 | Belgium, Canada, France, West Germany, Italy, Japan, the Netherlands, Switzerland, UK and US | Variability of the yearly percentage changes in the bilateral nominal and real exchange rates. | Zellner's Seemingly Unrelated Regression Estimator | Average yearly movements rates of bilateral exports between chosen countries | Insignificant result during fixed rate period and significant effect during floating period for real exchange rate variability. Nominal exchange rate variability has an insignificant effect. |
| Anderson and Garcia (1989) | 1975Q1–1985Q4 | US, Japan, Spain and France | Absolute percentage changes in quarter to quarter movements in the spot rate; absolute percentage difference between the current spot and the lagged forward rate. | Polynomial Distributed Lag Model | US exports of soybeans to Japan, France and Spain | All cases show a significant negative relationship with trade in Soybeans. |
| Koray and Lastrapes (1989) | 1959M1–1985M12 | US, UK, Germany, France, Japan and Canada | Twelfth-order moving average standard deviation | Vector Autoregressive (VAR) technique | Bilateral US imports | Weak relationship between variability and trade volume overall. Stronger relationship following the move to floating exchange rates. |

| Author | Sample period | Countries | Measure(s) of variability | Estimation technique | Dependent variable | Result |
|---|---|---|---|---|---|---|
| Perée and Steinherr (1989) | 1966–1985 (Annual Data) | US, UK, Belgium, Japan and West Germany | Disequilibrium measures incorporating short-run volatility and long-run misalignments of the exchange rate | OLS | Aggregate Export Volumes | Insignificant result overall. |
| Lastrapes and Koray (1990) | 1973M3–1987M12 | US | Moving Sample Standard Deviation of the movements of the real exchange rate | Vector Autoregressive (VAR) technique | Real multilateral US imports and exports | Significant but weak effect on trade. Effect of variability on trade is small compared to other determinants specified in the model, e.g. income. |
| Bini-Smaghi (1991) | 1976Q1–1984Q4 | Italy, France and West Germany | Standard deviation of the rate of change of the nominal exchange rate | OLS | Aggregate trade volumes and prices for manufactured exports | Overall significant negative influence on export volumes. For Germany volatility has a positive influence on export prices, for France and Italy a negative influence on export prices. |
| Chowdhury (1993) | 1973Q1–1990Q4 | Canada, France, West Germany, Italy, Japan, UK and US | Moving sample monthly standard deviation of the movements of the real exchange rate | Johansen Cointegration Procedure and Error Correction Model | Volume of aggregate real exports | Strong, significant negative effect. |

# 16 The Maastricht Treaty: EU convergence, unemployment and inflation

## E. KATSOULIE

## 16.1 Introduction

This chapter considers unemployment, EMU and convergence in the EU and examines the inflation:unemployment trade-off. The Maastricht Treaty signed on 7 February 1992, or more formally the 'Treaty on European Union', set out the following three stages for achieving Economic and Monetary Union (EMU). The terms of the treaty are considered initially. Thereafter each member state's inflation:unemployment experience is reviewed. Finally, a SURE estimation is made for each member and the union as a whole and policy implications considered.

*Stage 1*, commenced 1 January 1993: This refers to the creation of the 'Monetary Committee' (MC) which monitors and reviews all monetary matters in the EU, such as the integration of capital markets, the participation of all the member states of the EU in the Exchange Rate Mechanism (ERM), and the European Currency Unit (ECU) in EU transactions.

*Stage 2*, commenced 1 January 1994: This refers to the creation of the European Monetary Institute (EMI) which will be dealing with all matters necessary for the implementation of the single currency in the EU, such as the cooperation between the central banks of the member states, coordination of the various monetary policies, and monitoring the functioning of the European Monetary System (EMS).

*Stage 3*, commenced 1 January 1999: This refers to the transformation of the EMI into the European Central Bank (ECB) which deals with all matters relevant to the introduction of the single currency, the Euro, such as managing the official reserves of all the member states, the fixing of the exchange rates of the national currencies for all the member states, and the issue of banknotes throughout the EU.

For a member state to be eligible to join the EMS, it has to meet the following 'convergence criteria' (European Commission, 1997):

1. *Price stability*. A country's rate of price inflation should be no greater than 1.5% of the average rate of inflation of the three best-performing member states.

2. *Public sector finances*. A country's government deficit, i.e. budget deficit, should be no more than 3% of GDP at market prices, and the country's government debt, i.e. national debt, should be no more than 60% of GDP at market prices.

3. *Interest rates stability*. A country's nominal long-term interest rate levels should be no more than 2% of the interest rate levels of the countries with the lowest rates of price inflation.

4. *Exchange rates stability*. The exchange rate fluctuations of the country's currency within the ERM should not exceed specific predetermined margins for two years and should not be devalued against the currency of any other member state.

According to the Maastricht Treaty, convergence between the member states is a precondition for progress towards EMU. Convergence generally means the narrowing of differences in economic variables and characteristics, and it can be usually distinguished by three categories (Britton and Mayes, 1992):

1. *Nominal convergence*. This is the narrowing of differences in 'nominal' variables, such as price inflation, public finances, interest rates and exchange rates. The four convergence criteria for joining the EMS belong to this category.

2. *Real convergence*. This is the narrowing of differences in 'real' variables, such as labour productivity, living standards, unemployment rates, etc. Real convergence does not constitute a precondition for joining the EMU.

3. *Structural convergence*. This is the narrowing of differences in patterns of production and consumption and the assimilation of economic institutions referring mainly to financial markets and labour markets. Structural convergence does not constitute a precondition for joining the EMU.

The aim of this chapter is to examine how the price stability convergence criterion may affect real convergence, measured in terms of unemployment rates.

*The relationship between inflation and unemployment*. One of the most frequently cited papers in economics is Phillip's (1958) paper referring to the so-called Phillips curve, which shows the negative relationship between wage inflation and unemployment (Figure 16.1(a)), or the negative relationship between prices inflation and unemployment (Figure 16.1(b)).

The negative relationship of the Phillips curve, which is an empirical curve, associates the inflationary gap in the economy with high unemployment and similarly associates recessionary gaps of the economy with low unemployment. In other words, when unemployment is high the pressure for wage increases, and thus for price inflation, is low and conversely when unemployment is low the pressure for wage increases, and thus for price inflation, is high.

The trade-off between inflation and unemployment, shown in the negatively sloped Phillips curve, can also be explained in terms of economic policies. If the costs of inflation are believed to be high the government could intervene by regulating aggregate

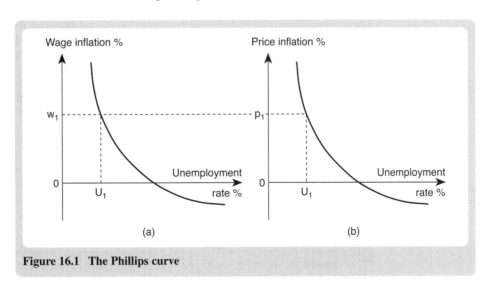

**Figure 16.1  The Phillips curve**

demand to lower levels, through either lower spending and/or tax increases, and/or decreases in money supply. However, higher unemployment, and lower inflation, result from this decrease in aggregate demand. Similarly, if the costs of inflation are believed to be low the government could intervene by regulating aggregate demand to higher levels, through either higher spending and/or tax cuts, and/or increases in money supply. However, higher inflation, and lower unemployment, are the result of this increase in aggregate demand.

## 16.2    An assessment of convergence among EU members

Although a convergence report (European Economy, 1999a) has been prepared recently in accordance with Article 109j(1) of the Treaty, assessing for all EU member states the four nominal convergence criteria, in this section we present the convergence situation for three major variables of member states: price inflation, unemployment rate, and growth rate of GDP. These variables were chosen in terms of measurability and availability. Price inflation refers to nominal convergence, the unemployment rate refers to real convergence, and the growth rate of GDP facilitates structural convergence measures.

To assess the convergence of these three variables, the data in Table 16.1, for price inflation, in Table 16.2, for unemployment rate, and in Table 16.3, for the growth rate of GDP, were used. Apart from specific time periods, and/or specific years, the following conclusions can be drawn for each member state:

*Belgium.* The average inflation rate showed a decrease from 8.78% in the 1970s to 1.4% in 1998, below the reference value of 2.7%, fulfilling therefore the criterion on price stability. By contrast with average inflation, average unemployment rates showed an increase from 2.52% in the 1970s to 8.50% in 1998, although less than 10.2% which was the average unemployment rate of the EU in 1998. The average GDP growth rate

**Table 16.1  Price deflator gross domestic product at market prices.**

|      | 71–75 | 76–80 | 81–85 | 86–90 | 91–95 | 96   | 97   | 98   |
|------|-------|-------|-------|-------|-------|------|------|------|
| B    | 8.78  | 5.62  | 5.88  | 3.10  | 3.00  | 1.60 | 1.50 | 1.40 |
| DK   | 10.62 | 8.84  | 7.66  | 3.92  | 1.92  | 1.90 | 2.70 | 2.70 |
| D    | 6.44  | 4.08  | 3.20  | 2.44  | 3.60  | 1.00 | 0.60 | 1.20 |
| EL   | 12.16 | 15.52 | 20.40 | 16.48 | 13.90 | 8.50 | 6.70 | 4.00 |
| E    | 12.18 | 18.16 | 11.52 | 7.40  | 5.44  | 3.10 | 2.20 | 2.40 |
| F    | 9.32  | 10.40 | 9.22  | 3.42  | 2.20  | 1.10 | 0.90 | 1.50 |
| IRL  | 13.08 | 14.72 | 11.04 | 3.24  | 1.92  | 1.10 | 2.40 | 2.20 |
| I    | 12.64 | 17.50 | 14.36 | 6.92  | 5.06  | 5.10 | 2.60 | 2.20 |
| L    | 6.66  | 6.56  | 6.44  | 2.26  | 2.50  | 0.00 | 3.10 | 2.80 |
| NL   | 9.14  | 6.06  | 3.22  | 0.82  | 2.16  | 1.30 | 2.00 | 2.20 |
| A    | 7.56  | 5.16  | 4.66  | 2.50  | 3.14  | 2.10 | 1.40 | 1.50 |
| P    | 11.48 | 21.08 | 21.86 | 13.40 | 7.94  | 2.40 | 2.00 | 2.80 |
| FIN  | 13.18 | 10.06 | 8.56  | 5.64  | 1.86  | 1.30 | 1.20 | 2.00 |
| S    | 9.02  | 10.30 | 8.42  | 7.00  | 3.48  | 1.00 | 1.20 | 2.00 |
| UK   | 13.20 | 14.94 | 6.96  | 5.56  | 3.68  | 3.00 | 2.60 | 2.30 |
| EU   | 10.22 | 11.36 | 8.50  | 4.88  | 3.84  | 2.40 | 1.80 | 1.90 |

*Source* adapted from European Economy (1999c).

**Table 16.2  Unemployment rate: Total.**

|      | 71–75 | 76–80 | 81–85 | 86–90 | 91–95 | 96    | 97    | 98    |
|------|-------|-------|-------|-------|-------|-------|-------|-------|
| B    | 2.52  | 6.60  | 10.64 | 8.68  | 8.54  | 9.80  | 9.50  | 8.50  |
| DK   | 1.82  | 5.54  | 8.36  | 6.40  | 8.62  | 6.90  | 6.10  | 5.40  |
| D    | 1.46  | 3.00  | 6.14  | 5.88  | 7.34  | 8.80  | 9.70  | 9.80  |
| EL   | 2.32  | 2.00  | 6.22  | 6.64  | 8.32  | 9.60  | 9.50  | 9.20  |
| E    | 3.30  | 5.14  | 18.02 | 18.92 | 20.94 | 22.10 | 20.90 | 19.70 |
| F    | 3.00  | 5.28  | 8.64  | 9.72  | 11.12 | 12.40 | 12.50 | 11.90 |
| IRL  | 6.52  | 8.86  | 13.94 | 15.52 | 14.48 | 11.60 | 10.20 | 8.40  |
| I    | 5.50  | 6.78  | 7.98  | 9.64  | 10.28 | 12.00 | 12.10 | 12.00 |
| L    | 0.00  | 1.68  | 2.86  | 2.12  | 2.52  | 3.30  | 3.70  | 3.90  |
| NL   | 2.88  | 5.82  | 9.62  | 7.38  | 6.40  | 6.30  | 5.30  | 4.40  |
| A    | 1.34  | 1.90  | 3.50  | 3.36  | 3.70  | 4.40  | 4.40  | 4.20  |
| P    | 2.74  | 7.38  | 7.90  | 6.06  | 5.64  | 7.30  | 6.40  | 6.20  |
| FIN  | 2.22  | 5.68  | 5.84  | 4.52  | 14.04 | 15.40 | 14.00 | 12.30 |
| S    | 2.26  | 2.00  | 3.32  | 2.08  | 7.52  | 10.00 | 10.20 | 9.10  |
| UK   | 2.64  | 5.02  | 10.58 | 9.02  | 9.52  | 8.20  | 7.10  | 6.50  |
| EU   | 2.92  | 5.14  | 8.98  | 8.94  | 10.04 | 10.90 | 10.70 | 10.20 |

*Source* adapted from European Economy (1999c).

**Table 16.3  Gross domestic product at 1990 market prices: annual percentage change.**

|      | 71–75 | 76–80 | 81–85 | 86–90 | 91–95 | 96    | 97    | 98   |
|------|-------|-------|-------|-------|-------|-------|-------|------|
| B    | 3.62  | 3.16  | 0.72  | 3.04  | 1.22  | 1.50  | 2.70  | 2.80 |
| DK   | 2.00  | 2.54  | 2.66  | 1.42  | 1.96  | 2.70  | 2.90  | 2.70 |
| D    | 2.22  | 3.26  | 1.16  | 3.36  | 2.10  | 1.40  | 2.20  | 2.60 |
| EL   | 5.16  | 4.40  | 1.36  | 1.88  | 1.14  | 2.60  | 3.50  | 3.80 |
| E    | 5.32  | 1.78  | 1.54  | 4.48  | 1.34  | 2.30  | 3.40  | 3.60 |
| F    | 3.48  | 3.12  | 1.52  | 3.22  | 1.12  | 1.50  | 2.40  | 3.00 |
| IRL  | 4.94  | 4.54  | 2.56  | 4.74  | 5.90  | 8.60  | 10.00 | 8.70 |
| I    | 2.78  | 4.46  | 1.52  | 2.98  | 1.12  | 0.70  | 1.50  | 2.40 |
| L    | 3.04  | 2.26  | 2.52  | 6.50  | 5.46  | 3.00  | 4.10  | 4.40 |
| NL   | 3.38  | 2.58  | 1.28  | 3.12  | 2.12  | 3.30  | 3.30  | 3.70 |
| A    | 3.94  | 3.34  | 1.42  | 3.20  | 1.96  | 1.60  | 2.50  | 2.80 |
| P    | 4.52  | 5.08  | 0.88  | 4.98  | 1.40  | 3.60  | 3.70  | 4.00 |
| FIN  | 4.12  | 2.84  | 2.84  | 3.42  | −0.46 | 3.60  | 5.90  | 4.60 |
| S    | 2.60  | 1.36  | 1.74  | 2.30  | 0.50  | 1.30  | 1.80  | 2.60 |
| UK   | 2.14  | 1.84  | 1.96  | 3.36  | 1.34  | 2.30  | 3.50  | 1.90 |
| EU   | 3.02  | 3.02  | 1.50  | 3.28  | 1.48  | 1.80  | 2.70  | 2.80 |

*Source* adapted from European Economy (1999c).

fluctuated around the rather moderate level of 3% for the 1970s and 80s, showing a steady increase in the 90s, and reaching the level of 2.80% in 1998 which was the average growth rate of the EU for this year.

*Denmark.* The average inflation rate showed a decrease from 10.62% in the 1970s to 2.7% in 1998, equal to the reference value of 2.7%, fulfilling therefore the criterion on price stability. By contrast with average inflation, average unemployment rates showed a moderate increase from 1.82% in the 1970s to 5.4% in 1998, well below the 10.2% average unemployment rate of the EU in 1998. The average GDP growth rate fluctuated around a rather low level of 2.5% for the 1970s and 80s, showing a steady increase in the 90s, and reaching the level of 2.70% in 1998 which was almost the average growth rate of the EU for this year.

*Germany*. The average inflation rate showed a decrease from 6.64% in the 1970s to 1.2% in 1998, much below the reference value of 2.7%, fulfilling therefore the criterion on price stability. By contrast with average inflation, average unemployment rates showed an increase from 1.46% in the 1970s to 9.8% in 1998, although less than 10.2% which was the average unemployment rate of the EU in 1998. The average GDP growth rate fluctuated around the rather moderate level of 2.5% during the whole period under investigation.

*Greece*. The average inflation rate showed a strong increase till the middle of the 1980s, reaching levels around 20%, and since then showed a slow decrease to 4% in 1998, above the reference value of 2.7%, not fulfilling therefore the criterion on price stability. By contrast with average inflation, average unemployment rates showed an increase from 2.32% in the 1970s to 9.2% in 1998, although less than 10.2% which is the average unemployment rate of the EU in 1998. The average GDP growth rate fluctuated around the high level of 5% in the 1970s, around the very low level of 1.5% in the 80s, showing a steady increase in late 90s, and reaching the level of 3.80% in 1998, much above the average growth rate of the EU for this year.

*Spain*. The average inflation rate showed a strong increase in the 1970s, reaching levels even around 20%, and since then showed a steady decrease to 2.4% in 1998, below the reference value of 2.7%, fulfilling therefore the criterion on price stability. On the contrary to average inflation, the average unemployment rate showed a very strong increase from 3.3% at the beginning of the 1970s to 19.7% in 1998, almost double the 10.2% average unemployment rate of the EU in 1998. The average GDP growth rate showed a decrease until the middle of the 1980s and then showed a steady increase in the 90s, reaching the level of 3.60% in 1998, much above the average growth rate of EU for this year.

*France*. The average inflation rate showed a decrease from 9.32% at the beginning of the 1970s to 1.5% in 1998, below the reference value of 2.7%, fulfilling therefore the criterion on price stability. By contrast with average inflation, average unemployment rates showed an increase from 3% at the beginning of the 1970s to 11.9% in 1998, higher than 10.2% which was the average unemployment rate of the EU in 1998. The average GDP growth rate fluctuated around the rather moderate level of 3% for the 1970s and 80s, showing a steady increase in the 90s, and reaching the level of 3% in 1998 which was just above the average growth rate of the EU for this year.

*Ireland*. The average inflation rate showed a decrease from 13.08% at the beginning of the 1970s to 2.2% in 1998, below the reference value of 2.7%, fulfilling therefore the criterion on price stability. By contrast with average inflation, average unemployment rates showed an increase from 6.52% at the beginning of the 1970s to 15.52% in the final years of the 90s, and decreasing in the 90s to 8.4% for 1998, being less than the 10.2% which was the average unemployment rate of EU in 1998. The average GDP growth rate, starting from 4.94% at the beginning of the 1970s, reached double values in the 90s, showing a steady increase and reaching the level of 8.7% in 1998, which was more than three times greater than the average growth rate of the EU for this year.

*Italy*. The average inflation rate showed a decrease from 17.5% in the late 1970s to 2.2% in 1998, below the reference value of 2.7%, fulfilling therefore the criterion on price stability. By contrast with average inflation, average unemployment rates showed an increase from 5.5% at the beginning of the 1970s to 12.0% in 1998, higher than 10.2% which was the average unemployment rate of the EU in 1998. Apart from the second half of the 1970s, average GDP growth rates fluctuated around the rather moderate level of 2.5% for all the period under investigation, taking the level of 2.4% in 1998 which was lower than average growth rate of the EU for this year.

*Luxembourg*. The average inflation rate showed a decrease from around 6% in the 1970s and middle 80s to 2.8% in 1998, almost the same as the reference value of 2.7%, fulfilling therefore the criterion on price stability. By contrast, the average unemployment rate showed a moderate increase from around 1.5% in the 1970s to 3.9% in 1998, which was much less than half the average unemployment rate of the EU in 1998. The average GDP growth rate showed generally an increase from 3.04% at the beginning of the 1970s, reaching the level of 4.4% in 1998 which was almost double the average growth rate of the EU for this year.

*Netherlands*. The average inflation rate showed a decrease from 9.14% at the beginning of the 1970s to 2.2% in 1998, below the reference value of 2.7%, fulfilling therefore the criterion on price stability. The average unemployment rate showed an increase until the mid-1980s and then a steady decrease to 4.4% in 1998, less than half of the 10.2% which was the average unemployment rate of the EU in 1998. The average GDP growth rate fluctuated around the rather moderate level of 3% during the whole period under investigation, reaching the level of 3.7% in 1998 which was more than the average growth rate of the EU for this year.

*Austria*. The average inflation rate showed a decrease from 7.56% at the beginning of the 1970s to 1.5% in 1998, below the reference value of 2.7%, fulfilling therefore the criterion on price stability. By contrast with average inflation, the average unemployment rate showed a moderate increase from 1.34% at the beginning of the 1970s to 4.2% in 1998, much less than half of the 10.2% which was the average unemployment rate of the EU in 1998. The average GDP growth rate fluctuated around the rather moderate level of 3% for the 1970s and the 80s, showing a steady increase in the 90s, and reaching the level of 2.80% in 1998 which was the average growth rate of the EU for this year.

*Portugal*. The average inflation rate showed a strong increase until the mid-1980s, reaching levels even around 20%, and since then showed a moderate decrease to 2.8% in 1998, around the reference value of 2.7%, fulfilling therefore the criterion on price stability. Similarly, average unemployment rate showed an increase until the mid-1980s, showing a fluctuation around the rate of 6% afterwards, and reaching the level of 6.2% in 1998, less than 10.2% which is the average unemployment rate of the EU in 1998. Apart from at the beginning of the 1980s the average growth rate fluctuated around a high level of 4.5% for the first two decades, showing a steady increase in 1990s, and reaching the level of 4% in 1998, much above the average growth rate of EU for this year.

*Finland*. The average inflation rate showed a decrease from 13.18% at the beginning of the 1970s to 2.0% in 1998, below the reference value of 2.7%, fulfilling therefore the criterion on price stability. By contrast, average unemployment rates showed an increase from 2.22% at the beginning of the 1970s to 12.3% in 1998, more than the 10.2% which was the average unemployment rate of the EU in 1998. The average GDP growth rate showed a moderate decrease until the end of the 1980s, and, apart from the beginning of the 1990s where the average growth rate was even negative, it increased to high levels for the rest of the 1990s, reaching the level of 4.6% in 1998 which was much more than the average growth rate of the EU for this year.

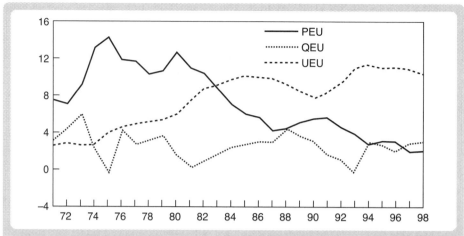

**Figure 16.2  Relationship between inflation rate, unemployment rate and GDP growth rate in the EU**

*Sweden*. The average inflation rate showed a decrease from 9.02% at the beginning of the 1970s to 2.0% in 1998, below the reference value of 2.7%, fulfilling therefore the criterion on price stability. By contrast, average unemployment rates showed a steady increase from 2.22% at the beginning of the 1970s to 9.1% in 1998, less than half the 10.2% which was the average unemployment rate of the EU in 1998. The average GDP growth rate fluctuated around the rather low level of 2% for all the period under investigation, reaching the level of 2.6% in 1998 which was just below the average growth rate of the EU for this year.

*United Kingdom*. The average inflation rate showed a decrease from 13.2% at the beginning of the 1970s to 2.3% in 1998, below the reference value of 2.7%, fulfilling therefore the criterion on price stability. The average unemployment rate showed an increase until the end of the 1980s and then a decrease, taking the level of 6.5% in 1998, much lower than the 10.2% which was the average unemployment rate for the EU in 1998. The average GDP growth rate fluctuated around the rather low level of 2.5% for all the period under investigation, reaching a level of 1.9% in 1998 which was below the average growth rate of the EU for this year.

*European Union*. The average inflation rate showed a decrease from 10.22% at the beginning of the 1970s to 1.9% in 1998. By contrast, average unemployment rates showed an increase from 2.92% at the beginning of the 1970s to 10.2% in 1998. The average GDP growth rate fluctuated around the rather moderate level of 3% for the 1970s, around the low level of 2.5% for the 1980s, and showing a steady increase in the 1990s from 1.48% at the beginning of the decade to 2.80% in 1998. The time series for the inflation rate, unemployment rate and GDP growth rate for EU are shown in Figure 16.2. It can be seen from Figure 16.2 that the inflation rate (PEU) is generally decreasing, the unemployment rate (UEU) is generally increasing, and the GDP growth rate (QEU) is generally stable, with its peaks being the opposite of the inflation rate peaks.

## 16.3    Estimating a price inflation equation for EU member states

From the times series behaviour presented in Section 16.3, the following observations can be derived:

- According to the trade-off between inflation and unemployment, the higher the unemployment rate, the lower the price inflation rate.

- According to changes in aggregate supply, a rise in aggregate supply causes a decrease in prices.

These two observations can be summarised in a (linear) price inflation equation model as follows:

$$P_{i,t} = \alpha + \beta U_{i,t} + \gamma Q_{i,t} + \delta P_{i,t-1} + \varepsilon_{i,t} \tag{16.1}$$

$$\frac{\partial P_{i,t}}{\partial U_{i,t}} = \beta \leq 0, \quad \frac{\partial P_{i,t}}{\partial Q_{i,t}} = \gamma \leq 0, \quad 0 \leq \frac{\partial P_{i,t}}{\partial P_{i,t-1}} = \delta \leq 1 \tag{16.2}$$

for $t = 1, 2, \ldots, T$ and $i = $ 1st, 2nd, $\ldots$, 15th member state

where:

$P_i$ = price inflation rate in member state $i$.
$U_i$ = unemployment rate in member state $i$.
$Q_i$ = rate of change of real GDP in member state $i$.
$\varepsilon_i$ = error term in equation $i$.

The model in (16.1) has been estimated by the method of seemingly unrelated regression equations (SURE), using Eviews 2.0, due to the implications of the main assumptions, namely that errors are correlated among equations. The data used cover the period 1971–1998, and are taken from European Economy (1999c). Specifically, the identification of the variables used is as follows:

$P_i$ = price deflator gross domestic product at market prices in member state $i$.
$U_i$ = total unemployment rate as percentage of civilian labour force in member state $i$.
$Q_i$ = annual percentage change of gross domestic product at 1990 market prices in member state $i$.

Final estimates of equation (16.1) are given for each member state in Table 16.4, where:

$R^2$ = coefficient of determination
DW = Durbin-Watson d statistic
[ ] = the numbers in brackets under the estimated coefficients represent the so-called t-ratios.

The results in Table 16.4 seem reasonable in all cases. All coefficients have the correct sign, according to the *a priori* restrictions set above, and, generally, all equations pass the usual statistical tests.

For comparison among the 15 member states and using the estimates in Table 16.4, Table 16.5 presents the price inflation elasticities, with respect to the three explanatory variables involved in equation (16.1), and the variables' sample means.

From the price inflation elasticities the member states could be categorised as follows:

With respect to unemployment rates:
*More inelastic countries* (less than the average EU elasticity, $|-0.61842|$): Greece, Luxembourg, Sweden, Finland, Denmark, Portugal, Spain, France, Germany
*More elastic countries* (greater than the average EU elasticity, $|-0.61842|$): Belgium, United Kingdom, Netherlands, Italy, Austria, Ireland

**Table 16.4  SURE for inflation equations (1971–1998): dependent variable $P_t$.**

|      | Constant             | $U_t$                | $Q_t$                  | $P_{t-1}$            | $R^2$   | DW      |
|------|----------------------|----------------------|------------------------|----------------------|---------|---------|
| B    | 6.782342 [6.01321]   | −0.456860 [4.67104]  | −0.443770 [4.53339]    | 0.530281 [6.63516]   | 0.72419 | 1.47196 |
| DK   | 4.343581 [5.90598]   | −0.410756 [5.48920]  | −0.310881 [4.23044]    | 0.800656 [15.3087]   | 0.90117 | 2.00761 |
| D    | 4.329473 [4.74908]   | −0.357795 [4.44572]  | −0.150710 [1.93176]    | 0.389578 [3.50097]   | 0.77201 | 1.52531 |
| EL   | 10.85288 [3.52870]   | −0.726418 [3.09655]  | −0.313887 [1.26451]    | 0.610928 [4.65924]   | 0.53157 | 2.20162 |
| E    | 8.794451 [4.21960]   | −0.306723 [4.26098]  | −0.190422 [1.09209]₂   | 0.626017 [7.64634]   | 0.86784 | 2.14437 |
| F    | 5.872393 [6.38205]   | −0.401364 [6.06184]  | −0.278346 [3.22126]    | 0.679833 [13.8740]   | 0.94533 | 1.33567 |
| IRL  | 22.65188 [7.95741]   | −1.067822 [7.01790]  | −0.976455 [6.09992]    | 0.358505 [4.07806]   | 0.72361 | 2.38867 |
| I    | 13.67023 [5.01846]   | −1.047532 [4.45015]  | −0.559279 [3.63390]₂   | 0.685087 [8.58245]   | 0.84685 | 1.49697 |
| L*⁺  | 5.828415 [2.14933]   | −0.661832 [0.80506]  | −0.379211 [1.90288]    | 0.379514 [1.88483]   | 0.43340 | 2.22665 |
| NL   | 4.666569 [4.81288]   | −0.485886 [5.00029]  | −0.251504 [2.20566]    | 0.731482 [12.5776]   | 0.89369 | 1.86512 |
| A    | 7.437445 [10.1363]   | −1.343421 [9.24596]  | −0.253756 [4.67626]    | 0.333433 [4.97069]   | 0.81706 | 1.54613 |
| P    | 8.718216 [3.48823]   | −1.023326 [2.47949]  | −0.526417 [2.80301]₂   | 0.955509 [10.1263]   | 0.76730 | 1.67073 |
| FIN  | 5.755389 [3.51548]   | −0.351386 [3.08614]  | −0.317143 [2.58093]₂   | 0.665085 [6.21122]   | 0.69178 | 1.85156 |
| S    | 6.952412 [5.39837]   | −0.520017 [4.16283]  | −0.100923 [0.88411]₂   | 0.331957 [2.95329]   | 0.70052 | 1.65668 |
| UK   | 11.79078 [6.72949]   | −0.816480 [5.12637]  | −0.633666 [3.76767]    | 0.461581 [5.77072]   | 0.73690 | 1.66491 |
| EU*  | 7.859793 [5.18952]   | −0.585438 [5.69211]  | −0.378303 [2.53919]    | 0.645680 [8.34883]   | 0.94456 | 1.75539 |

*Notes*: Estimates with Eviews; absolute values of t ratios in brackets.
\* OLS; + period 1977–1998; 2 variable lagged twice.

With respect to growth rates:

*More inelastic countries* (less than the average EU elasticity, $|-0.12975|$): Sweden, Spain, Greece, Germany, France, Denmark, Finland

*More elastic countries* (greater than the average EU elasticity, $|-0.12975|$): Portugal, Italy, Belgium, Austria, Netherlands, United Kingdom, Luxembourg, Ireland

**Table 16.5  Price inflation elasticities.**

|  | With respect to unemployment rate | With respect to growth rate | With respect to price inflation lagged once |
|---|---|---|---|
| B | −0.71242 | −0.21408 | 0.52734 |
| DK | −0.41076 | −0.11055 | 0.79316 |
| D | −0.51908 | −0.09894 | 0.37339 |
| EL | −0.27503 | −0.06072 | 0.62863 |
| E | −0.44318 | −0.05526 | 0.63119 |
| F | −0.51360 | −0.10925 | 0.67982 |
| IRL | −1.54614 | −0.60872 | 0.35449 |
| I | −0.84935 | −0.13183 | 0.69417 |
| L | −0.29369 | −0.32707 | 0.32140 |
| NL | −0.76230 | −0.16253 | 0.70396 |
| A | −0.91724 | −0.16100 | 0.32793 |
| P | −0.44802 | −0.13038 | 0.97781 |
| FIN | −0.35523 | −0.12291 | 0.66364 |
| S | −0.30674 | −0.02491 | 0.33174 |
| UK | −0.73149 | −0.16808 | 0.45908 |
| EU | −0.61842 | −0.12975 | 0.64489 |

With respect to price inflation rates lagged once:

*More inelastic countries* (less than average EU elasticity, 0.64489): Luxembourg, Sweden, Austria, Ireland, Germany, United Kingdom, Belgium, Greece, Spain

*More elastic countries* (greater than average EU elasticity, 0.64489): Finland, France, Italy, Netherlands, Denmark, Portugal

The categorisation of the economies according to sensitiveness to price inflation with respect to employment and production variables can be used as an index of real and structural economic divergence. To see this, consider, for example, the economies of Greece and Spain. In both economies the autonomous dynamics of inflation are more or less the same, as shown by the equality of the inflation elasticities with respect to inflation lagged once. Similarly, in the product market, supply affects prices by the same degree, taking into account that the elasticities of price inflation with respect to the rate of change of output are more or less equal. However, in the labour market things are not the same. Common policies aiming at decreasing unemployment rates by the same amounts have different effects on price inflation in these two countries. If for example, the policy aims at decreasing unemployment by 10%, price inflation in Greece will increase by 2.75% and in Spain by 4.43%.

## 16.4  Conclusions

The achievement of a high degree of nominal convergence between the economies of the EU member states facilitates the creation of economic policies referring to real and structural convergence. However, the sustainability of this convergence depends on the balance of real and structural policy mix. It is believed that once EMU is launched, member states will have more effective instruments available to promote employment policies and structural reforms at national levels (European Economy, 1999b).

Although price inflation convergence has been achieved among EU member states, a number of factors have contributed to the increase and persistence of unemployment in most EU member states. According to OECD (1994), the usual factors of technology and increased competition may not be crucial factors for rising unemployment in the EU. This is because:

1. It is not clear if technology destroys more jobs than it creates.
2. Imports from low wage countries are just a small part (about 1.5%) of total expenditure.
3. A loss of unskilled jobs due to increased competition from globalisation is offset by the creation of skilled jobs.

On the other hand, factors creating persistent unemployment in the EU are (European Economy, 1999b):

1. Economic growth has been less than or equal to the rate of increase in labour productivity.
2. Economic policies were not directed at maintaining and/or accelerating the pace of technological change.
3. Capital accumulation has slowed down in the EU.

Higher investment-supported economic growth is the crucial factor in achieving high employment rates in EU member states. The lowering of unemployment rates due to higher economic growth can also be derived from the estimated 'augmented Phillips curves' presented in Table 16.4. Considering that $P_{i,t} = P_{i,t-1} = P_i$ in function (16.1) and solving for $U_i$ for each member state estimated equation, Tables 16.6 and 16.7 present the unemployment rates for various levels of GDP growth rates and for two price inflation rate levels; 0%, i.e., non-inflation, and 2.5%, i.e., the Maastricht Treaty reference value for price convergence criterion.

By comparing the figures in Tables 16.6 and 16.7 we see the trade-off between inflation and unemployment for the various levels of GDP growth rates for all member states. Specifically, the figures in Table 16.6 present 'crude' estimates of the non-accelerating inflation rate of unemployment (NAIRU) because in this table the figures have been computed under the restriction that price inflation is zero. The following two interesting observations can be derived from the figures in Table 16.6:

**Table 16.6 Unemployment rates with respect to various GDP growth rates (Q) and 0% price inflation rate (NAIRU).**

| Q | B | DK | D | EL | E | F | IRL | I |
|---|---|----|---|----|---|---|-----|---|
| 0.00 | 14.85 | 10.57 | 12.10 | 14.94 | 28.67 | 14.63 | 21.21 | 13.05 |
| 1.00 | 13.87 | 9.82 | 11.68 | 14.51 | 28.05 | 13.94 | 20.30 | 12.52 |
| 2.00 | 12.90 | 9.06 | 11.26 | 14.08 | 27.43 | 13.24 | 19.38 | 11.98 |
| 3.00 | 11.93 | 8.30 | 10.84 | 13.64 | 26.81 | 12.55 | 18.47 | 11.45 |
| 4.00 | 10.96 | 7.55 | 10.41 | 13.21 | 26.19 | 11.86 | 17.56 | 10.91 |
| 5.00 | 9.99 | 6.79 | 9.99 | 12.78 | 25.57 | 11.16 | 16.64 | 10.38 |
| 6.00 | 9.02 | 6.03 | 9.57 | 12.35 | 24.95 | 10.47 | 15.73 | 9.85 |
| 7.00 | 8.05 | 5.28 | 9.15 | 11.92 | 24.33 | 9.78 | 14.81 | 9.31 |
| 8.00 | 7.07 | 4.52 | 8.73 | 11.48 | 23.71 | 9.08 | 13.90 | 8.78 |
| 9.00 | 6.10 | 3.76 | 8.31 | 11.05 | 23.08 | 8.39 | 12.98 | 8.24 |
| 10.00 | 5.13 | 3.01 | 7.89 | 10.62 | 22.46 | 7.70 | 12.07 | 7.71 |

**Table 16.7 Unemployment rates with respect to various GDP growth rates (Q) and 0% price inflation rate (NAIRU).**

| Q | L | NL | A | P | FIN | S | UK | EU |
|---|---|---|---|---|---|---|---|---|
| 0.00 | 8.81 | 9.60 | 5.54 | 8.52 | 16.38 | 13.37 | 14.44 | 13.42 |
| 1.00 | 8.23 | 9.09 | 5.35 | 8.00 | 15.48 | 13.17 | 13.66 | 12.78 |
| 2.00 | 7.66 | 8.57 | 5.16 | 7.49 | 14.57 | 12.98 | 12.89 | 12.13 |
| 3.00 | 7.09 | 8.05 | 4.97 | 6.98 | 13.67 | 12.79 | 12.11 | 11.49 |
| 4.00 | 6.51 | 7.53 | 4.78 | 6.46 | 12.77 | 12.59 | 11.34 | 10.84 |
| 5.00 | 5.94 | 7.02 | 4.59 | 5.95 | 11.87 | 12.40 | 10.56 | 10.19 |
| 6.00 | 5.37 | 6.50 | 4.40 | 5.53 | 10.96 | 12.20 | 9.78 | 9.55 |
| 7.00 | 4.80 | 5.98 | 4.21 | 4.92 | 10.06 | 12.01 | 9.01 | 8.90 |
| 8.00 | 4.22 | 5.46 | 4.02 | 4.40 | 9.15 | 11.82 | 8.23 | 8.26 |
| 9.00 | 3.65 | 4.95 | 3.84 | 3.89 | 8.26 | 11.62 | 7.46 | 7.61 |
| 10.00 | 3.08 | 4.43 | 3.65 | 3.37 | 7.35 | 11.43 | 6.68 | 6.96 |

1. The NAIRU depends on the level of growth for the economy. The higher the GDP growth rate, the lower the NAIRU.

2. The speed of decrease of the NAIRU with respect to the growth rate in the economy differs substantially among the member states. This possibly argues badly and brings difficulties in constructing common employment policies in EU.

In diagrammatic terms the first observation is seen in Figure 16.3, which refers to two Phillips curves for the EU economy as a whole.

In Figure 16.3, as also seen in the line for Q=2% in Table 16.7 for the EU, the NAIRU is equal to 12.13%. Under the assumption that the GDP growth rate remains constant at a level of 2%, any attempt to decrease the unemployment rate brings price inflation in the economy. If for example, the unemployment level decreases from 12.13% to 10.89%, then inflation increases from 0.0% to 2.5% (see also the line for Q=2% in Table 16.9 for the EU).

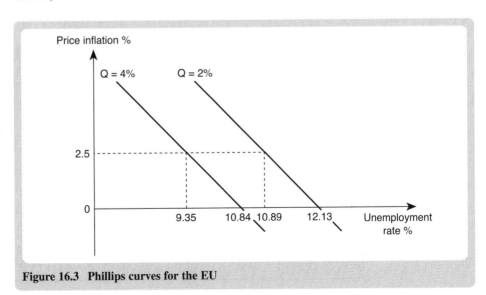

**Figure 16.3 Phillips curves for the EU**

**Table 16.8** Unemployment rates with respect to various GDP growth rates (Q) and 2.5% price inflation rate.

| Q | B | DK | D | EL | E | F | IRL | I |
|---|---|---|---|---|---|---|---|---|
| 0.00 | 12.28 | 9.36 | 7.84 | 13.60 | 25.62 | 12.64 | 19.71 | 12.30 |
| 1.00 | 11.30 | 8.60 | 7.41 | 13.17 | 25.00 | 11.94 | 18.80 | 11.76 |
| 2.00 | 10.33 | 7.85 | 6.99 | 12.74 | 24.38 | 11.25 | 17.88 | 11.23 |
| 3.00 | 9.36 | 7.09 | 6.57 | 12.30 | 23.76 | 10.56 | 16.97 | 10.70 |
| 4.00 | 8.39 | 6.33 | 6.15 | 11.87 | 23.14 | 9.86 | 16.05 | 10.16 |
| 5.00 | 7.42 | 5.58 | 5.73 | 11.44 | 22.52 | 9.17 | 15.14 | 9.63 |
| 6.00 | 6.45 | 4.82 | 5.31 | 11.01 | 21.90 | 8.48 | 14.22 | 9.09 |
| 7.00 | 5.48 | 4.06 | 4.89 | 10.58 | 21.28 | 7.78 | 13.31 | 8.56 |
| 8.00 | 4.50 | 3.31 | 4.47 | 10.41 | 20.66 | 7.09 | 12.40 | 8.03 |
| 9.00 | 3.53 | 2.55 | 4.04 | 9.71 | 20.04 | 6.40 | 11.48 | 7.49 |
| 10.00 | 2.56 | 1.79 | 3.62 | 9.28 | 19.42 | 5.70 | 10.57 | 6.96 |

The only way to decrease the unemployment rate without increasing the price inflation rate is to use economic policies that increase growth rates in the economy, i.e. economic policies that make the Q=2% Phillips curve in Figure 16.3 to shift to the left. If, for example, the GDP growth rate in the economy is Q=4%, then the Phillips curve shifts to the corresponding position in Figure 16.3, showing a NAIRU equal to 10.84% (see also the line for Q=4% in Table 16.7 for the EU) which is less than the NAIRU for the line corresponding to Q=2%. If price inflation was not at the level of 0.0%, but was at another level, say at a 2.5% reference value of convergence, then the corresponding level for the unemployment rate for Q=2% and Q=4% is 10.89% and 9.35% respectively. Generally speaking, the unemployment rate can lowered with higher investment-supported economic growth at any level of price inflation.

It must be noted here, that although the figures in Tables 16.6 and 16.7 show the levels of the NAIRU and the levels of unemployment rates for the inflation convergence reference values, at various GDP growth rates respectively, similar figures can be computed for

**Table 16.9** Unemployment rates with respect to various GDP growth rates (Q) and 2.5% price inflation rate.

| Q | L | NL | A | P | FIN | S | UK | EU |
|---|---|---|---|---|---|---|---|---|
| 0.00 | 6.46 | 9.38 | 4.30 | 8.39 | 14.00 | 10.16 | 12.79 | 12.44 |
| 1.00 | 5.89 | 8.79 | 4.11 | 7.87 | 13.09 | 9.96 | 12.02 | 11.67 |
| 2.00 | 5.32 | 8.20 | 3.92 | 7.36 | 12.19 | 9.77 | 11.24 | 10.89 |
| 3.00 | 4.74 | 7.61 | 3.73 | 6.85 | 11.29 | 9.58 | 10.46 | 10.12 |
| 4.00 | 4.17 | 7.02 | 3.54 | 6.33 | 10.39 | 9.38 | 9.69 | 9.35 |
| 5.00 | 3.60 | 6.43 | 3.35 | 5.82 | 9.48 | 9.19 | 8.91 | 8.57 |
| 6.00 | 3.02 | 5.84 | 3.16 | 5.31 | 8.58 | 8.99 | 8.14 | 7.80 |
| 7.00 | 2.45 | 5.25 | 2.97 | 4.80 | 7.68 | 8.80 | 7.36 | 7.02 |
| 8.00 | 1.88 | 4.66 | 2.78 | 4.28 | 6.78 | 8.61 | 6.58 | 6.25 |
| 9.00 | 1.31 | 4.07 | 2.60 | 3.77 | 5.87 | 8.41 | 5.81 | 5.48 |
| 10.00 | 0.73 | 3.48 | 2.41 | 3.26 | 4.97 | 8.22 | 5.03 | 4.70 |

various given levels of inflation and growth, using the estimated equations in Table 16.4. It is also important to notice that the speed of decrease of the unemployment rate, for the same conditions of inflation and growth, is different between member states. This observation makes questionable any EU-wide common strategy to achieve sustained, investment-supported, output growth and job creation over the medium term without inflationary tensions. However, this strategy contains the following three dimensions (European Economy, 1999b):

1. a stability-oriented monetary policy;

2. regulation of member states' public finances for consistency with the objectives of stability and growth;

3. nominal wage trends consistent with price stability objectives and real wage trends consistent with the labour productivity developments.

Finally, the approach using the augmented Phillips curve, to investigate trade-offs between price inflation convergence and unemployment rates, should involve further research in the context of complete wage – price – unemployment simultaneous equations models. Under such complete models, the effects of common policy strategies such as those stated can be investigated.

## Summary

- The Maastricht Treaty created stages for Monetary Union. All these stages related to convergence criteria.

- Categorising economies according to the degree of convergence means relating data for all economies to inherent sensitivities to inflation. Indices of real divergence are required. Experience from Spain and Greece links policy on inflation targets to unemployment effects.

- The EU experience links high investment with growth rates.

- NAIRU depends on the growth experience of the economy.

## Questions

1. Why is growth linked to investment ratios?

2. Why is NAIRU dependent on growth performance?

3. Why might there be a trade-off between unemployment and inflation?

4. Why does inflation reduce growth performance?

### Key concepts

| | |
|---|---|
| Maastricht Treaty | inflation |
| nominal growth | NAIRU |
| investment | convergence |
| SURE | real convergence |

# Bibliography

Atkinson, B., Livesey, F. and Milward, B. (eds) (1998) *Applied Economics*, London: Macmillan Business.

Britton, A. and Mayes, D. (1992) *Achieving Monetary Union in Europe*, London: Sage.

European Commission (1997) *Europe from A to Z: Guide to European Integration*, Luxembourg: Official Publications.

European Economy (1999a) 'Convergence Report', Commission, no. 8604.

European Economy (1999b) 'Growth and employment in the stability-oriented framework of EMU', Commission, no. 8605.

European Economy (1999c) 'Statistical Annex', Commission, no. 8606.

Griffiths, A. and Wall, S. (eds) (1997) *Applied Economics: An Introductory Course*, London: Longman, seventh edition.

Heather, K. (1994) *Modern Applied Economics*, New York: Harvester Wheatsheaf.

Lipsey, R. G., Courant, P. N., Purvis, D. D. and Steiner, P. O. (1993) *Economics*, New York: Harper Collins, tenth edition.

OECD (1994) *Jobs Study: facts, analysis and strategies*, Paris: OECD.

Parkin, M. and King, D. (1995) *Economics*, Wokingham: Addison-Wesley, second edition.

Phillips, A. W. (1958) 'The relation between unemployment and the rate of change of money wages in the United Kingdom, 1861–1957', *Economica*, vol. XXV, pp. 283–99.

Tresch, R. W. (1994) *Principles of Economics*, New York: West Publishing.

# PART FOUR

# Global issues

# 17 Global telecom development and Internet advertising

**M. LING and K. LAWLER**

## 17.1 Introduction

In the 1990s, the development of digital data transmission technology signalled major upheavals in the world telecommunications industry. Internet and wireless communications have dominated the telecommunications revolution in recent years and it is believed that they will produce a major impetus for a paradigm shift in world business. The present international economic environment is largely characterised by reduced growth and stagnant economic activity arising from the Asian crisis, downturns in Japan, and more recently the debt crisis in Brazil. The incidents give a clear signal that global recession is taking place. To maintain sustainability and competitiveness, firms realised the vital need to upgrade the use of communications and other advanced technologies. Full market liberalisation of the EU telecommunications industry began on 1 January 1998 which injected an extra boost for competition and large-scale consolidations.[1] The recent unprecedented spate of telecommunication takeovers was largely motivated by the liberalisation of world telecommunications set in motion by the Geneva World Trade Organisation meeting in 1997. Early momentum was introduced by a new Telecommunications Act in the USA in February 1996, which brought competition into local telecommunications services and video entertainment coupled with a series of privatisations of state-owned telecommunications companies in various countries between the mid-1980s and early 1990s (Table 17.1).

The elimination of these protective entry barriers is expected to generate a rigorous shake-out, sweeping away inefficient and capital-weak operators and leaving a handful of niche players. Most importantly, this process will attract an influx of dominant global players who possess the latest telecommunications technologies and significant amounts of international capital (Tables 17.2 and 17.3). The liberalisation of the European telecommunications market will certainly input extra operation capital for the global restructuring, and also stimulate the establishment of a full-blown liberal global environment for the digital communications era. The aggregate size of the telecommunications industry

**Table 17.1** Privatisation of state-owned telecommunications companies (1984–96).

|  | Less then US$1bn | US$1–2bn | US$2–5bn | Over US$5bn | Total |
|---|---|---|---|---|---|
| Aggregate market valuation | 2.962 | 15.155 | 25.57 | 114.529 | 158.216 |
| No. of countries | 19 | 10 | 8 | 4 | 41 |

*Source* adapted from ITU Privatisation Survey, Company Reports/Kelly (1996)

**Table 17.2 Top five M&A deals worldwide (deals announced between 1 Jan. and 30 Sept. 1998).**

| Target | Acquirer | Value ($bn) |
|---|---|---|
| Citicorp (US) | Travelers Group (US) | 72.558 |
| Ameritech (US) | SBC Communications (US) | 62.592 |
| Bank America (US) | NationsBank (US) | 61.633 |
| Tele-Communications (US) | AT&T (US) | 53.592 |
| GTE (US) | Bell Atlantic (US) | 53.414 |

*Source* adapted from IFR Securities Data/*Financial Times*, Lewis (1998)
Note: The snapshot is taken at the end of September 1998. Since then some mergers among global oil companies have been undertaken, namely Exxon Corp and Mobil ($257.8bn), Royal Dutch and Shell ($128.1bn) and BP and Amoco ($104bn) (Robert Corzine, *Financial Times*, 2 Dec. 1998). In February 2000, AOL acquired Time Warner with a total market capitalisation of $350 billion.

**Table 17.3 Emergence of the new US super-carrier.**

| | 1997 Revenue ($bn) | Growth Rate (%) | Market Capitalisation ($bn) |
|---|---|---|---|
| Bell Atlantic/GTE | 54.0 | 6.0 | 116 |
| AT&T | 51.3 | 1.6 | 93 |
| SBC/Ameritech | 40.8 | 6.3 | 123 |
| MCI WorldCom | 27.1 | 17.8 | 84 |
| BellSouth | 20.6 | 8.0 | 71 |
| Sprint | 14.9 | 5.9 | 30 |
| US West | 10.3 | 2.4 | 25 |

*Source* adapted from *Financial Times*, Waters (1998)

advanced at 15% in 1998, with about 4000 fixed-wire operators, mobile operators, satellite operators, equipment manufacturers, regulators and services providers at the moment (Cane, 1999a). According to Telegeography (1999), there are only 700m telephone lines on the globe for the world population of 6bn. However, telephone lines will increase to 2.3bn by 2002, which provides a promising picture for future development in global telecommunications.

Internet advertising may produce only marginal effects on sales at the moment. However, younger generations, who receive education and spend their leisure using Internet applications, will replace the less IT-literate generations. Ody (1999) emphasises that the boundary between 'shopping' and 'leisure' becomes increasingly blurred, and a similar thing might happen in cyberspace. Consequently, the sales of merchandise and services via the Internet will become more integrated. The use of Internet advertising will form an indispensable driving force enhancing commercialisation of the Internet. A recent report from Adknowledge indicates that the rate for newly established Web sites seeking advertisers increased by 38% in 1998 (Cyber Atlas, 1999). Global telecommunications are undergoing a distinct period of transition. According to Dean Witter, a Morgan Stanley investment banker, the whole world likes telecommunications so much, because demand is growing and costs are falling faster than prices (Cane, 1999b). The unprecedented speed of change in the telecommunications industry is backed by an armoury of new low-cost technologies. As noted by the Motorola Limited Chairman, David Brown, 'for many people, and the vast majority of users, technology is no longer an option, it is essential' (Cane, 1998a).

## 17.2 Restructuring and financing activities

Worldwide merger and acquisition (M&A) activities in 1998 were dominated by the telecommunications industry (Table 17.2). Among the top five M&A activities, telecommunications companies occupied two places, the second and fourth in the league table. Surprisingly, all the companies involved in the top five M&A deals are from the USA. US dominance has underlying reasons. Black (1998) argues that European companies are less fortunate than their US counterparts. This is due to the complicated regulations governing foreign investments in the USA. One of the obvious consequences is the failure of BT's earlier takeover bid for MCI. By contrast, the European telecommunications market liberalisation in 1998 introduced much more pressure on local operators. For instance, Deutsche Telekom was badly hit by increased foreign competition and is expected to shed 46,000 workers in three and half years and cut prices to sustain operational efficiency. Atkins (1998a) argued that the full liberalisation made Europe's telecoms the victim of 'one-sided, preferential treatment of competitors'. At any rate, European telecom firms would like to see level playing fields in the USA, Japan and the UK. However, hostile M&A activities do not only favour US telecoms. Table 17.4 displays the top cross-border M&A activities which were undertaken by non-US telecoms, ranking 6th, 7th and 9th among the top ten. This ranking has now changed as Vodafone AirTouch acquired Mannesmann in February 2000, creating the fourth largest company by market value behind Microsoft, General Electric and Cisco Systems. The takeover raises the market power of Vodafone so that it can take on challenges from other giants such as AT&T, NTT and Deutsche Telekom. This takeover was worth £113 billion.

For established US firms, looking for a financial partner in the US telecoms industry is possible; this is shown in the examples of recent hostile M&A activities. The results of these financial deals and recent restructuring processes generate an emerging group of new US super-carriers. However, in Europe, and elsewhere around the world, increased market liberalisation stimulated the explosive growth of new smaller companies. As the start-up costs for installation of networks require substantial capital and these newcomers lack credibility to seek sizeable bank funds, the most popular strategy for these new companies is to generate high-debt issues. Hence, there were huge amounts of high-loan issues in 1997 and 1998 (Jan.–July), which correspond to $1.8bn and $4.3bn (Cane, 1998). This financing trend reflects the fact that the risk premia involved are high.

**Table 17.4  Telecommunication industry activities among top 10 cross-border M&A deals (1 Jan.–30 Sep. 1998).**

| Ranking | Target | Acquirer | Value ($bn) |
|---|---|---|---|
| 6th | Bay Networks (US) | Northern Telecom/BCB Inc (Canada) | 9.2626 |
| 7th | Excel Communications (US) | Teleglobe (Canada) | 6.4072 |
| 9th | TELESP [Telebra] (Brazil) | Investor Group (Spain) | 4.9731 |

*Source* adapted from IFR Securities Data/*Financial Times*

Telecommunication companies are willing to try their luck in attempting to capture a slice of forecasted global aggregate revenue of $1,000bn. A selection of the high-yield debt issues from January to July 1998 are shown in Table 17.5.

In Eastern Europe, partial privatisations have taken place during the past few years. The selling of national strategic stakes to foreign operators is essential to bring finance and expertise into former Soviet countries requiring substantial modernisation and expansion of their telecommunication infrastructures. According to a report from Price Waterhouse, a total of $120bn are required to bring national fixed telephone line networks in Central and Eastern Europe up to parity with other competitors in Western Europe (Williamson, 1998). In line with worldwide liberalisation and resulting consolidation processes in recent years, wide-ranging privatisations and M&A activities occurred in Eastern Europe (Table 17.5).

In the Asia-Pacific region, the momentum for telecommunication restructuring was mainly sustained by the Japanese and Chinese economies. DoCoMo, the Japanese mobile telecommunications operator, raised around $19bn through a share issue which is the largest in world history for the telecommunications industry. This also makes DoCoMo the biggest mobile telecom in the world (Abrahams, 1998). In Hong Kong, the Special Administrative Region of China, China Telecom (Hong Kong) intends to pay $2.9bn to buy the mainland's biggest cellular networks from the parent company. Owing to the large market potential of the 1.2 billion population in China, foreign interest in the tele-communications industry, such as page services and data transmission, has increased. However, changing conditions concerning direct equity participation in telecommunica-tions operations limit foreign investment channels and restrict foreign market entry (Kynge, 1998a).

In Latin America, privatisation programmes introduced enormous impetus to the growth of the telecommunications industry. With a population of 460 million, around 11.8 million were connected to Internet services in the region. The total market transaction was worth US$1.4 billion in 1999. In four years' time, the total amount should reach the

**Table 17.5  Privatisation of national telecoms by selling a strategic stake.**

|  | Type of sales | Details |
| --- | --- | --- |
| Estonia | Strategic stake sold 1992 IPO of 51% in 1998 | 40% owned by Baltic Tele (Telia and Telecom Finland) |
| Hungary | Strategic Stake sold 1993 | Magyarcom (Ameritech & Deutsche Telekom) own 67.2% |
| Russia-Rostelcom | IPO of 49% in 1993 | 49% held by foreign/domestic investors 51% of Rostelcom still government owned |
| Czech Republic | Strategic stake sold 1995 IPO by 1999 | 27% owned by KPN & Swisscom consortium Sale of remaining stake expected by 1999 |
| Latvia | Strategic stake sold 1995 IPO when company formed into joint stock company | TILTS (Telecom Finland and Cable & Wireless to be sold when company reorganised into joint joint stock company) |
| Russia-Svyazinvest | Strategic stake sold 1997 IPO of 24% in 1998 Q2/Q3 | Mustcom Ltd own 25%, a further 24% of Svyazinvest to be sold in 1998 Q2/Q3 |

*Source* adapted from Price Waterhouse/*Financial Times*, Williamson (1998)

US$8.1 billion according to industry forecasts (Nua, 2000a). Some analysts feel scepticism about the sustainability of growth in Internet-related industries as Brazilian and Mexican economies suffered from the recent devaluation. As in other parts of the world, Internet stocks are hot assets, and the external effects on other associated industries such as banking and retailing are favourable. In most cases, as the related industries launch strategies relating to the Internet, share prices should pick up positively. However, the long-term growth in the region may rely on general economic growth to support purchasing power. Current income per capita is about $100 per week (Lapper, 2000). Moreover, to achieve a reasonable sustainable growth, the security issue is important, as postal services are unreliable and the rates of credit card fraud and theft are relatively high.

The increasing popularity of using the Internet in the Asia-Pacific region is demonstrated in Table 17.6. It is expected that an aggregate growth of 17.50 million new Internet users will occur within the next five years, representing a 218.75% increase. Generally speaking, all the economies listed are forecast to have more than 100% increase in Internet subscribers. Moreover, four out of 11 economies (Table 17.6) will experience an increase in Internet users by more than one million. The largest growth is expected from China (4.3m), Australia (3.25m) and Korea (1.7m). In terms of percentage growth, the Philippines (500%), Malaysia (450%) and India (475%) are expected to top the league. This rising forecasted number of Internet subscribers creates a favourable environment for the growth of the telecommunications industry and restructuring processes across East Asia.

Inspection of Table 17.7 indicates that the development of the telecommunications industry in Asia-Pacific is healthy. This can be demonstrated by the market capitalisation and the world rankings of telecommunications companies in that region. Although the ranking for NTT has dropped, it remains the biggest telecom operator in the world by market value. Moreover, the substantial share issue by DoCoMo stunned world markets. Owing to the currency crisis in Asia in 1997, the ranking of other Asian operators

**Table 17.6  Asia-Pacific Internet user forecasts (in millions).**

| | 1998 | 1999 | 2000 | 2001 | 2002 | 98–02 growth (%) | 98–02 growth (m) |
|---|---|---|---|---|---|---|---|
| Australia | 2.5 | 3.25 | 4.0 | 4.9 | 5.75 | 130 | 3.25 |
| China | 1.1 | 1.85 | 2.5 | 4.0 | 5.4 | 390 | 4.3 |
| Hong Kong | 0.95 | 1.25 | 1.55 | 1.8 | 2.0 | 110 | 1.05 |
| India | 0.33 | 0.5 | 0.8 | 1.3 | 1.9 | 475 | 1.57 |
| Indonesia | 0.12 | 0.16 | 0.23 | 0.32 | 0.45 | 275 | 0.33 |
| Korea | 0.5 | 0.85 | 1.15 | 1.8 | 2.2 | 340 | 1.7 |
| Malaysia | 0.2 | 0.35 | 0.55 | 0.8 | 1.1 | 450 | 0.9 |
| Philippines | 0.15 | 0.3 | 0.45 | 0.65 | 0.9 | 500 | 0.75 |
| Singapore | 0.5 | 0.8 | 1.05 | 1.2 | 1.3 | 160 | 0.8 |
| Taiwan | 1.5 | 2.2 | 3.0 | 3.5 | 4.0 | 166.7 | 2.5 |
| Thailand | 0.15 | 0.22 | 0.3 | 0.4 | 0.52 | 246.6 | 0.37 |
| Total | 8.00 | 11.70 | 15.60 | 20.70 | 25.50 | 218.75 | 17.50 |

*Source* adapted from Solomon Brothers, FT, 1998, www.iw.com.sg/main.htm

**Table 17.7  Market capitalisation value and world ranking of telecom companies 1996/97.**

|  | Capitalisation value ($m) | Ranking 1997 | Ranking 1996 |
|---|---|---|---|
| Nippon Telegraph & Telephone (Japan) | 146138.7 | 7 | 4 |
| Hitchison Whampoa (Hong Kong) | 38141.0 | 68 | 95 |
| Hong Kong Telecommunications (Hong Kong) | 26860.7 | 119 | 129 |
| Singapore Telecom (Singapore) | 26058.2 | 129 | 55 |
| Telekonumikasi Indonesia (Indonesia) | 11264.4 | 358 | 209 |
| Telecom Malaysia (Malaysia) | 9758.3 | 414 | 163 |
| Telecom Corp of New Zealand (New Zealand) | 9003.7 | 453 | 380 |
| Mahanagar (India) | 4235.1 | – | – |

*Source* adapted from 'The world's top 500 companies in 1997', *Financial Times*, 22 January 1998

dropped. Meanwhile, in Hong Kong, the scale of investment in the industry has been ever increasing. This is also partly due to the close ties with the Mainland Chinese market.

The global 500 table changed a lot in 1998 with more newcomers joining the telecommunications industry equipped with huge capital assets (Table 17.8). The change in the top 500 global companies is radical in the sense that most of the young communications companies had climbed up the league table. In particular, at the forefront of this tier are the companies conducting hostile acquisition and merger activities. A wave of new telecommunications giants, to a great extent, is consistent with the emergence of US super-carriers in the US telecommunications industry (Table 17.3).

These examples of merger and financing activities demonstrate that the worldwide industry structure is undergoing considerable change. According to Peter Rowell, managing director of the mergers specialists Regent Associates, merger activities on the Internet market will concentrate on three main areas: (1) Internet service providers (ISPs), in particular middle-tier ISPs are likely to be absorbed by telecoms operators; (2) equipment suppliers, e.g. between data network equipment and telephone equipment; and (3) among telecoms operators and Internet search engine companies (Black, 1998). The hostile M&A activities of the AT&T case have sparked off expectations of rising demand for merging among companies and rigorous competitive pressure on others in the same industry (Bloomberg, 1998). This is likely to bring forth more benefits to consumers. For many industries, the cost of information will become vastly cheaper with digital technology, as will the cost of operational changes and industrial restructuring (Jackson, 1998). This is compatible with the prediction of the loop system of the Structure-Conduct-Performance Paradigm. More importantly, with more finance being placed in the telecoms industry, the overall international efficiency in communication and telephone services will be enhanced. These resulting effects are significant for the worldwide advertising businesses. The use of direct marketing, online shopping and other advertising of communications via the Internet will increase the expected threshold impact of advertising messages, on which the advertising influences and economic values lie. There are clearly signs that ISPs are going to settle comfortably on an advertising-funded basis (Black, 1998). This creates a mutual dependency situation between the scale of potential advertising revenues and the ISP merger activities. Indeed, the global influence of the telecommunications industry is tremendous. This can be shown by the world ranking of companies engaged in the telecommunications and associated equipment industries. Of the top 100 companies worldwide by market capitalisation, there are 17 sizeable companies holding altogether

**Table 17.8  Market capitalisation value and world ranking of telecom companies 1997/98.**

| | Capitalisation value ($m) | Ranking 1998 | Ranking 1997 |
|---|---|---|---|
| Nippon Telegraph & Telephone (Japan) | 117,652.1 | 11 | 7 |
| AT&T (US) | 102,480 | 17 | 26 |
| Lucent Technology (US) | 90,985 | 21 | 45 |
| MCI WorldCom (US) | 86,214 | 24 | – |
| BT (UK) | 86,134 | 25 | 64 |
| Deutsche Telekom (Germany) | 83,724.1 | 27 | 44 |
| SBC Communications (US) | 81,529.7 | 30 | 35 |
| Bell Atlantic (US) | 75,246.4 | 33 | 29 |
| Bell South (US) | 74,196.5 | 35 | 38 |
| France Telecom (France) | 58,128.3 | 46 | – |
| GTE (US) | 52,978.3 | 51 | 61 |
| Ameritech (US) | 52,335 | 55 | 78 |
| TIM Spa (Italy) | 38,011.4 | 74 | 127 |
| Telefonica (Spain) | 36,747.2 | 77 | 101 |
| Telestra (Australia) | 35,845.6 | 79 | – |
| Telcom Italia (Italy) | 35,576.5 | 80 | 84 |
| Vodafone (UK) | 35,535.5 | 81 | 226 |
| Airtouch Communications (US) | 32,689.5 | 93 | 205 |
| Sprint (US) | 30,997.2 | 98 | 166 |
| US West (US) | 26,323.3 | 130 | 197 |
| Singapore Telecom (Singapore) | 24,956.3 | 139 | 129 |
| Hong Kong Telecommunications (Hong Kong) | 23,520.3 | 151 | 119 |
| Cable and Wireless (Hong Kong) | 22,677.6 | 153 | 187 |
| Hutchison Whampoa (Hong Kong) | 20,409.2 | 179 | 68 |
| China Telecom [Hong Kong] (Hong Kong) | 18,550.7 | 198 | – |
| BCE (Canada) | 17,844.0 | 208 | 192 |
| Telefonos de Mexico (Mexico) | 17,653.5 | 211 | 234 |
| KPN (Netherland) | 14,425.5 | 252 | 202 |
| Ote (Greece) | 11,884.0 | 314 | 359 |
| Orange (UK) | 11,385.5 | 332 | – |
| Tele Denmark A/S (Denmark) | 10,529.9 | 357 | – |
| NTT Data (Japan) | 10,380.4 | 364 | 351 |
| Cable and Wireless Communications (UK) | 10,024.1 | 382 | – |

*Source* adapted from 'The world's top 500 companies in 1998', Annual Review 1999, *Financial Times*, 28 January 1999

share values of more than $891 billion. Nevertheless, the externalities created by advanced telecommunications not only includes wealth creation, but also raise human consciousness of the applications of fast and vast movements of data and information. This will eventually exert enormous pressure on the advertising business. According to George Colong, the President of Forrester Research, companies need to adapt to the Internet economy as Web markets and selling experience evolve to a global business model (Taylor, 1998a). This induced dynamic trade model will match the reshaping of industrial relationships and technological infrastructures, and create a redefinition of internal processes of organisation. Following Houlder (1998a), these new imperatives for utilising IT are going to have profound effects on the emergence of new business metaphors such as 'virtual companies' and network organisations. Imagine that if the whole world was wired up by the Internet, messages could be passed from one end to another more reliably and efficiently, thus eliminating certain constraints found in postal and telefax services. The linkages between people, firms and society as a whole will be more efficiently handled without the usual geographical and time constraints. Hence, the dynamic global effects caused by increasing merger activities should result in more effective global knowledge transfer, where advertising is the activity socially beneficial in enhancing the transfer process.

## 17.3 Traffic control and advertising revenue

Economies of scales are essential for the survival of many businesses. The telecommunications industry is no exception. Recent mega-mergers, such as the $48bn acquisition of TCI by AT&T, and WorldCom Inc's $42bn takeover of MCI Communications Corp., are clear indications of hostile movements of dominant players. The lifting of federal regulations under a new set of US telecommunications laws had a profound impact on the US telecommunications industry. However, these massive takeover activities in the USA concern the EU. The EU competition minister, Karel Van Miert, recently objected to the danger of building excessive market power in Internet services resulting from the merger between WorldCom and MCI. The potential control over global Internet traffic and significant sales of high-speed communications in Europe have kept the EU regulators on the alert about the acquisition (Andrews, 1998). These aggressive mergers reflect the fact that the belief in stronger demand for data and information in global terms is virtually held by a few telecoms giants. Moreover, the aggregate advertising fees paid by agents are expected to rise to enormous levels. Market power is now highly concentrated.

The volume of Internet traffic is expected to experience a very rapid increase. The forecast for e-commerce volumes ($200–$300m) is regarded as too conservative by Techserver (1998), who generates a prediction of $1 trillion by 2002.[2] Based on the drastic increase in sheer size of the Internet, increased investment in Internet advertising by firms is inevitable. According to Black (1998), Houlder (1998b), Black (1998) and Taylor (1998b), there are concerns about the potential massive impact of e-commerce. However, agents cannot afford to stay out of investing in the Internet medium (Black, 1998). Inspection of Table 17.9 shows that advertising spending on the Internet is expected to increase 7.17 times, while the corresponding increase in e-commerce for consumer products/services may grow by 30 times. This means that there are business opportunities in Internet advertising to boost e-commerce. The effectiveness of Internet advertising outlays for generating sales is expected to rise between 1997 and 2002. These promising growth figures may imply a more favourable environment for greater potential increases

**Table 17.9  Some selected market trends.**

|  | 1997 | 2002 |
|---|---|---|
| No. of online users (m) | 100 | 216.6 |
| Volume of e-commerce ($bn) | 8–10 | 200–300 |
| Advertising revenue ($bn) | 0.9065 | 6.5 |
| Market for investing in information (%) | 15 | 42 |

*Source* adapted from Nua Report (1998), IAB (1998), Techserver (1998), Jupiter Communications (1998)

**Table 17.10  Online shopping volumes.**

| | 1998 | | 2003 | |
|---|---|---|---|---|
| | £(billion) | % of sale | £(billion) | % of global sales |
| UK | 0.23 | >0.2 | 3.1 | – |
| US | 7.7 | >0.5 | 1127** | – |
| Global | 9.28*** | – | 868–1928* | 5* |

*Source* adapted from Benjamin Ensor, Fletcher Research (1999)

\* Research Digest, *Financial Times*, 2 December 1998.

\*\* This figure is based on a projected growth of 200% p.a. according to the estimate from the Boston Consultancy Group (Englesham, 1999). However, the corresponding figure for 2001 generated by Forrester Research is only $206.8bn (£124.58bn; £=1.66$), representing 2.7% of US GDP (Nairn, 1999).

\*\*\* IDC/*Financial Times*, 13 February 1998, the corresponding figure in 2002 is $425bn (Table 17.11).

in the market for information investments, from 15% to an estimated 42% for the next five years (Table 17.9).

The aggregate momentum for e-commerce is tremendously supported by the volume of financial services. With many financial institutions starting trading via the Internet, business-to-business e-commerce will increase more quickly the greater the popularity of the Internet in world trade and retail industries. For instance, trade shares in 2003 for UK banking and stock-broking are expected to reach the £19bn level (Eaglesham, 1998). The corresponding volume of Internet shopping, excluding financial services, is expected to be worth £3.1bn (Table 17.10). Comparing Internet retailing between the USA and the UK, much higher retailing figures were achieved in the USA in 1998 than in the UK, which represents less than 0.5% of US total sales. Forecasts for 2003 show a much higher proportion of retailing to be realised by the Internet. This is likely to demand greater levels of advertising activity.

Apart from home shopping, Internet sales are likely to attract business away from various sectors. Radical effects on outsourcing, shipping and purchasing are expected (Nairn, 1999). Business-to-business commerce via the Internet is likely to continue to experience growth, rising from $20.8bn to $331.5bn between 1998 and 2002 respectively. The significance of business-to-business e-commerce is reflected by the estimated percentage growth in parentheses (Table 17.11).

These statistics imply that the use of electronic modes of telecommunication will create significant effects on global commerce both in the business and home sectors. However, business-to-business growth will outstrip home sales categories on all forecast estimates.

**Table 17.11  Volumes of e-commerce by sector.**

| | 1998 | | 2002 | |
|---|---|---|---|---|
| | $bn | % | $bn | % |
| Business | 20.8 | (65%) | 331.5 | (78%) |
| Home | 11.2 | (35%) | 93.5 | (22%) |
| Total | 32 | | 425 | |

*Source* adapted from IDC/Nairn (1999)

Many of the takeovers occurring in the USA and Europe in the telecommunications industry are classic examples of buying out a direct competitor (Farhi, 1998). However, there are other strategic implications of these mergers. For example, WorldCom aims to explore greater returns from Internet services. AT&T aims to enter local US phone markets. A media giant such as Disney aims to take over 43% of Infoseek, a popular search engine, to establish Web gateways (Hansell, 1998). The strategic intentions are explicit. Media groups seek to target Internet traffic control and consequently aim to transfer customers to the billboards that line the information highway. The ultimate missions are to capture a tempting share of advertising as well as investors' interest. According to Forrester Research, global Internet advertising revenue may grow from $1.5bn in 1998 to $15.2bn in 2003 (McGookin, 1998). This represents a 10 times growth rate in online advertising over the next five years. Based on the predicted 2002 figure in Table 17.9, the growth between 2002 and 2003 is expected to achieve around a 130% increase on the huge base figure. One induced commercial investment interest in global Internet advertising market is the development of several specialist online advertising companies. One key sideline business is traffic audits. This type of business has significantly flourished owing to the development of measurement technology such as 'cookies'. This technology enables Web sites to track movements to see which advertisement the visitor has assessed and to identify returning visitors. This creates significant value for increasing advertising influences on target groups, based on collected access information or purchasing patterns of Web users. With this 'footprint'-type electronic technology, it is not difficult to believe that the future growth of Internet advertising expenditure can rocket to $15.2bn in 2003.

Equally important, in the telecommunications equipment supplier market, is a new type of supplier emerging alongside the Internet advertising market. Rather than making the 'servers' which handle and supply data over the Internet, there exist 'routers', companies which dictate where data travels to. This leads to the creation of popular sites and artificial pre-determined priorities in downloading data. Consequently, this type of company also fosters the growth of the Internet advertising business with regard to complexity of segmentation and disseminating data. This further helps advertising agents, fulfils clients' target needs and provides enhanced advertising effectiveness.

Portals are increasingly seen as valuable assets for generating advertising and sponsorship revenues. A strategic trend of re-focusing strategies carried out by many telecom/IT players can be seen from the recent experience of Netscape and Microsoft, which provide Internet browser softwares. However, as 90% of the personal computer operating system market is dominated by Windows 95 which is owned by Microsoft, Netscape Communications Corp. has been shifting its focus from making browsers to operating portal sites. Netscape has launched an Internet portal called Netcenter, which aims to exploit the growth in business use of the Internet relating to the areas of e-commerce software and development of the digital marketplace (Price, 1998a). When more retailers participate in e-commerce, Web sites will become dominating powerhouses to funnel users to certain advertisers and help fulfil the tasks of searching for data/information that Internet users are looking for. To increase viewership, firms set up their Web sites with attractive names. Registration fees for a domain name ending with .com costs £80 in the UK. Recently, a small multimedia company paid £1.2m to buy the registered names Britain.com, London.com and England.com (Price, 1999). With many commercial Web sites existing in the market, it is very difficult for any new gateways to take on significant viewerships. In this competitive situation, brands become crucial in determining market share. This motivates media companies, for instance, Disney, to utilise its established name to attract Internet viewerships. According to Willman (1998), the brand is a promise

**Table 17.12  The increase in venture capital investment.**

| | Venture capital investment ($m) | Quarterly venture capital investment ($m) |
|---|---|---|
| 1995/1995 Q1 | 43 | 8 |
| 1997/1998 Q1 | 422 | 459 |

*Source* adapted from www.iw.com.sg/main.html

delivered, which commands higher prices, and an asset to differentiate it from others; during the market liberalisation process, rebranding is particularly useful for incumbents to defend themselves against competition.[3] Following the economic principles of vertical integration, it is a natural strategic move for Disney to explore further potential efficiency gains from a revolutionary mass medium by combining search and directory services with its entertainment, news, sports and family coverage. Combining the effects of radio and the Web can be seen from the success of the MediaRep Web Site Advertising Network. The portal site consists of 2000 radio stations, with more than 1500 affiliated stations, which altogether served over 150 million advertising impressions in October 1998. The loyalties of radio listeners are expected to generate one billion hits within the next 12 months (Cox, 1998a). Media giants not linked to any Web gateways regretted their late acquisition intentions as the market price of capitalisation for these popular gateways soared recently (Hansell, 1998). If this path of market share competition continues, there will be a growing trend for such strategic acquisition; despite high market prices, these Web sites may rocket dramatically. The increasing growth in capital on the Internet is shown in Table 17.12. These figures correspond to rapid aggressive strategic moves by players engaged in the telecommunications and media businesses.

Portals have been Internet stars on the stock market since 1995. However, M&A activities created different categories of portal targeting different market segments. The volumes of 'unique' visitors at top Web sites are shown in Table 17.13. The market leaders

**Table 17.13  Unique users of digital media/web properties.**

| | Unique visitors* (m) |
|---|---|
| AOL Network** | 53.8 |
| Yahoo! | 42.4 |
| Microsoft | 40.5 |
| Lycos | 30.3 |
| Excite@Home | 27.2 |
| Go Network | 21.3 |
| Amazon | 15.6 |
| NBC Internet | 14.9 |
| About.com | 12.6 |
| Time Warner Online | 12.2 |

*Source* adapted from *Financial Times*, Price (2000)
* The actual number of total users who visited the Web site once in the given month.
All unique visitors are unduplicated.
** Proprietary & WWW

are AOL, Yahoo! and Microsoft. These represent a total of 15% of all Internet traffic and 45% of all advertising revenue. This leaves little advertising income for second-tier portals, such as Lycos, Excite, Go and Amazon, which currently obtain 5% of total Internet advertising revenue. These second-tier companies have spent millions gaining reputations and increased market profiles via consolidation recently. Unfortunately, retailers turn to the top-tier portals. Industry analysts expect that the declining trend of Internet advertising earnings will continue to decline and may drop to 1% by 2004. By contrast, some niche markets may be increasingly occupied by smaller portals or portals in more focused segments. These are so-called 'vertical portals' or, 'affiliate sites'. According to Forrester Research, 57% of retailer advertising expenses will be achieved in these 'focused vertical portals'. These may gain in market share of total Internet advertising from 20% to 24% between 1999 and 2004 respectively (Nua, 2000b). This is why the media giant, Disney, recently moved its strategic focus from the broad-based portal markets to well-established entertainment markets. These changes show that after rapid market value creation, rationalisation processes in the Internet advertising market have reached a mature stage, where new growth is needed to satisfy retailers. Retailers will gradually move away from broad portals and seek cheaper channels. This market trend will certainly create a proliferation of product differentiation. Internet advertising media may yet see another round of market consolidation. Thus first- and second-tier portals will aim to extend their collections of media advertising distinctiveness. The economic implications are that the consumer-driven nature of the advertising industry and digital medium companies will aim to increase their goodwill by intensifying product differentiation to create more desirable functions for target advertisers. This first phase rationalisation mainly involves horizontal integration. As the market profile becomes more mature, the focus will shift to vertical integration and vertical product differentiation.

Tables 17.14 and 17.15 indicate the market capitalisations of selected search engines and the estimated values for some major Web sites. Inspection of Table 17.14 shows that market capitalisation is positively associated with the number of users for each search engine, with the exception of Lycos. The Internet traffic is dominated by Yahoo! which obtained a market value of $14.181bn, exceeding the entire sum of the remaining key navigation service companies. The corresponding value of Yahoo! was only $6.3bn in April 1998, which implies a 125% increase in value within a trading duration of six months.

The average share price in 1996 for the above navigation service companies was below $20. The figures in Table 17.16 show that the share prices of these firms experienced

**Table 17.14  Market capitalisation of selected search engines on 4 November 1998.**

|  | Number of users (millions) | Market capitalisation ($M) | User value |
|---|---|---|---|
| Yahoo! | 26.1 | 14,181 | 543 |
| Lycos | 17.6 | 1,929 | 109 |
| Excite | 16.6 | 1,997 | 121 |
| GeoCities | 15.5 | 1,035 | 67 |
| Infoseek | 11.0 | 959 | 87 |
| Total | 86.8 | 20,101 | 927 |
| Average | 17.36 | 4020.2 | 185.4 |

*Source* adapted from Harmon (1998) Internet Stock Report, Internet.com.

**Table 17.15 Estimated private market value of selected websites of different media companies on 4 November 1998.**

|  | Number of users (millions) | Market capitalisation ($M) | User value |
|---|---|---|---|
| AOL.com | 21.8 | 3,500 | 161 |
| Microsoft.com | 19.6 | 2,300 | 117 |
| Netscape.com | 16.3 | 2,000 | 123 |
| MSN.com/Hotmail | 15.6 | 2,100 | 135 |
| Disney.com | 10.4 | 1,350 | 129 |
| Total | 83.7 | 11,250 | 665 |
| Average | 16.74 | 2,250 | 133 |

*Source* adapted from Harmon (1998) Internet Stock Report, Internet.com.

**Table 17.16 A comparison of market capitalisation and user value index.**

|  | Share price in $ (end of April 1998) | User value index* |
|---|---|---|
| Yahoo! | 117 | 100 |
| Excite | 65 | 22 |
| Lycos | 55 | 20 |
| Infoseek | 30 | 16 |

*Source* adapted from *Financial Times* (30 April 1998), author computation
* The User index is set to 100 which equals to 543 (Yahoo!'s) as seen in Table 17.14

various levels of increase, ranging from 50% (Infoseek) to 485% (Yahoo!). Their combined market capitalisation value at the end of April 1998 was about $11bn which escalated to a level around $19bn on 4 November 1998. This reflects massive capital gains caused by the emerging attractiveness of navigation services. However, the combined valuation is significantly inflated by the rapid rise of the leading search engine, namely Yahoo!, which was valued at about 62 times the forecast 1999 revenue of $229m (Price, 1998b). The valuation of Yahoo! is very high. For international cellular companies, the corresponding calculation of market value is usually about 13 times the forecast earnings before interest, tax, depreciation and amortisation (Ridding, 1998). These escalating prices for search engine companies display the strong market belief in the huge potential value associated with Internet businesses. Recently, the flotation of a new US Internet company called Theglobe.coms set the record for the US stock market. On its first day of trading, share prices increased seven-fold (Cave, 1998a). This astonishing rise in opening prices shows that investors believe that huge income-generating potential will be captured by companies that help people create their own Websites.

## 17.4 Implications of competition

### 17.4.1 Overcapacity

Whatever the motives are, firms engaged in the telecommunications industry focus on scale development and pre-emptive strategy on the Internet battlefield. As argued by industry analysts, it is the scale that matters rather than skills required for new business activities. The $62.59bn SBC-Ameritech deal, the second largest corporate merger in history, was a typical strategic entry move and paved the way for a competitive edge in the long-distance businesses. This strategic move concerns the expansion of existing and traditional businesses instead of aiming at gaining wider spectrums of steering skills in other related telecommunications activities (PNE, 1998). When the global telecommunications market undergoes unprecedented massive restructuring processes, the pre-emptive strategy employed by giant players may generate lots of wasteful excess capacity during the transition period. A likely beneficial result is a reduction in service charges. Online advertising rates have displayed downward trends, as depicted in Table 17.17. According to Michele Schott, director of market communications at Adknowledge, the initial rates were set artificially high. The decreasing trends reflect the fact that businesses are now more knowledgeable as to how to get better value from online advertising rather than simply throwing money at the Internet. The rates charged by Web sites vary widely, ranging from CPM rates of more than $75, to as low as less than $1 CPM depending on the popularity commanded by Web sites (Nua, 1998). According to the Vice President for Marketing in Adknowledge, Kevin Wandryk, the decreasing trend in CPM is caused by the increase in Web space available for advertisers (Cyber Altas, ibid.).

The danger of excessive competition may occur if licensing and other network installations exceed the optimal levels. For instance, German authorities have issued 203 operating licences, with 130 new ones on the way to be added to services in Germany. To a certain extent, this helps force down service charges. However, it implies that another structural danger of market evolution is on the way, namely that future profits will largely rely on scale as margins crumble. Consequently, the resulting market shares will be in the hands of a few strong oligopolies.

Inspection of Table 17.18 indicates that the telecommunications giants will evolve to a form of 'deep pocket' competition. Six of the top ten telecommunication titans are based in the USA. Seven of the ten already exceed the $100bn benchmark in terms of market capitalisation. According to Cane (1998d), MCI and WorldCom intend to spend $800m to double their installed fibre optic network throughout Europe. The $500m per annum European project aiming to build a new high-capacity network carried out by Global One, the alliance of Deutsche Telekom, France Telecom and Sprint of the USA, is likely to

**Table 17.17 Online advertising rates (Nua/AdKnowledge, 1998, 1999, 2000a).**

|  | Advertising rates $CPM* |
|---|---|
| Feb. 2000 | 33.75 |
| Dec. 1998 | 35.13 |
| Sept. 1998 | 36.29 |
| Dec. 1997 | 37.21 |
| May 1997 | 37.84 |

* CPM refers to cost per thousand which is the most popular industry measurement standard for Internet advertising rates. Apart from the popularity of a Web site, the varying rates depend on the methods of operation in data mining, namely the registration approach or an open access approach. The former helps advertising agents to track movements through a Web site and store information. This eventually helps advertising agents target Web users with specific interests and deliver advertising messages to promote online sales.

**Table 17.18   The top ten telecommunications companies.**

| Company | Country | Market capitalisation ($ billion) |
| --- | --- | --- |
| *SBC/ Ameritech | US | 174.53 |
| AT&T | US | 148.35 |
| *Bell Atlantic | US | 143.85 |
| MCI WorldCom | US | 137.46 |
| NTT | Japan | 121.95 |
| *Vodafone AirTouch | UK/US | 110.00** |
| Deutsche Telekom | Germany | 105.25 |
| British Telecom | UK | 96.25 |
| Bell South | US | 90.94 |
| France Telecom | France | 89.27 |
| Total: | | 1217.85 |

*Source* adapted from Reuters/Global Business Outlook, *Financial Times*, 29 January 1999
* refers to planned mergers
** figure is provided by the company

create more transitional problems with excess capacity in Europe. However, there are optimistic players who argue that the spare installed capacity will easily be soaked up by increased demand for data and transmission. The increase in data transmitted is mainly due to the technical convergence in telecommunications. According to Cane (1999a), the concept of convergence is not new in telecommunications. The concept become more transparent recently as demand for information increased in different media and with every kind of information being gradually converted into binary digits, which is a computer-intrinsic benefit assisting transmission of data. Undoubtedly, such convergent phenomena will generate significant potential to deliver cost-effectiveness in new telecommunications services, alongside existing services. The development of convergent platforms facilitates firms to gain increasing cost advantages by merging different lines of service which become complementary to others.

## 17.4.2  Decreasing rates

Apart from intensified global competition in the telecommunications industry, there are solid grounds for believing that the volume of Internet traffic will grow rapidly. This is based on the fact that the International Telecommunication Union recently put forward new international policy forums for assessing prices charged by telephone companies.[4] The cost-based measurement and accounting reforms will favour new entrants competing with incumbents.[5] This helps promote lower costs of telecommunications services, hence stimulating wider use of Internet services. In turn, the rising volume of Internet traffic will raise the investment interests, including advertising businesses. Consequently, the competition in the telecommunications industry will produce beneficial welfare effects. In his remarks to the Annual Council of the Commonwealth Telecommunications Organisation, Dr Henry Chasia, the ITU Deputy Secretary-General, argued that the most important barrier holding up the realisation of new international telecommunications services is price, not a technical or regulatory one (Chasia, 1998). Table 17.19 indicates the potential reduction of international service pricing urged by the ITU. The significant potential reductions resulting from the proposed cost-based evaluation method reflects the extent of

**Table 17.19  Reduction targets for international settlement rates.**

| Country grouping | Required reduction (%) | Target year |
|---|---|---|
| Low | 14–30 | 2003 |
| Low to medium | 28–39 | 2001 |
| High | 50 | 1999 |

*Source* adapted from Wettemann *et al.* (1998)

direct cost savings. Higher-income countries were set up as pioneering groups to start the reduction process and are expected to reach the designated targets soon. This has co-incided with the recent reductions in long-distance telephone (IDD) rates in developed countries such as in the USA, the UK and other Western European countries. The tele-communications market liberalisation process occurring in advanced countries has kept up the downward pressure on the formation of lower price equilibria, which will be further rationalised by more competitive services provided by new entrants. For instance, the recently liberalised German telecoms market may force the existing telecommunications giant, Deutsche Telekom, to retaliate with drastic price cuts as high as 60% (Atkins, 1998).[6] Higher technical know-how associated with higher-income economies provides more favourable conditions for cuts in prices compared with less efficient lower-income countries.[7]

Despite this process of liberalisation, there still exist barriers to competition in the world telecommunications industry. In Table 17.20, substantial differences in inter-connection rates are displayed. The existing high connection costs in Japan discourage new telephone companies from entering the market as the cost of using existing networks becomes high. This eventually weakens potential competitors for international calls and other Internet-associated activities. There is rising pressure in the USA to force the Japanese NTT network to cut price by around 40% within a year. However, NTT have refused this dramatic cut. The data in Table 17.20 indicates that the Japanese rate is about

**Table 17.20  Telecom interconnection rates.**

| | Interconnection rate (Yen per minute) | % Lower than NTT rate |
|---|---|---|
| NTT (Japan) | 1.86 | – |
| Pacific Bell (US) | 0.48 | 74 |
| Ameritech (US) | 0.61 | 67 |
| France | 0.67 | 64 |
| BT-peak (UK) | 0.68 | 63 |
| Sweden | 0.99 | 47 |
| Denmark | 1.02 | 45 |
| Spain | 1.09 | 41 |
| Italy | 1.10 | 41 |
| Germany | 1.11 | 40 |

*Source* adapted from European Commission (Dept. of E-Commerce, Brussels)

**Table 17.21 Advertising spending by sector (annual compound growth rates (%)).**

|  | 1992–97 | 1997–2002 |
|---|---|---|
| TV | 6.1 | 6.1 |
| Radio | 9.3 | 9.3 |
| Daily newspaper | 6.2 | 7.2 |
| Consumer magazine | 7.0 | 6.25 |
| Business magazine | 8.0 | 9.2 |
| Outdoor | 7.6 | 8.4 |

*Source* adapted from Cox (1998b)

**Table 17.22 Advertising spending forecast ($bn).**

|  | World advertising spending | Online advertising spending |
|---|---|---|
| 1997 | 423.5 | 0.906 |
| 2002 | 613.7 | 6.500 |

*Source* adapted from Cox (1998)

74% higher than the American equivalent, or at least 40% higher than European standards. The higher rates in Japan seem to discourage aggressive entrants.

Lower Internet advertising rates and reductions in telecommunication service charges should favour the growth of the Internet to gain a larger share in overall global advertising. Table 17.21 shows the annual compound rate of increase in advertising for different media. The forecasts for 1997–2002 indicate that, despite increasing use of the cost-efficient Internet advertising medium, there is no sign of advertising shifting away from the traditional advertising media. Gapper (1999) found that between 1993 and 1997, media revenue grew by an average of 12.5% when new electronic media and Internet portals such as America Online (AOL) increased their strength rapidly. According to the estimations released by Vernois, Suhler & Association (VS&A) at the 12th annual Communications Industry Forecast, online advertising may reach $6.5bn in 2002, which is more than seven times the figure recorded in 1997. Moreover, the aggregate global advertising spend is expected to increase to $613.7bn in 2002 with an annual compound growth rate of 7.7% (Table 17.22). These trends indicate that Internet advertising will demonstrate an increasing importance for sales and play a supportive role complementing other media, instead of being a rival medium. The resulting economic externalities of Internet advertising are tremendous; however, as yet, they are difficult to quantify.

## 17.5 Development of mobile commerce and WAP technologies

The massive potential advertising revenue to be obtained by network operations can be enhanced by the development of the next generation industry-wide mobile handsets. This is supported by the convergent technical aspects for advanced data-transferring devices and wireless telecommunications. British Telecom in the UK argued that worldwide voice communications are going to be overtaken by data communications. The forecast in the

UK telecommunications market indicates that the data mode is increasing by 30% per annum compared to 5% for voice (Cane, 1998e). Parallel to the forecasted increase in demand for data communication, the focus of the equipment market for handling and receiving data will migrate to a new arena. The global telecommunications equipment market has an estimated value of £155bn p.a. (Walters, 1999). Industry analysts expect that about 15% of the estimated 600 million users will use mobile handsets as computers by 2002 (Reuters, 1998). The Asian emerging economic giant, China, which is regarded as the most important mobile telephone market worldwide, is expected to experience high growth rates of about one million subscribers per month (Kynge, 1998b).[8] This promising growth in mobile use motivates the development of the data-receiving handset market. Moreover, the use of Internet telephony may become yet another emerging telecommunications submarket.[9]

According to the statistics estimated by Ovum, a London-based consultancy, the growth of mobile connections will be dramatic across Europe, the USA and Asia-Pacific between 1998 and 2002 (Table 17.23).

In 1998, the greatest number of mobile users was recorded in Europe. According to Cane (1999c), the higher adherence to older analogue transmission in the USA enables Europe to take the lead at present. However, the relatively higher international telephone timed rates charged by local telephone companies in Europe, approximately three times higher than the Nordic rates or five times more expensive than the US ones, may allow the USA to take the leadership (Nua, 1999b). The Ovum forecast estimates that the fastest growth of wireless communication is to be found in the USA, reaching a growth rate of 106.41%. At the moment, scientists in the telecommunications industry have developed the third-generation mobile system in Europe, namely UMTS. This mobile system is another step forward based on the GSM system, a standard mobile system across the continent. In the USA, the digital technologies for mobile communications are called CDMA. The differences in mobile systems restrict mobile phone users to utilising wireless services when travelling across the Atlantic. The technical differences between these two major mobile systems are very small. The focal point is that one restricts the use of the other's system. This creates a vital technical barrier for consumers who demand easy communications across different geographical regions. The tempting rewards and market size may motivate system technologies to generate a global standard system.

The emerging effects of the convergent functions provided by computers and mobile technology can be seen by the intense commercial interests of the leading mobile companies, including Ericsson, Nokia and Motorola. These companies entered a collective deal with Psion plc, a British company which produces software for telephone-like devices enabling users to access Internet services, transmit e-mail and make phone

**Table 17.23  The number of mobile connections by region (millions).**

|              | 1998 | 2002 | % increase |
|--------------|------|------|------------|
| Europe       | 89   | 138  | 55.06      |
| US           | 78   | 161  | 106.41     |
| Asia-Pacific | 73   | 128  | 75.34      |
| Total        | 240  | 427  | 77.92      |

*Source* adapted from Cane (1999c)

calls. The collaborative work will certainly modify the data communication formats and habitual ties, currently dominated by desktop computer Internet station connections. According to Gapper (1998), a handheld electronic device incorporating a flat screen and voice phone will be an everyday object by 2002. In the long run, Shillingford (1998) argued that mobile phones will offer an unlimited supply of value-added services and become all-in-one tools, simply because mobiles will do what fixed phones can do. Mobiles are expected to integrate well with the Internet to provide tailored information for users. Moreover, locational-based information, voice-mail, voice-activated dialling and mobile wallets will provide added value to users. Blitz (1998) stresses that there will be enormous potential for mobiles' growth. Given that some countries have fixed phone penetration rates of around 65–70%, there is a considerable way to go before mobile phones penetrate world telephony currently occupied by fixed line services.

As the development of the Internet via the personal computer becomes more mature, the product life cycle of the Internet needs to generate greater power. Leading mobile phone makers such as Nokia and Ericsson are competing in terms of mobile Internet technology. Nokia is developing mobile handsets with a technology called the general packet radio system (GPRS) which enables faster flows of data in mobile networks. However, Ericsson will develop Bluetooth technology for networking systems via a type of short-range radio. Services provided by the Internet-enabled mobile phone may soon start from the integration of mobile voice-mail and e-mail, followed by more interactive Internet services, such as MP3 downloading devices. Nokia and others (3Com) will launch a combined PalmPilot organiser and mobile phone handset by 2001 (Shillingford, 2000). Moreover, Vodafone recently signed a £30 million sponsorship with Manchester United in February 2000. Advertising functions attached to Internet services will become more dynamic as Vodafone has ambitions to include Manchester United games via mobile phones.

With respect to fixed and mobile convergence, Claude Dechaux, vice-president of strategy at Alcatel's mobile communications division, believes that integration of fixed and mobile services will eventually lead to further integration of networks. The aggregate value of the integration in service is expected to reach $40–$50 billion in Europe and the USA (Costello, 1998). This will further attract media and mobile groups to explore the potential for interactive data transfer and telephone services. In turn, this market will create a new battlefield linked to Internet advertising businesses. Advertising fees may become a crucial source of finance for upgrading telephone infrastructures. At the moment, mobile operators spend significantly less resources on network maintenance and improvements than those spent on fixed wire services.[10] As suggested by Mr Malcom Ross, Head of telecommunications for the consultancy Arthur D. Little, mobile operators need to seek new sources of revenue, like advertising to ease out problems of inferior quantity and capacity compared to fixed wire counterparts (Cane, 1998).

The mobile phone sector requires significant capital inputs as it evolves. The substantial investment in the global mobile network is dominated by US players. For instance, the US-based group, Iridium, has invested $5bn for 66 satellites in orbit and established 12 ground stations. The development of the global mobile networks is primarily the result of extreme price pressure in the cellular market, where investors find little economic gains from further substantial investment. This is evident in the strategic moves by Iridium, which were originally planned to compete directly in the terrestrial mobile phone service market, after the recent appointment of Mr Ed Staiano, the Chief Executive of Iridium (Price, 1998c). Moreover, downward price trends for mobiles was caused by the US government (1994) deciding to auction wireless spectra to new entrants. The threat to the

Table 17.24 Mobile phone rates and phone set prices.

| | Talk-time rate per minute ($) | Phone set price ($) |
|---|---|---|
| Iridium | 1–2 (developing countries) | 3000 |
| | 2–7 (elsewhere) | |
| ICO | 3 (average) | 1000 |

*Source* adapted from Price (1998c)

US industry is that net earnings for some players may shrink to between 25 and 30% of revenue over the next few years (Cane, 1999c).

The development of global mobile networks has several important economic implications. First, it will provide efficient communications for various remote areas which are not covered by terrestrial networks, such as people working in off-shore oil rigs or remote mining areas. Secondly, it will reduce various transaction costs if highly mobile business travellers require multi-connections or want to switch networks frequently. Thirdly, it allows poor countries to develop their telecommunications infrastructures without investing hugely in sophisticated terrestrial networks. Moreover, bypassing this cost may ease the problems of getting government funding for other investment projects. This may generate wider socio-economic effects on other sectors such as medical and health services, education and other basic infrastructures. Lastly, the global mobile network may increase competition in global telecommunications as a whole, providing universal standards in the mobile phone business and eliminating the inefficiency arising from incompatible systems.

Global mobile network services are still a new market. Iridium seeks to conquer this battlefield. This aim is supported by an aggressive advertising strategy which is one of the largest ever, costing around $140m. To work out the global strategic links, Iridium has already signed agreements with 200 operators in 80 countries. However, no market is competition-proof. It is believed that two other global players, Globalstar and ICO, would like to compete in the satellite phone industry. The likely impact of this is a wider spectrum of services and lower phone rates.[11] Just like the gradually reducing international phone charges that have occurred in recent years, the competitive downward pressures on price are predicted in the global mobile phone market (Table 17.24).

## 17.6 Conclusions

The dynamics of the telecommunications industry has affected the world stock market capitalisation in recent years. By 2003, the Internet is expected to account for 90% of the world's bandwidth[12] (IWA, 1998). Undoubtedly, data will become a dominant source of traffic over telecommunications networks. Martin (1998) argued that for a global investor, the Internet provides a rival standard and a rival source of demand. Applications for advanced communications facilities have now become entrenched. The recent BT Electronic Business Award demonstrated the widespread application of the Internet and networking technologies in various industries. According to David Bowen, the editor of Net Profit Newsletter, the key theme of business nowadays is management of technology. However, managerially, there are difficulties given the differing levels of preparedness (Bowen, 1998).

Mobile Internet technology and other broadband services via cable may become more crucial. In Hong Kong, property builders installed broadband cable in apartments ready for the future growth of 'smart household appliances' such as fridges and microwaves, which can eventually be linked to the home computerised system via telephone lines. As the Internet functions via mobile phones and these smart household systems experience a dramatic increase, communication and network companies such as Cisco, Lucent Technologies and Nortel Networks will focus on the home network market using broadband optical technologies, which provide speeds much faster than conventional telephone lines.

The aggregate influences in the digital era are tightly related to the appealing functions of global standardised network service provision by and consumption of the Internet medium, which match the rising needs of efficient handling of data and access to various sorts of information. The resulting ease and comfort provided by convergent telecommunications technology are expected to continue to generate increased efficiency and welfare. At the firm level, the efficiency issue relating to cost savings is evident in British Telecom's £140m cost saving from using the intranet instead of paper as a means of communication (Cane, 1998f). Moreover, in 1995 British Petroleum introduced an advanced telecommunications system including desktop video conferencing systems, document scanning, electronic mail and the Internet; this generated benefits swiftly and repaid the initial cost of installation of the group online system. The savings include not only the reduction in travel bills, but also quicker decision processes (Houlder, 1998a). At the macro level, this stimulates job creation and contributes to GNP. For instance, in the UK, the number of people working for the digital media sector is more than 30,000, despite the fact that there are displacement losses in other sectors. The digital media industry which helps create and design the content of the Internet generates annual revenue of approximately £5bn and will create up to 80,000 new jobs in the UK by 2007 (Rawsthorn, 1998). Undoubtedly, the advertising industry will play a key role in shaping the way the world communicates. This will promote the conduct of business in more effective ways.

## Summary

- Internet technology and mobile commerce are complex technical products. The convergence of data and voice transmission is diffusing into every aspect of life. Consumers demand convenience and ease of handling. To a large extent, telecommunications companies and data carriers are actively working on technical developmental issues to gain first-mover advantages. Oligopolies normally employ pre-emptive strategies to maximise future business growth. However, as the size of the global market is huge, smaller and more flexible players can occupy niche markets. The second major attribute of the diffusion of Internet technology is consumer affordability. Without a proper level of consumption, the prospects for increased reinvestment are discouraged. Hence, Internet usage is an income-related phenomenon. This outcome is clearly reflected in the differences in the downloading charges in the USA and Europe. At the moment, the USA uses unmetered access for downloading.

- In the 1990s, the development of digital data transmission technology signalled major upheavals in the world telecommunications industry. Internet and wireless communications have dominated this revolution in recent years and it is believed that these will produce a major impetus for a paradigm shift in world business. To maintain sustainability and competitiveness, firms have realised the vital need to upgrade the availability of communications and related technologies. The full market liberalisation of the EU telecommunications industry began on 1 January 1998. This injected an extra boost to the impetus for competition and large-scale consolidation. The recent unprecedented spate of telecommunications takeovers was largely motivated by the liberalisation of world telecommunications set in motion by the Geneva World Trade Organisation meeting in 1997. Early momentum was achieved by a new Telecommunication Act in the USA in February 1996, which brought competition to local telecommunications services and video entertainment coupled with a series of large takeovers. The future of Web-commerce will be WAP technologies. The growth here is potentially large.

## Questions

1. Why did telecommunication liberalisation assist Internet growth and trade?
2. Which firms possess 'first mover' advantage in high-tech industry?
3. How does Internet retailing assist smaller firms?
4. Examine the welfare implications of Internet advertising.

### Key concepts

| | |
|---|---|
| globalisation | Internet commerce |
| strategy | WTO |
| global telecoms | oligopoly |
| Internet advertising | WAP technology |

## Notes

1. In Europe, effective from January 1998, 15 member states plus others such as Switzerland started a new phase of liberalised competition in their territories. Moreover, Belgium, Denmark, Germany, Ireland, Greece, the Netherlands and Portugal started allowing private sector participation in their main telecommunication operations since 1995 (Tarjanne, 1997).
2. According to Forrester Research, the Massachusetts-based market research firm estimates that e-commerce via the Internet could reach $3.2 trillion in 2003, which is equivalent to nearly 5% of all global sales (Taylor, 1998a). The $1 trillion volume is very high as the total volume of the American retail market only reached $2 trillion in 1997. The current industry statistics indicate that only 3% of users visiting a Web site actually made a purchase. To reach the $1 trillion benchmark, a very high purchase growth rate via the Internet is required in five years' time.
3. Willman (1998) discussed the importance of corporate brand names and associated economic impacts in various situations. A striking example of branding value is the £250,000 fee paid to Wolff Olins, the London corporate identity consultants, for choosing the name Diageo, for the recent merger between Guinness and Grand Metropolitan.
4. In March 1998, over 700 policy makers around the world met in Geneva at the ITU's Second World Telecommunications Policy Forum to discuss matters regarding WTO agreements on trade in telecommunication services, worldwide development of the telecommunications network and reforms for the current unstable accounting rates regimes. These discussions led to non-binding opinions in favour of building a more competitive global environment for telecommunications services.
5. Telecommunications trade is now a multinational affair. The corresponding agreements between operators to establish price is known as accounting rates (Tarjanne, 1997). The current

regime is called a revenue-sharing system which requires new operators to share the high cost structure of existing players. Ironically, new entrants should compete with existing players rather than sharing incumbent inefficiency cost. The proposed cost-based system refers to the payment regime according to the levels of calls terminated. This is more closely related to the real cost of provision of services for new entrants who inevitably originate more traffic than terminate calls at their stage of the business cycle (Chasia, ibid.).

6. The German telecommunications liberalised policies allow foreign competitors to link into the existing networks of Deutsche Telekom by paying a fee at 2.7 pfennigs a minute, which is low by international standards. Ron Sommer, the chief executive of Deutsche Telekom, expects to enter an escalating price war to regain the current loss of market share (14%) of long-distance business, which may reach 30% as suggested by industry analysts (Cane, 1998).

7. For instance, in the USA, AT&T and MCI intend to compete with Concert Communications, British Telecom's global super-carrier in the USA. Both AT&T and MCI/WorldCom are mega global players which represent the largest US long-distance operator and the fast-growing alternative carrier in the US respectively. One of the striking advantages obtained by WorldCom is its international network ownership. Hence, WorldCom can control its networks and set competing quality over its services supplied to users (Cane, 1998d).

8. The mobile telephone equipment market in China is worth about $7.5bn a year. For instance, Nokia sold $1.2bn telecoms equipment in 1997 in the Chinese market. The telecoms industry in China is expected to grow at 35% in 1998 (Kynge, 1998b).

9. According to a survey carried out on behalf of Motorola, 1 in 20 of the 1000 interviewees had used Internet telephony to make international calls (Cane, 1998f).

10. For instance, Deutsche Telekom could spend up to DM15bn per annum on fixed infrastructure. In Germany, a mobile operator may spend only DM7bn over a four-year scheme of network improvement. These lowlevel investments in networks may jeopardise the prosperity of using cellular phones to replace fixed line business (Cane, 1998).

11. In October, ICO stressed that it will compete with its rivals on price (Price, 1998c).

12. Some industry analysts even expect to see Internet bandwith use amounting to 99% (Martin, 1998).

## Bibliography

Abrahams, P. (1998) 'Docomo IPO will set world record', *Financial Times*, 12 October, p.25.

Andrews, E. (1998) 'EU backs WorldCom on MCI bid', *International Herald Tribune*, 20–21 June, p. 11.

Atkins, R. and Cane, A. (1998) 'A little local difficulty in the domestic market', *Financial Times*, 3 November, p. 28.

Atkins, R. (1998a) 'Deutsche Telekom fights rivals with price cut plan', *Financial Times*, 29 October, p. 28.

Blitz, J. (1998) 'Enormous potential for mobiles growth', *FT Telecoms 8*, *Financial Times*, 10 June.

Bloomberg, A. (1998) 'Telecom bulls bolster Wall Street', *International Herald Tribune*, 26 June, p. 14.

Bowen, D. (1998) 'Information technology electronic business awards: new media gets hard-headed', *Financial Times*, 14 October, p. 23.

Black, G. (1998) 'On the increase globally', *Financial Times*, Industry Issue 9, 10 June.

Cane, A. (1998a) 'Internet use highlighted', *Financial Times*, 10 November, p. 12.

Cane, A. (1998b) 'Mobile operators "spend too little" ', *Financial Times*, 15 October, p. 5.

Cane, A. (1998c) 'Telekom chief hits out on regulation', *Financial Times*, 3 November, p. 28.

Cane, A. (1998d) 'AT&T and MCI plan to compete on BT service', *Financial Times*, 12 November, p. 40.

Cane, A. (1998e) 'BT sees data overtake voice', *Financial Times*, 5 November, p. 26.

Cane, A. (1998f) 'It's good to talk with staff by e-mail', *Financial Times*, 10 November, p. 14.

Cane, A. (1998) 'Industry is switched on to a capital idea', *Financial Times*, Leverage Finance 4, October 9.

Cave, A. (1998) 'Internet float sets records on US stock market', *Daily Telegraph*, 16 November, p. 27.

Cane, A. (1999a) 'Internet represents both threats and opportunities', FT-IT Review 10, *Financial Times*, 13 January.

Cane, A. (1999b) 'Out with the old, in with the new', Global Business Outlook, *Financial Times*, III. 29 January.

Cane, A. (1999c) 'Mobile and going places', *Financial Times*, 7 January, p. 22.

Chasia, H. (1998) 'Accounting Rate Reform: The Current Debate, Annual Council of the Commonwealth Telecommunication Organisation', ITU, 1998, September, 29, www.itu.int/ti/papers/accrates/29septchasia.htm.

Costello, S. (1998) 'Hot topic with benefits for all', *Financial Times*, FT Telecom 10, 10 June.

Cox, B. (1998a) 'Nua Report – MediaRep launches advertising network', www.internetnews.com., 5 November.

Cox, B. (1998b) 'Nua Report – $6.5 billion in on-line ad spending in 2002', www.internetnews.com., 23 October.

Cyber Atlas (1999) 'Nua Internet Surveys: CPM's continue to fall', Nua Limited, vol. 4, no. 4, 1 February.

Eaglesham, J. (1999) 'Retailers warned over web delays', *Financial Times*, 7 January, p. 8.

European Commission, Dept. of E-Commerce, Brussels.

Farhi, P. and Mills, M. (1998) 'Deal to acquire cable-tv giants gives AT&T broader reach', *International Herald Tribune*, 25 June, p. 1.

Financial Times (1998) 'Research Digest: E-commerce surges ahead', *Financial Times*, 2 December.

Gapper, J. (1998) 'New battleground looms for mobile and media groups', *Financial Times*, 10 November, p. 12.

Gapper, J. (1999) 'Media: Focus on electronics', Financial Business Outlook, *Financial Times* IV, 29 January.

Harmon, S. (1998) 'Webdex spotlight: Microsoft goes hyper for linkexchange', the Internet Stock Report, Internet.com, http://www.internetnews.com/stocks/, 5 Nov.

Hansell, S. (1998) 'Median giants rush to set up Web "gateways" ', *International Herald Tribune*, 20–21 June.

Houlder, V. (1998) 'Fear and enterprise as the net closes in', *Financial Times*, 20 May, p. 18.

Houlder, V. (1998a) 'Spreading the message inside the organisation', *Financial Times*, 10 November, p. 14.

Houlder, V. (1998b) *Financial Times*, 10 January.

IAB (1998) 'On-line advertising revenue to hit US$2 billion in 1998', Internet Advertising Bureau, http://www.nua.ie/survey, 3 November.

ITU (1998) 'Conference report:- liberalisation of global telecoms: is it accomplished?', *Telecommunication Policy*, vol. 22, no. 7, pp. 631–33.

IWA (1998) 'Internet world Asia', http://www.iw.com.sg

Jackson, T. (1998) 'Plugged into the IT revolution', *Financial Times*, 13 October, p. 14.

Jupiter Communications (1998) 'Users will only pay for niche market content', http://www.nua.ie/survey, 23 October.

Kelly, T. (1996) 'Telecom privatisations: the new realism, ITU speeches and discussion papers – telecom privatisation', www.itu.int/it/papers/privatisation/realism.htm.

Kynge, J. (1998a) 'China cuts off foreign telecom investors' hope', *Financial Times*, 23 September, p. 4.

Kynge, J. (1998b) 'China Telecoms – Foreign companies out of favour in $7.5bn mobile telephone equipment market – Beijing gives "buy local" order', *Financial Times*, 5 November, p. 11.

Kynge, J. (1998) 'Telecoms minister hangs up on foreign investors', *Economist*, 5 November, p. 11.

Lapper, R. (2000) 'Tropical nets', *Financial Times*, 2 February, p. 18.

Martin, P. (1998) 'War waged on the net', *Financial Times*, 8 June, p. 23.

McGookin, S. (1998) 'Tapping into a new and growing audience', Annual Review – The Advertising Industry 2, *Financial Times*, 11 November.

Nairn, G. (1999) 'Electronic business-to-business trading: a vision of virtual commerce communities', FT-IT 2, *Financial Times*, 13 February.

Nua Internet Surveys (1998) 'On-line advertising rates are falling', Nua, http://www.nua.ie/surveys, 5 November.

Nua Internet Surveys (1999a) 'Nua's how many online?', Review Addition, Nua Ltd, 26 January.

Nua Internet Surveys (1999b) 'Editorial Review', vol. 4, no. 4 , Nua Ltd, 1 February.

Nua Internet Surveys (2000a) 'Latin American market continues to boom', vol. 5, no. 6, Nua Ltd, 7 February.

Nua Internet Surveys (2000b) 'Advertisers turn away from major portals', vol. 5, no. 6, Nua Ltd, 7 February.

Ody, K. (1999) FT Reviews, *Financial Times*, 13 January.

PNE (1998) 'Baby's next big step: SBC-Ameritech', *Public Network Europe*, vol. 8, no. 6, p. 12.

Price, C. (1998a) 'Bruised Netscape angles for corporate users', *Financial Times*, 8 June, p. 25.

Price, C. (1998b) 'Investors get live to attractions of internet groups', *Financial Times*, 30 April, p. 30.

Price, C. (1998c) 'Convenient, but not cheap', *Financial Times*, 30 September.

Price, C. (1999) 'Cybersquatters find wealth of names on the web', *Financial Times*, 10 March, p. 38.

Price, C. (2000) 'Portals re-evaluate their strategies', *Financial Times*, 2 February, p. 30.

Rawsthorn, A. (1998) 'Digital media could create 80,000 jobs by 2007', *Financial Times*, 3 November, p. 16.

Reuters (1998) 'Mobile-phone giants in computing deal', *International Herald Tribune*, 26 June, p. 15.

Ridding, J. (1998) 'CTHK unveils mainland buy', *Financial Times*, 29 April, p. 34.

Shillingford, J. (1998) 'Mobiles are becoming all-in-tools', *Financial Times*, Telecoms Business 9, 30 September.

Shillingford, J. (2000) 'Mobile leaders back the "Internet In Your Pocket" ', *Financial Times*, 2 February, Review 8.

Tarjanne, P. (1997) 'Telecommunications and trade, speeches and discussion papers, Forum ITA '97', Telecommunications and World Development: Forecasts, Technologies, and Services, 5 February, www.itu.int/ti/papers/moscow97/moscow97.htm.

Techserver (1998) 'E-commerce predicted to top 1 trillion by 2002', http://www.nua.ie/surveys, 27 October.

Taylor, P. (1998a) 'Internet set for 5% of sales', *Financial Times*, 10 November, p. 7.

Taylor, P. (1998b) 'Unique potential still untapped', *Financial Times*, 10 June.

Taylor, R. (1999) 'Yahoo! Figures provides a site for sore eyes', *Financial Times*, 14 January, p. 37.

Walters, R. and Taylor, R. (1999) 'Microsoft and Intel set to announce telecoms link-up', *Financial Times*, 15 March, p. 1.

Waters, R. (1998) 'US carriers seek leading role on the world stage', *Financial Times*, Review of the telecommunications industry, Part 1, 30 September.

Wettemann, R. and Kelly, T. (1998) 'The changing international telecommunications environment: country case studies', Geneva: ITU, ITU Strategic Planning Unit, March 8.

Williamson, J. (1998) '$120bn of investments needed', *Financial Times*, FT Telecoms 8, 8 June.

Willman, J. (1998) 'The sweet smell of earnings growth', Annual Review – The Advertising Industry 2, *Financial Times*, 11 November.

# 18 Trade and telecommunications in the Indian Ocean Region

**M. LING and K. LAWLER**

This chapter aims to discuss the current telecommunications environment in the countries stretched across the Indian Ocean Region. Available data shows diversities of communications services consumed by people, especially from the poorer and richer nations. Convergent technical advances promote cost-saving activities worldwide and technical improvements in telecommunications are expected to bring higher living standards for various economies in the region. Such an evolutionary period encompasses the drive towards market liberalisation in the areas. Moreover, the levels of telecommunications are related to success in trade performance, which is analysed using growth concepts. The extent to which telecommunications can give an impetus to the integration of this important infrastructural service for countries facing severe poverty are considered too.

## 18.1  Introduction

As the world moved closer to the millennium, takeover and consolidation activities in the global telecommunication industry have been increasing. Large players have been actively searching for new markets and revolutionary products to widen market potential. These phenomena have certainly improved the global environment for telecommunication services development to flourish at a greater pace. However, little attention has been focused on the less developed countries. Moreover, when global communication technologies advance at greater speed, less developed countries may find themselves exposed to yet another acute level of comparative disadvantage in economic development, such as international trade and efficiency in business, management, technological transfer and education. Within the Indian Ocean Region (IOR), there exists the advanced regions of Northern and Western Australia, newly industrial nations, Singapore and Malaysia, and large less developed countries, namely India and South and East African countries. Within this wide geographical expanse of countries, the varying levels of telecommunications facilities and infrastructure provide a good cross-section of the potential degree of convergence possible consequent on technological advance originating in the West.

In recent years, telecommunications developed to a convergent stage where data, sound and visual image can be transmitted by digital technologies (Blackman, 1998). In the past, communication networks were constructed to transmit different types of information separately; such as telephone networks (voice) and broadcasting networks (sound and vision). High-capacity digital compression techniques eliminate previous communication constraints and provide bandwidths for further development. In addition, the interactive multimedia services created by the telecommunications industry have demonstrated tremendous advances in various activities; such as Internet shopping, telebanking, interactive games and other forms of e-commerce. To build such high-tech telecommunication

314

infrastructures, huge financial investments are required. These exceed the capacity of any single country to sustain. Despite the fact that privatisation and liberalisation processes may bear on the countries in the IOR, to what extent can countries in the IOR gain the spillover benefits available from global restructuring and future advances in telecommunications? Will the costs of network development exceed the overall social benefits? Such questions should constitute the critical agenda for strategic state policy. Most countries in the IOR do not operate on the same basis as other telecommunication giants. However, they should learn from others' experience in terms of policy targeting, provision of service and implementation of regulations.

## 18.2 Profiling telecommunications environments

One of the fundamental problems confronting developing countries is the lack of telecommunication network development. A viable and sustainable network needs a well-developed customer base to support the large cost of maintenance and R&D. The scale of potential benefits derivable from technological spillovers is dependent on the size of the client base. Table 18.1 illustrates the various scales of telephone services operating in the various countries of the IOR.

Among the countries listed, India has the greatest number of main telephone lines, followed by Iran and Indonesia. Clearly, one of the large markets not listed is Australia, which, in terms of business computing, stands just behind the USA, Hong Kong and Canada according to the OECD. Based on a survey carried out by the Centre for Telemedia Strategy at the National University of Singapore, the Australian telecommunications environment is the second most competitive in Asia, after Japan. To produce a balanced picture of the general usage of telecommunications, the ratio of telephone lines to inhabitants is employed. Based on this evaluation, Singapore takes the lead and is well ahead of the second provider, Malaysia. While India and Indonesia rank high in absolute terms, they both have low teledensity, 1.53 and 2.13 respectively.[1] According to Table

**Table 18.1  Main phone lines 1996.**

| Country | In 000s | Teledensity (per 100 inhabitants) | Growth over previous year (%) |
|---|---|---|---|
| Bangladesh | 286.6 | 0.24 | 6.4 |
| India | 14450 | 1.53 | 20.6 |
| Indonesia | 4186 | 2.13 | 27.2 |
| Iran | 5825 | 9.53 | 14.4 |
| Malaysia | 3771.3 | 18.32 | 13.2 |
| Maldives | 16.6 | 6.30 | 19.4 |
| Myanmar | 178.6 | 0.39 | 13.2 |
| Oman | 197.7 | 8.59 | 16.3 |
| Pakistan | 2376.8 | 1.77 | 11.7 |
| Singapore | 1563 | 51.34 | 9.4 |
| Sri Lanka | 254.5 | 1.39 | 24.5 |
| Thailand | 4200.2 | 7.00 | 20.6 |
| Yemen | 204.7 | 1.29 | 9.4 |
| Asia | 206729 | 6.02 | 13.8 |

*Source* adapted from ITU, World Telecommunication Indicator Database.

18.1, the growth of density in 1996 based on 1995 data shows that Indonesia enjoys the highest growth rate (27.2%), followed by Sri Lanka (24.5%), Thailand and India (both of 20.6%) and the Maldives (19.4%). Most of the rest also experienced double digit increases, except Yemen, Bangladesh and Singapore. Certainly, Singapore historically has been very well established in teledensity, which leaves less scope for rapid growth.

Generally speaking, teledensity in the IOR is low (Table 18.1) and lags behind the world average of 12.8 (Table 18.2a) and is very different from the developed countries group average (54.3). This substantially limits economic growth and the right to communication. The idea of ensuring that people who suffer from poverty also have equal basic rights to communicate was proposed by Dr Pekka Targanne, Secretary-General of the International Telecommunication Union in 1996. The initiative eventually stimulated concerns about the maldistribution of access and opportunities in the fields of communication and information. In 1997, the United Nation's Administration Committee on Coordination issued a statement to highlight the importance of securing sustainable human development with respect to the objective of establishing universal access to basic communications for all.

Table 18.2b provides a snapshot contrast between the four Tiger economies in Asia, the G7 Asian economic powerhouse, Japan, and those recorded for the IOR. Japan and the Tiger economies were equipped with high levels of teledensity and managed to build telecommunications services with an average of 48.91 telephone lines per 100 inhabitants compared with only 6.02 recorded for the whole of Asia. Even in recent years, where

**Table 18.2a  Teledensity by income grouping.**

|  | Teledensity | | Household telephone penetration | |
| --- | --- | --- | --- | --- |
|  | 1996 | 2010 | 1996 | 2010 |
| World | 12.8 | – | 94.3 | – |
| Developed | 54.3 | – | 34.4 | – |
| Developing | 5.07 | 10 | 16.3 | >50 |
| Low income | 2.44 | 5 | 8.5 | >20 |
| Low income excluding China | 1.22 | – | 4.1 | – |

*Source* adapted from World Telecommunication Development Report 1998, http://info.itu/it/publications/WTDR98/index.html

**Table 18.2b  Main telephone lines per 100 inhabitants in South East Asia.**

|  | Telephone lines per 100 inhabitants |
| --- | --- |
| Hong Kong | 54.69 |
| Japan | 48.87 |
| Korea (Republic) | 43.04 |
| Singapore | 51.34 |
| Taiwan | 46.60 |
| Average of the above | 48.91 |
| Asia (average) | 6.02 |

*Source* adapted from ITU, World Telecommunication Indicator Database.

**Table 18.3  Website growth by period.**

|  | Number of Websites |
|---|---|
| June 1993 | 130 |
| Dec 1993 | 623 |
| June 1994 | 2,738 |
| Dec 1994 | 10,022 |
| June 1995 | 23,500 |
| Jan 1996 | 100,000 |
| June 1996 | 230,000 |
| Jan 1997 | 650,000 |

*Source* adapted from Web growth summary
[Http://www.mit.edu/people/mkgray/net/web-growth-summary.html]

all the economies in Table 18.2b suffered different levels of downturn; good communications infrastructure and high density telephone services have created the resources to improve living standards and the financial strength to withstand the recent currency turmoil. In particular, they are all involved significantly in exporting, and achieved success in manufacturing industries from the late 1970s to the early 1990s. Therefore it could be argued that sustainable growth relies on the cooperation and efficiency of various institutional and infrastructural factors which are enhanced by technical advance in telecommunications.

The Internet has achieved global success in recent years. None of the leading players in telecommunications considered the huge impacts created by Internet usage before 1994, when it was first commercially introduced. The phenomenal impact of its global influence can be seen in the rapid expansion of Website numbers since 1993 (Table 18.3). In 1998, the Internet attracted 129.8 million users worldwide. It is projected to reach the amazing amount of 413 millions in 2005 (Table 18.4). The Internet is popular in some IOR countries such as Australia, Singapore, Malaysia and India, whereas others such as East African countries and Bangladesh need time to catch up. According to Table 18.5, Internet users in Malaysia and Singapore are expected to increase to 2.2 m and 1.5m respectively. Australia, currently ranked sixth in the world in terms of Internet host distribution, is expected to increase its users from 3.6 million in 1998 to 5.76 million in 2002. More importantly, the Internet could generate attractive lump sums of investment within the region. This is demonstrated by available revenue forecasts, which range from $200

**Table 18.4  Internet users by region.**

|  | Subscribers on 1 July 1998* | Internet subscribers for 2005** Estimation in million |
|---|---|---|
| Canada & USA | 70 | 141 |
| Europe | 31.7 | 124 |
| Asia Pacific | 19.3 | 104 |
| ROW | 8.8 | 44 |
| Total | 129.8 | 413 |

*Source* adapted from * Various & Nua Internet Surveys, *Financial Times*, 30 September 1998.
** Company Data, CSFB, *Financial Times*, 10 June 1998

**Table 18.5   Internet users in selected countries in IOR (millions).**

|  | 1998 | 2000/2001/2002 |
|---|---|---|
| [δ]Africa | 0.8 to 1.0 | – |
| Australia | 3.6 | 5.76 |
| Bangladesh | 0.002 | – |
| India | 0.24 | 1.5 |
| Indonesia | 0.08 | – |
| Malaysia | 0.25 | 2.2 |
| Singapore | 0.25 | 1.5 |
| Sri Lanka | 0.014 | 0.05 |

*Source* adapted from Nua Internet Surveys. [δ]Jensen (1998)

million to $16 billion (Table 18.6). However, for the less developed countries depicted in Table 18.1 with low capital endowments and foreign inputs for telecommunication networks, widespread Internet usage cannot be expected in the near future, despite the fact that major cities in these regions have access to this interactive medium. Internet connectivity in Africa is very unevenly distributed. The total estimated number of users is between 0.8m and 1.0 m. However, about 0.7m users are located in South Africa. This leaves around 0.1m to 0.3m Internet connections for the remaining 700m population on the continent. Internet connectivity in areas other than South Africa is expected to be 1 in 5000 people, which is far lower than the world average of 1 in 40, lower than the developed world average of 4 in 6 (Jensen, 1998). Moreover, 46 out of 54 countries and territories in Africa have Internet access in capital cities which is a very commensurable example of the popularity of this global communications medium.

Household telephone penetration rates are expected to reach triple the rate recorded in 1996 for developing countries (Table 18.2b). This reflects a strong belief in the potential absorption for advanced telecommunication by these economies. More precisely, the overall teledensity in developing and low-income countries such as the East African nations and Bangladesh may experience more or less 100% increases. According to Table 18.4, the growth rates of Internet subscribers across the IOR can be derived from the data in categories, namely Asia/Pacific and ROW, which represent 5.39 and 5 times the 1998 statistics. Consumers in these regions who have experienced the first phase of telecommunication improvements may progressively demand more advanced services. Eventually, their influences and knowledge may spread out to the wider spectrum in societies. Most Asian countries are still experiencing the first wave of Internet development, while the USA is outperforming the rest of world in its third phase of Internet

**Table 18.6   Internet revenue forecasts (US$ billion).**

|  | 2001/2002 |
|---|---|
| Australia | 16 |
| Indonesia | 0.2 |
| Malaysia | 1 |
| Singapore | 0.8 |
| Thailand | 0.2 |

*Source* adapted from Nua Internet Surveys

growth, accompanied by Australia in the second phase of development (Skali, 1998). If this process continues to snowball, it will provide high-volume traffic for more international players which seek overseas footings. The forecast from Table 18.2b represents strong future potential demand-pull from these emerging markets.

## 18.3 Market liberalisations

Deregulation, privatisation and de-monopolisation are important for international investment. During the past decade, substantial structural changes in dominant telecommunication industries were experienced in various G7 industrial economies, such as AT&T in the USA, the privatisation of BT in the UK and even the de-monopolisation of the Japanese telecom NTT. These vigorous strategic moves have had a profound impact on international restructuring, particularly regarding focusing and competitive regimes. This can be demonstrated by the pursuit of organic growth and bolt-on acquisitions declared by Ericsson, the Swedish telecommunication group, under an entirely new strategy to cut losses in the fixed-line business and reform aggressively to exploit the convergence of telecoms and data networks on Internet access products (McIvor, 1998). Moreover, Ericsson abandoned the previous business area structure in favour of a new customer and regional organisations approach to raise responsiveness to rapid changes in the global communications arena. Relocating headquarters to London was considered to induce tax incentives for procurement as well as to match the new matrix organisation in three target categories (network operators, private consumers and commercial enterprises) rather than the existing structures comprising mobile systems, mobile phones and terminals (Burt, 1998). Blackman (ibid.) highlights that the liberalisation of telecommunications markets in Europe and around the world has been the driving force for reform in telecommunication policies in recent years. The process was started by the 1987 Green Paper for European markets, which had significant implications for the long-awaited occurrence of the global information society. In 1998, a global basic telecoms accord was reached in Geneva. This aimed to promote greater competition and liberalisation across 68 countries of the WTO, covering 90% of the world market. The outcome was an important victory, as was described by the WTO head Mr Renato Ruggiero; it was a big step forward after the deadlock experienced in 1996 between the USA, EU and Japan on the limited territory access commitments. However, access to the latest telecommunications technology has been largely enhanced by the recent breakthrough by Iridium's global mobile phones, which meet agreed standards recognised by about 100 members of the ITU (Cane, 1998). This boosts the hope of global convergence of services, including voice, data, fax, and paging services utilising constellations of orbiting satellites, to be consumed without geographical restrictions. This further confirms that consumers in the IOR have a fair chance of communicating on a global basis, provided they can afford the services.

Given the huge disparities in statistics shown between countries in the IOR, there should be a greater concern for the development of telecommunication services within the IOR. There are lots of international institutions that help the less developed countries to kick-start communication development projects. For instance, an amount of $0.5m for each of the 20 African countries was granted by the Leland Initiative to develop Internet connectivity. UNDP's Africa Bureau was granted a $6m project for Africa to improve Internet connectivity (Jensen, 1998). The fundamental need in these countries is to attract private consortiums to participate in improving the telecommunication industries. This requires governmental and associated departmental cooperation to create favourable business and legal environments to bring forth better commercial prospects.

Market liberalisation can be facilitated by joint ventures. This mode of operation allows some domestic providers to absorb foreign telecommunication techniques at lower costs, while foreign entrants can explore the domestic potential with their unique expertise. At the moment, Thailand and Indonesia have joint-venture partnerships with foreign tele-communication consortiums. However, the effects are not satisfactory as they operate with predetermined compensation systems that result in substandard market effects in consumption, including service quality, pricing and variety. To facilitate these inter-national alliances, government regulations should be freed from destructive political influence so as to favour a competitive environment to prevail. Trade liberalisation wins favour from economists. However, Sarntisart (1995) demonstrated that liberal trade regimes (combined with government financing such as through the use of direct taxation, external financing and indirect taxation) generated different redistributional effects and long-term repayment burdens based on the simulation analysis for Thailand.

Since 1987, Malaysian telecommunications have been liberalised to accommodate more private investment such as allowing private enterprises to use the latest satellite technologies to construct advanced telecommunications infrastructure and international service gateways to boost the efficiency and variety of telecommunications services. The success of practising competitive market systems can also be seen in India and Sri Lanka. Since competition was first brought into the basic telephony in India, the number of cable TV connections reached 25 million within 4 years by more than 800,000 private operators. This contrasts with only 5 million households with telephone services in the 114 years of the monopoly regime (Chowdary, 1998). In Thailand, zoning systems were laid down in the Master Plan launched in 1996 in order to promote efficiency (Cairns, 1998). However, there is a strong need for tighter suspension and non-linear pricing for Thai markets. In the Indian telecoms market, Internet access has been monopolised by VSNL, the state international carrier. On 7 November 1998, Internet access, which had 500,000 current users, was liberalised to allow foreign companies to enjoy stakes up to 49% in Internet Service Providers (ISP). At the time, more than 50 companies expressed interest in ISPs. According to the study in 1998 of the National Association of Software and Service Companies in India, about 20–25 companies are expected to apply for licences for ISPs immediately. Behari Vajpayee, the Prime Minister in India, expects the industry to operate with faster proliferation of quality Internet services. Although at the moment 80% of the Internet connections are linked through VSNL's gateway, the new policy allows new competitors running direct international gateway access. The software industry in India is expected to see unfettered and cheap Internet access, on which its growth essentially hinges. These liberal policy transformations will certainly provide greater impetus for the development of Internet telephony currently effected by com-plicated incomplete telecoms policies (Nicholson, 1998).

For those developing countries dominated by rural populations, the key issue is to pro-vide citizens with affordable telecommunications services. To achieve this, state-owned telecommunications or monopolised service providers should be liberalised in such a way as to allow more players to enter the markets and provide cheaper basic services. First, government or other funding bodies should focus on the development of the telenet-work by installing more major phone lines with optical fibre cables in both major cities and rural areas. Secondly, incentive schemes should be promoted by funding incumbents which allow entrants to run services via their existing cable networks and to cooperate in long-term service provision. This can significantly reduce entry costs, lower entry barriers and increase the likelihood of the provision of services at relatively lower cost. Hence, increases in accessibility to telecommunications services can be foreseen if sufficient cooperation and strategic alliances with experienced players are arranged in desirable ways.

The resulting momentum of economic liberalisation can be demonstrated by considering the large volume of capital liberated from leveraged finance and high-yield debt. In 1998, there were more than 180 debt issues, compared to only eight in 1992 (Cane, 1998). The recent unprecedented wave of capital flights reflects a high-risk premium as market winners are not yet decided. The world telecommunication revenue is estimated to $600 billion, or equivalent to 2% of GNP in 1995 (Raghavan, 1998). The revenue is expected to move towards $1,000 billion in future (Cane, 1998), which is the same as the forecast, 4% of world GNP over the next decade, by the WTO. The world's largest recent share issue was carried out by a Japanese mobile telecoms operator on 12 October 1998 (Abrahams, 1998). The impact on potential scale economies in the less developed countries of the IOR which could attract this level of service provision, the cost savings and the enhancement of efficiency can be achieved in the long run. To some extent, the less developed countries in the IOR can gain from being late starters in attracting FDI for telecommunications since they can acquire the latest technology in an industry subject to constant advances. For instance, the globalisation of telecommunications leads also to increase in efficiency and a surplus of manufacturing equipment and cables in developed countries, as argued by Chowdary (ibid.). This motivates global players to supply expensive high-tech capital to less developed countries, leading to global technological transfers. Moreover, these transfers determine the future trends of telecommunication development in developing countries. Such technological diffusion is only practical if developing countries can obtain sufficient finance to sustain capital investment. The widespread rapid increase in telecommunications services is largely driven by economies of scale. This is similar to semiconductor market prices; according to Moore's Law, as the performance of microchips increases twice about every 18 months, this pushes down the market prices of various types of telecommunications services and equipment in the global market, where imitation and development become more rapid. The fast penetration rates in the telephone market (Table 18.2b) demonstrate the emergent improvements in telecommunications in the IOR. However, as argued in the World Telecommunication Development Report 1998, the time required to reach a high level of teledensity varies immensely between nations. The earlier ITU data shows that attaining a teledensity of from 1 to 50 needs a time span of 50 years. The data also shows that achieving teledensity ratios of between one and ten may take 21 years on average. Unfortunately, there is a substantial proportion (a quarter) of ITU members with teledensity ratios below one for which it is impossible to predict the transition duration required to reach higher levels. This threshold hurdle restricts predictions for the low-income IOR countries such as Bangladesh and Myanmar, which in 1996 possessed a teledensity of 0.24 and 0.39 respectively (Table 18.1). These statistics on previous development trends generate a pessimistic view concerning the quick adaptation of advances in telecommunications services in the poorer IOR countries.

In the telecommunications industry, economic societal gains largely derive from its applications, and service adoption rather than production factors. Some writers argue that the diffusion of computerisation is more important than production. This provides a convincing view that the less developed country groups in the IOR may gain increasing revenues and catch up closer to world standards via non-production and non-R&D activities in the medium term despite the large gap between the higher- and lower-income countries in terms of services provided. This significance of government policy in assisting IT developments and telecommunications has been established for OECD countries (Hanna *et al.*, 1995). Countries in the IOR such as Singapore (Singapore One), Malaysia (Vision 2020) and Thailand (IT2000) have launched national initiatives to strengthen their own national information infrastructures. The use of the most sophisticated community-based approaches for individual broadband connection is encouraged by the Singaporean government to enhance its pro-Internet policies. In Thailand, based on the Build-Operate-Transfer (BOT) scheme implemented in 1991, teledensity has increased from 4 to 7 between 1993 and 1996, with installations of 4.1 million telephone lines in Bangkok and rural areas (ITU, 1998).

Following the implications of the traditional SCP paradigm, market liberalisation should lead to a series of structural influences on strategic conduct and performance. The present global market structure under rapid change reflects the urgent need for policy changes around the world to coordinate desirable outcomes. However, structure, as argued by Dosimoni (1984), provides only one set of dynamic variables which created the recent technological revolution in the market-led telecommunications industry. By contrast, Tirole (1988) and Cowling (1976) argue that strategic 'conduct' is generally more important. Indeed, during later stages of the evolutionary processes in this industry and especially in the IOR, 'conduct' chosen by key strategic players should generate great forces towards reshaping both the regional and global competitive frameworks. For instance, after rapid capital flights, mergers and new share issues, key entrants will have to re-target their corporate missions and aim to capture market share from incumbents throughout the IOR. They will need to capitalise returns and insulate themselves against the initial vast premia investments. In order to secure the 'battlefield' in regional and international terms, they will be willing to put capital investment into developing countries such as exist within the IOR

## 18.4    Growth: the theoretical implications

### 18.4.1  Growth perspectives

Within the IOR, countries exhibit wide disparities in living standards and respective GNPs. Studies by Baumol (1986) and Delong (1986) show evidence of the lack of convergent growth rates between the rich and the poor countries. This evidence counteracts predictions of the neo-classical growth models. However, digitalisation is likely to bring these poor countries to the new era of standardised/homogeneous and compatible industry platforms. Undoubtedly, the technical side of telecommunications has already reached a convergent state despite gaps in income levels. Surely barrier-free access to global information is a possibility for all, provided that they are connected to the Internet. The revolutionary Web-TV technology is expected to dominate household entertainment for the foreseeable future. These technological developments in telecommunications suggest that, if there exists efficient diffusion across countries, more convergent economic growth should be observed. However, this process largely depends on the speed of imitation processes facilitated by increased global knowledge exchange. When more information is available speedily, greater stocks of human capital and technological expertise can be accumulated more efficiently. This eventually leads to higher potential growth performance. The idea is equivalent to the controversial 'macro-endogenous growth models' within the new classical school explained by Romer (1986) and Lucas (1988). The welfare spin-offs may be large, especially when exposure to and adoption of efficient information resources can strengthen the productivity of physical and human capital. If countries in the IOR seek to make use of the diffused knowledge, the potential disparities in living standards will be reduced in the long run, since technological equilibrium and income equalisation go hand in hand. For less developed countries, technological growth via telecommunications should be the 'non-durable of growth'.

Using growth theory perspectives, there is evidence to show that the rates of technical change in telecommunication in developing countries originate from demand-pull forces, as shown by Grilliches (1957) and Schmookler (1962). The increase in demand for technology is more achievable given assistance from global organisations such as the WTO and UN, together with the pushful marketing campaigns led by profit-driven global telecommunication enterprises. Generally, consumers everywhere are motivated to try out new services. Moreover, suppliers are willing to provide tailor-made telecommunications technologies to match the needs of developing societies featuring large lower-income groups. These groups consist of customers with limited ideas about the forms of service provision derivable from advanced media, especially computer-literate consumers in the IOR. Evolutionary growth theorists such as Nelson and Winter (1975) argued that the search for better economic techniques is the driving force for growth. In the IOR, poorer countries, which suffer long-standing underdevelopment and poverty, always have stronger motivations to acquire higher levels of economic success. Hence, there exists driving needs to activate and transform economic activities, which naturally constitute an in-built mainspring momentum which seeks better communication techniques.

### 18.4.2 Trade-offs and externalities in IOR nations

One could argue that advances in telecommunication technology do not assist the alleviation of poverty, which is geographically concentrated in Asia and Africa, where food, nutrition and medical care are of more critical importance. However, to cure deep-rooted economic backwardness, effective communications media may have a significant role to play regarding effects on long-run efficiency. Despite this, most poor regions may not treat telecommunications as vital. Moreover, the stress on investment in telecommunication tends to favour the relatively rich and those living in major metropolitan areas. Debates relating to these issues are similar to the traditional arguments of efficiency vs. equity trade-off in policy making. Studies from Bardhan (1996) and Grossman (1992) show that increases in efficiency may not necessarily hinder the development of equity within poor countries. Thus, telecommunication infrastructures, as argued by Bardhan (1996), may introduce dynamic externalities, which may lead to increased 'social capital'. These externalities may result in better educational standards, the elimination of the 'brain drain' to the metropolitan areas, favourable decentralisation processes and improvements in the aggregate potential for productive investments and developments. According to the Washington-based Institute for International Economics, the welfare gains from worldwide communication liberalisation may exceed a trillion US dollars in a 14-year period. A corresponding forecast was believed to be around $220 billion in 1992/3 and $500 billion in December 1994 according to the World Bank and GATT respectively (Raghavan, 1998). In areas with surplus idle labour, the liberalisation of telecom activities, together with relaxation of excessive licensing charges, may reduce information costs, thus stimulating the growth of trade, thereby raising labour participation rates. This, in turn, passes on benefits to labour markets in low-income countries, as these usually comprise a high proportion of labour-intensive activities such as in agricultural and primary production sectors.

If one follows the precepts of neo-classical growth theorists (Solow, 1957), who place strong emphasis on technical progress, or the new growth theorists pioneered by Romer (ibid.) and Lucas (ibid.). They focused on R&D and the externalities of human capital accumulation, technical transfers and foreign investments in the telecommunications industry. This should generate spin-off effects beneficial to growth and capital formation in the IOR. The consequent induced increases in productivity for host countries arising from imported skills and FDI are discussed by Wang and Blonstrom (1992). Countries with low levels of technical 'know-how' are expected to capitalise more fundamental knowledge transfers in key sectors. If proper utilisation of this spill-over knowledge can be achieved across the IOR, together with R&D investments in crucial directions, then the productivity of resource endowments and human capital will be enhanced and generate greater positive externalities, reducing epidemic poverty found in Africa and Asia.

### 18.4.3 Trade regimes

Recent successes in the development of efficient telecommunications industries are evident given the experience of South East Asia. However, the lack of communications facilities in developing countries based on import-substitution trade regimes are also well evident (Kruger, 1998). Within the IOR, the outward-oriented exporting countries simultaneously feature with higher levels of telecommunications services, whereas those countries that rely on import-substitution activities experience relatively lower levels of telecommunication advance. This shows that differentials, in terms of economic advances and volume of inward FDI, may be affected by extant disparities in telecommunication capital investment.

Governmental attitudes towards FDI are crucial for long-term domestic development. Long-run effects follow the theoretical framework of endogenous growth models. In particular, the linkages interacting between FDI, trade policies and growth are central to the endogenous growth processes, and are shown in the recent studies by Greenaway and Sapsford (1994). Endogenous growth spin-offs are essential for poorer countries, striving to pursue progressive growth policies to alleviate long-standing poverty. Presently, countries with low telecommunication service provision such as Bangladesh, Indonesia, India, Ethiopia and Sri Lanka are practising import-substitution (IS) trade policies according to the World Bank Classifications (Stopford et al., 1991). Sapsford (1996) argues that countries that adopt inwardly oriented trade policies are relatively less successful in attracting FDI for promoting growth, compared to countries practising outwardly-oriented trade policies. Countries within the export-promoting (EP) category include Singapore, Malaysia and Thailand, which are trade neutral (neither using distortions nor artificial incentives for FDI). IS countries tend to employ government distortions when formulating trade regimes. Consequently, IS countries with complicated trade restrictions distort the incentives for potential FDI, and the adoption of contemporary and advanced technologies is limited. By contrast, EP countries stressing cost efficiency pull in more FDI. This may explain the low rates of teledensity and backward telecommunication infrastructures found in low-income countries in the IOR. If this 'closed-door' trade regime continues, poverty will remain and the income disparities will become more severe as other developed countries advance gradually. The long-run effects of this mis-allocation of resources and 'x'-efficiency can become more detrimental if the poor countries in the IOR do not tackle this problem urgently.

Inspection of Tables 18.1 and 18.2b shows that EP countries achieved greater levels of telecommunications services and teledensity. This implies that the level of technological advances may be significantly determined by the nature of trade polices. However, the reverse (causality) may apply in the endogenous growth process. Hence, greater incremental increases in telecommunications may be expected with the transformation from the IS to EP mode of trade regimes. This transformation is critical as FDI requires a conducive economic climate to breed positive effects on aggregate growth.[2] Hence, market liberation for telecommunications is a natural evolutionary step for the IS countries in the IOR to pursue greater economic successes. Kruger (1998) argues that liberalisation is the only element which effects the transition from IS to EP orientation. A liberalised market can facilitate more learning which is the key ingredient in the Romer (1986) and Lucas (1988) growth models. Moreover, the liberalisation regimes foster the rationalisation of resources and stimulate the reorientation of economic resources in favour of production sectors exhibiting greater efficiency (Sapsford, 1996). During transition periods, developing countries should put extra efforts on upgrading the capability of telecommunication networks to be ready to accommodate large changes or whatever may occur in future telecommunications technology.

## 18.5   Conclusions

A major fallacy in economics as argued by Stigler (1961) is that the best technological know-how is perceived as given and known by all people. This particularly stimulates controversial debate in the sphere of the economics of information. So, when technical advance demonstrates an incredible impact on digital activity and forms of market restructuring, the value of key information is widely recognised throughout the information society. Stigler (ibid.) also emphasises that knowledge is power and information is valuable. This is true especially when we consider recent crises in emerging markets such as the devaluation of the Russian rouble and the Asian contagion of currency crises. These crises are largely caused by asymmetric information problems between government/institutional authorities and investors. The resulting events show that the uninformed institutional weaknesses regarding debt-ridden financial systems, inconsistent interest rate regimes and exchange rates and the non-disclosures about incipient devaluations create domino effects on investors' asset values. These crises need more transparent policies from governmental/institutional measures to restore confidence. As mentioned by Wolf (1998), capital flows depend on confidence and the edifice between entrepreneurs and fund suppliers is 'faith'. To protect assets and avoid misuse of resources, effective flows of information in society are needed. This plea leaves a tremendous channel for the telecommunications industry to target. Advertising is a classic example of an information-producing industry. Recently, there has been increasing interest in Internet advertising, and this reflects the emerging informative functions of the telecommunication advances.[3] The volatility occurring in emerging markets in the 1990s makes investors reconsider ultimate trade-offs between riskiness and potential returns. Similarly, institutional problems may appear in the developing countries in the IOR, if precautionary measures are not taken in advance. Poorer countries are always regarded as passive observers on the global finance stage (Fidler and Balls, 1998). Indeed, there is a strong need for them to avoid the 'vicious' circle created by asymmetric information, uncertainty and moral hazard in handling FDI and future trade policies. There is an urgent need to call for a revolutionary phase in telecommunications improvement in the IOR. This is vital to enhance the efficient collection and distribution of information. The liberalisation process, which helps transform inward to outward orientation, is strongly believed to be conducive to growth. Dixon (1998) argue that the liberal process does provide favourable impacts on growth; however, the way is not straightforward, which may rely on a 'J curve' type adjustment process. Owing to the diversity of countries in terms of economic, political and social profiles within the IOR, it is not possible to discuss country-specific aspects for each country in the IOR in this chapter. However, detailed, country-specific analysis is definitely worthy of future research into the areas exploring the long-lasting effects on human beings arising from the contemporary trends revolutionising telecommunications globally.

## Summary

- Telecommunications environments throughout the IOR are diverse.
- Technical advances and cost cutting technology will increase teledensity in the next five years.
- Trade and telecommunications are likely to complement each other in the new trade scenarios being created by B2B and B2C commerce, and WAP technologies.
- Teledensity is an income-related phenomenon. Rising real incomes in Asia and IOR together with investment in infrastructure will be forces acting for convergence throughout the IOR.

## Questions

1. Discuss capital flows in the IOR in the context of market liberalisations.
2. Analyse the factors that should boost teledensities in countries in the IOR in the next five years.
3. How might B2B and B2C commerce develop in the IOR? Which countries will be at the forefront of this process?
4. Show how online trading can cut costs for buyers and sellers. (Hint: consider B2B or B2C auctions.)

## Key concepts

| | |
|---|---|
| IOR | convergence |
| telecoms liberalisation | capital flows |
| teledensity | new growth theory |
| telecoms infrastructure | |

## Notes

1. Teledensity is a common measure of telecommunication access and is represented by the number of main telephone lines per 100 inhabitants.
2. Korea, Hong Kong and Singapore are classified as high-income countries by the World Bank (World Bank, 1997). Taiwan, which has a higher income than Korea, is not listed in the World

Tables. All these economies achieved greater levels of living by utilising export-promoting trade policies and abandoning the import-substitution method since early 1960s (Kruger, 1998).

3. The details regarding the emerging functions of Internet advertising can be found in Ling *et al.* (1998).

# Bibliography

Abrahams, P. (1998) 'Japanese mobile telecoms operator will raise up to $19bn from share issue: Docomo IPO will set world record', *Financial Times*, 12 October, p. 25.

Bardhan, P. (1996) 'Efficiency, equity and poverty alleviation: policy issues in less developed countries', *Economic Journal*, vol. 106, pp. 1344–56.

Baumol, W. (1986) 'Productivity growth, convergence and welfare', *American Economic Review*, vol. 76, pp. 1072–85.

Blackman, C. (1998) 'Convergence between telecommunications and other media: how should regulation adapt?', *Telecommunications Policy*, vol. 22, no. 3, pp. 163–70.

Burt, T. (1998) 'Ericsson outlines new organisation', *Financial Times*, 9 September, p. 24.

Cairns, R. and Nikomborirak, D. (1998) 'An assessment of Thailand's new telecommunications plan', *Telecommunications Policy*, vol. 22, no. 2, pp. 145–55.

Cane, A. (1998) 'Industry is switched on to a capital idea', *Financial Times*, Special Supplement: Leveraged Finance 4, 9 October.

Cane, A. (1998) 'Global mobile phone, Iridium technology approved', *Financial Times*, 13 October, p. 10.

Chowdary, T. (1998) 'Telecom liberalisation and competition in developing countries', *Telecommunications Policy*, vol. 22, no. 4/5, pp. 259–65.

Cowling, K. and Waterson, M. (1976) 'Price-cost margins & market structure', *Economica*, vol. 43, pp. 267–74.

Delong, J. (1986) 'Productivity growth and welfare: comment', *American Economic Review*, vol. 78, pp. 1138–54.

Dixon, H. (1998) 'Controversy: trade liberalisation and growth; an introduction', *Economic Journal*, vol. 108, September, pp. 1511–12.

Donsimoni, M., Geroski, P. and Jacquemin, A. (1984) 'Concentration indices and market power: two views', *Journal of Industrial Economics*, vol. 32, pp. 419–34.

Fidler, S. and Balls, A. (1998) 'Feast or famine: are controls the answer?', *Financial Times*, 6 October, p. 12.

Greenaway, D. and Sapsford, D. (1994) 'What does liberalisation do for exports and growth?', *Welwirtschaftliches Archiv*, vol. 130, pp. 152–73.

Griliches, Z. (1957) 'Hybrid corn: an exploration in the economics of technical change', *Econometrica*, vol. 25, pp. 501–22.

Grossman, H. (1992) 'Robin Hood and the distribution of property income', IRIS Center Working Paper, 43, Maryland.

Hanna, N., Guy, K. and Arnold, E. (1995) 'The diffusion of information technology: Experience of industrial countries and lessons for developing countries', World Bank Discussion Paper, 281, Washington, DC: World Bank.

ITU (1998) World Telecommunication Development Report 1998, http://info.itu.int/ti/publications/WTDR_98/index.htm.

Jackson, T. (1998) 'Plugged into the IT revolution', *Financial Times*, 13 October, p. 14.

Jensen, M. (1998) 'An overview of Internet connectivity in Africa', 20 September, htttp://demiurge.wn.apc.org/africa/afstat.htm.

Kruger, A. (1998) 'Why trade liberalisation is good for growth', *Economic Journal*, vol. 108, September, pp. 1513–22.

Ling, M., Lawler, K., McBain, N. and Moscardini, A. (1998/9) *Economics of advertising: emerging functions of Internet advertising, Netnomics*, Baltzer Science Publishers BV (forthcoming).

Lucas, R. J. (1988) 'On the mechanics of economic development', *Journal of Monetary Economics*, vol. 22, pp. 3–42.

McIvor, G. (1998) 'Ericsson unveils Internet strategy', *Financial Times*, 13 October, p. 26.

Nelson, R. and Winter, S. (1975) 'Factor price changes & factor substitution in an evolutionary model', *Bell Journal of Economics*, vol. 6, pp. 466–86.

Nicholson, M. and Taylor, P. (1998) 'India throws market open to all comers to provide Internet access', *Financial Times*, 11 November, p. 6.

Raghavan, C. (1998) 'Telecoms liberalisation accord', http://www.southside.org.sg/souths/twn/souths/twn/title/tele-cn.htm.

Romer, P. (1986) 'Increasing returns and long run growth', *Journal of Political Economy*, vol. 94, pp. 1002–37.

Sapsford, D., Salisu, M. and Balasubramanyam, V. (1996) 'Foreign direct investment and growth in EP and IS countries', *Economic Journal*, vol. 106, no. 334, pp. 92–105.

Sarntisart, I. (1995) 'Trade liberalisation in Thailand: income distributional impact and financing problems', *Asian Economic Journal*, vol. 9, no. 3, pp. 251–92.

Schmookler, J. (1962) 'Determinants of industrial invention', in R. R. Nelson (ed.), *The Rate of Direction of Inventive Activity: Economic and Social Factors*, Princeton University Press.

Skali, P. R. (1998) 'The first international Alta Vista Asiawide user survey', Nua Internet Survey, 29 April.

Solow, R. (1957) 'Technical change and the aggregate production', *Review of Economics and Statistics*, vol. 39, pp. 312–20.

Stigler, G. (1961) 'The economics of information', *Journal of Political Economy*, vol. LXIX, no. 3, pp. 213–25.

Stopford, J., Strange, S. and Henley, J. (1991) *Rival states, rival firms: competition for world market shares*, Cambridge: Cambridge University Press.

Tirole, J. (1988) *The theory of industrial organisation*, Cambridge, Mass: MIT Press.

Wang, J. and Blonstrom, M. (1992) 'Foreign investment and technology transfer: a simple model', *European Economic Review*, vol. 36, pp. 137–55.

Wolf, M. (1998) 'Dangers of poor institutions, skill and moral hazard', *Financial Times*, 10 October, p. 12.

World Bank (1997) *World development report*, Oxford and New York: OUP.

# 19 The global brewers

**K. LAWLER and M. LING**

## 19.1 Introduction

The UK brewing industry has been attacked by many discount beers produced in the EU. The range spans premium beers from pretty Bohemian towns to lighter UK-brewed American beers. As the take-home beer market is expanding and foreign beers flood into the UK, market share expansion by UK brewers may be dramatically restricted. From a strategic perspective, UK brewers have to find ways to boost sales. Globalisation is likely to become an attractive option for aggressive or big brewers to develop their global shares. Basically, national brewers can afford a wide portfolio of globalisation programmes. However, different strategic views on global investment among the UK brewers has resulted in different levels of international reach. In global territory, methods and tactics of competition can be very different from what the UK brewers usually employ. Without doubt, as the international market environment evolves and globalisation with respect to brewing and distribution is intensified, brewers have to adapt to the new dynamics of competition.

## 19.2 The global strength of UK brewers

Within the European beer market, UK brewers have performed satisfactorily. Two UK brewers, Guinness and Bass, occupied the fifth and the seventh place respectively among the top seven European brewing groups in 1992 (Table 19.1).

In 1991, these two UK brewers were ranked the 17th and 18th largest brewing groups in the global ratings (Table 19.2). These comparisons and figures for the UK brewers do,

**Table 19.1 European sales of leading brewing groups (in million hectolitres).**

| Company | Country | 1992 | 1997 |
|---------|---------|------|------|
| Heineken | The Netherlands | 28.7 | 73.8 |
| Danone | France | 23.4 | 24.5 |
| Interbrew | Belgium | 15.4 | 34.7 |
| Carlsberg | Denmark | 15.2 | 35.3 |
| Guinness | Ireland | 13.9 | – |
| Foster's | Australia | 13.8 | 28.7 |
| Bass | UK | 13.6 | – |

*Source* adapted from Interbrew/Oram (1995a); BLRA Annual Report (1999)

**Table 19.2  Outputs of the world's leading brewers (in million hectolitres).**

| Brewer | Country of origin | 1991 output | 1997 output |
|---|---|---|---|
| Anheuser-Busch | US | 101.4 | 121.3 |
| Heineken | The Netherlands | 52.7 | 73.8 |
| Miller Brewing | US | 52 | 52.9 |
| South African Breweries | South Africa | 22.4 | 41.8 |
| Cervegaria Brahama | Brazil | 25.3 | 41.3 |
| Carlsberg | Denmark | 21.4 | 35.3 |
| Grupo Modelo | Mexico | 21.1 | 29.9 |
| Kirin | Japan | 34.0 | 29.2 |
| Foster's | Australia | 26.2 | 28.7 |
| Bavaria SA (Santo Domingo) | Columbia | – | 25.7 |
| Adolf Coors | US | 22.8 | 24.8 |
| BSN | France | 23.9 | – |
| Asahi | Japan | 16.4 | 23.5 |
| FEMSA Cerveza | Mexico | 20.0 | 21.8 |
| Antarctica Paulista | Brazil | 20.0 | 21.0 |
| Stroh | US | 18.5 | 18.6 |
| San Miguel | The Philippines | – | 14.2 |
| Cervejarias Kaiser | Brazil | – | 13.6 |
| Guinness | UK | 14.0 | – |
| Bass | UK | 13.6 | – |

*Source* adapted from BLRA Annual Reports (1995) and (1999)

however, not signify the extent of their globalisation strategies. However, these ratings indicate that UK brewers have potential in terms of production scale or financial power to establish global profiles. The volume of trade is a direct indicator of the overall involvement of a country in global markets. In Table 19.3, beer exports from the UK brewers to all countries showed a gradual increase. Between 1989 and 1994, the rate of increase was 106.23%. The increase is significantly affected by the big jump in exports to intra-EU members between 1993 and 1994; from 89.4 million litres to 166 million litres respectively. This reflects an 85.69% increase. However, between 1993 and 1994, exports to extra-EU countries experienced a decline from 128.3 million litres to 101.1 million litres. Research data in Table 19.3 indicates that, at the aggregate level, UK brewers have shown a balanced growth in beer exports to both intra-EU and extra-EU markets until 1993. Since 1993, with the elimination of economic barriers between EU member states, UK exporters took tax-free advantages and focused on exports to other EU markets which resulted in a near doubling in volumes of exports. Exports to extra-EU countries have fallen, however.

According to trade data in Table 19.4, more detailed dissection of the increase in intra-EU exports can be seen. Among all major export markets, the Irish Republic has a long record of significant volumes of UK beer absorption with about 28% of the total intra-EU exports. The increase in exports to the Irish Republic between 1993 and 1994 was 39.65%. Trade barrier elimination stimulated UK beer exports to France and Spain in 1994, which in total accounted for 29.71% of the export volume in 1994. Even the overall extra-EU exports from UK brewers showed a downward turn in 1994. However, UK brewers were still able to boost their sales in the USA and Canada. The export volumes to the USA were up by 1.52% from 68 million litres to 78.34 million litres (Table 19.5). The wider range of export markets, with increased volumes, is a clear sign showing that

**Table 19.3  A comparison of beer trade volumes: UK export to intra-EU and extra-EU countries (in litres).**

| Year | All countries | Intra-EC | Extra-EC |
|------|---------------|----------|----------|
| 1989 | 133,868,979<br>(61,230,000) | 63,923,123<br>(25,620,000) | 69,639,856<br>(35,610,000) |
| 1990 | 162,390,040<br>(80,854,000) | 81,031,207<br>(37,748,000) | 81,358,833<br>(43,106,000) |
| 1991 | 184,202,125<br>(95,640,000) | 92,359,762<br>(46,559,000) | 91,842,363<br>(49,081,000) |
| 1992 | 208,384,687<br>(116,046,000) | 109,067,948<br>(59,117,000) | 99,346,739<br>(56,929,000) |
| 1993 | 217,716,468<br>(127,557,000) | 89,400,123<br>(52,003,000) | 128,316,345<br>(75,555,000) |
| 1994 | 276,081,772<br>(175,449,000) | 166,006,566<br>(87,726,000) | 101,075,206<br>(87,723,000) |

*Source* adapted from Overseas trade statistics of the United Kingdom with the World 1993–1994, Business Monitor, HM Customs & Excise Tariff & Statistical Office.
( ) refer to the corresponding nominal valuation in £

**Table 19.4  Major intra-EU markets for UK beer exports (in litres).**

| Year | Irish Republic | Italy | Netherlands | France | Spain |
|------|----------------|-------|-------------|--------|-------|
| 1989 | 30,974,129<br>(12,366,000) | 6,648,896<br>(3,259,000) | ~ | ~ | ~ |
| 1990 | 38,346,012<br>(18,683,000) | ~ | ~ | ~ | ~ |
| 1991 | 48,380,675<br>(25,865,000) | ~ | 11,447,988<br>(5,655,000) | ~ | ~ |
| 1992 | 61,514,185<br>(36,055,000) | ~ | ~ | ~ | ~ |
| 1993 | 45,447,619<br>(28,223,000) | 14,143,656<br>(7,889,000) | ~ | ~ | ~ |
| 1994 | 63,467,890<br>(30,066,000) | 23,686,738<br>(11,080,000) | ~ | 32,173,834<br>(25,708,000) | 17,150,807<br>(7,434,000) |

*Source* adapted from Overseas trade statistics of the United Kingdom with the World 1993–1994, Business Monitor, HM Customs & Excise Tariff & Statistical Office.
( ) – refer to the corresponding nominal valuation in £
~ – official figures are not available because those transactions are below the minimum threshold size

UK brewers expanded their overseas markets. The UK is currently the second highest beer duty nation within the EU. Simon Ward, Whitbread's Strategic Affairs Director, referred to the high UK beer duty (almost 31p) as a self-imposed problem. Ian Prosser, Chairman of Bass, was disappointed by the Chancellor who took no action to pull down beer duty in the UK (Buxton, 1995).

**Table 19.5   Major extra-EU markets for UK beer exports (in litres).**

| Year | USA | Russia | Canada |
|------|-----|--------|--------|
| 1989 | 47,626,297 (23,933,000) | ~ | ~ |
| 1990 | 53,661,369 (27,684,000) | ~ | ~ |
| 1991 | 53,121,846 (29,407,000) | ~ | 10,646,713 (5,311,000) |
| 1992 | 59,290,458 (34,927,000) | ~ | ~ |
| 1993 | 67,996,757 (43,274,000) | 23,411,019 (7,653,000) | ~ |
| 1994 | 78,336,233 (50,923,000) | 22,353,912 (7,191,000) | 4,950,415 (3,525,000) |

*Source* adapted from Overseas trade statistics of the United Kingdom with the World 1993–1994, Business Monitor, HM Customs & Excise Tariff & Statistical Office.
( ) – refer to the corresponding nominal valuation in £
~ – official figures are not available because those transactions are below the minimum threshold size

## 19.3   Global entry in practice

Globalisation is attractive to brewers as it can generate benefits through economies of scale and economies of scope. Most brewers start their global ambitions by exporting beers to other countries. Export activity increases brewers' capacity utilisation and efficiency which eventually generates higher profits and allows larger scales of global marketing activity and advertising investment to be executed. Another popular way to globalise beer products is via licensed production. Often, once a brand has established its foundation and gained a level of popularity in a new market, licensed production can be used to further expand actual market shares. Licensed production in a new market is usually in the form of a joint venture. This allows new entrants in the market to gain more local management expertise from well-established local partners. Labatt's management skills in Canada's mature beer market was one of the crucial factors behind Interbrew's takeover of Labatt (Pilling, 1995). Finally, if sales volumes reach a threshold large enough to facilitate rearrangement of company capital structures, purchases of equity stakes in key markets is another practical route to enhance market power. These market penetration procedures were used by Heineken and Guinness. Most large brewers adopt similar strategies to achieve their global ambitions (Oram, 1995b). But sometimes the first step is the acquisition of an equity stake in a local outfit. Bass has purchased a 34% stake in Prague Breweries, which brews Staropramen. The beer is now selling in the UK, Sweden and Germany (Mingay, 1994). Interbrew, the Belgium brewer, purchased John Labatt in Canada to gain a key market position for Stella Artois in North America (Oram, Middlemann, and Simon, 1995). The deal turned Interbrew into the world's third biggest brewing group after Anheuser-Busch (US) and Heineken (Holland) (AFX, 1995).

Risk and uncertainty in new markets are key factors considered by global investors. No matter how strong a financial background a brewing group has, the associated risks of its investment profile must be monitored closely. For instance, Mr Michael Iuul, Head of Carlsberg International Operations, indicates that Carlsberg has been operating in the UK for a long time and is comfortable with the UK market. He also admits that Carlsberg likes to spread risks.[1] In general, there are risks when entering a new market. Ironically, however, globalisation is also a crucial factor for a brewing group to spread risks in the long run. To tackle the globalisation investment issue, it may be more appropriate for brewers to choose a 'step-wise' approach.[2] Otherwise, instead of spreading risks, global players may end up holding too many risky cards in a given international portfolio.

## 19.4    The global focus: the market for beer in China

China is a huge country which has an amazingly large population of 1.2 billion people. The Chinese market, currently served by 850 local Chinese brewers, has an extremely low per capita beer consumption, at approximately 15 litres a year. Per capita consumption is relatively low in China compared with the West European markets' average of 100 litres. Annual consumption is well below the international market average (Table 19.6).

However, the beer market in China is believed to be the world's fastest-growing market, which encourages global brewers to rush into the market with a hope of fulfilling their Asian dreams. Miller, part of Phillip Morris, has invested heavily in recent years in China (Oram, 1994). Bass has spent $40m on a joint venture with the Chinese-owned Ginsber Beer Group which brews Tennet's lager (Oram, 1995b). Foster's, an Australian brewer, sold Courage's breweries to Scottish & Newcastle for £425m to finance its strategic move into the Asian beer market, and has already created three Chinese joint ventures (Oram and Jacques, 1995).

**Table 19.6  International consumption comparisons.**

| Country | 1970 | 1980 | 1990 | 1994 | 1998 |
|---|---|---|---|---|---|
| Czech Republic | – | – | – | 161.1 | 162.9* |
| Germany | 141.1 | 145.9 | 142.8 | 139.5 | 127.4 |
| Ireland | 101.0 | 121.7 | 123.9 | 112.6 | 124.2 |
| Austria | 98.7 | 101.9 | 121.3 | 116.6 | 108.1 |
| Denmark | 108.5 | 130.7 | 127.2 | 126.7 | 107.7 |
| UK | 103 | 118.3 | 113.2 | 103.7 | 99.4 |
| Belgium and Luxembourg | 131.8 | 131.0 | 120.8 | 107.2 | 98.8 |
| Australia | 119.4 | 132.3 | 111.6 | 99.0 | 94.7* |
| US | 70.4 | 91.1 | 91.2 | 85.2 | 83.2 |
| Venezuela | 49.5 | 74.0 | 66.2 | 71.0 | 72.1* |
| Canada | 74.0 | 86.1 | 78.2 | 68.2 | 64.8* |
| Brazil | 10.6 | 18.9 | 46.2 | 38.8 | 54.2* |
| Japan | 28.7 | 39.0 | 53.7 | 59.9 | 53.9* |
| China | – | – | 6.7 | 11.5 | 15.0* |

*Source* adapted from BLRA (1999)
* refers to 1997 figures

The people of mainland China have their own distinctive culture which is, from the point of view of Westerners, still not easy to understand. To work out an effective marketing strategy, the culture of Chinese consumers constitutes the prime consideration and risk.

Hong Kong and China have inseparable links because of both the political factors and geographical reasons. Being on the doorstep of China, Hong Kong has significantly influenced various consumption trends in many consumer good industries. Frequent contact between Hong Kong and China due to ever-increasing business commuters and family ties concludes the inseparable cultural influence. As a colonial city under the British Government, Hong Kong has already evolved as a modernised international financial centre, with a good blend of Westernised and traditional Chinese lifestyles. By contrast, mainland China is still under communist rule even though concepts of democracy and capitalism are gradually emerging in China. With economic booms catalysed by various large-scale joint ventures with foreign partners, Western aspirations and values have been injected and mixed into daily lives. The best and most direct way to satisfy their materialistic needs is to 'smuggle' goods from Hong Kong. More specifically, they usually encourage relatives and friends in Hong Kong to bring in their long-awaited foreign consumer items.

Purchasing power parity does not exist in practical terms in China. Very often, huge and excessive tax rates are imposed on all imported items, which make foreign products too expensive to be consumed by the mainland Chinese. Eventually, because of import restrictions and the long-suppressed living standards in mainland China, Hong Kong naturally becomes the local paradise for a better quality of life. This creates a stereotyped influx of foreign consumer goods from Hong Kong to mainland China. Hence, it is an habitual characteristic for mainland Chinese to imitate Hong Kong fashion trends and follow hot topics in leisure.

The same principles apply to the cultural influence in markets for beer in China. Drinkers in China are affected by beer consumption in Hong Kong. Back in the 1970s, the Hong Kong beer market was dominated by Chingto Beer, a well-established brand supplied from China, and San Miguel, a foreign brand from the Philippines but brewed in Hong Kong. As living standards before the early 1970s were relatively low in Hong Kong, foreign beers were treated as luxury consumer items. Since the major economic upswing that started in the mid-1970s in Hong Kong, this 'Eastern Pearl' has experienced non-stop growth both in light manufacturing and in tertiary industry. More and more foreign brands can be found in Hong Kong to suit the rise in living standards. However, the domestic-brewed San Miguel, being welcomed by the lower working class, which accounted for the majority of the population before the 1980s, has been a constant companion of Hong Kong drinkers. Moreover, with the heavy use of well-designed theme slogans shown on main media advertising, the image of San Miguel has been well placed in Hong Kong people's minds.

Image and the translated Chinese name of San Miguel also favoured sales. San Miguel has sponsored major sporting functions in Hong Kong and even in mainland China. The brand is portrayed as the backbone of sports sponsorship in Hong Kong and China. Financial support and provocative advertising messages have become a part of community involvement. The wider the involvement in the local community, the better is the resulting brand image. Most importantly, consumer ignorance is largely eliminated and a special relationship has been successfully built between the brand and the consumers. Undoubtedly, San Miguel, like a baby, grew up with the community in Hong Kong. Based on the distinctive link in consumption preferences between Hong Kong and China, San Miguel is a natural-born winner among foreign brands in mainland China.

The people in mainland China love the translated Chinese name of San Miguel, which stands for energy and instinct, bringing forward new and prosperous lives. Generally, the Chinese care much more about immaterial aspects of future fortunes than people in the West. A good Chinese brand name, to an extent, favours product promotion, say at wedding banquets and other celebratory occasions, where beer consumption can be massive. The Chinese are more apt to choose a drink with easily imagined meanings. Because San Miguel has a very simple but fortune-oriented Chinese brand name, most consumers in Hong Kong and China, especially business people, are more likely to drink a beer with special connections to fortune.

Globalisation in Asian countries is not easy and straightforward. Foreign beer brands which are used to promote Western cultures with humour or cheeky characters may be offensive to the Chinese and may create negative impacts. Global players, therefore, have to understand target consumers and adjust entry strategies tactically to match variations in local market environments and cultural backgrounds. Quite simply, a Chinese marketing and business approach has to be identified first.

Since 1998, Carlsberg, the Danish giant, has been trying hard to promote beer brands in mainland China. Carlsberg has already obtained control of a springboard, the Hong Kong beer market, into the Chinese beer market. Its subsidiary Danbrew has built ten breweries within mainland China (Jackson, 1994). However, it lacks a long history of community involvement and an impressive Chinese name for its brand. Technically, global players such as Foster's and Bass have found proper business methods to enter the Chinese market by entering into joint ventures with local establishments, which provide valuable insights for the required development in a Chinese society. In the end, consumer goods need to flourish and must be accepted by local consumers. Hence, Chinese culture and beliefs form a crucial factor in gaining success. For instance, Guinness has been pouring millions into advertising stouts. Advertised messages always focus on an image of Guinness as a drink for macho types. Since dark drinks are very easy for Chinese people to relate to their dark herbal medicine soups, the related uncomfortable feelings discourage many consumers. This can be classified as a cultural mismatch which directly hinders Guinness's market potential in China.

## 19.5    Non-price determinants for global market entry

Globalisation can occur almost everywhere in the world. An increase in globalisation implies an extension of vigorous competition in markets between local and foreign players. Generally speaking, competition displays two major formats: price and non-price competition. When a local market is invaded by a foreign brand, existing brands react accordingly. Faced with international brands which can afford extensive marketing activities and advertising investment, dominant local brands can choose to counter-attack or simply accommodate them. For financially weaker local brands, survival depends very much on competitive pricing.

One big management challenge for ambitious global brewers is brand building. For international dominant brewers, brand building may be an easier task. Global brewers such as Heineken, Guinness and Carlsberg have already gained significant consumer confidence and produced worldwide prestige images. Image and brand names have complementary influences on each other. In the early stages of a product's life, a well-designed image helps a brand to build up some intangible features to assist promotion and increase its explicit market power. When a product reaches maturity, the brand carries an in-built image which helps to relate consumer desires with the brand. In global markets, a well-known beer brand may give a specific distinctive reputation. But a reputable brand does not necessarily mean that successful entry follows.[3] Again, culture differences and local market environments can determine the survival of a brand. Obviously, an international brand of beer possesses a principal corporate image. Sometimes, this image is related to the origin of the beer brand, which is the so-called national identity.[4] To work out an effective market entry, a global beer brand wearing a national image has to tactically adjust its image in a local market to cater for local tastes. It is believed that the more national taste differences across global markets, the harder will be the globalisation for a brand. Giant international food labels like McDonald's, Pizza Hut and KFC have also to provide tailor-made menus to appeal in different overseas markets with respect to national taste differences. Similarly, global brewers may select different brands with suitable flavours to suit local consumers. When flavour and alcoholic content come close between rivals, excluding the price effect at this stage, images for a brand have much to do to stand out from close competitors.

Image has an intricate quality. Image may refer to a wide spectrum of elements. These include the overall appearance in different advertising and marketing media, the actual display and impression on consumption at retail levels, the perceived character of the brand and the interpreted values in lifestyle. All these eventually create a 'chemical reaction' in a market, particularly in fashions. To successfully enter a market, the image of a beer brand should be fascinating, which has a potential to associate leisure with a new value or some amusing ideas.[5]

When a local market is challenged by foreign global brands, the structure of the local beer market is altered. Referring to demand and supply analysis, as total market supply increases, assuming that market demand remains the same, market equilibrium will occur at a lower section of the demand curve. This means that demand for beer becomes more elastic with respect to price. When the process of globalisation is intensified as time goes by, momentums of price competition may become more dominant. The market response to the invasion of global players is consistent with general demand theory. In fact, the second law of demand indicates that as time horizon increases, more substitute products can be available for consumption which results in a more intense competition and more elastic demand response.

When brewers, both local and foreign, gather in a beer market, they always conduct a considerable amount of advertising to fight for better market shares. The initial market equilibrium is therefore not only upset by a quantity-induced phenomenon but also non-price influences, mainly coming from advertising investments. Quality characteristics, including flavour, clearness and amount of gaseous bubbles, are obviously another important non-price determinant. To a large extent, when a foreign beer brand penetrates a new market, consumers will be first influenced by advertising. Qualitative aspects of a beer may become a secondary influence. For non-specialist drinkers, quality differences across brands may not be easily identified. It may, therefore, be logical to reach a conclusion that beers are basically perceived as homogeneous products but beer brands are significantly differentiated by advertising messages.

## 19.6    The product range and competition

Product range development is significant to feed changes in market tastes and stimulate consumer interest. Technical advances in brewing can upgrade brewing strength and allow brewers to adjust the flavour and quality of beers. Continuous research on technical aspects is crucial for global brewers to widen their future manufacturing prospects, especially brand portfolio development and brewing efficiency. Modern technology, therefore, constitutes a crucial factor affecting the potential and the long-term market power of global brewers. Modern brewing technology determines productivity differences between brewers. The resulting operational efficiency can affect the fate of a brewer in terms of its ability to stand fierce competition. Modern technology enables America to be more efficient than Germany and Japan in brewing (The Economist, 1993). In comparing unit labour productivity, Japanese workers produce 31% less than the USA. Japanese brewers basically may enjoy higher productivity and economies of scale, but their government protects smaller breweries from competition (Jackson, 1993). When divergences in productivity between brewers exist, such as between Japanese and US brewers, efficient American brewers can adjust and afford a stronger selling force. More resources can be bought to develop beers which directly improves their competitiveness in international markets. The productivity differences partly explains why Budweiser, the leading world brand from the USA, is more popular than the Japanese brand, Kirin, in international beer markets. However, socio-economic factors such as government intervention and associated competition policies, such as the competition laws exerted on the EU, may affect industry concentration and the resulting productivity variations.

When global brewers enter a new market, they are always confronted by some other problematic issues. Smaller local brewers, being less able to afford expensive advertising, tend to undercut dominant brands on price. Fierce price competition within the cheap beer subsector implies that the overall market share distribution in the subsector will be decided by cost-effective operations.[6] The introduction of foreign brands in new markets will certainly widen product ranges. In order to maintain a coherent global strategy, some dominant global brewers like Heineken and Guinness concentrate their resources to market a few big volume brands. Most probably, global brewers try to introduce their most reputable brands first when they enter a new market.[7] This produces two predictable outcomes. The first is that the premium quality beer ranges in the market face more intense competition. More advertising campaigns can be predicted. Existing middle range brewers, which are afraid of losing their potential top-end market share, may also enter the quality challenge and enlarge their brand portfolios. Increased advertising campaigns may push up beer prices charged by local brewers. Under this circumstance, price competition among top brands may become less extreme. Contenders are likely to adjust their retail prices within a narrower limit. Having said that, it does not imply that price competition is not vigorous at all. A small reduction in price is still possible to induce consumers to buy more. This depends on the degree of consumer responsiveness to a change in relative prices across associated brands. As demonstrated by Ling *et al.* (1997), it is important to stress the relative strength of price and advertising elasticities in analysing demand conditions in premium beer markets.[8]

While lower quality beers or smaller budget brewers may stress 'cheapie' images and extend their budget beer ranges to draw consumer attention and hopefully stabilise their lower-end market shares, in a mature market, it is easy to foresee that more and more lower price brands will enter the market. For instance, the UK market has been stagnant since the 1990s, as more sales have gone through off-licences and there is a sign that more consumers are satisfied with bulk-purchase low-price brands supported by bootlegged transactions and imports from European countries. This generated a vicious circle so that UK brewers, who face high beer duties, have to pull down average beer prices in order to attract sales.[9] The overall picture in the global beer market is characterised by finer distinctive market segmentations. As a result, increased globalisation may broaden the scope for product differentiation in beer markets.

## 19.7 Conclusions

Competition in beer markets is intensified by product range developments and fierce price competition, after global brands are introduced. As a market becomes more competitive, profit margins are greatly reduced. Global brewers may have to invest a lot but they eventually earn profits. It prompts the question as to why global brewers are still very eager to commit global strategies. One rational economic reason is that global brewers are interested in making profits and diversifying their assets' strengths. However, it is important to understand that global brewers do not enter every beer market in the world. They tend to select certain target markets. One thing in common is that global brewers like to invest in growing rather than mature markets. As mentioned by Mr Iuul, 'in growing markets, you have a lot of people with social aspirations. And when it comes to beer, most (international) brands reflect higher quality as well.'[10] In mature beer markets, price stimulation is more crucial. Lower profit margins make global brands financially unfeasible when executing big-budget advertising strategies. This explains why many global brewers have been keeping their eyes on, or have even entered, the Chinese as well as the Brazilian market.[11]

From the UK export data, UK brewers have already enlarged their profiles to increase their overall long-run export volumes. A culturally rich national character may help to create an initial focal point for UK beer products. But whether they can flourish in a foreign market depends on image building and commercial profiles in managing target markets, which are full of cultural variations.

## Summary

- Product differentiation and advertising are key features in global brewing.
- Oligopolisitc competition is largely focused on global brands.
- Cross-cultural issues and language difficulties, religions and tastes affect the world demand for beers.
- UK and continental brewers now operate with very large export volumes for top brands.
- Absolute and relative concentration ratios for brewing are on the increase in the UK and the EU generally. This tendency is likely to continue on a Pan-European basis as mergers, takeovers, joint ventures and strategic alliances develop.
- Economies of scale are critical determinants of market power in brewing. Export volumes are linked to economies of scale and market shares in national markets.

### Questions

1. Why is product differentiation a barrier to entry in brewing?
2. What determines the market power of global brewers?
3. Why is advertising activity a crucial determinant of success in 'global markets for beers'?

4. What are the main strategies employed by global brewers to gain enhanced market shares?

## Key concepts

oligopoly

global brewers

advertising

target markets

oligopolistic competition

concentration levels

brand naming strategy

brand growth

## Notes

1. Although its UK market contributes an estimated 50% of the group's worldwide profit, Carlsberg also has brewing business in China, Vietnam, Thailand and Russia. When Carlsberg enters a country like Vietnam, its knowledge of local conditions is bound to be more superficial (Jackson, 1994).
2. Mr John Purnell, Chief Executive of Anheuser-Busch's international subsidiary, believes in a step-by-step approach, used by global brewers such as Heineken and Guinness, and dislikes the idea of attacking the world at once (Oram, 1995b).
3. According to John Murphy, Head of Interbrand, the branding consultancy, brands are not a licence to print money (Lorenz and Alexander, 1994).
4. Mac Cato, Chairman of the Cato strategic image consultancy, which has worked with drink brands 7-up and Heineken, emphasises that the value of the national badge is very important for those attempting to build global brands (Summers, 1995).
5. Image consultant Stephen Bayley indicates that there is an increasing global phenomenon in business and industry of people falling back on ideas (Richards, 1994).
6. Mr Iuul believes cheap beer brands will undercut dominant brewers on price and never go away once they gain some volume. This will lead to a shake-out in production cost (Jackson, 1994). Fitzgerald points out that if a business is not cost-effective, it will not generate the resource to invest in marketing, innovation and so on (Lorenz and Alexander, ibid.).
7. Interbrew tries to tempt the world with its premium lager, Stella Artois, and at the same time market some 20 other distinctive beers (Oram, 1995a).
8. Mr Hans Meerlos, Interbrew's Chief Executive, said that the days of going for volume were over (Oram, 1995a). People are not spending more on each drink. This encourages brewers to invest more on advertising to build up attractive images for their premium beers.
9. Mr Roy Burry, beverage and tobacco analyst at Kidder Peabody in New York, says that the discounters have forced the brands to cut prices (Lorenz and Alexander, ibid.)
10. On the contrary, Mr Iuul indicates that cheap own-label products are more likely to move in some mature markets (Jackson, 1994).
11. The Brazilian beer market is the world's fastest-growing beer market after the Chinese one. Anheuser-Busch, the leading brewing group in the world, has shown great interest in the Brazilian market and has set up a joint venture to produce and distribute Budweiser in Brazil (Foster, 1995).

## Bibliography

AFX (1995) 'International Company News: Interbrew woos potential investors for fresh funds (496)', *Financial Times*, 19 September.

Boland, V. (1995) 'Survey of Czech Finance, Industry and Investment (15): Global profile eludes the brewers – The beer industry has yet to realise its potential', *Financial Times*, 2 June.

Brewers and Licenced Retailers Association Annual Reports (1995) and (1999), London.

Buxton, A. (1995) 'And other ways to peel the onion/Three ways to go global', *The Economist*, vol. 334, 7 January.

*Financial Times* (1994) 'Budget 94 (Tax): Big business gives its verdict', 30 November, p. 22.

Foster, A. (1995) 'International Company News: Brazil's potential draws Anheuser – Several global brewers are eyeing the market', *Financial Times*, 28 February.

Jackson, T. (1993) 'Report dents Japan's image as highly efficient manufacturer', *Financial Times*, 22 October, p. 2.

Jackson, T. (1994) 'Survey of Danish Food Industry 3: Carlsberg sees China as top market – The global reach of a brewer that (probably) exports more than 80% of its output', *Financial Times*, 7 June.

Ling M., Lawler, K. and Abbott, A. (1997) 'Advertising investment in the UK brewing industry: an empirical analysis', *Economic Issues*, vol. 2. Part I, pp. 55–66.

Lorenz, A. and Alexander, G. (1994) 'Brands fight back; Business Focus', *The Sunday Times*, 3 April.

Mingay, H. (1994) 'FT exporter (4): Attempting to take on the west – Helen Mingay examines the way the emphasis on pre-war excellence is having marked success in attracting international business/Czech manufacturers/Strategy, industrial reform, global sourcing of car components and technology transfer arrangement demand a variety of approaches to exporting', *Financial Times*, 7 July.

Oram, R. (1994) 'A consuming interest in China: Big manufacturers of branded goods are fighting over a potential market of 1.2 billion people', *Financial Times*, 28 September.

Oram, R. (1995a) 'Reassuringly expansive – the Stella strategy: Roderick Oram explains why Belgium's Interbrew is counting on premium lagers and Cherry beers', *Financial Times*, 20 January.

Oram, R. and Jacques, B. (1995), 'Foster's Asian dreams', *Financial Times*, 19 May.

Oram, R. (1995b) 'A few more for the road abroad: A look at the increasingly international nature of the beer trade as premium brands make inroads (1407)', *Financial Times*, 6 July.

Oram, R., Middlemann, C. and Simon, B. (1995) 'Interbrew takes time to improve Labatt flavour: A new collaborative management structure struggles to prove its competitors wrong (1085)', *Financial Times*, 16 October.

Pilling, D. (1995) 'International Company News: Argentine brewer aims to tap Latin American neighbours – Despite losing Canada's John Labatt to rival bidder Interbrew, Quilmes is still seeking to expand/Latin American brewing (1077)', *Financial Times*, 24 November.

Richards, S. (1994) 'UK plc.: trapped in a time warp?', Cover story, *The Sunday Times*, 30 October.

Summers, D. (1995) 'When it's all in the label – Diane Summers examines the value of national badges and their importance to building global brands', *Financial Times*, 3 August.

*The Economist* (1993) 'Economics focus: workers of the world unite – is greater global competition the best way to erode differences in labour productivity between countries?', vol. 329, 23 October.

# 20 Emerging markets and convergence

**K. LAWLER and M. LING**

## 20.1 Introduction

Traditional studies of economic convergence have usually been based on investigations of comparative national income trends and manufacturing outputs. Recent studies, however, by Sala-i-Martin (1996), Durlauf (1996) and Romer (1994) have revisited key controversial issues regarding economic growth. Indeed, a plethora of arguments focused on endogenous and exogenous growth models are available. According to Romer (1986), the implications of convergence models depend very much on the assumption of externalities and increasing returns to scale. Lucas (1988) also introduced further theoretical developments into endogenous growth mechanisms. By contrast, new growth models exclude the concept of diminishing returns. Hence, in the mid-1980s, new growth models' forecasts could track lack of convergence more efficiently than the neo-classical models (Sala-i-Martin, 1996). Romer (1994) provides a comprehensive discussion regarding fundamental belief in endogenous growth models and discusses criticisms of these. Moreover, models investigating divergence across countries with different initial situations and controlling variables, including saving rates and population growth rates, were examined by Barro (1991) and Mankiw *et al.* (1992). However, others such as Barro (1991), Quah (1996a, b) and Durlauf and Johnson (1995) use various econometric modelling methods to show different convergence mechanisms in their empirical studies. To some extent, to move the debate regarding comparative growth issues forward, a new approach is required. Therefore, this chapter employs data from the brewing industries in the EU and East Asia to assess relative market conditions and estimate the degree of relative convergence based on statistical analysis of comparative industrial performance in the EU and East Asia. Beer is a traditional and standard alcoholic beverage across European countries. Owing to cultural affinities, beer consumption and production should, to some extent, reflect a European nation's economic momentum; whereas in Asian markets, beer has not yet developed a strong cultural 'socialising' influence in public perception. Nonetheless, beer production and consumption have increased significantly in recent years. This produces interesting issues with respect to EU and Asian beer markets, worthy of examination.

Since the 1970s, beer consumption and production patterns in the EU and Asia have experienced varying levels of change and development. Hence Table 20.1, shows that production in the EU achieved positive growth until 1990. The strongest growth rates were recorded in the early 1970s. By contrast, in Asian markets, strongest growth trends are to be found between 1985 and 1990. This is also matched by the peak growth rates (107.52%) in consumption during the same period. As with production, the largest rise in consumption in the EU was achieved in the period 1970–75. Since then, growth rates have deteriorated and suffered negative changes throughout the 1980s.

**Table 20.1  Growth rates for beer consumption and production in EU and Asia (%).**

|  | 70–75 | 75–80 | 80–85 | 85–90 | 90–91 | 91–92 | 92–93 |
|---|---|---|---|---|---|---|---|
| **Production** | | | | | | | |
| EU | 15.51 | 4.41 | 0.67 | 6.67 | −2.28 | 0 | −1.59 |
| Asia◊ | 36.10 | 35.37 | 47.74 | 72.21 | 12.22 | 9.20 | 8.73 |
| **Consumption** | | | | | | | |
| EU | 18.20 | 4.40 | −1.69 | −7.11 | −2.02 | 0.96 | −3.35 |
| Asia◊ | 25.62 | 23.46 | 4.09 | 107.52 | −3.54 | 4.09 | 2.95 |

*Source* adapted from *Statistical Handbook*, Brewers and Licensed Retailers Association (1995)
◊ – The Asian grouping includes Japan, China, Korea and the Philippines

**Table 20.2  The average production of global brewers (million hectolitres).**

|  | 1991 | 1993 |
|---|---|---|
| Top 10 world brewers | 38.21 | 40.96 |
| Top 20 world brewers | 27.26 | 27.90 |
| Top eight international brewers in the EU | 17.84 | 19.28 |
| Top three international brewers in Asia | 20.93 | 22.00 |
| Top 20 brewers in Asia | / | 6.15 |

*Source* adapted from Brewers and Licensed Retailers Association (1995) and Key Note Report (1994)

When the worldwide recession set in during the early 1990s, beer production and consumption in Asian markets was buoyant compared with the growth rates experienced within the EU. That East Asia is an impressive market environment for beer is illustrated by the comparative production figures depicted in Table 20.2. The average production for the top three brewers in Asia in 1991 and 1993 exceeds the corresponding data for the top eight international brewers in the EU. This result rests largely on the muscular performance of Japanese brewers who still dominate markets throughout Asia.

The relative strength of the Japanese beer market is also reflected in its dominant position as the leading importer as a percentage of total consumption (Table 20.3). The Japanese import statistics exceed the corresponding average percentage levels of all other Asian countries. Apart from the leading Asian beer markets, the data for other Asian countries indicate that these countries too experienced rising production, which contrasts sharply with the shrinking average production levels in the EU. Ironically, the increase in imported volumes, together with the slow or negative aggregate growth in the EU, implies that the EU is nearing saturation levels. Major international brewers in the EU, seeking expansion and healthy growth, should therefore target the consumers with rising beer consumption patterns found in Asia. The rising average consumption and production levels in Asia and the corresponding trends in the EU are revealed in Table 20.3.

## 20.2  Growth

Growth is a phenomenon of particular importance for governments and entrepreneurs. For economists, theoretical models emphasise growth processes and linkages to the factors

**Table 20.3  Some comparative statistics between the EU and Asia.**

|  | 1991 | 1993 |
|---|---|---|
| Average alcoholic consumption (litres/head of 100% alcohol) | EU: 9.59<br>Asia[φ]: 3.66 | EU: 9.27<br>Asia[φ]: 3.8 |
| Average beer consumption (litres/head) | EU: 85.55<br>Asia[φ]: 31.15 | EU: 83.45<br>Asia[φ]: 31.43 |
| Average beer production (m hectolitres) | EU: 26.92<br>Asia[φ]: 45.9<br>Asia*: 14.21 | EU: 26.49<br>Asia[φ]: 54.5<br>Asia*: 17.09 |
| Import as a % of total consumption | EU: 7.20<br>Japan: 1.66 | EU: 7.36<br>Japan: 1.66 |

*Source* adapted from Brewers and Licensed Retailers Association (1995) and Key Note Report (1994)
* – includes the following Asian nations: Japan, China, Korea, the Philippines, Cambodia, Hong Kong, India, Indonesia, South Korea, Malaysia, Singapore, Taiwan, Thailand and Vietnam.
φ – denotes the four major Asian producer and consumption countries under study: Japan, China, Korea and the Philippines.

creating economic development. International trade and globalised activities are encouraged by the establishment of trading organisations such as NAFTA (1994), the Single Market of the EU (1993), and perhaps even the formation of ASEAN in 1967. These associations aim to increase the number of favourable environments for trade and to facilitate exchange of technological advances and vital commercial information. The influence of technology transfer for economic convergence is emphasised by Romer (1993). However, based on neo-classical models, technology is treated as an exogenous variable in a Cobb-Douglas production function. The derived benefits of the 'diffusion' and international 'transfer' processes can accelerate the stimulus of endogenous economic variables and introduce more exogenous elements into the growth process. Depending on rates of transformation and current asset stocks, different economies in a region may experience increases or decreases in convergent tendencies. This study employs a different view of industrial entrepreneurship and performance to investigate trends in convergence and emerging market forces. This deviates, however, from mainstream growth theory which relies on analysis using macroeconomic indicators such as income and gross national production attainments.

Following the tenets of classical growth theory methodologies, this analysis is based on δ-convergence. The criteria for δ-convergence is shown by the following representation.

$$\delta_{t+1} < \delta_t$$

where $\delta_t$ – standard deviation ($\sigma$) for a growth indicator at time t
$\delta_{t+1}$ – standard deviation for a growth indicator at time t−1

In this data set, if beer consumption or production experienced a continuous decrease in standard deviation through time for the sample period, convergence is said to have occurred within a beer market grouping. Figure 20.1 indicates per capita consumption data in the EU. Between 1970 and 1980, the standard deviations of beer consumption within the EU increased, whereas in 1980, convergence in beer consumption is clearly shown by the declining trend in the standard deviations.

By contrast, Figure 20.2 shows the trend of major beer consumption among major Asian nations. Here δs have increased since 1975 with exceptions in 1989, 1991 and

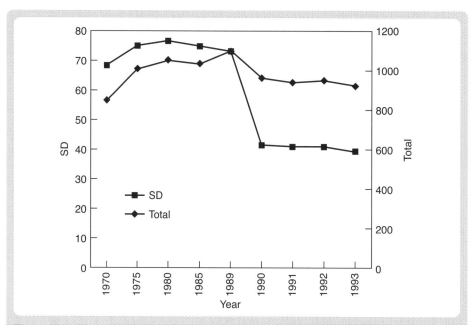

**Figure 20.1  The total consumption and standard deviations in consumption within the EU**

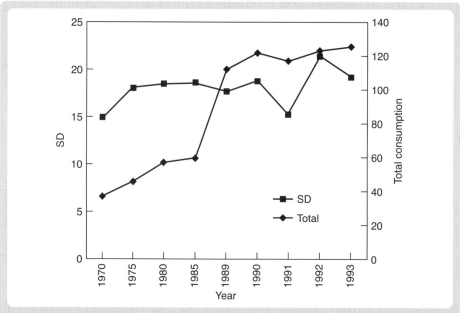

**Figure 20.2  The total consumption and standard deviations in consumption within the Asian Countries Group**

1993, although this trend is not continuous and consistent throughout the time period. However, inspection of statistical trends shows a diverging consumption pattern among Asian nations. This is clearly seen by merely comparing beer consumption since 1990 with that before. Since the 1978 Open Door Policy implemented in mainland China, economic growth there has been rocketing. This phenomenon introduced an extraordinary acceleration process building consumer purchasing power. This factor may significantly affect the magnitude of the divergent trends. However, if the data for China is excluded from the standard deviation calculation, the divergence still exists. This means that Chinese economic development is a key factor in the resulting divergence pattern, but not the only crucial force at work.

The standard deviations for beer production in the EU fluctuated greatly between 1970 and 1990. The lack of consistent movements for beer production implies that convergence in EU brewing is not likely. Some European brewers and international market leaders such as Heineken (The Netherlands), Brau and Brunnen (Germany), Guinness (the UK), Interbrew (Belgium) and Cruz del Camp (Spain) are national brewers which claim significant global market shares. Changes in world market conditions and relative competitiveness can introduce large variations in production patterns. Export activities are a dominant strategic feature for the key European players. When domestic or EU consumption becomes stagnant, as is demonstrated by the decreases in the corresponding δ in Figure 20.1, more production effort will target potentially unexploited markets. EU brewers have experienced substantial variations in beer production year by year. Increases in beer exports from the EU mean that production variations are no longer subject to domestic competition but depend greatly on the success attained in penetrating new markets. Consequently, different levels and rates of change in international trade results in the random and inconsistent trends in standard deviations in EU beer production (Figure 20.3).

Moreover, the distribution of standard deviations shown in Figure 20.3 is rather trend-free but remains at a particularly high level (30m hl). However, the spread of standard deviations between 1970 and 1993 is rather small (1.12), but the corresponding data for the period 1989–1993 is even smaller (0.70). If exports to foreign markets become ever more prominent, the production variations should be ever higher. This is understandable since beer production is inherently bulky and heavy. Shipping a container load of beer

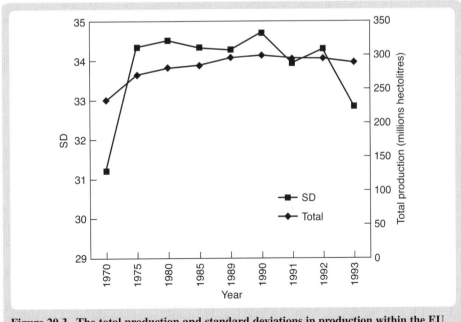

**Figure 20.3 The total production and standard deviations in production within the EU**

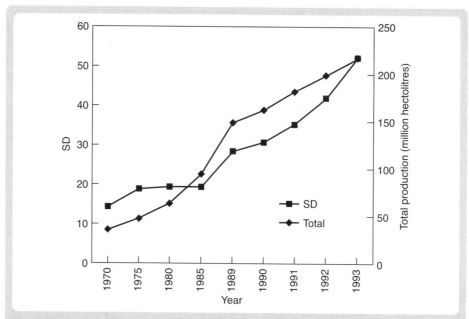

**Figure 20.4  The total production and standard deviations in production within the Asian Countries Group**

is equivalent to the transportation of water. When overseas demand is relatively limited, shipments of beer are relatively uneconomical. However, when overseas demand increases to sufficiently high levels, domestic production in overseas markets is an attractive alternative. This in turn sets limits for fluctuations in production in the EU as foreign investments such as strategic alliances and foreign production facilities can replace traditional exporting when these operations become economically viable. According to the trends shown in Figure 20.4, it is very clear that there was no convergence in beer production within Asian countries. An upward $\delta$ trend indicates divergence occurring among Asian brewers. The range of $\delta_s$ for beer production between 1970 and 1993 is (12.67), whereas, for the period 1989 to 1993, the spread remains high, but at a lower level of (9.61). Comparing the spread of $\delta_s$ in the EU and in Asia, rather explosive growth rates in production were recorded in Asia. However, inconsistent but stable production conditions with small fluctuations are seen in the mature EU markets.

## 20.3    Empirical findings and estimations

To assess the structural impact of income on the demand for beer in the EU and Asia, two representative nations were selected for comparison. Based on the study carried out by Lawler *et al.* (1997), empirical findings on the UK beer market indicate that income is a dominant factor influencing changes in aggregate beer consumption in the long run. The long-run consumption changes in Japan were estimated using the normalised long-run coefficient of (1.57) obtained from the above study. The data in the Table 20.4 shows the estimation based on three different income indicators for Japan.

Clearly, no country in the world behaves exactly the same as any other; however, the Japanese beer consumption trends projected from the long-run income elasticity deviates from actual figures, especially for the period between 1989 and 1991. However, induced

**Table 20.4  Estimation of changes in beer consumption in Japan.**

| Year | Actual change in consumption | | Estimation | |
|------|------|------|------|------|
| | (%) | (Based on per capita income) | (Based on real GDP) | (Based on real GNP) |
| 1989 | 5.18 | 9.12 | 7.39 | 7.55 |
| 1990 | 8.05 | 10.53 | 7.55 | 7.55 |
| 1991 | 3.54 | 8.49 | 6.76 | 6.76 |
| 1992 | 3.06 | 1.10 | 1.73 | 2.04 |
| 1993 | −1.92 | 0.16 | −0.31 | −0.31 |

income responses roughly indicate that the rate of change in consumption, especially the estimated negative growth rates recorded in 1993, matched actual consumption trends (Figure 20.5). Moreover, the comparatively larger growth rates experienced between 1989 and 1991 show that income indicators can assist consumption predictions, but do not explain all the fluctuations in the Japanese beer market. Inspection of Table 20.4 shows that beer consumption trends in Japan are better tracked by real GNP and real GDP figures. Based on this result, consumption trends for the other three Asian countries were estimated by use of corresponding real GNP data. Comparative resulting estimations are shown in Table 20.5. However, estimated trends are very different from the actual consumption changes. This implies that relying simply on the income elasticity variable in estimating consumption fails to capture the true fluctuations. According to industry analysts, beer consumption in the Philippines is shown to link closely with the changes in disposable income. The failure to track the fluctuation here does not directly deny the sensitive response of beer consumption to income changes. In China, the estimated changes are all well below the actual figures. This, to certain extent, captures the nature of the fast growth of economic activity seen in China in recent years. However, consumption in China is not only internally driven by increases in domestic income levels, but is also affected by the explosive growth in foreign investment. Secondly, as

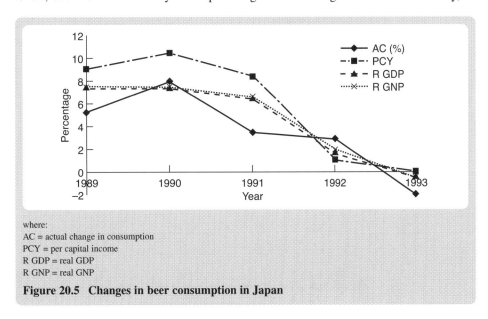

where:
AC = actual change in consumption
PCY = per capital income
R GDP = real GDP
R GNP = real GNP

**Figure 20.5  Changes in beer consumption in Japan**

**Table 20.5  Estimation of changes in beer consumption in China, Korea and the Philippines (%).**

|  | China | | Korea | | Philippines | |
|---|---|---|---|---|---|---|
| 1989 | 17.9 | (6.76) | – | – | | |
| 1990 | 24.7 | (7.07) | 7.47 | (12.89) | 9.96 | (6.13) |
| 1991 | 28.4 | (15.25) | 20.20 | (14.15) | −14.77 | (0.786) |
| 1992 | 27.9 | (22.32) | −1.10 | (7.86) | −12.60 | (2.52) |
| 1993 | 31.7 | (20.91) | −4.74 | (8.96) | 12.61 | (3.30) |

Figures in parentheses are estimated values based on the normalised income elasticities in the UK.

cumulative growth in wealth increases dramatically, the impact of changes in current income may soon reach a level that produces reduced induced effects on beer consumption. This is equivalent to a shift in living standards (the change in autonomous consumption bundles) and adjustments in marginal propensity to consume. These two combined effects make predictions difficult in the emerging markets.

In Figure 20.6, a higher income elasticity of consumption is represented by the steeper line AB. Consumers accumulate wealth (savings) up to a specific level and then consumption may follow a new income–consumption pattern, represented by a more gently sloping line (CD). The growth of consumption levels with respect to income change (E) is F. At G, the growth rates of consumption predicted by two consumption models are the same. However, autonomous fixed consumption (e.g. consumer inertia or habitual consumption patterns) is different. The difference between the two intercept values can be regarded as the changes in basic level of maintenance expected by individuals. As consumers accumulate wealth (implicitly assuming people save a proportion of what they could earn), they adjust their basic autonomous standard of living (which is indicated by

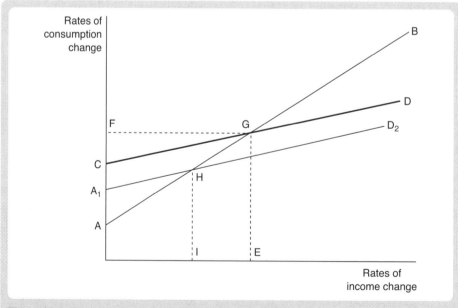

**Figure 20.6  Rates of consumption and rates of income change**

a Y-intercept value). When an economy starts achieving sustained strong growth, agents may revise their views on expected minimum living standards. This issue is consistent with permanent income hypothesis. As people revise their belief, they alter their expectations on marginal propensity to consume or even the autonomous consumption to match their new expectation on living standard. The pioneering work on this field was done by Milton Friedman (1957). The change in consumption forecast by using income elasticity from well-developed nations is equivalent to the regression line CD. This means that using a G7 member's income–consumption relationship may underestimate the emerging force of a typical Asian developing beer market. This is illustrated by the vertical distance between GD and GB. Hence, in using an identical income elasticity from a developed market, the resulting estimation is likely to be inappropriate in capturing crucial changes within growing beer markets (Craigwell and Rock, 1991).

In short, consumption changes are influenced by two significant factors, namely wealth stocks (stocks at a specific time) and flows (income levels). The slope of a regression line reflects the influences introduced by income changes, while expectations about the stock of wealth dictate the magnitude of the intercept value along the vertical axis. If expectations over autonomous consumption are increased but income growth rates remain high (beyond I), the income response still generates underprediction. This is indicated by the section $HD_2$ of the line $A_1D_2$. The diagram shows that if the income responses in the mature developed markets remain roughly the same and estimation of consumption changes follow a regression relationship pattern like CD, the only accurate forecast when autonomous consumption increases in developing beer markets is a point like G, at which the two lines intersect each other. When the differences in the slope values and the autonomous values between the EU and Asia become closer, better predictions based on developed market income elasticities are possible. As increases in autonomous consumption accelerate and income response slows down simultaneously, the line AB will tilt clockwise until it overlaps the regression line CD. This transformation process may take a considerable period of time, which corresponds to the evolutionary process of an emerging market towards a mature economy.

## 20.4 Globalisation

In emerging markets, economic activities follow endogenous growth models. Growth in economic activities may create more and more economic by-products such as business travelling and tourism. These economically induced by-products of societal prosperity also contribute to increased beer consumption in emerging Asian beer markets. Tourism used to be a major source of income for the Philippines. However, owing to the economic and political instability in the early 1990s, the growth rates in beer markets have plummeted. This economic downfall is reflected by the negative growth in beer consumption shown in Table 20.5. However, in recent years, as economic development in the Philippines became more stable, the dominant brewer, San Miguel, took advantage of the booming Asia-Pacific markets. The outlook for the beer market in the Philippines is now more optimistic. Thus San Miguel has brewing assets in Hong Kong, China, Vietnam and Indonesia. In stretching into the Chinese market, San Miguel has spent more than $260 million to create four major joint ventures in a country with a quarter of the world's population. The choice of destination for substantial investment is a good indicator of the degree of emerging market trends. Chinese and Vietnamese beer markets have been very popular for aggressive brewers. Industry analysts expected to see a 20% annual rise in beer consumption in Vietnam, with a population of 77 million by 2001. The per capita consumption is forecast to reach 26 litres in 2010 and total production of 4.98 m hl by 2001. This is because the potential market size in these unexplored markets is huge. Presently, consumption levels are not as appealing as in EU countries, but rising living standards steadily increase the demand, plus the large population base potentially creates sufficiently large market sizes to accommodate large brewing operations. The fundamental issue of economies of scale in brewing is largely due to the homogeneous nature of beer production. The significance of brewing economies is discussed by Tremblay (1987) and Scherer (1996). To achieve successful market diversification, brewers from mature EU markets seek potential and viable markets to maximise internationalisation developments. Market entry is not straightforward and free of regulation. To overcome this hurdle and get a tangible grip on unfamiliar business environments, foreign brewers favour the use of joint ventures. Obviously, in some emerging markets, such as China and Vietnam, local business practices and rules and regulations are full of uncertainty and unsophisticated compared with Western standards. Performing activity with local joint venture partners is unavoidable. According to Dahringer and Muhlbacher (1991), regarding the market entry process in high-risk markets, to join forces with a local partner is desirable in order to reduce political risk and manage an unfamiliar political environment.

In developed nations, competition for market share is vigorous and non-price competition is an important strategic weapon which helps brewers maintain sensible price-cost margins for long-term profits, avoiding excessive price cutting. To cope with domestic and dynamic globalised competition, advertising was shown as a key non-price strategic weapon in the UK. Similar influences in consumption can be found in different EU countries and even some emerging Asian countries. A cointegration analysis from the study written by Ling *et al.* (1997) indicates that advertising affects demand. Case studies for other EU countries, for instance Kioulafas (1985), also found that advertising can create statistically significant accumulative impact on the demand for beer. However, the relative impact of non-price competition depends very much on the variety and commercial impact of different advertising media. In developed nations and cities like Japan, Singapore and Hong Kong, advertising media are well developed. Here the effectiveness of advertising could be similar to the UK. However, in less developed areas such as Cambodia, Vietnam and China, the advertising business is relatively inefficient and more primitive in providing strategic weapons. If advertising elasticity can be accurately estimated, beer consumption in different societies can be forecasted efficiently.

## 20.5    Conclusions

This study has compared relative trends in beer production and consumption in mature markets in the EU and emerging markets in Asia. The fundamental conclusion is that income elasticity-based estimations of demand trends are reasonably reliable in established markets in the EU but must remain suspect in emerging markets like China and Vietnam where wealth effects, resulting from explosive growth rates, swamp estimates based on incremental movements of the consumption function. Therefore, wealth-savings and induced consumption patterns in emerging markets nullify the case sometimes advanced for standardised convergence criteria. All in all, this study reveals that investigating consumption and production trends in mature EU beer markets may lead the way in establishing reliable forecasting practices and procedures in emerging markets. Statistical tests of convergence based on real GNP data/variables produce distorted or misleading patterns of potential growth convergence at industry levels of aggregation. This industry-based study reveals the significance of wealth effects on consumption/production levels in emerging markets, where the contrasts revealed by comparison with mature markets are striking.

## Summary

- EU beer consumption trends indicate strong convergence for member states. For Asia the large variations in production and consumption indicate strong growth potential.

- An evaluation of emerging market forces based purely on income data does not reflect real relative strengths of industrial performance.

- Beer production and consumption trends in the EU and emerging markets in Asia differ dramatically. Within Asia, trends are divergent for a number of reasons.

- The potential growth of beer consumption in emerging Asian markets is likely to be driven by strong wealth effects.

## Questions

1. What is meant by convergence in emerging markets?
2. Can income data alone be reliably used for analysis for convergent trends between nations?
3. How might wealth effects in Asia enhance beer consumption over time?
4. Why are consumption trends convergent in the EU beer markets?

## Key concepts

| | |
|---|---|
| convergence | wealth effects |
| per capita income | beer markets |
| global trends | GNP per capita |
| standard deviation | growth effects |

## Bibliography

Barro, R. (1991) 'Economic growth in a cross section of countries', *Quarterly Journal of Economics*, vol. 106, no. 2 (May), pp. 407–43.

Brewers and Licensed Retailers Association Annual Report (1995).

Craigwell, R. and Rock, L. (1991) 'An aggregate consumption function for Canada: a cointegration approach', *Applied Economics*, vol. 27, pp. 239–49.

Dahringer, L. and Muhlbacher, H. (1991) *International Marketing – A Global Perspective*, Addison-Wesley Publication Company, USA.

Durlauf, S. (1996) 'On the convergence and divergence of growth rates: an introduction', *Economic Journal*, vol. 106, no. 437, pp. 1016–18.

Durlauf, S. and Johnson, P. (1995) 'Multiple regimes and cross-country growth behaviour', *Journal of Applied Econometrics*, vol. 10, pp. 365–84.

Friedman, M. (1957) *A Theory of the Consumption Functions*, Princeton, NJ: Princeton University Press.

Key Note Report (1994) CD-Rom.

Kioulafas, K. (1983) 'An application of multiple regression analysis to the Greek beer market', *Journal of Operational Research Society*, vol. 36, no. 8, pp. 689–96.

Lawler, K., Abbott, A. and Ling, M. (1998) 'An empirical analysis of the effects of the Monopolies and Mergers Commission Beer Orders (1989) on the UK brewing industry', *Applied Economics*, January.

Ling, M., Lawler, K. and Abbott, A. (1997) 'Advertising investment in the brewing industry: an empirical analysis', *Economic Issues*, vol. 2, Part 1, March, pp. 55–66.

Lucas, R. (1988) 'On the mechanics of economic development', *Journal of Monetary Economics*, vol. 22, no. 3 (June), pp. 3–42.

Mankiw, N., Romer, D. and Weil, D. (1992) 'A contribution to the empirics of economic growth', *Quarterly Journal of Economics*, vol. 107, pp. 407–37.

Quah, D. (1996a) 'Convergence empirics with (some) capital mobility', *Journal of Economic Growth*, vol. 22, no. 3, pp. 19–28.

Quah, D. (1996b) 'Aggregate and regional disaggregate fluctuations', *Empirical Economics*, vol. 12, no. 2, pp. 23–39.

Romer, P. (1986) 'Increasing returns and long run growth', *Journal of Political Economy*, vol. 99 (June), pp. 500–21.

Romer, P. (1994) 'The origins of endogenous growth', *Journal of Political Perspectives*, vol. 8, no. I, pp. 3–22 (winter).

Sala-i-Martin, X. (1996) 'The classical approach to convergence analysis', *Economic Journal*, vol. 106, no. 437, pp. 1019–36.

Scherer, F. (1996) *Industry Structure, Strategy and Public Policy*, HarperCollins, USA.

Tremblay, V. (1987) 'Scale economies, technological changes, and firm-cost asymmetries in the US brewing industry', *Quarterly Review of Economics and Business*, Summer.

# 21 Foreign direct investment and multinational enterprise

## G. DE VITA

## 21.1 Introduction

Foreign direct investment (FDI) is at the core of the process of globalisation and has now become even more important than trade as a vehicle for international economic transactions.

FDI is inextricably linked to the activities of multinational enterprises (MNEs), defined as companies which own and control productive facilities in more than one country.

FDI and MNEs have always attracted much attention, and their effects on home and host countries, being the subject of great controversy, have generated heated debates in the literature.

In the Marxist tradition, foreign investments by MNEs represent the tangible expression of capitalist oppression; the manifestation of the economic exploitation inherent in the capitalist system of production. Today, however, FDI by MNEs is largely seen, by both governments and academic writers, as a critical catalyst in the globalisation process through which growth, economic development and technological innovation are diffused across countries.

This chapter starts by examining the recent trends and geographical patterns of FDI. This is followed by a review and critical evaluation of FDI theories. The impacts of FDI on home and host countries are then discussed. Finally, an assessment of recent policy developments is provided.

## 21.2 What is FDI?

Foreign direct investment (FDI) can be defined as an investment involving the setting up of a new overseas operation (greenfield investment[1]) or the acquisition of a controlling interest in an already existing foreign company (by purchasing a majority of the shares).

In terms of the latter, the proportion of equity ownership necessary to allow the investor to exercise control cannot but vary from case to case,[2] depending on how widely dispersed the remaining ownership is. If the extent of ownership of a foreign company is insufficient to allow the investor to exert a significant degree of influence on the management of the company resident in the other economy (lack of control), then this investment is classified as foreign portfolio investment rather than FDI.

## 21.3 Recent trends and geographical patterns of FDI

Although cross-border investment activity has been a long-standing feature of the international economic environment, since the early 1980s world FDI flows (now attributable to almost 60,000 MNEs operating through over 500,000 foreign affiliates) have grown at a much faster pace than either world output or world exports. The strong expansion recorded in the past two decades has been driven by several interrelated factors. These include rapid technological change, the adoption of investment liberalisation policies by many countries, privatisation and de-monopolisation activities, and the switch of emphasis by firms from product to geographical diversification.

As shown in Table 21.1, in 1998, world FDI inflows and outflows (which should, theoretically, be equal to each other but due to differences in national estimation methodologies always tend to show discrepancies) reached record levels of $644 billion and $649 billion, respectively. Hence, in spite of the adverse global economic conditions witnessed in 1998 (the Asian financial crisis, declining world trade, reduced privatisation activity, etc.) which could have led to a reduction in FDI, inflows and outflows grew by approximately 39% and 37%, respectively.

This dramatic growth of FDI in 1998 can be explained by the fact that a growing number of firms opted for mergers and acquisitions (M&As) as a mode of overseas expansion or consolidation in the increasingly competitive global environment. Indeed, the value of M&As activity, at $411 billion, was $175 billion higher than in 1997.[3] The average size in value of M&As is also growing. Some of the deals closed in 1998 in fact involve record amounts (see Table 21.2).

An analysis by sector would reveal that M&As continue to occur across many industries: oil, automobiles, pharmaceuticals, electric, gas and water utilities, banking and telecommunications, to name but a few. Some industries have fewer deals but these deals are larger. Generally, the highest average value deals take place in capital-intensive sectors such as natural resources, utilities, the automobile industry and the banking sector. Less capital-intensive sectors tend to record deals of lower average values.

In terms of geographical patterns, as can be seen from Table 21.3, FDI remains heavily concentrated in developed countries. Although 'developing countries' share of FDI inflows rose from 26 per cent in 1980 to 37 per cent in 1996, and their share in total outflows rose from 3 per cent in 1980 to 14 per cent in 1997' (Mallampally and Sauvant, 1999, p. 3), 1998 saw a reversal in the trend. This is primarily due to the spectacular FDI performance of the developed countries (and the EU in particular) which now account for

**Table 21.1  Selected indicators of FDI, 1991–98.**

| | Value at current prices ($ billion) | | | Annual growth rate (%) | | | |
|---|---|---|---|---|---|---|---|
| | 1996 | 1997 | 1998 | 1991–1995 | 1996 | 1997 | 1998 |
| FDI inflows | 359 | 464 | 644 | 19.6 | 9.1 | 29.4 | 38.7 |
| FDI outflows | 380 | 475 | 649 | 15.9 | 5.9 | 25.1 | 36.6 |
| FDI inward stock | 3,086 | 3,437 | 4,088 | 9.6 | 10.6 | 11.4 | 19 |
| FDI outward stock | 3,145 | 3,423 | 4,117 | 10.5 | 10.7 | 8.9 | 20.3 |
| Cross-border M&As | 163 | 236 | 411 | 30.2 | 15.5 | 45.2 | 73.9 |
| GDP at factor cost | 29,024 | 29,360 | ... | 6.4 | 2.5 | 1.2 | ... |
| GFCF[a] | 6,072 | 5,917 | ... | 6.5 | 2.5 | −2.5 | ... |
| Exports of goods and non-factor services | 6,523 | 6,710 | 6,576 | 9.3 | 5.7 | 2.9 | −2.0 |

*Source* adapted from UN, World Investment Report (1999)
[a] Gross fixed capital formation

Table 21.2  The five largest M&A deals announced in 1998.

| Industry | Acquiring company | Home economy | Acquired company | Host economy | Value ($billion) |
|---|---|---|---|---|---|
| Petrolium | British Petroleum Co PLC | (UK) | Amoco Corp. | (US) | 55.0 |
| Automotive | Daimler-Benz AG | (Germany) | Chrysler Corp. | (US) | 40.5 |
| Pharmaceuticals | ZENECA Group PLC | (UK) | Astra AB | (Sweden) | 31.8 |
| Pharmaceuticals | Hoechst AG | (Germany) | Rhône-Poulenc SA | (France) | 21.2 |
| Utilities | Scottish Power PLC | (UK) | Pacif Corp. | (US) | 12.6 |

*Source* adapted from UN, World Investment Report (1999)

Table 21.3  Regional distribution of FDI inflows and outflows, 1987–98.

| Regions as a share of totals | Inflows (percentage) | | | | | | |
|---|---|---|---|---|---|---|---|
| | 1987–1992 | 1993 | 1994 | 1995 | 1996 | 1997 | 1998 |
| Developed countries[a] | 78.7 | 61 | 57.7 | 63.4 | 58.8 | 58.9 | 71.5 |
| Developing countries[b] | 20.4 | 35.9 | 48 | 32.3 | 37.7 | 37.1 | 25.8 |
| Central and East Europe[c] | 0.9 | 3.1 | 2.3 | 4.3 | 3.5 | 4.0 | 2.7 |
| *World* | 100 | 100 | 100 | 100 | 100 | 100 | 100 |

| | Outflows (percentage) | | | | | | |
|---|---|---|---|---|---|---|---|
| | 1987–1992 | 1993 | 1994 | 1995 | 1996 | 1997 | 1998 |
| Developed countries[a] | 93 | 83.8 | 84.9 | 85.3 | 84.2 | 85.6 | 91.6 |
| Developing countries[b] | 7 | 16.1 | 15 | 14.6 | 15.5 | 13.7 | 8.1 |
| Central and East Europe[c] | 0 | 0.1 | 0.1 | 0.1 | 0.3 | 0.7 | 0.3 |
| *World* | 100 | 100 | 100 | 100 | 100 | 100 | 100 |

*Source* adapted from UN, World Investment Report (1999)

[a] Western Europe, United States, Japan and other developed countries.

[b] Africa, Latin America and the Caribbean, Developing Europe, Asia, the Pacific.

[c] Albania, Belarus, Bulgaria, Czech Republic, Estonia, Hungary, Latvia, Lithuania, Moldova, Republic of Poland, Romania, Russian Federation, Slovakia, Ukraine.

about 71% and 92% of world FDI inflows and outflows, respectively. These data suggest a tendency toward a regionalisation of international production primarily concentrated within the three major regional blocks of the 'Triad' (the US, the EU and Japan) rather than a movement towards truly global production relations. If these trends persist, this intra-regional growth of FDI (influenced strongly by neighbourhood effects) should lead to a further consolidation of the Triad members.

As noted by Kozul-Wright and Rowthorn (1998), the extent to which similar regional dynamics will emerge in the developing world largely depends on the developing countries' ability to close the gap on advanced industrial economies. The FDI performance of Asia (South, East and South East) justified by the rapid economic growth in these economies (only temporarily slowed down by the Asian financial crisis) is a confirmation of the regionalisation of production hypothesis. Indeed, the share of developing countries in the total FDI outflows from the Asian region has increased from 60% in 1987 to about 90% in 1997 and, in terms of stock, more than 80% of FDI from this region is in developing countries, with more than 90% of it being invested within the Asian region (United Nations, World Investment Report, 1999).

## 21.4 The theories of FDI

Conventional international trade theory, though insightful in terms of trade flows among countries, is clearly incapable of providing an explanation of FDI. The H-O-S model (reviewed earlier in the book), for example, cannot shed any light on the very existence of FDI since the model assumes that factors of production (including capital) cannot move between countries. Since the early 1970s, however, a number of new theories have emerged seeking to explain the 'why', 'how' and 'where' of international production. The sub-sections that follow review and assess the most important hypotheses that have been put forward.

### 21.4.1 The market imperfections theory of FDI

The 'market imperfections' theory states that due to market failures or imperfections in product or factor markets, some firms enjoy advantages not shared by rivals which allow them to obtain rents in foreign markets. Firms therefore invest overseas to capitalise on such advantages. Hymer (1970, 1976) argued that this conduct by firms (which often results in 'swallowing up' or 'pre-empting' competition) affects the structure of markets and allows MNEs to exploit monopoly or oligopoly powers.

The aggressive and defensive behaviours of firms operating in imperfect markets have also been examined by Knickerbocker (1973), who concluded that it is the interdependence and uncertainty which characterise the nature of oligopoly that explains the observed clustering of FDI in such industries.

The market imperfections approach was extended further by Buckley and Casson (1976) who focused on the gains from internalisation available in imperfect markets. Internalisation entails the acquisition of control over activities previously carried out by intermediate markets through vertical integration (either to ensure stability and quality of supplies or distribution and marketing channels). Under this view, MNEs derive market power through their ability to efficiently internalise market transactions for intermediate products.

Both firm-specific and internalisation-incentive advantages constitute two key pillars of the eclectic theorem of international production which is examined later in this chapter.

### 21.4.2 The Uppsala internationalisation model

Although the market imperfections approach provides a rationale for international production, it does not explain why FDI is the best vehicle to harness the advantages possessed by the firm and, most importantly, it does not shed light on the process by which a firm engages in international activities.

The internationalisation process has received much attention in the literature and most conceptualisations of the dynamic path through which a local firm becomes an MNE can be traced back to the seminal work conducted by the Scandinavian researchers Johanson, Vahlne and Wiedersheim-Paul (commonly referred to as the Uppsala School).

In examining the increasing outward involvement of four Swedish organisations, Johanson and Wiedersheim-Paul (1975) identified a four-step sequence leading to international production. Firms begin by serving the domestic market, then foreign markets are penetrated through exports; after a time, sales outlets are established in overseas markets until, finally, overseas production facilities are set up.

Johanson and Vahlne (1977) qualified the underlying logic of this sequential internationalisation process, arguing that this stepwise development is based on the gradual acquisition of knowledge of the foreign market, and use of foreign-based sources of intelligence. It is this process of incremental, experiential learning that justifies and determines successively greater levels of commitment to foreign markets.

Although some studies have confirmed the gradual process of firms' international involvement (e.g. Yoshihara, 1978), the Uppsala internationalisation model has not escaped criticism. Millington and Bayliss (1990), for example, found that the postulated stepwise development did not reflect the actual process of internationalisation of UK companies in the EC. This is because knowledge based on experiential learning can be translated across countries and product markets, and these economies of scope allow firms to bypass some or all of the intermediate steps of the postulated 'sequential' process. It has also been argued (Kozul-Wright and Rowthorn, 1998) that the model neglects the potentially disruptive influence of policy on the described sequence leading to international production. Most importantly, however, the notions of 'experiential learning' and 'gradual acquisition of knowledge', which are at the heart of the model, cannot provide an all-encompassing explanation of the 'why' of international production since these notions do not allow for the possibility of a reverse process, a process which is often experienced by firms that undergo retrenchment. Since learning and the acquisition of knowledge are not reversible processes, there must be additional factors that influence investment and divestment decisions.

### 21.4.3   Vernon's product-cycle hypothesis

The model developed by Vernon (see Chapter 12), which builds on both the earlier anatomies of the product life cycle conducted by Kuznetz (1953) and Hirsch (1965), and the imitation-gap theory developed by Posner (1961), provides an integrated framework for the analysis of international trade patterns and FDI.

The hypothesis explains how a product may emerge as a developed country export and go through the life cycle to ultimately be produced in developing countries and thus become a developed country import. Vernon's hypothesis was, at the time of its inception, found to account for the concentration of innovations in, and technological superiority of, developed countries (the USA in particular), the tendency of firms to become MNEs at the maturity stage of their products' life cycle, and the transfer of (often outdated) technology from developed to developing economies.

Although the theory enjoyed widespread recognition and acceptance during the 1960s and 1970s, it is now regarded by many as largely anachronistic on at least two counts. First, the product-life extension which characterises the maturity phase is inconsistent, or at least difficult to reconcile with MNEs' tendency to produce the new product where costs are at their lowest from the start, and opt for a contemporaneous launch and introduction phase of the product in many countries. Second, as acknowledged by Vernon himself (1979), the technological gap between the USA and other developed countries (most notably Europe and Japan) is reducing.

### 21.4.4   Aliber's explanation of FDI

Aliber (1970) put forward two distinct hypotheses to explain the existence of FDI.

The first hypothesis states that the imposition of trade barriers (e.g. import tariffs) will lead to an increase in FDI inflows. The underlying rationale is that by producing directly in the countries concerned, FDI can serve as a vehicle to overcome trade restrictions and penetrate otherwise barred markets.

Corden (1974) examined the possible exceptions to the postulated positive relationship between trade barriers and inward FDI, and concluded that, under certain conditions (e.g. when the restricted imports are complementary to FDI outputs), import restrictions may actually reduce FDI inflows.

Aliber's argument, however, remains by and large still valid and appears to be particularly cogent whenever the countries concerned are part of a customs union, in which case the potential market goes much beyond that of the member state in question.[4]

Aliber's second explanation of FDI is based on the idea that weak-currency countries will attract FDI due to the high purchasing power of investors operating from a strong-currency country. As pointed out by Dunning (1991) though, currency valuation considerations, being short-term considerations in nature, can at best explain the 'when' or timing of FDI. Moreover, as argued by John *et al.* (1997), currency valuation considerations are at best pertinent to FDI through acquisition of already existing foreign companies rather than greenfield FDI, since the latter entails a medium- to long-term gestation period unlikely to be affected by short-term issues related to currency valuation.

Aliber (1993) also stressed the role of real macroeconomic variables as key factors affecting FDI location decisions. Here, particular emphasis is placed upon the positive relationship between the rate of growth of the host country and inward FDI; a relationship widely supported by the empirical literature. Indeed, with the exception of the findings reported by Scaperlanda and Mauer (1969), all the empirical studies to date have confirmed the statistical significance of the growth variable as a determinant of inward FDI (see, for example, Wheeler and Mody, 1992).

### 21.4.5   Dunning's eclectic paradigm

In search of an holistic framework capable of explaining the 'why', 'how' and 'where' of FDI, Dunning (1979, 1981, 1988) developed what he called an eclectic paradigm of international production. The paradigm states that firms will engage in FDI if, and only if, ownership-specific, internalisation-incentive and location-specific advantages (often referred to as OLI advantages) co-exist.

Ownership advantages (like those discussed by Hymer) are firm-specific and refer to the core competencies[5] that give the company a competitive advantage vis-à-vis rivals in the alien environment, and which more than offset the advantages that host country firms have already developed (e.g. market knowledge). Examples of ownership advantages include patents, trademarks, managerial capabilities, particular organisational and marketing skills, innovatory capacity and know-how. They have also been expressed in terms of technological sophistication (Buckley and Casson, 1976; Cantwell, 1991) in which case measurement can be based on factor productivity.[6] By granting, at least for a period of time, competitive advantage over companies already serving foreign markets, such assets or capabilities explain the 'why' of international production.

The existence of ownership advantages can, under certain conditions, provide an internalisation incentive in that, whenever transactions can be made at lower cost within the company, it must be beneficial for a company possessing these advantages to use them itself rather than sell them or lease them to foreign companies. The 'how' of such internalisation gains is based on the extension of value-added chains within the ownership and governance of the company (rather than outsourcing or licensing the corresponding activities). This usually takes the form of vertical integration, either backward (toward the source of supply) or forward (toward the buyer).

Ownership-specific and internalisation-incentive advantages are both necessary but not sufficient to justify international production. As far as the theory goes, there must additionally exist location-specific factors which favour overseas production as opposed to production in domestic locations. Typical advantages which determine the location dimension of the FDI decision, i.e. the 'where' of international production, can be found in the availability, cost and productivity of factor inputs (e.g. labour), the quality of the transport and communication systems (infrastructure), favourable host government policies (e.g. lower corporate tax rates) and attractive macroeconomic conditions.[7] If there are no location-specific advantages to be gained by producing overseas, then the company is better off by expanding domestic production and serving foreign markets through exports.

It should be emphasised at this stage that ownership, internalisation and location advantages are interrelated by nature and that, ultimately, location decisions will depend upon the character of ownership advantages and the extent to which one location offers greater internalisation incentives than another. Any question concerning the relative importance of the variables of 'the OLI triad' is best answered by referring to Dunning's analogy of the three-legged-stool: 'each leg is supportive of the other, and the stool is only functional if the three legs are evenly balanced' (Dunning, 1998, p. 45).

By virtue of its eclectic nature, which combines elements of various approaches, Dunning's hypothesis can be said to be the most comprehensive framework to examine the geographical, sectoral and industrial patterns of FDI.

## 21.5    The impact of FDI

First, MNEs, by efficiently organising international production, can considerably increase world output. Indeed, 25% of world output is now attributable to the output under the common governance of MNEs (United Nations, World Investment Report, 1999).

Another impact of FDI is that on employment, in both the home and host country. In terms of the home country, the loss of domestic jobs resulting from outward investment is seen as a drawback of FDI, these being jobs that are essentially exported. The counter-argument of course is that, had the investment remained at home, the jobs created would have soon been lost to more efficient foreign-based rivals. With respect to inward FDI, its impact on employment in the host country is generally believed to be positive, with considerable gains in terms of direct and indirect[8] employment creation. Yet, it should be noted that a significant increase in inward FDI, by increasing domestic wages, may, through a process of 'corrective' capital/labour substitution undertaken by domestic firms, generate a reduction in domestic employment. Driffield (1999) estimated the indirect employment substitution effect of inward investment in the UK over the period 1986–1992, and concluded that the extent of job reduction was approximately one-fifth of all the jobs created by inward investment.

MNEs may also absorb finance and skilled labour in the host country, thus preventing these factors from being used to establish local firms. This is the so-called 'crowding out' effect in factor markets which is said to prevent the development of indigenous industries. This potential drawback, however, may be more than offset by the gains to be made by the host country through externalised (to other firms) and internalised (to affiliates) FDI technology transfers.

**Table 21.4  Wider effects of FDI: evidence from the UK. In 1994 the Department of Trade and Industry (DTI) commissioned PA Cambridge Economic Consultants (PACEC) to conduct a study of the wider effects of FDI in manufacturing in the UK (DTI, 1995). The specific aims included the assessment of impacts on suppliers, competitors and customers of inward investors as well as how practices adopted by inward investors had affected performance of other UK-based firms. The (random) sample comprised 30 inward investors in manufacturing industries that located in the UK between the mid-1970s and early 1990s and employed a minimum of 250 people at the time of the study, and approximately 300 supplier, customer and competitor companies to the selected inward investors. The research design consisted of case study analyses, interviews with all parties, fieldwork and surveys. The main findings of the study are summarised in the table.**

| | |
|---|---|
| Impact on suppliers | Nearly 75% of suppliers recognised impacts of inward investors on their business practices. The strongest effects were on quality, product development activities, reducing costs and improvements to delivery methods. Approximately 60% of suppliers acknowledged effects on their competitive advantage, especially in terms of client responsiveness, reputation, speed of service and price. Additional positive impacts included increases in sales profitability and productivity. The most important transmission mechanism for these transfers of benefits were the value of purchases, agreements on product specification, quality assurance and cost reduction pressures. Impacts were transmitted relatively quickly. By and large, suppliers felt that the presence of inward investors had been a critical stimulus for the transmission and enhancement of practices and only a small minority would have improved their practices anyway within the same time-scale. There was little evidence of negative impacts. |
| Impact on competitors | Apart from an increase in competition in shared product markets, only few adverse effects were identified. These included increased wage pressures and reduced access to institutional R&D facilities. Approximately 40% of competitors reported that positive changes to their strategies and practices took place in response to the inward investors' presence. These included product adjustment and development, emphasis on reductions in costs and prices as well as quality improvements. The key transmission mechanism here was said to be the general 'competitive spur'. About 50% of the competitors reported that effects were transmitted within 12 months, though for the remainder of firms effects fed through much more slowly. The overall impact reflected a balance of adverse effects and positive effects (resulting from the changes made). In most cases, however, it was felt that improvements would have taken place even if inward investors were located elsewhere outside the UK. |
| Impact on customers | A total of 70% of customers experienced benefits of improved inputs from inward investors through the combined effects of reduced prices, better quality, enhanced technologies and availability of new products and designs. Additional benefits included the demonstration effect of better working practices with significant effects on purchasing practices, product development, marketing and sales activities. The major impacts on performance were on profitability, productivity, costs and prices. The main mechanism for transmission was the informal sharing of views and ideas. Seventy per cent of companies reported that effects fed through within two years. Customers reckoned that only 40% of the identified benefits would have occurred anyway if the inward investor had not located in the UK. |

*Source* adapted from 'Assessment of the Wider Effects of Foreign Direct Investment in the UK', DTI publications, URN 96/535, DTI Regional Policy Directorate.

Indeed, MNEs can bring modern technologies not available to host countries in the absence of FDI; technologies which can raise the efficiency with which existing technologies are being used. Where host countries possess domestic research skills, and scientific resources and infrastructure, MNEs may also set up R&D facilities which can upgrade technologies as innovations emerge, thus improving the content of the technology transfer. The hypothesis that the higher the level of a country's scientific resources, the higher is the level of R&D investments by foreign-owned MNEs in the country, has found unanimous support in the empirical literature (see, for example, the recent study on the level of R&D activity performed by US MNEs, conducted by Muralidharan and Phatak, 1999).

FDI also has an impact on the balance of payments of both the home and host country. If the investment is financed by borrowing in the home capital market, then the initial capital outflow will lead to a worsening of the balance of payments of the home country and an improvement in that of the host country. As profits flow back to the investing country, however, the effect on the balance of payments of home and host country will be reversed. FDI may also affect a country's balance of payments via MNEs' control over imports and exports of inputs, components and semi-finished products at both inter- and intra-MNE level.

In addition to the direct effects of MNEs in terms of their output, employment creation, technology transfers, etc., the impact of FDI can be assessed in terms of the wider effects on host-country-based suppliers, competitors and customers. In order to measure these wider effects it is necessary to weigh up the benefits and adverse impacts on supplier, competitor and customer firms that result from the presence of the inward investor. In this context, it is also important to assess the transmission mechanisms by which the effects feed through, and the time lag of these effects. Finally, it is necessary to estimate the potential effect on host-country-based suppliers, competitors and customers, had the foreign investor located elsewhere. Table 21.4 reports on evidence of the wider effects of FDI on the UK.

## 21.6    Policy responses and developments

Host governments have rarely held a neutral position toward FDI. Some governments, perceiving the net effects as negative, have sought to restrict FDI through the establishment of various barriers, while others, conscious of the potential role that FDI can play in accelerating growth, have offered incentives in order to attract inward investment.

Since the mid-1980s we have witnessed a shift in policy towards the latter approach. Indeed, many countries that had traditionally opted for widespread controls on FDI undertook often drastic revisions in their investment regimes with a view to removing existing barriers and adopting a range of positive measures aimed at facilitating and promoting inward FDI. The vast majority of countries now permit inward investment, and many actively court foreign-owned MNEs.

As shown in Table 21.5, of a total of 895 regulatory changes concerning FDI made during the period 1991–98, only 52 were in the direction of greater restriction, while 94% were aimed at creating a more favourable environment for inward investment by foreign-owned MNEs.

The most important liberalisation measures were in terms of greater promotion through incentives (grants, tax concessions, loans, etc.) and more liberal operational conditions.

Perhaps the best illustrative example of this shift in policy regimes is that given by the policy changes implemented by the Canadian government over the past 35 years.

Table 21.5  National regulatory changes, 1991–98.

| | 1991 | 1992 | 1993 | 1994 | 1995 | 1996 | 1997 | 1998 |
|---|---|---|---|---|---|---|---|---|
| Number of countries that introduced changes | 35 | 43 | 57 | 49 | 64 | 65 | 76 | 60 |
| Number of regulatory changes of which: | 82 | 79 | 102 | 110 | 112 | 114 | 151 | 145 |
| – More favourable to FDI | 80 | 79 | 101 | 108 | 106 | 98 | 135 | 136 |
| – Less favourable to FDI | 2 | – | 1 | 2 | 6 | 16 | 16 | 9 |

*Source* adapted from UN, World Investment Report (1999)

By and large during the 1960s, the Canadian policy agenda was to control inward investment with many policy measures directed at all categories of FDI. In 1963, for example, the Canadian government introduced a new tax regime requiring foreign-owned MNEs to be taxed at a much higher rate than Canadian corporations. This restrictive attitude toward foreign-ownership continued through the 1970s. In 1974, the Foreign Investment Review Act (FIRA) established that an 'application-process' review was necessary for any proposed acquisition or greenfield investment by foreign-owned MNEs. Under FIRA, approval was granted only to those foreign investors who had satisfied the government that the investment was of 'significant benefit' to Canadians. As reported by Globerman and Shapiro (1999), the Canadian rejection rate was relatively high compared to that experienced by other countries (e.g. Australia) implementing a similar policy over the same period. The Investment Canada Act ratified in 1985, however, marked a major shift in government policy towards the facilitation of FDI. Exemptions, especially with respect to greenfield investments, were granted to several sectors, and the 'review' process of 'significant benefit' was replaced by 'notification' of 'net benefit'; a policy shift which resulted in an increase in the level of inward FDI. Further liberalisation of the FDI environment was achieved through the Free Trade Pact between the USA and Canada (implemented as FTA in 1989) later culminating in the North American Free Trade Agreement (NAFTA) which contains numerous provisions aimed at protecting and encouraging FDI among signing parties.

The national trends shown in Table 21.5 and the policy shift illustrated by the Canadian experience are echoed by the developments taking place at the international level.

The constantly rising number of Bilateral Investment Treaties (BITs), for example, is a good indicator of the greater willingness of countries to enhance cooperation on foreign investment and promote FDI flows. In particular, some 170 new BITs were signed in 1998 alone (of which only 36% were between developed and developing countries), bringing the total number of BITs in existence at the end of 1998 to 1726.

At the regional level too, several new initiatives have been launched with the aim of encouraging, facilitating and protecting FDI. These include the Framework Agreement on the ASEAS Investment Area, the proposed regional agreement among the member states of the Economic Cooperation Organisation (ECO), and the Community Charter on Investment set out by the Central African Economic Community and Monetary Union (CEMAC).

## Summary

- FDI is an investment involving the setting up of a new overseas operation or the acquisition of controlling interest in an already existing foreign company.

- In recent years there has been a dramatic growth in FDI due to a number of factors. These include rapid technological change, the adoption of investment liberalisation policies, privatisation and de-monopolisation activities, and the switch of emphasis from product to geographical diversification via mergers and acquisitions.

- In terms of geographical patterns, FDI remains heavily concentrated in developing countries. Recent data on the regional distribution of FDI inflows and outflows also suggest a tendency towards a regionalisation of production within the major blocks of the 'Triad' rather than truly global production relations.

- Since the early 1970s, many theories have emerged in order to explain the 'why', 'how', 'where' and 'when' for international production. Dunning's hypothesis can be said to be the most comprehensive framework to examine the geographical, sectoral and industrial patterns of FDI.

- The impact of FDI activity by MNEs has a direct effect on world output, and on employment, technology and the balance of payments of both the home and host country. The impact of FDI can also be assessed in terms of the wider effects on host-country-based suppliers, competitors and customers.

- Since the mid-1980s, most countries that had traditionally opted for widespread controls on FDI have undertaken drastic revisions in their policy regimes with the aim of promoting and facilitating inward foreign investment.

## Questions

1. What are the location-specific advantages of *your* country of origin?
2. What are the direct and indirect effects of FDI on employment?
3. What is meant by the 'crowding out' effect?
4. Discuss the recent policy developments concerning FDI at both national and international levels.

### Key concepts

| | |
|---|---|
| technical progress | core competencies |
| internalisation advantages | vertical integration |
| capital/labour substitution | direct investment |
| outsourcing | retrenchment |
| portfolio investment | technological gap |
| market imperfections | multinational enterprise (MNE) |
| factor productivity | regionalisation of international production |

## Notes

1. Strictly defined, greenfield FDI involves a company building a new production facility abroad financed by capital raised in the home country.
2. In the USA, a good indicative threshold for the control of assets is an equity capital stake of 10% of shares (or voting power). In other countries, however, such as the UK, a stake of 20% or more is a more appropriate indicative threshold.
3. It should be noted that the establishment of M&As as the primary entry mode for overseas expansion also means that the ratio of FDI to gross fixed capital formation (usually used as a

proxy for measuring the net contribution by foreign companies to domestic investment in host countries) is now better interpreted as a measure of ownership and control turnover over countries' firms among shareholders located in different countries (World Investment Report, 1999).

4. Evidence presented by Blair (1987) provides support to Aliber's hypothesis by suggesting that in the case of FDI in the UK the potential market is perceived as the whole of the EU.

5. Firm-specific advantages that grant a company competitive advantage and which are difficult to imitate or copy either because it is illegal to do so or because of their intangible and tacit nature.

6. Davies and Lyons (1991) measured the factor productivity gap stemming from technological differences in the UK and concluded that the foreign-owned sector had a productivity advantage of 20% over the domestic sector.

7. For a recent empirical analysis of the factors affecting the location of FDI see Billington (1999).

8. The employment created in local firms that are suppliers, subcontractors or service providers to the inward investor.

## Bibliography

Aliber, R. Z. (1970) 'A theory of direct foreign investment'. In C. P. Kindleberger (ed.), *The International Corporation*, MIT Press, Cambridge, MA.

Aliber, R. Z. (1993) *The Multinational Paradigm*, MIT Press, Cambridge, MA.

Billington, N. (1999) 'The location of foreign direct investment: an empirical analysis', *Applied Economics*, vol. 31, no. 1, pp. 65–81.

Blair, A. R. (1987) 'The relative distribution of the US direct investment: the UK/EEC experience', *European Economic Review*, vol. 31, pp. 1137–44.

Buckley, P. and Casson, M. C. (1976) *The future of the Multinational Enterprise*, Macmillan, London.

Cantwell, J. A. (1991) 'The international agglomeration of R&D', in M. C. Casson (ed.), *Global Research Strategy and International Competitiveness*, Basil Blackwell, Oxford.

Corden, W. M. (1974) *Trade Policy and Economic Welfare*, Oxford University Press, Oxford.

Davies, S. W. and Lyons, B. R. (1991) 'Characterising relative performance: the productivity advantage of foreign owned firms in the UK', *Oxford Economic Papers*, vol. 43, pp. 584–95.

DTI Regional Policy Directorate (1995) *Assessment of the Wider Effects of Foreign Direct Investment in the UK*, DTI publications, URN 96/535.

Driffield, N. (1999) 'Indirect employment effects of foreign direct investment into the UK', *Bulletin of Economic Research*, vol. 51, no. 3, pp. 207–21.

Dunning, J. H. (1979) 'Explaining patterns of international production: In defence of the eclectic theory', *Oxford Bulletin of Economics and Statistics*, vol. 41, no. 4, pp. 269–95.

Dunning, J. H. (1981) *International Production and the Multinational Enterprise*, Allen & Unwin, London.

Dunning, J. H. (1988) 'The eclectic paradigm of international production: A restatement of some possible extensions', *Journal of International Business Studies*, vol. 19, no. 1, pp. 1–29.

Dunning, J. H. (1991) 'The eclectic paradigm of international production: a personal perspective', in C. N. Pitelis and R. Sugden (eds), *The Nature of the Transnational Firm*, Routledge, London.

Dunning, J. H. (1998) 'Location and the multinational enterprise: A neglected factor?', *Journal of International Business Studies*, vol. 29, no. 1, pp. 45–66.

Globerman, S. and Shapiro, D. M. (1999) 'The impact of government policies on foreign direct investment: The Canadian experience', *Journal of International Business Studies*, vol. 30, no. 3, pp. 513–31.

Hirsch, S. (1965) 'The United States electronic industry in international trade', *National Institute Economic Review*, vol. 24, pp. 92–7.

Hymer, S. (1970) 'The efficiency (contradictions) of multinational corporations', *American Economic Review*, vol. 60, pp. 441–8.

Hymer, S. (1976) *The International Operations of National Firms: A Study in DFI*, MIT Press, Cambridge MA.

Johanson, J. and Vahlne, J.E. (1977) 'The internationalisation process of the firm', *Journal of International Business Studies*, vol. 8, pp. 23–32.

Johanson, J. and Wiedersheim-Paul, F. (1975) 'The internationalisation of the firm: four Swedish cases', *Journal of Management Studies*, vol. 12, no. 3, pp. 305–22.

John, R., Letto-Gillies, G. and Grimwade, N. (1997) *Global Business Strategy*, International Thomson Business Press, London.

Kozul-Wright, R. and Rowthorn, R. (1998) 'Spoilt for choice: multinational corporations and the geography of international production', *Oxford Review of Economic Policy*, vol. 14, no. 2, pp. 74–93.

Knickerbocker, F. T. (1973) *Oligopolistic Reaction and Multinational Enterprise*, Graduate School of Business Administration, Harvard University, Cambridge, MA.

Kuznetz, S. (1953) *Economic Change*, Norton, New York.

Mallampally, P. and Sauvant, K. P. (1999) 'Foreign direct investment in developing countries', *Finance and Development*, vol. 36, no. 1, pp. 34–7.

Millington, A. I. and Bayliss, B. T. (1990) 'The process of internationalisation: UK companies in the EC', *Management International Review*, vol. 30, no. 2, pp. 151–61.

Muralidharan, R. and Phatak, A. (1999) 'International R&D activity of US MNCs: An empirical study with implications for host government policy', *Multinational Business Review*, vol. 7, no. 2, pp. 97–105.

Posner, M. (1961) 'International trade and technical change', *Oxford Economic Papers*, vol. 13, pp. 323–41.

Scaperlanda, A. E. and Mauer, L. J. (1969) 'The determinants of US direct investment in the EEC', *European Economic Review*, vol. 59, pp. 558–68.

United Nations, World Investment Report (1999) *Foreign Direct Investment and the Challenge of Development*, UNCTAD.

Vernon, R. (1966) 'International investment and international trade in the product cycle', *Quarterly Journal of Economics*, vol. 80, pp. 190–207.

Vernon, R. (1979) 'The product cycle hypothesis in a new international environment', *Oxford Bulletin of Economics and Statistics*, vol. 41, pp. 255–67.

Wheeler, D. and Mody, A. (1992) 'International investment location decisions: the case of US firms', *Journal of International Economics*, vol. 33, pp. 57–36.

Yoshihara, K. (1978) 'Determinants of Japanese investment in South-East Asia', *International Social Science Journal*, vol. 30, no. 2, pp. 1–20.

# 22 Foreign direct investment in China since 1978

**M. LING and K. LAWLER**

In 1979, China opened its economy to foreign direct investment (FDI). Investors from Hong Kong, Taiwan and the United States have led the list with European investors contributing less than 10% of the overall FDI. In recent years, the British government increasingly recognises the shift in the dynamism of the world economy from the Atlantic to the Pacific and its benefits for the West. A growing number of British enterprises are confident that the twenty-first century will be an Asian century. Recent data show that Britain is China's most important partner in terms of FDI within the European Union.

This chapter examines the issue of British direct investment (BDI) in China from the British perspective. It seeks to investigate the success of China's Open Door Policy and the part of UK corporations within it. By recounting organisational experiences, it hopes to provide some indications of best practice to be adopted in formulating and implementing strategies for penetrating the Chinese market.

## 22.1 The Chinese initiative to attract foreign investment

The Chinese government has long been aware of the fact that China had technologically fallen far behind the developed countries, perhaps by as much as 10 to 30 years. Absorption of foreign direct investment, especially, was seen as a desirable solution to the lack of funds for investment and the low level of technology. In fact, China had been isolated from advanced technology for so long that its industry had little chance of reaching world levels without inviting in foreign manufacturers.

Opening up to Western investment was nevertheless perceived as a radical move, even though China was familiar with operating joint ventures with foreign countries. In the 1950s, China had set up state-owned joint companies with the Soviet Union, but tensions between the two countries heightened, followed by the withdrawal of Soviet aid in the 1960s.

The primary objectives in opening China up to foreign investment are to bring in foreign capital, advanced technology, management skills and urban construction, and generally to catch up with the developed countries. Preference is given to foreign projects that are consistent with the long-term development plans of the Chinese national economy, and priorities have been assigned in the following areas:

- machinery and electronic products;
- export-oriented products;
- import substitutes;
- communication, energy and transportation sectors;
- agriculture, particularly machinery and cultivation chemicals.

In 1995, the Chinese government formulated a series of new policies. Under the new policies, foreign trade, retailing sales, financial services, civil aviation, real estate, information services, and so on, have been partly opened to foreign investment. Other fields opened to foreign investment under the new policies are leasing, accounting, advertising, consulting, engineering, industrial designing, schools and training centres.

The Law on Joint Ventures Using Chinese and Foreign Investment was announced in 1979. But it was brief and vague, with only 14 articles. However, Chinese officials emphasised the need to fill in the gaps in the Law with contractual clauses to give greater flexibility, which would appeal to foreign investors. Under the joint ventures system, the Chinese partners normally supply land, plant, labour, infrastructure and some machinery, as well as materials. Foreign partners are expected to provide technology, capital, marketing and management expertise, and possibly some raw materials.

The major developments which have occurred since the inception of the Open Door Policy are shown in Table 22.1. One of the most significant of these developments was the establishment of the Special Economic Zones (SEZs), designed as political, cultural, educational and technological centres. The main features of the policies applied within the SEZs are:

- 15% corporation taxes and a tax holiday;

- cheap land and services (relative to Hong Kong);

- low labour costs (although higher than elsewhere in China);

**Table 22.1  The chronology of China's 'Open Door Policy'.**

| | |
|---|---|
| 1979 | 'Open door' policy announced and Law on Joint Ventures. |
| 1980 | China joined World Bank and International Money Fund. |
| 1980 | Special Economic Zones established (four initially). |
| 1982 | Debt crisis enhanced the attractiveness of foreign capital. |
| 1983 | Joint venture regulation – permission granted to sell products in the domestic market (as opposed to exporting entire output) if 'urgently needed . |
| 1984 | Patents legislation. |
| | Fourteen coastal sites opened. |
| | Licence Import regulations and foreign exchange retention rules. |
| 1985 | Nominal tariff rates reduced on exports. |
| | Tightened access to imports. |
| | Three Open Economic Zones established. |
| 1986 | Joint Venture Foreign Exchange Balance Provisions and Provisions for the Encouragement of Foreign Investment – collectively covering remittance of funds, tax and other incentives, and the hiring and firing of workers. |
| | The 13th Communist Party Conference proclaimed the need for China to join the world economy through the utilisation of foreign capital, technology and raw materials. |
| | Law on Enterprises Operating Exclusively with foreign capital – introduced with more relaxed controls. |
| | Technical Economic Development Areas established in twelve coastal cities. |
| 1987 | Application to join GATT. |
| 1988 | Austerity Programme to reduce inflation – firmer control over credit creation and tax reforms. |
| | Bankruptcy Laws introduced. |
| | Restrictions on economic relations with other countries loosened. |
| 1989 | The Tian-an-men Square Incident followed by a Credit squeeze and devaluation. |

- greater freedom in labour management;
- zero or low customs duties;
- simplified entry/exit and other formalities;
- increased access to imports and the internal Chinese market.

Administrative features included the setting up of the China International Trust and Investment Corporation (CITIC), and the Ministry of Foreign and Economic Relations and Trade (MOFERT). These constitute the approval body for foreign and Chinese enterprises, respectively. Foreign businesses considering a joint venture in China are required to contribute a minimum of 25% of the necessary total investment.

## 22.2 Foreign direct investment

China's strategy behind its 'open door policy' to attract foreign direct investment to the country has proved extremely successful. From 1979 to 1994 the total pledged investment was $275bn, and actual investment reached $85.1bn. In 1994 only, materialised foreign investment was $34bn, which represents about half of all FDI to developing countries worldwide; contractual commitment of foreign investment was $81bn (Figure 22.1). More than 210,000 foreign founded ventures were approved from 1979 to the end of September 1994 (Figure 22.2). China was second only to the USA in attracting foreign investment. The top countries and regions investing in China are Hong Kong, Taiwan, the United States, Japan, Singapore, the UK, Germany, Thailand, France and Canada (Figure 22.3).

Although this immense inflow of foreign investment capital was not surprisingly, dominated by ethnic Chinese investors from Hong Kong and Taiwan, as well as Japan and the USA, Britain was still number six in the top ten investors' list, which is quite impressive amongst European Union countries. As the largest investor among EU countries (Figure 22.4), Britain leads the table, ahead of Germany, France and Italy, with pledged investment and utilised investments amounting to US$3,013 million. In 1993 alone, contractual British investments in China were US$1,990 million in total.

In a report, however, the Commission of the European Union (1994) suggested that, between 1986 and 1992, only 10% of the FDI to Asia came from the European Union

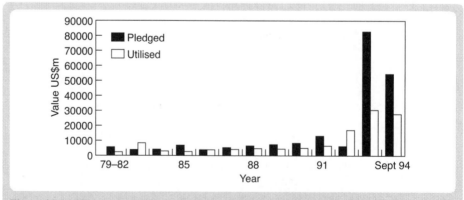

**Figure 22.1  Pledged and utilised foreign investment in China (1979–94)**

*Source* adapted from Almanac of China's Foreign Economic Relations and Trade (CFERT), FT, November 1994; Agency France Press English Wire, 8 July 1994

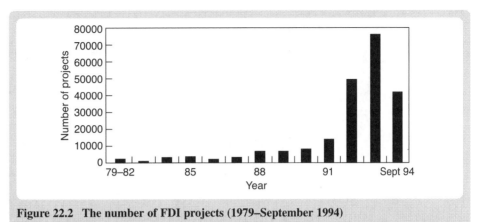

**Figure 22.2  The number of FDI projects (1979–September 1994)**

*Source* adapted from Almanac of China's Foreign Economic Relations and Trade (CFERT), FT, November 1994; Agency France Press English Wire, 8 July 1994

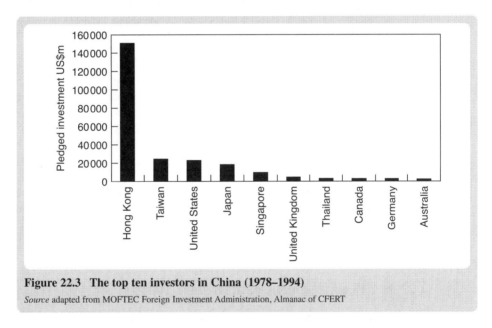

**Figure 22.3  The top ten investors in China (1978–1994)**

*Source* adapted from MOFTEC Foreign Investment Administration, Almanac of CFERT

(EU). Britain contributed only a small share of FDI in China over this period. Compared with the total direct investment of US$110bn in China in the period between 1979 and 1993, companies from Britain committed themselves to a total of 616 direct investment projects with pledged investment and utilised investments amounting to US$3,013 million, contributing only 3.5% of total actual investment in China.

The relatively small stake by British investors being held in Sino-foreign projects is surprising as Britain was, according to figures for 1993, the fifth biggest provider of FDI worldwide, accounting for some US$11bn. Furthermore, given that China was receiving the second biggest share of all FDI in 1993 (US$26bn), the under-representation of BDI into China becomes obvious. Since 1993 a sharp increase in the willingness of British enterprises to invest in China can be identified, together with increased capital inflows from Germany, Singapore and South Korea. At the same time, investment from Hong Kong and Taiwan has been decreasing.

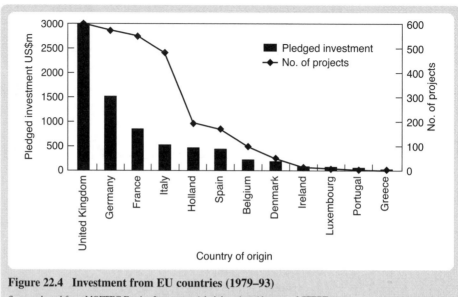

**Figure 22.4  Investment from EU countries (1979–93)**

*Source* adapted from MOFTEC Foreign Investment Administration, Almanac of CFERT

It should be mentioned that there is a discrepancy between the pledged and actual investment. According to figures released by MOFERT, for example, for the period 1978–1985, actual investment was estimated at only US$460m. Alternative figures published by the World Bank indicate that of US$720m pledged up to June 1985, only US$350m had actually been invested (World Bank, 1988). Compared with that of other countries and regions, however, the discrepancy is relatively small, and it has been narrowing since 1990.

It is also worth mentioning that the lack of reliable and comprehensive statistical and market information in China has created a host of problems. As Pomfret has commented, in China there is 'no strong tradition of reporting economic statistics'. The data available probably understate the true situation.

## 22.3    The investment pattern since 1986

The years 1986 and 1987 saw the first surge in the number of FDI projects as a result of the introduction of policies to encourage FDI in the productive sectors, especially those involving advanced technology. The actual number of projects decreased during the period 1990–1992 due to the after-effects of the 1989 Tiananmen incident, but the level of investment in these three years was still higher than the pre-1986–87 era. With the restoration and consolidation of investment confidence by Deng's tour to the South in spring 1992, British investment jumped dramatically in 1993, when investment numbers almost doubled that of 1987. Project numbers rose further in 1994 (Figure 22.5). The strong British interest in the Chinese market and its confidence in the future prospect of that market are also illustrated by our survey. Among the 125 British firms responding to the survey, over a third of them plan to invest in China within the next couple of years, while the rest said they have already invested in China.

It has been suggested, elsewhere, that China's coastal areas were the first regions targeted for the country's economic development. They absorbed, up to 1992, more than

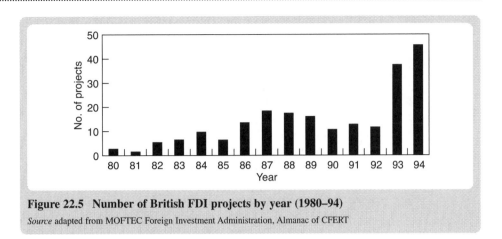

**Figure 22.5  Number of British FDI projects by year (1980–94)**

*Source* adapted from MOFTEC Foreign Investment Administration, Almanac of CFERT

80% of the total worldwide inward FDI to China. Only 9.5% of all FDI in China was located in China's inland provinces (Vogel, 1989). Whilst foreign investors generally emphasise the South and Southeast coastal provinces of Guangdong, Jiangsu, Fujian, Shandong and Shanghai, the majority of British companies have approached the urban centres of industry, such as Beijing and Shanghai, as locations for their joint ventures. The examination of the current version of the investment guide of the *China Mirror* supports the above observation. Up to January 1994, 25% of all British-funded companies' representatives and Sino-British joint ventures in China were located in Shanghai, and more than 46% of them were located in Beijing (Far Eastern Economic Review, 1993). The remaining 29% of all British investment projects were located in the Chinese coastal and inland provinces. The number of projects in Shanghai and Beijing are presented in Table 22.2.

As far as industrial distribution is concerned, most of the joint ventures established in China are found to be engaged in the exploitation of natural fuels, labour-intensive manufacturing or tourism, as well as infrastructure projects, including highways, railways and port developments. In addition, foreign investors engage in the textile, medicine, food, motorcycle, electronics, automotive, chemical, machinery and coal industries. This study also found that manufacturing, as well as construction and services, were the industries

**Table 22.2  Regional distribution of British direct investment in China.**

| Location | Companies' representatives and JVs | | Sino-British joint ventures | | Total number | |
|---|---|---|---|---|---|---|
| | (No) | (%) | (No) | (%) | (No) | (%) |
| Shanghai | 65 | 24.53 | 30 | 26.09 | 95 | 25.00 |
| Beijing | 154 | 58.11 | 21 | 18.26 | 175 | 46.05 |
| Rest | 46 | 17.36 | 64 | 55.65 | 110 | 28.95 |
| Total | 265 | 100 | 115 | 100 | 380 | 100 |

*Source* adapted from Almanac of China's Foreign Economic Relations and Trade (CFERT), FT., Nov. 1994; Agency France Press English Wire, 8 July 1994.

which received the most foreign investment and that the proportion to manufacturing dropped slightly in 1992, whereas estate and services increased by 40%. This chapter further suggests a considerable increase in the establishment of high-tech projects by UK multinational companies seeking a long-term commitment in China. Furthermore, foreign investors are increasingly interested in infrastructure projects such as power stations, motorways and railways. This trend will intensify over the next five years.

The reason for this has been found in China's priority for new investment to improve its poor infrastructure. In 1995, for instance, new incentive guidelines are aiming at directing investment towards high-tech and infrastructure projects. Thus, the proportion of telecommunications and power-generating industries is about to increase rapidly within the next decade, as the Asia Pacific region is likely to spend more on telephones and power than any other region in the world.

In general, the investment pattern by industry roughly corresponds to the economy's exporting structure (Pomfret, 1991). The majority of British investors, primarily multinationals represent industries such as mechanical engineering (27%), textiles (23%), electronics (9%) and chemicals and pharmaceuticals (9%), industries which face a structural and cost crisis in Britain (Wilpert and Scharpf, 1990).

Foreign-funded ventures in China contribute considerably to the export volume of the specific Chinese economy. In 1994, for instance, the 100,000 foreign-funded enterprises operating in China generated exports worth some US$87.65bn, 30.7% more than the previous year, thereby accounting for 37% of China's total exports (34.3% in 1993). In 1991, they accounted for only US$12.1bn (16.7%), an increase by 54% compared with the previous year (12.6%) (Yang, 1990).

The growth rate of 54% was distinctly higher than the overall growth rate of all Chinese exports by 15.8%. Foreign-funded ventures, which contribute primarily to the increase of Chinese exports, can be founded in textiles, chemicals and electronics, all of which are heavily represented by BDI. In 1993, 111 of the total 616 Sino-British ventures (18%) exported more than 80% of their output from mainland China (Walker and Done, 1994).

## 22.4    The UK investors' experience

The response of Western businesses generally to the opportunities presented by the Chinese incentives has not been as enthusiastic as the host country initially hoped for; a fact which is now openly acknowledged. What success has been recorded is largely a result of China's low labour costs, huge and underdeveloped domestic market, abundant material reserves and, not least, because of the overall enthusiasm displayed by the Chinese themselves.

Investors have encountered many problems such as infrastructure deficiencies, obtaining a share of the domestic market, getting assistance from the relevant authorities and overcoming the managerial style differences involved. Moreover, there is no doubt that the political power struggle in China shakes confidence among investors, plus the fact that, given the length of time China was cut off from international markets, UK investors feel that there has been a severe underestimation of 'how much they would have to improve their infrastructure, upgrade cadre training, and fundamentally alter their way of thinking to be competitive with other countries' (Far Eastern Economic Review, 1993).

## 22.5    Case studies

The special UK experience can be illustrated by case studies. In the case of all but one, this investment has taken the form of joint ventures. The exception is Cherry Valley, which operates a compensation trade arrangement.

### 22.5.1  Cable & Wireless

Cable & Wireless (C&W) has a long-established association with China going back to the early part of the twentieth century, and currently has two equity joint ventures operating there. The Huaying Nanhai Oil Telecommunication Service Company Limited is a £5m, 15-year contract providing off-shore domestic and international telecommunication services for oil and oil-field support companies engaged in development of the South China Sea oil-field. However, reduction in the scale of oil exploitation activities in the area has now made the company relatively insignificant.

C&Ws' other project is the Shenda Telephone Company Limited, which provides local and international telephone services in the Shenzhen SEZ, which borders Hong Kong. C&W holds 49% of the equity, with the balance being in the hands of the public sector Shenzhen Telecommunications Development Company. C&W was considered a suitable partner by the Chinese because of its strong presence in Hong Kong, and its positive attitude towards helping the Chinese authorities. In the early stages of the project, C&W imported engineering expertise from its Hong Kong subsidiary, whilst Chinese were sent to Hong Kong for training. C&W, being a service-based company rather than a manufacturer, helped the Chinese design the specifications with tenders from France, Japan and the USA. In return the Chinese authorities supplied free land use and a tax holiday.

The tariff for telephone calls is set according to the international rate. Since China receives more calls than it makes, and since most of the transactions are paid for in US dollars, the Chinese side can earn foreign exchange to repay its share of the equipment costs. The return on investment is around 15–20%, which C&W considers unsatisfactory. The company's expenditure to date (including loans to their Chinese partner) has been substantial, around US$50m, which it is anxious to recoup eventually. The company has also found Chinese investment procedures lengthy and bureaucratic. It was found very difficult to arrive at a common goal through negotiations, especially with the large number of people that had to 'pass' a project in order for it to be approved. The most useful technique was found to be to get everybody together, but cultural differences made this very difficult to arrange. Problems have reduced over the years with increasing experience, but C&W still wants to see more improvements relating to screening and approval. Furthermore, the laws on investment are brief and vague, and more clarification is needed.

### 22.5.2  The Tootal Group

Tootal has been operating in forms of trade other than direct investment in Shanghai since 1949. It is currently involved in two joint ventures and a management contract in China. Both joint ventures are spinning mills and are situated in the coastal area.

The decision to go into China was a strategic move. In order to supply the area, to fight off competitors, and to complement and reinforce the group's other manufacturing bases nearby, the establishment of manufacturing bases in China seemed only logical, given the existing long-term relationship with the Chinese, and the very attractive offerings that were provided by the host country. The equity shareholdings were agreed through discussions and resulted in Tootal owning 42.5% of the equity in both the joint ventures established. This was provided in the form of capital (in foreign currency) and high-tech equipment brought in from Switzerland, Germany and Britain.

The export-oriented nature of Tootal's operations suits China's ultimate goal of generating foreign exchange, and it has accordingly guaranteed both the supply of raw materials and an uninterrupted supply of power. Tootal has found penetration of the local market difficult, and recently concentration has been upon greater value added products. The Chinese foreign balance requirement has done little to help Tootal's two ventures, since equipment is paid for in foreign exchange. A policy of tight cash control has had to be enforced. Trust built up among the partners has helped the businesses to run smoothly, and understanding the Chinese philosophy of 'always placing personal qualities above rules and regulations' (Wilpert and Scharpf, 1990) has helped formulate the right tactics.

### 22.5.3 Pilkington

Pilkington was one of five partners who set up the Shanghai Yaohua Pilkington Glass Company Limited in March 1983. The joint venture was to be 100% equity funded, with the three Chinese partners taking 75%, and Pilkington taking half the remaining 25%. Eventually, funding was 40% equity and 60% loan from the Bank of China.

The project was initiated by the Chinese side, who wanted to update their huge glass industry. They had concluded that the best way to do this was to set up an operation under licence from Pilkington. The first meeting was held in June 1980, but 16 rounds of negotiations ensued before the company was formally established in December 1980, mainly due to State Planning Commission delays.

Other problems encountered were:

- clearance of the chosen site was a major source of delay, with resettlement of people living on the site taking an unexpectedly long time;
- rent for the land was high given that vacant possession was not immediately available;
- ground conditions were much worse than expected from interpretation of the geological surveys; piles were needed to strengthen the site and a diaphragm wall required for excavation;
- whilst local engineers and workers were competent, project management was inefficient;
- most raw materials had to be transported by water;
- the quality and volume of soda ash available locally was inadequate, and materials had to be imported;
- labour quality was low and required extensive training (85 managers and operators were sent to the UK for eight weeks before production began);
- own power generators were required because of the risk of interruption in electricity supply to what is essentially a continuous process.

The increase in total investment (from a budgeted 165.2m Renminbi to an eventual 432m) made the original projected 15% return on investment unrealistic, and the proposed export levels were not enough to cover the loans, royalties and dividends remittable increased to 50% of production (due also to the poor state of the Chinese domestic economy, leading to low local sales whilst there was high demand abroad).

Since the third year of production the operation has been in profit, and Pilkington's existence shows that trust, firm commitment and good working relations are very important in making a successful operation. Indeed, the Chinese side is so proud of the venture that a tour of the plant has become a virtual 'must' for every visiting foreign dignitary.

### 22.5.4  Cherry Valley Farms

Cherry Valley, based in Lincoln, is considered to be the leading duck-breeding operation in the world in terms of technology and stock. Cherry Valley supplies parent breeding stock, technology and marketing expertise, and then deducts its share of the profits from the earnings, with the balance going to the Chinese. The Chinese side is happy with this arrangement, since they earn foreign currency from the export sales. Equipment for the process, such as incubators and cold stores, can be obtained both locally and from abroad, although the latter is often preferred because both the local equipment and information thereon are generally in short supply.

The quality of feed is sometimes not as high as Cherry Valley would like, and must be supplemented through the use of vitamins and prompt rectification to prevent serious afflictions developing in the stock. In addition to the supply of technology, Cherry Valley also provides in-house training either in the UK or in China. Many problems are associated with this, since it is known that some trainees are looking for perks in the UK rather than training. The language barrier poses a serious problem, and this has been solved by employing a part-time translator in Chinese. Qualified trainees are subsequently sent back to China to train other Chinese in turn.

Serious problems were also created by transportation and power supply difficulties. Quick and efficient transport is essential to the transportation of livestock; whilst a small, but constant, supply of power is required for the incubators and cold stores, and the east coast does suffer from power disruptions from time to time.

Cherry Valley ensures that at any one time there is at least one UK representative in China. Cherry Valley is very confident about China, although the rate of growth is not the same as before the Tiananmen Square incident (UK personnel were repatriated within two weeks of 10 June 1989). The company has great pride in its technology and does not like to sell it separately. It considers this part of its recipe for success.

### 22.5.5  McVitie's Cakes

Part of United Biscuits holdings, McVitie's joint venture set up in Shekou was the group's first contract with the Chinese, and is its latest addition to reinforce its Asian markets (following cooperative projects in Taiwan, Singapore and Malaysia). The joint venture, United Biscuits Guangjin (China) Limited, is owned 80% by McVitie's, and was set up to produce a limited range of products to keep production costs low.

All raw materials are sourced domestically and at local prices. However, the quality and variety of materials are limited, which means that the quality of products is restricted to Asian standards, which does not permit of export to the West.

The start-up time for production to reach an acceptable level of efficiency was 'normal'. However, a lot of teething troubles were both expected and encountered, relating mainly to organisation and management. Approximately half the products are for export to Hong Kong, with the rest being sold domestically, and whilst there have been no difficulties experienced with the Hong Kong market, with the Chinese market problems have arisen mainly due to the poor sales distribution system. For example, purchases by wholesalers tend to be erratic, making planning difficult. McVitie's response has been to adopt a posture of very rapid response to sudden orders and yet simultaneously to attempt to keep stocks to a minimum. Prices for products exported to Hong Kong are set according to the market price in order to make them competitive. For locally consumed products, the price is usually set according to what the market will bear.

The plant is labour intensive, and the cost of production is reduced greatly by using existing imported technology and the extremely low local wages. The venture uses a UK manager at the top level and Chinese managers elsewhere. The UK manager is there simply to organise and assist in the running of the business, and most of the decisions are made by the Chinese team. McVitie's believes this use of Chinese management will encourage true commitment and minimise communication problems.

## 22.6    Summary of findings

A number of clues for commercial success in China emerge from the company case studies. The form of enterprise appears significant, with the joint venture being particularly favoured (Swain, 1991). It is preferred by China and, from the foreign partner's point of view, this makes it easier to obtain assistance from the Chinese authorities.

All the operations examined comprised an element of technology transfer from the foreign partners. In the case of the transfer of 'soft' technology, due to the shortage of skilled labour, training is invariably necessary, depending upon the degree of sophistication of the 'hard' technology involved. Since it is expensive to send either a group of UK instructors to China, or Chinese workers to the UK, an appropriate technique appears to be to train a small group of Chinese who are then used to train their fellows.

Every operation that involves obtaining raw materials locally has experienced difficulties in one or a combination of the following areas (Stavis and Gang, 1988): quality, volume, delivery and variety. The only successful solution to this problem so far identified is to import the necessary materials from abroad. Local conditions have made it difficult to bring products up to the companies' normal quality standards. In part this due to the quality of local raw materials, but it is also explained by the fact that the Chinese have not previously been exposed to such high quality standards.

All the enterprises have had to handle their foreign exchange balances carefully, and whilst, so far, major problems have not arisen, this is only because it has been possible to sell at least part of the output for hard currencies which can subsequently be used to cover external expenditures (the Renminbi remaining inconvertible). The use of Chinese management seems to be the norm in every case examined. This is beneficial to the operation in terms of managing the human resource to greatest economic benefit. Trust is perceived as very important in running the businesses, and the use of Chinese in the management decision-making process is seen as the best way to avoid conflict between work practices and management styles. This approach also exploits every potential for the benefit of the organisation and avoids many of the problems which have been experienced by expatriates, in terms of adapting to the way of living, and having to cope with the cultural differences, of a foreign country.

Almost all the operations examined had experienced infrastructure problems to varying degrees. Whilst in developed countries energy, transport and housing are taken for granted, no such assumption should be made about China, even within the relatively favoured environment of the SEZs. The most common problems encountered have been inadequate transportation and power cuts. These problems had been foreseen in most cases and their effects minimised by locating plants near their markets and installing their own generators.

A further common problem has been delays in bringing production on stream. This is attributed (variously) to poor organisation, local project management deficiencies, and the very high degree of bureaucracy associated with the Communist system. As an illustration of this problem, it has been reported that it took one company two years and 173 stamps of approval to import a single piece of machinery (Walker, 1994). Whilst no easy solution has been found to the bureaucracy problem, any prospective investor would be well advised to carry out a thorough investigation of the structure of Chinese officialdom if some of the more protracted potential delays are to be avoided. The art of cultivating a personal relationship with those in power, known as *guanxi*, is essential, and potential investors are well advised to develop this skill.

## 22.7 Conclusions

China's Open Door Policy still brings great opportunities for foreign investors to penetrate the Chinese and the extended Asian market. Britain's role as an investor in China is steadily growing. Despite the problems British companies face when establishing projects in China, investing in this country remains an essential tool for penetrating the vast Chinese market as long as other means of doing business with China, such as exporting, licensing and other cooperative forms, are not available.

Difficulty has, nevertheless, been experienced in introducing radical change into an economy cut off for so long from commercial and technological developments occurring elsewhere. Although a vast number of foreign investors bringing in substantial foreign capital has been as fruitful as anticipated, most investors have experienced numerous problems related to the inadequate investment environment, complicated procedures, and the difficulty of negotiating with the Chinese.

British investors also face cultural dissimilarities, which result in difficulties in managing production, personnel and marketing issues (Islam, 1994). Although it is the Chinese who benefit from British-Chinese business relations, especially in terms of trade, it should always be recognised that whoever wants to succeed in the Chinese market must be willing to understand the Chinese way of living, must be patient and must focus on the future.

Not all companies have experienced the difficulties mentioned, and experience suggests that once the initial hurdles have been overcome, the majority of joint venture investments seem to operate reasonably successfully (*Financial Times*, 1995).

The attitude of the Chinese government itself has been crucial in providing an impetus to overcoming the problems imposed by an inconvertible currency, exchange control regulations and a general management ethos seriously out of line with twentieth-century requirements. Mere investment incentives and policy changes of themselves would have been insufficient to achieve even the limited success that has occurred. Whilst many problems remain, corporations have been able to develop strategies which enhance their possibility of success. A study of the problems those corporations have encountered and the responses they have developed provides useful clues to success for those wishing to invest in China.

## Summary

- Data analysis shows that the UK is an important partner for China in terms of FDI.
- The trends in UK direct investment in China are a direct result of the Open Door Policy.

- The distribution of UK FDI in China is largely focused on Beijing and Shanghai. UK experience in China is examined via case studies.
- All UK FDI in China comprises an element of technology transfer.
- Most projects have run into management and local production problems caused largely by cross-cultural issues and quality problems.

## Questions

1. Using an appropriate case study, indicate how China gains from FDI.
2. 'Technology transfer and growth are complementary factors.' Explain and discuss.
3. Why are strategic alliances crucial for success in Chinese markets?
4. What types of technological transfer should the Chinese government seek to attract to maximise growth?

### Key concepts

the Chinese market                     technology transfer
management efficiency                  open door policy
product quality                        globalisation
FDI

## Bibliography

Commission of European Communities (1994) 'Towards a new Asia strategy', Brussels, 13 July. The report was proposed by Sir Leon Brittan, the European Commissioner for External Trade Relations, as a thorough Review of the European Union's Asia policy as stated in the *Financial Times*, 9 November.

*Far Eastern Economic Review* (1993) 'Switching into High Gear', 30 September, p. 44.

*Financial Times* (1995) 'Bayer in China venture', 9 March, p. 9.

Islam, S. (1994) 'Wake-up call', *Far Eastern Economic Review*, 4 August, pp. 18–19.

Pomfret, R. (1991) *Investing in China: Ten Years of the 'Open Door' Policy*, Hemel Hempstead: Harvester Wheatsheaf, p. 103.

Stavis, B. and Gang, Y. (1988) 'A survey of Shanghai joint ventures', *China Business Review*, March/April, pp. 46–8.

Swain, J. (1991) 'Shanghai surprise', *The Sunday Times Magazine*, Business World Supplement, 10 November, p. 38.

Vogel, E. F. (1989) *One Step Ahead in China: Guangdong Under Reform*, Cambridge, MA: Harvard University Press, p. 125.

Walker, T. (1994) 'Ready for China to westernise', *Financial Times*, 19 July, p. 18.

Walker, T. and Done, K. (1994) 'Chinese roads paved with gold', *Financial Times*, 23 November, p. 18.

Wilpert, B. and Scharpf, S. Y. (1990) 'Tercultural management – joint ventures in the People's Republic of China', *Journal of Psychology*, vol. 48, no. 1, pp. 257–74.

World Bank (1988) 'China: external trade and capital', *World Bank*, p. 54.

Yang, L. P. (1990) 'Business in China – current information sources', *Asia Pacific Journal of Management* , vol. VII, pp. 137–45.

# 23 China and world trade

## K. LAWLER AND H. SEDDIGHI

## 23.1  Introduction

Chinese trade expansion is expected to become more dynamic when accession to the WTO materialises. China passed a large hurdle when the USA agreed to accept China's entry to the WTO. Therefore, final entry to the WTO is a matter of time. WTO entry may result in dynamic effects. However, there will exist short-run costs as structural changes in the Chinese economy inevitably occur. The WTO is regarded by many countries as a 'global club'. Indeed, as the global trade system has progressed, this has caused an impetus to globalisation processes. Moreover, market entry and geographical barriers are now largely breaking down by applications of Internet technology. Thus, market distances are shortened and exchange processes become easier. These factors have created a desirable environment for the reformist leaders in China. Thus China can adjust trade directions and restructure domestic economic activities to capture gains from WTO membership. The Chinese government is likely to take on the challenge to liberalise the economy to increase trade flows.

Clearly, living standards in China have increased markedly since the Open Door Policy was initiated in 1978. GDP per capita increased from $571.1 to $772.2 between 1995 and 1997 respectively. However, per capita income in rural areas still remains approximately 40–50% of the urban level. As inflation subsided during the same period, increases in real purchasing power occurred. During the late 1990s, given the Asian turmoil and as the lagged effects of the recession in the Asian region gathered momentum, economic growth fell. Surprisingly, however, manufacturing sectors still experienced growth. For instance, more than 20% increases in growth rates for exports were experienced between 1995 and 1997. The corresponding growth in the current account balance remain strong. In 1997 and 1998, the current account balance was around 3% of China's nominal GDP, which is equivalent to US$29bn. These favourable trade conditions helped China accumulate foreign exchange reserves, which increased from less than US$75 in 1995 to US$145 in 1999.

In terms of sectoral growth, GDP data show that China experienced tremendous growth in different sectors (Table 23.1). These growth indicators reflect expanded production in various areas. The Chinese economy appears to have achieved balance growth in different sectors. As evident from Table 23.2, absolute consumption levels for the domestic market are restrained by relatively low purchasing power. The majority of products were exported to obtain foreign exchange. However, trade statistics indicate that China imported significantly more from overseas, representing approximately one-third of aggregate consumption values. Eventual WTO membership should further amplify this trend as tariffs are reduced and quotas expanded. For instance, in agriculture, under the deal with the USA, China has to reduce tariffs on agricultural produce to 14.5% by 2004.

**Table 23.1  GDP performance by sector in China.**

| Growth (%) | 1995 | 1996 | 1997 | 1998 |
|---|---|---|---|---|
| GDP | 10.0 | 9.7 | 8.8 | 8.0* |
| Agriculture | 4.5 | 5.1 | 4.5* | 4.5* |
| Industry | 13.6 | 12.3 | 11.9* | 9.2* |
| Services | 8.0 | 8.2 | 8.0* | 8.0* |

*Source* adapted from The World Economic Factbook 1999; Asian Development Outlook 1999
* Authors' estimate

**Table 23.2  Consumption and trade statistics in China.**

| | 1995 | 1996 | 1997 |
|---|---|---|---|
| Consumption (US$bn) | 315.4 | 379.8 | 435.1 |
| Consumption per capita (US$) | 258.2 | 307.8 | 349.2 |
| Total exports (US$bn) | 148.8 | 151.5 | 189.5 |
| Total imports (US$bn) | 129.1 | 135.6 | 166.8 |

*Source* adapted from The World Economic Factbook 1999

According to WTO rules for the car manufacturing industry, tariffs levied on imported vehicles have to be cut to 25%.

The economic development in China is closely associated with trade performance. Since the Open Door Policy, China has been actively promoting joint ventures and strategic alliances. This mode of investment allows large pools of funds and foreign expertise to be injected. Foreign direct investment (FDI) in China soared dramatically from merely US$2.3bn to US$43bn between 1987 and 1997 respectively (Euromonitor, 1998). The inflow of capital transformed key areas in the Chinese economy, such as power supply, chemicals, food, transportation and other high-tech equipment. In 1998, the Chinese government launched a US$750 billion project to improve infrastructure development in China. These development projects should facilitate entrepreneurs to bolster sales and distribution, telecommunications and other essential supporting networks required for manufacturing and exporting.

Privatisation is an effective way of eliminating inefficient operations and releasing idle resources for better production. To liberalise markets occupied by state-owned enterprises and to restructure the centrally planned economic system in China, privatisation processes were put high on the agenda at the 15th Party Congress in 1997. Privatisation theoretically should create more efficient structures and increase asset flows. Between 1998 and 1999, some small debt-ridden state enterprises were sold at low or zero prices. The underlying rationale for selling assets at low costs were that the associated provinces would get rid of financial burdens such as huge unpaid pension and medical insurance debts. Owing to bankruptcy and inability to pay employees, some enterprises decided to liquidate and distributed all shares to employees in compensation for long-owed wage payments. However, these events indicate that provincial leaders wanted to avoid financial liabilities, but they did not intend to improve the manufacturing environment. Given such negative externalities, the central government responded by limiting 'disposals' of state enterprises as well as using closer monitoring. In the years ahead, it is likely that the Chinese

**Table 23.3  China's share in US and EU clothing and textile imports.**

| | 1974 | | | 1981 | | | 1994 | | | 1997 | | |
|---|---|---|---|---|---|---|---|---|---|---|---|---|
| | $bn | % | World Rank | $bn | % | World Rank | $bn | % | World Rank | $bn | % | World Rank |
| **Textile** | | | | | | | | | | | | |
| US | 0.03 | 1.7 | 13 | 0.26 | 8.4 | 3 | 1.11 | 11.5 | 2 | 1.43 | 11.5 | 3 |
| EU | 0.12 | 1.1 | 13 | 0.38 | 2.0 | 7 | 1.13 | 2.8 | 6 | 1.42 | 2.6 | 5 |
| **Clothing** | | | | | | | | | | | | |
| US | – | – | – | 0.46 | 5.6 | 4 | 6.67 | 17.2 | 1 | 7.77 | 15.4 | 1 |
| EU | – | – | – | 0.31 | 1.7 | 11 | 4.40 | 7.4 | 2 | 6.64 | 8.3 | 2 |

*Source* adapted from WTO Annual Report (1995–1999)

government will promote more large-scale mergers and acquisitions among state-owned enterprises. This may bring in sufficient private funds to restructure operations and to alter dated business cultures.

Chinese export trades were primarily focused on textiles, clothing and other lower-value merchandise before 1980. Textiles and clothing were an important issue under the Multi-Fibre Arrangement. China's increased market share in the USA and EU is shown in Table 23.3. In recent years, trade has become more diversified. However, in total Chinese world market shares are in aggregate less than 3% of world trade. In certain particular sectors, Chinese trade did well (Table 23.4). For instance, around 25% of all toys made in the world are manufactured in China and one-eighth of all footwear and clothing are

**Table 23.4  China's share of world imports and exports in selected merchandise.**

| | % share in world exports | | | | % share in world imports | | | |
|---|---|---|---|---|---|---|---|---|
| | 1980 | 1990 | 1994 | 1997 | 1980 | 1990 | 1994 | 1997 |
| Food | 1.4 | 2.5 | 3.2 | 2.8 | 1.4 | 1.4 | 1.3 | 1.5 |
| Chemicals | 0.8 | 1.3 | 1.6 | 2.1 | 2.0 | 2.2 | 3.1 | 3.8 |
| Iron & steel | – | 1.2 | – | 3.2 | – | 2.5 | – | 4.4 |
| Machinery & transport equipment | – | – | – | – | 1.0 | 1.8 | 3.2 | 2.4 |
| Office machines & telecom equipment | 0 | 1.3 (17.4) | 2.1 (8.3) | 3.2 (23.9) | 0.7 | 1.4 (40.3) | 2.5 (10.2) | 2.6 (37.0) |
| Automotive products | – | – | 0.1 (0.4) | – | 0.2 | 1.3 | 1.1 (3.8) | – |
| Textiles | 4.6 | 6.9 (11.6) | 9.2 (9.8) | 8.9 (7.6) | 1.9 | 4.8 (9.9) | 6.9 (8.1) | 7.8 (8.6) |
| Clothing | 4.0 | 9.0 (15.6) | 17.0 (19.6) | 18.0 (17.4) | – | – | – | – |
| World merchandise Trade | – | – | 2.9 | 3.3 | – | – | 2.7 | 2.5 |

*Source* adapted from WTO Annual Report (1990–1999)
Note: Figures in parentheses indicate the share in China's total merchandise trade

produced in the Mainland. In recent decades, China has gradually moved away from the low-cost labour-intensive assembly operations, however, by employing more advanced technology. The rising importance of chemicals, office machinery and telecom equipment in China's exports and world exports is clear evidence (Table 23.4). Chinese trade is also concentrated with certain trade partners. In Table 23.5, the data indicates that the USA is the second largest trading partner after Japan. In the past decade, US trade has been limited by barriers in the USA. Generally, China is a major trading nation in the South East Asian region, as evident by significant trade shares in Japan, South Korea, Taiwan and Hong Kong. By contrast, China's preferences in the EU and Latin America are relatively small.

More than a quarter of total Chinese trade involves foreign-funded enterprises. Significant gains from trade have contributed directly to the development of the Chinese economy. Given the high volume of FDI and perverse income distribution effects, the 'true' gains from trade may fall if replacement investment and procurements go abroad. In view of this, the Chinese government launched specific measures to tackle these problems and to improve the investment climate. For instance, the Chinese government allowed *yuan* convertibility on the Current Account in 1996. This aims to foster the growth of FDI. As manufacturing industries consume power, frequent interruptions in workplaces due to the shortage of electricity are common in China. To improve this manufacturing environment for exporters, the State Planning Commission in China has allowed FDI projects (more than 40% in 1996) for energy provision and other key services such as transportation and telecommunications. To prevent the domestic market from overheating, China continues to practise tight control over fixed asset investment in state-owned enterprises. The combined effects of careful policy administration, liberalisation and prudent macroeconomic strategies are destined to promote a stable economy to enhance international trade and boost economic growth.

All countries can benefit from trade by utilising assets in line with the classical theory of comparative advantage. China used to be dominated by primary production and low-value-added industries. This was mainly due to abundant cheap labour, which still contributes to relative and absolute advantages of Chinese trade. In moving towards the market economy and away from central planning, more economic rationalisation and transformation are expected. FDI inflows have been important for China's development.

**Table 23.5  Trade share of China's trading partners.**

| Major Export Destinations 1997 | (% share) |
| --- | --- |
| Hong Kong | 21.8 |
| Japan | 16.4 |
| USA | 16.1 |
| EU (12) | 12.0* |
| South Korea | 5.0 |
| **Major Import Sources 1997** | |
| Japan | 21.0 |
| US | 11.6 |
| Taiwan | 8.9 |
| South Korea | 8.4 |

*Source* adapted from The World Economic Outlook 1999
* Authors' estimate

By actively promoting FDI in the past two decades, China's successful enterprises also create FDI outflows abroad. These reverse FDI flows reflect the potential economic power of China. The interaction of FDI movements will certainly increase the diffusion of technology and the accumulation of fixed assets for China. Eventual WTO membership should enhance trade flows too. The emergent philosophy of capitalism in Mainland China may create conflicts for those who benefit from socialism, perhaps especially those 50 million workers in state-owned enterprises who may become redundant. Given the noise of globalisation around the world, China cannot hide from the common mechanism of multilateralism if she is to advance.

## 23.2 China's import demand function: a cointegration study

### 23.2.1 Introduction

In the past two decades, the world has witnessed the emergence of the People's Republic of China (PRC) as a major economic power. From 1980 to 1992, China had an average annual growth rate (adjusted for inflation) of 9%, and by 1993 had the tenth largest GDP in the world (The World Economic Factbook, 1996/97). However, China was only ranked 157th in terms of per capita GDP at US$433.8 (see Figure 23.1).

As a result of this rapid expansion in economic growth, the average per capita income growth rate during the 1980s and 1990s reached approximately 7.4%, which is remarkable by any standard. Furthermore, there has been a significant shift in the composition of output from agricultural products in favour of industrial.

Trade with the outside world has also increased rapidly during the last two decades. By 1995, with a population of 1.2 billion people (the largest in the world), China not only had one of the highest GDPs, but was also the 13th largest importer (US$97,000 million) and the 12th largest exporter in the world (US$95,000 million) (The World Economic Factbook, 1994/95).

There are two key issues in this field, namely that of Sekiguchi (1990) and Yuan (1994). In these papers, the authors tried to model the PRC's import function using various determinants. For instance, Sekiguchi modelled both linear and log-linear functions

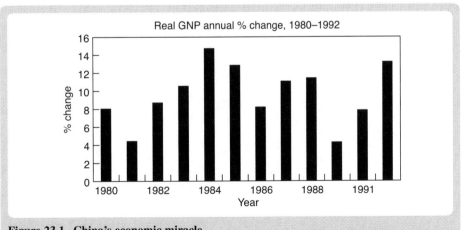

**Figure 23.1  China's economic miracle**
*Source* adapted from State Statistical Bureau (PRC 1980–95)

of disaggregated components of aggregate demand for both China and Japan, whilst Yuan (1994) used real industrial output, foreign exchange rates and price ratios as the determinants of real imports.

Given the importance of trade with China for the West, this section provides empirical analysis of the China's import function using the Johansen (1988) and Johansen and Juselius (1990) cointegration method.

We aim to examine the responsiveness of China's aggregate imports to key determinants in the long run and short run.

This section is organised as follows: first, we sketch a brief account of China's recent economic development with reference to foreign trade, and then deal with the theoretical model. Next, results are presented. Finally, we provide a summary and conclusions.

### 23.2.2 Recent economic development

Not long ago China, with a growing population, began massive economic reforms under Deng Xiao Ping. Therefore, China slowly proceeded along a well-trodden path of market reforms undertaken by others. When had this transformation taken place?

Between 1940 and 1970, foreign trade played only a small role in China's economic development. During the 1950s and 60s, the total value of foreign trade was only 2% of GNP. In the 1970s, trade grew rapidly but still amounted to just 6% of GNP in 1979 (Figure 23.2).

As a result of China's policy of self-reliance, both imports and exports have been used mainly to improve existing production and earn foreign exchange. Imports from 1960 to 1985 were mostly of an industrial nature (Table 23.6).

Imports of machinery and equipment and industrial raw materials have increased from about US$10,880 million and US$482 million in 1955 to about US$12,291 million and US$15,274 million in 1986 respectively. On the other hand, even though food and consumer goods increased considerably, they only constituted a small amount of total imports compared to industrial goods.

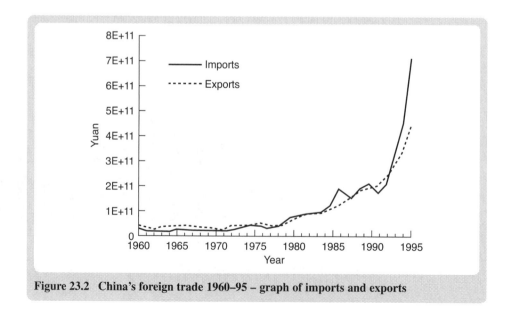

**Figure 23.2  China's foreign trade 1960–95 – graph of imports and exports**

**Table 23.6  China's levels of annual imports (US$ 100 million).**

|      | Machinery and equipment | Industrial raw materials | Raw materials for agriculture | Food and consumer goods |
|------|------|------|------|------|
| 1955 | 10.88 | 4.82 | 0.56 | 1.07 |
| 1960 | 9.7 | 8.13 | 0.8 | 0.9 |
| 1965 | 3.58 | 8.08 | 1.76 | 6.75 |
| 1970 | 3.69 | 13.36 | 2.2 | 4.01 |
| 1975 | 24.06 | 34.17 | 5.7 | 10.94 |
| 1980 | 53.75 | 86.2 | 14.25 | 41.3 |
| 1981 | 51.05 | 76.69 | 14.09 | 52.99 |
| 1982 | 33.94 | 75.96 | 13.82 | 51.06 |
| 1983 | 32.54 | 95.37 | 17.84 | 39.55 |
| 1984 | 51.96 | 132.61 | 20.87 | 48.12 |
| 1985 | 109.65 | 159.83 | 14.91 | 58.92 |
| 1986 | 122.91 | 152.74 | 9.09 | 46.08 |

*Source* adapted from UN Statistical Year Book, Annual Abstract, 1990

Exports have also grown and are a major contributor to China's growth (Table 23.7). From 1955, agricultural exports declined from 46.1% to about 17.5% in 1985, while exports of heavy industrial goods and textiles increased from 22.7% and 11.7% in 1955 to about 42.8% and 19.7% in 1985 respectively.

Primary product exports consisted of five categories: foodstuffs, beverages and tobacco, non-food raw materials and minerals.

In Figure 23.3, we see that primary products constituted about 45–50% of exports during the early 1980s, but had begun to decline steadily after that. On the other hand, the share of manufactured products rose rapidly from half to over three-quarters of exports by 1991. This change was fuelled by the increase in the production of manufactured products such as textiles and other apparel, which reflected China's comparative advantage in labour-intensive commodities.

Oil also becomes an important export commodity during the late 1970s and early 80s. During this period, China exported 47 million tons of crude oil to Japan alone. All in all, exports of crude oil and petroleum products rose from 12 to 36 million tons by 1988 (Kleinburg, 1990).

**Table 23.7  The composition of export products (%).**

|      | Agricultural, sideline | Light industries | Textiles | Heavy industrial |
|------|------|------|------|------|
| 1955 | 46.1 | 19.5 | 11.7 | 22.7 |
| 1960 | 31 | 17.1 | 29.1 | 22.8 |
| 1965 | 33.1 | 23.4 | 20.1 | 23.4 |
| 1970 | 36.4 | 26.2 | 21.4 | 15.7 |
| 1975 | 29.6 | 23.9 | 17.9 | 28.6 |
| 1980 | 18.7 | 24 | 17.9 | 39.4 |
| 1985 | 17.5 | 20 | 19.7 | 42.8 |

*Source* adapted from Almanac of China's Foreign Economic Relations and Trade, 1987, p 401.

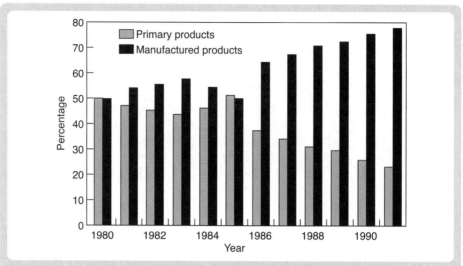

**Figure 23.3   The commodity composition of Chinese exports, 1980–91 (%)**

*Sources* adapted from State Statistical Bureau, Chinese Statistical Abstracts (Beijing: Statistical Publishing House) 1983,
1985, 1986, 1987, 1988, 1990, 1991, Mincai, Z. (1992) 'China's foreign economic and trade relations continue to develop',
*Renmin Ribao*, 31 January

China's main trading partners in the past three decades have been Western industrial countries which have the technology and capital China needs for its industrialisation programme (Table 23.8)

China's exports during this period were mainly in crude oils (to Japan), as well as in traditional goods like soybeans and minerals. Exports of oil and textiles to Japan grew, and imports of industrial and capital goods increased as well.

Hong Kong, on the other hand, has been reliant on China as its main supplier of food and foodstuffs. In addition, Hong Kong has been a principal link for indirect exports as well as a ready market for goods processed and assembled in China after 1978. For example, re-exports of Chinese goods in 1980 was valued at US$1.68 billion. (Hsu, 1983). Trade with Hong Kong further increased in the 1980s as Hong Kong itself became China's major re-export centre for its manufactured products, such as textiles and light industrial goods. In exchange, Hong Kong exported raw materials and semi-finished

**Table 23.8   Total value of trade with industrial countries (US$100,000).**

|      | Japan   | W. Germany | USSR   | USA    | Hong Kong |
|------|---------|------------|--------|--------|-----------|
| 1950 | 472     | 194        | 3,384  | 2,381  | 1,512     |
| 1955 | 833     | 192        | 17,898 | –      | 1,894     |
| 1960 | 2       | 1,137      | 16,639 | –      | 2,083     |
| 1965 | 4,543   | 1,266      | 4,074  | –      | 4,636     |
| 1970 | 8,065   | 2,750      | 472    | –      | 5,925     |
| 1975 | 37,955  | 8,155      | 2,972  | 4,707  | 16,835    |
| 1980 | 92,011  | 20,433     | 4,924  | 48,113 | 49,231    |
| 1985 | 164,344 | 30,720     | 18,814 | 70,250 | 108,941   |
| 1986 | 138,640 | 37,544     | 26,377 | 59,935 | 115,184   |

*Source* adapted from Almanac of China's Foreign Economic Relations and Trade, 1984, 1987

products to assembly factories in China. As China's third largest trading partner, the USA imports textiles, clothing, raw and crude materials (petroleum), whilst exporting, before 1979, grain (wheat and corn) and after 1979, machinery and transportation equipment. Furthermore, the USA had begun to export advanced technology to China as restrictions on such trade were eased. As a result of increased exports of textiles from China, the USA ran trade deficits with China after 1985 and had to negotiate a four-year bilateral trade agreement, in 1988, to limit exports from China to an annual growth of 3% (*Wall Street Journal*, 1988). Furthermore, the imposition of market restrictions and the problems of dealing with the two non-convertible currencies served to exacerbate strains between the two nations.

### 23.2.3 An empirical model

In recent years (Giovannetti, 1989 and Abbott, 1996) have studied the import function using principal components of final expenditure in the import demand function. That is, consumption, investment and exports, as the main determinants of import demand. It has been found that the individual components do have a separate impact and a significant influence on final import demand, the underlying assumption being that each component of final expenditure has a separate impact on imports. The empirical model is thus specified as follows:

$$M_t = b_0 + b_1 C_t + b_2 I_t + b_3 X_t + b_4 PP_t + e_t \quad e_t \sim NID(0, \sigma^2)$$

Where: $M_t$ = Real imports
$C_t$ = Total consumption (private and government)
$I_t$ = Gross domestic investment
$X_t$ = Total exports
$PP_t$ = A price ratio (price of imports relative to the price of domestic substitutes)

All variables are measured in logarithmic forms. The data is annualised in constant 1980 prices, from 1960 to 1994 (World Tables of Economic and Social Indicators, 1995).

### Findings

In this section, we report the results of the unit root test carried out on each variable using the Pesaran and Pesaran (1995) Microfit V4.0 software package. For this purpose, we have conducted DF and ADF tests, using a random walk with drift model. (A drift term was added since Microfit results are biased in equations without a drift term.)

DF test: $\Delta X_t = a_0 + a_1 X_{t-1} + u_t$

ADF test: $\Delta X_t = a_0 + a_1 X_{t-1} + \sum_{i=1}^{k} \Delta X_{t-i} + e_t$

Table 23.9 presents a summary of the results obtained.

From Table 23.9, we can see that all variables are I(1) processes. First differencing is necessary to make the series stationary.

Before testing for cointegration, we need to determine the lag length of the VAR equation:

$$M_t = M_{t-1} + M_{t-2} + \dots M_{t-n} \quad \text{where n is the lag length}$$

Using the maximum likelihood ratio test, we were able to determine the lag length as 3. In accordance with the cointegration tests proposed by Johansen (1988) and Johansen

**Table 23.9  DF and ADF test results.**

| Variable | DF test | ADF test | Lag length of ADF test |
|---|---|---|---|
| M | 1.9069 | 1.5336 | 2 |
| GDP | 1.3342 | 1.3578 | 4 |
| PP | −0.76162 | −1.4924 | 5 |
| C | 0.6377 | −0.3463 | 4 |
| I | −0.354 | −1.2656 | 3 |
| X | −1.4388 | 0.2906 | 11 |

M = import demand, GDP = Gross Domestic Product, PP = Price ratio, C = Private plus government consumption, I = Gross domestic investment and X = Exports. Critical value of ≅2.95 from Fuller (1976).

**Table 23.10  Cointegration LR test based on maximal eigenvalue of the stochastic matrix.**

| Null | Alternative | 95% CV | 90% CV | Statistic |
|---|---|---|---|---|
| r = 0 | r = 1 | 33.319 | 30.841 | 45.9268 |
| r <= 1 | r = 2 | 27.136 | 24.783 | 19.4376 |
| r <= 2 | r = 3 | 21.074 | 18.904 | 11.7911 |
| r <= 3 | r = 4 | 14.9 | 12.912 | 8.8635 |

**Table 23.11  Cointegration LR test based on trace of the stochastic matrix.**

| Null | Alternative | 95% CV | 90% CV | Statistic |
|---|---|---|---|---|
| r = 0 | r >= 1 | 70.598 | 66.486 | 89.7148 |
| r <= 1 | r >= 2 | 48.28 | 45.229 | 43.788 |
| r <= 2 | r >= 3 | 31.525 | 28.709 | 24.3504 |
| r <= 3 | r >= 4 | 17.953 | 15.663 | 12.5593 |

and Juselius (1990), the two test statistics, $\lambda_{max}$ and $\lambda_{trace}$, were then carried out to determine the number of cointegrating vectors (Tables 23.10 and 23.11). These are shown in Table 23.10.

From Table 23.11 we see that there is a unique cointegrating vector. The long-run coefficients are reported in Table 23.12. The long run relationship can thus be expressed as:

$$M = 26.2097 - 17.4209I - 3.3382X - 6.8416PP$$

Looking at the long-run relationship again, we see that the consumption coefficient is very large indeed, implying that for every 1% change in aggregate consumption, imports to China are likely to increase by 26%. This information has significant implications for Western exporters who are engaged in exports of consumer goods to China. The elasticity of imports with respect to investment goods is also high (−17.4). Similarly, development of the Renmini would lead to a collapse in imports.

The negative sign implies that as investments in manufacturing and industry expand, aggregate imports in the long run are likely to fall significantly. The same also appears to

**Table 23.12  Estimated cointegrating vector in Johansen estimation (normalised in brackets).**

| | Eigenvector | | | |
|---|---|---|---|---|
| **M** | **C** | **I** | **X** | **PP** |
| −0.13526 | 3.5452 | −2.3564 | −0.45155 | −092543 |
| | **Normalised** | **Coefficients** | | |
| −1.0000 | 26.2097 | −17.4209 | −3.3382 | −6.8416 |

be the case for exports with the estimated elasticity of −3.3. The expansion of exports generates additional resources which are then used to reduce imports in the long run.

Using the likelihood ratio test, it was found that each variable was statistically significant at the 5% level of significance (Table 23.13).

We also carried out a test to see whether the elasticity of imports with respect to each component of the aggregate is the same.

Consider the import function: $M = b_0 + b_1C + b_2I + b_3X + b_4PP$.

We test the hypothesis:

$H_0$: $b_1 = b_2 = b_3$

$H_1$: $H_0$ is not true.

The restricted equation is as follows:

$M = 0.67899C + 0.67899I + 0.67899X - 1.1941PP$

Decision rule: the Chi-sq. value of 24.2112 is way above the 5% critical value of 5.99. Therefore, we reject the null hypothesis and conclude that each coefficient of the import function is independent. A short-run ECM model can be specified using residuals saved from the cointegrating vector, of the form:

$$\Delta M_t = a_0 + \sum_{i=0}^{k}\Delta C_{t-i} + \sum_{i=0}^{k}\Delta I_{t-i} + \sum_{i=0}^{k}\Delta X_{t-i} + \sum_{i=0}^{k}\Delta PP_{t-i} + RES\,2_{t-1}$$

In order to determine a parsimonious model, the AIC (Akaike Information Criterion) was used. Omitting insignificant regressors, the following is an estimation of the short-run model:

**Table 23.13  Chi-sq. values for each variable of the import function.**

| Variable | d.f. | Chi-sq. value | 5% CV |
|---|---|---|---|
| C | 1 | 21.3204 | 3.84 |
| I | 1 | 26.0551 | 3.84 |
| X | 1 | 13.9696 | 3.84 |
| PP | 1 | 10.0393 | 3.84 |

$$\Delta M_t = -23.1285 - 3.5514\Delta C_{t-2} + 1.4287\Delta I_{t-1} + 1.2796\Delta I_{t-3} + 0.19334\Delta X_t$$
$$\phantom{\Delta M_t =} (-2.5777) \quad (-2.0771) \qquad (2.2542) \qquad\quad (2.1553) \qquad\quad (1.9225)$$

$$+ 0.83992\Delta X_{t-1} + 0.61331\Delta X_{t-2} + 0.21265\Delta X_{t-3} - 0.7827\Delta PP_{t-2}$$
$$\phantom{+} (3.2883) \qquad\qquad (2.9789) \qquad\qquad (2.1374) \qquad\quad (-1.8051)$$

$$+ 1.2798\Delta PP_{t-3} - 0.21875\Delta RES2_{t-1}$$
$$\phantom{+} (2.0706) \qquad\qquad (-2.5876)$$

$R^2 = 0.78877$      DW $= 1.8455$      $F_{sc} = 0.028894$      $F_{ff} = 1.912$
$F_h = 0.89356$

The short-run elasticities appear to be significantly smaller than their long-run counterparts. Moreover, imports respond to changes in consumption and investment expenditures with significant lags. Furthermore, the short-run model seems to track the data well ($R^2 = 0.788$), and has satisfied all diagnostic tests.

## Conclusion

Given the importance of foreign trade with China and China's key role in global change, this study was motivated by the need for empirical analysis of the determinants of China's aggregate imports. For this purpose we carried out cointegration analysis to examine the long-run relationship between aggregate imports and the main components of final expenditure. Our empirical investigation suggests that there exists a long-run relationship between aggregate imports and the main components of final expenditure. Moreover, there are significant differences between the long-run partial elasticities of imports with respect to different macro components of final expenditure. Consumption expenditure, in particular, appears to be the major determinant of China's imports, with the imports' elasticity of over 26%. These results have profound implications for Western exporters of goods and services to China and their delivery and pricing strategies. Generally, even small changes in relative prices create large adjustments in all import categories. In the short run, an error correction model which embodies disaggregated demand variables appears to perform well, providing an appropriate framework for forecasting the short-run fluctuations in China's aggregate demand for imports.

## Summary

- China's entry into world trade in the past decade has been remarkable, with growth rates in trade flows averaging 10–12% per annum since 1992. Hence China's case for entry into the WTO is based on sheer scale and potential dominance in East Asia given its overwhelmingly large internal market.
- GDP per annum has grown at 9–13% per annum since 1994.
- The sheer scale of the economy indicates the size of the potential markets for exporters.
- China's import function is very elastic as the cointegration coefficients are large for small changes in price.

## Questions

1. Why is China's import function highly price elastic?
2. To what extent could China meet the conditions necessary for (a) the Metzler paradox or (b) immiserising growth, in the future?

3. What would happen to imports if China's growth rate slowed?

4. Discuss the structure and composition of China's imports; how might this change in the future?

## Key concepts

| | |
|---|---|
| cointegration | import functions |
| ECMs | unit roots |
| ADF | elasticities |

## Bibliography

Abbott, A. J. and Seddighi, H. R. (1996) 'Aggregate imports and expenditure components in the UK: an empirical analysis,' *Applied Economics*, September, vol. 28, pp. 1119–25.

Army Area Handbook (1994) US department of the Army at gopher.umsl.edu.

Asian Economic Bank (1997) *Asian Development Outlook 1999*, OUP, pp. 47–54.

Euromonitor (1998) *The World Economic Factbook 1999, China*, Euromonitor plc, pp. 127–8.

Fuller, W. A. (1976) *Introduction to statistical time series*, Wiley: New York.

Giovannetti, G. (1989) 'Aggregate imports and expenditure components in Italy: An econometric analysis', *Applied Economics*, vol. 21, pp. 957–71.

Hsu, J. C. (1983) 'Hong Kong in China's foreign trade: A changing role', in A. J. Young (ed.) *China and Hong Kong; The economic Nexus*, Hong Kong: Oxford University Press, p. 175.

Johansen, S. (1988) 'Statistical analysis of cointegrating vectors', *Journal of Economic Dynamics and Control*, vol. 17, pp. 231–54.

Johansen, S. and Juselius, K. (1990) 'Maximum likelihood estimation and inference on cointegration with application to the demand for money', *Oxford Bulletin of Economics and Statistics*, vol. 52, pp. 169–209.

Kleinburg, R. (1990) *China's opening to the outside world: The experiment with foreign capitalism*, Westview Press, Chapters 5 and 6.

Maddala, G. S. (1992) *Introduction to Econometrics*, Macmillan.

Pesaran, M. H. and Pesaran, B. (1995) *Microfit 3: An interactive Econometrics Package*, Oxford University Press.

Sims, C. A. (1980) 'Macroeconomics and reality', *Econometrica*, vol. 48, pp. 1–48.

Sekiguchi, S. (1990) 'Foreign trade in Chinese economy prices and price responsiveness', *The Developing Economies*, December, vol. 28, part 4, pp. 390–417.

State Statistical Bureau, *Chinese Statistical Abstracts*, Beijing: Statistical Publishing House, vol. 2.

*The World Economic Factbook 1994/5*, Euromonitor plc, 1994.

The World Economic Outlook 1999, IMF Report, vol. 50, New York.

UN Statistical Year Book, Annual Abstract, 1990, New York.

World Tables of Economic and Social Indicators, 1960–1992, at www.lib.virginia.edu.

World Tables of Economic and Social Indicators, UN, 1995.

*Wall Street Journal*, 1 February, 1988.

WTO (1995) *International Trade 1995: Trends and Statistics*, World Trade Organisation, prepared by The Economic Research & Analysis Division & The Statistics and Information Systems Division.

WTO (1990–1999) WTO Annual Report, WTO, 1990–1999.

Yuan, M. and Kochhar, K. (1994) *China's imports: An empirical analysis using Johansen's Cointegration approach*, IMF working paper, December, pp. 1–24.

# Index

Note: entries in **bold** appear as key terms in the text.